D1709685

Consequentialism

The International Research Library of Philosophy
Series Editor: John Skorupski

Metaphysics and Epistemology

Identity *Harold Noonan*   **Infinity** *A.W. Moore*
Personal Identity *Harold Noonan*   **Scepticism** *Michael Williams*
Future Volumes: Space and Time; Substance and Causation; Necessity; The Existence and Knowability of God; Faith, Reason and Religious Language; Knowledge and Justification; Truth.

The Philosophy of Mathematics and Science

Future Volumes: Mathematical Objects and Mathematical Knowledge; Proof and its Limits; Probability; The Ontology of Science; Theory, Evidence and Explanation; The Philosophy of the Life Sciences; The Philosophy of History and the Social Sciences; Rational Choice.

The Philosophy of Logic, Language and Mind

Understanding and Sense, Vols I and II *Christopher Peacocke*
Metaphysics of Mind *Peter Smith*
Future Volumes: Truth and Consequence; Modality, Quantification, High-order Logic; Reference and Logical Form; The Nature of Meaning; Functionalism; Interpretation; Intentionality and Representation; Reason, Action and Free Will.

The Philosophy of Value

Consequentialism *Philip Pettit*   **Duty and Virtue** *Onora O'Neill*
Punishment *Antony Duff*   **Environmental Ethics** *Andrew Brennan*
Future Volumes: Meta-ethics; Medical Ethics; Aesthetics; The Foundations of the State; Justice; Liberty and Community.

Consequentialism

Edited by

Philip Pettit
The Australian National University, Canberra

Dartmouth
Aldershot · Brookfield USA · Hong Kong · Singapore · Sydney

© Philip Pettit, 1993. For copyright of individual articles please refer to the Acknowledgements.
All rights reserved. No part of this publication may be reproduced, stored in a retrieval system,
or transmitted in any form or by any means, electronic, mechanical, photocopying, recording, or
otherwise without the prior permission of Dartmouth Publishing Company Ltd.

Published by
Dartmouth Publishing Company Limited
Gower House
Croft Road
Aldershot
Hants GU11 3HR
England

Dartmouth Publishing Company
Old Post Road
Brookfield
Vermont 05036
USA

A CIP catalogue record for this book is available from the British Library

Library of Congress Cataloging-in-Publication Data
Consequentialism / [edited by] Philip Pettit.
    p. cm. — (The International research library of philosophy)
    Includes bibliographical references.
    ISBN 1-85521-304-4 : $99.95
    1. Consequentialism (Ethics) I. Pettit, Philip, 1945-
II. Series.
BJ1031.C594 1993
171'.5—dc20

92-36095
CIP

ISBN 1 85521 304 4

Printed in Great Britain by Galliard (Printers) Ltd, Great Yarmouth

Contents

Acknowledgements

The editor and publishers wish to thank the following for permission to use copyright material.

American Philosophical Quarterly for essays: R. Eugene Bales (1971), 'Act Utilitarianism: Account of Right–Making Characteristics or Decision–Making Procedure?', *American Philosophical Quarterly*, **8**, pp. 257–65, and Joel J. Kupperman (1981), 'A Case for Consequentialism', *American Philosophical Quarterly*, **18**, pp. 305–13.

The Aristotelian Society for essays: Michael Slote (1984), 'Satisficing Consequentialism', *Proceedings of the Aristotelian Society*, **58**, pp. 139–63. Reprinted by courtesy of the Editor of the Aristotelian Society: copyright © (1984) and Philip Pettit (1984), 'Satisficing Consequentialism', *Proceedings of the Aristotelian Society*, **58**, pp. 165–76. Reprinted by courtesy of the Editor of the Aristotelian Society: copyright © (1984).

Australasian Journal of Philosophy for essays: Allan F. Gibbard (1965), 'Rule–Utilitarianism: Merely an Illusory Alternative?', *Australasian Journal of Philosophy*, **43**, pp. 211–20; David Lewis (1972), 'Utilitarianism and Truthfulness', *Australasian Journal of Philosophy*, **50**, pp. 17–19, and Philip Pettit and Geoffrey Brennan (1986), 'Restrictive Consequentialism', *Australasian Journal of Philosophy*, **64**, pp. 438–55.

Blackwell Publishers for essays: Lars Bergström (1971), 'Utilitarianism and Alternative Actions', *Noûs*, **5**, pp. 237–52, and J.J.C. Smart (1956), 'Extreme and Restricted Utilitarianism', *Philosophical Quarterly*, **6**, pp. 344–54. Reprinted in Philippa Foot (ed.), *Theories of Ethics*, pp. 171–83, Oxford: Oxford University Press.

The British Academy for the essay: Derek Parfit (1979), 'Prudence, Morality and the Prisoner's Dilemma', *Proceedings of the British Academy*, **65**, pp. 539–64. Copyright © The British Academy 1979. Reprinted by permission from Proceedings of the British Academy, Volume **65**, (1979).

Cambridge University Press for essays: James Griffin (1992), 'The Human Good and the Ambitions of Consequentialism', *Social Philosophy and Policy*, **9**, pp. 118–32, and Alan P. Hamlin (1989), 'Rights, Indirect Utilitarianism, and Contractarianism', *Economics and Philosophy*, **5**, pp. 167–87.

The Journal of Philosophy for essays: Robert Merrihew Adams (1976), 'Motive Utilitarianism', *The Journal of Philosophy*, **73**, pp. 467–81; Amartya Sen (1979), 'Utilitarianism and Welfarism', *The Journal of Philosophy*, **76**, pp. 463–89, and Michael Stocker (1976), 'The Schizophrenia of Modern Ethical Theories', *The Journal of Philosophy*, **76**, pp. 453–66.

Series Preface

The International Research Library of Philosophy collects in book form a wide range of important and influential essays in philosophy, drawn predominantly from English-language journals. Each volume in the Library deals with a field of inquiry which has received significant attention in philosophy in the last 25 years, and is edited by a philosopher noted in that field.

No particular philosophical method or approach is favoured or excluded. The Library will constitute a representative sampling of the best work in contemporary English-language philosophy, providing researchers and scholars throughout the world with comprehensive coverage of currently important topics and approaches.

The Library is divided into four series of volumes which reflect the broad divisions of contemporary philosophical inquiry:

- Metaphysics and Epistemology
- The Philosophy of Mathematics and Science
- The Philosophy of Logic, Language and Mind
- The Philosophy of Value

I am most grateful to all the volume editors, who have unstintingly contributed scarce time and effort to this project. The authority and usefulness of the series rests firmly on their hard work and scholarly judgement. I must also express my thanks to John Irwin of the Dartmouth Publishing Company, from whom the idea of the Library originally came, and who brought it to fruition; as also to his colleagues in the Editorial Office, whose care and attention to detail are so vital in ensuring that the Library provides a handsome and reliable aid to philosophical inquirers.

John Skorupski
General Editor
University of St. Andrews
Scotland

Introduction[1]

Roughly speaking, consequentialism is the theory that the way to tell whether a particular choice is the right choice for an agent to have made is to look at the relevant consequences of the decision: to look at the relevant effects of the decision on the world. In directing us to consequences the theory is teleological in focus; the term comes from the Greek work *telos*, meaning end or goal. It is opposed to any sort of deontological approach; this term comes from the Greek work *deon*, meaning obligation or duty. Where consequentialism would assess a choice by looking at its consequences, a deontological approach would assess it by looking at how the choice measured up to the obligations incumbent on the agent.

Consequentialism has been at the centre of ethical and meta-ethical debate over the past quarter of a century and more. This collection of essays is designed to highlight the questions raised in relation to consequentialism and to provide suitable readings on each question. I distinguish nine major questions that have come up again and again in those debates and I have organized the table of contents around them. Perhaps the best thing for me to do in introducing the volume is to comment in turn on each of these issues.

The first question is the basic one of why one should be a consequentialist rather than a deontologist; these options may not be exhaustive but they are the salient possibilities. Surprisingly, there has been very little discussion of this question in the literature. Consequentialists tend to assume that, if one is to be rational about the enterprise of moral assessment, then there is no alternative to looking at the consequences – the consequences, neutrally or impersonally characterized – of the choices assessed. How could it be rational, they ask, to neglect any such consequences? They assume that, if deontologists think otherwise, that is because of an unquestioning commitment to a theological or a commonsense viewpoint. A theological viewpoint might suggest that human agents ought to fulfil prescribed obligations and let God look after the consequences. And a commonsense viewpoint might support the attitude that the important thing in moral decision making is to look after one's own moral standing, to keep one's own hands clean, and not to worry overmuch, except perhaps in exceptional circumstances, about any bad consequences that may follow on this.

There is also a second reason why consequentialists may not have concerned themselves much with providing a defence of their position. Consequentialists are a mixed bunch, for they differ among themselves on the question of which substantive sorts of consequences are the ones by reference to which choices ought to be assessed. For example, they divide into utilitarians and non-utilitarians, depending on whether or not they accept the view that it is only consequences that bear on the utility of sentient beings which matter: only consequences that affect the happiness or preference-satisfaction of such beings. Being a mixed bunch, consequentialists tend each to be concerned more with arguing for their particular view of what consequences count than with arguing for the shared consequentialist credo that it is indeed consequences that matter, and not the sort of thing on which deontologists focus.

But if consequentialists have not done much by way of arguing for their position, what have been the issues debated between them and deontologists? These have mainly had to do with how far consequentialism can support firm commonsense intuitions about what is morally right. Deontologists typically object to consequentialism that, in one way or another, it would undermine otherwise compelling moral attitudes. Rather than providing positive reasons for adopting their position, consequentialists have often been content to try to deal with those objections or to try to argue that, while the points made are valid, they are not as important as deontologists make them seem.

The issues between consequentialists and deontologists are often explicated by reference to a distinction between agent-neutrally justified and agent-relatively justified choices. It may be useful to comment briefly on this. As already suggested, the consequentialist counts only neutrally or impersonally characterized consequences as relevant to whether a choice is right. Such consequences will be characterized without reference to particular individuals and therefore without reference back to the person making the choice; it is a relevant consequence that happiness will be increased, or that life will thrive, but not that the chooser will have kept his promise, or that he or his will benefit in some way. Thus the consequentialist holds that a choice is right only if it is neutrally and, in particular, agent-neutrally justified. The deontologist opposes this claim. He sticks by commonsense intuitions that some promises should be kept, come what may; some rights respected, no matter what the results; some loyalties honoured, regardless of the effects; and so on. And in maintaining that a person may be bound to keep a promise, or respect a right, or be loyal to a friend, regardless of the fact that the consequences of that choice are relatively undesirable, he is saying that a choice may be right in virtue of an agent-relative justification: it enables the agent to keep *his* promise, honour this right invoked against *him*, and be loyal to *his* friend, and so on.

Because the first question has not been prominent in recent debate, I have only reprinted one essay relevant to the question. I have selected this essay because it may serve to explain and motivate the consequentialist presumption that there is really no alternative to looking at consequences – neutrally characterized consequences – in the assessment of choice.

The next three questions in my list of nine concern the nature of consequentialism, rather than its rationale. Question two is whether consequentialism should be seen as a theory of the right or a theory of the good. To say that something is good is to hold that it has a certain value, in particular a certain positive value. To say that something is right is to hold that, in some relevant choice, it is what ought to be chosen. Only options or potential options can be right or wrong; any sort of entity, option or not, can be good or bad. And, to complicate things further, rightness and goodness may come apart with options. An option that is wrong may yet be an object of great value; it may be wrong simply because another option is an object of even greater value. An option that is right, on the other hand, may not be something of great value; it may be right, simply because it is the least bad option among a very poor set of alternatives. A theory of good, a theory of value, would enable us to determine the values of different entities, options included. A theory of the right would enable us to determine, for any set of options, or at least for any set of options in a certain category, which alternative or sub-set of alternatives is the right one.

When I speak of what is good, and of what has value, I have in mind an impersonal or agent-neutral conception of goodness and value. Something is agent-neutrally valued just in case the basis on which it is valued can be articulated without reference back to the valuer. Something is agent-relatively valued just in case this is not so. If I value a prospect for the increase of happiness it promises, or even for a particular effect it will have, say on planet

Earth, then I value it agent-neutrally. If I value it for the benefits it will have for me or mine, or for the fact that it will keep my hands clean, or for any reason of that self-referential kind, then I value it agent-relatively. The theory of the good, or the theory of the valuable, refers to the theory of what ought to be agent-neutrally valued.

Does consequentialism present itself as a theory of the good or as a theory of the right, or as something involving commitments in both areas? That is the second question on my list. Consequentialists themselves tend to say that the theory is concerned only with the right, not with the good. But that position has required argument, as consequentialists and deontologists tend to focus on different values and may seem to be in essential conflict here. The majority of consequentialists have been utilitarians who think that something can be of value only so far as it bears on the happiness or preference satisfaction of sentient beings. Many deontologists are unwilling to talk about what is agent-neutrally good; they claim to offer a theory of the right that is independent of any theory of the good. But those who commit themselves explicitly on what is agent-neutrally valuable concentrate on different sorts of goods from most consequentialists: goods to do with honouring promises, for example, keeping faith with friends and respecting people. And even those who do not commit themselves explicitly invite the ascription of similar non-utilitarian commitments: they hold that it is right for this or that person to keep a promise or respect a right and, by universalization, commit themselves to believing that it is right for anyone in such a position to keep that sort of promise or respect that sort of right; they acknowledge as agent-neutrally good or valuable the universal state of affairs in which those promises are kept, those rights respected. This divergence on matters of value has suggested to some that consequentialism and deontology offer different views of what is good, as well as different views on what makes an option right.

The standard consequentialist line is that this suggestion is misleading. From the point of view of consequentialists, the question as to what makes for the value of different states of affairs is quite distinct from the question of what makes for the rightness of a particular option. The consequentialist holds that an option is right just in case it is associated with better relevant consequences than alternatives, however the superiority of those consequences is to be judged: whether by reference to a utilitarian theory of the good, for example, or by reference to some other theory. Henceforth I shall assume in my discussion that this line is defensible and that consequentialism is uncommitted in the theory of the good; it amounts only to a theory of the right.

Question three is the second of the three questions that bear on the nature of consequentialism. This is the question as to whether consequentialism is just a theory for determining which choice is the right one for an agent or agency to have made or whether it is also meant to be a theory whereby the decision maker reaches a conclusion.

There is a long tradition among the opponents of consequentialist doctrines, in particular the opponents of utilitarianism, of suggesting that consequentialists are committed to holding that every choice should be made in a highly calculative, actuarial mode. F.H. Bradley made the point in the last century, writing about the utilitarian approach: 'So far as my lights go, this is to make possible, to justify, and even to encourage, an incessant practical casuistry; and that, it need scarcely be added, is the death of morality.'[2] Consequentialists have almost always resisted this charge. Thus Henry Sidgwick in the last century, and J.J.C. Smart in this, have argued forcibly that utilitarianism does not require that agents all make their decisions by explicit reference to how the options will do by the promotion of happiness.[3] The point they have wanted to make was nicely summed up early in the nineteenth century by the jurisprude, John Austin, in defending the utilitarian thinker: 'Though he approves of love because it accords with his principle, he is far from maintaining that the general good ought to be the motive of the lover. It was never contended or conceived by a sound, orthodox utilitarian, that the lover should kiss his mistress with an eye to the common weal.'[4]

As recent consequentialists have almost all taken the view that consequentialism is a theory of the right, not a theory of the good, so they have nearly unanimously argued that it is a theory for assessing the right option for an agent or an agency to have made, not necessarily a useful theory to be applied in decision making. The sort of point which is made in this literature, including the literature selected here, is that making one's decison by reference to which option has the best consequences may be a way of making one's decision that does not itself have the best consequences. Suppose one is concerned with one's own pleasure, for example. It is notorious that the agent who makes her decisions by reference to which option will promote the most pleasure may actually enjoy less pleasure than someone who makes her decisions in a more spontaneous fashion; say, by reference to certain rules of thumb.

Perhaps the question most hotly debated about the nature of consequentialism is question four on our list. This is the question as to whether consequentialism is a theory for evaluating any option that an agent or agency faces, or just a theory for evaluating abstract rules with which options may comply or fail to comply. Suppose I consider the choice between two rules of action: say, the rule of always being hospitable to neighbours or the rule of only being hospitable when inclination leads that way. I may decide that, as between these rules, the better one to follow – it will probably be the one that produces the most happiness in my neighbourhood – is the first. But does that mean that any action I perform in compliance to that rule is the right option to have chosen in the particular circumstances on hand? In particular, does it mean this, even if in those circumstances it would have been better to make an exception and infringe the rule?

Rule-consequentialists hold that it is appropriate only to assess abstract rules by reference to consequences – that whether this or that rule is the right one to follow is determined by consequences – and that the rightness of more particular options is determined by whether they comply with the right rules. Act-consequentialists – option-consequentialists, as I prefer to call them – argue that there is no reason to restrict the range of consequentialism in this way. They hold that, if one is a consequentialist, one should in consistency be a consequentialist about assessing, not just abstract rules, but also any option that an agent or agency is likely to face. Sometimes option-consequentialists have argued, not only that their position is the more coherent, but that rule-consequentialism proves on examination not really to be a distinct alternative.[5] The more or less standard view nowadays is that while option-consequentialism is more uniformly consequentialist in its approach to assessment – in that sense it may be more coherent than rule-consequentialism – rule-consequentialism does represent a real alternative.

I said earlier that I would assume henceforth, as the standard line has it, that consequentialism is a theory of the right, not a theory of the good. I will assume, equally, that it is a theory of evaluation, not a theory of deliberation; and that it is a theory for assessing all options that can face an agent or agency, not just a theory for assessing abstract rules of choice. This takes me to question five. The question is whether consequentialism is a collectively satisfactory theory, and it is closely related to the last issue discussed; indeed it has not always been sharply distinguished from that issue in the literature. A collectively satisfactory theory is a theory such that it is not forced to evaluate the choices of individuals positively in any case where those choices collectively lead to a result that is worse by the relevant theory of the good than other possible collective outcomes. Suppose we had a society of utilitarians, each of whom acted in a way that utilitarians would approve. Is it possible that the collective result of their so acting might be worse than the collective result of actions that did not individually earn utilitarian approval? Is it possible, in particular, that the collective result might be worse in utilitarian terms: that it might actually lead to less human happiness or preference satisfaction than certain alternatives?[6]

Opinions are divided on the answer to this question. Some are happy to say that a consequentialist theory can be self-defeating in this way; they hold that, if agents try to do what it best by the theory, or succeed in doing what is best by the theory, then the collective results may still be worse in their own terms than it might have been.[7] Others will want to deny this, arguing that, where that result appears to hold, it usually transpires that one of the options before the individuals is not being taken into account: say, the option of exploring possibilities of cooperation with others, rather than acting unilaterally, or the option of seeking further information on the prospects facing the agent.[8] Among those who admit the possibility that a consequentialist theory may be collectively unsatisfactory, opinions are equally divided on how far this is damaging to consequentialism. The prisoner's dilemma is often taken to show that what is individually rational may not be collectively rational: each of two prisoners confesses to a crime because, whatever the other does, confessing promises a better result than refusing to confess; yet each would be better off by both refusing to confess than they are by both confessing. Why should it not be the case, so these thinkers will argue, that what is individually right may not be collectively right; that what individuals unilaterally combine to do is not what it would be right for the collectivity, did the collectivity have the status of an agent, to do?

Questions six, seven and eight bear on matters of some detail that are discussed within the ranks of consequentialists. They are important matters, as the essays selected should indicate, but they are matters of in-house debate.

Question six bears on how we should identify the alternatives to be evaluated in any decision. Should an agent do A or B, we ask. A, we answer, because its consequences do better on the relevant theory of the good. But what if there is some other option C which the agent might have chosen instead and which would have itself been better than A? This sort of example alerts us to the fact that in the consequentialist assessment of any choice we have to be clear about what are the relevant alternatives to bring into consideration. The question about alternatives has not received as much attention as it deserves in the literature but I include two essays relevant to the matter, on the grounds of its inherent importance.[9]

Question seven has been more widely debated in consequentialist circles. This is the issue as to whether, in looking at the decision an agent or agency ought to have made, we consider the actual consequences of the option chosen and the consequences that would have followed on alternatives; or whether, rather, we look at the expected consequences at the time of choice.[10] If the answer is that we should look at expected rather than actual consequences, then the question is whether we should look at the subjectively expected consequences – in the manner of decision theory – or whether we should look at the consequences that were in some sense objectively expected.

Suppose that a doctor prescribes a drug for a non-fatal skin condition, which has the following features: there is a 10 per cent chance that it will kill the patient, an 80 per cent chance that it will make no difference, and a 10 per cent chance that it will cure her complaint. Imagine that the drug works and the complaint is cured. Does consequentialism take its cue from actual consequences and say that the doctor made the right choice? Or does it look to expected consequences, whether subjectively or objectively expected, and say that the doctor made the wrong choice? That is the issue here.

The third more or less in-house issue, question eight, is whether consequentialism should hold that the right option is that which does best by relevant consequences – that which is optimific – or whether it is sufficient for an option to be right that it does well enough, as we might say, by the relevant consequences. Some theories of rationality are maximizing theories, requiring rational agents to maximize some function, whereas others are satisficing theories: these require rational agents just to perform satisfactorily by some relevant criterion. The question here is whether consequentialism should not take the softer, satisficing line, rather than the stern, maximizing one.[11]

This takes us, finally, to the last question, whether consequentialism conflicts with commonsense morality. This issue, in one form or another, is at the core of much of the consequentialist literature of the past quarter of a century and many of the essays included under the other questions are concerned with it; in particular, they are concerned to argue that consequentialism does not run into any damaging conflict with common sense. For that reason, the essays that I have selected on this question mainly represent the opposition line. They all suggest, in one way or another, that consequentialism fails to preserve important commonsense intuitions: intuitions, it is alleged, which few of us would be prepared to give up.

The intuitions involved come in three broad categories.[12] First of all, there is an intuition that we are not always obliged to do what is best: that, in some cases, it is perfectly all right to do less than the best, though it would be an act of heroism to do the best. Second, there is an intuition that, if we are to be virtuous, then often we must act without regard to overall, impersonal goals: we must act in a way that shows us to be a friend, a person of integrity, a keeper of promises, or whatever. Third, perhaps most tellingly, there is an intuition that the rights of other people bind us in certain ineluctable ways: there are certain harms we may not cause them, regardless of the good that would come of it. The essays selected raise these and other, related, matters.

The debate between consequentialism and deontology goes on. But the discussions of the last quarter-century or so have made for real gains and, while there has not been much convergence in the field, there is at least a greater degree of clarity about the issues involved. I hope that the essays selected for reprinting here will bear out my belief that in this regard the philosophical debate about consequentialism has generated real progress.

Notes

1   I am grateful for comments received from Ian Ravenscroft, Michael Smith and John Skorupski.
2   F.H. Bradley (1876) (1962), *Ethical Studies*, Oxford: Oxford University Press.
3   See Henry Sidgwick (1966), *The Methods of Ethics*, New York: Don Press; J.J.C. Smart and Bernard Williams (1973), *Utilitarianism: For and Against*, Cambridge: Cambridge University Press.

4 John Austin (1832) (1954), *The Province of Jurisprudence*, ed. H.L.A. Hart, London: Weidenfeld, p. 108.
5 See David Lyons (1965), *Forms and Limits of Utilitarianism*, Oxford: Oxford University Press.
6 See D.H. Hodgson (1967), *Consequences of Utilitarianism*, Oxford: Oxford University Press.
7 See Derek Parfit (1984), *Reasons and Persons*, Oxford: Oxford University Press.
8 See D.H. Regan (1980), *Utilitarianism and Cooperation*, Oxford: Oxford University Press.
9 See Lars Bergstrom (1966), *The Alternatives and Consequences of Actions*, Stockholm: Almqvist and Wiksell.
10 See C.I. Lewis (1969), *Values and Intentions*, Stanford: Stanford University Press.
11 See Michael Slote (1985), *Common-Sense Morality and Consequentialism*, London: Routledge, and (1989), *Beyond Optimizing: A Study of Rational Choice*, Cambridge, Mass.: Harvard University Press.
12 See Amartya Sen and Bernard Williams (eds) (1982), *Utilitarianism and Beyond*, Cambridge: Cambridge University Press; Sam Scheffler (1982), *The Rejection of Consequentialism*, Oxford: Oxford University Press; R.G. Frey (ed.) (1984), *Utility and Rights*, Oxford: Blackwell; and Sam Scheffler (ed.) (1988), *Consequentialism and its Critics*, Oxford: Oxford University Press.

Part I
Why Consequentialism?

[1]

AMERICAN PHILOSOPHICAL QUARTERLY
Volume 18, Number 4, October 1981

V. A CASE FOR CONSEQUENTIALISM

JOEL J. KUPPERMAN

CONSEQUENTIALISM is one of the most keenly, and least adequately debated theories in the history of philosophy.[1] Much of the existing debate has been carried on by means of discussion of apparent counter-examples. There are two glaring defects in this. (1) Unless the nature of the theory under discussion is made very clear, there is usually ample room for doubt as to whether it yields the results its detractors allege. (2) When a result alleged to be yielded by consequentialism is said to be inadequate or incorrect, the basis for this judgment is usually not spelled out. There has been a good deal of loose talk about "intuition," either the intuitions of particular philosophers or of right-thinking people. But rarely is anything said to distinguish "intuition" from "snap judgment," and snap judgments are especially likely to be influenced by how a situation or dilemma is described. The same moral problem can evoke very different responses depending on which factors are articulated or highlighted in its description.

The aim of this paper is both very general and limited. A case will be given for thinking that *some* form of consequentialism is correct. What will be supplied will be a line of argument, with some branching arguments indicated: it will be impossible of course to anticipate all objections or alternatives to consequentialism. Some parts of the argument will be given rather fully; but, because of limitations of space, some will only be sketched. I do not claim that anything that I supply or might supply amounts to proof. In philosophy one can be happy with considerations that can justify the agreement of some reasonable people. Nor will it be argued that a certain form of consequentialism is the correct or ideal one. It is important thus to bear in mind that there are very many forms of consequentialism. Consequentialism is most usually considered to be utilitarianism when it is conjoined with hedonism (and the conjunction of what Amartya Sen has called "welfarism" with sum ranking).[2] Richard Miller has argued that both Aristotle and Marx are "non-utilitarian

consequentialists," citing (for the first half of this) their rejection of hedonism.[3] His argument seems to me convincing with respect to Marx, and to establish at least that Aristotle's view is compatible with consequentialism. It can be argued that both Aristotle and Marx reject the conjunction of welfarism with sum-ranking, thus not qualifying as utilitarians even by Sen's standard. Consequentialism can base judgments of rightness on judgments of the consequences of individual actions (act consequentialism), or on judgments of the consequences of general observance of certain moral rules (rule consequentialism); there is room for other alternatives, including one along the lines of what Robert Merrihew Adams calls "motive utilitarianism."[4] Or one can hold a consequentialism based on Aristotle's ethics, in which the primary evaluations are of the consequences, both for the agent's own life and for others, not of individual acts or observance of lawlike moral rules, but rather of institutions and systems of attitudes. (It is arguable that a desirable system of attitudes would have some degree of flexibility but not unlimited flexibility, and thus this kind of consequentialism would be different from both act consequentialism and rule consequentialism, and—in so far as one thinks of attitudes as including far more than wants and desires—different from the consequentialism suggested by Adams' paper.) There will be, however, little discussion in this paper of rival forms of consequentialism. The argument will be merely that some form of consequentialism is correct.

This means that I shall not argue for any single, seemingly definite statement of moral policy such as the familiar "One should always do what has the best consequences". Many consequentialists would not accept this statement. Instead the argument has to be for the following.

Proposition C. In any case in which it is not true that one should do what has the best consequences, the reason for this has to be based on some judgment of consequences.

¹ For a discussion of misunderstandings and of gaps in arguments, cf. my "Vulgar Consequentialism", *Mind*, vol. 89 (1980).
² Cf. Amartya Sen, "Utilitarianism and Welfarism", *The Journal of Philosophy*, vol. 76 (1979).
³ Richard W. Miller, "Marx and Aristotle: The Unity of Two Opposites", *Proceedings of the American Political Science Association*, 1978.
⁴ Robert Merrihew Adams, "Motive Utilitarianism", *The Journal of Philosophy*, vol. 73 (1976).

In this, and in subsequent discussion, it is assumed that the term "consequences of X" means the set which includes X itself and physical and psychological events that are concomitant with, or follow from, X; it is assumed also (as part of the characteristic consequentialist treatment of consequences) that in no form of consequentialism can a particular consequence automatically override all others or be given infinite weight. Proposition C is the claim that some form of consequentialism is correct, that the only valid reason for not doing what has the best consequences (understood with the stipulations just mentioned) is that the optimific act in question is ruled out by some moral rule, motive, or system of attitudes which itself is shown to be desirable by virtue of its consequences (understood with the stipulation just mentioned).

This paper will have two parts. In the first part I shall lay out a general line of argument for Proposition C. The argument will be defensive in that it will seek to undermine likely anti-consequentialist lines of argument, showing in each case that what seems an anti-consequentialist position is plausible only if it rests on some judgment of consequences. The second part of the paper will consist of a general positive argument for Proposition C. This will require some discussion of the epistemological status of consequentialism, discussion of which has been disappointingly scanty in the recent literature.

I

In real life we never are sure of what all the consequences will be of actions that are open to us. We also may not be entirely sure of what the alternatives are that are open to us. As a number of writers have pointed out, there is a kind of moral creativity in difficult situations that consists in thinking of alternatives besides the obvious ones. Let me immediately grant all of these points. They show that consequentialism, in any form, is far less precise, and far more difficult to apply, than it may seem. This does not mean, however, that consequentialism can never be applied or that it is so vague as to be totally useless. In real life we may make rough non-quantitative judgments of degrees of importance, and we may balance prospective gains (for others and for ourselves) against risks. Consequentialist policies, of various sorts, can be pursued in the face of uncertainty and imprecision; but they make sense only if some general consequentialist proposition, statable without reference to uncertainty and imprecision, is correct. It makes sense to balance prospective gains against

risks only if there is some correct general proposition about doing what has the best consequences in the abstracted and unreal case in which we know what has the best consequences. Let us begin then with the simplest, and seemingly most straightforward, consequentialist proposition.

Proposition AC. One should always do what has the best consequences.

There are a number of factors that give proposition AC immediate plausibility, besides its generality and simplicity. It advocates acting responsibly: instead of adopting the attitude of "I made a moral choice; it fell to earth I know not where," one adopts the attitude of caring about the results of one's actions. Further, if something (happiness, satisfaction of desires, or moral virtue) is of value, there is an obvious point in bringing about as much of it as is possible. Proposition AC also has the virtue of giving us at least some independence from cultural biases and indictrination: instead of basing our morality on a received vision of what is "fitting" (e.g. what used to be perceived as the fittingness of the poor deferring to the wealthy), we have a chance to arrive at a more matter of fact morality which rests on observation of how certain practices actually work.

Why then should we not simply seek to do what has the best consequences? There are two main lines of deviation from Proposition AC.

Deviation 1: To accept AC and to try to lead one's life on its basis would be to opt for an undesirable personal character. Therefore AC is to be rejected.
Deviation 2: In some cases the alternative that has the best consequences happens to be morally wrong. Therefore AC is to be rejected.

Each of these lines of deviation from AC has three especially attractive or likely forms. Thus we can examine six forms of deviation from AC, as follows.

D_1a. To accept AC and to try to lead one's life on its basis would be to be an excessively calculating and unspontaneous person.

D_1b. To follow AC would be to feel one's policies and commitments as more provisional than should be the case for a decent, reliable person.

D_1c. To follow AC would be to be, first and foremost, altruistic. But it is better (more satisfying, more estimable) to be independent and oriented toward personal projects than to be an altruist. Everyone should look out for, first and foremost, himself or herself.

D2a. What AC recommends in some cases is wrong, in that some of its recommendations violate valid moral rules.

D2b. What AC recommends in some cases is wrong, in that some of its recommendations call for an agent to violate the rights of others.

D2c. What AC recommends in some cases is wrong, period: the wrongness is, as it were, intrinsic, and does not need to be derived from moral rules or from statements that certain rights are not to be violated.

Let us consider *D1a.* A *locus classicus* for this deviation is a philosophical joke, told by John Rawls. Jeremy Bentham says, "When I run to the other wicket after my partner has struck a good ball I do so because it is best on the whole."[5] An act consequentialist might reasonably reply with the story of Isaac Newton, who, asked why he had been hit on the head by a ball while playing in the field, replied with an exposition of the Law of Gravity. In both physics and ethics, it might be said, to account for everyday and easy cases by direct reference to fundamental and abstract laws is not only unnecessary but also comically pompous. There is, however, a difference between the cases of Bentham and Newton. It is clear that Newton does not have to be constantly mindful of the Law of Gravity in order to be governed by it; this is open to question in the case of Bentham and the Utilitarian Principle. But a consequentialist can reasonably say, as J. J. C. Smart has, that the policy of not thinking about consequences during normal sporting activity (and presumably during other kinds of normal everyday activity) has good consequences, and on that account is to be adopted.[6]

The point is that D1a can rest on an appeal to consequences: the undesirable consequences for one's own spontaneity of keeping something like AC in mind. There is only one way in which D1a can emerge as a non-consequentialist objection to AC. That is, if the objector maintains that it is better to be spontaneous than constantly to think of consequences, even if the bad consequences for others of one's spontaneity outweigh any good consequences for oneself. To advocate this is to advocate what we customarily term irresponsibility: most of us who believe in the value of spontaneity customarily in fact distinguish areas of life in which the effects of our actions on others are not likely to be serious enough to outweigh the value of spontaneity from other areas in which this is not the case. When we become aware that some of our actions have serious consequences, we normally consider it appropriate to reflect on them. Jeremy Bentham will reflect on the greatest good of the greatest number, after his partner has struck a good ball, if the opposing bowler has threatened suicide. Someone who is enjoyably casual and carefree in most situations of life ought to become reflective when his or her actions impinge on the extreme vulnerability of others. It is hard to imagine a human life in which the majority of actions have major effects on others—such a life would be very different from any of ours—but we would hope that such a person would be careful, and not too carefree and spontaneous. To speak as we have been doing of "irresponsibility" is of course not to refute the non-consequentialist version of D1a; it is merely to point out that the only immediately plausible version of D1a is a consequentialist one. And that is enough for our present purposes.

We now turn to *D1b.* This represents the inside view of the point made by those who ask, "Who would take seriously a promise made by a consequentialist"? Consequentialists sometimes attempt to meet this point by pointing to the side-effects of breaking promises, violating commitments, or letting down those who depend upon one. There are likely bad effects on one's future attitudes and behavior, on personal relationships, and on the general atmosphere of trust some degree of which is necessary to society. These side effects are often significant enough so that, if a philosopher asks about a case in which a net of 1,000 units of good (mainly for a promisee) would be brought about by keeping a promise, and a net of 1,001 units of good would be brought about by breaking the promise, one knows that in this case some major harm would be prevented (or good brought about) by breaking the promise, in order to bring about even a slight surplus.[7] The philosopher has neglected to say what this major factor is, and until it is specified we are in no position to make a judgment.

Nevertheless there is something to be said for this general line of attack on AC. It is widely recognized that promises ought to be broken if keeping them will bring about serious harm, or will prevent great good; and in this sense commitments in general are not inviolable. But there is something unsettling about being associated with people who are in a state of

[5] John Rawls. "Two Concepts of Rules", *The Philosophical Review*, vol. 64 (1955), p. 27n.
[6] J. J. C. Smart. "Benevolence as an Overriding Attitude", *Australasian Journal of Philosophy*, vol. 55 (1977).
[7] Cf. Sir David Ross, *The Right and the Good* (Oxford: 1930), pp. 38–9.

readiness to break commitments, and it should be even more unsettling to be such a person. A consequentialist can recognize this. There are good consequences attached to having an attitude of not thinking about the consequences of keeping one's commitments, except in extreme circumstances. Thus there is a very plausible consequentialist form of D1b. Is there a plausible non-consequentialist form? If the world were such that promise keeping and other forms of fidelity to commitments brought about misery or other bad consequences, would we (or should we) still prize such a character? A world as different from ours as that one would have to be is hard to imagine; but it seems plausible to say that in such a world virtues that we now regard as central would come (and should come) to seem anachronistic. *D1c.* This line of deviation from AC represents a moderate egoism. Much philosophical ink has been spilled about the more extreme forms of egoism, but they are not represented here: arguably they are not moral views, but rather the refusal to enter into moral reflection or judgment at all. There is no arguing with a person who says simply "I want what I want"; such a person may mimic the terminology of moral discussion, and say, "My interests ought to be considered above everyone else's"; but we can agree with Hume that to make a genuine moral judgment is to make an implicit appeal for the agreement of others (an appeal which thus must rest on impersonally statable considerations), and with Hare that moral judgments are subject to the logical requirement of universalizability. The moderate egoism of D1c passes these tests.

One can consistently, of course, prefer one's own interests to those of others as long as one accords the same right to others. It is frequently pointed out, indeed, that some policy along these lines will have better consequences than a policy of single-minded, continuous altruism. We are much better equipped, the argument runs, to look out for our own interests than to look out for those of others; indeed, others may not always appreciate our unflinching concern. This leads to a common sense policy which many well-meaning people would assent to: one looks out for one's own interests first, and assumes that others will do likewise, but in cases in which actions look likely to have major effects on the well-being of others one's policy is to try to give everyone's interests equal weight.

There are two difficulties with this. One is that it is

no longer possible (if it ever was) to seal off areas of one's life in which one's actions have a drastic effect on others from other areas of life. One always could be doing more to help famine victims in poor countries: as Glover points out, even the decision to read a novel or buy a concert ticket is a decision not to spend the time working for (or not to donate the money to) Oxfam.[8] This suggests that some forms of consequentialism, including classic utilitarianism, might entail a very heavy moral burden on us: Loren Lomasky has pointed out the existence of "moral black holes," examples of which are aged parents and Cambodia. His argument is that zealous utilitarianism would make anything like normal human life impossible.[9]

A second, independent difficulty is that, even if we maintain some shred of a distinction between areas of life in which our actions have some direct, immediate, and visible effect on others, and areas in which our actions do not, it is not clear that in the former areas one can be expected to give everyone's interests entirely equal weight. Andrew Oldenquist has brought out this difficulty very effectively, in the course of an argument against Hare's universalizability principle.[10] Oldenquist argues that I can accept "I ought to save my child first" without being logically committed (if we now imagine Harry alone near the two drowning children) to accepting "Harry ought to save his child first." My own view is that the universalizability principle survives this attack. "I ought to save my child first" can be glossed as meaning roughly the combination of "I very much want to save my child first (and indeed would be inhuman if I did not)" with "I have a perfect right to save my child first." The universalizability principle tells me that Harry, also, has a perfect right to save his child first, but it cannot be said that, in the situation envisioned, I very much want him to do it, and thus "I ought to save my child first" does not logically commit me to "Harry ought to save his child first."

Nevertheless Oldenquist has an important point. We commonly organize our sense of responsibility so that we feel more responsible to family and friends than to strangers, to those nearby than to those far away. We do not commonly give everyone's interests exactly equal weight, even in important matters. At the center of most people's concern is themselves, and even well-meaning people consider it proper to give their own interests preference even in some situations

[8] Jonathan Glover, *Causing Death and Saving Lives* (Harmondsworth, 1977), pp. 92-112, 292-3.
[9] Loren Lomasky, "A Refutation of Utilitarianism", paper read at the University of Connecticut, October 1979.
[10] Andrew Oldenquist, "Universalizability and the Self", unpublished manuscript.

in which the results for others will be important. An example would be the case in which two people are competing for a job, and the loser will be unemployed, or the case in which two people are competing for an attractive marriage partner and the loser will be depressed and lonely.

There is a consequentialist solution to both difficulties. One has to choose attitudes and policies with an eye to consequences, and in reckoning consequences we must take into account human psychology, and especially our own psychology. Most of us are capable of more self-denial than we exercise, but few of us have an infinite capacity. Consequentialist policies have to be workable over the long haul, which means that they can ask only what can be sustained. But we must carefully limit the context, and also the degree of preference. We may think it right that a man save his child before another, but wrong if he save his child from injury before saving another from death, and wrong also if he gives the child preference in a banking or hiring decision. It seems appropriate for people to compete freely for jobs or for marriage partners, but there are cases in which we might judge that competition for scarce resources such as food ought to be limited. The phrase that comes to mind is "the rules of the game": standards for when and how it is appropriate to pursue one's private interest. The present rules of the game may work badly, as in the Jean Renoir film with that title; it is also true that the rules of the game evolve, and that we are shocked by practices, such as slavery and the subjection of women, which failed to shock Aristotle and many other worthies of the past. It is reasonable to ask what practices which similarly seem normal and acceptable to us might (justifiably) shock people in the future.

The point is that a consequentialist can consistently maintain (a) that it is useful for us to make a rough distinction between moments and occasions in which we are highly accountable for the effects of our actions on others and moments in which we are not, and (b) that it is useful for us to adopt policies that encourage some degree of preference for our own interests and the interests of those close to us in some kinds of circumstances. A consequentialist can maintain that some ways of drawing the line between the self-regarding and other-regarding parts of our lives have better consequences than others, and thus are to be preferred; a consequentialist can make a similar claim about some policies circumscribing the kind and degree of preference for our own interests as opposed to others, and thus is not committed to endorsing the policies actually followed by most

decent and well-meaning people nowadays. All of this is to say that the line of deviation from AC under discussion can be given a very plausible consequentialist basis. If a policy of continuous single-minded altruism is impossible for the very great majority of people to sustain, and if it would tend to deprive people of the motivation for various kinds of achievement, then there are consequentialist reasons for recommending policies that incorporate some degree of moderate egoism.

Are there plausible non-consequentialist grounds for recommending moderate egoism? The most plausible contender might involve removing the burden of proof from moderate egoism, by regarding altruism as a deviation (requiring special justification) from egoism rather than the reverse. This might be done by someone who claims that individual rights provide a justification for pursuing one's own interest which make this kind of behavior a norm rather than a deviation. This presupposes however that there is a plausible non-consequentialist account of rights; I shall indicate shortly grounds for scepticism.

Because of limitations of space I shall merely sketch consequentialist lines of argument for D2a, D2b, and D2c.

First answer *D2a.* Some consequentialists would argue that it is a useful policy to adhere to generally good moral rules even in cases in which the probable consequences are slightly worse than those of one or more alternatives. It might also be a useful policy in relation to certain moral rules that we not even be prepared to consider whether a case at hand is an exception to them: such a policy would protect us from slippery slopes and the danger of corruption. Thus there are plausible consequentialist versions of D2a. Is there a plausible non-consequentialist version? Such a version would seem to require that there is an inherent power in moral rules, at least in some moral rules, so that regardless of consequences one should have a policy of adhering to them. At this point there are two alternatives for the non-consequentialist. The non-consequentialist can claim that moral rules have this power because they *are* moral rules: that it is bound up with respect for moral rules as such. Or the non-consequentialist can claim that *some* moral rules (say those governing loss of life) have this power because they are especially important.

The first alternative seems inseparable from rigorism. If moral rules do have exceptions, it is hard to resist the view that our judgments of consequences determine which cases count as exceptions. But rigorism can be made plausible only if those who believe that there can be a valid, exception-free moral code actually produce such a code. So far this has not been done.

The second alternative has different problems. Why should some moral rules have a special claim? It is hard to resist the view that this is because what they govern is important, and that this importance is intimately connected with the dangers of loose conduct with regard to them.

Let us turn to *D2b*. It has been noted by a number of writers that there are good consequentialist reasons not only for recognizing rights, but also for regarding rights as in some sense "trump cards."[11] Thus if it is objected to AC that it can lead to violations of rights that ought to be respected, a consequentialist can agree and can furnish a consequentialist basis for the objection.

Is there a plausible non-consequentialist version of D2b? In order for there to be one, two conditions would have to be met. One is that a non-consequentialist way of demonstrating what someone's rights are would have to be produced. This is perhaps less easy than it might seem. It seems obvious to us that certain beings have certain rights in certain situations; but not only is this intuitive obviousness the result of a historical process, as is the concept of "rights" itself (a relative newcomer as moral concepts go), but also it is very hard to disengage the intuitive obviousness from the fact that recognition of certain rights has very good consequences. One has to offer more here than intuitive appeal.

Secondly, a plausible non-consequentialist version of D2b would require that certain rights would obtain, and should be respected, even in a world in which recognition of and respect for such rights did not have generally good consequences. Thus, it might appear, the crucial test between consequentialist and non-consequentialist versions of D2b involves thought experiments with worlds in which recognition of and respect for certain rights no longer had good consequences. However such thought experiments are not always easy to construct, and there are reasons to have doubts about their reliability in some cases. John Stuart Mill denied in *On Liberty* that there was a general human right to have children, and (whatever one thinks of this in relation to our world) one can certainly imagine a world in which the consequences of recognizing such a right are bad and most of us would not want to recognize it. But it is far more difficult to imagine, in adequate detail, a world in which the consequences of recognizing a general human right to have enough to eat, or not to be

tortured, would be bad. Such a world would be so different from ours that it is open to question whether it would be compatible with what we think of as human life. Furthermore, even if we could imagine such a world adequately, our responses to it and judgments of it will reflect inevitably the outlooks and mental sets of people who are used to our world, in which deep abhorrence of certain practices has good consequences.

All of this is to say that we may not be in a good position to decide between consequentialist and non-consequentialist versions of D2b by means of thought experiments. But there are reasons, all the same, for linking the validity of rights to consequences. We can see this if we look at instances in which the consequences of not waiving a particular right are overwhelmingly disastrous. These instances are difficult to imagine but less difficult to imagine than the worlds in which fundamental human rights would lack utility, in that all one is required to imagine is a peculiar set of circumstances, not a peculiar context of human life. Virtually no one holds that there is any right which ought to be respected in a case in which a clear result would be the destruction of all or virtually all human life; although specific cases of such a stark choice are bound to sound fanciful, and in any case should not be dwelt upon. (A fascination with extreme cases that provide exceptions is dangerous in that it promotes a tendency to look for exceptions in less extreme cases.) There are good consequentialist grounds, outlined by Mill and others, for treating certain rights as being, for practical purposes, generally valid. It is hard to see what the non-consequentialist grounds would be, especially if it is conceded that there is no right that obtains in all imaginable cases. It is valuable that we recognize rights; but it must be said also that these are the sophisticated modern counterparts of taboos, and perhaps all one is left with, after analysis, is a *feeling* of something glowing with mysterious force. A consequentialist can account for why we do, and should, have this feeling.

We come now to *D2c*. This line of deviation inevitably involves the most direct appeal to "intuition." The claim is that an action which AC would seem to endorse in fact is wrong, and that it is wrong not because—or perhaps not just because—it violates a moral rule or someone's rights, but rather is wrong intrinsically.

But any reasonable person will take as a start, not an end, to reflection the sense that an action is

[11] Cf. especially D. W. Haslett, "The General Theory of Rights", *Social Theory and Practice*, vol. 5 (1980), also David Lyons, "Human Rights and the General Welfare", *Philosophy and Public Affairs*, vol. 6 (1977).

intrinsically wrong. One may reasonably begin by inquiring into the roots of this sense. Does it simply mirror the moral indoctrination one received while young, or the current attitudes of one's social class or caste? Is it instead (or also) connected with some deep and less parochial tendency, such as the tendency to avoid producing suffering in others? The answers to questions like these should determine the weight one gives to one's moral first responses. If this is so, then we can arrive at the following generalization: that an action endorsed by AC seems intrinsically wrong counts against AC only if the sense of intrinsic wrongness grows out of tendencies of thought that generally have good consequences. If the tendencies of thought that lead someone to regard an action endorsed by AC as intrinsically wrong are not themselves useful tendencies, then it is hard to see why the sense of wrongness they yield cannot be dismissed as misleading and based on prejudice.

II

Let us turn now to the positive justification of Proposition C. The argument thus far has been that plausible deviations from the simplest form of consequentialism (AC) all have consequentialist grounds. This argument, while general, is still defensive in character. It shows how consequentialism can accommodate likely objections, so that lines of thought which seem to start out as non-consequentialist take their most plausible development in a consequentialist form. But this is not enough. We need some positive argument for consequentialism. This in turn requires some clarification of the epistemological status of consequentialism. Consequentialism is an ethical theory (in a familiar but very broad sense of the word "theory"); but that by itself tells us very little unless we know what an ethical theory is, and how it may be similar to, or different from, scientific theories.

Recent work in philosophy of science can help us here. It has increased awareness that scientific theories have many functions besides that of enabling us to make predictions. Scientific theories also help to shape our perceptions, so that the character of the data which may support or disconfirm a scientific theory is itself influenced by that theory. We also now know that scientific theories are typically more sinuous than used to be thought, so that disconfirmation of a theory is often a more complicated job than that of finding

one counter-example. Might consequentialism have features somewhat similar to these?

The sinuousness of consequentialism has been illustrated by much of the discussion of this paper. We can see better the role of consequentialism in shaping the character of ethical judgments (which in turn might seem to confirm or disconfirm it) if we look more closely at the relation of consequentialism to common sense morality. The ethical education of almost all of us begins with general rules. A consequentialist can endorse this as in fact the most useful starting point in ethical education.[12] But at a certain point a thoughtful person may come to realize, as Aristotle and Confucius realized long ago, that no collection of general moral rules will be by themselves adequate to all moral tasks. The record of success gives us no reason to think that casuistry can fill the gap, or that someone will be able to spell out a valid moral code composed completely of exceptionaless general rules.

This leaves us with the question of what we are to do in cases in which various abnormal factors give us a sense that familiar moral rules might not be adequate to tell us what ought to be done. Both Aristotle and the Confucians speak of judgment, sharpened by experience. Even from a consequentialist point of view, choosing the right alternative can be more like an art than a science, so that it does seem appropriate here to speak of judgment, and to comment on the value of experience, or the need for discernment. But we still may wonder what experience is supposed to teach us, and what we are supposed to discern.

A reasonable answer may depend on the case. In looking at any case, we may want to ponder the effect of an action on our own character. Even the character of an Aristotelian philosopher or a Confucian sage is not entirely static; new habits or temptations may be possible; and such a person can attempt to gauge the psychological results of having done a certain kind of thing. There may also be an assumption, based on a wide fund of experience, that there is a natural harmony between a certain kind of character and the social world: that the normal way of acting of a philosopher or sage will produce more happiness than unhappiness for others, and will strengthen social trust. On this basis, the philosopher or sage might be entitled to assume that the solution to a variety of moral problems will lie simply in one's acting in character, in being natural.[13] In difficult or especially problematic cases, sensitivity to others may be

---

[12] Cf. my "Inhibition", *Oxford Review of Education*, vol. 4 (1978).

[13] Cf. my "Confucius and the Problem of Naturalness", *Philosophy East and West*, vol. 18 (1968).

required. We may need to know how likely it is that those around us will be hurt or scarred by things we might do, or conversely how encouraging or strengthening our actions are likely to be. Finally, if we are in a position of political responsibility, we will need to know the likely effect on our community, state, or society of various courses of action. For this we need a sense of how others are likely to react to our action, and what effects their actions in turn are likely to have. We also need a sense of what the likely effects of our policies will be when they are imitated by others.

These considerations are consequentialist. They involve estimation of the consequences of sets of attitudes, of policies or of actions, with attention paid to the development of our own character, the feelings and adjustments of others, and the broader social consequences. Someone who is not in any formal and reflective way a consequentialist will still want to pay attention to all this, and to decide difficult moral cases accordingly. An explicit consequentialism can help to make consideration of consequences systematic and comprehensive.

To sum up this part of the argument: a large part of the value and justification of consequentialism as an ethical theory resides in its heuristic role, in guiding estimation of ethically problematic situations, organizing ethical data, and solving problems. One does not want to overstate this role. As an ethical theory consequentialism is highly general. In much of the ordinary conduct of life we need explicit appeal to consequentialism no more than we need explicit reference to gravitational acceleration of heavy bodies while making decisions in baseball. But informally in problematic cases we look at consequences, and in especially difficult or important cases formal reliance on the theory may help us to know what we are doing.

The claim also is that consequentialism is heuristically very helpful, not that an intelligent and sincere consequentialist can solve all problems. It is frequently pointed out as a defect of consequentialism that, if it is true, there are many cases (especially cases in which what we do clearly will have important social consequences) in which no one is in a position to claim to know what the right choice is. In my view, that is a merit of consequentialism rather than a defect. In difficult cases we can judge more intelligently if we systematically estimate consequences, but to have a better chance of making the right decision

is not to be sure that one is making it. An ethical theory which tells people making such decisions that they can be sure their decisions are right is both false and dangerous.

Not only does consequentialism function well in the heuristic role one expects a theory to play, but also it functions better than any alternative. What indeed are the alternatives? Ethical common sense not bolstered by consequentialism leaves us merely with our inhibitions and our prejudices. Our inhibitions serve us well in cases of ordinary temptation to murder or to steal, etc.; but in difficult and unusual cases, we may well lack the flexibility that we ought to have. In such cases, as Confucius says, "Your honest countryman is the spoiler of morals."[14] One may try to give common sense morality depth and flexibility by reading into it, as Alan Donagan has done, a principle of respect for rational beings.[15] This is a very useful addition, and arguably with it common sense morality can rival consequentialism in dealing with cases in which the major worry is one of doing harm to, or violating the rights of, others. In many moral cases, though, the primary consideration is one of doing good, rather than avoiding harm. There, arguably, what Donagan calls the "Hebrew-Christian tradition", which provides the core of our common sense, is deficient. John Stuart Mill observes of Christian morality that "Its ideal is negative rather than positive; passive rather than active; innocence rather than nobleness; abstinence from evil rather than energetic pursuit of good; in its precepts (as has been well said) 'thou shalt not' predominates over 'thou shalt'."[16] This observation suggests that consequentialism fulfills the heuristic function of a theory better in an important range of cases than does common sense morality regarded as an implicit theory.

A word finally should be said about the interplay between ethical theory and our pretheoretical moral responses. An ethical theory which simply summarized or codified these responses would be about as useful as a scientific theory which simply summarized our ordinary perceptions. On the other hand, an ethical theory which as often as not ran counter to our pretheoretical moral responses would seem most implausible. Enough has been said to indicate that consequentialism falls at neither of these extremes. It harmonizes well with our general pretheoretical sense that we ought to be responsible for our actions, our policies, and our habits of mind, and that to be

[14] *The Analects of Confucius*, trans. W. E. Soothill (London, 1955), Book XVII, Chapter XIII, p. 193.
[15] Cf. Alan Donagan, *The Theory of Morality* (Chicago, 1977).
[16] J. S. Mill, *On Liberty*, ed. E. Rappaport (Indianapolis, 1978), Chapter II, para. 36, p. 47.

responsible is to be prepared to consider consequences. On the other hand, most forms of consequentialism yield a much stronger sense of our duties to those in need than we normally have. Jonathan Glover has very effectively brought out how consequentialist lines of thought could transform our sense of our moral responsibilities. Consequentialism can accom- plish this transformation partly because, like any good theory, it makes sense of tendencies of thought that have some pretheoretical appeal. By making sense of the way in which we look at the consequences of our actions, policies, and habits of mind, conse- quentialism makes it possible to give moral reflection a more coherent and systematic quality.

University of Connecticut

Received May 27, 1980

Part II
A Theory of the Right or the Good?

[2]

THE JOURNAL OF PHILOSOPHY

VOLUME LXXVI, NO. 9, SEPTEMBER 1979

UTILITARIANISM AND WELFARISM *

"SOME of the unacceptable features of utilitarianism," argues Bernard Williams, "are to be traced to its general character as a form of consequentialism." [1] In this paper I shall be concerned with those features which *cannot* be traced to consequentialism. The intention is to provide a critique of utilitarianism without disputing the acceptability of consequentialism.

The scope of such a critique will, naturally, depend on how narrowly the consequences are characterized and how broadly utility is defined. It is possible to define things in a way that makes a teleologist necessarily a utilitarian in a broad sense, as in the following statement of David Lyons: "Teleologists claim that the rightness of acts depends solely upon their utility, that is, upon their contribution towards intrinsically good states of affairs." [2] In contrast, in this paper I shall be concerned with investigating the relationship between goodness of states of affairs and the utility characteristics of those states. Utility will be taken to stand for a person's conception of his own well-being, and although this would still permit alternative interpretations in terms of "pleasure" and "desire," there is no definitional link with the "goodness of states of affairs." That link will be treated as an open moral issue.

In section 1 various utilitarian structures will be examined. A principle that seems to be shared by all variants of utilitarianism (such as act and rule utilitarianism) identifies the goodness of a

---

* I have greatly benefited from many illuminating discussions with Derek Parfit, from the comments on an earlier draft by Ronald Dworkin and Richard Hare, and from helpful remarks by Jonathan Glover, Martin Hollis, Frederic Schick, and Charles M. Taylor.
[1] "A Critique of Utilitarianism," in Williams and J. J. C. Smart, *Utilitarianism: For and Against* (New York: Cambridge, 1973), p. 79. Williams explains that in this essay he is "particularly concerned with" the features referred to.
[2] *Forms and Limits of Utilitarianism* (New York: Oxford, 1965), Preface.

0022-362X/79/7609/0463$02.70

state of affairs (or outcome) with the sum total of individual utilities in that state, and this will be called "outcome utilitarianism." Outcome utilitarianism will be itself factorized into more elementary requirements, which will be examined in turn in the sections that follow.

Section II is concerned with "sum-ranking," i.e., with the *addition* of individual utilities as the appropriate method of aggregation. Section III will deal with "welfarism," i.e., the principle that the goodness of a state of affairs depends ultimately on the set of individual utilities in that state, and—more demandingly—can be seen as an increasing function of that set. Welfarism implies that any two states of affairs that are identical in terms of individual utility characteristics must be judged to be equally good no matter how different they are in nonutility respects, and also that any state that has more utility for someone and no less utility for anyone in comparison with another state is a better state than the other. This last characteristic is sometimes called "Paretianism."

A weak version of Paretianism requires that if one state has more utility for *everyone* than another, then it is a better state; this may be called "weak Paretianism." [3] Section IV is devoted to a critique of weak Paretianism, and it is argued that the principle deserves rejection in its general form. Since weak Paretianism is a mild version of welfarism, this consolidates the critique of welfarism.

I. OUTCOME UTILITARIANISM AND COMPLEX UTILITARIAN STRUCTURES

Take act utilitarianism. This is the morality that says that, in choosing one among various alternative acts, one should choose an act that yields at least as high a sum total of utilities as any other alternative act. This assertion can be derived from combining the following two principles:

Act Consequentialism: An action α is right if and only if the state of affairs x resulting from α is at least as good as each of the alternative states of affairs that would have resulted respectively from the alternative feasible acts.

Outcome Utilitarianism: Any state of affairs x is at least as good as an alternative state of affairs y if and only if the sum total of individual utilities in x is at least as large as the sum total of individual utilities in y.

Act consequentialism establishes a correspondence between the rightness of acts and the goodness of resulting states of affairs (in-

---

[3] See Kenneth J. Arrow, *Social Choice and Individual Values* (New York: Wiley, 2nd ed., 1963), p. 96.

cluding the value of the performed acts).[4] Outcome utilitarianism is a method of judging the goodness of states of affairs. Act consequentialism can be easily combined with a different "outcome morality," judging goodness of states of affairs in some other way, e.g., in terms of the utility levels of the worst-off group of persons.[5] Similarly, outcome utilitarianism can be combined with consequentialism applied to instruments other than acts, e.g., rules or motives, which can differ substantially from act consequentialism.

It could be asked whether outcome utilitarianism is a *moral* principle at all. On its own it asserts nothing about rightness of actions. But, combined with some way of relating actions to states of affairs (e.g., act consequentialism or rule consequentialism), it does contribute to the moral assessment of actions.

Even on its own, outcome utilitarianism asserts something of moral interest. If it is said that the volcanic eruption in Krakatoa in 1883, which killed many and made many others homeless, was a tragedy, and that the meteorite fall in Siberia in 1908 on uninhabited land was not a tragedy, something of substance is being asserted.[6] Outcome utilitarianism provides a sufficient basis for such judgments. It is, of course, possible to translate this into *as if* choices, e.g., if one *could have* chosen not to have the Krakatoa disaster, one *should have* chosen not to, but it does not seem very helpful to interpret the tragedy of Krakatoa as "ultimately" one

---

[4] Cf. "Standardly, the action will be right in virtue of its causal properties, of maximally conducing to good states of affairs . . . even a situation . . . in which the action itself possesses intrinsic value is one in which the rightness of the act is derived from the goodness of a certain state of affairs—the act is right *because* the state of affairs which consists in its being done is better than any other state of affairs accessible to the agent" (Williams, *op. cit.*, pp. 86/7).

[5] See John Rawls, *A Theory of Justice* (Cambridge, Mass.: Harvard, 1971), pp. 76/7. It may be important to mention here that, although Rawls considers the claim of the *minimal* element of utilities as against that of *total* utility, his "Difference Principle" focuses directly on the minimal availability of "social primary goods" and not on minimal utility as such.

[6] Although Sidgwick argued that "the Good investigated in Ethics is limited to Good in some degree attainable by human effort; accordingly knowledge of the end is sought in order to ascertain what actions are the right means to its attainment" [*The Method of Ethics* (London: Macmillan, 7th edition, 1907), p. 3], this is a statement on where the main interest in a principle like outcome utilitarianism would lie, and not a denial of its independent status. Indeed, Sidgwick made frequent use of outcome utilitarianism, even though he defined utilitarianism as "the ethical theory, that the conduct which under any given circumstances, is objectively right, is that which will produce the greatest amount of happiness on the whole" (411). In a different context, Sidgwick even asserted that "Bentham's dictum must be understood merely as making the conception of ultimate end precise . . . not as directly prescribing the rules of conduct by which this end will be best attained" (432).

of rightness of action. Similarly, intertemporal comparisons of "social welfare" based on, say, real national income,[7] are primarily judgments of states of affairs and not of actions.

It is possible to combine outcome utilitarianism with nonconsequentialist moralities, but I shall not explore that avenue in this paper, since the utilitarian approach is typically combined with some variant or other of consequentialism. Act consequentialism is perhaps the simplest case of consequentialism (and is sometimes taken to be the only proper case). Outcome utilitarianism provides a way of assessing alternative "histories" of what can happen, and for a consequentialist approach of any variety, that must be the ultimate basis of evaluation. But different entities—such as acts, or rules, or motivations, or dispositions—can be varied to influence such "histories."

A utilitarian moral structure consists of the central element of outcome utilitarianism combined with some consequentialist method of translating judgments of outcomes into judgments of actions. The most comprehensive consequentialist structure would require that the *combination* of all influencing variables be so chosen that the result is the *best feasible* state of affairs according to outcome utilitarianism. However, the literature on utilitarian ethics displays a preference for dealing with one influencing variable at a time, e.g., one act from a set of acts, or one rule from a set of rules. This may be called "single-influence consequentialism," of which act utilitarianism, rule utilitarianism, etc., are special cases with the influencing variable being, respectively, an act or a rule, etc. There are various strategic issues to be considered in evaluating the efficacy of these different utilitarian moral structures, and it is easy to construct examples such that each of these limited structures fails to achieve the best outcome that could have resulted from a comprehensive structure.[8] But in this paper I shall not go into these strategic issues, since my main concern is with outcome utilitarianism as an outcome morality.

---

[7] Cf. my "Real National Income," *Review of Economic Studies*, XLIII, 1 (February 1976): 19–39.

[8] For examples of the failure of act utilitarianism to deliver the best outcome, see Allan Gibbard, "Rule Utilitarianism: A Merely Illusory Alternative?," *Australasian Journal of Philosophy*, XLIII, 2 (August 1965): 211–219, and John Harsanyi, "Rule Utilitarianism and Decision Theory," *Erkenntnis*, XI (1977). I have tried to argue elsewhere that such failures apply not merely to act utilitarianism but to all single-influence consequentialism, including some versions of rule utilitarianism, while other versions of rule utilitarianism can lead to sub-optimal outcomes for other—clearly specifiable—reasons ("Welfare and Rights," text of Hägerström Lectures, delivered at Uppsala University in April 1978, to be published).

The translation from the "best outcome" to the "right action" is affected not merely by such strategic considerations, but also by qualifications about what is or is not within a person's or an agent's control. For example, it may be possible to identify which type of "personal disposition" is most effective in achieving the best state of affairs according to the chosen outcome morality (in this case, outcome utilitarianism), but this need not point immediately to a best course of action, since personal dispositions are not entirely controllable by the person in question.

This problem arises particularly sharply with what Robert Merrihew Adams has called "motive utilitarianism." There is little difficulty with his characterization of this as the theory that "one pattern of motivation is morally better than another to the extent that the former has more utility that the latter." [9] This is obtained by combining "outcome utilitarianism" with what we may call "motive consequentialism," i.e., single-influence consequentionalism applied to the set of possible motivations. [10] There is, however, more difficulty with his further characterization of motive utilitarianism as the theory that "the morally perfect person, on this view, would have the most useful desires, and have them in exactly the most useful strengths; he or she would have the most useful among the patterns of motivation that are causally possible for human beings" (470). One can indeed rank *motives* as such in terms of the combination of motive consequentialism and outcome utilitarianism, but this does not in itself yield a method of ranking *persons*, or identifying "the morally perfect person."

There are indeed two separate difficulties with using motive utilitarianism to rank persons in terms of "moral perfectness." First, the choice over motivation may not be in the person's control. As Adams points out, "motive utilitarianism is not about what motives one ought to foster and promote, or *try* to have, but about what motives one ought to *have*" (474). This is indeed so, but it is by no means obvious that one must accept the moral superiority of the *person* who happens to have the best motives "without really trying" over the person who does his damnedest best to develop the best motives. Second, even if the motives are entirely within

---

[9] "Motive Utilitarianism," this JOURNAL, LXXIII, 14 (Aug. 12, 1976): 467–481, p. 470.

[10] There is an additional issue, however, as to whether the motivation in question is that of a given person (which motivation of this person would lead to the best outcome *given* the motivations of the others?) or that of all members of the community (which motivation. if *shared* by members of this community, would lead to the best outcome?).

the person's control, it is arguable whether the rightness of the motive may be fully translatable into the goodness of the person. If, for example, it were to turn out that the motivation of merciless profit maximization happens, in fact, to produce the highest utility sum, though it would be clearly right in terms of motive utilitarianism to describe that as the best motivation, the judgment of the moral worth of the person capable of such ruthlessness would remain a separate issue, requiring a treatment of its own.

II. OUTCOME UTILITARIANISM AND SUM-RANKING

Since outcome utilitarianism is common to different varieties of utilitarianism, any criticism of outcome utilitarianism applies to all these variants.[11] I shall confine my discussion to only two types of difficulties with outcome utilitarianism, but they can be seen as applying respectively to two "weaker" requirements into which outcome utilitarianism can be factorized.

Welfarism: The judgment of the relative goodness of alternative states of affairs must be based exclusively on, and taken as an increasing function of, the respective collections of individual utilities in these states.

Sum-ranking: One collection of individual utilities is at least as good as another if and only if it has at least as large a sum total.

It is easily checked that welfarism and sum-ranking together are exactly equivalent to outcome utilitarianism. I am concerned with sum-ranking in this section and will go into welfarism in the next. Sum-ranking can be criticized from the moral perspective of egalitarianism, and John Rawls's "Difference Principle" was partly a response to the characteristic of utilitarianism of being "indifferent as to how a constant sum of benefits is distributed" (*A Theory of Justice*, p. 77). That sum-ranking is completely insensitive to the inequality of utilities is obvious enough. I have tried to discuss elsewhere the unpalatable implications of sum-ranking,[12] and rather than repeat that discussion I shall confine myself to a few additional remarks only.

First, it is possible to define individual utilities in such a way that the only way of aggregating them is by summation. By confining his attention to utilities defined in that way, John Harsanyi

---

11 I am not concerned in this paper with the problem of population being a variable, so that the distinction between "classical utilitarianism" and "average utilitarianism" does not arise.

12 *On Economic Inequality* (New York: Oxford, 1973), pp. 15-22.

has denied the credibility of "nonlinear social welfare functions."[13] That denial holds perfectly well for the utility measures to which Harsanyi confines his attention, but has no general validity outside that limited framework.[14] Thus, sum-ranking remains an open issue to be discussed in terms of its moral merits—and in particular, our concern for equality of utilities—and cannot be "thrust upon" us on grounds of consistency.[15]

Second, if interpersonal comparisons of utility are given only normative interpretations, without any independent descriptive content, then it is possible to have a "dual" representation such that in terms of one representation the utility sum is maximized while in terms of the other representation the specified conditions of "equity" are met.[16] Although this remarkable result is of very considerable analytical interest, it does not resolve the conflict between sum-ranking and equity when utility comparisons do have *descriptive* content, as is assumed by the typical utilitarian.

Third, that great utilitarian, Henry Sidgwick, was himself acutely aware of the fact that "the Utilitarian formula seems to supply no answer" to the question "whether any mode of distributing a given quantum of happiness is better than any other" (*The Method of Ethics*, 416). He declared his support for "pure equality" as "the only one which does not need a special justification" (417; see also 447). This would go against sum-ranking and also against outcome utilitarianism, but Sidgwick did not seem to entertain any possibility of trade-offs between the size of the utility sum and the equality of the utility distribution. Indeed, one gets the impression that the

---

[13] "Nonlinear Social Welfare Functions: Do Welfare Economists Have a Special Exemption from Bayesian Rationality?" *Theory and Decision* VI, 3 (August 1975): 311–332.

[14] See my "Welfare Inequalities and Rawlsian Axiomatics," *Theory and Decision*, VII, 4 (October 1976): 243–262; reprinted in R. Butts and J. Hintikka eds., *Foundational Problems in the Special Sciences* (Boston: Reidel, 1977).

[15] For some moral arguments on the two sides, see Harsanyi, "Nonlinear Social Welfare Functions: A Rejoinder to Professor Sen," and my "Non-linear Social Welfare Functions: A Reply to Professor Harsanyi," in Butts and Hintikka, eds., *op. cit.* For the axiomatic structure of "utilitarianism" (in fact, of outcome utilitarianism), see C. d'Aspremont and L. Gevers, "Equity and the Informational Basis of Collective Choice," *Review of Economic Studies*, XLIV (1977); R. Deschamps and Gevers, "Leximin and Utilitarian Rules: A Joint Characterization," *Journal of Economic Theory*, XVII (1978); Eric Maskin, "A Theorem on Utilitarianism" *Review of Economic Studies*, XLV (1978); Kevin Roberts, "Interpersonal Comparability and Social Choice Theory," mimeographed, 1977, forthcoming in *Review of Economic Studies*.

[16] See Peter Hammond, "Dual Interpersonal Comparisons of Utility and the Welfare Economics of Income Distribution," *Journal of Public Economics*, VII (1977).

strict ordering of the sum total would have lexicographic priority over the consideration of equality in Sidgwick's system, which could make the violation of sum-ranking very marginal indeed. The "classical utilitarian," as Rawls observed, "appeals to equality only to break ties" (77). It is not surprising that people who argue for equality don't find this good enough.

Finally, an important question on distributional equity concerns the correspondence between our attitudes toward two kinds of distribution: between different persons, and between different time-periods in the life of the same person. Utilitarians have the same attitude to both, believing that (i) equality of utility distribution between persons has no more intrinsic value than equality of utility distribution at different points of time for the same person, and (ii) that value is negligible (used only for breaking ties, if it is used at all). Derek Parfit has forcefully argued that this utilitarian attitude becomes more plausible—though by no means obligatory—if we reject what he calls "the simple view" about the nature of personal identity.[17] On this view, which he believes that most of us implicitly hold, personal identity is a peculiarly deep further fact, over and above the facts of bodily or psychological continuity. I accept that personal identity may be less deep than we commonly assume, and agree that the effect of realizing this is to weaken the claim that "a person's burden, while it can be morally outweighed by benefit to him, cannot ever be outweighed by mere benefits to others" (Parfit, 1973, p. 156). My difficulty with Parfit's argument that the rejection of the "simple view" provides some defense for the utilitarian unconcern with *inter*personal distribution arises partly from the belief that the moral intuitions dealing with *intra*personal distribution which are referred to in this defense depend heavily on the acceptance of the "simple view." When we reject the "simple view," the case for revising our moral beliefs on *intra*personal distribution is very strong. Thus, we could move *toward* (i) but *against* (ii). This would provide a different way, unlike that of the utilitarians, of making our attitudes to *inter*personal and *intra*personal distribution correspond closely to each other.

Even in terms of moral beliefs that can be found among people who take the "simple view," it is, in fact, not the case that no importance is attached to *intra*personal distributions. The tragedy of

17 "Later Selves and Moral Principles," in A. Montefiore, ed., *Philosophy and Personal Relations* (London: Routledge, 1973). See also his "Personal Identity," *Philosophical Review*, LXXX, 1 (January 1971): 3-27, and "Against Prudence," mimeographed 1977, ch. III.

King Lear's fate is not thought to be effectively blunted because Lear was unusually fortunate in the earlier parts of his long life. Similarly, the typical economic judgment on the undesirability of "poverty" or "inequality" looks at a "snapshot picture" of the economy at a point of time, and the poverty of a person is not weighed up or down in terms of the deal that he has got in the past or is expected to get in the future. I am not arguing that these judgments will be fully vindicated by further moral reflection, but only that it is not true that there is a general acceptance of the moral irrelevance of *intra*personal inequality. And this is already the case even for those who take the "simple view" of personal identity which Parfit attacks. The "equilibrium" moral beliefs if we reject that view may well involve further emphasis being put on *intra*personal distribution.

III. WELFARISM AS OUTCOME MORALITY

I turn now to welfarism, which is the other—and in some ways, more fundamental—element in simple utilitarianism. This can be seen as imposing an "informational constraint" in making moral judgments about alternative states of affairs.[18] If all the personal-utility information about two states of affairs that can be known is known, then they can be judged without any other information about these states. This need not stop us from using non-utility information as "surrogates" for utility information when utility information is scarce (e.g., using the availability of "primary social goods" as an index of utility in one—apocryphal—interpretation of Rawls's approach), but the non-utility information then has no status of its own independent of the indications it gives of the utility picture.

A very general approach within the structure of welfarism is that of maximizing the sum of some particular concave transformation of each person's utilities. This approach has been used by James Mirrlees.[19] The kind of egalitarian considerations we discussed in the last section can be easily accommodated within the Mirrleesian approach, of which simple utilitarianism and the utility-based ver-

---

[18] See my "On Weights and Measures: Informational Constraints in Social Welfare Analysis," *Econometrica*, XLV (1977). "Welfarism" is defined there a bit less demandingly, viz., moral goodness of states being a function just of the *n*-tuple of individual utilities but not *necessarily* an *increasing* function. The informational constraint operates nevertheless.

[19] "An Exploration in the Theory of Optimal Income Taxation," *Review of Economic Studies*, XXXVIII (1971). See also A. B. Atkinson, "On the Measurement of Inequality," *Journal of Economic Theory*, II (1970).

sion of the Rawlsian difference principle will be special cases.[20] But welfarism also covers cases that are not within the Mirrleesian approach, e.g., judging the welfare of the society in terms of the utility of the "median" person in the utility ranking. This section is concerned with a critique of welfarism as such, and in the arguments to be presented nothing more will be used than the informational constraint asserting the *sufficiency* of utility information for judgments of states of affairs.

It is perhaps also worth remarking that welfarism is, in an important way, less demanding that the Aristotelian notion of "eudaimonism," which has been recently discussed by Bernard Williams and others. Eudaimonism has clear affinities with welfarism, but they are not the same, since eudaimonism is concerned with judging *actions*, whereas welfarism is an approach for judging *states of affairs*. "To say . . . that the system is *eudaimonistic* is to say that what it regards as the desirable feature of actions is that they should increase or maximize people's *happiness*" (*op. cit.*, 79). This characterization of eudaimonism is in line with Aristotle's own action-centered introduction to the subject: "let us discuss what is that which is aimed at by politics and what is the highest of all goods achievable by *action*." [21] On this characterization of eudaimonism, it corresponds to welfarism in a way similar to the correspondence between consequentialist utilitarian structures and outcome utilitarianism. But it is also clear that Aristotle was, in fact, greatly concerned with examining the claims of what we have been calling welfarism, in much the same way as someone may be concerned with outcome utilitarianism as a basis for complex utilitarian structures.

Welfarism is essentially an informational constraint for moral judgments about states of affairs. In order to scrutinize it, we may

[20] See also Arrow's "Some Ordinalist-Utilitarian Notes on Rawls's Theory of Justice," this JOURNAL, LXX, 9 (May 10, 1973): 245–263, and 13: 422; in which this entire approach is called "utilitarian." Arrow is, thus, led to the view that the Rawlsian maximin is a "limiting case" of utilitarianism. For the cardinal utility framework underlying the use of utilitarianism, this is, strictly speaking, inaccurate, since the strictly concave *exponential* transformations considered by Arrow are not permissible. Arrow's statement applies, thus, to the class of additive social-welfare functions rather than to utilitarianism as such. On the particular form of the limiting case (i.e., whether pure maximin *or* lexicographic maximin should prevail as the degree concavity is taken to the limit), see Hammond, "A Note on Extreme Inequality Aversion," *Journal of Economic Theory*, XI (1975).

[21] *The Nichomachean Ethics*, translated by H. G. Apostle (Dordrecht: Reidel, 1975), p. 3.

consider *two* pairs (x,y) and (a,b) of states of affairs which have *identical* utility information (x has the same as a and y has the same as b), but differ in other respects. Welfarism would require that x must be ranked vis-à-vis y in exactly the same way as a is ranked vis-à-vis b, irrespective of the non-utility descriptions.

Consider first the pair (x,y). Let there be two persons r (rich) and p (poor), and let the difference between x and y rest in the fact that in x there is no redistributive taxation, whereas in y some money obtained by taxing r has been passed on to p, even though r continues to remain richer than p. The utility values of the two persons in the two states are the following:

		states	
		x (no tax)	y (redistributive tax)
utilities	r	10	8
	p	4	7

Outcome utilitarianism must rank y above x. So must the utility-based variant of the Rawlsian difference principle. So must all criteria that combine considerations of *total* utility with the *equality* of utility distribution.[22] But this isn't what I am concerned with here, since my focus must be on the correspondence between the ranking of two pairs, of which (x,y) is one.

For considering states of affairs a and b, let r be a romantic dreamer and p a miserable policeman. In b the policeman tortures the dreamer; in a he does not. The dreamer has a happy disposition ("the future is ours") and also happens to be rich, in good health, and resilient, while the policeman is morose, poor, ill, and frustrated, getting his simple pleasures out of torturing. The utility values for p and r happen to be the same as in x and y.

		states	
		a (no torture)	b (torture of r by p)
utilities	r	10	8
	p	4	7

Welfarism leaves us free to rank a over b or the other way round (or as indifferent), just as it leaves us free to rank x vis-à-vis y in

---

[22] A class of such synthetic criteria have been investigated by C. Blackorby and D. Donaldson, "Utility vs. Equity: Some Plausible Quasi-orderings," *Journal of Public Economics*, VI (1977).

either way, when we consider these rankings separately. However, it requires that *x* and *y* be ranked *in exactly the same way* as *a* and *b*, respectively. That is, welfarism would insist that the state of affairs with redistributive taxation (*y*) is better than that without taxation (*x*) *if and only if* the state of affairs with the torture (*b*) is better than that without torture (*a*). Many people would, however, hold that the case involving redistributive taxation is better (i.e., *y* *is* better than *x*) but the case involving torture is not (i.e., *b* is not better than *a*). One is free to hold such a view only by rejecting welfarism. To discriminate between the two pairs would bring in non-utility information, which can have no role of its own under welfarism.

Before I consider the example further, I would like to point out certain claims that welfarism does *not* require us to make. It is important to emphasize the claims that are not being made if we are to avoid being influenced against welfarism through misunderstanding of its content.

First, to say that the state of affairs with torture is better than that without it, is not the same as saying that the policeman *p* *should* undertake this torture. That would be a judgment about actions, not about states of affairs as such, and the link between the two must depend on whether a consequentialist view is taken, and even if consequentialism were accepted, it would depend on the *version* of consequentialism to be used. To say that the state of affairs with torture is better does not even amount to asserting that the policeman would not be acting wrongly by indulging in his simple pleasures. (An act consequentialist who accepts welfarism—for brevity, an "act welfarist"—must do this translation if this torture has no other consequences, but a welfarist need not be an act consequentialist.)

Second, to say that the state of affairs with torture is better than the one without it, does not even remotely imply that the policeman is being a *good man* in torturing the romantic dreamer. Indeed, even an act consequentialist does not have to translate the judgment about states of affairs into a judgment about the goodness of the person undertaking the action in question. Indeed, an act consequentialist who supports both taxation and torture in the two cases as respectively the "right" actions, is not even obliged to accept the torture as "good action," if he characterizes "good action" as "what a good man would do, even if not right." [23]

23 R. M. Hare, "Ethical Theory and Utilitarianism," in H. D. Lewis, ed., *Contemporary British Philosophy*, IV (London: Allen & Unwin, 1976), p. 126.

If we find the welfarist position unacceptable, we have to make sure that this finding does not arise from a misunderstanding of it as identified with these other claims. This is particularly important if we are to avoid falling into the trap of what R. M. Hare calls "the commonest trick of the opponents of utilitarianism." Hare distinguishes between "level-1" thinking at an immediate intuitive level and "level-2" thinking at a more critical level. "Level-1" principles are for use in "practical moral thinking especially under conditions of stress," and "they have to be general enough to be impartable by education (including self-education), and to be 'of ready application in the emergency'," while "level-2 principles are what would be arrived at by leisured moral thought in completely adequate knowledge of facts, as the right answer in a specific case" (122/3).

> The commonest trick of the opponents of utilitarianism is to take examples of such [level-2] thinking, usually addressed to fantastic cases, and confront them with what the ordinary man would think. It makes the utilitarian look like a moral monster. The anti-utilitarians have usually confined their own thought about moral reasoning (with fairly infrequent lapses which often go unnoticed) to what I am calling level-1, the level of everyday moral thinking of ordinary, often stressful, occasions in which information is sparse (123).

Hare's distinction between level-1 and level-2 thinking is clearly important, and one has to be careful that in evaluating applications of utilitarianism—more generally, of welfarism—that go against one's moral intuition, one is not being caught in the trap of the roughness of level-1 immediacy rather than exercising level-2 wisdom. Hare would presumably think that that is exactly what is happening in the taxation-and-torture correspondence, since he is persuaded that "the thinking of our archangel"—uncompromisingly level-2—will be of "a specific rule-utilitarian sort," which is "practically equivalent to universalistic act-utilitarianism"; this clearly will incorporate outcome utilitarianism. Departures from this would reflect, at best, "the thinking of ordinary people whom he [the archangel] has educated," reflecting "good general principles," which they use "in ordinary level-1 moral thinking especially in situations of stress" (124/5).

It seems a bit immodest to have to claim that one's rejection of welfarism does not reflect "the thinking of ordinary people" indulging in level-1 cogitation. But perhaps a few cautious defensive statements could be made.

First, there is little difficulty in accepting the proposition that *if* the "archangel" *were* utilitarian, he may encourage people to have a hostile attitude toward torture, since such an attitude can be an effective *means* to utilitarian ends. But that is not the same thing as saying that one's disapproval of torture arises *only* from such indirect reasons. Whether giving "equal weight to the equal interests of all the parties in a situation," to use Hare's formula (116), requires one to attach the same weight to a person's enjoyment of food or shelter or personal liberty as to his joy from torturing is surely subject to critical questioning. The utilitarian archangel, since he must accept outcome utilitarianism, has to put *b* (with torture) above *a* (without torture), even though, when it comes to choosing "general principles" for the "ordinary people," he will include a principle against torture as a good means to the utilitarian end. But an archangel who has not taken such a simple interpretation of giving "equal weight to equal interests" need not be a utilitarian, nor a welfarist. If one finds after "leisured moral thought" that one is unable to attach the same level of "urgency" [24] to utilities arising from different sources, this need not be put down as the result of some archangelic cunning in implanting moral education in pursuit of goals that do not discriminate among different sources of utility.

Second, to be of practical use, level-1 principles must be of rather simple kind, e.g., torture is always bad, or give "no weight at all or a negative weight" to such desires (see Hare, 122). Welfarism contradicts not only such straightforward rules, but also rather less simple principles; e.g., utility from torture should get less weight than utility from other sources (this weight can be positive, negative, or zero). If someone is inclined to take such a position, it is unlikely that all he is doing is to express his level-1 prejudice. Indeed one could even claim that to attach the same importance

---

[24] See T. M. Scanlon, "Preference and Urgency," this JOURNAL, LXXII, 19 (Nov. 6, 1975): 655–669. Note also that Rawls's specification of "the measurement of benefit" being in terms of "an index of social primary goods," including "rights, liberties and opportunities, income and wealth, and the social bases of self-respect," uses a notion of "urgency" that differs from intensities of utilities. The "difference principle" under this interpretation has the advantage of not being tied to welfarism (as the utility-based difference principle must be), and can discriminate between the cases of taxation (*x,y*) and torture (*a,b*). This is particularly important if one rejects the "priority" of Rawls's "principle of liberty" over his "difference principle" as untenable, since that priority is another way of distinguishing the two cases. For a powerful critique of that "priority" argument, see H. L. A. Hart, "Rawls on Liberty and Its Priority," *University of Chicago Law Review*, XL (1973); reprinted in Norman Daniels, ed., *Reading Rawls* (Oxford: Blackwell, 1975).

to all types of utility irrespective of source as a rough-and-ready principle has some appeal for intuitive level-1 thinking, but not at the critical level-2 when there is time and leisure to consider principles more complex than the simple welfarist rules such as the utilitarian rule.

Third, welfarism and outcome utilitarianism are directly concerned not with judging action, but with ranking *states of affairs*. This is, in a significant sense, at some distance from one's immediate intuitions on *action*, with which level-1 thinking must be primarily concerned. Since welfarism would not by itself assert— as explained earlier—in the example about taxation and torture that "policeman *p* will not be acting wrongly in torturing the romantic dreamer, if the redistributive taxation is justified," a denial of welfarism does not turn on this issue at all. Moral thinking about judgments on ordering states of affairs requires one to move some distance from attitudes toward actions as such, and would necessitate the use of one's critical faculty.

It is, however, possible that a person making a judgment on outcome utilitarianism or welfarism might not precisely understand what he is doing, and his revulsion at the policeman's *act* of torture at this level-1 thinking could be "infecting" his judgment in ordering the states of affairs.[25] In order to avoid this, the example can be somewhat changed so that neither party brings the situation about through some positive action. Let *r* be the rider of a motor cycle—joyful, rich, in good health and resilient—while *p* is a pedestrian—morose, poor, ill in health, and frustrated. In state *m* the rider gleefully goes by; in state *n* he falls inadvertently into a ditch, breaking his bike and getting bruised badly. The rider is worse off in *n* than in *m*, while the pedestrian, who has not caused the accident in any way, thoroughly enjoys the discomfiture and discomfort of the rider ("I could kill myself laughing looking at that crestfallen Angel!"). The utility values of *r* and *p* are the same in this case as in the earlier two cases.

	states	
	m (no accident)	*n* (accident)
r	10	8
p	4	7

utilities

[25] I am grateful to Derek Parfit for drawing my attention to this possibility. The example that follows, which tries to avoid any scope of such an "infection," owes much to my discussions with him.

Welfarism would require us to say that if the state of affairs with taxation (*y*) is better than the one without it (*x*), then the state of affairs with the rider in the ditch (*n*) is better than the one without the accident (*m*). If on reflection one would like to deny this—as I would—maintaining that one can distinguish between sources of utility in deciding on the moral weights to be put on them, there is no danger of this judgment being due to any "infection" from a level-1 judgment about acts like torture where one person inflicts harm on another, since no such act is involved.

It is perhaps worth emphasizing that a nonwelfarist view that suggests that "*m* may not be ranked vis-à-vis *n* in exactly the same way as *x* is ranked vis-à-vis *y*" need *not* be based on attaching *zero or negative* weight to the pedestrian *p*'s pleasure (because it arises from someone else's discomfort or discomfiture). It is adequate that the utility of poor *p* from more income through redistributive taxation be treated differently from the utility of *p* from enjoying the tragic fate of *r*. It is indeed possible to maintain without any inconsistency that a much larger utility gain of *p* or a much smaller utility loss of *r* from the accident might have made the state with the accident better than the state without it. All that is being denied is that a coincidence of the utility picture of (*m*,*n*) vis-à-vis (*x*,*y*) must necessitate that (*m*,*n*) be ranked in exactly the same way as (*x*,*y*).

Welfarism is an exacting demand, ruling out essential use of any non-utility information (the use of non-utility information being confined to instrumental analysis or as surrogate for utility information when the latter is incomplete). In this paper the non-utility information that has been most discussed relates to different *sources* of utility and the motivation underlying it, but similar difficulties can arise from the relevance of other kinds of non-utility information as well. An outcome morality incorporating such principles as "equal pay for equal work," or elimination of "exploitation," or priority for feeding the hungry, requires essential use of non-utility information. An outcome utilitarian (or a welfarist) who defends such principles must do so on some instrumental grounds, i.e., in terms of their favorable influence on outcomes judged rigidly in the utilitarian (or some other welfarist) scale, and this misses those discriminations which can be achieved by making these principles have some role in the outcome morality itself. The informational constraints imposed by welfarism restrict the scope of moral discrimination of outcomes very severely indeed. The limitations can be brought out by looking at correspondences between judgments in different cases that are identical on the utility space but not in terms of particular non-utility information (as in the method of argument used in this section).[26]

IV. WEAK PARETIANISM AS OUTCOME MORALITY

Welfarism asserts unconditionally the adequacy of utility information for outcome morality. Weak Paretianism asserts this adequacy conditionally, viz., for the special case in which everyone's utility ranking happens to coincide.

Weak Paretianism: If state of affairs *x* is higher than state of affairs *y* in everyone's utility ranking, then *x* is a better state than *y*.

This is indeed a mild-looking component of welfarism and outcome utilitarianism, and if weak Paretianism is to be rejected, then the adequacy of utility information would be denied in what might appear to be the most straightforward case. Indeed, weak Paretianism is typically regarded as the least controversial of the criteria used in welfare economics for judging states of affairs.[27]

Does the criticism of welfarism in the last section apply to weak Paretianism? The immediate answer is no, since the cases considered involved *conflicts* in individual utility rankings (with *p* and *r* having opposite rankings). But a more probing question can be posed. Is it possible that the type of considerations that led us to question welfarism by attaching different importance to utility from different sources can also provide a case for violating even the shared utility ranking of all? If the possibility of differential importance of utility according to source is conceded, because of the relevance of non-utility considerations, is it not possible that the resulting outcome morality could go even against everyone's total utility ranking, thereby violating the weak Pareto principle?

This type of question relates closely to the issues underlying the problem of the "Paretian Libertarian" which I have analyzed elsewhere.[28] Libertarian values require that particular importance be

---

[26] For some indirect implications of welfarism and related conditions, see my "On Weights and Measures," *op. cit.* The impossibility theorems of the type pioneered by Arrow (*Social Choice and Individual Values, op. cit.*) can also be shown to result from combining welfarism with *poor* utility information.

[27] See Paul Samuelson, *Foundations of Economic Analysis* (Cambridge, Mass.: Harvard, 1947), ch. 8; J. de V. Graaff, *Theoretical Welfare Economics* (New York: Cambridge, 1957), pp. 9/10; I. M. D. Little, *A Critique of Welfare Economics* (New York: Oxford, 1957), pp. 84/5.

[28] *Collective Choice and Social Welfare* (San Francisco: Holden-Day, 1970), ch. 6, and "Liberty, Unanimity and Rights," *Economica*, XLIII (1976).

attached to each person's desires over pairs that are, in an obvious
sense, "personal" to him, e.g., what he should read. If two states of
affairs *x* and *y* differ from each other only in some such private
features related to a particular person, and are in other respects
identical, then the ranking of *x* vis-à-vis *y* may be thought to be-
long to that person's "personal domain" or "protected sphere."
Libertarianism may be seen, thus, to require that that person's
utility ranking should prevail in the outcome-morality ranking of
such pairs in each person's "protected sphere." It can be shown
that such a condition of libertarianism, *even* in the very limited
form of demanding a nonempty "personal domain" for just two
persons, can easily conflict with the weak Pareto principle in terms
of the inter-pair consistency of outcome morality.[29]

I shall not go here into the formal aspects of this impossibility
result, but refer only to an example that was used to illustrate the
conflict. There is a book thought to be pornographic and disap-
proved of by prude *P* but not by lewd *L*. (My first presentation of
the problem is clearly dated by the fact that I chose *Lady Chatter-
ley's Lover* as the controversial book in question—a choice that
may now appear puzzling.) The states of affairs *p*, *l*, and *o* differ
from each other in the respect that in *p* the prude reads the book,
in *l* the lewd reads the book, and in *o* nobody reads the book. The
utility ranking of the prude in descending order is: *o* ("great
escape"), *p* ("sad to have to read that muck"), *l* ("much more awful
to think of that depraved lewd gloating over this terrible stuff").
The lewd's utility ranking in descending order is: *p* ("true delight
in thinking of the discomfort of that pompous prude suffering the
consequences of his absurd disposition"), *l* ("good fun"), *o* ("waste
of a good book"). The orderings, thus, are:

P's utility ranking	*L's utility ranking*
o	*p*
p	*l*
l	*o*

The outcomes do not differ in any other respect, e.g., through

---

[29] *Collective Choice and Social Welfare*, Theorems 6•1, 6•2, and 6•3. There
are also related problems of internal consistency of libertarian values, on which
see Gibbard, "A Pareto-consistent Libertarian Claim," *Journal of Economic
Theory*, VII (1974); M. J. Farrell, "Liberalism in the Theory of Social Choice,"
Review of Economic Studies, XLIII (1976); Sen, "Liberty, Unanimity and Rights,"
pp. 234/5 and 243/4; Kotaro Suzumura, "On the Consistency of Libertarian
Claims," *Review of Economic Studies*, XLV (1978).

the influence of one's reading on one's actions or dispositions or capacities,[30] and no indirect effects need be considered.

An outcome morality that is both libertarian and weak Paretian then faces the following dilemma. Clearly, *o* is better than *p* on libertarian grounds, since the difference between the two states consists in whether the prude has to read the book or not (the lewd is not directly involved), and the prude has no desire to read it since he suffers from reading it. Similarly, *l* is better than *o*, since the difference in this case consists in whether the lewd reads the book or not (the prude is not directly involved), and the lewd desires to read the book and gains from it. But on Paretian grounds *p* is better than *l*, since both have more utility from *p* than from *l*. *Every* state is worse than some other in this Paretian and libertarian outcome morality.

Various ways of avoiding this conflict have been proposed in the literature. Some methods, proposed by Allan Gibbard, Julian Blau, and others, preserve the Pareto principle and make the libertarian principle conditional.[31] Others, including Robert Nozick and—amidst exploring other solutions—Michael Farrell, have responded to the problem by retaining the Pareto principle in the outcome morality, resting the burden of safeguarding liberty on *nonconsequentialist* judgments of action.[32] And some have proposed relaxing the weak Pareto principle by making it conditional, retaining

---

[30] Cf. "An adolescent ploughs through D. H. Lawrence in pursuit of pornographic matter and comes to acquire a taste for writing that is more passionate, original and imaginative than the works of Ian Fleming," Anthony Quinton, *Utilitarian Ethics* (London: Macmillan, 1973), p. 57.

[31] Gibbard, "A Pareto-consistent Libertarian Claim," *op. cit.*; Blau, "Liberal Values and Independence," *Review of Economic Studies*, XLII (1975); P. Bernholz, "Is a Paretian Liberal Really Impossible?" *Public Choice*, XIX (1974); Christian Seidl, "On Liberal Values," *Zeitschrift für Nationalöconomie*, XXXV (1975); Jerry Kelly, "Rights-exercising and a Pareto-consistent Libertarian Claim," *Journal of Economic Theory*, XIII (1976); John A. Ferejohn, "The Distribution of Rights in Society," in H. W. Gottinger and W. Leinfellner, *Decision Theory and Social Ethics: Issues in Social Choice* (Boston: Reidel, 1978); Wulf Gaertner and Lorenz Kruger, "From Hand-cuffed Paretians to Self-consistent Libertarians: A New Possibility Theorem," forthcoming in *Economica*; Edi Karni, "Collective Rationality, Unanimity and Liberal Ethics," *Review of Economic Studies*, XLV (1978).

[32] Nozick, *Anarchy, State and Utopia* (Oxford: Blackwell, 1974), pp. 164/5; Farrell, "Liberalism in the Theory of Social Choice," pp. 9/10; C. R. Perelli-Minetti, "Nozick on Sen: A Misunderstanding," *Theory and Decision*, VIII, 4 (October 1977): 387–393.

482   THE JOURNAL OF PHILOSOPHY

the libertarian principle in the outcome morality.[33] Still other avenues have been explored.[34]

I have tried to discuss elsewhere the merits of the proposed solutions,[35] and will refrain from doing this here. By varying the exact non-utility description of the conflict but retaining the same utility rankings, persuasive arguments can be produced *either* in favor of relaxing the weak Pareto principle *or* in favor of relaxing the libertarian principle. It is not my intention to deny this plurality. Rather to assert it. The plurality shows how a variation of non-utility description can precipitate different moral judgments even when the utility description is unaltered,[36] and this is, of course, contrary to the essence of welfarism. Non-utility information relating to *how* "personal" the choices are,[37] what *motivation* the per-

[33] Farrell, *op. cit.*, pp. 3–8; Sen, "Liberty, Unanimity and Rights," pp. 235–7 and 243/4; and Suzumura, *op. cit.*, pp. 330–334. This line was examined also in my original presentation of the problem in *Collective Choice and Social Welfare*, pp. 83–85.

[34] The scope of solving the problem by taking a nonbinary approach to social evaluation has been investigated by R. N. Batra and P. K. Pattanaik, "On Some Suggestions for Having Non-binary Social Choice Functions," *Theory and Decision*, III, 1 (October 1972): 1–11, establishing that the problem reappears in the nonbinary context. The scope of "domain restriction" was explored by Blau, *op. cit.*, and also by F. Breyer, "The Liberal Paradox, Decisiveness over Issues, and Domain Restrictions," *Zeitschrift für Nationalökonomie*, XXXVII (1977). Other aspects of the problem have been studied in some other contributions, e.g., James Buchanan, "An Ambiguity in Sen's Alleged Proof of the Impossibility of the Paretian Libertarian," mimeographed paper, Virginia Polytechnic, 1976.

[35] "Liberty, Unanimity and Rights," and also "Personal Utilities and Public Judgements: Or What's Wrong with Welfare Economics?," *Economic Journal*, LXXXIX (1979). The latter also evaluates another line of reasoning that has been advocated, which seeks a "solution" to the problem by arguing that the "libertarian" outcome of the lewd reading the book cannot be an "equilibrium," since both parties would gain from passing on the book to the prude on condition that he read it. Thus the libertarian outcome is "unfeasible," and the chosen position must be Pareto optimal. This overlooks the possibility that the lewd or the prude, if libertarian, would not offer such a contract, and the assumption that each *must* do whatever maximizes his personal utility simply abstracts from the moral issue that is under discussion. The absence of an "equilibrium" with the "libertarian" outcome *if everyone were* to behave in a way that maximizes his personal utility provides no "solution" to the problem at hand. (It is also the case that such a contract may not be offered by the lewd on the prudential—rather than moral—ground that he may not be able to ensure that the prude will, in fact, read the book once it has been handed over to him.)

[36] Contrast the two descriptions of the "Edwin-Angelina" case given respectively in Gibbard's "A Pareto-consistent Libertarian Claim," pp. 398/9, and in my "Liberty, Unanimity and Rights," pp. 225/6.

[37] Cf. Ronald Dworkin's distinction between "personal" and "external" preferences, in *Taking Rights Seriously* (London: Duckworth, 1978), pp. 234–238.

sons have behind their utility rankings, whether the interdependence arises from liking or disliking the others' physical *acts* (in this case, the reading of the book) or from the *joys and sufferings* of the others, etc., may well be found to be relevant in deciding which way to resolve the conflict. If so, then the adequacy of utility information is denied. More particularly, the existence of circumstances that would lead to the moral rejection of the outcome supported by the weak Pareto principle would indicate that welfarism even in this apparently mild form can be too demanding.

Can this criticism of Paretianism be softened by invoking Richard Hare's distinction between "level-1" ("intuitive") and "level-2" ("critical") moral thinking? There is, of course, no difficulty in *conceiving* of an archangelic outcome-utilitarian (or—more generally—an archangelic welfarist, or—even more generally—an archangelic weak Paretian) supporting libertarian intuitions for day-to-day quick decisions, and even of a domesticated archangel bent on the task "to bring up his children"—sticking to the Harean analogy (*op. cit.*, p. 124)—with fostered libertarian values. But can the tension not be interpreted in exactly the opposite line to this? Paretianism does seem to have immense immediate appeal; it is very much a level-1 winner. Insofar as Paretianism is based on catering to everyone's interests—on a very simple interpretation of interests—its immediate appeal is not difficult to explain. Nor is it in general a bad quick rule to follow even from the libertarian point of view: conflicts of the kind captured in the example above (and more generally in the Pareto-libertarian impossibility theorems) may well be rare. Libertarian values, on the other hand, require rather complex distinctions to be made, e.g., between *sources* of happiness, between *domains* of personal affairs, and between different conceptions of a person's *interest*. It seems, therefore, not unplausible that an intuitive (level-1) Paretianism may go with a critical (level-2) libertarianism.

In the conversation that follows—between a libertarian outcome moralist and an outcome utilitarian—I have tried to demonstrate the plausibility of such a combination. It may seem that I have put Richard Hare on his head—exactly reversing the correspondence of utilitarian and non-utilitarian positions vis-à-vis "critical" and "intuitive" moral thoughts. But I would like to emphasize that the argument has the "Harean" feature of invoking the distinction, which seems to me to be important, between these two levels. More specifically, the general principle that is used as the main criterion is the Harean one of "giving equal weight to the

equal interests of the occupants of all the roles in the situation"
(116). The difference arises from the interpretation of a person's
"interest," disputing its identification with utility—either as desire-
fulfilment or as happiness.

I have to report that it was a little difficult to get an outcome
libertarian for the dialogue, since libertarians tend to be anti-
consequentialist and ferociously "deontic," but by a lucky coincidence the prude *P* in the example considered earlier, confessed to
being an outcome libertarian. He was dispatched to talk to the
utilitarian, who found (not to his surprise, since he had read his
Hare) that his adversary had "usually confined" his "own thought
about moral reasoning (with fairly infrequent lapses which often
go unnoticed) to . . . level-1, the level of everyday moral thinking
of ordinary, often stressful, occasions in which information is
sparse" (123). *P* was himself acutely aware of his own condition,
and eagerly met the utilitarian healer—Doctor *U*—in the latter's
surgery for diagnosis and advice.

U: I understand you experience moral intuitions. When do you get
   them?
P: At night, doctor, and also during the day. I am much bothered by
   them.
U: I bet you are, but don't worry, we are here to help you.
P: Shall I tell you about my moral intuitions?
U: Yes, yes, please do so. I am resigned to hearing them; people are
   always telling me about their moral intuitions. But I must later explain to you that what is important is not what moral intuitions you
   have, but what moral intuitions you *ought* to have.
P: I am truly relieved to hear that, doctor, since I am much bothered by
   my immediate moral intuitions.
U: Don't worry at all; that's a good sign. I take it that your immediate
   moral intuitions relate to fantastic cases which make the utilitarian
   look like a moral monster? I know that ailment well.
P: Actually, doctor, my immediate moral intuitions are typically
   utilitarian, and certainly invariably Paretian.
U: So what seems to be the problem?
P: Just that when I have one of my fairly infrequent lapses into thinking
   critically about my Paretian and utilitarian moral intuitions, I find I
   cannot sustain them.
U: Obviously, you must think critically *differently*. But first tell
   me about this Lawrence book—which I understand you find
   pornographic.
P: A truly revolting book, doctor. What I have heard about it is enough.
   I certainly wouldn't wish to go so far as to read it.

U: Yes, but I gather that you desire that the lewd shouldn't read it either?

P: How can I desire anything else, doctor? I would suffer so immensely from the thought of his gloating over it. Imagine his face, doctor! Or worse. No, no, I desire even less that he should read that stuff.

U: I understand that he too desires that you rather than he should read the book.

P: Exactly. And so my immediate moral intuition is that it is better that I should read the book rather than he. *Must be* good, I hear myself saying when I am in a hurry, since it increases everybody's utility!

P: Have you made sure that there are no indirect effects? You must consider them too.

P: I have. There are none. No, my reading the book, stopping the lewd from reading it, will make everyone happier.

U: So what's the problem? What's wrong with you reading it rather than the lewd?

P: Simply that I *detest* the book and he *loves* it! When I think about it coolly, I ask myself: why should I have to read something I hate, while he is stopped from reading something he would so much enjoy reading?

U: But, don't you see, P, that he would *enjoy even more* your reading the book, and you would have *even more pain* from his reading the book. The net gain in utility of both is positive from your reading the book.

P: Yes, so far as the *total* utility of each is concerned. But should the lewd's pleasure in meddling in my affairs or my discomfort from my nosiness about what he does, have the same weight in the moral accounting as his own reading pleasure or my own reading discomfort?

U: Perhaps you are trying to say that it is morally wrong for you to have these nosy feelings. Perhaps you are really worried that the world would be a less happy place if everyone were nosy about other's tastes. If so, I am inclined to think that I can help you to build a more sophisticated argument involving universalization.

P: But, doctor, I haven't been able to see that it is morally wrong for me to have these nosy feelings. Indeed, I would never forgive myself if I were not revolted by the lewd's detestable reading pleasures! I am not saying that I shouldn't have these nosy feelings, but only that these nosy feelings shouldn't count in the moral weighing of what the lewd ends up reading—at least not count as much as his own feelings about his reading. The lewd has the right to enjoy reading what he likes; I have the right to feel revolted by it; and the only reason his pleasure has a different moral status from my pleasure, in this particular case, is that it is *his* reading that we are talking about.

U: And you wouldn't find it odd to recommend something that makes everyone unhappier than he need be?

P: My immediate intuitions are, of course, offended by it. But thinking
    about it more critically, I can see that such a recommendation must
    follow from agreeing that it is morally better that the lewd be
    able to read what he likes than that I have to read something I
    detest. What is at stake is our interests in the form of our ability to
    do with our own lives what we want. This covers our ability to read
    what we like and avoid reading what we don't like. Our interests are
    less clearly involved in the power to stop others from reading what
    they like or to make them read what they detest. Do you see what I
    am trying to say?

U: Of course, I follow your simple thoughts, but I have to tell you that
    you have just replaced one set of moral intuitions by another. You
    are still stuck at level 1, and will, I guess, stay there until your critical
    thinking takes you in a different direction. If you want to defend
    libertarian values critically, you would find better ground by intro-
    ducing indirect effects, and by considering the problems posed by
    universalization, and you can then be a utilitarian too, I am happy
    to say.

P: That's a nice thought; I would have loved to be a utilitarian, since
    my immediate intuitions *are* rather utilitarian. But reflection reveals
    that in this case utilitarianism—even Paretianism—will conflict with
    acknowledging that it is morally better that the lewd—rather than
    I—should read the book he loves and I detest. And I am thus forced
    to reject utilitarianism—even Paretianism. The lewd also agrees with
    this moral judgment, as it happens.

U: He does, does he? What would you say, then, if someone suggested
    that you are *already* a Paretian—possibly even a utilitarian, since
    both of you think that the lewd reading the book is better. You are
    thus recommending what everyone desires and what is in everyone's
    interest.

P: I would say, quoting Hare, please "do not confuse the issue, as some
    do, by introducing moral considerations into this prudential ques-
    tion" as to "what are someone's true interests," i.e., "by alleging
    that becoming morally better, or worse, in itself affects a man's
    interests" (Hare, 118).

U: Despite your poor ability to absorb what you read, you do show good
    taste in your reading. But, I am afraid, you have a long way to go,
    and much more to read.

P: I know that, doctor. I will, in fact, read more utilitarian literature if
    I get the time.

U: Now, there! You have just given—at long last—a good reason why
    the lewd—and not you—should read that other book, which he loves
    and you detest. You need the time to read utilitarian literature, and
    that will increase everyone's utility. Good critical thinking, P, and a
    fine indirect utilitarian justification of your intuitive libertarian
    feelings!

I leave them there, and end this section with a clarificatory remark. Corresponding to the distinction between pleasure-based utilitarianism and desire-based utilitarianism, both welfarism and Paretianism can be defined in either way. It is, therefore, worth noting that the difficulties with Paretianism discussed here (and those with welfarism discussed in the last section) apply to interpretations based on desires as well as to pleasure-based interpretations. The descriptions given can be taken in either sense, or both, without eliminating the problem. In fact, both the interpretations were explicitly invoked in the dialogue.

V. CONCLUDING REMARKS

I end with a few general remarks, to put the discussion in perspective.

First, an "outcome morality" is a morality dealing with judging states of affairs. Any utilitarian moral structure, e.g., act utilitarianism, rule utilitarianism, or motive utilitarianism, is made up of such an outcome morality, viz., "outcome utilitarianism," and some version of consequentialism causally relating other entities (e.g., acts, rules, or motives) to states of affairs, which are assessed through outcome utilitarianism. Since outcome utilitarianism is common to all these structures, any limitation of it applies to these structures without exception (section I). This is independent of how we decide to assess actions, e.g., whether by contrasting one act with another, or one rule with another.

Second, outcome utilitarianism can be split into "welfarism" and "sum-ranking" (section II). Welfarism asserts that the goodness of states of affairs depends ultimately only on the personal utilities in the respective states, and sum-ranking asserts that the appropriate way of combining personal utilities to assess goodness is by addition.

Third, sum-ranking makes it difficult to accommodate egalitarian values, when personal utility measures are taken to have independent descriptive content rather than being defined in terms of the *moral* valuation of the respective individual situations. This limitation remains substantial even after what Parfit calls the "simple view" of personal identity (section III) is rejected.

Fourth, welfarism is a more limited approach than it might appear at first sight. Its limitations can be properly brought out only by considering *correspondences* between different judgments, and not by considering each such judgment on its own (section III).

Fifth, Hare's distinction between "intuitive" level-1 and "criticial" level-2 thinking is both important and useful, but it is not easy to sustain the claim that intuitive difficulties with the implications of the utilitarian (and, more generally, welfarist) approaches would tend to be resolved at the critical level (section III). Indeed, the exact opposite can be the case, and an *intuitive utilitarian* (or welfarist) position may go with a *critical non-utilitarian* (or non-welfarist) position (section IV).

Sixth, considerations of liberty and rights have been viewed here as parts of the structure of outcome morality itself (sections III and IV). This contrasts with treating them as constraints on, or nonconsequentialist judgments of, actions, as in the systems proposed by, say, Nozick (*op. cit.*). This shift is possible because of the departure from the tradition—often implicit—of identifying *consequences* with *utility consequences* (and of basing the description of states of affairs entirely on utility information regarding these states). But a tortured body, an unfed belly, a bullied person, or unequal pay for equal work, is as much a part of the state affairs as the utility and disutility occurring in that state.[38] A teleological approach can, therefore, give more than an instrumental role to rights.[39]

Seventh, the weak Pareto principle can be viewed as a mild version of welfarism. Even this mild version raises serious consistency problems with elementary considerations of personal liberty, and a case can be made for the rejection of the unconditional use of the weak Pareto principle (section IV). A critical issue relates to whether a person's "interests" are best represented by his or her utility level (interpreted either in terms of pleasure and pain, or as desire satisfaction), *irrespective* of the source of utility and the non-utility characteristics of states of affairs.

Finally, since (i) any utilitarian moral structure implies outcome utilitarianism (but not vice versa), (ii) outcome utilitarianism im-

---

[38] I have tried to argue elsewhere that certain moral problems, e.g., the responsibility of person 1 when strong-armed 2 beats up person 3, can be much more easily analyzed in a system that incorporates rights in the outcome morality itself rather than just in nonconsequentialist evaluation of, or constraints on, actions ("Liberty, Unanimity and Rights," pp. 229–231, and more extensively in my Hägerström Lectures, "Welfare and Rights").

[39] It may also be worth remarking that there is no reason why a nonwelfarist outcome morality (incorporating rights) cannot be combined with assessing actions in a non-fully-consequentialist way (incorporating rights in some way not captured by the first route). The status of rights in both these methods will be, in an important sense, more primitive than the instrumental status that rights enjoy in a consequentialist and welfarist moral structure (e.g., under act or rule utilitarianism).

plies welfarism (but not vice versa), (iii) welfarism implies Paretianism (but not vice versa), and (iv) Paretianism implies weak Paretianism (but not vice versa), a rejection of weak Paretianism has
rather far-reaching consequences, affecting *all* utilitarian moralities, *and* a great many others.

AMARTYA SEN

Nuffield College, Oxford University

[3]

THE HUMAN GOOD AND THE AMBITIONS
OF CONSEQUENTIALISM

By James Griffin

I want to look at one aspect of the human good: how it serves as the basis for judgments about the moral right. One important view is that the right is always derived from the good. I want to suggest that the more one understands the nature of the human good, the more reservations one has about that view.

I. One Route to Consequentialism

Many of us think that different things make a life good, with no one deep value underlying them all. My own list includes: enjoyment, accomplishing something with one's life, deep personal relations, certain sorts of understanding, and the elements of a characteristically human existence (autonomy, liberty).[1]

Most of us also think that moral right and wrong are based, in some way or other, in how well individual lives go, and that the moral point of view is, in some sense or other, impartial between lives. Utilitarianism is a prominent, but not the only, way of spelling out this intuition. There is no reason why an account of the human good needs to be confined, in the classical utilitarian way, to happiness or to fulfillment of desire (on the usual understanding of that notion). Nor is there any reason why impartiality has to be confined to maximizing the good, counting everybody for one and nobody for more than one. We may generalize.

Let us broaden the notion of the good. We might say, for instance, that though happiness is a good, so are the other items on my list. But though broadened, this notion of the good stays within the confines of individual goods; it still has to do with human well-being, with what promotes the quality of one person's life.

But it may be that further features of consequences—say, that individual goods are distributed equally or that no human rights are violated—also help to determine right and wrong. Let us broaden the notion of the good further: we add to individual goods such moral goods as equality and respect for human rights. When we look at consequences, we now

---

[1] I start where other discussions finish. See, for example, my book *Well-Being* (Oxford: Clarendon Press, 1986), pt. I, and a more recent article, "Against the Taste Model," in *Interpersonal Comparisons of Well-Being*, ed. Jon Elster and John Roemer (Cambridge: Cambridge University Press, 1991).

118 © 1992 Social Philosophy and Policy Foundation. Printed in the USA.

Social Philosophy & Policy, vol. 9, no. 2 (1992), pp. 118–132

look not just at the quantity of individual goods but also, say, at their pattern of distribution.

Now, an intuitive feature of the word 'consequences' is that the consequences of an act flow from, and thus follow, the act. But that restriction excludes goods that make essential reference to what precedes the act — for instance, the fact that a certain act would keep a (past) promise, or that it would bring a just distribution seen over life as a whole (past, present, or future), or that it is what persons deserve given what they have done (in the past). Therefore, let us now broaden the word 'consequences' to include any state of affairs that makes up a history (past, present, or future), and thereby broaden the word 'good' to include desert, promise-keeping, historical conceptions of justice, and so on.[2]

We have said nothing so far about another feature of classical utilitarianism: that it uses the maximization of good as the standard of right and wrong. But the 'maximum' is the greatest quantity, and once the notion of the good grows to include, say, promise-keeping, there is no obvious quantity to be maximized. But there is a more general notion than the maximum, namely the 'optimum'. The optimum could be, but need not be, the greatest in size. We could say, then, that consequentialism is the view that it is wrong to produce less than the optimum. But why confine the consequentialist standard to the optimum? One might regard as morally right the first available action whose consequences score above a certain level of aspiration.[3] Therefore, let us broaden the standard of the right by linking it not to the optimum but to the 'satisfactory' or 'good enough', interpreted in such a way that one option is that only the optimum is good enough.[4]

Where does this leave us? It leaves us at what we now call 'consequentialism'.[5] Consequentialists, on this wide and commonly accepted defi-

[2] Derek Parfit, for instance, takes this step in his definition of 'consequentialism' in *Reasons and Persons* (Oxford: Clarendon Press, 1984), p. 26.

[3] Michael Slote does this in his book *Common-Sense Morality and Consequentialism* (London: Routledge, 1985), ch. 3. He there develops Herbert Simon's 'satisficing' model of rational strategy. On this model, one should: (1) fix an aspiration level, (2) enumerate one's options, (3) evaluate them as one proceeds, and (4) accept the first option to meet one's aspiration level. See, for example, Herbert Simon, "A Behavioral Model of Rationality" in his *Models of Bounded Rationality* (Cambridge: MIT Press, 1982).

[4] This step takes us beyond what a lot of our contemporaries *say* about 'consequentialism': it is common to make optimizing part of the word's definition. See, for example, Samuel Scheffler, *The Rejection of Consequentialism* (Oxford: Clarendon Press, 1982), p. 1; and Parfit, *Reasons and Persons*, p. 24. However, Michael Slote argues for including the 'satisficing' standard within the bounds of consequentialism. See his *Common-Sense Morality and Consequentialism*, pp. 36–37. But these authors are unlikely to resist my broadening of the standard of the right; it contradicts nothing important in what they say.

[5] See, for example, Parfit, *Reasons and Persons*, section 10; Scheffler, *The Rejection of Consequentialism*, pp. 1–2; Shelly Kagan, *The Limits of Morality* (Oxford: Clarendon Press, 1989), pp. xi, 7; and Philip Pettit, "Consequentialism," in *A Companion to Ethics*, ed. P. Singer (Oxford: Blackwell, 1991). This is a big change from what Elizabeth Anscombe meant when she coined the term in 1958 in "Modern Moral Philosophy," *Philosophy*, vol. 33 (1958). On her

120   JAMES GRIFFIN

nition, are those who derive the right from the good in this sense: moral
prohibitions on, or permissions to, an individual agent — the *do's, don't's,*
and *may do's* that are addressed to a particular person — are derived from
judgments about the amount of good (in this broadened sense of 'good')
in the consequences (in this broadened sense of 'consequences') of his
possible actions. In contrast, nonconsequentialists are those who hold
that some *do's, don't's,* and *may do's* are not derived from the good, even
in this broadened sense. In short, consequentialists hold that all goods are
to be promoted, while nonconsequentialists hold that some goods are to
be honored.[6] An innocent person's right not to be killed is one of the
goods (in the broadened sense). Consequentialists respond to this good
by bringing about its respect by agents generally — that is, by promoting
it. Nonconsequentialists respond simply by respecting it themselves in
their own actions as individuals — that is, by honoring it.[7]

II. BACKING UP: A THREAT OF EMPTINESS

I think that there is something deeply puzzling about consequentialism,
on this wide definition of it. The puzzle, for me, centers on how one is
supposed to move from the expanded notion of the good to the right. It
is not especially puzzling how a utilitarian makes the move. A utilitarian
starts with a more or less comprehensible account of the good, which is
supposed to be independent of the right, and then adds rules for deriving the right from the good. But once we expand the good in the way that
we have just seen, many of the goods that are added do not lend themselves easily to this derivation. It is hard even to understand what it is to
'promote' them.

---

account, nonconsequentialists hold that certain acts are ruled out morally whatever the results; on the current use, they hold merely that some acts are ruled out morally on grounds
other than their results.

 [6] I borrow Philip Pettit's handy way of summarizing the distinction. See his "Consequentialism."

 [7] I prefer summarizing the distinction between consequentialism and nonconsequentialism in terms of 'promoting' and 'honoring' values, rather than in the more widespread terms
of 'agent-neutral' and 'agent-relative' obligations. Derek Parfit suggests that consequentialism gives to all agents common moral aims and is, thus, agent-neutral, while nonconsequentialism gives different agents different aims and is, thus, agent-relative (see his *Reasons and
Persons,* p. 27). But some nonconsequentialist *do's* and *don't's,* such as "Do no murder," are
also given to all agents. What Parfit means, of course, is that for me that prohibition is statable as "Griffin, do no murder," and for him it is statable as "Parfit, do no murder." This
merely brings out a feature of *do's* and *don't's.* The feature in question, however, does not
go morally very deep. Consequentialists, too, may hold that agents must be given *do's* and
don't's; they may even hold that our decision procedures will be largely constituted by *do's*
and *don't's.* The important difference is that for a consequentialist these *do's* and *don't's* derive from the promotion of the good, while for a nonconsequentialist some of them do not.
A nonconsequentialist says that some *do's* and *don't's* are not the creatures of the promotion
of the good and, thus, are not challengeable merely by its more efficient promotion, even
though they may be overrideable by it when a sufficient amount of it turns out to be at stake.

Take what I suppose is a limiting case. On the wide interpretation of consequentialism, morality itself could be regarded as a good and, therefore, could be given either the consequentialist or nonconsequentialist treatment. Consequentialists would act so as to bring about the most, or a satisfactory degree of, moral behavior in the world at large. Nonconsequentialists would, so far as possible, act morally themselves.

Look more closely at consequentialists. They have a good before them — acting morally — which they put into their formula for the derivation of the right: the morally right act is the one that most (or, at least, satisfactorily) promotes morally right acts. But this formula is empty. The good that consequentialists start with is supposed to give content to the right, but since the good that they start with in this case *is* the right, no content enters. This problem does not face utilitarians, who are supposed to form one species of consequentialist. It is true that utilitarians start with a good, namely the quality of life, and that they, too, can put content into the notion of the right only if they put content into the (far from crystalline or substantial) notion of the quality of life. One might ask: Then why are consequentialists any different? They too, one might say, need to put content into their notion of acting morally, but, once they do, the problem disappears. After all, utilitarians go outside the immediate bounds of the derivation of the right from the good to find content for their notion of the quality of life. But the two cases are not analogous in the way needed. Consequentialists are supposed to derive a contentful standard of the right from a substantive good, but some of these added goods that appear in the course of the expansion we have just traced, cannot play this role, while the notion of the quality of life can.

I do not offer this as a fatal objection to consequentialism; it is not. It is only the first of a series of puzzling features. In any case, one cannot rest too much weight on such a marginal example of a good as acting morally. The extended good that consequentialists themselves usually cite includes such things as keeping promises, not lying, acting justly, and respecting rights. The threat of emptiness is not necessarily avoided, though, just by shifting to more specific goods such as acting justly and respecting rights. The notions of justice and rights both have great elasticity: they are sometimes used to cover the whole of morality and sometimes only a part of it. The more broadly they are interpreted, the more emptiness threatens.

True, there are other goods that fall under the expanded notion of the good, such as keeping promises and not lying, that have content of their own. Let us turn to them now.

III. BACKING UP FURTHER: AN ODD PICTURE OF AGENCY

In turning to these other goods, the puzzles do not disappear, but merely change.

122   JAMES GRIFFIN

There is an unclarity in act descriptions. Do I keep my promise only if I act to some extent voluntarily, or do I also keep it if, kicking and screaming, I am forced to do what I said I would do? Consequentialists aim at producing optimum (or, at least, satisfactory) promise-keeping overall. But do they have in mind a voluntary act or mere conformity of action? Either answer is puzzling. If they mean a voluntary act, then they are adopting an odd conception of agency. If they mean mere conformity, then it is hard to see why they regard such actions as moral goods in the first place. Let me take up the alternatives in turn.

It is within the realm of possibility for one person to break a promise in a way that gets many others autonomously to keep theirs. George, let us say, a prominent politician, is fed up with his colleagues' regularly welching on their word and finds himself in a position to welch on them so spectacularly that they would decide that the rules of the game had to be changed. He might be able to work a kind of conversion. But how often are such conversions within one's power? It would probably be a unique chance for George, so it would be unreasonable of him to elevate his response to this one case to a policy for his whole moral life. I doubt that I have ever been in such a position; nor, I suspect, have most people. Normal agents are not. If I, situated as I am, were to break a promise in order to bring about more cases of autonomous promise-keeping, then, unlike George, I should merely be dropping my act into a causal stream in which so many other eddies and currents and undertows are at work that I could have, at best, only the faintest hope of producing the desired effect. Thus, though such conversions are not psychologically impossible, they are so rare, so unlikely ever to present themselves in the course of a life, so much a fluke of fate, as, for all practical purposes, not to figure in the formation of goals in life. In a certain loose sense, 'ought' implies 'can'. All moral theories work implicitly with a picture of what lies within human capacity. The limits of human capacity help to define the limits of moral obligation. But acts like maximizing the universal observance of promise-keeping or of fairness are simply not in our repertoire. Our moral life is not so much a matter of what we do as of what we choose to do. What I choose to do has to be, roughly speaking, within my power. I do not have to be 100 percent sure of bringing it off; I can, for instance, choose to go to London first thing tomorrow morning, although British Rail might let me down. But if the chances are only one in several million of my carrying something off, then I cannot be said to choose to do it. I can choose to have a flutter on the Irish Sweepstake, but not to win. Winning may enter my hopes and plans but not my intentions. The chances of my promise-breaking making others (plural) autonomously keep their promises approach Irish Sweepstake proportions. There is, therefore, something quite unreal in consequentialists' choosing as one of their goals in life, "Promote promise-keeping impartially." It is not the sort of action-guiding goal that one would ever give to, or adopt as, an agent.

Still, breaking one's own promise is not the only means at one's disposal for promoting promise-keeping. One can persuade or indoctrinate. But this addition to our causal resources does not much change our prospects of success. Few of us are in a position effectively to persuade or indoctrinate. I was when my children were young, but a person's moral character is pretty much fixed in childhood and little, certainly not sermons or lectures, is likely to change it afterward. George's making a speech in favor of probity in public life would have little chance of success. My making a similar speech would have even less. The strangeness of the goal remains.

What is strange is, precisely, consequentialists' choosing as goals in life the promotion of acts of promise-keeping, acts of justice, and the like. It is not strange that opportunities for conversions are rare. After all, opportunities for saving babies who fall face down into puddles are rare, too: normal agents will probably never have such an opportunity in their lives. One can choose as a goal helping others in distress when the cost to oneself is small. Saving a baby in a puddle fits under this heading. Although that particular case is rare, cases of that kind certainly are not, and acts of compliance with the principle are within our powers. What makes a moral principle strange, however, is not the rarity of one particular instantiation of the kind of situation it regulates (there is nothing strange in that) but the unlikelihood of being able to comply with it at all. Why choose a standard for moral action so remotely connected to what one can do? Of course, 'strange' does not imply 'wrong'. But 'ought' implies 'can'. Action-guiding principles must fit human capacities, or they become strange in a damaging way: pointless.

Perhaps the promotion of promise-keeping is not meant as an action-guiding principle. There is a familiar distinction between a decision procedure (what we appeal to in deciding how to act) and a criterion (what makes an act right or wrong). Perhaps a doctor is best advised to follow certain procedures in diagnosing and treating patients – best advised because those procedures have the best results overall, though not necessarily in each case. But the criterion for successful medical practice is clear and independent of any diagnostic procedures: namely, health. Perhaps, similarly, the promotion of promise-keeping should be regarded, not as the immediate goal that we use in our thought and action, but as the criterion of moral practice.

It is not clear whether, or how much, this reply solves the earlier puzzles. Although criterion and decision procedure can diverge, they should not, I think, get too far apart from one another. Our decision procedures must take account of our capacities, but any criterion for a human practice cannot become too remote from our capacities without losing its point even as a criterion. Health is a reasonable criterion for medical practice because doctors can, directly or indirectly, act to bring it about. In contrast with that, a very demanding moral criterion (say, Jesus's "Be ye therefore perfect") may go too far even to be a moral criterion. Take perfection to be counting one person's interests as much as any other's. Some philosophers think that, as long as we can try to be perfect, although we are bound to fail, the principle is not pointless. But I am inclined to think that if such perfection is (as I believe) well outside our reach, it loses interest even as a criterion. In certain respects, the promotion of promise-keeping is more remote from human capacities than is perfection. In seeking perfection, the problem is making one's own reluctant will conform. In promoting promise-keeping, the problem is making an altogether more independent world conform. If it is strained to say that one "intends" to promote promise-keeping, it is also strained to say that one will "try" to promote it. Unless one can afford to buy a great number of tickets, one cannot "try" to win the Irish Sweepstake either.

Suppose, then, that consequentialists adopt the other reading of "keeping my promise"—not voluntary promise-keeping, but mere conformity. Here, too, there clearly are cases in which one can break one's promise and consequently force others, in some sense or other, to keep theirs. I have promised my two children, let us say, not to interfere any more in their lives, but then they each promise their mother to stay at home one evening and, just as they are about to sneak out, I lock them in. I have broken my (one) promise, but they, kicking, screaming, and trying to get out, are keeping their (two) promises. Or are they? It is misleading to say that they "keep their promise," even misleading to say that they are "staying in," when they are being kept in. And why should we classify mere conformity as a moral good? What is the intuitive justification for considering a world with more cases of mere conformity as being morally better than a world with fewer? We might sometimes be able to explain why the first world is better than the second by appealing to the narrower sort of consequentialism that I shall shortly recommend, a form of consequentialism that uses the term 'good' to refer only to individual goods and couples this conception of the good with some conception or other of equal respect. If one falls back on this narrower form of consequentialism, though, one abandons the aim of promoting acts of promise-keeping (or of fairness, or of respect for rights) that is characteristic of the wider form. The narrower form of consequentialism explains why the world with more cases of mere conformity is better than the world with fewer, by appealing to the pattern and extent of the satisfaction of interests (which has some intuitive force), rather than, as the wider form would, by appealing to the number of merely conforming actions (which, to my mind, does not have intuitive appeal).

This leads to a further puzzle. Does one promote promise-keeping just by acting to maximize the number of promises kept, or to minimize the number of promises broken, regardless of whether what is at stake is trivial or important? That would be a very odd goal. But if not that, then what? Can we rank cases of broken promises, except perhaps by ranking the interests at stake in the various cases? Can we rank the interests at stake without undermining the status of promise-keeping as one of the goods added to produce the expanded notion of the good? Do I really minimize promise-breaking by bringing it about that there are only *n* breakings rather than the *n* + 10 that there would otherwise have been, although the *n* violations seriously damage the lives of the persons affected, whereas the *n* + 10 are not especially damaging? Could I maximize promise-keeping by setting up the following sort of promising teams? Your team makes and keeps several trivial promises to the members of mine, whereupon we turn around and do the same to the members of your team, and so on. As this example shows, it is puzzling to regard promise-keeping as the sort of thing to be promoted. The same is true of justice, honesty, and respect for rights. It is odd to seek to promote acts of fairness; it is more natural to seek to promote one's own or other persons' interests fairly (or unfairly).

There is a bad fit between the idea of *general promotion of the good* and these *moral* goods that were added in the expansion of the notion of the good that we traced at the start. That bad fit is at the center of the wide definition of 'consequentialism' now commonly accepted, and is a good enough reason, I think, to abandon the definition for a different one. It is not that no taxonomy of moral positions should allow any position to be odd or incorrect, but that it is better if all positions are plausible enough to be interesting.

IV. WHERE DOES THIS LEAVE US?

How might we amend consequentialism? It has to retain the derivation of the right from the good; otherwise it would not be consequentialism. Its live option is to reverse the expansion of the notion of the good that we traced at the start. But how far? I think that we have to bring the notion of the good back to such notions as well-being, the quality of life, human interests — back to what I have been calling 'individual goods'. Whether this is to bring it all the way back to the notion of utility depends upon what we think 'utility' means.[8]

---

[8] Amartya Sen thinks that there are two "traditional meanings of utility," namely "happiness" and "desire-fulfillment," and he gives narrow interpretations to both. See his *On Ethics and Economics* (Oxford: Blackwell, 1987), p. 3. I do not think that it does violence to the term 'utilitarian' to let it cover pluralist and objective value theories. But for our present purposes, my suggestion is that we let the class of the good contract to individual goods, on any account of what they are. We may leave open whether that means that the notion of the good will be reduced to the notion of utility.

Whether or not this move to limit the notion of the good is a retreat to utility, it is clearly not a retreat all the way back to utilitarianism. For there are many derivations of the right from the good besides utilitarian ones. The right could be what maximizes the good, or achieves a satisfactory level of good, or distributes the good equally except when inequalities are to the advantage of the worst off, or brings everyone up to some minimum level of good above which obligations cease, and so on. Though it is not clear exactly where to draw the line between utilitarian and nonutilitarian positions, some of the ones I have just listed are nonutilitarian. There are two characteristic features of all these positions: they assess outcomes in terms of individual goods and they derive the right through a function representing equal respect. Certain elements of justice enter into the derivation with the function representing equal respect: for example, counting everybody for one, nobody for more than one; or being governed by the difference principle; or maintaining a minimum acceptable level of welfare.[9] But these conceptions of justice enter into the process of derivation and not into the list of goods. Agents are directed to distribute according to one of those standards, not to promote the universal observance of the standard.

If, in this way, we shrink the class of goods used in the wide account of consequentialism, we shall get, to my mind, a more interesting distinction between consequentialism and nonconsequentialism.

V. THE FAILURE OF PURE CONSEQUENTIALISM

However, that does not end the troubles. I wonder whether we do not have to give up the distinction between consequentialism and nonconsequentialism altogether.

No one could plausibly claim that the right is derivable solely from the good. One would have to claim, instead, that it is derivable from the good through some function interpreting the requirement of equal respect: maximizing, achieving a satisfactory level, equalizing, and so on. No form of consequentialism yields any judgments of moral right without the aid of some conception of equal respect. But a conception of equal respect is, on the face of it, an abstract moral view, a high-level principle of right.

---

[9] Should 'consequentialism' encompass even an interpretation of equal respect that allows partiality—for example, the view that equal respect requires only that agents render to others what is 'due' them (my children, say, are due more from me than strangers, and so on)? There is a problem with this interpretation: does 'due' mean something other than 'right,' in which case it is not, after all, a function for deriving the right from the good. Still, the doubts about consequentialism that I am in the process of raising apply as well to nontrivial versions of this view; this view regards what is 'due' as an expression of the moral notion of equal respect, and I shall argue that what is 'due' others is often determined by a partly arbitrary picture of human agency. I shall, however, concentrate on interpretations of equal respect that require some sort of impartial promotion of the good: maximizing, equalizing, and so on.

It would seem, therefore, that no form of consequentialism can derive the right except from the good plus at least one key element of the right.

There are pure consequentialists, I think, who would resist this conclusion. They would allow that some of those functions do indeed express moral requirements (for instance, equalizing, or equalizing except when inequalities help the worst off), but others represent irresistible nonmoral requirements of rationality (for instance, maximizing or achieving a satisfactory level—there is dispute as to which of these two does represent the requirement of rationality[10]). Thus, pure consequentialists can claim to derive the right from the good plus a morally neutral standard of rationality.

But I think that pure consequentialism is untenable. I have argued elsewhere that, at least in morality, maximization is not a requirement of a thin, irresistible form of rationality.[11] If it is a rational requirement at all, it is a requirement of a fairly thick conception of rationality that already incorporates certain judgments about what are good moral reasons—for instance, whether one has more reason to maximize than to equalize. Maximization can look as if it were only a thin requirement because it can be taken to hold merely that, as enjoyment (say) is good, more is better. On that weak interpretation, though, maximization is a standard for ranking outcomes; it has not yet left the domain of the good for that of the moral right. To enter the domain of the right, one has to take a fateful decision as to when benefiting one person justifies harming another. One can adopt a maximizing standard there, too, but it is hardly any longer thin and irresistible. Consequentialism is a moral view. The only tenable form of consequentialism is an impure one in which lower level judgments about the right are derivable from the good plus at least one high-level principle of the right. The right and the good cannot be kept on opposite sides of a line of inference.

VI. Human Good and Human Agents

There is a further way in which the human good and human agency raise trouble for consequentialism. There are many forces at work shaping moral norms. One force is the human good itself. Recall the list: deep personal relations, accomplishment, understanding, and so on. Most of these goods involve commitment to particular persons or causes. Commitment reduces freedom: one cannot take up and put aside this sort of life at will.[12]

A second force is the limits of the will. Our biological nature ties us to certain individuals. Our conception of a good life strengthens those ties

[10] See note 3.

[11] See my *Well-Being*, ch. 9.

[12] See *ibid.*, ch. 10, section 2; see also my paper "On the Winding Road from Good to Right," in *Value, Welfare, and Morality*, ed. R. G. Frey and C. Morris, forthcoming, section 1a.

and leads us to make many more. How much freedom is left to us? 'Ought' implies 'can'. Where are the limits of the will—and, especially, where are the limits of our capacity for impartiality? These are crucial, complicated, and neglected empirical questions. We know that these limits shift. One can do more for strangers if their plight becomes vivid to one. One can make greater sacrifices if one is stirred enough by the cause. But in the end, I think, there are important limits to the will: one cannot be completely impartial[13]—at least, not if one is living the kind of life that realizes the human good.

A third force shaping moral norms is the demands of social life. Our social life requires us to hit upon, or at least to take part in, stable patterns of cooperation. Sometimes we explicitly strike a bargain, but many key social institutions emerge without conscious calculation and choice. Institutions of property, for instance, are shaped by deep forces. They may be a human correlate of animal territoriality. They are probably influenced by not fully conscious beliefs about the limits of the will—about, for instance, the strength of one's commitments to one's family. Moreover, many social institutions generate rights and obligations: if it is your property, I must keep hands off. The rights and obligations generated are important; the institutions that generate them produce most of the major goods of our lives.[14]

A fourth force is the limits of knowledge. Some information is beyond our intellectual capacity, not just for now but forever. What set of norms would, if they were dominant in our society, maximize utility impartially? What set of dispositions would, if they were ours, lead us to behave in a utility-maximizing way over the course of our lives?[15] The answers are beyond me. There are, of course, degrees of ignorance. Sometimes we know enough to be able to estimate probabilities: for instance, such-and-such is as likely to maximize utility as so-and-so. But at other times we know too little even for that. The daunting questions that I just asked are no doubt answerable, at least in probabilistic terms, when we must judge between two sets of norms-*cum*-dispositions that are far apart in quality. But there will be a wide range in which they are closer in quality and in which our ignorance defeats even judgments of likelihood. We are often as ignorant about an individual social institution as we are about institutions collectively. How far can we assess an institution of property? We can assess egregiously bad forms of it. We can assess this or that part of decent forms of it. But institutions of property in advanced societies are

---

[13] Shelly Kagan denies this in his book *The Limits of Morality*. See my review of the book in *Mind*, vol. 99 (1990); the views expressed there are developed further in my "On the Winding Road from Good to Right," section 1c.

[14] See my *Well-Being*, ch. 10, sections 1 and 2; see also my "On the Winding Road from Good to Right," section 1d.

[15] One finds this question asked, for example, by R. B. Brandt, *A Theory of the Good and the Right* (Oxford: Clarendon Press, 1979), chs. 9–10.

so complex that there will be a wide range of acceptable forms that no doubt differ in quality among themselves, but that we have no hope of ranking. If our institution falls within this range, what is behind the claim that we ought to do this or that is not (that is, not entirely) the promotion of interests but also the fact that this is the institution that we happen to have. Another piece of information permanently beyond us is where the limits of the will are. We can rule out some implausible views on the subject, but here, too, there is a wide range of views that we cannot rank even probabilistically. Since there will be no morality at all until we take a view on the subject, we simply adopt one. The view we adopt is bound to be arbitrary to some degree, and our moral norms will share in this arbitrariness. For instance, we adopt (fairly arbitrarily) a view about how much a typical moral agent can deprive his own children to help distant strangers; having done so, we can work out a policy (which will inherit the arbitrariness) on giving to charity. When our knowledge runs out, contingency and arbitrariness enter to fix what we morally ought to do.[16]

Consequentialism, I have proposed, is the view that the right is derived from the good through a function interpreting equal respect. The four forces I have discussed (and others) push any such consequentialist principle well into the background of moral life. In the foreground, in our everyday moral thinking, are principles such as "Hands off the property of others," "Look after your own children," and so on. Most consequentialists nowadays accept that their principle, "Promote the good impartially," belongs in the background, but that it still plays an enormously important role there, justifying and systematizing all the norms in the foreground. Consequentialists often appeal to the distinction we considered earlier between a decision procedure and a criterion. Although these four forces, they say, make the moral decision procedure (largely) nonconsequentialist, the forces leave the criterion fully consequentialist. The impartial promotion of the good, the consequentialists claim, remains the sole criterion or right-making feature of morality. But these four forces seem to me more powerful than that.

One familiar reason for resisting the consequentialist claim that promotion of the good is the sole right-making feature of morality, is that there are further, deontological right-making features. I want to leave that matter aside. I want to suggest that, quite apart from any possible deontological features, the correct conception of the human good and of human agency lead us to resist this consequentialist claim.

There are interpretations of the claim on which it may well be right. If, for instance, some feature of our institution of property were known to promote the good less well than an available alternative, then, without special reasons, it may not produce a morally authoritative norm. It is

---

[16] See my "On the Winding Road from Good to Right," section 1e.

130   JAMES GRIFFIN

plausible that an issue is *moral* only if the promotion of individual good
is at stake. It is also plausible to think of the whole apparatus of morality as having an object, namely, to make our lives go better than they otherwise would. Still, although the promotion of the good may be the sole
right-making feature in some senses of that phrase, it is not in another:
that is, it is not the only consideration that ultimately determines a moral
reason for action. In this last sense, there are further right-making features: for instance, the limits of the will and the institutions that happen
to have emerged in our society. These further right-making features give
us such moral reasons for action as "It's her property" and "He's my
son."

The promotion of the good cannot play the strong justifying and systematizing role that consequentialists assign it. It plays the role with some
norms but not with all. The fact that certain money is yours, say, has
moral weight in my life. It does so partly because our institution of property helps promote the good, but also because that is the institution of
property in my society and I respect it. The respect I give it does not rest
on a case-by-case calculation of its promotion of good, so I will not normally resort to a case-by-case calculation of interests to decide when to
put the institution's norms aside. The institution generates a norm of a
rough-and-ready nature—"Hands off the property of others." Since the
norm is not justified by case-by-case estimates, it can be set aside only in
extreme cases. The norms of property lose authority when following
them conflicts with the whole object of morality: for instance, a government may seize property for national defense. The norms lose authority
when following them is beyond human capacity: for instance, I may seize
property to save my child's life. It is not that a norm of property does not
get authority from its promoting the good; it is just that it does not get
all of its authority in that way. A norm of property also gets authority
from the fact that it is part of *our* institution, and from the fact that adherence to it (except in extreme cases) is the best that limited agents like us
can do.

Consequentialists think that we can do better, that we can extend the
rationality of promoting the good into the selection of norms, policies,
and dispositions. For instance, rule utilitarians say that we should act in
accordance with the nicely elaborated rules (or in accordance with simpler first-order rules for everyday life, and probably fairly complex
second-order rules to resolve conflicts) that would best promote the good
impartially and in the long run. Motive utilitarians say that we should follow the finely tuned dispositions that would have the same result. But I
doubt that we could perform the large-scale calculations of what is best
that they require, or even determine reasonable approximations of what
is best. I have acknowledged that we can make these judgments when
faced with extreme alternatives—say, when a set of rules or dispositions
is quite bad—and that we can make judgments about this or that feature

of a nonextreme set. But there will be a wide range in which we cannot make judgments, and there will have to be something else at work in those cases to carry us to a determinate norm. Moral norms must be tailored to fit the human moral torso. They are nothing but what such tailoring produces. There are no moral norms outside the boundary set by our capacities. There are not some second-best norms — norms made for everyday use by agents limited in intelligence and will — and then, behind them, true or ideal norms — norms without compromises to human frailty. Moral norms regulate human action; a norm that ignores the limited nature of human agents is not an "ideal" norm, but no norm at all.

But have I really taken the distinction between a decision procedure and a criterion seriously enough? The distinction seems to be at times useful: for instance, as I said earlier, in medical practice. In medicine, though, the criterion (health) is not so remote that it cannot actually be applied: in time, doctors learn whether their treatments work. In parts of moral life, we can also learn how the major interests at stake have been affected, but, in many other parts, we never do. What most promotes interests is often permanently beyond our reach. Then a "criterion" like that can play no role, not even that of criterion.

Consequentialists say that moral norms are justified, perhaps indirectly, by their impartially promoting the good. My suggestion is that moral norms arise from various sources: for example, from solutions to cooperation problems and from commitments to family. They also arise from important values, such as life itself: "Do not deliberately kill the innocent." These norms are not, and could not be, justified by long-term effects on the promotion of the good. Even the norm "Do not deliberately kill the innocent" derives directly from the importance of life, not from the unmanageable calculation of the effects of our adopting this norm rather than any other possible one. Consequentialism assumes that morality is more thoroughly determined by the promotion of the good — and less determined by convention, arbitrariness, and the needs of very limited agents — than it is. In this way, consequentialism is too ambitious: it tries to derive all moral norms from the promotion of the good plus equal respect. Wide though that base may be, it is not wide enough. Consequentialism tries to rationalize morality more than it can be rationalized. Norms are not always fully rationalizable.[17] That does not create problems: we are not bereft of norms. Many norms are present in our lives independently of our deliberation and choice. We treat certain norms as authoritative even though they are not backed by the rationality of individual good. Such reasons can be used to criticize and change those norms, but they do not create or authorize them.

---

[17] We should have found further support for this conclusion if we found irresolvable conflict between moral norms. In another paper, I work out the consequences for moral conflicts of the four forces I have been talking about here; see "Mixing Values," *Proceedings of the Aristotelian Society*, Supplementary Volume 65 (1991), section 4.

132   JAMES GRIFFIN

VII. CONSEQUENTIALISM AND NONCONSEQUENTIALISM

Many of us start by thinking that any account of the good can be incorporated into consequentialism, but that seems not to be true. Once we understand the nature of human goods, once we see the good life that they describe, once we recognize the sort of agent who can live that life, we find it hard to accept certain claims of consequentialism. It is not, I think, that we have to abandon much of what is intuitively appealing about consequentialism (for instance, the belief that in some, perhaps indirect way the moral right rests on the individual good, that nothing can be right or wrong independently of effects on interests), but perhaps we have to abandon enough to want also to give up the name. Nevertheless, I do not think that distancing oneself from consequentialism takes one toward deontology. The firm ground, I think, lies in neither position.

Philosophy, University of Oxford

Part III
A Theory of Evaluation
or Deliberation?

[4]

AMERICAN PHILOSOPHICAL QUARTERLY
Volume 8, Number 3, July 1971

IV. ACT-UTILITARIANISM: ACCOUNT OF RIGHT-MAKING CHARACTERISTICS OR DECISION-MAKING PROCEDURE?

R. EUGENE BALES

IN this paper I want to stress the importance of maintaining a sharp distinction between (a) decision-making procedures, and (b) accounts of what makes right acts right. In particular, I want to show how the failure to keep the distinction clearly in mind has given a type of argument against act-utilitarianism a currency it does not deserve.

The question at issue may be considered to be one of what we take the purpose of an ethical theory to be, or of what we expect of an ethical theory.

To make my intentions quite clear, I should like to emphasize a couple of points at the outset. First, I do not pretend that I am in a position to legislate for anyone what he ought to take the purpose of an ethical theory to be, or what he ought to expect of an ethical theory. More specifically, I do not pretend to be in a position to legislate for anyone what he ought to take the purpose of act-utilitarianism to be, or what he ought to expect of act-utilitarianism.

Secondly, I do not intend to underestimate the difficulties stressed by the type of argument I shall challenge. I do intend to show that these difficulties do not have the disastrous implications for act-utilitarianism some critics claim they have.

Thirdly, I am not concerned, in this paper, to defend act-utilitarianism against all comers. I am not concerned to show that act-utilitarianism is true, or that it is more nearly true than any other ethical theory, or even that it is more nearly true than any other form of utilitarianism. I am concerned only to show that one type of argument against act-utilitarianism—a type of argument which enjoys some popularity nowadays—is not a good type of argument.

Fourthly, I shall speak of act-utilitarianism as that normative doctrine which maintains that a particular act (as opposed to a type of act or a class of acts) is right if and only if its utility—that

is, its contribution toward intrinsically good states of affairs—is no less than that of some alternative. At best this is a rough and ready formulation of one form of act-utilitarianism. However, the type of argument I wish to challenge is supposed to apply to a great many forms of act-utilitarianism. My critique should apply whenever such arguments are used against act-utilitarianism as a theory of objective rightness, i.e., as a theory which maintains that all and only right acts are those whose actual consequences (as opposed to expectable consequences) are, e.g., optimally contributive toward intrinsically good states of affairs.

Arguments of the type I shall challenge in this paper are characterized by an emphasis on practical difficulties involved in, or paradoxes arising out of, the attempt to apply act-utilitarian theory to concrete moral situations. The arguments themselves take several forms. "Weaker" forms are used to attempt to establish that, because of difficulties involved in determining which of the acts open to us at a given time would contribute toward intrinsically good states of affairs no less than any alternative, the attempt to act as an act-utilitarian is impracticable or self-defeating. "Stronger" forms are used to attempt to establish that, if any really serious attempt were made to deliberate along act-utilitarian lines, the deliberator would be trapped in a vicious regress. In still other forms a generalization test, "What would happen if everyone deliberated along act-utilitarian lines?" is employed. My thesis is that a systematic confusion runs throughout all such arguments and that at least some of the problems they stress are spurious. I believe that by keeping clearly in mind the distinction between decision-making procedures and accounts of what makes right acts right, we can see both that arguments of this type are not good arguments and why they are not good arguments.

A "weak" form of the type of argument I am

considering might proceed as follows. Calculating the consequences of even insignificant acts is an exceedingly complex task. Calculating and comparing the consequences of alternative acts obviously compounds the complexity. Often we have so little information at our disposal, or are so personally involved, that we cannot calculate with any degree of reliability even if we try. Furthermore, calculating and comparing the relative utilities of alternative acts may be very time-consuming. Indeed, in some cases, circumstances may be such that if we attempt to calculate and compare the utilities of alternative acts, we virtually choose one of the alternatives: the familiar case of the drowning man, and the case of a promise to have done a certain thing by a time that is now in the very near future, are examples of this kind of situation. For if we take the time to attempt to calculate and compare the relative utilities of various helping-the-drowning-man acts and various not-helping-the-drowning-man acts, we virtually choose not to help him. If we take the time to attempt to calculate and compare the relative utilities of various promise-keeping acts and various promise-breaking acts, we virtually choose to break the promise. Therefore, if there occur cases in which an act which is right by act-utilitarian standards must be performed quickly if it is to be performed at all—and surely such cases do occur— attempting to apply act-utilitarian theory to these cases is tantamount to choosing, by default, to perform an act which is wrong by act-utilitarian standards.

Other situations are not of this kind, however. In some cases nothing in the nature of the situation would prevent us from deliberating more or less indefinitely. But, the argument proceeds, unless some act-utilitarian justification can be given for cutting deliberation short, every possible alternative act, ". . . however trivial, might become, and on some views ought to be, a subject of utilitarian calculation: not only those actions about which I commonly do think a little, but others which I could bring under deliberate control if I set myself to do so."[1] Surely, however, it would be absurd to deliberate about trivial alternatives, including those I could perform "if I set myself to do so." Should I take one step to the left? Two steps to the left? One step to the right and one back? Twiddle my thumbs counter-clockwise? Indefinitely many trivial alternatives are open to us at any given time. Must all of them be a subject of

act-utilitarian calculation? If so, it would seem that any really serious attempt to put act-utilitarian theory into practice virtually guarantees that act-utilitarian theory will not be put into practice: that we would perform acts no less contributive toward intrinsically good states of affairs than any alternatives, if we sat around dreaming up alternatives and attempting to calculate and compare their consequences, seems unlikely.

A "strong" form of this type of argument sometimes is developed in the following way. We consider a case of the second kind mentioned above, viz., one in which decision is postponable. For the sake of simplicity, we begin by supposing that two acts, A and B, are open to the agent. Which should he perform? If the agent is a consistent act-utilitarian, the argument goes, he will estimate and compare the probable consequences of A and B and perform the one with the better probable consequences. In brief, he will calculate. But the act of calculating is itself an act which the agent may or may not choose to perform. Thus, a third act, C, the act of calculating, has entered the picture. Shall the agent, then, simply perform A, or shall he perform B, or shall he perform C? If the agent is a consistent act-utilitarian, these alternatives, too, provide an occasion for calculating, and a fourth alternative presents itself, D, which is the act of calculating the probable consequences of A, B, and C. But of course D is an alternative itself subject to calculation, and the agent is caught in a vicious regress.

The regress may be generated in a slightly different way: because at any given time uncountably many acts, both non-trivial and trivial, are open to us, we may deliberate more or less indefinitely about which of the acts to perform. We agree that indefinite deliberation would be absurd, but if the act-utilitarian must deliberate about whether to cut deliberation short—and apparently he must, if he is to justify cutting deliberation short on act-utilitarian grounds—he is, again, caught in a vicious regress.

Usually these forms of the type of argument I am considering are used to emphasize the indispensability of rules to moral decision-making. The weaker form emphasizes the practical indispensability of rules, the stronger their theoretical indispensability; hence the distinction between "weak" and "strong" forms.

In the face of arguments such as these, act-utilitarians typically introduce the notion of "rules-

[1] A. Duncan-Jones, "Utilitarianism and Rules," *The Philosophical Quarterly*, vol. 8 (1957), p. 366.

of-thumb," rules which are practically indispensable guidelines to behavior, and which we more or less habitually follow, but which in no theoretical sense are determinative of the rightness or wrongness of acts. Act-utilitarians can (and do) argue that by experience we discover that keeping promises, telling the truth, helping one's neighbor when he is in distress, etc., are kinds of actions which generally conduce to better states of affairs than, e.g., refraining from such actions whenever it is convenient to do so. To facilitate decision and action, we devise rules-of-thumb such as "Don't tell lies," "Don't break promises," "Help your neighbor," etc., which we generally are justified, on act-utilitarian grounds, in following. We are justified in following them for the very reasons emphasized by critics in arguments like the above. Of course no act-utilitarian claims that the rightness or wrongness of an act derives from a rule-of-thumb, or that rules-of-thumb define or establish one's obligations. In the final analysis, only the question of whether a particular act contributes toward intrinsically good states of affairs no less than would any alternative is relevant to the question of its rightness or wrongness. Nevertheless, the act-utilitarian may agree with his critics that rules are practically indispensable.

> It is true that we may choose to habituate ourselves to behave in accordance with certain rules, such as to keep promises, in the belief that behaving in accordance with these rules is generally optimific, and in the knowledge that we most often just do not have time to work out individual pros and cons. When we act in such an habitual fashion we do not of course deliberate or make a choice. The act utilitarian will, however, regard these rules as mere rules of thumb, and will use them only as rough guides. Normally he will act in accordance with them when he has no time for considering probable consequences or when the advantages of such a consideration of consequences are likely to be outweighed by the disadvantage of the waste of time involved.[2]

Critics, however, can and do reply that the act-utilitarian introduction of rules-of-thumb merely shifts the problem. The act-utilitarian speaks of the use of rules-of-thumb *in general*. But in the particular case he still must deliberate about whether to follow a rule-of-thumb or to calculate. If he does not deliberate in the particular case, it is difficult to see how he can justify following the rule-of-

thumb in that case. But if he does deliberate, the problem of the vicious regress reappears.[3]

A third form of the type of argument I am considering employs a generalization test, "What would happen if everyone deliberated along act-utilitarian lines?". In *Ethical Theory*, R. B. Brandt develops what I take to be an argument of this form; rather, he develops a series of arguments which culminates in an argument of this form.

Brandt begins by asking us to consider the case of the act-utilitarian Frenchman resident in wartime England who is faced with the decision of whether to conform to the governmental directive to conserve gas and electricity by having a maximum temperature of 50° F. in his home, or to use more gas and electricity to keep his temperature up to 70° F. We suppose that he reasons as follows: "The vast majority of Englishmen will conform with the governmental directive. Thus the war effort will not suffer if only a few people (myself included) use enough gas and electricity to keep their homes warm but it will make a lot of difference in their comfort. Thus the general good will be increased if I use enough gas and electricity to keep my home warm; that state of affairs in which a few people are warm is better than one in which no one is. Therefore, I ought to use the gas and electricity." Brandt says this is a perfectly valid argument according to the act-utilitarian theory and suggests that it reveals a serious flaw in act-utilitarianism, viz., that act-utilitarianism cannot account for our duty to assume our fair share of the burden when a cooperative sacrifice has to be made for the general good. For the sake of easy reference, I propose to refer to this argument as "Brandt's argument from the maximization of good."

Brandt continues by suggesting that the example discloses a further difficulty. Let us suppose the Frenchman goes on to reason as follows: "If enough other people decide to use gas and electricity, so that the war is lost, my abstaining won't have made any difference to the war effort, but it will have made a lot of difference in my comfort. Thus the general harm will be decreased if I use enough gas and electricity to keep my home warm. Therefore, I ought to use the gas and electricity." Brandt seems to believe this argument also is valid and that it also reveals a serious flaw in the act-utilitarian theory, viz., that act-utilitarianism will

[2] J. J. C. Smart, *Outline of a System of Utilitarian Ethics* (New York, 1962), p. 30.
[3] In their recently published textbook, *Moral Philosophy*, R. T. Garner and Bernard Rosen of Ohio State University develop an elaborate argument along these lines. A. Duncan-Jones, *op. cit.*, mentions in passing the possibility of such a regress.

justify self-indulgent behavior whenever any substantial benefit accrues to the agent as a result of such behavior. I propose to refer to this argument as "Brandt's argument from the minimization of harm."

Thus far, Brandt's point seems to be that, in cases where general cooperation is required to achieve a desired result, the act-utilitarian comes out with a justification for self-indulgent behavior whatever the assumed outcome. In the Frenchman's case, if the war is won anyway, he will have maximized the general good by increasing his own welfare, and if the war is lost, he will have minimized the general harm. Thus, given either outcome—defeat or victory—he ought to use the gas and electricity.

These arguments are interesting in their own right, but whether they are forms of the type of argument I am challenging is not clear. However, they set the stage for what seems to me to be a third form of that type of argument.

Brandt now asks us to suppose that every Englishman reasons the way the Frenchman does. Then everybody will come out with a justification for self-indulgent behavior and the war will be lost. Brandt concludes that "if everybody follows this act-utilitarian reasoning, the war will be lost, with disastrous effects for everybody. Thus, universal obedience of the act-utilitarian directive to seek the public good may well cause great public harm."[4] Here Brandt's point seems to be that the act-utilitarian theory is to be rejected because everyone's *reasoning* in this act-utilitarian fashion could well lead to harm and injustice. I shall refer to this argument as "Brandt's argument from universal act-utilitarian reasoning."

When J. J. C. Smart, in defense of act-utilitarianism, discusses Brandt's argument from universal act-utilitarian reasoning, he objects that Brandt ". . . fails to recognize that the Frenchman would have used as an empirical premiss in his calculation the proposition that very few people would be likely to reason as he does. They would presumably be adherents of a traditional, non-utilitarian morality."[5] Smart agrees, however, that in a society composed entirely of act-utilitarians, the Frenchman would be in trouble. Because he would not be able to depend on his fellow act-utilitarians to follow blindly the governmental directive, and

because he needs premises about what other people will do to calculate the probable consequences of alternative acts open to him, he will not be able to plan his course of action. Moreover, each of his fellow act-utilitarians is in the same boat: each needs premises about what other people (including the Frenchman) will do to carry out *his* calculation. "There is a circularity in the situation," Smart writes, "which cries out for the technique of game theory."[6]

In the passages which follow, Smart proposes a game-theoretical solution to the Frenchman's problem in the all act-utilitarian society. He admits that ". . . the matter is of little practical importance," but maintains that ". . . it is of interest for the theoretical understanding of ethics."[7]

I confess I see little point in outlining here Smart's ingenious and interesting appeal to game theory, for I see no difference, that would affect the present discussion, between the appeal to game theory and the appeal to rules-of-thumb. Both are attempts to overcome the objection that "act-utilitarian reasoning" or "act-utilitarian deliberation" is self-defeating, and I am convinced that a clever critic, if he were intent on doing so, could devise an argument purported to show that an act-utilitarian's attempting to use game theory would be just as impracticable, self-defeating, or paradoxical as is his attempt to use rules-of-thumb.

My thesis is that all these arguments from so-called "act-utilitarian reasoning" or "act-utilitarian deliberation" are mistaken, not in detail, but in conception. That is, I believe they share a common confusion, a confusion which demands clarification, and I propose to cut the Gordian knot by posing a simple and straightforward question: What do we take the purpose of ethical theories in general and act-utilitarianism in particular to be? What do we expect of an ethical theory? What do we think an ethical theory is supposed to do?

One time-honored answer to my question is that an ethical theory may be expected to provide an account of right-making characteristics, good-making characteristics, or the like. That is, an ethical theory is supposed to provide an account of that characteristic, or perhaps that very complex set of characteristics, which all and only right acts have by virtue of which they are right, or which all and only good things or states of affairs have

[4] R. B. Brandt, *Ethical Theory* (Englewood Cliff., 1959), p. 390.
[5] *Op. cit.*, pp. 42 f.
[6] *Ibid.*, p. 43.
[7] *Loc. cit.*

by virtue of which they are good, and so on. Philosophers who expect this sort of thing of an ethical theory probably will tend to look to act-utilitarianism as an account of right-making characteristics.

However, some philosophers apparently expect something different, or something more, of an ethical theory. For example, when Smart appeals to game theory, he seems to be seeking a procedure which, if followed, would provide us in practice with correct and helpful answers to questions like, "Ought I in this particular case to use enough gas and electricity to keep my home warm?". The key word here is "helpful," for if act-utilitarianism provides a correct account of right-making characteristics, it does provide a correct answer, of a kind, to such questions. The answer to the above question would be, "If and only if doing so would maximize utility." Unfortunately, this answer may seem singularly unhelpful, and one might be inclined to reply, "Yes, but that isn't what I want to know. I want to know *which* alternative to perform, and you haven't told me that." But, of course, the act-utilitarian has told us. He has not told us whether in fact the utility of using the gas and electricity in this case would be less than that of not using the gas and electricity, but he has told us which alternative, under one description, to perform: the one which would maximize utility. Whether what he says is true is another matter, of course. But even if it is, we should like to have a procedure which would help us signal out, in the particular case *and under an immediately helpful description*, which alternative would in fact maximize utility. In short, we should like to have a decision-making *procedure*. Here, then, is another task we might expect an ethical theory to perform: to provide a decision-making procedure.

These are not the only options open to us. We might expect an ethical theory to provide an account of the considered moral judgments of informed, mature persons in their disinterested, reflective moments: in "Some Merits of One Form of Rule-Utilitarianism,"[8] Brandt seems to expect his "Ideal Moral Code" theory to provide this kind of account. Other philosophers seem to expect an ethical theory to provide an account of the modes of moral reasoning employed by ordinary men, or to reflect the moral opinions of ordinary men, or to provide an analysis of the meanings of terms which are an essential part of the language of our moral discourse.

I concede that there may be no reason *a priori* why a single ethical theory could not fulfill all these expectations, although to my knowledge none has ever done so as a matter of fact. I believe there are good reasons for believing that no ethical theory can fulfill all these expectations in one breath, as it were, but perhaps a theory comprised of a series of conjuncts could—with one conjunct being an account of right-making characteristics, another conjunct being an account of good-making characteristics, another being a decision-making procedure, and so on. I am willing to concede, moreover, that given certain plausible assumptions, we might be able to derive, say, an account of right-making characteristics from an account of the considered moral judgments of informed, mature persons in their disinterested, reflective moments. But providing an account of right-making characteristics still is not *the same thing* as providing an account of the considered moral judgments of informed, mature persons in their disinterested, reflective moments, nor is it the same thing as providing a decision-making procedure.

The point I wish to emphasize—and the point which constitutes the backbone of my argument—is that a theory (like act-utilitarianism) could satisfy one of the expectations enumerated above, and do it very nicely, and yet fail to satisfy others of the expectations. A striking example of what I have in mind is the analytic proposition that all and only right acts are those having the characteristic of rightness. This is a proposition which specifies a characteristic which all and only right acts have by virtue of which they are right. It is hardly a useful decision-making guide for our Frenchman trying to decide whether he ought to use gas and electricity to keep his home warm, however; for that matter, it isn't a very interesting account of right-making characteristics, either.

I am concentrating on the distinction between ethical theories conceived of as accounts of right-making characteristics, good-making characteristics, etc., and ethical theories conceived of as decision-making procedures, because the arguments I am challenging gain their plausibility from playing the one off against the other. My claim is that a proposed ethical theory—and I have act-utilitarianism in mind—*could* provide a correct account of right-making characteristics *without* spelling out a procedure which, if followed, would crank out in practice a correct and immediately helpful answer to questions like, "Ought

[8] In *University of Colorado Studies, Series in Philosophy*, vol. 3 (1967), pp. 39–65.

I in this case to use enough gas and electricity to keep my home warm?"

An appropriate question at this point is, "What do act-utilitarians themselves expect of their ethical theory? Do they expect it to provide an account of right-making characteristics, or a decision-making procedure, or both, or something else?" Unfortunately, it isn't clear what the correct answer to this question should be. Every formulation of act-utilitarianism I have seen states that an act is right if and only if it would contribute no less than would any alternative toward intrinsically good states of affairs, or something like this. This surely looks like an account of right-making characteristics to me. I cannot see that such a claim even pretends to tell us how to determine in practice which are those acts which in fact would maximize utility. Nevertheless, act-utilitarians frequently do recommend a particular decision-making procedure, the procedure of estimating and comparing probable consequences of alternative particular acts, and certainly this is the decision-making procedure most frequently associated with act-utilitarianism, by act-utilitarians and critics alike. Indeed, Smart maintains that act-utilitarianism is intended, at least in part, *to be* a decision-making procedure. He writes, "The utilitarian criterion, then, is *designed* to help a person who could do various things if he chose to do them, to decide which of these things he should do."[9] And in another passage he writes ". . . act utilitarianism is *meant to give a method of deciding* what to do in those cases where we do indeed decide what to do."[10]

Earlier I said that I do not pretend to be in a position to legislate for anyone what he ought to take the purpose of act-utilitarianism to be, or what he ought to expect of act-utilitarianism. Obviously, however, both those philosophers who have advanced arguments of the type I am challenging, and those who have attempted to counter them, either *do* expect act-utilitarianism to provide both an account of right-making characteristics and a decision-making procedure, or believe that it claims to provide both.

Weak forms of this type of argument are used to attempt to show that one kind of decision-making procedure, the procedure of estimating and comparing probable consequences of alternative acts, is an impracticable or self-defeating procedure to use to try to determine, from the alternatives open

to us at a given time, the one or ones—under immediately helpful descriptions—which would be pronounced right by the act-utilitarian account of right-making characteristics. Strong forms of this type of argument are used to attempt to show that any serious attempt to use such a procedure traps the user in a vicious regress.

The three arguments from Brandt are rather more difficult to assess. Brandt places his arguments in the mouth of the Frenchman, as it were, so it is not clear whether we should interpret them as critiques of the act-utilitarian account of right-making characteristics, or of the procedure of estimating and comparing probable consequences of alternative acts, or of both. The distinction may not be important to our evaluation of Brandt's arguments from the maximization of good and the minimization of harm, but it is essential to our evaluation of his argument from universal "act-utilitarian reasoning." One interpretation requires one treatment of this argument; the other interpretation requires a different treatment.

Suppose we interpret the argument from the maximization of good in the following way. We take as premisses the proposition that in fact the vast majority of Englishmen will conform with the governmental directive, the proposition that the war effort in fact will not suffer if only a few people use enough gas and electricity to keep their homes warm, and the proposition that that state of affairs in which a few people have warm homes is better than one in which no one has. These propositions, together with the act-utilitarian account of right-making characteristics, do seem to me to imply that it would be right for a few people to use the gas and electricity; the Frenchman could be one of the few. And if the act-utilitarian account of right-making characteristics in fact has this implication, I agree with Brandt that a serious flaw has been revealed. Certainly the notion that that kind of parasitic behavior should be morally right does not sit well with me. A similar interpretation of Brandt's argument from the minimization of harm seems to me to reveal similarly a serious flaw in the act-utilitarian account of right-making characteristics. But under this kind of interpretation, Brand't argument from universal "act-utilitarian reasoning" will not work. For it simply cannot—*logically* cannot—be the case that in fact the war effort will not suffer if every Englishman uses enough gas and electricity to keep

[9] *Op. cit.*, p. 33. My italics.
[10] *Ibid.*, p. 31. My italics.

his home warm, if in fact every Englishman's using enough gas and electricity to keep his home warm would result in the war's being lost.

But now suppose that we interpret the arguments in a different way. We begin with Brandt's argument from the maximization of good. We assume that the Frenchman is faced with the decision of whether to use the gas and electricity. He attempts to use, as his decision-making procedure, the procedure of estimating and comparing probable consequences of alternatives open to him, and he carries out the following bit of reasoning: "It seems reasonable to assume, the English character being what it is, that the vast majority of Englishmen will conform with the governmental directive. It seems reasonable to assume that the war effort will not suffer if only a few people, myself included, use enough gas and electricity to keep their homes warm. It seems reasonable to assume that the general good will be increased if I use the gas and electricity. On the basis of these reasonable assumptions and the act-utilitarian account of right-making characteristics, I conclude that it would be right for me to use the gas and electricity." If this interpretation of the argument is what Brandt has in mind, then I agree that the Frenchman's use of the procedure of estimating and comparing probable consequences of alternative acts has permitted him to exempt himself from assuming his fair share of the burden of what ought to be a cooperative sacrifice. I agree that, given a similar interpretation, Brandt's argument from the minimization of harm suggests that the Frenchman's use of that decision-making procedure permits him ostensibly to justify self-indulgent behavior. I agree, moreover, that it is quite possible for every Englishman to carry out the same bit of reasoning the Frenchman carried out, and with just those disastrous results Brandt points out. But on this interpretation, Brandt's argument from universal "act-utilitarian reasoning" is seen to be just a generalized version of the weak form of the type of argument I am criticizing.[11]

The three forms of the type of argument I am challenging may be telling critiques of the decision-making procedure most frequently associated with act-utilitarianism, *as* a decision-making procedure

for act-utilitarianism, but I cannot see that they are even relevant to the question of whether act-utilitarianism, as it is usually formulated, is true. For certainly it could be the case *both* that all and only right acts are those which contribute no less than would any alternative toward intrinsically good states of affairs, *and* that the procedure of estimating and comparing the probable consequences of alternative acts is an impracticable or self-defeating procedure for singling out, under immediately helpful descriptions, right acts so characterized.

The assumption which seems to underlie the arguments we are considering, an assumption apparently shared by act-utilitarians and critics alike, is that acceptance of the act-utilitarian account of right-making characteristics somehow commits one *a priori* to a particular decision-making procedure: the procedure of estimating and comparing probable consequences of alternative acts. This is an erroneous assumption. The act-utilitarian account of right-making characteristics attempts to specify that characteristic, or perhaps that very complex set of characteristics, which all and only right acts have by virtue of which they are right. From the alternatives open to us in concrete situations, we shall want to isolate, under immediately helpful descriptions, the one (or ones) having that characteristic or set of characteristics—provided, of course, we believe that the act-utilitarian account is true and we want to perform the morally right act—but the account itself places no *a priori* restrictions whatever on the procedures we use to isolate that alternative.

"But," someone may object, "how can the act-utilitarian *know*, in each and every case, which of the acts open to him would maximize utility unless he estimates and compares their probable consequences?" How can he know indeed! Perhaps he should roll dice, as Smart suggests.[12] Perhaps he should always follow rules, as Moore suggests.[13] David Gauthier suggests cutting a deck of cards.[14] Perhaps he should pray or consult his horoscope or gypsy fortune teller. I confess I don't know how he is to determine in each and every case which of the acts open to him in fact would maximize utility. I do have a word of advice for him, how-

[11] Someone may object that I have distorted Brandt's intent. His formulation of act-utilitarianism in *Ethical Theory* is, after all, couched in terms of "maximum net *expectable* utility," and he explicitly says that he opts for such a formulation rather than one couched in terms of "maximum net *actual* utility." My reply is that Brandt also explicitly says that the arguments he adduces ". . . in criticism of the theory are effective in whichever way we interpret it. . . ." (Fn. 2, p. 381.)

[12] *Op. cit.*, p. 43.

[13] G. E. Moore, *Principia Ethica* (Cambridge, 1962), p. 164.

[14] D. Gauthier, "Rule-Utilitarianism and Randomization," *Analysis*, vol. 25 (1964–1965), pp. 68–69.

ever: look and see what kind of procedure has tended to work in given kinds of situations. If he doesn't have a foolproof procedure for determining in each and every case which of the acts open to him would maximize utility, at least he can look to those procedures which have tended to be reliable in the past, and he can look to strategists for reliable procedures to use in the future. I take it that Smart's appeal to game theory at the various appeals to rules-of-thumb are just such moves. But they are moves toward a decision-making procedure. As such, their success or failure will tend not at all to show that the act-utilitarian account of right-making characteristics is true or false. Indeed, the very notion of a successful or unsuccessful decision-making procedure for act-utilitarianism presupposes the act - utilitarian account of right-making characteristics. For what would be a successful decision-making procedure for act-utilitarianism be, if not one that enables us successfully to single out, under immediately helpful descriptions, which of the acts open to us in concrete situations would be pronounced right by the act-utilitarian account of right-making characteristics?

Although the act-utilitarian's account of right-making characteristics places no *a priori* limitations on the decision-making procedures he adopts, there is a sense in which his account does dictate his procedures. His account dictates his procedures insofar as, but only insofar as, the procedures are or are not reliable methods for singling out, under immediately helpful descriptions, which of the acts open to him at a given time would maximize utility. Here I echo the claim, frequently made by act-utilitarians, that use of rules-of-thumb, game theory, or the like, may be justified on act-utilitarian grounds. But by failing to point out that acceptance of the act-utilitarian account of right-making characteristics commits one *a priori* no more to the procedure of estimating and comparing probable consequences of alternative acts than it does to any other decision-making procedure, the act-utilitarian has left himself open to further harassment from advocates of the type of argument I have been criticizing in this paper.

In conclusion, I should like to anticipate and respond to two possible objections. Someone may object, first, that the distinction I am drawing between the act-utilitarian account of right-making characteristics and the decision-making procedure of estimating and comparing probable consequences of alternative acts is illegitimate on

historical grounds. After all, act-utilitarians typically have held that act-utilitarianism provides us with a reasonable way to decide what we ought to do in particular cases, and they have urged us to look to the facts of particular situations rather than to "worship" rules. My reply is that if act-utilitarians have conflated logically independent procedures, that of providing an account of right-making characteristics and that of providing a decision-making procedure, they have conflated them, and someone needs to point that out. I don't see why act-utilitarians should continue to be weighed down with confusions of the past.

Another objection may be that I have failed even to mention the one thing we expect most of an ethical theory: help in making moral decisions. In light of this, we expect an account of right-making characteristics *to be* a decision-making procedure. The distinction I have drawn is illegitimate because it is artificial; I have drawn a distinction where in fact there is none to be drawn.

My reply to the first part of the objection is that I agree that we expect an ethical theory to provide help in making moral decisions, but I see no reason to believe that the help we reasonably can expect from an ethical theory is as immediate or direct as the objection suggests it should be. We expect scientific theories to help us cope with the world around us, but as far as I know, no one has objected that if we had to calculate the mass of the physical bodies involved, when we wanted to know whether we would fall if we jumped from a second-story window of a blazing building, we would be burned to death; and that, therefore, Newton's Laws are of no help at all in coping with the world around us. I do not wish to suggest that there are no differences between a scientific theory and an ethical theory. I do wish to suggest that theories of any kind may be too general to provide the immediately practical kind of help the objection suggests an ethical theory should provide. Anyway, having a true account of right-making characteristics could be of considerable practical help, even if the account were general. Although it probably would not tell us how to single out, from the acts open to us at a given time, those which in fact have the morally relevant features, it at least could tell us what to look for. It could provide a standard against which to measure the success or failure of rules-of-thumb and moral codes: those are successful the adoption of which tends to maximize the performance of acts pronounced right by the account.

My reply to the second part of the objection is only that it seems transparently obvious to me that the claim, that what makes right acts is that they maximize utility, is not equivalent to the claim, that the way to pick out the right acts so characterized from the alternatives open to us at a given time is to estimate and compare the probable consequences of the alternatives. If I am right, and the two claims are not equivalent, then the distinction is neither artificial nor illegitimate. And if, as I believe, the arguments from "act-utilitarian reasoning" or "act-utilitarian deliberation" gain their plausibility from playing one claim off against the other, the distinction seems to me to be one well worth keeping in mind.[15]

Stanford University and the University of Warsaw

Received May 22, 1970

---

[15] Another version of this paper is forthcoming, in Polish translation, in *Etyka*, vol. 8. Still earlier versions, under the title, "Act-Utilitarianism: Ethical Theory or Decision-Making Procedure?", were read before the Philosophy Club, California State College at Hayward, and the American Philosophical Association, Western Division, at its convention in Portland, Oregon.

[5]

MOTIVE UTILITARIANISM *

PHILOSOPHERS have written much about the morality of traits of character, much more about the morality of actions, and much less about the morality of motives. [By "motives" here I mean principally wants and desires, considered as giving rise, or tending to give rise to actions. A desire, if strong, stable, and for a fairly general object (e.g., the desire to get as much money as possible), may perhaps constitute a trait of character; but motives are not in general the same, and may not be as persistent, as traits of character.] Utilitarian theories form a good place to begin an investigation of the relation between the ethics of motives and the ethics of actions, because they have a clear structure and provide us with familiar and comprehensible, if not always plausible, grounds of argument. I believe that a study of possible treatments of motives in utilitarianism will also shed light on some of the difficulties surrounding the attempt to make the maximization of utility the guiding interest of ethical theory.

I

What would be the motives of a person morally perfect by utilitarian standards? It is natural to suppose that he or she would be completely controlled, if not exclusively moved, by the desire to maximize utility. Isn't this ideal of singlemindedly optimific motivation demanded by the principle of utility, if the principle, as Bentham puts it, "states the greatest happiness of all those whose interest is in question, as being the right and proper, and only right and proper and universally desirable, end of human action"? [1]

But there is a good utilitarian objection to such singlemindedness: it is not in general conducive to human happiness. As Sidgwick says, "Happiness [general as well as individual] is likely to be better attained if the extent to which we set ourselves consciously to aim at it be carefully restricted." [2] Suggestions of a utilitarian theory about motivation that accommodates this objection can be found in both Bentham and Sidgwick.

The test of utility is used in different theories to evaluate differ-

* The largest part of my work on this paper was supported by a fellowship from the National Endowment for the Humanities. I am indebted to several, and especially to Gregory Kavka, Jan Narveson, and Derek Parfit, for helpful discussion and comments on earlier versions.

1 Jeremy Bentham, *An Introduction to the Principles of Morals and Legislation* (New York: Hafner, 1961) (referred to hereafter as *Introduction*, with page number), p. 1n.

2 Henry Sidgwick, *The Methods of Ethics*, seventh edition (New York: Dover, 1966) (referred to hereafter as *Methods*, with page number), p. 405.

ent objects. It is applied to acts in act utilitarianism and to roles, practices, and types of action in the various forms of rule utilitarianism. In the view about motives stated in the first paragraph above, the test is not applied at all: nothing is evaluated for its utility, but perfect motivation is identified with an all-controlling desire to maximize utility. The test of utility could be applied in various ways in the evaluation of motives.

It could be applied directly to the motives themselves, and is so applied by Bentham, when he says,

> If they [motives] are good or bad, it is only on account of their effects: good, on account of their tendency to produce pleasure, or avert pain: bad, on account of their tendency to produce pain, or avert pleasure (*Introduction*, 102).

Alternatively, we could apply the test directly to objects of desire and only indirectly to the desires, saying that the best motives are desires for the objects that have most utility. Sidgwick seems to take this line when he says,

> While yet if we ask for a final criterion of the comparative value of the different objects of men's enthusiastic pursuit, and of the limits within which each may legitimately engross the attention of mankind, we shall none the less conceive it to depend upon the degree in which they respectively conduce to Happiness (*Methods*, 406).

Or we could apply the test of utility to the acts to which motives give rise (or are likely to give rise) and, thence, indirectly to the motives; the best motives would be those productive of utility-maximizing acts.[3]

Another approach, also endorsed by Bentham, is to evaluate motives by the intentions to which they give rise: "A motive is good, when the intention it gives birth to is a good one; bad, when the intention is a bad one" (*Introduction*, 120). The value of an intention to do an act, he regards as depending, in turn, on whether "the consequences of the act, had they proved what to the agent they seemed likely to be, *would* have been of a beneficial nature" or the opposite (*Introduction*, 93). This approach seems inconsistent with Bentham's insistence that the test of utility must be applied to everything that is to be evaluated—that

> Strictly speaking, nothing can be said to be good or bad, but either in itself; which is the case only with pain or pleasure: or on account

---

[3] This too may find some support in Sidgwick. Cf. *Methods*, 493, on the praise of motives conceived to prompt to felicific conduct.

of its effects; which is the case only with things that are the causes or preventives of pain and pleasure (*Introduction*, 87; cf. 102).

Bentham would presumably defend the evaluating of intentions by the utility of expected consequences of the intended act rather than the utility of the intentions themselves in the same way that he defends a similar method of evaluating dispositions. That is, he would appeal to the assumption "that in the ordinary course of things the consequences of actions commonly turn out conformable to intentions" (*Introduction*, 133), so that there is no practical difference between the utility of the intention and the utility of the expected consequences of the intended action. This assumption is plausible as regards the short-term consequences of our actions, though even there it yields at best a very rough equivalence between utility of intentions and utility of expected consequences. It is wildly and implausibly optimistic as regards our ability to foresee the long-term consequences of our actions.[4]

Bentham similarly regards the evaluating of motives by the value of intentions arising from them as consistent with (or even practically equivalent to) a direct application of the test of utility to motives, on the ground that the intention resulting from a motive is responsible for "the most material part of [the motive's] effects" (*Introduction*, 120). His position will still be inconsistent, however, unless he maintains (falsely, I believe) that the resulting intentions to act are responsible for *all* the relevant effects of having a motive.

If the moral point of view, the point of view from which moral evaluations are made, is dominated by concern for the maximization of human happiness, then it seems we must revert to the thesis that the test of utility is to be applied directly to everything, including motives. This is the conclusion toward which the following argument from Sidgwick tends:

> Finally, the doctrine that Universal Happiness is the ultimate *standard* must not be understood to imply that Universal Benevolence is the only right or always best *motive* of action. For . . . if experience shows that the general happiness will be more satisfactorily attained if men frequently act from other motives than pure universal philanthropy, it is obvious that these other motives are reasonably to be preferred on Utilitarian principles (*Methods*, 413).

---

[4] Also, as Gregory Kavka has pointed out to me, the utility of *having* an intention (e.g., to retaliate if attacked) may be quite different from the utility (actual or expected) of *acting* on it. I shall be making a similar point about motives, below.

Accordingly, the theory that will be my principal subject here is that one pattern of motivation is morally better than another to the extent that the former has more utility than the latter. The morally perfect person, on this view, would have the most useful desires, and have them in exactly the most useful strengths; he or she would have the most useful among the patterns of motivation that are causally possible for human beings.[5] Let us call this doctrine *motive utilitarianism*.

II

It is distinct, both theoretically and practically, from act utilitarianism. It can be better, by motive-utilitarian standards, to have a pattern of motivation that will lead one to act wrongly, by act-utilitarian standards, than to have a motivation that would lead to right action. Even if there is no difference in external circumstances, the motivational pattern that leads to more useful actions is not necessarily the more useful of two motivational patterns, on the whole. For the consequences of any acts one is thereby led to perform are not always the only utility-bearing consequences of being influenced, to a given degree, by a motive.[6]

This can be seen in the following fictitious case. Jack is a lover of art who is visiting the cathedral at Chartres for the first time. He is greatly excited by it, enjoying it enormously, and acquiring memories which will give him pleasure for years to come. He is so excited that he is spending much more time at Chartres than he had planned, looking at the cathedral from as many interior and exterior angles, and examining as many of its details, as he can. In fact, he is spending too much time there, from a utilitarian point of view. He had planned to spend only the morning, but he is spending the whole day; and this is going to cause him considerable inconvenience and unpleasantness. He will miss his dinner, do several hours of night driving, which he hates, and have trouble finding a place to sleep. On the whole, he will count the day well spent, but some of the time spent in the cathedral will not produce as much utility as would have been produced by departing that

---

[5] It is difficult to say what is meant by the question, whether a certain pattern of motivation is causally possible for human beings, and how one would answer it. I shall sidestep these issues here, for I shall be making comparative evaluations of motives assumed to be possible, rather than trying to determine the most useful of all causally possible motivations.

[6] I am here denying, as applied to motives, what Bernard Williams rather obscurely calls the "act-adequacy premise" [A Critique of Utilitarianism," in J. J. C. Smart and Williams, *Utilitarianism, For and Against* (New York: Cambridge, 1975), pp. 119–130].

much earlier. At the moment, for example, Jack is studying the sixteenth to eighteenth century sculpture on the stone choir screen. He is enjoying this less than other parts of the cathedral, and will not remember it very well. It is not completely unrewarding, but he would have more happiness on balance if he passed by these carvings and saved the time for an earlier departure. Jack knows all this, although it is knowledge to which he is not paying much attention. He brushes it aside and goes on looking at the choir screen because he is more strongly interested in seeing, as nearly as possible, everything in the cathedral than in maximizing utility. This action of his is therefore wrong by act-utilitarian standards, and in some measure intentionally so. And this is not the only such case. In the course of the day he knowingly does, for the same reason, several other things that have the same sort of act-utilitarian wrongness.

On the other hand, Jack would not have omitted these things unless he had been less interested in seeing everything in the cathedral than in maximizing utility. And it is plausible to suppose that if his motivation had been different in that respect, he would have enjoyed the cathedral much less. It may very well be that his caring more about seeing the cathedral than about maximizing utility has augmented utility, through enhancing his enjoyment, by more than it has diminished utility through leading him to spend too much time at Chartres. In this case his motivation is right by motive-utilitarian standards, even though it causes him to do several things that are wrong by act-utilitarian standards.

Perhaps it will be objected that the motive utilitarian should say that Jack ought indeed to have been as interested in the cathedral as he was, but ought to have been even more interested in maximizing utility. Thus he would have had as much enjoyment from the more rewarding parts of the cathedral, according to the objector, but would not have spent too much time on the less rewarding parts. The weak point in this objection is the assumption that Jack's enjoyment of the things he would still have seen would not be diminished in these circumstances. I think, and I take it that Sidgwick thought too,[7] that a great concern to squeeze out the last drop of utility is likely to be a great impediment to the enjoyment of life. Therefore it seems plausible to suppose that from a motive-utilitarian point of view Jack ought not only to have been as

[7] I believe this is the most natural reading of Sidgwick, but it may be barely possible to construe him as meaning only that the perpetual *consciousness* of such a concern would be an impediment. See *Methods*, 48f.

strongly interested in seeing the cathedral as he was, but also to
have been as weakly interested in maximizing utility as he was.

In describing this case I have been treating the maximization of
utility as a unitary end which Jack might have pursued for its own
sake. Perhaps it will be suggested that, although an all-controlling
desire for that end would have diminished utility by dulling Jack's
enjoyment, he could have had undimmed enjoyment without wrong
action if he had had the maximization of utility as an *inclusive
end*—that is, if he had been moved by desire for more particular
ends for their own sakes, but in exact proportion to their utility.[8]
But this suggestion is not plausible. While he is in the cathedral
Jack's desire to see everything in it is stronger, and his desire for
the benefits of an early departure is weaker, than would be proportionate to the utility of those ends. And a stronger desire for
an early departure would probably have interfered with his enjoyment just as much as a stronger desire for utility maximization as
such. We are likely in general to enjoy life more if we are often
more interested in the object of an enthusiastic pursuit, and less
concerned about other ends, than would be proportionate to their
utility. It follows that failing (to some extent) to have utility maximization as an inclusive end is often right by motive-utilitarian
standards, and may be supposed to be so in Jack's case.

In order to justify the view that motive utilitarianism implies
something practically equivalent to act utilitarianism one would
have to show that the benefits that justify Jack's motivation by
motive-utilitarian standards also justify his spending time on the
choir screen by act-utilitarian standards. But they do not. For they
are not consequences of his spending time there, but independent
consequences of something that caused, or manifested itself in, his
spending time there. It is not that deciding to devote only a cursory
inspection to the choir screen would have put him in the wrong
frame of mind for enjoying the visit. It is rather that, being in the
right frame of mind for enjoying the visit, he could not bring
himself to leave the choir screen as quickly as would have maximized utility.

III

The act utilitarian may try to domesticate motive utilitarianism,
arguing (A) that motive utilitarianism is merely a theorem of act

---

[8] The terminology of "dominant" and "inclusive" ends was developed by
W. F. R. Hardie, "The Final Good in Aristotle's Ethics," *Philosophy*, XL, 154
(October 1965): 277–295; Rawls makes use of it. J. S. Mill seems to treat the
maximization of utility as an inclusive end in *Utilitarianism*, ch. 4, §§ 5–8.

utilitarianism, and denying (B) that behavior like Jack's inspection of the choir screen, if resulting from obedience to the dictates of motive utilitarianism, can properly be called wrong action.

(A) Since act utilitarianism implies that one ought to do whatever has most utility, it implies that, other things equal, one ought to foster and promote in oneself those motives which have most utility. And that, it may be claimed, is precisely what motive utilitarianism teaches.

(B) Jack was once, let us suppose, an excessively conscientious act utilitarian. Recognizing the duty of cultivating more useful motives in himself, he took a course of capriciousness training, with the result that he now stands, careless of utility, before the choir screen. It would be unfair, it may be argued, to regard what Jack is now doing as a wrong action by utilitarian standards. Rather, we must see it as only an inescapable part of a larger, right action, which began with his enrolling for capriciousness training—just as we do not say that a person rightly jumped from a burning building, saving his life, but wrongly struck the ground, breaking his leg. It is unreasonable, on this view, to separate, for moral evaluation, actions that are causally inseparable.

Both of these arguments are to be rejected. The second (B) involves deep issues about the individuation of actions and the relation between causal determination and moral responsibility. It seems clear enough, however, that Jack's staying at the choir screen is separable from his earlier efforts at character reform in a way that striking the ground is not separable from jumping out of a building. Once you have jumped, it is no longer in your power to refrain from striking the ground, even if you want to. If you are sane and well informed about the situation, you have only one choice to make: to jump or not to jump. There is no further choice about hitting the ground, and therefore it is inappropriate to separate the impact from the leap, as an object of moral evaluation. But even after Jack has taken capriciousness training, it is still in his power to leave the choir screen if he wants to; it is just that he does not want to. His choice to stay and examine it is a new choice, which he did not make, years ago, when he decided to reform. He did decide then to become such that he would sometimes make nonutilitarian choices, but it may not even have occurred to him then that he would ever be in Chartres. It seems perfectly appropriate to ask whether the choice that he now makes is morally right or wrong.

It is plausible, indeed, to say that Jack is not acting wrongly in acting on the motivation that he has rightly cultivated in himself. But I think that is because it is plausible to depart from act utilitarianism at least so far as to allow the rightness or wrongness of Jack's action in this case to depend partly on the goodness or badness of his motive, and not solely on the utility of the act. It is noteworthy in this connection that it would be no less plausible to acquit Jack of wrongdoing if he had always been as easygoing as he now is about small increments of utility, even though there would not in that case be any larger action of character reform, of which Jack's present scrutiny of the choir screen could be regarded as an inescapable part.

A similar irrelevant emphasis on doing something about one's own motivational patterns also infects the attempt (A) to derive motive utilitarianism from act utilitarianism. Motive utilitarianism is not a theorem of act utilitarianism, for the simple reason that motive utilitarianism is not about what motives one ought to foster and promote, or *try* to have, but about what motives one ought to *have*. There is a preconception to be overcome here which threatens to frustrate from the outset the development of any independent ethics of motives. I refer to the assumption that "What should I (try to) do?" is *the* ethical question, and that we are engaged in substantive *ethical* thinking only insofar as we are considering *action*-guiding principles.[9] If we hold this assumption, we are almost bound to read "What motives should I have?" as "What motives should I try to develop and maintain in myself?"

There are other questions, however, that are as fundamental to ethics as "What should I do?" It is characteristic of moral as opposed to pragmatic thinking that, for example, the question, "Have I lived well?" is of interest for its own sake. In pragmatic self-appraisal that question is of interest only insofar as the answer may guide me toward future successes. If I am personally concerned, in more than this instrumental way, and not just in curiosity, about whether I have lived well, my concern is not purely pragmatic, but involves at least a sense of style, if not of morality.

If the question is "Have I lived well?" the motives I have *had* are relevant, and not just the motives I have *tried* to have. If I

---

[9] Cf. Jan Narveson, *Morality and Utility* (Baltimore, Md.: John Hopkins, 1967), p. 105: "Let us begin by recalling the primary function of ethical principles: to tell us what to do, i.e., to guide action. Whatever else an ethical principle is supposed to do, it must do that, otherwise it could not (logically) be an ethical principle at all."

tried to have the right motive, but nonetheless had the wrong one
—if I tried to love righteousness and my neighbors, but failed and
did my duty out of fear of hellfire for the most part—then I did
not live as well as I would have lived if I had *had* the right motive.

Suppose, similarly, that Martha is an overscrupulous utilitarian,
completely dominated by the desire to maximize utility. She has
acted rightly, by act-utilitarian standards, just as often as she could.
Among her right actions (or attempts at right action) are many
attempts to become strongly interested in particular objects—more
strongly, indeed, than is proportionate to their utility. For she
realizes that she and her acquaintances would be happier if she
had such interests. But all these attempts have failed.

Mary, on the other hand, has not had to work on herself to develop such nonutilitarian interests, but has always had them; and,
largely because of them, her motivational patterns have had more
utility, on the whole, than Martha's. The motive utilitarian will
take this as a reason (not necessarily decisive) for saying that
Martha has *lived less well* than Mary. This censure of Martha's
motives is not derivable from act utilitarianism, for her actions
have been the best that were causally possible for her. (If you are
tempted to say that Martha's conscientiousness is better than Mary's
more useful motives, you are experiencing a reluctance to apply
the test of utility to motives.)

IV

I have argued that right action, by act-utilitarian standards, and
right motivation, by motive-utilitarian standards, are incompatable
in some cases. It does not immediately follow, but it may further
be argued, that act utilitarianism and motive utilitarianism are
incompatible theories.

One argument for this conclusion is suggested, in effect, by Bernard Williams. He does not formulate or discuss motive utilitarianism, but he holds that it is inconsistent of J. J. C. Smart, following
Sidgwick, "to present direct [i.e., act] utilitarianism as a doctrine
merely about justification and not about motivation." Williams's
argument is,

> There is no distinctive place for *direct* utilitarianism unless it is,
> within fairly narrow limits, a doctrine about how one should decide
> what to do. This is because its distinctive doctrine is about what acts
> are right, and, especially for utilitarians, the only distinctive interest
> or point of the question what acts are right, relates to the situation
> of deciding to do them (*op. cit.*, 128).

The doctrine about motives that Williams believes to be implied by act utilitarianism is presumably the doctrine, discarded at the beginning of my present essay, that one ought always to be controlled by the desire or purpose of maximizing utility. And this doctrine, if conjoined with plausible empirical beliefs illustrated in section II above, is inconsistent with motive utilitarianism.

There are two questionable points in Williams's argument. One is the claim that for utilitarians the only use of the question, What acts are right? is for guidance in deciding what to do. He defends this claim, arguing that "utilitarians in fact are not very keen on people blaming themselves, which they see as an unproductive activity," and that they therefore will not be interested in the question, "Did he (or I) do the right thing?" (124). I am not convinced by this defense. Blame is a self-administered negative reinforcement which may perhaps cause desirable modifications of future behavior. The retrospective question about the evaluation of one's action is a question in which one can hardly help taking an interest if one has a conscience; one who desires to act well will naturally desire to *have* acted well. And the desire to act well, at least in weighty matters, will surely be approved on motive-utilitarian grounds.

But suppose, for the sake of argument, we grant Williams that the point of act-utilitarian judgments, when they have a point, is to guide us in deciding what to do. His argument still rests on the assumption that the act utilitarian is committed to the view that it is generally useful to ask what acts are right, and that one ought always or almost always to be interested in the question. Why should the act utilitarian be committed to this view? If he is also a motive utilitarian, he will have reason to say that, although it is indeed useful to be guided by utilitarian judgments in actions of great consequence, it is sometimes better to be relatively uninterested in considerations of utility (and so of morality). "For everything there is a season and a time for every matter under heaven: . . . a time to kill, and a time to heal; a time to break down, and a time to build up," said the Preacher (Ecclesiastes 3:1, 3 RSV). The act-and-motive utilitarian adds, "There is a time to be moral, and a time to be amoral." (The act-and-motive utilitarian is one who holds both act and motive utilitarianism as *theories*. He does not, for he cannot, always satisfy the demands of both theories in his acts and motives.)

Perhaps it will be objected that this reply to Williams overlooks the utility of conscientiousness. Conscience is, in part, a motive:

the desire to act or live in accordance with moral principles. If the moral principles are mainly sound, it is so useful a motive that it is important, from a motive-utilitarian standpoint, not to undermine it. This consideration might make a motive utilitarian reluctant to approve the idea of "a time to be amoral," lest such "moral holidays" weaken a predominantly useful conscience.

The question facing the act-and-motive utilitarian at this point is, what sort of conscience has greatest utility. We have seen reason to believe that an act-utilitarian conscience that is scrupulous about small increments of utility would have bad effects on human happiness, smothering many innocent enjoyments in a wet blanket of excessive earnestness. A more useful sort of conscience is probably available to the act-and-motive utilitarian. It would incorporate a vigorous desire to *live well,* in terms of the over-all utility of his life, but not necessarily to *act rightly* on every occasion. Having such a conscience, he would be strongly concerned (1) not to act in ways gravely detrimental to utility, and (2) not to be in a bad motivational state. If he performs a mildly unutilitarian action as an inevitable consequence of the most useful motivation that he can have, on the other hand, he is still living as well as possible, by his over-all utilitarian standards; and there is no reason why such action should undermine his determination to live well. A conscience of this sort seems as possible, and at least as likely to be stable, as a conscience that insists on maximizing utility in every action. Thus the act-and-motive utilitarian has good motive-utilitarian reasons for believing that he should sometimes be, in relation to his act-utilitarian principles, amoral.

v

But this conclusion may be taken, quite apart from Williams's argument, as grounds for thinking that act utilitarianism and motive utilitarianism are incompatible in the sense that holding the latter ought reasonably to prevent us from holding the former as a *moral* theory. The incompatibility has to do with moral seriousness. The problem is not just that one cannot *succeed* in living up to the ideals of both theories simultaneously. It is rather that the motive utilitarian is led to the conclusion that it is morally better on many occasions to be so motivated that one will not even *try* to do what one ought, by act-utilitarian standards, to do. If the act-and-motive utilitarian accepts this conclusion, however, we must wonder whether all his act-utilitarian judgments about what one ought to do are really judgments of *moral* obligation. For it is commonly made a criterion for a theory's being a theory of *moral* obligation, that it claim a special seriousness for its judgments of obligation. By this criterion, act utilitarianism cannot really be a theory of moral obligation (as it purports to be) if it is conjoined with the view that some of its dictates should be taken as lightly as motive utilitarianism would lead us to think they should be taken.

This argument depends on the triviality of any reasonable human interest in some of the obligations that act utilitarianism would lay on us. And the triviality is due to the totalitarian character of act utilitarianism, to its insistence that, as Sidgwick puts it, "it is *always* wrong for a man knowingly to do *anything* other than what he believes to be most conducive to Universal Happiness" (*Methods*, 492, italics mine).

Without this triviality a conflict between the ethics of actions and the ethics of motives need not destroy the seriousness of either. Maybe *no* plausible comprehensive ethical theory can avoid all such conflicts. Are there *some* circumstances in which it is best, for example, in the true morality of motives, to be unable to bring oneself to sacrifice the happiness of a friend when an important duty obliges one, in the true morality of actions, to do so? I don't know. But if there are, the interests involved, on both sides, are far from trivial, and the seriousness of both moralities can be maintained. If one fails to perform the important duty, one ought, seriously, to feel guilty; but one could not do one's duty in such a case without having a motivation of which one ought, seriously, to be ashamed. The situation presents a tragic inevitability of moral disgrace.

There are, accordingly, two ways in which the utilitarian might deal with the argument if he has been trying to combine act and motive utilitarianism and accepts the view I have urged on him about the kind of conscience it would be most useful to have. (A) He could simply acknowledge that he is operating with a modified conception of moral obligation, under which a special seriousness attaches to some but not all moral obligations.[10] He would claim that his use of "morally ought" nonetheless has enough similarity, in other respects, to the traditional use, to be a reasonable extension of it.

(B) The other, to my mind more attractive, way is to modify the act-utilitarian principle, eliminating trivial obligations, and limit-

---

[10] It may be thought that Sidgwick has already begun this modification, by holding that good actions ought not to be praised, nor bad ones blamed, except insofar as it is useful to praise and blame them. See *Methods*, 428 f., 493.

ing the realm of duty to actions that would be of concern to a conscience of the most useful sort. Under such a limitation it would not be regarded as morally wrong, in general, to fail to maximize utility by a *small* margin. One's relatively uninfluential practical choices would be subject to moral judgment only indirectly, through the motive-utilitarian judgment on the motives on which one acted (and perhaps a character-utilitarian judgment on the traits of character manifested by the action). Some acts, however, such as shoplifting in a dime store or telling inconsequential lies, would still be regarded as wrong even if only slightly detrimental in the particular case, because it is clear that they would be opposed by the most useful sort of conscience. I leave unanswered here the question whether a conscience of the most useful kind would be offended by some acts that maximize utility—particularly by some utility-maximizing violations of such rules as those against stealing and lying. If the answer is affirmative, the position we are considering would have approximately the same practical consequences as are commonly expected from rule utilitarianism. This position—that we have a *moral duty* to do an act, if and only if it would be demanded of us by the most useful kind of conscience we could have—may be called "conscience utilitarianism," and is a very natural position for a motive utilitarian to take in the ethics of actions.

The moral point of view—the point of view from which moral judgments are made—cannot safely be defined as a point of view in which the test of utility is applied directly to all objects of moral evaluation. For it is doubtful that the most useful motives, and the most useful sort of conscience, are related to the most useful acts in the way that the motives, and especially the kind of conscience, regarded as right must be related to the acts regarded as right in anything that is to count as a morality. And therefore it is doubtful that direct application of the test of utility to everything results in a system that counts as a morality.

VI

Considered on its own merits, as a theory in the ethics of motives, which may or may not be combined with some other type of utilitarianism in the ethics of actions, how plausible is motive utilitarianism? That is a question which we can hardly begin to explore in a brief paper, because of the variety of forms that the theory might assume, and the difficulty of stating some of them. The exploration might start with a distinction between individualistic and universalistic motive utilitarianism, analogous to the distinction between act and rule utilitarianism.

Individualistic motive utilitarianism holds that a person's motivation on any given occasion is better, the greater the utility of *his* having it on *that* occasion. This seemed to Bentham, on the whole, the least unsatisfactory view about the moral worth of motives:

> The only way, it should seem, in which a motive can with safety and propriety be styled good or bad, is with reference to its effects *in each individual instance* (*Introduction*, 120, italics mine).

This doctrine seems liable to counterexamples similar to those which are commonly urged against act utilitarianism. An industrialist's greed, a general's bloodthirstiness, may on some occasions have better consequences on the whole than kinder motives would, and even predictably so. But we want to say that they remain worse motives.

Universalistic motive utilitarianism is supposed to let us say this, but is difficult to formulate. If we try to state it as the thesis that motives are better, the greater the utility of *everybody's* having them on *all* occasions, we implausibly ignore the utility of diversity in motives. A more satisfactory view might be that a motivation is better, the greater the average probable utility of *anyone's* having it on *any* occasion. This formulation gives rise to questions about averaging: do we weigh equally the utility of a motive on all the occasions when it could conceivably occur, or do we have some formula for weighing more heavily the occasions when it is more likely to occur? There are also difficult issues about the relevant description of the motive. One and the same concrete individual motive might be described correctly as a desire to protect Henry Franklin, a desire to protect (an individual whom one knows to be) one's spouse, a desire to protect (an individual whom one knows to be) the chief executive of one's government, and a desire to protect (an individual whom one knows to be) a betrayer of the public trust; these motive types surely have very different average utilities. If one makes the relevant description of the motive too full, of course, one risks making universalistic motive utilitarianism equivalent to individualistic.[11] If the description is not full enough, it will be hard to get any determination of average utility at all. Bentham's principal effort, in his discussion of the ethics of mo-

---

[11] By a process similar to that by which David Lyons, in his *Forms and Limits of Utilitarianism* (New York: Oxford, 1965), has tried to show that rule utilitarianism is equivalent to act utilitarianism.

tives, is to show, by a tiresome profusion of examples, that the application of the test of utility to sorts of motive yields no results, because "there is no sort of motive but may give birth to any sort of action" (*Introduction,* 128); his argument depends on the use of very thin descriptions of sorts of motive.

The doctrine that a type of motive is better, the greater the utility of commending or fostering it in a system of moral education, might seem to be another version of universalistic motive utilitarianism, but is not a form of motive utilitarianism at all. For in it the test of utility is directly applied not to motives or types of motive, but to systems of moral education.

I am not convinced (nor even inclined to believe) that any purely utilitarian theory about the worth of motives is correct. But motive-utilitarian considerations will have some place in any sound theory of the ethics of motives, because utility, or conduciveness to human happiness (or more generally, to the good), is certainly a great advantage in motives (as in other things), even if it is not a morally decisive advantage.

                                              ROBERT MERRIHEW ADAMS
University of California, Los Angeles

[6]

PETER RAILTON

Alienation, Consequentialism, and the Demands of Morality

INTRODUCTION

Living up to the demands of morality may bring with it alienation—from one's personal commitments, from one's feelings or sentiments, from other people, or even from morality itself. In this article I will discuss several apparent instances of such alienation, and attempt a preliminary assessment of their bearing on questions about the acceptability of certain moral theories. Of special concern will be the question whether problems about alienation show consequentialist moral theories to be self-defeating.

I will not attempt a full or general characterization of alienation. Indeed, at a perfectly general level alienation can be characterized only very roughly as a kind of estrangement, distancing, or separateness (not necessarily consciously attended to) resulting in some sort of loss (not necessarily consciously noticed).[1] Rather than seek a general analysis I will rely upon examples to convey a sense of what is involved in the sorts of alienation with which I am concerned. There is nothing in a word, and the phenomena to be discussed below could all be considered while avoid-

1. The loss in question need not be a loss of something of value, and *a fortiori* need not be a bad thing overall: there are some people, institutions, or cultures alienation from which would be a boon. Alienation is a more or less troubling phenomenon depending upon what is lost; and in the cases to be considered, what is lost is for the most part of substantial value. It does not follow, as we will see in Section V, that in all such cases alienation is a bad thing on balance. Moreover, I do not assume that the loss in question represents an actual *decline* in some value as the result of a separation coming into being where once there was none. It seems reasonable to say that an individual can experience a loss in being alienated from nature, for example, without assuming that he was ever in communion with it, much as we say it is a loss for someone never to receive an education or never to appreciate music. Regrettably, various relevant kinds and sources of alienation cannot be discussed here. A general, historical discussion of alienation may be found in Richard Schacht, *Alienation* (Garden City, NY: Doubleday, 1971).

135   *Alienation,*
                                       Consequentialism,
                                       and Morality

ing the controversial term 'alienation.' My sense, however, is that there
is some point in using this formidable term, if only to draw attention to
commonalities among problems not always noticed. For example, in the
final section of this article I will suggest that one important form of
alienation in moral practice, the sense that morality confronts us as an
alien set of demands, distant and disconnected from our actual concerns,
can be mitigated by dealing with other sorts of alienation morality may
induce. Finally, there are historical reasons, which will not be entered
into here, for bringing these phenomena under a single label; part of the
explanation of their existence lies in the conditions of modern "civil society," and in the philosophical traditions of empiricism and rationalism—
which include a certain picture of the self's relation to the world—that
have flourished in it.

Let us begin with two examples.

I. JOHN AND ANNE AND LISA AND HELEN

To many, John has always seemed a model husband. He almost invariably
shows great sensitivity to his wife's needs, and he willingly goes out of
his way to meet them. He plainly feels great affection for her. When a
friend remarks upon the extraordinary quality of John's concern for his
wife, John responds without any self-indulgence or self-congratulation.
"I've always thought that people should help each other when they're in
a specially good position to do so. I know Anne better than anyone else
does, so I know better what she wants and needs. Besides, I have such
affection for her that it's no great burden—instead, I get a lot of satisfaction out of it. Just think how awful marriage would be, or life itself,
if people didn't take special care of the ones they love." His friend accuses
John of being unduly modest, but John's manner convinces him that he
is telling the truth: this is really how he feels.

Lisa has gone through a series of disappointments over a short period,
and has been profoundly depressed. In the end, however, with the help
of others she has emerged from the long night of anxiety and melancholy.
Only now is she able to talk openly with friends about her state of mind,
and she turns to her oldest friend, Helen, who was a mainstay throughout.
She'd like to find a way to thank Helen, since she's only too aware of
how much of a burden she's been over these months, how much of a
drag and a bore, as she puts it. "You don't have to thank me, Lisa," Helen

replies, "you deserved it. It was the least I could do after all you've done for me. We're friends, remember? And we said a long time ago that we'd stick together no matter what. Some day I'll probably ask the same thing of you, and I know you'll come through. What else are friends for?" Lisa wonders whether Helen is saying this simply to avoid creating feelings of guilt, but Helen replies that she means every word—she couldn't bring herself to lie to Lisa if she tried.

II. What's Missing?

What is troubling about the words of John and Helen? Both show stout character and moral awareness. John's remarks have a benevolent, consequentialist cast, while Helen reasons in a deontological language of duties, reciprocity, and respect. They are not self-centered or without feeling. Yet something seems wrong.

The place to look is not so much at what they say as what they don't say. Think, for example, of how John's remarks might sound to his wife. Anne might have hoped that it was, in some ultimate sense, in part for *her* sake and the sake of their love as such that John pays such special attention to her. That he devotes himself to her because of the characteristically good consequences of doing so seems to leave her, and their relationship as such, too far out of the picture—this despite the fact that these characteristically good consequences depend in important ways on his special relation to her. She is being taken into account by John, but it might seem she is justified in being hurt by the way she is being taken into account. It is as if John viewed her, their relationship, and even his own affection for her from a distant, objective point of view—a moral point of view where reasons must be reasons for any rational agent and so must have an impersonal character even when they deal with personal matters. His wife might think a more personal point of view would also be appropriate, a point of view from which "It's my wife" or "It's Anne" would have direct and special relevance, and play an unmediated role in his answer to the question "*Why* do you attend to her so?"

Something similar is missing from Helen's account of why she stood by Lisa. While we understand that the specific duties she feels toward Lisa depend upon particular features of their relationship, still we would not be surprised if Lisa finds Helen's response to her expression of gratitude quite distant, even chilling. We need not question whether she has

Alienation,
Consequentialism,
and Morality

strong feeling for Lisa, but we may wonder at how that feeling finds expression in Helen's thinking.[2]

John and Helen both show alienation: there would seem to be an estrangement between their affections and their rational, deliberative selves; an abstract and universalizing point of view mediates their responses to others and to their own sentiments. We should not assume that they have been caught in an uncharacteristic moment of moral reflection or after-the-fact rationalization; it is a settled part of their characters to think and act from a moral point of view. It is as if the world were for them a fabric of obligations and permissions in which personal considerations deserve recognition only to the extent that, and in the way that, such considerations find a place in this fabric.

To call John and Helen alienated from their affections or their intimates is not of itself to condemn them, nor is it to say that they are experiencing any sort of distress. One may be alienated from something without recognizing this as such or suffering in any conscious way from it, much as one may simply be uninterested in something without awareness or conscious suffering. But alienation is not mere lack of interest: John and Helen are not *uninterested* in their affections or in their intimates; rather, their interest takes a certain alienated form. While this alienation may not itself be a psychological affliction, it may be the basis of such afflictions—such as a sense of loneliness or emptiness—or of the loss of certain things of value—such as a sense of belonging or the pleasures of spontaneity. Moreover, their alienation may cause psychological distress in others, and make certain valuable sorts of relationships impossible.

However, we must be on guard lest oversimple categories distort our diagnosis. It seems to me wrong to picture the self as ordinarily divided into cognitive and affective halves, with deliberation and rationality belonging to the first, and sentiments belonging to the second. John's alienation is not a problem on the boundary of naturally given cognitive and affective selves, but a problem partially constituted by the bifurcation of his psyche into these separate spheres. *John's* deliberative self seems remarkably divorced from his affections, but not all psyches need be so divided. That there is a cognitive element in affection—that affection is not a mere "feeling" that is a given for the deliberative self but rather

2. This is not to say that no questions arise about whether Helen's (or John's) feelings and attitudes constitute the fullest sort of affection, as will be seen shortly.

involves as well certain characteristic modes of thought and perception—
is suggested by the difficulty some may have in believing that John really
does love Anne if he persistently thinks about her in the way suggested
by his remarks. Indeed, his affection for Anne does seem to have been
demoted to a mere "feeling." For this reason among others, we should
not think of John's alienation from his affections and his alienation from
Anne as wholly independent phenomena, the one the cause of the other.[3]
Of course, similar remarks apply to Helen.

III. THE MORAL POINT OF VIEW

Perhaps the lives of John and Anne or Helen and Lisa would be happier
or fuller if none of the alienation mentioned were present. But is this a
problem for *morality*? If, as some have contended, to have a morality is
to make normative judgments from a moral point of view and be guided
by them, and if by its nature a moral point of view must exclude considerations that lack universality, then any genuinely moral way of going
about life would seem liable to produce the sorts of alienation mentioned
above.[4] Thus it would be a conceptual confusion to ask that we never be
required by morality to go beyond a personal point of view, since to fail
ever to look at things from an impersonal (or nonpersonal) point of view
would be to fail ever to *be* distinctively moral—not immoralism, perhaps,
but amoralism. This would not be to say that there are not other points
of view on life worthy of our attention,[5] or that taking a moral point of

3. Moreover, there is a sense in which someone whose responses to his affections or
feelings are characteristically mediated by a calculating point of view may fail to know
himself fully, or may seem in a way unknowable to others, and this "cognitive distance"
may itself be part of his alienation. I am indebted here to Allan Gibbard.

4. There is a wide range of views about the nature of the moral point of view and its
proper role in moral life. Is it necessary that one actually act on universal principles, or
merely that one be willing to universalize the principles upon which one acts? Does the
moral point of view by its nature require us to consider everyone alike? Here I am using
a rather strong reading of the moral point of view, according to which taking the moral
point of view involves universalization and the equal consideration of all.

5. A moral point of view theorist might make use of the three points of view distinguished
by Mill: the moral, the aesthetic, and the sympathetic. "The first addresses itself to our
reason and conscience; the second to our imagination; the third to our human fellow-
feeling," from "Bentham," reprinted in *John Stuart Mill: Utilitarianism and Other Writings*, ed. Mary Warnock (New York: New American Library, 1962), p. 121. What is morally
right, in his view, may fail to be "loveable" (e.g., a parent strictly disciplining a child) or
"beautiful" (e.g., an inauthentic gesture). Thus, the three points of view need not concur
in their positive or negative assessments. Notice, however, that Mill has divided the self

139   *Alienation,*
                                        Consequentialism,
                                        and Morality

view is always appropriate—one could say that John and Helen show no
moral defect in thinking so impersonally, although they do moralize to
excess. But the fact that a particular morality requires us to take an
impersonal point of view could not sensibly be held against it, for that
would be what makes it a morality at all.

This sort of position strikes me as entirely too complacent. First, we
must somehow give an account of practical reasoning that does not merely
multiply points of view and divide the self—a more unified account is
needed. Second, we must recognize that loving relationships, friendships,
group loyalties, and spontaneous actions are among the most important
contributors to whatever it is that makes life worthwhile; any moral theory
deserving serious consideration must itself give them serious consideration. As William K. Frankena has written, "Morality is made for man,
not man for morality."[6] Moral considerations are often supposed to be
overriding in practical reasoning. If we were to find that adopting a particular morality led to irreconcilable conflict with central types of human
well-being—as cases akin to John's and Helen's have led some to suspect—then this surely would give us good reason to doubt its claims.[7]

For example, in the closing sentences of *A Theory of Justice* John
Rawls considers the "perspective of eternity," which is impartial across
all individuals and times, and writes that this is a "form of *thought and
feeling* that rational persons can adopt in the world." "Purity of heart,"
he concludes, "would be to see clearly and act with grace and self-com-
mand from this point of view."[8] This may or may not be purity of heart,

---

into three realms, of "reason and conscience," of "imagination," and of "human fellow-
feeling"; notice, too, that he has chosen the word 'feeling' to characterize human affections.

6. William K. Frankena, *Ethics*, 2d ed. (Englewood Cliffs, NJ: Prentice-Hall, 1973), p.
116. Moralities that do not accord with this dictum—or a modified version of it that includes
all sentient beings—might be deemed alienated in a Feuerbachian sense.

7. Mill, for instance, calls the moral point of view "unquestionably the first and most
important," and while he thinks it the error of the moralizer (such as Bentham) to elevate
the moral point of view and "sink the [aesthetic and sympathetic] entirely," he does not
explain how to avoid such a result if the moral point of view is to be, as he says it ought,
"paramount." See his "Bentham," pp. 121f.

Philosophers who have recently raised doubts about moralities for such reasons include
Bernard Williams, in "A Critique of Utilitarianism," in J.J.C. Smart and B. Williams, *Utilitarianism: For and Against* (Cambridge: Cambridge University Press, 1973), and Michael
Stocker, in "The Schizophrenia of Modern Ethical Theories," *Journal of Philosophy* 73
(1976): 453–66.

8. John Rawls, *A Theory of Justice* (Cambridge: Harvard University Press, 1971), p. 587,
emphasis added.

but it could not be the standpoint of actual life without radically detaching the individual from a range of personal concerns and commitments. Presumably we should not read Rawls as recommending that we adopt this point of view in the bulk of our actions in daily life, but the fact that so purely abstracted a perspective is portrayed as a kind of moral ideal should at least start us wondering.[9] If to be more perfectly moral is to ascend ever higher toward *sub specie aeternitatis* abstraction, perhaps we made a mistake in boarding the moral escalator in the first place. Some of the very "weaknesses" that prevent us from achieving this moral ideal—strong attachments to persons or projects—seem to be part of a considerably more compelling human ideal.

Should we say at this point that the lesson is that we should give a more prominent role to the value of non-alienation in our moral reasoning? That would be too little too late: the problem seems to be the way in which morality asks us to look at things, not just the things it asks us to look at.

IV. THE "PARADOX OF HEDONISM"

Rather than enter directly into the question whether being moral is a matter of taking a moral point of view and whether there is thus some sort of necessary connection between being moral and being alienated in a way detrimental to human flourishing, I will consider a related problem the solution to which may suggest a way of steering around obstacles to a more direct approach.

One version of the so-called "paradox of hedonism" is that adopting as one's exclusive ultimate end in life the pursuit of maximum happiness may well prevent one from having certain experiences or engaging in certain sorts of relationships or commitments that are among the greatest sources of happiness.[10] The hedonist, looking around him, may discover that some of those who are less concerned with their own happiness than

9. I am not claiming that we should interpret all of Rawls' intricate moral theory in light of these few remarks. They are cited here merely to illustrate a certain tendency in moral thought, especially that of a Kantian inspiration.

10. This is a "paradox" for individual, egoistic hedonists. Other forms the "paradox of hedonism" may take are social in character: a society of egoistic hedonists might arguably achieve less total happiness than a society of more benevolent beings; or, taking happiness as the sole social goal might lead to a less happy society overall than could exist if a wider range of goals were pursued.

Alienation,
                                     Consequentialism,
                                     and Morality

he is, and who view people and projects less instrumentally than he does, actually manage to live happier lives than he despite his dogged pursuit of happiness. The "paradox" is pragmatic, not logical, but it looks deep nonetheless: the hedonist, it would appear, ought not to be a hedonist. It seems, then, as if we have come across a second case in which mediating one's relations to people or projects by a particular point of view— in this case, a hedonistic point of view—may prevent one from attaining the fullest possible realization of sought-after values.

However, it is important to notice that even though adopting a hedonistic life project may tend to interfere with realizing that very project, there is no such natural exclusion between acting for the sake of another or a cause as such and recognizing how important this is to one's happiness. A spouse who acts for the sake of his mate may know full well that this is a source of deep satisfaction for him—in addition to providing him with reasons for acting internal to it, the relationship may also promote the external goal of achieving happiness. Moreover, while the pursuit of happiness may not be the reason he entered or sustains the relationship, he may also recognize that if it had not seemed likely to make him happy he would not have entered it, and that if it proved over time to be inconsistent with his happiness he would consider ending it.

It might be objected that one cannot really regard a person or a project as an end as such if one's commitment is in this way contingent or overridable. But were this so, we would be able to have very few commitments to ends as such. For example, one could not be committed to both one's spouse and one's child as ends as such, since at most one of these commitments could be overriding in cases of conflict. It is easy to confuse the notion of a commitment to an end *as such* (or *for its own sake*) with that of an *overriding* commitment, but strength is not the same as structure. To be committed to an end as such is a matter of (among other things) whether it furnishes one with reasons for acting that are not mediated by other concerns. It does not follow that these reasons must always outweigh whatever opposing reasons one may have, or that one may not at the same time have other, mediating reasons that also incline one to act on behalf of that end.

Actual commitments to ends as such, even when very strong, are subject to various qualifications and contingencies.[11] If a friend grows too

---

11. This is not to deny that there are indexical components to commitments.

predictable or moves off to a different part of the world, or if a planned life project proves less engaging or practical than one had imagined, commitments and affections naturally change. If a relationship were highly vulnerable to the least change, it would be strained to speak of genuine affection rather than, say, infatuation. But if members of a relationship came to believe that they would be better off without it, this ordinarily would be a non-trivial change, and it is not difficult to imagine that their commitment to the relationship might be contingent in this way but nonetheless real. Of course, a relationship involves a shared history and shared expectations as well as momentary experiences, and it is unusual that affection or concern can be changed overnight, or relationships begun or ended at will. Moreover, the sorts of affections and commitments that can play a decisive role in shaping one's life and in making possible the deeper sorts of satisfactions are not those that are easily overridden or subject to constant reassessment or second-guessing. Thus a sensible hedonist would not forever be subjecting his affections or commitments to egoistic calculation, nor would he attempt to break off a relationship or commitment merely because it might seem to him at a given moment that some other arrangement would make him happier. Commitments to others or to causes as such may be very closely linked to the self, and a hedonist who knows what he's about will not be one who turns on his self at the slightest provocation. Contingency is not expendability, and while some commitments are remarkably non-contingent—such as those of parent to child or patriot to country—it cannot be said that commitments of a more contingent sort are never genuine, or never conduce to the profounder sorts of happiness.[12]

Following these observations, we may reduce the force of the "paradox of hedonism" if we distinguish two forms of hedonism. *Subjective hedonism* is the view that one should adopt the hedonistic point of view in

12. It does seem likely to matter just what the commitment is contingent upon as well as just how contingent it is. I think it is an open question whether commitments contingent upon the satisfaction of egoistic hedonist criteria are of the sort that might figure in the happiest sorts of lives ordinarily available. We will return to this problem presently.

Those who have had close relationships often develop a sense of *duty* to one another that may outlast affection or emotional commitment, that is, they may have a sense of obligation to one another that is less contingent than affection or emotional commitment, and that should not simply be confused with them. If such a sense of obligation is in conflict with self-interest, and if it is a normal part of the most satisfying sorts of close relationships, then this may pose a problem for the egoistic hedonist.

143   *Alienation,*
                                             Consequentialism,
                                             and Morality

action, that is, that one should whenever possible attempt to determine
which act seems most likely to contribute optimally to one's happiness,
and behave accordingly. *Objective hedonism* is the view that one should
follow that course of action which would in fact most contribute to one's
happiness, even when this would involve *not* adopting the hedonistic
point of view in action. An act will be called *subjectively hedonistic* if it
is done from a hedonistic point of view; an act is *objectively hedonistic*
if it is that act, of those available to the agent, which would most contribute
to his happiness.[13] Let us call someone a *sophisticated hedonist* if he
aims to lead an objectively hedonistic life (that is, the happiest life available to him in the circumstances) and yet is not committed to subjective
hedonism. Thus, within the limits of what is psychologically possible, a
sophisticated hedonist is prepared to eschew the hedonistic point of view
whenever taking this point of view conflicts with following an objectively
hedonistic course of action. The so-called paradox of hedonism shows
that there will be such conflicts: certain acts or courses of action may be
objectively hedonistic only if not subjectively hedonistic. When things
are put this way, it seems that the sophisticated hedonist faces a problem
rather than a paradox: how to act in order to achieve maximum possible
happiness if this is at times—or even often—*not* a matter of carrying out
hedonistic deliberations.

The answer in any particular case will be complex and contextual—it
seems unlikely that any one method of decision making would always
promote thought and action most conducive to one's happiness. A sophisticated hedonist might proceed precisely by looking at the complex
and contextual: observing the actual modes of thought and action of those
people who are in some ways like himself and who seem most happy. If

13. A few remarks are needed. First, I will say that an act is available to an agent if he
would succeed in performing it if he tried. Second, here and elsewhere in this article I
mean to include quite "thick" descriptions of actions, so that it may be part of an action
that one perform it with a certain intention or goal. In the short run (but not so much the
long run) intentions, goals, motives, and the like are usually less subject to our deliberate
control than overt behavior—it is easier to say "I'm sorry" than to say it and mean it. This,
however, is a fact about the relative availability of acts to the agent at a given time, and
should not dictate what is to count as an act. Third, here and elsewhere I ignore for
simplicity's sake the possibility that more than one course of action may be maximally
valuable. And fourth, for reasons I will not enter into here, I have formulated objective
hedonism in terms of actual outcomes rather than expected values (relative to the information available to the agent). One could make virtually the same argument using an
expected value formulation.

our assumptions are right, he will find that few such individuals are subjective hedonists; instead, they act for the sake of a variety of ends as such. He may then set out to develop in himself the traits of character, ways of thought, types of commitment, and so on, that seem common in happy lives. For example, if he notes that the happiest people often have strong loyalties to friends, he must ask how he can become a more loyal friend—not merely how he can seem to be a loyal friend (since those he has observed are not happy because they merely seem loyal)—but how he can in fact be one.

Could one really make such changes if one had as a goal leading an optimally happy life? The answer seems to me a qualified *yes*, but let us first look at a simpler case. A highly competitive tennis player comes to realize that his obsession with winning is keeping him from playing his best. A pro tells him that if he wants to win he must devote himself more to the game and its play as such and think less about his performance. In the commitment and concentration made possible by this devotion, he is told, lies the secret of successful tennis. So he spends a good deal of time developing an enduring devotion to many aspects of the activity, and finds it peculiarly satisfying to become so absorbed in it. He plays better, and would have given up the program of change if he did not, but he now finds that he plays tennis more for its own sake, enjoying greater internal as well as external rewards from the sport. Such a person would not keep thinking—on or off the court—"No matter how I play, the only thing I really care about is whether I win!" He would recognize such thoughts as self-defeating, as evidence that his old, unhelpful way of looking at things was returning. Nor would such a person be self-deceiving. He need not hide from himself his goal of winning, for this goal is consistent with his increased devotion to the game. His commitment to the activity is not eclipsed by, but made more vivid by, his desire to succeed at it.

The same sort of story might be told about a sophisticated hedonist and friendship. An individual could realize that his instrumental attitude toward his friends prevents him from achieving the fullest happiness friendship affords. He could then attempt to focus more on his friends as such, doing this somewhat deliberately, perhaps, until it comes more naturally. He might then find his friendships improved and himself happier. If he found instead that his relationships were deteriorating or his happiness declining, he would reconsider the idea. None of this need be

145   *Alienation,*
                                                       Consequentialism,
                                                       and Morality

hidden from himself: the external goal of happiness reinforces the internal goals of his relationships. The sophisticated hedonist's motivational
structure should therefore meet a *counterfactual condition*: he need not
always act for the sake of happiness, since he may do various things for
their own sake or for the sake of others, but he would not act as he does
if it were not compatible with his leading an objectively hedonistic life.
Of course, a sophisticated hedonist cannot guarantee that he will meet
this counterfactual condition, but only attempt to meet it as fully as
possible.

Success at tennis is a relatively circumscribed goal, leaving much else
about one's life undefined. Maximizing one's happiness, by contrast, seems
all-consuming. Could commitments to other ends survive alongside it?
Consider an analogy. Ned needs to make a living. More than that, he
needs to make as much money as he can—he has expensive tastes, a
second marriage, and children reaching college age, and he does not have
extensive means. He sets out to invest his money and his labor in ways
he thinks will maximize return. Yet it does not follow that he acts as he
does solely for the sake of earning as much as possible.[14] Although it is
obviously true that he does what he does because he believes that it will
maximize return, this does not preclude his doing it for other reasons as
well, for example, for the sake of living well or taking care of his children.
This may continue to be the case even if Ned comes to want money for
its own sake, that is, if he comes to see the accumulation of wealth as
intrinsically as well as extrinsically attractive.[15] Similarly, the stricture
that one seek the objectively hedonistic life certainly provides one with
considerable guidance, but it does not supply the whole of one's motives
and goals in action.

My claim that the sophisticated hedonist can escape the paradox of
hedonism was, however, qualified. It still seems possible that the happiest
sorts of lives ordinarily attainable are those led by people who would

14. Michael Stocker considers related cases in "Morally Good Intentions," *The Monist*
54 (1970): 124–41. I am much indebted to his discussion.

15. There may be a parallelism of sorts between Ned's coming to seek money for its own
sake and a certain pattern of moral development: what is originally sought in order to live
up to familial or social expectations may come to be an end in itself.

It might be objected that the goal of earning as much money as possible is quite unlike
the goal of being as happy as possible, since money is plainly instrumentally valuable even
when it is sought for its own sake. But happiness, too, is instrumentally valuable, for it
may contribute to realizing such goals as being a likeable or successful person.

reject even sophisticated hedonism, people whose character is such that if they were presented with a choice between two entire lives, one of which contains less total happiness but nonetheless realizes some other values more fully, they might well knowingly choose against maximal happiness. If this were so, it would show that a sophisticated hedonist might have reason for changing his beliefs so that he no longer accepts hedonism in any form. This still would not refute objective hedonism as an account of the (rational, prudential, or moral) *criterion* one's acts should meet, for it would be precisely in order to meet this criterion that the sophisticated hedonist would change his beliefs.[16]

V. The Place of Non-Alienation Among Human Values

Before discussing the applicability of what has been said about hedonism to morality, we should notice that alienation is not always a bad thing, that we may not want to overcome all forms of alienation, and that other values, which may conflict with non-alienation in particular cases, may at times have a greater claim on us. Let us look at a few such cases.

It has often been argued that a morality of duties and obligations may appropriately come into play in familial or friendly relationships when the relevant sentiments have given out, for instance, when one is exasperated with a friend, when love is tried, and so on.[17] 'Ought' implies 'can' (or, at least, 'could'), and while it may be better in human terms when we do what we ought to do at least in part out of feelings of love, friendship, or sympathy, there are times when we simply cannot muster these sentiments, and the right thing to do is to act as love or friendship or sympathy would have directed rather than refuse to perform any act done merely from a sense of duty.

But we should add a further role for unspontaneous, morally motivated action: even when love or concern is strong, it is often desirable that people achieve some distance from their sentiments or one another. A spouse may act toward his mate in a grossly overprotective way; a friend may indulge another's ultimately destructive tendencies; a parent may favor one child inordinately. Strong and immediate affection may over-

16. An important objection to the claim that objective hedonism may serve as the *moral* criterion one's acts should meet, even if this means not believing in hedonism, is that moral principles must meet a *publicity* condition. I will discuss this objection in Section VI.

17. See, for example, Stocker, "The Schizophrenia of Modern Ethical Theories."

147   *Alienation,*
                                       Consequentialism,
                                       and Morality

whelm one's ability to see what another person actually needs or deserves. In such cases a certain distance between people or between an individual and his sentiments, and an intrusion of moral considerations into the gap thus created, may be a good thing, and part of genuine affection or commitment. The opposite view, that no such mediation is desirable as long as affection is strong, seems to me a piece of romanticism. Concern over alienation therefore ought not to take the form of a cult of "authenticity at any price."

Moreover, there will occur regular conflicts between avoiding alienation and achieving other important individual goals. One such goal is autonomy. Bernard Williams has emphasized that many of us have developed certain "ground projects" that give shape and meaning to our lives, and has drawn attention to the damage an individual may suffer if he is alienated from his ground projects by being forced to look at them as potentially overridable by moral considerations.[18] But against this it may be urged that it is crucial for autonomy that one hold one's commitments up for inspection—even one's ground projects. Our ground projects are often formed in our youth, in a particular family, class, or cultural background. It may be alienating and even disorienting to call these into question, but to fail to do so is to lose autonomy. Of course, autonomy could not sensibly require that we question all of our values and commitments at once, nor need it require us to be forever detached from what we are doing. It is quite possible to submit basic aspects of one's life to scrutiny and arrive at a set of autonomously chosen commitments that form the basis of an integrated life. Indeed, psychological conflicts and practical obstacles give us occasion for reexamining our basic commitments rather more often than we'd like.

At the same time, the tension between autonomy and non-alienation should not be exaggerated. Part of avoiding exaggeration is giving up the Kantian notion that autonomy is a matter of escaping determination by any contingency whatsoever. Part, too, is refusing to conflate autonomy with sheer independence from others. Both Rousseau and Marx emphasized that achieving control over one's own life requires participation in certain sorts of social relations—in fact, relations in which various kinds of alienation have been minimized.

Autonomy is but one value that may enter into complex trade-offs with

18. Williams, "Critique."

non-alienation. Alienation and inauthenticity do have their uses. The alienation of some individuals or groups from their milieu may at times be necessary for fundamental social criticism or cultural innovation. And without some degree of inauthenticity, it is doubtful whether civil relations among people could long be maintained. It would take little ingenuity, but too much of the reader's patience, to construct here examples involving troubling conflicts between non-alienation and virtually any other worthy goal.

VI. REDUCING ALIENATION IN MORALITY

Let us now move to morality proper. To do this with any definiteness, we must have a particular morality in mind. For various reasons, I think that the most plausible sort of morality is consequentialist in form, assessing rightness in terms of contribution to the good. In attempting to sketch how we might reduce alienation in moral theory and practice, therefore, I will work within a consequentialist framework (although a number of the arguments I will make could be made, *mutatis mutandis*, by a deontologist).

Of course, one has adopted no morality in particular even in adopting consequentialism unless one says what the good is. Let us, then, dwell briefly on axiology. One mistake of dominant consequentialist theories, I believe, is their failure to see that things other than subjective states can have intrinsic value. Allied to this is a tendency to reduce all intrinsic values to one—happiness. Both of these features of classical utilitarianism reflect forms of alienation. First, in divorcing subjective states from their objective counterparts, and claiming that we seek the latter exclusively for the sake of the former, utilitarianism cuts us off from the world in a way made graphic by examples such as that of the experience machine, a hypothetical device that can be programmed to provide one with whatever subjective states he may desire. The experience machine affords us decisive subjective advantages over actual life: few, if any, in actual life think they have achieved all that they could want, but the machine makes possible for each an existence that he cannot distinguish from such a happy state of affairs.[19] Despite this striking advantage, most rebel at the

19. At least one qualification is needed: the subjective states must be psychologically possible. Perhaps some of us desire what are, in effect, psychologically impossible states.

149   *Alienation,*
                                       Consequentialism,
                                       and Morality

notion of the experience machine. As Robert Nozick and others have
pointed out, it seems to matter to us what we actually *do* and *are* as well
as how life *appears* to us.²⁰ We see the point of our lives as bound up
with the world and other people in ways not captured by subjectivism,
and our sense of loss in contemplating a life tied to an experience machine, quite literally alienated from the surrounding world, suggests where
subjectivism has gone astray. Second, the reduction of all goals to the
purely abstract goal of happiness or pleasure, as in hedonistic utilitarianism, treats all other goals instrumentally. Knowledge or friendship may
promote happiness, but is it a fair characterization of our commitment
to these goals to say that this is the only sense in which they are ultimately
valuable? Doesn't the insistence that there is an abstract and uniform
goal lying behind all of our ends bespeak an alienation from these particular ends?

Rather than pursue these questions further here, let me suggest an
approach to the good that seems to me less hopeless as a way of capturing
human value: a pluralistic approach in which several goods are viewed
as intrinsically, non-morally valuable—such as happiness, knowledge,
purposeful activity, autonomy, solidarity, respect, and beauty.²¹ These

20. Robert Nozick, *Anarchy, State, and Utopia* (New York: Basic Books, 1974), pp. 42ff.
21. To my knowledge, the best-developed method for justifying claims about intrinsic
value involves thought-experiments of a familiar sort, in which, for example, we imagine
two lives, or two worlds, alike in all but one respect, and then attempt to determine whether
rational, well-informed, widely-experienced individuals would (when vividly aware of both
alternatives) be indifferent between the two or have a settled preference for one over the
other. Since no one is ideally rational, fully informed, or infinitely experienced, the best we
can do is to take more seriously the judgments of those who come nearer to approximating
these conditions. Worse yet: the best we can do is to take more seriously the judgments
of those we *think* better approximate these conditions. (I am not supposing that facts or
experience somehow entail values, but that in rational agents, beliefs and values show a
marked mutual influence and coherence.) We may overcome some narrowness if we look
at behavior and preferences in other societies and other epochs, but even here we must
rely upon interpretations colored by our own beliefs and values. Within the confines of this
article I must leave unanswered a host of deep and troubling questions about the nature
of values and value judgments. Suffice it to say that there is no reason to think that we
are in a position to give anything but a tentative list of intrinsic goods.
It becomes a complex matter to describe the psychology of intrinsic value. For example,
should we say that one values a relationship of solidarity, say, a friendship, *because it is* a
friendship? That makes it sound as if it were somehow instrumental to the realization of
some abstract value, friendship. Surely this is a misdescription. We may be able to get a
clearer idea of what is involved by considering the case of happiness. We certainly do not
value a particular bit of experienced happiness because it is instrumental in the realization
of the abstract goal, happiness—we value the experience for its own sake because it is a

goods need not be ranked lexically, but may be attributed weights, and
the criterion of rightness for an act would be that it most contribute to
the weighted sum of these values in the long run. This creates the possibility of trade-offs among values of the kinds discussed in the previous
section. However, I will not stop here to develop or defend such an
account of the good and the right, since our task is to show how certain
problems of alienation that arise in moral contexts might be dealt with
if morality is assumed to have such a basis.

Consider, then, Juan, who, like John, has always seemed a model
husband. When a friend remarks on the extraordinary concern he shows
for his wife, Juan characteristically responds: "I love Linda. I even *like*
her. So it means a lot to me to do things for her. After all we've been
through, it's almost a part of me to do it." But his friend knows that Juan
is a principled individual, and asks Juan how his marriage fits into that
larger scheme. After all, he asks, it's fine for Juan and his wife to have
such a close relationship, but what about all the other, needier people
Juan could help if he broadened his horizon still further? Juan replies,
"Look, it's a better world when people can have a relationship like ours—
and nobody could if everyone were always asking themselves who's got
the most need. It's not easy to make things work in this world, and one
of the best things that happens to people is to have a close relationship
like ours. You'd make things worse in a hurry if you broke up those close
relationships for the sake of some higher goal. Anyhow, I know that you
can't always put family first. The world isn't such a wonderful place that
it's OK just to retreat into your own little circle. But still, you need that
little circle. People get burned out, or lose touch, if they try to save the
world by themselves. The ones who can stick with it and do a good job
of making things better are usually the ones who can make that fit into
a life that does not make them miserable. I haven't met any real saints
lately, and I don't trust people who think they *are* saints."

---

happy experience. Similarly, a friendship is itself the valued thing, the thing of a valued
kind. Of course, one can say that one values friendship and therefore seeks friends, just
as one can say one values happiness and therefore seeks happy experiences. But this
locution must be contrasted with what is being said when, for example, one talks of seeking
things that make one happy. Friends are not "things that make one achieve friendship"—
they partially constitute friendships, just as particular happy experience partially constitute
happiness for an individual. Thus taking friendship as an intrinsic value does not entail
viewing particular friendships instrumentally.

151   *Alienation,*
                                       Consequentialism,
                                       and Morality

If we contrast Juan with John, we do not find that the one allows moral considerations to enter his personal life while the other does not. Nor do we find that one is less serious in his moral concern. Rather, what Juan recognizes to be morally required is not by its nature incompatible with acting directly for the sake of another. It is important to Juan to subject his life to moral scrutiny—he is not merely stumped when asked for a defense of his acts above a personal level, he does not *just* say "Of course I take care of her, she's my wife!" or "It's Linda" and refuse to listen to the more impersonal considerations raised by his friend. It is consistent with what he says to imagine that his motivational structure has a form akin to that of the sophisticated hedonist, that is, his motivational structure meets a counterfactual condition: while he ordinarily does not do what he does simply for the sake of doing what's right, he would seek to lead a different sort of life if he did not think his were morally defensible. His love is not a romantic submersion in the other to the exclusion of worldly responsibilities, and to that extent it may be said to involve a degree of alienation from Linda. But this does not seem to drain human value from their relationship. Nor need one imagine that Linda would be saddened to hear Juan's words the way Anne might have been saddened to overhear the remarks of John.[22]

Moreover, because of his very willingness to question his life morally, Juan avoids a sort of alienation not sufficiently discussed—alienation from others, beyond one's intimate ties. Individuals who will not or cannot allow questions to arise about what they are doing from a broader perspective are in an important way cut off from their society and the larger world. They may not be troubled by this in any very direct way, but even so they may fail to experience that powerful sense of purpose and meaning that comes from seeing oneself as part of something larger and more enduring than oneself or one's intimate circle. The search for such a sense of purpose and meaning seems to me ubiquitous—surely much of the impulse to religion, to ethnic or regional identification (most strikingly, in the "rediscovery" of such identities), or to institutional loyalty stems from this desire to see ourselves as part of a more general, lasting,

22. If one objects that Juan's commitment to Linda is lacking because it is contingent in some ways, the objector must show that the *kinds* of contingencies involved would destroy his relationship with Linda, especially since moral character often figures in commitments—the character of the other, or the compatibility of a commitment with one's having the sort of character one values—and the contingencies in Juan's case are due to his moral character.

and worthwhile scheme of things.[23] This presumably is part of what is meant by saying that secularization has led to a sense of meaninglessness, or that the decline of traditional communities and societies has meant an increase in anomie. (The sophisticated hedonist, too, should take note: one way to gain a firmer sense that one's life is worthwhile, a sense that may be important to realizing various values in one's own life, is to overcome alienation from others.)

Drawing upon our earlier discussion of two kinds of hedonism, let us now distinguish two kinds of consequentialism. *Subjective consequentialism* is the view that whenever one faces a choice of actions, one should attempt to determine which act of those available would most promote the good, and should then try to act accordingly. One is behaving as subjective consequentialism requires—that is, leading a *subjectively consequentialist life*—to the extent that one uses and follows a distinctively consequentialist mode of decision making, consciously aiming at the overall good and conscientiously using the best available information with the greatest possible rigor. *Objective consequentialism* is the view that the criterion of the rightness of an act or course of action is whether it in fact would most promote the good of those acts available to the agent. Subjective consequentialism, like subjective hedonism, is a view that prescribes following a particular mode of deliberation in action; objective consequentialism, like objective hedonism, concerns the outcomes actually brought about, and thus deals with the question of deliberation only in terms of the tendencies of certain forms of decision making to promote appropriate outcomes. Let us reserve the expression *objectively consequentialist act (or life)* for those acts (or that life) of those available to the agent that would bring about the best outcomes.[24] To complete

23. I do not mean to suggest that such identities are always matters of choice for individuals. Quite the reverse, identities often arise through socialization, prejudice, and similar influences. The point rather is that there is a very general phenomenon of identification, badly in need of explanation, that to an important extent underlies such phenomena as socialization and prejudice, and that suggests the existence of certain needs in virtually all members of society—needs to which identification with entities beyond the self answers.

Many of us who resist raising questions about our lives from broader perspectives do so, I fear, not out of a sense that it would be difficult or impossible to lead a meaningful life if one entertained such perspectives, but rather out of a sense that our lives would not stand up to much scrutiny therefrom, so that leading a life that *would* seem meaningful from such perspectives would require us to change in some significant way.

24. Although the language here is causal—'promoting' and 'bringing about'—it should be said that the relation of an act to the good need not always be causal. An act of learning

153   *Alienation,*
                                       Consequentialism,
                                       and Morality

the parallel, let us say that a *sophisticated consequentialist* is someone who has a standing commitment to leading an objectively consequentialist life, but who need not set special stock in any particular form of decision making and therefore does not necessarily seek to lead a subjectively consequentialist life. Juan, it might be argued (if the details were filled in), is a sophisticated consequentialist, since he seems to believe he should act for the best but does not seem to feel it appropriate to bring a consequentialist calculus to bear on his every act.

Is it bizarre, or contradictory, that being a sophisticated consequentialist may involve rejecting subjective consequentialism? After all, doesn't an adherent of subjective consequentialism also seek to lead an objectively consequentialist life? He may, but then he is mistaken in thinking that this means he should always undertake a distinctively consequentialist deliberation when faced with a choice. To see his mistake, we need only consider some examples.

It is well known that in certain emergencies, the best outcome requires action so swift as to preclude consequentialist deliberation. Thus a sophisticated consequentialist has reason to inculcate in himself certain dispositions to act rapidly in obvious emergencies. The disposition is not a mere reflex, but a developed pattern of action deliberately acquired. A simple example, but it should dispel the air of paradox.

Many decisions are too insignificant to warrant consequentialist deliberation ("Which shoelace should I do up first?") or too predictable in outcome ("Should I meet my morning class today as scheduled or should I linger over the newspaper?"). A famous old conundrum for consequentialism falls into a similar category: before I deliberate about an act, it seems I must decide how much time would be optimal to allocate for this deliberation; but then I must first decide how much time would be

---

may non-causally involve coming to have knowledge (an intrinsic good by my reckoning) as well as contributing causally to later realizations of intrinsic value. Causal consequences as such do not have a privileged status. As in the case of objective hedonism, I have formulated objective consequentialism in terms of actual outcomes (so-called "objective duty") rather than expected values relative to what is rational for the agent to believe ("subjective duty"). The main arguments of this article could be made using expected value, since the course of action with highest expected value need not in general be the subjectively consequentialist one. See also notes 13 and 21.

Are there any subjective consequentialists? Well, various theorists have claimed that a consequentialist must be a subjective consequentialist in order to be genuine—see Williams, "Critique," p. 135, and Rawls, *Theory of Justice*, p. 182.

optimal to allocate for this time-allocation decision; but before that I must decide how much time would be optimal to allocate for *that* decision; and so on. The sophisticated consequentialist can block this paralyzing regress by noting that often the best thing to do is not to ask questions about time allocation at all; instead, he may develop standing dispositions to give more or less time to decisions depending upon their perceived importance, the amount of information available, the predictability of his choice, and so on. I think we all have dispositions of this sort, which account for our patience with some prolonged deliberations but not others.

There are somewhat more intriguing examples that have more to do with psychological interference than mere time efficiency: the timid, put-upon employee who knows that if he deliberates about whether to ask for a raise he will succumb to his timidity and fail to demand what he actually deserves; the self-conscious man who knows that if, at social gatherings, he is forever wondering how he should act, his behavior will be awkward and unnatural, contrary to his goal of acting naturally and appropriately; the tightrope walker who knows he must not reflect on the value of keeping his concentration; and so on. People can learn to avoid certain characteristically self-defeating lines of thought—just as the tennis player in an earlier example learned to avoid thinking constantly about winning—and the sophisticated consequentialist may learn that consequentialist deliberation is in a variety of cases self-defeating, so that other habits of thought should be cultivated.

The sophisticated consequentialist need not be deceiving himself or acting in bad faith when he avoids consequentialist reasoning. He can fully recognize that he is developing the dispositions he does because they are necessary for promoting the good. Of course, he cannot be preoccupied with this fact all the while, but then one cannot be *preoccupied* with anything without this interfering with normal or appropriate patterns of thought and action.

To the list of cases of interference we may add John, whose all-purpose willingness to look at things by subjective consequentialist lights prevents the realization in him and in his relationships with others of values that he would recognize to be crucially important.

Bernard Williams has said that it shows consequentialism to be in grave trouble that it may have to usher itself from the scene as a mode of decision making in a number of important areas of life.[25] Though I think

25. Williams, "Critique," p. 135.

155   *Alienation,*
                                       Consequentialism,
                                       and Morality

he has exaggerated the extent to which we would have to exclude consequentialist considerations from our lives in order to avoid disastrous
results, it is fair to ask: If maximizing the good were in fact to require
that consequentialist reasoning be *wholly* excluded, would this refute
consequentialism? Imagine an all-knowing demon who controls the fate
of the world and who visits unspeakable punishment upon man to the
extent that he does not employ a Kantian morality. (Obviously, the demon
is not himself a Kantian.) If such a demon existed, sophisticated consequentialists would have reason to convert to Kantianism, perhaps even
to make whatever provisions could be made to erase consequentialism
from the human memory and prevent any resurgence of it.

Does this possibility show that objective consequentialism is self-defeating? On the contrary, it shows that objective consequentialism has
the virtue of not blurring the distinction between the *truth-conditions*
of an ethical theory and its *acceptance-conditions* in particular contexts,
a distinction philosophers have generally recognized for theories concerning other subject matters. It might be objected that, unlike other
theories, ethical theories must meet a condition of publicity, roughly to
the effect that it must be possible under all circumstances for us to
recognize a true ethical theory as such and to promulgate it publicly
without thereby violating that theory itself.[26] Such a condition might be
thought to follow from the social nature of morality. But any such condition would be question-begging against consequentialist theories, since
it would require that one class of actions—acts of adopting or promul-
gating an ethical theory—*not* be assessed in terms of their consequences.
Moreover, I fail to see how such a condition could emanate from the
social character of morality. To prescribe the adoption and promulgation
of a mode of decision making regardless of its consequences seems to
me radically detached from human concerns, social or otherwise. If it is
argued that an ethical theory that fails to meet the publicity requirement
could under certain conditions endorse a course of action leading to the
abuse and manipulation of man by man, we need only reflect that no
psychologically possible decision procedure can guarantee that its widespread adoption could never have such a result. A "consequentialist demon" might increase the amount of abuse and manipulation in the world

26. For discussion of a publicity condition, see Rawls, *Theory of Justice*, pp. 133, 177–
82, 582. The question whether a publicity condition can be justified is a difficult one,
deserving fuller discussion than I am able to give it here.

in direct proportion to the extent that people act according to the categorical imperative. Objective consequentialism (unlike certain deontological theories) has valuable flexibility in permitting us to take consequences into account in assessing the appropriateness of certain modes of decision making, thereby avoiding any sort of self-defeating decision procedure worship.

A further objection is that the lack of any direct link between objective consequentialism and a particular mode of decision making leaves the view too vague to provide adequate guidance in practice. On the contrary, objective consequentialism sets a definite and distinctive criterion of right action, and it becomes an empirical question (though not an easy one) which modes of decision making should be employed and when. It would be a mistake for an objective consequentialist to attempt to tighten the connection between his criterion of rightness and any particular mode of decision making: someone who recommended a particular mode of decision making regardless of consequences would not be a hard-nosed, non-evasive objective consequentialist, but a self-contradicting one.

VII. Contrasting Approaches

The seeming "indirectness" of objective consequentialism may invite its confusion with familiar indirect consequentialist theories, such as rule-consequentialism. In fact, the subjective/objective distinction cuts across the rule/act distinction, and there are subjective and objective forms of both rule- and act-based theories. Thus far, we have dealt only with subjective and objective forms of act-consequentialism. By contrast, a *subjective rule*-consequentialist holds (roughly) that in deliberation we should always attempt to determine which act, of those available, conforms to that set of rules general acceptance of which would most promote the good; we then should attempt to perform this act. An *objective rule*-consequentialist sets actual conformity to the rules with the highest acceptance value as his criterion of right action, recognizing the possibility that the best set of rules might in some cases—or even always—recommend that one not perform rule-consequentialist deliberation.

Because I believe this last possibility must be taken seriously, I find the objective form of rule-consequentialism more plausible. Ultimately, however, I suspect that rule-consequentialism is untenable in either form, for it could recommend acts that (subjectively or objectively) accord with

Alienation,
                                           Consequentialism,
                                           and Morality

the best set of rules even when these rules are *not* in fact generally
accepted, and when as a result these acts would have devastatingly bad
consequences. "Let the rules with greatest acceptance utility be followed,
though the heavens fall!" is no more plausible than *"Fiat justitia, ruat
coelum!"*—and a good bit less ringing. Hence, the arguments in this
article are based entirely upon act-consequentialism.

Indeed, once the subjective/objective distinction has been drawn, an
act-consequentialist can capture some of the intuitions that have made
rule- or trait-consequentialism appealing.[27] Surely part of the attraction
of these indirect consequentialisms is the idea that one should have
certain traits of character, or commitments to persons or principles, that
are sturdy enough that one would at least sometimes refuse to forsake
them even when this refusal is known to conflict with making some
gain—perhaps small—in total utility. Unlike his subjective counterpart,
the objective act-consequentialist is able to endorse characters and commitments that are sturdy in just this sense.

To see why, let us first return briefly to one of the simple examples of
Section VI. A sophisticated act-consequentialist may recognize that if he
were to develop a standing disposition to render prompt assistance in
emergencies without going through elaborate act-consequentialist deliberation, there would almost certainly be cases in which he would perform
acts worse than those he would have performed had he stopped to deliberate, for example, when his prompt action is misguided in a way he
would have noticed had he thought the matter through. It may still be
right for him to develop this disposition, for without it he would act rightly
in emergencies still less often—a quick response is appropriate much
more often than not, and it is not practically possible to develop a disposition that would lead one to respond promptly in exactly those cases
where this would have the best results. While one can attempt to cultivate
dispositions that are responsive to various factors which might indicate
whether promptness is of greater importance than further thought, such
refinements have their own costs and, given the limits of human resources, even the best cultivated dispositions will sometimes lead one
astray. The objective act-consequentialist would thus recommend cultivating dispositions that will sometimes lead him to violate his own criterion of right action. Still, he will not, as a trait-consequentialist would,

27. For an example of trait-consequentialism, see Robert M. Adams, "Motive Utilitarianism," *Journal of Philosophy* 73 (1976): 467–81.

shift his criterion and say that an act is right if it stems from the traits it would be best overall to have (given the limits of what is humanly achievable, the balance of costs and benefits, and so on). Instead, he continues to believe that an act may stem from the dispositions it would be best to have, and yet be wrong (because it would produce worse consequences than other acts available to the agent in the circumstances).[28]

This line of argument can be extended to patterns of motivation, traits of character, and rules. A sophisticated act-consequentialist should realize that certain goods are reliably attainable—or attainable at all—only if people have well-developed characters; that the human psyche is capable of only so much self-regulation and refinement; and that human perception and reasoning are liable to a host of biases and errors. Therefore, individuals may be more likely to act rightly if they possess certain enduring motivational patterns, character traits, or *prima facie* commitments to rules in addition to whatever commitment they have to act for the best. Because such individuals would not consider consequences in all cases, they would miss a number of opportunities to maximize the good; but if they were instead always to attempt to assess outcomes, the overall result would be worse, for they would act correctly less often.[29]

28. By way of contrast, when Robert Adams considers application of a motive-utilitarian view to the ethics of actions, he suggests "conscience utilitarianism," the view that "we have a *moral duty* to do an act, if and only if it would be demanded of us by the most useful kind of conscience we could have," "Motive Utilitarianism," p. 479. Presumably, this means that it would be morally wrong to perform an act contrary to the demands of the most useful sort of conscience. I have resisted this sort of redefinition of rightness for actions, since I believe that the most useful sort of conscience may on occasion demand of us an act that does not have the best overall consequences of those available, and that performing this act would be wrong.

Of course, some difficulties attend the interpretation of this last sentence. I have assumed throughout that an act is available to an agent if he would succeed in performing it if he tried. I have also taken a rather simple view of the complex matter of attaching outcomes to specific acts. In those rare cases in which the performance of even one exceptional (purportedly optimizing) act would completely undermine the agent's standing (optimal) disposition, it might not be possible after all to say that the exceptional act would be the right one to perform in the circumstances. (This question will arise again shortly.)

29. One conclusion of this discussion is that we cannot realistically expect people's behavior to be in strict compliance with the counterfactual condition even if they are committed sophisticated consequentialists. At best, a sophisticated consequentialist tries to meet this condition. But it should be no surprise that in practice we are unlikely to be morally ideal. Imperfections in information alone are enough to make it very improbable

159   *Alienation,*
                                       Consequentialism,
                                       and Morality

We may now strengthen the argument to show that the objective act-consequentialist can approve of dispositions, characters, or commitments to rules that are sturdy in the sense mentioned above, that is, that do not merely supplement a commitment to act for the best, but sometimes override it, so that one knowingly does what is contrary to maximizing the good. Consider again Juan and Linda, whom we imagine to have a commuting marriage. They normally get together only every other week, but one week she seems a bit depressed and harried, and so he decides to take an extra trip in order to be with her. If he did not travel, he would save a fairly large sum that he could send OXFAM to dig a well in a drought-stricken village. Even reckoning in Linda's uninterrupted malaise, Juan's guilt, and any ill effects on their relationship, it may be that for Juan to contribute the fare to OXFAM would produce better consequences overall than the unscheduled trip. Let us suppose that Juan knows this, and that he could stay home and write the check if he tried. Still, given Juan's character, he in fact will not try to perform this more beneficial act but will travel to see Linda instead. The objective act-consequentialist will say that Juan performed the wrong act on this occasion. Yet he may also say that if Juan had had a character that would have led him to perform the better act (or made him more inclined to do so), he would have had to have been less devoted to Linda. Given the ways Juan can affect the world, it may be that if he were less devoted to Linda his overall contribution to human well-being would be less in the end, perhaps because he would become more cynical and self-centered. Thus it may be that Juan should have (should develop, encourage, and so on) a character such that he sometimes knowingly and deliberately acts contrary to his objective consequentialist duty. Any other character, of those actually available to him, would lead him to depart still further from an objectively consequentialist life. The issue is not whether staying home would *change* Juan's character—for we may suppose that it would not—but whether he would in fact decide to stay home if he had that

---

that individuals will lead objectively consequentialist lives. Whether or when to *blame* people for real or apparent failures to behave ideally is, of course, another matter.

Note that we must take into account not just the frequency with which right acts are performed, but the actual balance of gains and losses to overall well-being that results. Relative frequency of right action will settle the matter only in the (unusual) case where the amount of good at stake in each act of a given kind—for example, each emergency one comes across—is the same.

character, of those available, that would lead him to perform the most beneficial overall sequence of acts. In some cases, then, there will exist an objective act-consequentialist argument for developing and sustaining characters of a kind Sidgwick and others have thought an act-consequentialist must condemn.[30]

VIII. Demands and Disruptions

Before ending this discussion of consequentialism, let me mention one other large problem involving alienation that has seemed uniquely troubling for consequentialist theories and that shows how coming to terms with problems of alienation may be a social matter as well as a matter of individual psychology. Because consequentialist criteria of rightness are linked to maximal contribution to the good, whenever one does not perform the very best act one can, one is "negatively responsible" for any shortfall in total well-being that results. Bernard Williams has argued that to accept such a burden of responsibility would force most of us to abandon or be prepared to abandon many of our most basic individual

---

30. In *The Methods of Ethics*, bk. IV, chap. v, sec. 4, Sidgwick discusses "the Ideal of character and conduct" that a utilitarian should recognize as "the sum of excellences or Perfections," and writes that "a Utilitarian must hold that it is always wrong for a man knowingly to do anything other than what he believes to be most conducive to Universal Happiness" (p. 492). Here Sidgwick is uncharacteristically confused—and in two ways. First, considering act-by-act evaluation, an objective utilitarian can hold that an agent may simply be wrong in believing that a given course of action is most conducive to universal happiness, and therefore it may be right for him knowingly to do something other than this. Second, following Sidgwick's concern in this passage and looking at enduring traits of character rather than isolated acts, and even assuming the agent's belief to be correct, an objective utilitarian can hold that the ideal character for an individual, or for people in general, may involve a willingness knowingly to act contrary to maximal happiness when this is done for the sake of certain deep personal commitments. See Henry Sidgwick, *The Methods of Ethics*, 7th ed. (New York: Dover, 1966), p. 492.

It might be thought counterintuitive to say, in the example given, that it is not right for Juan to travel to see Linda. But it must be kept in mind that for an act-consequentialist to say that an action is not right is not to say that it is without merit, only that it is not the very best act available to the agent. And an intuitive sense of the rightness of visiting Linda may be due less to an evaluation of the act itself than to a reaction to the sort of character a person would have to have in order to stay home and write a check to OXFAM under the circumstances. Perhaps he would have to be too distant or righteous to have much appeal to us—especially in view of the fact that it is his spouse's anguish that is at stake. We have already seen how an act-consequentialist may share this sort of character assessment.

commitments, alienating ourselves from the very things that mean the most to us.[31]

To be sure, objective act-consequentialism of the sort considered here is a demanding and potentially disruptive morality, even after allowances have been made for the psychological phenomena thus far discussed and for the difference between saying an act is wrong and saying that the agent ought to be blamed for it. But just *how* demanding or disruptive it would be for an individual is a function—as it arguably should be—of how bad the state of the world is, how others typically act, what institutions exist, and how much that individual is capable of doing. If wealth were more equitably distributed, if political systems were less repressive and more responsive to the needs of their citizens, and if people were more generally prepared to accept certain responsibilities, then individuals' everyday lives would not have to be constantly disrupted for the sake of the good.

For example, in a society where there are no organized forms of disaster relief, it may be the case that if disaster were to strike a particular region, people all over the country would be obliged to make a special effort to provide aid. If, on the other hand, an adequate system of publicly financed disaster relief existed, then it probably would be a very poor idea for people to interrupt their normal lives and attempt to help—their efforts would probably be uncoordinated, ill-informed, an interference with skilled relief work, and economically disruptive (perhaps even damaging to the society's ability to pay for the relief effort).

By altering social and political arrangements we can lessen the disruptiveness of moral demands on our lives, and in the long run achieve better results than free-lance good-doing. A consequentialist theory is therefore likely to recommend that accepting negative responsibility is more a matter of supporting certain social and political arrangements (or rearrangements) than of setting out individually to save the world. Moreover, it is clear that such social and political changes cannot be made unless the lives of individuals are psychologically supportable in the meanwhile, and this provides substantial reason for rejecting the notion that we should abandon all that matters to us as individuals and devote ourselves solely to net social welfare. Finally, in many cases what matters

---

31. Williams, "Critique," sec. 3.

most is *perceived* rather than actual demandingness or disruptiveness, and this will be a relative matter, depending upon normal expectations. If certain social or political arrangements encourage higher contribution as a matter of course, individuals may not sense these moral demands as excessively intrusive.

To speak of social and political changes is, of course, to suggest eliminating the social and political preconditions for a number of existing projects and relationships, and such changes are likely to produce some degree of alienation in those whose lives have been disrupted. To an extent such people may be able to find new projects and relationships as well as maintain a number of old projects and relationships, and thereby avoid intolerable alienation. But not all will escape serious alienation. We thus have a case in which alienation will exist whichever course of action we follow—either the alienation of those who find the loss of the old order disorienting, or the continuing alienation of those who under the present order cannot lead lives expressive of their individuality or goals. It would seem that to follow the logic of Williams' position would have the unduly conservative result of favoring those less alienated in the present state of affairs over those who might lead more satisfactory lives if certain changes were to occur. Such conservativism could hardly be warranted by a concern about alienation if the changes in question would bring about social and political preconditions for a more widespread enjoyment of meaningful lives. For example, it is disruptive of the ground projects of many men that women have begun to demand and receive greater equality in social and personal spheres, but such disruption may be offset by the opening of more avenues of self-development to a greater number of people.

In responding to Williams' objection regarding negative responsibility, I have focused more on the problem of disruptiveness than the problem of demandingness, and more on the social than the personal level. More would need to be said than I am able to say here to come fully to terms with his objection, although some very general remarks may be in order. The consequentialist starts out from the relatively simple idea that certain things seem to matter to people above all else. His root conception of moral rightness is therefore that it should matter above all else whether people, insofar as possible, actually realize these ends.[32] Consequentialist

32. I appealed to this "root conception" in rejecting rule-consequentialism in Section VII. Although consequentialism is often condemned for failing to provide an account of morality

163   *Alienation,*
                                      Consequentialism,
                                      and Morality

moralities of the sort considered here undeniably set a demanding standard, calling upon us to do more for one another than is now the practice.
But this standard plainly does not require that most people lead intolerable
lives for the sake of some greater good: the greater good is empirically
equivalent to the best possible lives for the largest possible number of
people.[33] Objective consequentialism gives full expression to this root
intuition by setting as the criterion of rightness actual contribution to the
realization of human value, allowing practices and forms of reasoning to
take whatever shape this requires. It is thus not equivalent to requiring
a certain, alienated way of thinking about ourselves, our commitments,
or how to act.

Samuel Scheffler has recently suggested that one response to the problems Williams raises about the impersonality and demandingness of consequentialism could be to depart from consequentialism at least far enough
to recognize as a fundamental moral principle an agent-centered prerogative, roughly to the effect that one is not always obliged to maximize
the good, although one is always permitted to do so if one wishes. This
prerogative would make room for agents to give special attention to personal projects and commitments. However, the argument of this article,
if successful, shows there to be a firm place in moral practice for prerogatives that afford such room even if one accepts a fully consequentialist
fundamental moral theory.[34]

---

consistent with respect for persons, this root conception provides the basis for a highly
plausible notion of such respect. I doubt, however, that any fundamental ethical dispute
between consequentialists and deontologists can be resolved by appeal to the idea of respect
for persons. The deontologist has his notion of respect—e.g., that we not use people in
certain ways—and the consequentialist has *his*—e.g., that the good of every person has an
equal claim upon us, a claim unmediated by any notion of right or contract, so that we
should do the most possible to bring about outcomes that actually advance the good of
persons. For every consequentially justified act of manipulation to which the deontologist
can point with alarm there is a deontologically justified act that fails to promote the well-
being of some person(s) as fully as possible to which the consequentialist can point, appalled.
Which notion takes "respect for persons" more seriously? There may be no non-question-
begging answer, especially once the consequentialist has recognized such things as autonomy or respect as intrinsically valuable.

33. The qualification 'empirically equivalent to' is needed because in certain empirically
unrealistic cases, such as utility monsters, the injunction "Maximize overall realization of
human value" cannot be met by improving the lives of as large a proportion of the population
as possible. However, under plausible assumptions about this world (including diminishing
marginal value) the equivalence holds.

34. For Scheffler's view, see *The Rejection of Consequentialism: A Philosophical Investigation of the Considerations Underlying Rival Moral Conceptions* (Oxford: Clarendon

IX. ALIENATION FROM MORALITY

By way of conclusion, I would like to turn to alienation from morality itself, the experience (conscious or unconscious) of morality as an external set of demands not rooted in our lives or accommodating to our perspectives. Giving a convincing answer to the question "Why should I be moral?" must involve diminishing the extent that morality appears alien.

Part of constructing such an answer is a matter of showing that abiding by morality need not alienate us from the particular commitments that make life worthwhile, and in the previous sections we have begun to see how this might be possible within an objective act-consequentialist account of what morality requires. We saw how in general various sorts of projects or relationships can continue to be a source of intrinsic value even though one recognizes that they might have to undergo changes if they could not be defended in their present form on moral grounds. And again, knowing that a commitment is morally defensible may well deepen its value for us, and may also make it possible for us to feel part of a larger world in a way that is itself of great value. If our commitments are regarded by others as responsible and valuable (or if we have reason to think that others should so regard them), this may enhance the meaning or value they have for ourselves, while if they are regarded by others as irresponsible or worthless (especially, if we suspect that others regard them so justly), this may make it more difficult for us to identify with them or find purpose or value in them. Our almost universal urge to rationalize our acts and lives attests our wish to see what we do as defensible from a more general point of view. I do not deny that bringing a more general perspective to bear on one's life may be costly to the self—it may cause reevaluations that lower self-esteem, produce guilt, alienation, and even problems of identity. But I do want to challenge the simple story often told in which there is a personal point of view from which we glimpse meanings which then vanish into insignificance when we adopt a more general perspective. In thought and action we shuttle back and forth from more personal to less personal standpoints, and both play an

Press, 1982). The consequentialist may also argue that at least some of the debate set in motion by Williams is more properly concerned with the question of the relation between moral imperatives and imperatives of rationality than with the content of moral imperatives as such. (See note 42.)

165   *Alienation,*
                                       Consequentialism,
                                       and Morality

important role in the process whereby purpose, meaning, and identity are generated and sustained.[35] Moreover, it may be part of mature commitments, even of the most intimate sort, that a measure of perspective beyond the personal be maintained.

These remarks about the role of general perspectives in individual lives lead us to what I think is an equally important part of answering the question "Why should I be moral?": reconceptualization of the terms of the discussion to avoid starting off in an alienated fashion and ending up with the result that morality still seems alien. Before pursuing this idea, let us quickly glance at two existing approaches to the question.

Morality may be conceived of as in essence selfless, impartial, impersonal. To act morally is to subordinate the self and all contingencies concerning the self's relations with others or the world to a set of imperatives binding on us solely as rational beings. We should be moral, in this view, because it is ideally rational. However, morality thus conceived seems bound to appear as alien in daily life. "Purity of heart" in Rawls' sense would be essential to acting morally, and the moral way of life would appear well removed from our actual existence, enmeshed as we are in a web of "particularistic" commitments—which happen to supply our *raisons d'être*.

A common alternative conception of morality is not as an elevated purity of heart but as a good strategy for the self. Hobbesian atomic individuals are posited and appeal is made to game theory to show that pay-offs to such individuals may be greater in certain conflict situations—such as reiterated prisoners' dilemmas—if they abide by certain constraints of a moral kind (at least, with regard to those who may reciprocate) rather than act merely prudentially. Behaving morally, then, may be an advantageous policy in certain social settings. However, it is not likely to be the *most* advantageous policy in general, when compared to a strategy that cunningly mixes some compliance with norms and some non-compliance; and presumably the Hobbesian individual is interested only in maximal self-advantage. Yet even if we leave aside worries about how far such arguments might be pushed, it needs to be said that morality

35. For example, posterity may figure in our thinking in ways we seldom articulate. Thus, nihilism has seemed to some an appropriate response to the idea that mankind will soon destroy itself. "Everything would lose its point" is a reaction quite distinct from "Then we should enjoy ourselves as much as possible in the meantime," and perhaps equally comprehensible.

as such would confront such an entrepreneurial self as an alien set of demands, for central to morality is the idea that others' interests must sometimes be given weight for reasons unrelated to one's own advantage.

Whatever their differences, these two apparently antithetical approaches to the question "Why should I be moral?" have remarkably similar underlying pictures of the problem. In these pictures, a presocial, rational, abstract individual is the starting point, and the task is to construct proper interpersonal relations out of such individuals. Of course, this conceit inverts reality: the rational individual of these approaches is a social and historical *product*. But that is old hat. We are not supposed to see this as any sort of history, we are told, but rather as a way of conceptualizing the questions of morality. Yet why when conceptualizing are we drawn to such asocial and ahistorical images? My modest proposal is that we should keep our attention fixed on society and history at least long enough to try recasting the problem in more naturalistic terms.[36]

As a start, let us begin with individuals situated in society, complete with identities, commitments, and social relations. What are the ingredients of such identities, commitments, and relations? When one studies relationships of deep commitment—of parent to child, or wife to husband—at close range, it becomes artificial to impose a dichotomy between what is done for the self and what is done for the other. We cannot decompose such relationships into a vector of self-concern and a vector of other-concern, even though concern for the self and the other are both present. The other has come to figure in the self in a fundamental way—or, perhaps a better way of putting it, the other has become a reference point of the self. If it is part of one's identity to be the parent of Jill or the husband of Linda, then the self has reference points beyond the ego, and that which affects these reference points may affect the self in an unmediated way.[37] These reference points do not all fall within the circle

36. I do not deny that considerations about pay-offs of strategies in conflict situations may play a role in cultural or biological evolutionary explanations of certain moral sentiments or norms. Rather, I mean to suggest that there are characteristic sorts of abstractions and simplifications involved in game-theoretic analysis that may render it blind to certain phenomena crucial for understanding morality and its history, and for answering the question "Why should I be moral?" when posed by actual individuals.

37. Again we see the inadequacy of subjectivism about values. If, for example, part of one's identity is to be Jill's parent, then should Jill cease to exist, one's life could be said to have lost some of its purpose even if one were not aware of her death. As the example of the experience machine suggested earlier, there is an objective side to talk about purpose.

167   *Alienation,*
                                         Consequentialism,
                                         and Morality

of intimate relationships, either. Among the most important constituents
of identities are social, cultural, or religious ties—one is a Jew, a South-
erner, a farmer, or an alumnus of Old Ivy. Our identities exist in relational,
not absolute space, and except as they are fixed by reference points in
others, in society, in culture, or in some larger constellation still, they are
not fixed at all.[38]

There is a worthwhile analogy between meaning in lives and meaning
in language. It has been a while since philosophers have thought it helpful
to imagine that language is the arrangement resulting when we hook
our private meanings up to a system of shared symbols. Meaning, we are
told, resides to a crucial degree in use, in public contexts, in referential
systems—it is possible for the self to use a language with meanings
because the self is embedded in a set of social and historical practices.
But ethical philosophers have continued to speak of the meaning of life
in surprisingly private terms. Among recent attempts to give a foundation
for morality, Nozick's perhaps places greatest weight on the idea of the
meaning of life, which he sees as a matter of an individual's "ability to
regulate and guide [his] life in accordance with some overall conception
[he] chooses to accept," emphasizing the idea that an individual creates
meaning through choice of a life plan; clearly, however, in order for choice
to play a self-defining role, the options among which one chooses must
already have some meaning independent of one's decisions.[39]

38. Here I do not have in mind identity in the sense usually at stake in discussions of
personal identity. The issue is not identity as principle of individuation, but as *experienced*,
as a sense of self—the stuff actual identity crises are made of.

39. Nozick, *Anarchy*, p. 49. (I ignore here Nozick's more recent remarks about the
meaning of life in his *Philosophical Explanations* [Cambridge: Harvard University Press,
1981].) The notion of a "rationally chosen life plan" has figured prominently in the literature
recently, in part due to Rawls' use of it in characterizing the good (see Rawls, *Theory of
Justice*, ch. VII, "Goodness as Rationality"). Rawls' theory of the good is a complex matter,
and it is difficult to connect his claims in any direct way to a view about the meaning of
life. However, see T. M. Scanlon, "Rawls' Theory of Justice," *University of Pennsylvania
Law Review* 121 (1973): 1020–69, for an interpretation of Rawls in which the notion of an
individual as above all a rational chooser—more committed to maintaining his status as a
rational agent able to adopt and modify his goals than to any particular set of goals—
functions as the ideal of a person implicit in Rawls' theory. On such a reading, we might
interpolate into the original text the idea that meaning derives from autonomous individual
choice, but this is highly speculative. In any event, recent discussions of rationally chosen
life plans as the bearers of ultimate significance or value do not appear to me to do full
justice to the ways in which lives actually come to be invested with meaning, especially
since some meanings would have to be presupposed by any rational choice of a plan of life.

It is not only "the meaning of life" that carries such presuppositions. Consider, for example, another notion that has played a central role in moral discourse: respect. If the esteem of others is to matter to an individual those others must themselves have some significance to the individual; in order for their esteem to constitute the sought-after respect, the individual must himself have some degree of respect for them and their judgment.[40] If the self loses significance for others, this threatens its significance even for itself; if others lose significance for the self, this threatens to remove the basis for self-significance. It is a commonplace of psychology and sociology that bereaved or deracinated individuals suffer not only a sense of loss owing to broken connections with others, but also a loss in the solidity of the self, and may therefore come to lose interest in the self or even a clear sense of identity. Reconstructing the self and self-interest in such cases is as much a matter of constructing new relations to others and the world as it is a feat of self-supporting self-reconstruction. Distracted by the picture of a hypothetical, presocial individual, philosophers have found it very easy to assume, wrongly, that in the actual world concern for oneself and one's goals is quite automatic, needing no outside support, while a direct concern for others is inevitably problematic, needing some further rationale.

It does not follow that there is any sort of categorical imperative to care about others or the world beyond the self as such. It is quite possible to have few external reference points and go through life in an alienated way. Life need not have much meaning in order to go on, and one does not even have to care whether life goes on. We cannot show that moral skepticism is necessarily irrational by pointing to facts about meaning, but a naturalistic approach to morality need no more refute radical skepticism than does a naturalistic approach to epistemology. For actual people, there may be surprisingly little distance between asking in earnest "Why should I take any interest in anyone else?" and asking "Why should I take any interest in myself?"[41] The proper response to the former is not

40. To be sure, this is but one of the forms of respect that are of importance to moral psychology. But as we see, self-respect has a number of interesting connections with respect for, and from, others.

41. This may be most evident in extreme cases. Survivors of Nazi death camps speak of the effort it sometimes took to sustain a will to survive, and of the importance of others, and of the sense of others, to this. A survivor of Treblinka recalls, "In our group we shared everything; and at the moment one of the group ate something without sharing it, we knew it was the beginning of the end for him." (Quoted in Terrence Des Pres, *The Survivor: An Anatomy of Life in the Death Camps* [New York: Oxford University Press, 1976], p. 96.)

169   *Alienation,*
                                       Consequentialism,
                                       and Morality

merely to point out the indirect benefits of caring about things beyond
the self, although this surely should be done, but to show how denying
the significance of anything beyond the self may undercut the basis of
significance for the self. There is again a close, but not exact parallel in
language: people can get along without a language, although certainly
not as well as they can with it; if someone were to ask "Why should I
use my words the same way as others?" the proper response would not
only be to point out the obvious benefits of using his words in this way,
but also to point out that by refusing to use words the way others do he
is undermining the basis of meaning in his own use of language.

These remarks need not lead us to a conservative traditionalism. We
must share and preserve meanings in order to have a language at all, but
we may use a common language to disagree and innovate. Contemporary
philosophy of language makes us distrust any strict dichotomy between
meaning, on the one hand, and belief and value, on the other; but there
is obviously room within a system of meanings for divergence and change
on empirical and normative matters. Language itself has undergone considerable change over the course of history, coevolving with beliefs and
norms without in general violating the essential conditions of meaningfulness. Similarly, moral values and social practices may undergo change
without obliterating the basis of meaningful lives, so long as certain
essential conditions are fulfilled. (History does record some changes, such
as the uprooting of tribal peoples, where these conditions were not met,
with devastating results.)

A system of available, shared meanings would seem to be a precondition
for sustaining the meaningfulness of individual lives in familiar sorts of
social arrangements. Moreover, in such arrangements identity and self-
significance seem to depend in part upon the significance of others to
the self. If we are prepared to say that a sense of meaningfulness is a
precondition for much else in life, then we may be on the way to answering the question "Why should I be moral?" for we have gone beyond
pure egocentrism precisely by appealing to facts about the self.[42] Our

---

Many survivors say that the idea of staying alive to "bear witness," in order that the deaths
of so many would not escape the world's notice, was decisive in sustaining their own
commitment to survival.

42. One need not be a skeptic about morality or alienated from it in any general sense
in order for the question "Why should I be moral?" to arise with great urgency. If in a
given instance doing what is right or having the best sort of character were to conflict

earlier discussions have yielded two considerations that make the rest of the task of answering this question more tractable. First, we noted in discussing hedonism that individual lives seem most enjoyable when they involve commitments to causes beyond the self or to others as such. Further, we remarked that it is plausible that the happiest sorts of lives do not involve a commitment to hedonism even of a sophisticated sort. If a firm sense of meaningfulness is a precondition of the fullest happiness, this speculation becomes still more plausible. Second, we sketched a morality that began by taking seriously the various forms of human non-moral value, and then made room for morality in our lives by showing that we can raise moral questions without thereby destroying the possibility of realizing various intrinsic values from particular relationships and activities. That is, we saw how being moral might be compatible (at least in these respects) with living a desirable life. It would take another article, and a long one, to show how these various pieces of the answer to "Why should I be moral?" might be made less rough and fitted together

head-on with acting on behalf of a person or a project that one simply could not go against without devastating the self, then it may fail to be reasonable from the agent's standpoint to do what is right. It is always *morally* wrong (though not always morally blameworthy) to fail to perform morally required acts, but in certain circumstances that may be the most reasonable thing to do—not because of some larger moral scheme, but because of what matters to particular individuals. Therefore, in seeking an answer to "Why should I be moral?" I do not assume that it must always be possible to show that the moral course of action is ideally rational or otherwise optimal from the standpoint of the agent. (I could be more specific here if I had a clearer idea of what rationality is.) It would seem ambitious enough to attempt to show that, in general, there are highly desirable lives available to individuals consistent with their being moral. While we might hope for something stronger, this could be enough—given what can also be said on behalf of morality from more general viewpoints—to make morality a worthy candidate for our allegiance as individuals.

It should perhaps be said that on an objective consequentialist account, being moral need not be a matter of consciously following distinctively moral imperatives, so that what is at stake in asking "Why should I be moral?" in connection with such a theory is whether one has good reason to lead one's life in such a way that an objective consequentialist criterion of rightness is met as nearly as possible. In a given instance, this criterion might be met by acting out of a deeply felt emotion or an entrenched trait of character, without consulting morality or even directly in the face of it. This, once more, is an indication of objective consequentialism's flexibility: the idea is to *be* and *do* good, not necessarily to *pursue* goodness.

I am grateful to a number of people for criticisms of earlier drafts of this paper and helpful suggestions for improving it. I would especially like to thank Marcia Baron, Stephen Darwall, William K. Frankena, Allan Gibbard, Samuel Scheffler, Rebecca Scott, Michael Stocker, Nicholas Sturgeon, Gregory Trianoski-Stillwell, and Susan Wolf.

171   *Alienation,*
                                       Consequentialism,
                                       and Morality

into a more solid structure. But by adopting a non-alienated starting
point—that of situated rather than presocial individuals—and by showing
how some of the alienation associated with bringing morality to bear on
our lives might be avoided, perhaps we have reduced the extent to which
morality seems alien to us by its nature.

[7]

RESTRICTIVE CONSEQUENTIALISM

Philip Pettit and Geoffrey Brennan

1. Introduction

Restrictive consequentialism is a variant of the standard consequentialist doctrine. It is not an unknown variant, since it has been widely endorsed in the past, but it is infrequently explicated and less often defended. This paper offers both explication and defence.

Standard consequentialism is a theory of decision. It attempts to identify, for any set of alternative options, that which it is right that an agent should take or should have taken.[1] The theory is characterised by three propositions.

1. Every relevant state of the world, realised or not, has an evaluator-neutral value.
2. The right option in any decision is a function of the value to be realised in the world: as the function is usually understood, it is that which maximises objectively probable value, that which promotes the best objectively probable consequences.[2]
3. The function which determines what is the right decision is also the function which ought to be applied in decision-making: it serves at once to evaluate options, and to select them.

For each of these three assumptions, there is a non-standard variety of consequentialism in which that assumption is lifted. The first is lifted in the evaluator-relative sort of consequentialism recently explored by Amartya

---

[1] This role in assessing decisions should not be confused with the other functions that ethical doctrines serve in the assessment of agents, actions and the like. A bad agent may choose the right option. And the right option may result in the wrong action: that is, in an action which is inferior to the action that would have come of a different choice. We think that a great deal of confusion has come of failing to distinguish the concern with options from the concern with actions: the failure is marked by the ambiguity often attendant on the phrase 'act-consequentialism'. For some relevant distinctions see Anthony Quinton, *Utilitarian Ethics* Macmillan, London, 1973, p. 49.

[2] These phrases are meant to suggest that the value of the option is to be computed in a manner parallel to the computation of expected utility: see Ellery Eells, *Rational Decision and Causality*, Cambridge University Press, 1982, Chapters 1 and 3, for a survey of some approaches to that computation. The suggestion is standard: see J. J. C. Smart's comments on page 42 in Smart and Bernard Williams, *Utilitarianism: For and Against*, Cambridge University Press, 1973. The suggestion needs further explication however, since we do not mean to insinuate for example that a consequentialist's evaluative ordering must satisfy the conditions for being representable in a real-valued utility function: on such conditions, see for example H. A. John Green, *Consumer Theory*, rev.ed., Macmillan, London, 1976. In a forthcoming paper, Frank Jackson argues that the subjectively right option is that which maximises subjectively probable value. On related matters, see Hugh Mellor, 'Objective Decision-Making', *Social Theory and Practice* 9, (1983).

438

Australasian Journal of Philosophy
Vol. 64, No. 4; December 1986

Sen.[3] The second is relaxed, more famously, in the sort of doctrine known as universalistic or rule-consequentialism: here the right option is that type of option which is such that if everyone chose it or took steps to choose it, then that would maximise objectively probable value.[4]

Restrictive consequentialism lifts the third standard assumption. It suggests that while it may be appropriate to evaluate options by the criterion of maximising probable value, it need not be sensible to select them on that basis. The idea is that the way to satisfy the criterion of evaluation may often be to restrict or forswear its application, relying rather on some other criterion of choice.

Opponents of consequentialism have traditionally alleged that the doctrine cannot go restrictive. The allegation is turned against consequentialism, for it is said that no theory can be plausible if it compels agents to ignore ingrained habits, spontaneous motives and principled commitments, forcing them always to choose on the basis of calculation over outcomes. F. H. Bradley put the objection nicely. 'So far as my lights go, this is to make possible, to justify, and even to encourage, an incessant practical casuistry; and that, it need scarcely be added, is the death of morality'.[5]

More sympathetic expositors of the consequentialist approach have usually taken a different view. They have suggested that with the choice of actions in particular, consequentialism need not require explicit application of the criterion of option evaluation. It may allow people to accelerate and avoid deliberation, taking their guidance from more homely maxims or motives. It will permit this if that generally seems to be the way of actually achieving the best probable consequences.

Sidgwick was explicit on the point. 'It is not necessary that the end which gives the criterion of rightness should always be the end at which we consciously aim: and if experience shows that the general happiness will be more satisfactorily attained if men frequently act from other motives than pure universal philanthropy, it is obvious that these other motives are reasonably to be preferred on utilitarian principles'.[6]

Nor was Sidgwick alone. Austin writes in richer vein but to similar effect in The Province of Jurisprudence. 'Of all the pleasures bodily or mental, the pleasures of mutual love, cemented by mutual esteem, are the most enduring and varied. They therefore contribute largely to swell the sum of well-being, or they form an important item in the account of human

---

[3] See Amartya Sen 'Rights and Agency', *Philosophy and Public Affairs* 11, (1982), p. 30.

[4] See David Lyons, *The Forms and Limits of Utilitarianism*, Oxford University Press, 1965, Ch. 4. See too R. M. Adams 'Motive Utilitarianism', *Journal of Philosophy* 73, (1976), p. 480. Often universalistic consequentialism is characterised as an ethic of action rather than decision. Sometimes the phrase 'rule-consequentialism' is used loosely, like the phrase 'indirect consequentialism', to encompass the sort of approach that we describe as restrictive.

[5] F. H. Bradley, *Ethical Studies*, Oxford University Press, 1962, p. 109. See too Bernard Williams in Smart and Williams *op. cit.*, pp. 118-135.

[6] Henry Sidgwick, *The Methods of Ethics*, Dover, New York, 1966, p. 413. See too James Griffin 'Modern Utilitarianism', *Revue Internationale de Philosophie*, 36, (1982), p. 347; R. M. Hare *Moral Thinking*, Oxford University Press, 1981, pp. 35-40; David Lyons *op. cit.*, p. 149; and Smart in Smart and Williams *op. cit.*, pp. 42-57.

happiness. And, for that reason, the well-wisher of the general good, or the adherent of the principle of utility, must, in that character, consider them with much complacency. But, though he approves of love because it accords with his principle, he is far from maintaining that the general good ought to be the motive of the lover. It was never contended or conceived by a sound, orthodox utilitarian, that the lover should kiss his mistress with an eye to the common weal'.[7]

We think that the supporters of consequentialism are in the right on the issue dividing them from their opponents; but that with some recent exceptions, they have not done enough to argue their restrictive point of view; and that without exception, they have done too little to develop it.[8] Our paper is designed to show how the fault may begin to be remedied. It may also serve, we hope, to draw attention to a significant research programme for applied consequentialist ethics.

2. The Argument for Restrictive Consequentialism

The possibility of restrictive consequentialism is rooted in the fact, more or less ignored in our introduction, that the options which consequentialists are concerned to evaluate are not limited just to behavioural ones. In particular, they also include the psychological options of whether to encourage this or that trait, this or that motive, this or that policy, and so on.[9] Such non-behavioural options are significant, because the choice of a trait or motive or policy is likely to pre-empt certain decisions between act-options.

Psychological profiles which threaten such pre-emption are all predispositions in the following, stipulative sense: they are states whose manifestation in action means that the action is not chosen on a fully calculative or deliberative basis. These predispositions are to be distinguished from ordinary dispositions such as the belief that something is the case, or the desire that it should be so. One may encourage a certain belief or desire in oneself, and do so on conseqentialist grounds, without being thereby inhibited from calculating over the choice of any actions.[10]

If a consequentialist were concerned just with isolated decisions between act-options, then he would be inevitably calculating.[11] He would select what

---

[7] John Austin, *The Province of Jurisprudence Determined* (ed. H. L. A. Hart), London, 1954, pp. 107-108. We are indebted to Thomas Mautner for drawing our attention to this passage.

[8] The exceptions mentioned certainly include R. M. Adams *op. cit.*; R. M. Hare *op. cit.*; Derek Parfit *Reasons and Persons*, Oxford University Press, 1984; and J. J. C. Smart 'Benevolence is an overriding attitude', *Australasian Journal of Philosophy* 55, (1977). See to Brian Ellis 'Retrospective and Prospective Utilitarianism', *Nous* 15, (1981). An important background piece is R. Eugene Bales 'Act-Utilitarianism: Account of Right-Making Characteristics or Decision-Making Procedure?', *American Philosophical Quarterly* 8, (1971).

[9] They also include more. See Joel J. Kupperman, *The Foundations of Morality*, Allen and Unwin, London, 1983, Ch. 7 for an insightful overview.

[10] The one sort of exception will be a belief that is inconsistent with the second standard consequentialist assumption. See footnote 31 below. We are not concerned in this paper with that sort of case.

[11] A choice between psychological predispositions might be represented as itself a choice or set of choices between act-options. If it were, then our point would have to be recast. The contrast between predisposition-options and act-options would have to be replaced by a contrast between those act-options which affect calculation over other act-options and those which do not.

he did in each case on the calculated ground that it maximised probable value. But as a matter of fact he must also be concerned with his own predispositions. He must ask himself whether he ought to preserve or promote this or that trait or motive or policy, as well as asking whether he ought to perform this or that action. That means that he has to be open to the possibility of deciding to restrict calculation in some areas of action. For to opt for a predisposition will be to accept that some actions — those that manifest the predisposition — will be uncalculatingly generated.

The reasoning, more formally stated, is this.

1. It is possible that the consequentialist agent will opt for (preserving and/or promoting) some predispositions as well as opting for (performing) various actions.
2. If he does opt for such predispositions, then he will not calculate over the choice of the particular actions which they generate.
3. Thus he will be a restrictive consequentialist; he will forswear calculation over some options; specifically, over those actions which manifest the predispositions.

An example will help to clarify the possibility. Suppose that a consequentialist agent finds that he is by temperament inclined to involve himself unselfconsciously in his activities. He will naturally be concerned, not just with what he ought to do in this or that situation, but also with whether he ought to preserve this predisposition. Suppose now that he applies the criterion of option evaluation to the choice of predisposition and decides in favour of keeping it. He must then accept that the actions which manifest that predisposition will not be selected by him on the calculated ground provided by that criterion. Having made a calculated decision in favour of the predisposition, he is bound to forswear calculation in regard to the actions which it generates.

The possibility that a consequentialist may have to go restrictive is of some importance. It means that he may have to choose in a manner which fails to guard against taking less than the best option. The restrictive consequentialist trusts himself in the field of moral action to the control of relatively unseeing predispositions: predispositions which, in the nature of things, are not fine-tuned to the requirements of the circumstances on hand. Inevitably then, he is going to act occasionally in a non-optimific manner. That is the cost he must pay for seeking out optimific predispositions as well as optimific actions.[12]

We have argued for the possibility that the consequentialist will have to go restrictive. We must now identify the conditions under which that possibility will materialise. In order to do this, we need to examine the strategies by which a consequentialist might hope to circumvent the need for

---

[12] The risk of taking less than the best option will not concern a satisficing consequentialist such as Michael Slote describes. See his *Common-Sense Morality and Consequentialism*, Routledge and Kegan Paul, London, 1985. For a critical notice which rejects Slote's relevant claims see Philip Pettit 'Slote on Consequentialism', *Philosophical Quarterly*, forthcoming.

restriction. If we know those strategies, then we can tell the conditions under which they will fail; and those conditions are precisely the circumstances where restrictive consequentialism becomes more than a mere possibility.

Consider a predisposition P whose presence promises the realisation of a benefit B. There are two ways in which the consequentialist agent might envisage taking B into account without ceding control of his actions to P. These are the strategies by which he might hope to promote the consequences associated with the predisposition without having to pay the cost of restricting his calculative sovereignty.

First of all, he might imagine that having recognised the value of B, there is nothing to stop him from ignoring the predisposition with which it is normally associated, concentrating on the issue of how he ought to act in order to promote B and, more generally, to maximise probable value. On such grounds he might hope to be able to focus on the selection of act-options alone. Why should he think of committing himself to the care of more or less coarse-grained predispositions, if all the benefits that such commitments might promote could be taken into account in a programme of calculating over every action?

If this recourse is to be blocked, so that restrictive consequentialism is a real possibility, then the benefit B must be such that it cannot be attained under the calculative choice of action. It must be calculatively elusive, as we will say. The lustre which unselfconscious involvement gives to behaviour is an example of a calculatively elusive consequence. It is a benefit which is reliably produced by the unselfconscious predisposition but which evaporates under a regime of sustained action-calculation.

Blocked in this way, the consequentialist who recoils from any restriction on calculation might consider a second course. He might envisage adopting P – or at least going through the motions of adopting it – but allowing it to issue in action only when calculative monitoring reveals that the action is indeed for the best. The idea behind this project is that the benefit B which P produces can be equally well produced by the monitored counterpart.

If this second recourse is also to be closed then the consequence B must have a further feature over and beyond being calculatively elusive. It must be unavailable, not just when each action is calculatively chosen, but even when the predisposition which normally produces that action is calculatively monitored. It must be vulnerable to the presence of calculation, even in a supervisory role. The benefit attendant on unselfconscious involvement is calculatively vulnerable in this sense, and not just calculatively elusive. It is destroyed as readily by calculative supervision of the involvement as it is by calculative choice of each action.

In summary: if the argument for the possibility of restrictive consequentialism is to have concrete significance, then the benefits which are thought to motivate a choice of certain calculation-inhibiting predispositions must have two distinctive features. They must be calculatively elusive and, more strongly, they must be calculatively vulnerable. If the benefits do not have these features, then the consequentialist cannot be persuaded to relinquish calculative control of his actions; the risk of achieving less than the best will be an effective deterrent.

In the remainder of this paper we will be looking at examples of benefits which appear to meet these two requirements. In section three we consider a well recognised case but one which does not readily generalise. In section four we turn to a case that is also commonly recognised but which has the added attraction that it suggests a variety of parallels. Section five is devoted to a taxonomy of those parallels, a taxonomy which suggests that there are many different areas where the consequentialist may be required to go restrictive.

3. A Less Interesting Case of Restrictive Consequentialism

A person's tendency to throw himself unselfconsciously into his activities provides an example of a predisposition with elusive benefits. Examples similar to it abound. They are predispositions which raise the psychological returns to an agent of the actions which they select: the actions become more rewarding than they would have been had they been chosen in a calculating way. Examples are available wherever some form of enthusiasm or dedication or even obsessiveness has the effect of giving an agent greater pleasure in his achievements than he would have if he had been more calculating and detached.

This sort of example will provide a first case where the consequentialist may have to go restrictive, provided that the consequences are calculatively vulnerable as well as elusive. We suggested that they are vulnerable in the case of our unselfconsciousness example. We believe that they are calculatively vulnerable for all examples of this kind.

Suppose that one could monitor the operation of such predispositions, suspending them where necessary for the maximisation of probable value. It is not obvious that such monitoring would necessarily undermine the relevant effects of the dispositions. Nevertheless the effects are calculatively vulnerable. For what is true is that predispositions of the type in question are not such as can be suspended by calculative monitoring. Genuinely to instantiate predisposition is to be more or less incapable, in the particular instance, of inhibiting their operation. The dispositions have a pathological aspect.

This pathological character of the predispositions makes their relevant consequences calculatively vulnerable in a special sense. It means that effective monitoring would cancel the consequences, as vulnerability requires, but this is because the availability of such monitoring would involve the absence of the dispositions. It is not that if an agent could both have a predisposition and monitor it, then the monitoring would destroy the relevant effects. It is rather that if an agent was in a position to monitor and control the predisposition, that would undermine its realisation and thereby the realisation of its effects.

We have found a first case where a consequentialist may be rationally led to forswear calculation. It is not unfamiliar, since it is the sort of case that has led various writers to argue the merits of motive utilitarianism.[13] The thought behind such a doctrine is that certain predispositions generate results which make them worth having; that the results are not available under a strategy of calculation, or even of calculative monitoring; and that the right thing for a consequentialist to do therefore may be to put himself in thrall to the dispositions. He will encourage the development of those characteristics in the knowledge that he will thereby lose calculative control over certain actions. And he will do this because he believes that that is the way for him to realise the consequentialist optimum.

This case is interesting, but it does not suggest any very general lessons. It shows that there are some predispositions which allow the argument for restrictive consequentialism to assume significance. But it does not indicate how that argument can be borne out more generally. The illustration is available only for dispositions with the highly distinctive character that they are difficult to monitor and suspend.

4. A More Interesting Case of Restrictive Consequentialism

A second case of predispositions with calculatively elusive and vulnerable consequences has been longer recognised in the literature. It is of greater interest, because the predispositions in question do not have to be difficult to suspend. This means that the case may allow of extrapolation to a variety of dispositions. We attempt to sketch some lines of extrapolation in the next section.

The case has been recognised both by utilitarian philosophers and by certain decision theorists. It arises with predispositions to take various calculative short-cuts that have the benefit of saving the agent time and trouble. In order to establish that this sort of case is one where the requirements for restrictive consequentialism are met we need to demonstrate that the time-saving consequence is calculatively elusive and calculatively vulnerable. The demonstration is not difficult.

The consequence is calculatively elusive, because it is not a result mediated by action. What saves time for the agent with a predisposition to take calculative short-cuts is not the action which his predisposition selects. Rather it is the exercise of that disposition itself. Where full calculation would take considerable time, the exercise of the predisposition is likely to consume little. There is no way that the benefit procured by this means could be obtained by someone who followed a calculative route, even if that route led to the same actions.

But is the time-saving consequence also calculatively vulnerable? It certainly is in those cases where the calculative short-cuts spring from habits which, like the predispositions discussed in the last section, are more or less pathological in character.[15] But it turns out to be a vulnerable consequence

---

[13] See for example Adams *op. cit.*, Hare *op. cit.*, pp. 36 ff, and Parfit *op. cit.*, section 2.
[14] See Smart *op. cit.*, p. 42 and H. A. Simon 'A Behavioral Model of Rational Choice', *Quarterly Journal of Economics* 69, (1955).
[15] See Hare *op. cit.*, p. 38.

too, even when the short-cut involves a calculative strategy which can be suspended at will.

The most obvious example of such a strategy is the disposition to satisfice: that is, to set a level of aspiration in advance of choosing, and in the absence of full knowledge of available options, and to adopt the first alternative that is expected to reach that level. This predisposition can be suspended at will by someone who instantiates it and yet the time-saving which it produces is calculatively vulnerable. That vulnerability can be established by a form of regress argument.[16]

Suppose that a satisficer is persuaded that he ought to monitor his disposition and allow it to control what he does only when it seems likely to maximise probable value. He will commit himself then to a sort of second order maximisation. Presented with a decision situation, he will ask whether at a first order level he ought to satisfice or to maximise: that is, to calculate the probable value of each action and choose the most valuable. He will decide the question by a higher order maximising procedure: he will calculate the probable value of each first order strategy and select the strategy with the higher value. But this monitoring – this higher order maximisation – will cancel out, or at least reduce, the sort of benefit which unmonitored satisficing would have procured. It will involve time costs of exactly the kind that satisficing was designed to avoid.

In the case mentioned in the last section, the consequences which justify the choice of a predisposition are calculatively vulnerable for a special reason: calculative monitoring is incompatible with the disposition itself and for that reason incompatible with its effects. Here in the satisficing case we have a disposition which has more straightforwardly vulnerable consequences. The disposition secures the benefit of saving time and any attempt to monitor it for the importance of that effect, even one which endorses the strategy, will ensure that the effect is not realised, or not realised in the same measure.

In view of its calculatively elusive and vulnerable consequences, the satisficing strategy – and indeed any time-saving maxim – will often attract the commitment of the consequentialist. He will make that commitment in any range or sphere of activity where it seems likely that time costs will be important relative to other considerations. An initial, schematic calculation will usher further calculation from the scene – subject perhaps to periodic review – and will put the agent on automatic pilot, submitting him to the more or less mechanical direction of the appropriate maxim.

The metaphor of the automatic pilot is appropriate in a further respect that is worth specifying. Just as an automatic pilot will be disengaged in emergencies, so the maxim is subject to escape clauses. Thus if the agent comes to learn in any instance that the best thing for him to do there is after all to break with the maxim, then he can have no ground for not doing so. Equally, if it becomes clear to the agent that the situation is out of the ordinary run, say because it involves some sort of emergency, then he must avoid

---

[16] See Philip Pettit 'Satisficing Consequentialism' *Proceedings of the Aristotelian Society*, Supp. Vol. 58, (1984), where this argument is presented.

an unthinking reliance on the general rule. The consequentialist satisficer is not wedded to his maxim; he espouses it only so far as it promises to deliver optimal results. Where that promise is withdrawn, he has no reason for remaining faithful.

5. The Possibility of Generalising the Second Case

In the satisficing case, the consequence which is liable to justify choice of the predisposition — the fact that it saves time — is deliberatively fragile. It cannot be pursued in direct calculation over actions, nor in calculative monitoring of the disposition to satisfice. Any such pursuit would be self-defeating. It would itself consume time, and would eliminate or reduce the benefit on offer.

This single feature of satisficing explains both why its potentially justifying consequence is calculatively elusive and why it is calculatively vulnerable. The observation is useful, for it suggests that we can expect to find cases where the argument for restrictive consequentialism applies wherever we can identify predispositions which have such deliberatively fragile results. The results are liable to justify selection of the predispositions and eschewal of calculation over the actions to which one is thereby predisposed.

We have a method of extrapolating our second case in prospect, for the notion of deliberatively fragile results is a familiar one.[17] We have only to find such deliberatively fragile results as attach to predispositions and we will have new cases where consequentialists should go restrictive. The dispositions to which we will particularly look are commitments to follow certain maxims; such commitments are the paradigm of non-pathological predispositions that can be suspended on particular occasions.

In view of the currency of the phrase in consequentialist circles, it is tempting to think of the maxims which we shall be identifying as rules of thumb. But care is needed, for this phrase is sometimes used to pick out merely presumptive maxims, not properly restrictive or pre-emptive ones.

A presumptive maxim tells an agent to make a presumption in favour of doing a certain act A under conditions C, when he is calculating what to do in such circumstances. It does not prohibit the agent from applying the consequentialist criterion of option evaluation when he is selecting the action. It just prescribes that he should be loath to trust evidence that suggests doing anything other than A.[18]

---

[17] For a virtuoso review see Jon Elster, *Sour Grapes*, Cambridge University Press, 1983, Ch. 2.
[18] It is not clear to us whether any consequentialists are counselling a presumptive rule approach in advocating selectional rules of thumb. If their only reason for prescribing rules of thumb is a belief that agents in the field are calculatively fallible, then this probably is what they are recommending. But in any case we do not think that the approach is significantly distinct from that of just applying the evaluation criterion in selecting inputs. It is not the sort of line for which we shall be arguing.
Bernard Williams foists something like the presumptive rule approach on his opponents. In Smart and Williams *op. cit.*, p. 127 he writes as follows of the rules that they recommend: 'it is important that I treat them as rules of thumb, which means not only that if I do discover that this is an exceptional case, then I treat it as an exception, but also — and importantly — that I keep a utilitarian eye open for signs that a case may be exceptional'.

A restrictive or pre-emptive maxim tells an agent to do A under conditions C, given at least that there is no (loosely specified sort of) emergency.[19] The rule pre-empts the agent's calculating in accordance with the criterion of option evaluation, for while the conditions C may be of various kinds, they cannot — on pain of making the rule redundant — include the condition that the agent calculates that A is for the best. The rule directs the agent to ascertain that circumstances C obtain, and that the escape condition is unrealised, but not to bother with any information beyond that: in particular, not to try to identify and weigh the pro's and con's of doing A in that particular instance of C.

But to return now to the main business, we want to identify various predispositions, consisting of commitments to pre-emptive maxims, which are distinguished by the fact that they have desirable but deliberatively fragile outcomes.

Our original case, exemplified by satisficing, is one where the deliberation involved in calculatively monitoring a predisposition, or in replacing it by straight calculation over action, itself undermines a benefit which the unmonitored disposition would have. That case suggests three analogues. In each of these a consequence of the deliberation, not the deliberation itself, destroys that benefit. In the first the destructive consequence is the agent's becoming aware of deliberating; in the second, other people's becoming aware of his deliberating; and in the third, his acting on the basis of the deliberation.

In the remainder of the section we will illustrate this range of cases. The illustration may be of interest in its own right. Mainly, however, it should serve to reveal further avenues for research, indicating the rich resources of restrictive consequentialism.

The original case

The original case is already well illustrated by the satisficing example. But we would like to offer one further instance, in particular an instance with a less technical aspect. The example is provided by the maxims which serve to produce virtue, at least on one particular conception of virtue.

On that conception, a characteristic feature of the virtues — or in any case of the virtues to which the conception applies — is that they require the eschewal of a certain kind of calculation. There may be various background qualifications to be entered but within the limits which these set, to possess one of the virtues is to be able to hearken to certain considerations, while remaining deaf to others. This filtering of attention may be principled,

---

[19] The restrictive rule approach is clearly what David Lyons ascribes to consequentialists when he writes *op. cit.*, p. 148: 'follow the rules, indeed, but not when you know or are quite certain that breaking one will have better effects on the whole than keeping to it'. We shall see at the end of section 6 that one sort of plausible restrictive rule does not even require this escape clause. While C cannot sensibly include the clause that the agent has not calculated and found that some action other than A is best, they may in some cases include a weaker calculative condition: for example, a condition to the effect that the agent has not calculated and found that A falls by more than a certain margin below the optimum available. Such a possibility is raised in Samuel Scheffler, *The Rejection of Consequentialism*, Oxford University Press, 1982, Ch. 2.

requiring renewed commitment, or ingrained, being a matter of established habit.

To be honourable, so the story then goes, is to find one's commitments obligating and motivating – albeit they may be overridden – without first having to see whether their fulfilment is for the best in some impersonal or global scheme. To be courageous is to have the ability to be galvanised by a venture on hand without the prior assurance that it is worth the danger to oneself involved in its pursuit. To be generous is to enjoy the capacity to respond to certain demands made by others without weighing up the cost to oneself in time or money. And to be a person of integrity, as Bernard Williams argues, is to have the gumption that enables one uncalculatingly to manifest one's deepest, even self-defining, attachments in the bulk of one's normal behaviour.[20]

We assume that some such virtues are indeed worth having. That is not unreasonable, since they all have the aspect of powers. They are capacities to be motivated by considerations which it is easy to lose sight of; capacities which make one proof against weakness of the will, the pale cast of thought, and other such ailments of practical reason. In some approaches indeed the virtues are capacities with a cognitive dimension: they are necessary even for a person to become attuned to the considerations on which they bear.[21]

By some accounts fidelity to appropriate maxims is sufficient to constitute virtue. By all accounts it is sufficient to cause virtue eventually to appear: this, through leading to the formation of corresponding habits. In either case we can say that virtues of the kind surveyed are consequences of a commitment to suitable maxims. And the question then is whether they are calculatively elusive and vulnerable consequences.

The reason that virtue can come as a consequence of committing one-self to appropriate maxims is that such a commitment enforces the calculative discipline associated with virtue. It allows a place in deliberation only to those considerations that should count with the virtuous agent. This practice of ratiocinative exclusion is what constitutes virtue or causes it to appear.

Given the reason why fidelity to suitable maxims may produce corresponding virtues, the production of those virtues is bound to be calculatively elusive and vulnerable. The agent who calculates consequentially over every action is certainly not going to exhibit or pick up the virtuous habits in question. And neither is the person who goes through the motions of virtue but stops to check every manifestation for its consequentialistic sense. If the consequentialist agent wants to develop virtuous patterns of thought, then he has no choice but to go restrictive. He must forswear the sort of practical reasoning that is classically associated with his ethic.

---

[20] See Bernard Williams *Moral Luck*, Cambridge University Press, 1981, Ch. 3. See too Michael Stocker 'Values and Purposes: The Limits of Teleology and the Ends of Friendship', *Journal of Philosophy* 78, (1981).

[21] John McDowell 'Virtue and Reason' *The Monist* 62, (1979).

The first derived case

So much for the original sort of case: the case where deliberation itself undermines a benefit that may serve to justify choice of a predisposition. We now turn to three derived cases, in each one of which a consequence of deliberation destroys the effect. In the first the consequence is the agent's awareness of deliberating, in the second other people's awareness of his doing so and in the third his acting on the basis of his deliberation.

The first of these further cases is of a familiar kind. It arises when the potentially justifying consequence of fidelity to some maxim is a state of the agent which requires a degree of unselfconsciousness. This requirement means that if the result enters the arena of deliberation, whether in calculation proper or in calculative monitoring, then the fact that deliberation generates selfconsiousness jeopardises the result. If you want the consequence on offer therefore, you had better bind yourself to the maxim that produces it and forswear further calculation.

The primary example of such a result is unselfconsciousness itself, since this is often prized for its own sake. Other instances are states in which unselfconsciousness is a component or for which it is a precondition. Spontaneity is one example, being relaxed another.[22]

Suppose you wish, among other things, to be in such a state. If you try to calculate over actions to determine whether the achievement of the state justifies choice of one rather than another, then inevitably you will become conscious of deliberating. Similarly if you try to monitor a maxim — say, 'Act first, ask questions after' — which on its own would produce the state. Either way you will destroy whatever chance you had of getting the desired result. You will condemn yourself to its absence.

It follows that if you reckon that the state is generally of great importance in a certain sphere of activity — perhaps only a limited one, such as a game provides — then you should be prepared to eschew all calculative control there. You should trust yourself to a maxim like that advising the postponement of questions. Only by going on automatic pilot in this way, can you achieve your desired result. The state will be realised by fidelity to such a maxim, but in a calculatively elusive and vulnerable manner. It cannot spring from action that is chosen with calculation and consciousness. And similarly it cannot issue from attachment to a maxim, if that attachment is subject to conscious supervision.

The second derived case

The second of our three derived cases is of potentially greater importance than the first. It arises when I can get another to believe that I am following a certain maxim in my behaviour towards him only if I do actually follow that maxim; where his believing this produces some desired effect; and where his believing that I calculated, or calculatively monitored, every move would not do so. In such a case I will secure the effect only if I follow the maxim. Thus the effect will be calculatively elusive and calculatively vulnerable.

---

[22] See J. J. C. Smart 'Benevolence is an over-riding attitude'.

A first, uncomplicated illustration is provided by the security which lovers or friends produce in one another by being guided, and being seen to be guided, by maxims of virtually unconditional fidelity. Adherence to such maxims is justified by this prized effect, since any retreat from it will undermine the effect, being inevitably detectable within a close relationship. This is so whether the retreat takes the form of intruding calculation or calculative monitoring. The point scarcely needs emphasis.[23]

The example lends itself to a general pattern of analysis, if it is conceptualised with the help of the idea of loyalty. The definition of loyalty presupposed in the analysis is stipulative; those who reject it may replace the term by another.

1. If you are loyal to family, friends or associates, then you will not weigh their claims on you in a standard consequentialist way. You will be committed to the fulfilment of such claims independently of whether fulfilling them turns out to be the optimific action; and this, though you may decide on occasion that other considerations override the commitment.

2. Because such a commitment will inevitably be visible to your contacts, it will be a source of security for them. It will be an assurance that they matter to you, since their claims provide you with an independent motivation to action: that is, a motivation which does not depend on the discovery that fulfilling the claims is impersonally optimific.

3. This effect of the commitment is bound to be calculatively elusive and vulnerable. It will be obvious to your beneficiaries if you calculate over your responses to them, or if you calculatively monitor those responses, and once they see this, they will see that they do not matter to you in a way that they would expect of someone loyal. You will not be thought loyal, merely conscientious.

4. The security of immediate contacts is likely to concern you and so, if you are a consequentialist, you should be prepared to forswear calculation and calculative monitoring in favour of the commitments — in effect, maxims — distinctive of loyalty.

The benefit of analysing our initial example in this way is that it suggests a further, more significant illustration of the second derived case. Instead of loyalty and the special claims which correspond to it, this illustration involves respect for persons and the rights acknowledged under a regimen of respect.

In parallel to our earlier analysis, the analogy suggests the following argument:

1. If you respect a person then you will regard certain of the claims he makes as privileged: that is, as claims which block goals whose realisation you would otherwise see as more important than the

---

[23] The case for loyalties is more fully explored in Philip Pettit 'Social Holism and Moral Theory', *Proceedings of the Aristotelian Society* 86, (1985-86). See too Philip Pettit and Robert Goodin 'The Possibility of Special Duties', *Canadian Journal of Philosophy*, forthcoming.

    fulfilment of those claims. The claims will count as rights in the sense in which rights are distinguished by their trumping role.[24]

2. Such respect invests the beneficiary with dignity. Since your attitude will be obvious to him, and probably to people at large, it means that he can enjoy a certain sort of discretion over your behaviour; specifically, the discretion to stop you sacrificing his interest to the achievement of something that you regard as a greater objective good.[25]

3. This dignity is a calculatively elusive and vulnerable consequence. You cannot achieve it if you are known to calculate over your treatment of the individual, or to monitor that treatment, because the fact of deliberating in such a manner means that you do not yield any controlling discretion to him. And if you do actually calculate or calculatively monitor your responses to the individual, then that will inevitably become known.

4. The dignity of the people with whom you deal is likely to be important to you and so if you are a consequentialist you should be prepared to forswear calculation and calculative monitoring in favour of the commitments — in effect, maxims — distinctive of respect for persons.

This consequentialist argument for the importance of respect and of the rights recognised under the dispensation of respect is in significantly greater need of elaboration and defence than the corresponding argument for loyalty.[26] For present purposes however, it may stand in its austere form. It serves in tandem with the loyalty argument to demonstrate the potential significance of our second derived case. Clearly there is a real possibility that if a consequentialist is concerned about dignity then he will have to take rights seriously, restricting his own calculative impulses. That is a prospect sufficient on its own to make restrictive consequentialism worth exploring.[27]

The third derived case:

And now, finally, to the third derived case. This arises where deliberation undermines a potentially justifying consequence of adhering to a maxim, not by its nature, nor because of the awareness it generates, but because of the action to which it leads.

    The sort of example which we propose in illustration of this possibility is an effect of maxim-fidelity which materialises only over a considerable period of time. Suppose that the effect is forthcoming from behaving in

---

[24] For this view of rights see Robert Nozick, *Anarchy, State, and Utopia*, Basic Books, New York, 1974, pp. 28-30 and Ronald Dworkin, *Taking Rights Seriously*, Duckworth, London, 1977, pp. 90-94. See to Philip Pettit, 'Rights, Constraints and Trumps', *Analysis*, forthcoming.

[25] See Joel Feinberg, *Rights, Justice, and the Bounds of Liberty*, Princeton University Press, 1980, Ch. 7.

[26] One of us has elaborated the case elsewhere. See Philip Pettit 'A Consequentialist Case for Rights' in Denis Galligan and Charles Sampford, eds, *Law, Rights and the Welfare State*, Croom Helm, London, forthcoming and 'The Consequentialist Can Recognise Rights', *Philosophical Quarterly*, forthcoming.

[27] For a different line see David Lyons 'Utility and Rights', *Nomos* 24, (1982).

accordance with the maxim over a certain period; that each act of compliance with the maxim is troublesome; and that no one act on its own makes the difference between the achievement and non-achievement of the effect. In that case deliberation would undermine the effect, because it would select non-compliance in each instance.

The maxim in question might be a trivial one, such as that of washing one's teeth after every meal. Sticking to a maxim like this over one's lifetime would ensure dental health; so at least we may assume. But the effect is both calculatively elusive and calculatively vulnerable. It would be undermined by the actions to which instance-by-instance deliberation must lead.

Suppose that I were to calculate after every meal whether to clean my teeth. On the negative side I would count the non-trivial cost of going to the trouble required. What would I count on the positive? The temptation is to say: the importance of the cleaning for my dental health. But the fact is that the significance of each individual cleaning for my oral well-being is negligible or next to negligible. No individual cleaning is sufficient to make the difference between having healthy teeth and not having healthy teeth; this is because dental health is a vaguely defined gestalt. Thus, other things being equal, calculation after every meal would always fail to elicit a walk to the bathroom; the result would be, bad teeth.[28]

Dental health then is a calculatively elusive consequence of adherence to a certain maxim. In order to achieve it, one must forswear calculation over individual actions. Better find a rule and stick to it. Wash after every meal, or wash every day, or wash when some regular chance event occurs. Do anything other than weigh the pro's and con's in every instance. Othewise you will never resist the opportunity to free ride on your future selves, and you will fail to ensure that you maintain your teeth.

We have laboured the fact that dental health is a calculatively elusive consequence of adherence to the maxim. The other question is whether it is also a consequence of a calculatively vulnerable sort.

Consider again the situation of deciding whether or not to wash my teeth now. If we agree that other things being equal, strict calculation of the pro's and con's would not galvanise me to action, then equally it must be admitted that a calculatively monitored maxim would fail to do so. The unmonitored maxim would certainly have the desired effect. But it would be robbed of all its power, once subjected to the question of whether adherence in this particular instance is strictly for the best. The question would be an immediate stimulus to free riding.

The dental health example is trivial but it stands proxy for many other illustrations of the third derived case where our argument for uncalculating consequentialism applies. We find similar examples wherever there is a good which has the following characteristics: it emerges over a period from

---

[28] For some discussion of intertemporal, intrapersonal free riding, see Richard Tuck 'Is there a free rider problem?' in Ross Harrison, ed., *Rational Action*, Cambridge University Press, 1979. If principle C10 in Derek Parfit *op. cit.*, p. 77 is accepted, then an analogue will block the temptation to free ride in this way. For more on free riding see Philip Pettit 'Free Riding and Foul Dealing', *Journal of Philosophy*, forthcoming.

independent actions; each of those actions is relatively burdensome; and none of the actions makes the difference between the appearance and non-appearance of the good. Under any such circumstances the person will be tempted at each moment to free ride on future efforts. Even where the good is a matter of the deepest self-interest therefore, the agent may be sure of achieving it only if he commits himself to an appropriate maxim.

In concluding discussion of this final case, it is worth noting that the case is exceptional in an important regard. It does not satisfy an otherwise general rule: viz. that the consequentialist will remain faithful to a maxim only if he does not independently come to believe that breaking it is actually for the best in the instance on hand. The consequentialist will abandon the sort of maxim that produces virtue, or unselfconsciousness, or loyalty, if that is known in a given instance to be genuinely for the best. In such an event — however unlikely — he will even violate the maxim that ensures respect and rights. But he will not defect from the maxim in our third derived case, even when he knows that doing so secures the optimal result.

It is not surprising that this case should be exceptional, for the damage done there by deliberation is due precisely to the fact that deliberation selects the option with the best probable results. If the restrictive consequentialist has found reason for submitting himself to some maxim in such a case, then knowing that following the maxim in a particular instance produces less than the best will not deprive him of that reason. It is precisely that sort of knowledge which motivate his adherence to the maxim in the first place.

Still, there is a paradox here. The consequentialist endorses the criterion of option evaluation associated with best probable consequences but in this sort of case he operates with an option selection criterion that is inconsistent in each instance, and is known to be inconsistent, with the achievement of the best probable consequences. How can that be?

The answer has to do with temporal perspective. The selection criterion for each option is inconsistent with the criterion of evaluation as applied to that particular option but not with the criterion of evaluation as applied to the series of options over which selection has to be made. In order to secure the best result overall therefore, the agent has to be sure that he does not pursue the best result in each case. Like Ulysses he must tie his hands. But he must do so to protect himself from his rational impulses, not from any irrational visitation.

6. Conclusion

We have tried to show that there is good reason why the consequentialist may want to go restrictive in certain areas of action and that those areas abound. The upshot is a fresh view of the possibilities of consequentialism, albeit one which squares with the traditional emphasis of defenders of the doctrine on the need for indirection. The view is worthy of further exploration, we believe, for we have done little more than provide some scattered illustrations of the need for consequentialists to go restrictive. It holds out the prospect of a consequentialism which fits better than many other variants with common sense intuitions about morality.[29]

There are two objections which will certainly be brought against the line which we have argued and we would like to end the paper by mentioning these and indicating why we think that they do not succeed.

The first objection is that our approach is not of any significance, representing a trivial variation on the consequentialist themes. The suggestion is that a consequentialist who proclaims the importance of restrictive rules still fits the familiar picture. He differs from the old-style image of the consequentialist only on matters of detail, not in his essential attitudes.

In his essential evaluative attitudes it is true that our consequentialist fits the standard profile. But we maintain that the difference on questions of selection makes for a real discontinuity. There is nothing trivial about the change in outlook demanded by accepting the points that we have made.

Amartya Sen has observed that moral principles can be usefully distinguished on the basis of the sort of information whose use they exclude.[30] Utilitarian rules render information on the identity of those who benefit from an action irrelevant; rules drawn from natural rights make information on the overall outcome of respecting a right redundant; and so on. Different moral principles are different informational constraints.

This observation connects illuminatingly with our approach. At the level of evaluation the consequentialist endorses the sort of informational constraint which we would expect; all that is relevant to the assessment of an input is how the world promises to lie in its wake. But if our approach is adopted, then at the level of selection quite different informational constraints may prevail. The essence of the approach is to say that often the consequentialist has reason to restrict the sort of information-use by which his position is distinguished.

What we have argued then is that in the field of action the best thing for the consequentialist to do may be to forsake his established moral persona. This thesis can scarcely be dismissed as insignificant. There could hardly be a more demanding amendment of consequentialism than to require that it should be self-effacing in this manner.

The second objection to our approach is that it endorses self-deception and even deception of others. It will be said that you are recommended self-deception in being told that while you should strive to bring about your own virtue or unselfconsciousness, you should do so by a path that involves not thinking about those goals. Equally it will be held that you are prescribed dishonesty in being instructed to promote the security or dignity of your beneficiaries by making it seem that your choice of action is not dictated by a concern for that good.

[29] We do not claim that all such intuitions are accommodated. For example we believe that for all we have said, consequentialism lacks the resources to provide an appropriately strong prohibition on interpersonal free riding. See Pettit 'The Prisoner's Dilemma and Social Theory', *Politics* 20, 1985, pp. 9-10.

[30] See Amartya Sen 'Informational Analysis of Moral Principles' in Ross Harrison *op. cit.*

The charge of dishonesty is obviously misplaced. You may make it clear to your beneficiary that your choice of maxim, and ultimately therefore your choice of action, is motivated by a concern for his security or dignity. What you are required to do is to make it equally clear that acting on the maxim does not involve weighing the importance of that effect in the scale of pro's and con's. There is no deception of others involved here.

And neither in the other cases is there any deception of self. I do not have to hide from myself the fact that following such and such a maxim is designed to produce my virtue or unselfconsciousness or whatever. I can retain a keen awareness of that goal, provided that in my choice of particular actions I stick to the maxim and keep the goal out of deliberative play. What is required is not self-deception, only self-discipline.

In order to emphasise that point, consider the contrast between the sorts of goals which we have mentioned and a goal like that of believing something. A belief is a route-specific state, in the sense that you can coherently aspire to instantiate it, only if you aspire to achieve it along a particular path: specifically, by being rationally persuaded that it is true. There would be something self-deceived about cleaving to a maxim with the goal of inducing a particular belief in yourself. But there is no such self-deception involved in the oblique pursuit of the goals mentioned in our examples. Goals like virtue and unselfconsciousness are not route-specific. You can aspire to exhibit them without aspiring to achieve them along any particular path.[31]

The upshot is that the restrictive consequentialist can be both ingenuous and reflective. He can keep all his aspirations in the open, so long as he is capable of insulating them from his decision-making processes. What is required of him may not be easy to attain but it is not a dissonant or unattractive cast of mind. It may even be an essential part of moral wisdom.[32] [33]

Australian National University   Received May 1985
                                                          Revised January 1986

---

[31] The belief case shows that we should add a further category to the calculatively elusive and vulnerable consequences already distinguished. These are the sort of consequences which are vulnerable even to strategic planning: to pre-calculation, as we might say.

[32] Perhaps the part emphasised in the tradition of Zen Buddhism. See Elster *op. cit.* In this connection it is worth mentioning that one of the effects of adopting a restrictive form of consequentialism will be to make room for an emphasis on the non-mechanical, non-actuarial character of moral judgment.

[33] We are grateful for helpful comments provided when this paper was read at the Dept of Philosophy, Faculty of Arts, Australian National University and at the Dept of Philosophy, University of Adelaide. We are also grateful for comments received from Stanley Benn, Jerry Dworkin, Peter Forrest, Jerry Gaus, Loren Lomasky, Hugh Mellor, Graham Nerlich, Huw Price, Christina Slade and Kim Sterelny.

Part IV
A Theory of Option-Evaluation
or Just Rule-Evaluation?

[8]

TWO CONCEPTS OF RULES*

IN THIS paper I want to show the importance of the distinction between justifying a practice [1] and justifying a particular action falling under it, and I want to explain the logical basis of this distinction and how it is possible to miss its significance. While the distinction has frequently been made,[2] and is now becoming commonplace, there remains the task of explaining the tendency either to overlook it altogether, or to fail to appreciate its importance.

To show the importance of the distinction I am going to defend utilitarianism against those objections which have traditionally been made against it in connection with punishment and the obligation to keep promises. I hope to show that if one uses the distinction in question then one can state utilitarianism

---

* This is a revision of a paper given at the Harvard Philosophy Club on April 30, 1954.

[1] I use the word "practice" throughout as a sort of technical term meaning any form of activity specified by a system of rules which defines offices, roles, moves, penalties, defenses, and so on, and which gives the activity its structure. As examples one may think of games and rituals, trials and parliaments.

[2] The distinction is central to Hume's discussion of justice in *A Treatise of Human Nature*, bk. III, pt. II, esp. secs. 2–4. It is clearly stated by John Austin in the second lecture of *Lectures on Jurisprudence* (4th ed.; London, 1873), I, 116ff. (1st ed., 1832). Also it may be argued that J. S. Mill took it for granted in *Utilitarianism;* on this point cf. J. O. Urmson, "The Interpretation of the Moral Philosophy of J. S. Mill," *Philosophical Quarterly*, vol. III (1953). In addition to the arguments given by Urmson there are several clear statements of the distinction in *A System of Logic* (8th ed.; London, 1872), bk. VI, ch. xii pars. 2, 3, 7. The distinction is fundamental to J. D. Mabbott's important paper, "Punishment," *Mind*, n.s., vol. XLVIII (April, 1939). More recently the distinction has been stated with particular emphasis by S. E. Toulmin in *The Place of Reason in Ethics* (Cambridge, 1950), see esp. ch. xi, where it plays a major part in his account of moral reasoning. Toulmin doesn't explain the basis of the distinction, nor how one might overlook its importance, as I try to in this paper, and in my review of his book (*Philosophical Review*, vol. LX [October, 1951]), as some of my criticisms show, I failed to understand the force of it. See also H. D. Aiken, "The Levels of Moral Discourse," *Ethics*, vol. LXII (1952), A. M. Quinton, "Punishment," *Analysis*, vol. XIV (June, 1954), and P. H. Nowell-Smith, *Ethics* (London, 1954), pp. 236–239, 271–273.

THE PHILOSOPHICAL REVIEW

in a way which makes it a much better explication of our considered moral judgments than these traditional objections would seem to admit.[3] Thus the importance of the distinction is shown by the way it strengthens the utilitarian view regardless of whether that view is completely defensible or not.

To explain how the significance of the distinction may be overlooked, I am going to discuss two conceptions of rules. One of these conceptions conceals the importance of distinguishing between the justification of a rule or practice and the justification of a particular action falling under it. The other conception makes it clear why this distinction must be made and what is its logical basis.

I

The subject of punishment, in the sense of attaching legal penalties to the violation of legal rules, has always been a troubling moral question.[4] The trouble about it has not been that people disagree as to whether or not punishment is justifiable. Most people have held that, freed from certain abuses, it is an acceptable institution. Only a few have rejected punishment entirely, which is rather surprising when one considers all that can be said against it. The difficulty is with the justification of punishment: various arguments for it have been given by moral philosophers, but so far none of them has won any sort of general acceptance; no justification is without those who detest it. I hope to show that the use of the aforementioned distinction enables one to state the utilitarian view in a way which allows for the sound points of its critics.

For our purposes we may say that there are two justifications of punishment. What we may call the retributive view is that punishment is justified on the grounds that wrongdoing merits punishment. It is morally fitting that a person who does wrong

---

[3] On the concept of explication see the author's paper *Philosophical Review*, vol. LX (April, 1951).

[4] While this paper was being revised, Quinton's appeared; footnote 2 supra. There are several respects in which my remarks are similar to his. Yet as I consider some further questions and rely on somewhat different arguments, I have retained the discussion of punishment and promises together as two test cases for utilitarianism.

TWO CONCEPTS OF RULES

should suffer in proportion to his wrongdoing. That a criminal should be punished follows from his guilt, and the severity of the appropriate punishment depends on the depravity of his act. The state of affairs where a wrongdoer suffers punishment is morally better than the state of affairs where he does not; and it is better irrespective of any of the consequences of punishing him.

What we may call the utilitarian view holds that on the principle that bygones are bygones and that only future consequences are material to present decisions, punishment is justifiable only by reference to the probable consequences of maintaining it as one of the devices of the social order. Wrongs committed in the past are, as such, not relevant considerations for deciding what to do. If punishment can be shown to promote effectively the interest of society it is justifiable, otherwise it is not.

I have stated these two competing views very roughly to make one feel the conflict between them: one feels the force of *both* arguments and one wonders how they can be reconciled. From my introductory remarks it is obvious that the resolution which I am going to propose is that in this case one must distinguish between justifying a practice as a system of rules to be applied and enforced, and justifying a particular action which falls under these rules; utilitarian arguments are appropriate with regard to questions about practices, while retributive arguments fit the application of particular rules to particular cases.

We might try to get clear about this distinction by imagining how a father might answer the question of his son. Suppose the son asks, "Why was J put in jail yesterday?" The father answers, "Because he robbed the bank at B. He was duly tried and found guilty. That's why he was put in jail yesterday." But suppose the son had asked a different question, namely, "Why do people put other people in jail?" Then the father might answer, "To protect good people from bad people" or "To stop people from doing things that would make it uneasy for all of us; for otherwise we wouldn't be able to go to bed at night and sleep in peace." There are two very different questions here. One question emphasizes the proper name: it asks why J was punished rather than someone else, or it asks what he was punished for. The other question asks why we have the institution of punish-

5

THE PHILOSOPHICAL REVIEW

ment: why do people punish one another rather than, say, always forgiving one another?

Thus the father says in effect that a particular man is punished, rather than some other man, because he is guilty, and he is guilty because he broke the law (past tense). In his case the law looks back, the judge looks back, the jury looks back, and a penalty is visited upon him for something he did. That a man is to be punished, and what his punishment is to be, is settled by its being shown that he broke the law and that the law assigns that penalty for the violation of it.

On the other hand we have the institution of punishment itself, and recommend and accept various changes in it, because it is thought by the (ideal) legislator and by those to whom the law applies that, as a part of a system of law impartially applied from case to case arising under it, it will have the consequence, in the long run, of furthering the interests of society.

One can say, then, that the judge and the legislator stand in different positions and look in different directions: one to the past, the other to the future. The justification of what the judge does, *qua* judge, sounds like the retributive view; the justification of what the (ideal) legislator does, *qua* legislator, sounds like the utilitarian view. Thus both views have a point (this is as it should be since intelligent and sensitive persons have been on both sides of the argument); and one's initial confusion disappears once one sees that these views apply to persons holding different offices with different duties, and situated differently with respect to the system of rules that make up the criminal law.[5]

One might say, however, that the utilitarian view is more fundamental since it applies to a more fundamental office, for the judge carries out the legislator's will so far as he can determine it. Once the legislator decides to have laws and to assign penalties for their violation (as things are there must be both the law and the penalty) an institution is set up which involves a retributive conception of particular cases. It is part of the concept of the criminal law as a system of rules that the application

---

[5] Note the fact that different sorts of arguments are suited to different offices. One way of taking the differences between ethical theories is to regard them as accounts of the reasons expected in different offices.

6

TWO CONCEPTS OF RULES

and enforcement of these rules in particular cases should be justifiable by arguments of a retributive character. The decision whether or not to use law rather than some other mechanism of social control, and the decision as to what laws to have and what penalties to assign, may be settled by utilitarian arguments; but if one decides to have laws then one has decided on something whose working in particular cases is retributive in form.[6]

The answer, then, to the confusion engendered by the two views of punishment is quite simple: one distinguishes two offices, that of the judge and that of the legislator, and one distinguishes their different stations with respect to the system of rules which make up the law; and then one notes that the different sorts of considerations which would usually be offered as reasons for what is done under the cover of these offices can be paired off with the competing justifications of punishment. One reconciles the two views by the time-honored device of making them apply to different situations.

But can it really be this simple? Well, this answer allows for the apparent intent of each side. Does a person who advocates the retributive view necessarily advocate, as an *institution*, legal machinery whose essential purpose is to set up and preserve a correspondence between moral turpitude and suffering? Surely not.[7] What retributionists have rightly insisted upon is that no man can be punished unless he is guilty, that is, unless he has broken the law. Their fundamental criticism of the utilitarian account is that, as they interpret it, it sanctions an innocent person's being punished (if one may call it that) for the benefit of society.

On the other hand, utilitarians agree that punishment is to be inflicted only for the violation of law. They regard this much as understood from the concept of punishment itself.[8] The point of

---

[6] In this connection see Mabbott, *op. cit.*, pp. 163–164.

[7] On this point see Sir David Ross, *The Right and the Good* (Oxford, 1930), pp. 57–60.

[8] See Hobbes's definition of punishment in *Leviathan*, ch. xxviii; and Bentham's definition in *The Principle of Morals and Legislation*, ch. xii, par. 36, ch. xv, par. 28, and in *The Rationale of Punishment*, (London, 1830), bk. I, ch. i. They could agree with Bradley that: "Punishment is punishment only when it is deserved. We pay the penalty, because we owe it, and for no other reason; and if punishment is inflicted for any other reason whatever than because it is

THE PHILOSOPHICAL REVIEW

the utilitarian account concerns the institution as a system of rules: utilitarianism seeks to limit its use by declaring it justifiable only if it can be shown to foster effectively the good of society. Historically it is a protest against the indiscriminate and ineffective use of the criminal law.[9] It seeks to dissuade us from assigning to penal institutions the improper, if not sacrilegious, task of matching suffering with moral turpitude. Like others, utilitarians want penal institutions designed so that, as far as humanly possible, only those who break the law run afoul of it. They hold that no official should have discretionary power to inflict penalties whenever he thinks it for the benefit of society; for on utilitarian grounds an institution granting such power could not be justified.[10]

The suggested way of reconciling the retributive and the utilitarian justifications of punishment seems to account for what both sides have wanted to say. There are, however, two further questions which arise, and I shall devote the remainder of this section to them.

First, will not a difference of opinion as to the proper criterion of just law make the proposed reconciliation unacceptable to retributionists? Will they not question whether, if the utilitarian principle is used as the criterion, it follows that those who have broken the law are guilty in a way which satisfies their demand

---

merited by wrong, it is a gross immorality, a crying injustice, an abominable crime, and not what it pretends to be." *Ethical Studies* (2nd ed.; Oxford, 1927), pp. 26–27. Certainly by definition it isn't what it pretends to be. The innocent can only be punished by mistake; deliberate "punishment" of the innocent necessarily involves fraud.

[9] Cf. Leon Radzinowicz, *A History of English Criminal Law: The Movement for Reform 1750–1833* (London, 1948), esp. ch. xi on Bentham.

[10] Bentham discusses how corresponding to a punitory provision of a criminal law there is another provision which stands to it as an antagonist and which needs a name as much as the punitory. He calls it, as one might expect, the *anaetiosostic*, and of it he says: "The punishment of guilt is the object of the former one: the preservation of innocence that of the latter." In the same connection he asserts that it is never thought fit to give the judge the option of deciding whether a thief (that is, a person whom he believes to be a thief, for the judge's belief is what the question must always turn upon) should hang or not, and so the law writes the provision: "The judge shall not cause a thief to be hanged unless he have been duly convicted and sentenced in course of law" (*The Limits of Jurisprudence Defined*, ed. C. W. Everett [New York, 1945], pp. 238–239).

8

TWO CONCEPTS OF RULES

that those punished deserve to be punished? To answer this difficulty, suppose that the rules of the criminal law are justified on utilitarian grounds (it is only for laws that meet his criterion that the utilitarian can be held responsible). Then it follows that the actions which the criminal law specifies as offenses are such that, if they were tolerated, terror and alarm would spread in society. Consequently, retributionists can only deny that those who are punished deserve to be punished if they deny that such actions are wrong. This they will not want to do.

The second question is whether utilitarianism doesn't justify too much. One pictures it as an engine of justification which, if consistently adopted, could be used to justify cruel and arbitrary institutions. Retributionists may be supposed to concede that utilitarians *intend* to reform the law and to make it more humane; that utilitarians do not *wish* to justify any such thing as punishment of the innocent; and that utilitarians may appeal to the fact that punishment presupposes guilt in the sense that by punishment one understands an institution attaching penalties to the infraction of legal rules, and therefore that it is logically absurd to suppose that utilitarians in justifying *punishment* might also have justified punishment (if we may call it that) of the innocent. The real question, however, is whether the utilitarian, in justifying punishment, hasn't used arguments which commit him to accepting the infliction of suffering on innocent persons if it is for the good of society (whether or not one calls this punishment). More generally, isn't the utilitarian committed in principle to accepting many practices which he, as a morally sensitive person, wouldn't want to accept? Retributionists are inclined to hold that there is no way to stop the utilitarian principle from justifying too much except by adding to it a principle which distributes certain rights to individuals. Then the amended criterion is not the greatest benefit of society *simpliciter*, but the greatest benefit of society subject to the constraint that no one's rights may be violated. Now while I think that the classical utilitarians proposed a criterion of this more complicated sort, I do not want to argue that point here.[11] What I want to show is that

---

[11] By the classical utilitarians I understand Hobbes, Hume, Bentham, J. S. Mill, and Sidgwick.

THE PHILOSOPHICAL REVIEW

there is *another* way of preventing the utilitarian principle from justifying too much, or at least of making it much less likely to do so: namely, by stating utilitarianism in a way which accounts for the distinction between the justification of an institution and the justification of a particular action falling under it.

I begin by defining the institution of punishment as follows: a person is said to suffer punishment whenever he is legally deprived of some of the normal rights of a citizen on the ground that he has violated a rule of law, the violation having been established by trial according to the due process of law, provided that the deprivation is carried out by the recognized legal authorities of the state, that the rule of law clearly specifies both the offense and the attached penalty, that the courts construe statutes strictly, and that the statute was on the books prior to the time of the offense.[12] This definition specifies what I shall understand by punishment. The question is whether utilitarian arguments may be found to justify institutions widely different from this and such as one would find cruel and arbitrary.

This question is best answered, I think, by taking up a particular accusation. Consider the following from Carritt:

> . . . the utilitarian must hold that we are justified in inflicting pain always and only to prevent worse pain or bring about greater happiness. This, then, is all we need to consider in so-called punishment, which must be purely preventive. But if some kind of very cruel crime becomes common, and none of the criminals can be caught, it might be highly expedient, as an example, to hang an innocent man, if a charge against him could be so framed that he were universally thought guilty; indeed this would only fail to be an ideal instance of utilitarian 'punishment' because the victim himself would not have been so likely as a real felon to commit such a crime in the future; in all other respects it would be perfectly deterrent and therefore felicific.[13]

Carritt is trying to show that there are occasions when a utilitarian argument would justify taking an action which would be generally condemned; and thus that utilitarianism justifies too much. But the failure of Carritt's argument lies in the fact that

---

[12] All these features of punishment are mentioned by Hobbes; cf. *Leviathan*, ch. xxviii.

[13] *Ethical and Political Thinking* (Oxford, 1947), p. 65.

TWO CONCEPTS OF RULES

he makes no distinction between the justification of the general system of rules which constitutes penal institutions and the justification of particular applications of these rules to particular cases by the various officials whose job it is to administer them. This becomes perfectly clear when one asks who the "we" are of whom Carritt speaks. Who is this who has a sort of absolute authority on particular occasions to decide that an innocent man shall be "punished" if everyone can be convinced that he is guilty? Is this person the legislator, or the judge, or the body of private citizens, or what? It is utterly crucial to know who is to decide such matters, and by what authority, for all of this must be written into the rules of the institution. Until one knows these things one doesn't know what the institution is whose justification is being challenged; and as the utilitarian principle applies to the institution one doesn't know whether it is justifiable on utilitarian grounds or not.

Once this is understood it is clear what the countermove to Carritt's argument is. One must describe more carefully what the *institution* is which his example suggests, and then ask oneself whether or not it is likely that having this institution would be for the benefit of society in the long run. One must not content oneself with the vague thought that, when it's a question of *this* case, it would be a good thing if *somebody* did something even if an innocent person were to suffer.

Try to imagine, then, an institution (which we may call "telishment") which is such that the officials set up by it have authority to arrange a trial for the condemnation of an innocent man whenever they are of the opinion that doing so would be in the best interests of society. The discretion of officials is limited, however, by the rule that they may not condemn an innocent man to undergo such an ordeal unless there is, at the time, a wave of offenses similar to that with which they charge him and telish him for. We may imagine that the officials having the discretionary authority are the judges of the higher courts in consultation with the chief of police, the minister of justice, and a committee of the legislature.

Once one realizes that one is involved in setting up an *institu-*

THE PHILOSOPHICAL REVIEW

tion, one sees that the hazards are very great. For example, what check is there on the officials? How is one to tell whether or not their actions are authorized? How is one to limit the risks involved in allowing such systematic deception? How is one to avoid giving anything short of complete discretion to the authorities to telish anyone they like? In addition to these considerations, it is obvious that people will come to have a very different attitude towards their penal system when telishment is adjoined to it. They will be uncertain as to whether a convicted man has been punished or telished. They will wonder whether or not they should feel sorry for him. They will wonder whether the same fate won't at any time fall on them. If one pictures how such an institution would actually work, and the enormous risks involved in it, it seems clear that it would serve no useful purpose. A utilitarian justification for this institution is most unlikely.

It happens in general that as one drops off the defining features of punishment one ends up with an institution whose utilitarian justification is highly doubtful. One reason for this is that punishment works like a kind of price system: by altering the prices one has to pay for the performance of actions it supplies a motive for avoiding some actions and doing others. The defining features are essential if punishment is to work in this way; so that an institution which lacks these features, e.g., an institution which is set up to "punish" the innocent, is likely to have about as much point as a price system (if one may call it that) where the prices of things change at random from day to day and one learns the price of something after one has agreed to buy it.[14]

---

[14] The analogy with the price system suggests an answer to the question how utilitarian considerations insure that punishment is proportional to the offense. It is interesting to note that Sir David Ross, after making the distinction between justifying a penal law and justifying a particular application of it, and after stating that utilitarian considerations have a large place in determining the former, still holds back from accepting the utilitarian justification of punishment on the grounds that justice requires that punishment be proportional to the offense, and that utilitarianism is unable to account for this. Cf. *The Right and the Good*, pp. 61–62. I do not claim that utilitarianism can account for this requirement as Sir David might wish, but it happens, nevertheless, that if utilitarian considerations are followed penalties will be proportional to offenses in this sense: the order of offenses according to seriousness can be paired off

TWO CONCEPTS OF RULES

If one is careful to apply the utilitarian principle to the institution which is to authorize particular actions, then there is *less* danger of its justifying too much. Carritt's example gains plausibility by its indefiniteness and by its concentration on the particular case. His argument will only hold if it can be shown that there are utilitarian arguments which justify an institution whose publicly ascertainable offices and powers are such as to permit officials to exercise that kind of discretion in particular cases. But the requirement of having to build the arbitrary features of the particular decision into the institutional practice makes the justification much less likely to go through.

II

I shall now consider the question of promises. The objection to utilitarianism in connection with promises seems to be this: it is believed that on the utilitarian view when a person makes a promise the only ground upon which he should keep it, if he should keep it, is that by keeping it he will realize the most good on the whole. So that if one asks the question "Why should I keep *my* promise?" the utilitarian answer is understood to be that doing so in *this* case will have the best consequences. And this answer is said, quite rightly, to conflict with the way in which the obligation to keep promises is regarded.

Now of course critics of utilitarianism are not unaware that one defense sometimes attributed to utilitarians is the consideration involving the practice of promise-keeping.[15] In this connec-

---

with the order of penalties according to severity. Also the absolute level of penalties will be as low as possible. This follows from the assumption that people are rational (i.e., that they are able to take into account the "prices" the state puts on actions), the utilitarian rule that a penal system should provide a motive for preferring the less serious offense, and the principle that punishment as such is an evil. All this was carefully worked out by Bentham in *The Principles of Morals and Legislation*, chs. xiii–xv.

[15] Ross, *The Right and the Good*, pp. 37–39, and *Foundations of Ethics* (Oxford, 1939), pp. 92–94. I know of no utilitarian who has used this argument except W. A. Pickard-Cambridge in "Two Problems about Duty," *Mind*, n.s., XLI (April, 1932), 153–157, although the argument goes with G. E. Moore's version of utilitarianism in *Principia Ethica* (Cambridge, 1903). To my knowledge it does not appear in the classical utilitarians; and if one interprets their view correctly this is no accident.

THE PHILOSOPHICAL REVIEW

tion they are supposed to argue something like this: it must be admitted that we feel strictly about keeping promises, more strictly than it might seem our view can account for. But when we consider the matter carefully it is always necessary to take into account the effect which our action will have on the practice of making promises. The promisor must weigh, not only the effects of breaking his promise on the particular case, but also the effect which his breaking his promise will have on the practice itself. Since the practice is of great utilitarian value, and since breaking one's promise always seriously damages it, one will seldom be justified in breaking one's promise. If we view our individual promises in the wider context of the practice of promising itself we can account for the strictness of the obligation to keep promises. There is always one very strong utilitarian consideration in favor of keeping them, and this will insure that when the question arises as to whether or not to keep a promise it will usually turn out that one should, even where the facts of the particular case taken by itself would seem to justify one's breaking it. In this way the strictness with which we view the obligation to keep promises is accounted for.

Ross has criticized this defense as follows:[16] however great the value of the practice of promising, on utilitarian grounds, there must be some value which is greater, and one can imagine it to be obtainable by breaking a promise. Therefore there might be a case where the promisor could argue that breaking his promise was justified as leading to a better state of affairs on the whole. And the promisor could argue in this way no matter how slight the advantage won by breaking the promise. If one were to challenge the promisor his defense would be that what he did was best on the whole in view of all the utilitarian considerations, which in this case *include* the importance of the practice. Ross feels that such a defense would be unacceptable. I think he is right insofar as he is protesting against the appeal to consequences in general and without further explanation. Yet it is extremely difficult to weigh the force of Ross's argument. The kind of case imagined seems unrealistic and one feels that it needs to be described. One is inclined to think that it would

---

[16] Ross, *The Right and the Good*, pp. 38–39.

TWO CONCEPTS OF RULES

either turn out that such a case came under an exception defined by the practice itself, in which case there would not be an appeal to consequences in general on the particular case, or it would happen that the circumstances were so peculiar that the conditions which the practice presupposes no longer obtained. But certainly Ross is right in thinking that it strikes us as wrong for a person to defend breaking a promise by a general appeal to consequences. For a general utilitarian defense is not open to the promisor: it is not one of the defenses allowed by the practice of making promises.

Ross gives two further counterarguments:[17] First, he holds that it overestimates the damage done to the practice of promising by a failure to keep a promise. One who breaks a promise harms his own name certainly, but it isn't clear that a broken promise always damages the practice itself sufficiently to account for the strictness of the obligation. Second, and more important, I think, he raises the question of what one is to say of a promise which isn't known to have been made except to the promisor and the promisee, as in the case of a promise a son makes to his dying father concerning the handling of the estate.[18] In this sort of case the consideration relating to the practice doesn't weigh on the promisor at all, and yet one feels that this sort of promise is as binding as other promises. The question of the effect which breaking it has on the practice seems irrelevant. The only consequence seems to be that one can break the promise without running any risk of being censured; but the obligation itself seems not the least weakened. Hence it is doubtful whether the effect on the practice ever weighs in the particular case; certainly it cannot account for the strictness of the obligation where

---

[17] Ross, *ibid.*, p. 39. The case of the nonpublic promise is discussed again in *Foundations of Ethics*, pp. 95–96, 104–105. It occurs also in Mabbott, "Punishment," *op. cit.*, pp. 155–157, and in A. I. Melden, "Two Comments on Utilitarianism," *Philosophical Review*, LX (October, 1951), 519–523, which discusses Carritt's example in *Ethical and Political Thinking*, p. 64.

[18] Ross's example is described simply as that of two men dying alone where one makes a promise to the other. Carritt's example (cf. n. 17 supra) is that of two men at the North Pole. The example in the text is more realistic and is similar to Mabbott's. Another example is that of being told something in confidence by one who subsequently dies. Such cases need not be "desert-island arguments" as Nowell-Smith seems to believe (cf. his *Ethics*, pp. 239–244).

THE PHILOSOPHICAL REVIEW

it fails to obtain. It seems to follow that a utilitarian account of the obligation to keep promises cannot be successfully carried out.

From what I have said in connection with punishment, one can foresee what I am going to say about these arguments and counterarguments. They fail to make the distinction between the justification of a practice and the justification of a particular action falling under it, and therefore they fall into the mistake of taking it for granted that the promisor, like Carritt's official, is entitled without restriction to bring utilitarian considerations to bear in deciding whether to keep *his* promise. But if one considers what the practice of promising is one will see, I think, that it is such as not to allow this sort of general discretion to the promisor. Indeed, the point of the practice is to abdicate one's title to act in accordance with utilitarian and prudential considerations in order that the future may be tied down and plans coordinated in advance. There are obvious utilitarian advantages in having a practice which denies to the promisor, as a defense, any general appeal to the utilitarian principle in accordance with which the practice itself may be justified. There is nothing contradictory, or surprising, in this: utilitarian (or aesthetic) reasons might properly be given in arguing that the game of chess, or baseball, is satisfactory just as it is, or in arguing that it should be changed in various respects, but a player in a game cannot properly appeal to such considerations as reasons for his making one move rather than another. It is a mistake to think that if the practice is justified on utilitarian grounds then the promisor must have complete liberty to use utilitarian arguments to decide whether or not to keep his promise. The practice forbids this general defense; and it is a purpose of the practice to do this. Therefore what the above arguments presuppose—the idea that if the utilitarian view is accepted then the promisor is bound if, and only if, the application of the utilitarian principle to his own case shows that keeping it is best on the whole—is false. The promisor is bound because he promised: weighing the case on its merits is not open to him.[19]

---

[19] What I have said in this paragraph seems to me to coincide with Hume's important discussion in the *Treatise of Human Nature*, bk. III, pt. II, sec. 5; and also sec. 6, par. 8.

TWO CONCEPTS OF RULES

Is this to say that in particular cases one cannot deliberate whether or not to keep one's promise? Of course not. But to do so is to deliberate whether the various excuses, exceptions and defenses, which are understood by, and which constitute an important part of, the practice, apply to one's own case.[20] Various defenses for not keeping one's promise are allowed, but among them there isn't the one that, on general utilitarian grounds, the promisor (truly) thought his action best on the whole, even though there may be the defense that the consequences of keeping one's promise would have been *extremely* severe. While there are too many complexities here to consider all the necessary details, one can see that the general defense isn't allowed if one asks the following question: what would one say of someone who, when asked why he broke his promise, replied simply that breaking it was best on the whole? Assuming that his reply is sincere, and that his belief was reasonable (i.e., one need not consider the possibility that he was mistaken), I think that one would question whether or not he knows what it means to say "I promise" (in the appropriate circumstances). It would be said of someone who used this excuse without further explanation that he didn't understand what defenses the practice, which defines a promise, allows to him. If a child were to use this excuse one would correct him; for it is part of the way one is taught the concept of a promise to be corrected if one uses this excuse. The point of having the practice would be lost if the practice did allow this excuse.

It is no doubt part of the utilitarian view that every practice should admit the defense that the consequences of abiding by it would have been extremely severe; and utilitarians would be inclined to hold that some reliance on people's good sense and some concession to hard cases is necessary. They would hold that a practice is justified by serving the interests of those who take part in it; and as with any set of rules there is understood a background of circumstances under which it is expected to be applied and which need not—indeed which cannot—be fully stated. Should these circumstances change, then even if

[20] For a discussion of these, see H. Sidgwick, *The Methods of Ethics* (6th ed.; London, 1901), bk. III, ch. vi.

THE PHILOSOPHICAL REVIEW

there is no rule which provides for the case, it may still be in accordance with the practice that one be released from one's obligation. But this sort of defense allowed by a practice must not be confused with the general option to weigh each particular case on utilitarian grounds which critics of utilitarianism have thought it necessarily to involve.

The concern which utilitarianism raises by its justification of punishment is that it may justify too much. The question in connection with promises is different: it is how utilitarianism can account for the obligation to keep promises at all. One feels that the recognized obligation to keep one's promise and utilitarianism are incompatible. And to be sure, they are incompatible if one interprets the utilitarian view as necessarily holding that each person has complete liberty to weigh every particular action on general utilitarian grounds. But must one interpret utilitarianism in this way? I hope to show that, in the sorts of cases I have discussed, one cannot interpret it in this way.

III

So far I have tried to show the importance of the distinction between the justification of a practice and the justification of a particular action falling under it by indicating how this distinction might be used to defend utilitarianism against two long-standing objections. One might be tempted to close the discussion at this point by saying that utilitarian considerations should be understood as applying to practices in the first instance and not to particular actions falling under them except insofar as the practices admit of it. One might say that in this modified form it is a better account of our considered moral opinions and let it go at that. But to stop here would be to neglect the interesting question as to how one can fail to appreciate the significance of this rather obvious distinction and can take it for granted that utilitarianism has the consequence that particular cases may always be decided on general utilitarian grounds.[21] I want to

---

[21] So far as I can see it is not until Moore that the doctrine is expressly stated in this way. See, for example, *Principia Ethica*, p. 147, where it is said that the statement "I am morally bound to perform this action" is identical with the statement "*This* action will produce the greatest possible amount of good in

TWO CONCEPTS OF RULES

argue that this mistake may be connected with misconceiving the logical status of the rules of practices; and to show this I am going to examine two conceptions of rules, two ways of placing them within the utilitarian theory.

The conception which conceals from us the significance of the distinction I am going to call the summary view. It regards rules in the following way: one supposes that each person decides what he shall do in particular cases by applying the utilitarian principle; one supposes further that different people will decide the same particular case in the same way and that there will be recurrences of cases similar to those previously decided. Thus it will happen that in cases of certain kinds the same decision will be made either by the same person at different times or by different persons at the same time. If a case occurs frequently enough one supposes that a rule is formulated to cover that sort of case. I have called this conception the summary view because rules are pictured as summaries of past decisions arrived at by the *direct* application of the utilitarian principle to particular cases. Rules are regarded as reports that cases of a certain sort have been found on *other* grounds to be properly decided in a certain way (although, of course, they do not *say* this).

There are several things to notice about this way of placing rules within the utilitarian theory.[22]

the Universe" (my italics). It is important to remember that those whom I have called the classical utilitarians were largely interested in social institutions. They were among the leading economists and political theorists of their day, and they were not infrequently reformers interested in practical affairs. Utilitarianism historically goes together with a coherent view of society, and is not simply an ethical theory, much less an attempt at philosophical analysis in the modern sense. The utilitarian principle was quite naturally thought of, and used, as a criterion for judging social institutions (practices) and as a basis for urging reforms. It is not clear, therefore, how far it is necessary to amend utilitarianism in its classical form. For a discussion of utilitarianism as an integral part of a theory of society, see L. Robbins, *The Theory of Economic Policy in English Classical Political Economy* (London, 1952).

[22] This footnote should be read after sec. 3 and presupposes what I have said there. It provides a few references to statements by leading utilitarians of the summary conception. In general it appears that when they discussed the logical features of rules the summary conception prevailed and that it was typical of the way they talked about moral rules. I cite a rather lengthy group of passages from Austin as a full illustration.

John Austin in his *Lectures on Jurisprudence* meets the objection that deciding

in accordance with the utilitarian principle case by case is impractical by saying that this is a misinterpretation of utilitarianism. According to the utilitarian
view ". . . our conduct would conform to *rules* inferred from the tendencies of
actions, but would not be determined by a direct resort to the principle of
general utility. Utility would be the test of our conduct, ultimately, but not
immediately: the immediate test of the rules to which our conduct would conform, but not the immediate test of specific or individual actions. Our rules
would be fashioned on utility; our conduct, on our rules" (vol. I, p. 116). As
to how one decides on the tendency of an action he says: "If we would try the
tendency of a specific or individual act, we must not contemplate the act as if
it were single and insulated, but most look at the class of acts to which it belongs. We must suppose that acts of the class were generally done or omitted,
and consider the probable effect upon the general happiness or good. We must
guess the consequences which would follow, if the class of acts were general;
and also the consequences which would follow, if they were generally omitted.
We must then compare the consequences on the positive and negative sides,
and determine on which of the two the *balance* of advantage lies. . . . If we
truly try the tendency of a specific or individual act, we try the tendency of the
class to which that act belongs. The *particular* conclusion which we draw, with
regard to the single act, implies a *general* conclusion embracing all similar
acts. . . . To the rules thus inferred, and lodged in the memory, our conduct
would conform *immediately* if it were truly adjusted to utility" (*ibid.*, p. 117).
One might think that Austin meets the objection by stating the practice conception of rules; and perhaps he did intend to. But it is not clear that he has
stated this conception. Is the generality he refers to of the statistical sort? This
is suggested by the notion of tendency. Or does he refer to the utility of setting
up a practice? I don't know; but what suggests the summary view is his subsequent remarks. He says: "To consider the specific consequences of single or
individual acts, would *seldom* [my italics] consist with that ultimate principle"
(*ibid.*, p. 117). But would one ever do this? He continues: ". . . this being admitted, the necessity of pausing and calculating, which the objection in question supposes, is an imagined necessity. To preface each act or forbearance by
a conjecture and comparison of consequences, were clearly *superfluous* [my
italics] and mischievous. It were clearly superfluous, inasmuch as the *result of
that process* [my italics] would be embodied in a known *rule*. It were clearly
mischievous, inasmuch as the *true* result would be expressed by that rule,
whilst the process would probably be faulty, if it were done on the spur of the
occasion" (*ibid.*, pp. 117–118). He goes on: "If our experience and observation
of particulars were not *generalized*, our experience and observation of particulars would seldom avail us in *practice*. . . . The inferences suggested to our minds
by repeated experience and observation are, therefore, drawn into *principles*, or
compressed into *maxims*. These we carry about us ready for use, and apply to
individual cases promptly . . . without reverting to the process by which they
were obtained; or without recalling, and arraying before our minds, the numerous and intricate considerations of which they are *handy abridgments* [my italics].
. . . True theory is a *compendium* of particular truths. . . . Speaking then, generally, human conduct is inevitably *guided* [my italics] by *rules*, or by *principles*
or *maxims*" (*ibid.*, pp. 117–118). I need not trouble to show how all these remarks incline to the summary view. Further, when Austin comes to deal with

TWO CONCEPTS OF RULES

cases "of comparatively rare occurrence" he holds that specific considerations may outweigh the general. "Looking at the reasons from which we had inferred the rule, it were absurd to think it inflexible. We should therefore dismiss the *rule;* resort directly to the *principle* upon which our rules were fashioned; and calculate *specific* consequences to the best of our knowledge and ability" (*ibid.*, pp. 120–121). Austin's view is interesting because it shows how one may come close to the practice conception and then slide away from it.

In *A System of Logic*, bk. VI, ch. xii, par. 2, Mill distinguishes clearly between the position of judge and legislator and in doing so suggests the distinction between the two concepts of rules. However, he distinguishes the two positions to illustrate the difference between cases where one is to apply a rule already established and cases where one must formulate a rule to govern subsequent conduct. It's the latter case that interests him and he takes the "maxim of policy" of a legislator as typical of rules. In par. 3 the summary conception is very clearly stated. For example, he says of rules of conduct that they should be taken provisionally, as they are made for the most numerous cases. He says that they "point out" the manner in which it is least perilous to act; they serve as an "admonition" that a certain mode of conduct has been found suited to the most common occurrences. In *Utilitarianism*, ch. ii, par. 24, the summary conception appears in Mill's answer to the same objection Austin considered. Here he speaks of rules as "corollaries" from the principle of utility; these "secondary" rules are compared to "landmarks" and "direction-posts." They are based on long experience and so make it unnecessary to apply the utilitarian principle to each case. In par. 25 Mill refers to the task of the utilitarian principle in adjudicating between competing moral rules. He talks here as if one then applies the utilitarian principle directly to the particular case. On the practice view one would rather use the principle to decide which of the ways that make the practice consistent is the best. It should be noted that while in par. 10 Mill's definition of utilitarianism makes the utilitarian principle apply to morality, i.e., to the rules and precepts of human conduct, the definition in par. 2 uses the phrase "actions are right in *proportion* as they *tend* to promote happiness" [my italics] and this inclines towards the summary view. In the last paragraph of the essay "On the Definition of Political Economy," *Westminster Review* (October, 1836), Mill says that it is only in art, as distinguished from science, that one can properly speak of exceptions. In a question of practice, if something is fit to be done "in the majority of cases" then it is made the rule. "We may . . . in talking of árt *unobjectionably* speak of the *rule* and the *exception*, meaning by the rule the cases in which there exists a preponderance . . . of inducements for acting in a particular way; and by the exception, the cases in which the preponderance is on the contrary side." These remarks, too, suggest the summary view.

In Moore's *Principia Ethica*, ch. v, there is a complicated and difficult discussion of moral rules. I will not examine it here except to express my suspicion that the summary conception prevails. To be sure, Moore speaks frequently of the utility of rules as generally followed, and of actions as generally practiced, but it is possible that these passages fit the statistical notion of generality which the summary conception allows. This conception is suggested by Moore's taking the utilitarian principle as applying directly to particular actions (pp. 147–148) and by his notion of a rule as something indicating which

THE PHILOSOPHICAL REVIEW

1. The point of having rules derives from the fact that similar cases tend to recur and that one can decide cases more quickly if one records past decisions in the form of rules. If similar cases didn't recur, one would be required to apply the utilitarian principle directly, case by case, and rules reporting past decisions would be of no use.

2. The decisions made on particular cases are logically prior to rules. Since rules gain their point from the need to apply the utilitarian principle to many similar cases, it follows that a particular case (or several cases similar to it) may exist whether or not there is a rule covering that case. We are pictured as recognizing particular cases prior to there being a rule which covers them, for it is only if we meet with a number of cases of a certain sort that we formulate a rule. Thus we are able to describe a particular case as a particular case of the requisite sort whether there is a rule regarding *that* sort of case or not. Put another way: what the *A*'s and the *B*'s refer to in rules of the form 'Whenever *A* do *B*' may be described as *A*'s and *B*'s whether or not there is the rule 'Whenever *A* do *B*', or whether or not there is any body of rules which make up a practice of which that rule is a part.

To illustrate this consider a rule, or maxim, which could arise in this way: suppose that a person is trying to decide whether to tell someone who is fatally ill what his illness is when he has been asked to do so. Suppose the person to reflect and then decide, on utilitarian grounds, that he should not answer truthfully; and suppose that on the basis of this and other like occasions he formulates a rule to the effect that when asked by someone fatally ill what his illness is, one should not tell him. The point to notice is that someone's being fatally ill and asking what his illness is, and someone's telling him, are things that can be described as such whether or not there is this rule. The performance of the action to which the rule refers doesn't require the stage-setting of a practice of which this rule is a part. This is

---

of the few alternatives likely to occur to anyone will generally produce a greater total good in the immediate future (p. 154). He talks of an "ethical law" as a prediction, and as a generalization (pp. 146, 155). The summary conception is also suggested by his discussion of exceptions (pp. 162–163) and of the force of examples of breaching a rule (pp. 163–164).

TWO CONCEPTS OF RULES

what is meant by saying that on the summary view particular cases are logically prior to rules.

3. Each person is in principle always entitled to reconsider the correctness of a rule and to question whether or not it is proper to follow it in a particular case. As rules are guides and aids, one may ask whether in past decisions there might not have been a mistake in applying the utilitarian principle to get the rule in question, and wonder whether or not it is best in this case. The reason for rules is that people are not able to apply the utilitarian principle effortlessly and flawlessly; there is need to save time and to post a guide. On this view a society of rational utilitarians would be a society without rules in which each person applied the utilitarian principle directly and smoothly, and without error, case by case. On the other hand, ours is a society in which rules are formulated to serve as aids in reaching these ideally rational decisions on particular cases, guides which have been built up and tested by the experience of generations. If one applies this view to rules, one is interpreting them as maxims, as "rules of thumb"; and it is doubtful that anything to which the summary conception did apply would be called a *rule*. Arguing as if one regarded rules in this way is a mistake one makes while doing philosophy.

4. The concept of a *general* rule takes the following form. One is pictured as estimating on what percentage of the cases likely to arise a given rule may be relied upon to express the correct decision, that is, the decision that would be arrived at if one were to correctly apply the utilitarian principle case by case. If one estimates that by and large the rule will give the correct decision, or if one estimates that the likelihood of making a mistake by applying the utilitarian principle directly on one's own is greater than the likelihood of making a mistake by following the rule, and if these considerations held of persons generally, then one would be justified in urging its adoption as a general rule. In this way *general* rules might be accounted for on the summary view. It will still make sense, however, to speak of applying the utilitarian principle case by case, for it was by trying to foresee the results of doing this that one got the initial estimates upon which acceptance of the rule depends. That one is

taking a rule in accordance with the summary conception will show itself in the naturalness with which one speaks of the rule as a guide, or as a maxim, or as a generalization from experience, and as something to be laid aside in extraordinary cases where there is no assurance that the generalization will hold and the case must therefore be treated on its merits. Thus there goes with this conception the notion of a particular exception which renders a rule suspect on a particular occasion.

The other conception of rules I will call the practice conception. On this view rules are pictured as defining a practice. Practices are set up for various reasons, but one of them is that in many areas of conduct each person's deciding what to do on utilitarian grounds case by case leads to confusion, and that the attempt to coordinate behavior by trying to foresee how others will act is bound to fail. As an alternative one realizes that what is required is the establishment of a practice, the specification of a new form of activity; and from this one sees that a practice necessarily involves the abdication of full liberty to act on utilitarian and prudential grounds. It is the mark of a practice that being taught how to engage in it involves being instructed in the rules which define it, and that appeal is made to those rules to correct the behavior of those engaged in it. Those engaged in a practice recognize the rules as defining it. The rules cannot be taken as simply describing how those engaged in the practice in fact behave: it is not simply that they act as if they were obeying the rules. Thus it is essential to the notion of a practice that the rules are publicly known and understood as definitive; and it is essential also that the rules of a practice can be taught and can be acted upon to yield a coherent practice. On this conception, then, rules are not generalizations from the decisions of individuals applying the utilitarian principle directly and independently to recurrent particular cases. On the contrary, rules define a practice and are themselves the subject of the utilitarian principle.

To show the important differences between this way of fitting rules into the utilitarian theory and the previous way, I shall consider the differences between the two conceptions on the points previously discussed.

TWO CONCEPTS OF RULES

1. In contrast with the summary view, the rules of practices
are logically prior to particular cases. This is so because there
cannot be a particular case of an action falling under a rule of a
practice unless there is the practice. This can be made clearer as
follows: in a practice there are rules setting up offices, specifying
certain forms of action appropriate to various offices, establishing penalties for the breach of rules, and so on. We may think of
the rules of a practice as defining offices, moves, and offenses. Now
what is meant by saying that the practice is logically prior to
particular cases is this: given any rule which specifies a form of
action (a move), a particular action which would be taken as
falling under this rule given that there is the practice would not
be *described as* that sort of action unless there was the practice.
In the case of actions specified by practices it is logically impossible to perform them outside the stage-setting provided by
those practices, for unless there is the practice, and unless the
requisite proprieties are fulfilled, whatever one does, whatever
movements one makes, will fail to count as a form of action
which the practice specifies. What one does will be described in
some *other* way.

One may illustrate this point from the game of baseball. Many
of the actions one performs in a game of baseball one can do by
oneself or with others whether there is the game or not. For example, one can throw a ball, run, or swing a peculiarly shaped
piece of wood. But one cannot steal base, or strike out, or draw
a walk, or make an error, or balk; although one can do certain
things which appear to resemble these actions such as sliding into
a bag, missing a grounder and so on. Striking out, stealing a base,
balking, etc., are all actions which can only happen in a game.
No matter what a person did, what he did would not be described as stealing a base or striking out or drawing a walk unless
he could also be described as playing baseball, and for him to be
doing this presupposes the rule-like practice which constitutes
the game. The practice is logically prior to particular cases: unless there is the practice the terms referring to actions specified
by it lack a sense.[23]

---

[23] One might feel that it is a mistake to say that a practice is logically prior
to the forms of action it specifies on the grounds that if there were never any

25

THE PHILOSOPHICAL REVIEW

2. The practice view leads to an entirely different conception of the authority which each person has to decide on the propriety of following a rule in particular cases. To engage in a practice, to perform those actions specified by a practice, means to follow the appropriate rules. If one wants to do an action which a certain practice specifies then there is no way to do it except to follow the rules which define it. Therefore, it doesn't make sense for a person to raise the question whether or not a rule of a practice correctly applies to *his* case where the action he contemplates is a form of action defined by a practice. If someone were to raise such a question, he would simply show that he didn't understand the situation in which he was acting. If one wants to perform an action specified by a practice, the only legitimate question concerns the nature of the practice itself ("How do I go about making a will?").

This point is illustrated by the behavior expected of a player in games. If one wants to play a game, one doesn't treat the rules of the game as guides as to what is best in particular cases. In a game of baseball if a batter were to ask "Can I have four strikes?" it would be assumed that he was asking what the rule was; and if, when told what the rule was, he were to say that he meant that on this occasion he thought it would be best on the whole for him to have four strikes rather than three, this would be most kindly taken as a joke. One might contend that baseball would be a better game if four strikes were allowed instead of three; but one cannot picture the rules as guides to what is best on the whole in particular cases, and question their applicability to particular cases as particular cases.

3 and 4. To complete the four points of comparison with the summary conception, it is clear from what has been said that

---

instances of actions falling under a practice then we should be strongly inclined to say that there wasn't the practice either. Blue-prints for a practice do not make a practice. That there is a practice entails that there are instances of people having been engaged and now being engaged in it (with suitable qualifications). This is correct, but it doesn't hurt the claim that any given particular instance of a form of action specified by a practice presupposes the practice. This isn't so on the summary picture, as each instance must be "there" prior to the rules, so to speak, as something from which one gets the rule by applying the utilitarian principle to it directly.

TWO CONCEPTS OF RULES

rules of practices are not guides to help one decide particular cases correctly as judged by some higher ethical principle. And neither the quasi-statistical notion of generality, nor the notion of a particular exception, can apply to the rules of practices. A more or less general rule of a practice must be a rule which according to the structure of the practice applies to more or fewer of the kinds of cases arising under it; or it must be a rule which is more or less basic to the understanding of the practice. Again, a particular case cannot be an exception to a rule of a practice. An exception is rather a qualification or a further specification of the rule.

If follows from what we have said about the practice conception of rules that if a person is engaged in a practice, and if he is asked why *he* does what *he* does, or if he is asked to defend what he does, then his explanation, or defense, lies in referring the questioner to the practice. He cannot say of *his* action, if it is an action specified by a practice, that he does it rather than some other because he thinks it is best on the whole.[24] When a man engaged in a practice is queried about his action he must assume that the questioner either doesn't know that he is engaged in it ("Why are you in a hurry to pay him?" "I promised to pay him today") or doesn't know what the practice is. One doesn't so much justify one's particular action as explain, or show, that it is in accordance with the practice. The reason for this is that it is only against the stage-setting of the practice that one's particular action is described as it is. Only by reference to the practice can one *say* what one is doing. To explain or to defend one's own action, as a particular action, one fits it into the practice which defines it. If this is not accepted it's a sign that a different question is being raised as to whether one is justified in accepting the practice, or in tolerating it. When the challenge is to the practice, citing the rules (saying what the practice is) is naturally to no avail. But when the challenge is to the particular action defined by the practice, there is nothing one can do but refer to the rules. Concerning particular actions

[24] A philosophical joke (in the mouth of Jeremy Bentham): "When I run to the other wicket after my partner has struck a good ball I do so because it is best on the whole."

THE PHILOSOPHICAL REVIEW

there is only a question for one who isn't clear as to what the practice is, or who doesn't know that it is being engaged in. This is to be contrasted with the case of a maxim which may be taken as pointing to the correct decision on the case as decided on *other* grounds, and so giving a challenge on the case a sense by having it question whether these other grounds really support the decision on this case.

If one compares the two conceptions of rules I have discussed, one can see how the summary conception misses the significance of the distinction between justifying a practice and justifying actions falling under it. On this view rules are regarded as guides whose purpose it is to indicate the ideally rational decision on the given particular case which the flawless application of the utilitarian principle would yield. One has, in principle, full option to use the guides or to discard them as the situation warrants without one's moral office being altered in any way: whether one discards the rules or not, one always holds the office of a rational person seeking case by case to realize the best on the whole. But on the practice conception, if one holds an office defined by a practice then questions regarding one's actions in this office are settled by reference to the rules which define the practice. If one seeks to question these rules, then one's office undergoes a fundamental change: one then assumes the office of one empowered to change and criticize the rules, or the office of a reformer, and so on. The summary conception does away with the distinction of offices and the various forms of argument appropriate to each. On that conception there is one office and so no offices at all. It therefore obscures the fact that the utilitarian principle must, in the case of actions and offices defined by a practice, apply to the practice, so that general utilitarian arguments are not available to those who act in offices so defined.[25]

---

[25] How do these remarks apply to the case of the promise known only to father and son? Well, at first sight the son certainly holds the office of promisor, and so he isn't allowed by the practice to weigh the particular case on general utilitarian grounds. Suppose instead that he wishes to consider himself in the office of one empowered to criticize and change the practice, leaving aside the question as to his right to move from his previously assumed office to another. Then he may consider utilitarian arguments as applied to the practice; but

TWO CONCEPTS OF RULES

Some qualifications are necessary in what I have said. First, I may have talked of the summary and the practice conceptions of rules as if only one of them could be true of rules, and if true of any rules, then necessarily true of *all* rules. I do not, of course, mean this. (It is the critics of utilitarianism who make this mistake insofar as their arguments against utilitarianism presuppose a summary conception of the rules of practices.) Some rules will fit one conception, some rules the other; and so there are rules of practices (rules in the strict sense), and maxims and "rules of thumb."

Secondly, there are further distinctions that can be made in classifying rules, distinctions which should be made if one were considering other questions. The distinctions which I have drawn are those most relevant for the rather special matter I have discussed, and are not intended to be exhaustive.

Finally, there will be many border-line cases about which it will be difficult, if not impossible, to decide which conception of rules is applicable. One expects border-line cases with any concept, and they are especially likely in connection with such involved concepts as those of a practice, institution, game, rule, and so on. Wittgenstein has shown how fluid these notions are.[26] What I have done is to emphasize and sharpen two conceptions for the limited purpose of this paper.

IV

What I have tried to show by distinguishing between two conceptions of rules is that there is a way of regarding rules which allows the option to consider particular cases on general utilitarian grounds; whereas there is another conception which does not admit of such discretion except insofar as the rules themselves authorize it. I want to suggest that the tendency while doing philosophy to picture rules in accordance with the sum-

---

once he does this he will see that there are such arguments for not allowing a general utilitarian defense in the practice for this sort of case. For to do so would make it impossible to ask for and to give a kind of promise which one often wants to be able to ask for and to give. Therefore he will not want to change the practice, and so as a promisor he has no option but to keep his promise.

[26] *Philosophical Investigations* (Oxford, 1953), I, pars. 65-71, for example.

mary conception is what may have blinded moral philosophers
to the significance of the distinction between justifying a practice
and justifying a particular action falling under it; and it does so
by misrepresenting the logical force of the reference to the rules
in the case of a challenge to a particular action falling under a
practice, and by obscuring the fact that where there is a practice,
it is the practice itself that must be the subject of the utilitarian
principle.

It is surely no accident that two of the traditional test cases of
utilitarianism, punishment and promises, are clear cases of practices. Under the influence of the summary conception it is natural to suppose that the officials of a penal system, and one who
has made a promise, may decide what to do in particular cases
on utilitarian grounds. One fails to see that a general discretion
to decide particular cases on utilitarian grounds is incompatible
with the concept of a practice; and that what discretion one does
have is itself defined by the practice (e.g., a judge may have
discretion to determine the penalty within certain limits). The
traditional objections to utilitarianism which I have discussed
presuppose the attribution to judges, and to those who have
made promises, of a plenitude of moral authority to decide particular cases on utilitarian grounds. But once one fits utilitarianism together with the notion of a practice, and notes that punishment and promising are practices, then one sees that this attribution is logically precluded.

That punishment and promising are practices is beyond question. In the case of promising this is shown by the fact that the
form of words "I promise" is a performative utterance which
presupposes the stage-setting of the practice and the proprieties
defined by it. Saying the words "I promise" will only be promising given the existence of the practice. It would be absurd to
interpret the rules about promising in accordance with the summary conception. It is absurd to say, for example, that the rule
that promises should be kept could have arisen from its being
found in past cases to be best on the whole to keep one's promise;
for unless there were already the understanding that one keeps
one's promises as part of the practice itself there couldn't have
been any cases of promising.

It must, of course, be granted that the rules defining promising

30

are not codified, and that one's conception of what they are necessarily depends on one's moral training. Therefore it is likely that there is considerable variation in the way people understand the practice, and room for argument as to how it is best set up. For example, differences as to how strictly various defenses are to be taken, or just what defenses are available, are likely to arise amongst persons with different backgrounds. But irrespective of these variations it belongs to the concept of the practice of promising that the general utilitarian defense is not available to the promisor. That this is so accounts for the force of the traditional objection which I have discussed. And the point I wish to make is that when one fits the utilitarian view together with the practice conception of rules, as one must in the appropriate cases, then there is nothing in that view which entails that there must be such a defense, either in the practice of promising, or in any other practice.

Punishment is also a clear case. There are many actions in the sequence of events which constitute someone's being punished which presuppose a practice. One can see this by considering the definition of punishment which I gave when discussing Carritt's criticism of utilitarianism. The definition there stated refers to such things as the normal rights of a citizen, rules of law, due process of law, trials and courts of law, statutes, etc., none of which can exist outside the elaborate stage-setting of a legal system. It is also the case that many of the actions for which people are punished presuppose practices. For example, one is punished for stealing, for trespassing, and the like, which presuppose the institution of property. It is impossible to say what punishment is, or to describe a particular instance of it, without referring to offices, actions, and offenses specified by practices. Punishment is a move in an elaborate legal game and presupposes the complex of practices which make up the legal order. The same thing is true of the less formal sorts of punishment: a parent or guardian or someone in proper authority may punish a child, but no one else can.

There is one mistaken interpretation of what I have been saying which it is worthwhile to warn against. One might think that the use I am making of the distinction between justifying a practice and justifying the particular actions falling under it in-

THE PHILOSOPHICAL REVIEW

volves one in a definite social and political attitude in that it
leads to a kind of conservatism. It might seem that I am saying
that for each person the social practices of his society provide the
standard of justification for his actions; therefore let each person
abide by them and his conduct will be justified.

This interpretation is entirely wrong. The point I have been
making is rather a logical point. To be sure, it has consequences
in matters of ethical theory; but in itself it leads to no particular
social or political attitude. It is simply that where a form of action
is specified by a practice there is no justification possible of the
particular action of a particular person save by reference to the
practice. In such cases the action is what it is in virtue of the
practice and to explain it is to refer to the practice. There is no
inference whatsoever to be drawn with respect to whether or not
one should accept the practices of one's society. One can be as
radical as one likes but in the case of actions specified by practices the objects of one's radicalism must be the social practices
and people's acceptance of them.

I have tried to show that when we fit the utilitarian view together with the practice conception of rules, where this conception is appropriate,[27] we can formulate it in a way which saves
it from several traditional objections. I have further tried to
show how the logical force of the distinction between justifying
a practice and justifying an action falling under it is connected
with the practice conception of rules and cannot be understood
as long as one regards the rules of practices in accordance with
the summary view. Why, when doing philosophy, one may be
inclined to so regard them, I have not discussed. The reasons for
this are evidently very deep and would require another paper.

Cornell University   JOHN RAWLS

---

[27] As I have already stated, it is not always easy to say where the conception
is appropriate. Nor do I care to discuss at this point the general sorts of cases
to which it does apply except to say that one should not take it for granted that
it applies to many so-called "moral rules." It is my feeling that relatively few
actions of the moral life are defined by practices and that the practice conception is more relevant to understanding legal and legal-like arguments than
it is to the more complex sort of moral arguments. Utilitarianism must be
fitted to different conceptions of rules depending on the case, and no doubt the
failure to do this has been one source of difficulty in interpreting it correctly.

[9]

EXTREME AND RESTRICTED UTILITARIANISM[1]

J. J. C. SMART

I

UTILITARIANISM is the doctrine that the rightness of actions is to be judged by their consequences. What do we mean by 'actions' here? Do we mean particular actions or do we mean classes of actions? According to which way we interpret the word 'actions' we get two different theories, both of which merit the appellation 'utilitarian'.

(1) If by 'actions' we mean particular individual actions we get the sort of doctrine held by Bentham, Sidgwick, and Moore. According to this doctrine we test individual actions by their consequences, and general rules, like 'keep promises', are mere rules of thumb which we use only to avoid the necessity of estimating the probable consequences of our actions at every step. The rightness or wrongness of keeping a promise on a particular occasion depends only on the goodness or badness of the consequences of keeping or of breaking the promise on that particular occasion. Of course part of the consequences of breaking the promise, and a part to which we will normally ascribe decisive importance, will be the weakening of faith in the institution of promising. However, if the goodness of the consequences of breaking the rule is *in toto* greater than the goodness of the consequences of keeping it, then we must break the rule, irrespective of whether the goodness of the consequences of *everybody's* obeying the rule is or is not greater than the consequences of *everybody's* breaking it. To put it shortly, rules do not matter, save *per accidens* as rules of thumb and as *de facto* social institutions with which the utilitarian has to reckon when estimating consequences. I shall call this doctrine 'extreme utilitarianism'.

(2) A more modest form of utilitarianism has recently become

From *Philosophical Quarterly*, Vol. 6 (1956), pp. 344–54. Reprinted, with emendation, by permission of the author and the *Philosophical Quarterly*.

[1] Based on a paper read to the Victorian Branch of the Australasian Association of Psychology and Philosophy, October 1955. [The article is discussed in H. J. McCloskey, 'An Examination of Restricted Utilitarianism' *Philosophical Review* (1957); also by D. Lyons, *Forms and Limits of Utilitarianism* (Clarendon Press, Oxford, 1965). Ed.]

172   J. J. C. SMART

fashionable. The doctrine is to be found in Toulmin's book *The Place of Reason in Ethics*, in Nowell-Smith's *Ethics* (though I think Nowell-Smith has qualms), in John Austin's *Lectures on Jurisprudence* (Lecture II), and even in J. S. Mill, if Urmson's interpretation of him is correct (*Philosophical Quarterly*, Vol. 3, pp. 33–39, 1953). Part of its charm is that it appears to resolve the dispute in moral philosophy between intuitionists and utilitarians in a way which is very neat. The above philosophers hold, or seem to hold, that moral rules are more than rules of thumb. In general the rightness of an action is *not* to be tested by evaluating its consequences but only by considering whether or not it falls under a certain rule. Whether the rule is to be considered an acceptable moral rule, is, however, to be decided by considering the consequences of adopting the rule. Broadly, then, actions are to be tested by rules and rules by consequences. The only cases in which we must test an individual action directly by its consequences are (a) when the action comes under two different rules, one of which enjoins it and one of which forbids it, and (b) when there is no rule whatever that governs the given case. I shall call this doctrine 'restricted utilitarianism'.

It should be noticed that the distinction I am making cuts across, and is quite different from, the distinction commonly made between hedonistic and ideal utilitarianism. Bentham was an extreme hedonistic utilitarian and Moore an extreme ideal utilitarian, and Toulmin (perhaps) could be classified as a restricted ideal utilitarian. A hedonistic utilitarian holds that the goodness of the consequences of an action is a function only of their pleasurableness and an ideal utilitarian, like Moore, holds that pleasurableness is not even a necessary condition of goodness. Mill seems, if we are to take his remarks about higher and lower pleasures seriously, to be neither a pure hedonistic nor a pure ideal utilitarian. He seems to hold that pleasurableness is a necessary condition for goodness, but that goodness is a function of other qualities of mind as well. Perhaps we can call him a quasi-ideal utilitarian. When we say that a state of mind is good I take it that we are expressing some sort of *rational preference*. When we say that it is pleasurable I take it that we are saying that it is enjoyable, and when we say that something is a higher pleasure I take it that we are saying that it is more truly, or more deeply, enjoyable. I am doubtful whether 'more deeply enjoyable' does not just mean 'more enjoyable, even though not more enjoyable on a first look', and so I am doubtful whether quasi-ideal utilitarianism, and possibly ideal utilitarianism too, would not collapse into hedonistic utilitarianism

EXTREME AND RESTRICTED UTILITARIANISM   173

on a closer scrutiny of the logic of words like 'preference', 'pleasure', 'enjoy', 'deeply enjoy', and so on. However, it is beside the point of the present paper to go into these questions. I am here concerned only with the issue between extreme and restricted utilitarianism and am ready to concede that both forms of utilitarianism can be either hedonistic or non-hedonistic.

The issue between extreme and restricted utilitarianism can be illustrated by considering the remark 'But suppose everyone did the same'. (Cf. A. K. Stout's article in *The Australasian Journal of Philosophy*, Vol. 32, pp. 1–29) Stout distinguishes two forms of the universalization principle, the causal forms and the hypothetical form. To say that you ought not to do an action A because it would have bad results if everyone (or many people) did action A may be merely to point out that while the action A would otherwise be the optimific one, nevertheless when you take into account that doing A will probably cause other people to do A too, you can see that A is not, on a broad view, really optimific. If this causal influence could be avoided (as may happen in the case of a secret desert island promise) then we would disregard the universalization principle. This is the causal form of the principle. A person who accepted the universalization principle in its hypothetical form would be one who was concerned only with what would happen *if* everyone did the action A: he would be totally unconcerned with the question of whether in fact everyone would do the action A. That is, he might say that it would be wrong not to vote because it would have bad results if everyone took this attitude, and he would be totally unmoved by arguments purporting to show that my refusing to vote has no effect whatever on other people's propensity to vote. Making use of Stout's distinction, we can say that an extreme utilitarian would apply the universalization principle in the causal form, while a restricted utilitarian would apply it in the hypothetical form.

How are we to decide the issue between extreme and restricted utilitarianism? I wish to repudiate at the outset that milk and water approach which describes itself sometimes as 'investigating what is implicit in the common moral consciousness' and sometimes as 'investigating how people ordinarily talk about morality'. We have only to read the newspaper correspondence about capital punishment or about what should be done with Formosa to realize that the common moral consciousness is in part made up of superstitious elements, of morally bad elements, and of logically confused elements. I address myself to good hearted and benevolent people and so I hope that if we rid ourselves of the logical confusion the superstitious and morally bad elements will largely fall away. For even among good hearted and benevolent people it is possible to find superstitious and morally bad reasons for moral beliefs. These superstitious and morally bad reasons hide behind the protective screen of logical confusion. With people who are not logically confused but who are openly superstitious or morally bad I can of course do nothing. That is, our ultimate pro-attitudes may be different. Nevertheless I propose to rely on *my own* moral consciousness and to appeal to *your* moral consciousness and to forget about what people ordinarily say. 'The obligation to obey a rule', says Nowell-Smith (*Ethics*, p. 239), 'does not, *in the opinion of ordinary men*', (my italics), 'rest on the beneficial consequences of obeying it in a particular case'. What does this prove? Surely it is more than likely that ordinary men are confused here. Philosophers should be able to examine the question more rationally.

II

For an extreme utilitarian moral rules are rules of thumb. In practice the extreme utilitarian will mostly guide his conduct by appealing to the rules ('do not lie', 'do not break promises', etc.) of common sense morality. This is not because there is anything sacrosanct in the rules themselves but because he can argue that probably he will most often act in an extreme utilitarian way if he does not think as a utilitarian. For one thing, actions have frequently to be done in a hurry. Imagine a man seeing a person drowning. He jumps in and rescues him. There is no time to reason the matter out, but usually this will be the course of action which an extreme utilitarian would recommend if he did reason the matter out. If, however, the man drowning had been drowning in a river near Berchtesgaden in 1938, and if he had had the well known black forelock and moustache of Adolf Hitler, an extreme utilitarian would, if he had time, work out the probability of the man's being the villainous dictator, and if the probability were high enough he would, on extreme utilitarian grounds, leave him to drown. The rescuer, however, has not time. He trusts to his instincts and dives in and rescues the man. And this trusting to instincts and to moral rules can be justified on extreme utilitarian grounds. Furthermore, an extreme utilitarian who knew that the drowning man was Hitler would nevertheless praise the rescuer, not condemn him. For by praising the man he is strengthening a courageous and benevolent disposition of mind, and in general this disposition has great positive utility. (Next time, perhaps, it will be

EXTREME AND RESTRICTED UTILITARIANISM 175

Winston Churchill that the man saves!) We must never forget that an extreme utilitarian may praise actions which he knows to be wrong. Saving Hitler was wrong, but it was a member of a class of actions which are generally right, and the motive to do actions of this class is in general an optimific one. In considering questions of praise and blame it is not the expediency of the praised or blamed action that is at issue, but the expediency of the praise. It can be expedient to praise an inexpedient action and inexpedient to praise an expedient one.

Lack of time is not the only reason why an extreme utilitarian may, on extreme utilitarian principles, trust to rules of common sense morality. He knows that in particular cases where his own interests are involved his calculations are likely to be biased in his own favour. Suppose that he is unhappily married and is deciding whether to get divorced. He will in all probability greatly exaggerate his own unhappiness (and possibly his wife's) and greatly underestimate the harm done to his children by the break up of the family. He will probably also underestimate the likely harm done by the weakening of the general faith in marriage vows. So probably he will come to the correct extreme utilitarian conclusion if he does not in this instance think as an extreme utilitarian but trusts to common sense morality.

There are many more and subtle points that could be made in connexion with the relation between extreme utilitarianism and the morality of common sense. All those that I have just made and many more will be found in Book IV Chapters 3–5 of Sidgwick's *Methods of Ethics*. I think that this book is the best book ever written on ethics, and that these chapters are the best chapters of the book. As they occur so near the end of a very long book they are unduly neglected. I refer the reader, then, to Sidgwick for the classical exposition of the relation between (extreme) utilitarianism and the morality of common sense. One further point raised by Sidgwick in this connexion is whether an (extreme) utilitarian ought on (extreme) utilitarian principles to propagate (extreme) utilitarianism among the public. As most people are not very philosophical and not good at empirical calculations, it is probable that they will most often act in an extreme utilitarian way if they do not try to think as extreme utilitarians. We have seen how easy it would be to misapply the extreme utilitarian criterion in the case of divorce. Sidgwick seems to think it quite probable that an extreme utilitarian should not propagate his doctrine too widely. However, the great danger to humanity comes nowadays on the plane of public morality—not private morality. There is a greater danger to humanity from the hydrogen

176   J. J. C. SMART

bomb than from an increase of the divorce rate, regrettable though
that might be, and there seems no doubt that extreme utilitarianism
makes for good sense in international relations. When France walked
out of the United Nations because she did not wish Morocco discussed,
she said that she was within her rights because Morocco and Algiers
are part of her metropolitan territory and nothing to do with U.N.
This was clearly a legalistic if not superstitious argument. We should
not be concerned with the so-called 'rights' of France or any other
country but with whether the cause of humanity would best be served
by discussing Morocco in U.N. (I am not saying that the answer to
this is 'Yes'. There are good grounds for supposing that more harm
than good would come by such a discussion.) I myself have no hesi-
tation in saying that on extreme utilitarian principles we ought to
propagate extreme utilitarianism as widely as possible. But Sidgwick
had respectable reasons for suspecting the opposite.

   The extreme utilitarian, then, regards moral rules as rules of
thumb and as sociological facts that have to be taken into account
when deciding what to do, just as facts of any other sort have to be
taken into account. But in themselves they do not justify any action.

                              III

   The restricted utilitarian regards moral rules as more than rules of
thumb for short-circuiting calculations of consequences. Generally,
he argues, consequences are not relevant at all when we are deciding
what to do in a particular case. In general, they are relevant only to
deciding what rules are good reasons for acting in a certain way in
particular cases. This doctrine is possibly a good account of how the
modern unreflective twentieth century Englishman often thinks about
morality, but surely it is monstrous as an account of how it is most
rational to think about morality. Suppose that there is a rule R and
that in 99% of cases the best possible results are obtained by acting in
accordance with R. Then clearly R is a useful rule of thumb; if we have
not time or are not impartial enough to assess the consequences of an
action it is an extremely good bet that the thing to do is to act in
accordance with R. But is it not monstrous to suppose that if we *have*
worked out the consequences and if we have perfect faith in the impartiality of our calculations, and if we *know* that in this instance to
break R will have better results than to keep it, we should nevertheless
obey the rule? Is it not to erect R into a sort of idol if we keep it when
breaking it will prevent, say, some avoidable misery? Is not this a form

of superstitious rule-worship (easily explicable psychologically) and not the rational thought of a philosopher?

The point may be made more clearly if we consider Mill's comparison of moral rules to the tables in the nautical almanack. (*Utilitarianism*, Everyman Edition, pp. 22–23). This comparison of Mill's is adduced by Urmson as evidence that Mill was a restricted utilitarian, but I do not think that it will bear this interpretation at all. (Though I quite agree with Urmson that many other things said by Mill are in harmony with restricted rather than extreme utilitarianism. Probably Mill had never thought very much about the distinction and was arguing for utilitarianism, restricted or extreme, against other and quite non-utilitarian forms of moral argument.) Mill says: 'Nobody argues that the art of navigation is not founded on astronomy, because sailors cannot wait to calculate the Nautical Almanack. Being rational creatures, they go to sea with it ready calculated: and all rational creatures go out upon the sea of life with their minds made up on the common questions of right and wrong, as well as on many of the far more difficult questions of wise and foolish . . . . Whatever we adopt as the fundamental principle of morality, we require subordinate principles to apply it by'. Notice that this is, as it stands, only an argument for subordinate principles as rules of thumb. The example of the nautical almanack is misleading because the information given in the almanack is in all cases the same as the information one would get if one made a long and laborious calculation from the original astronomical data on which the almanack is founded. Suppose, however, that astronomy were different. Suppose that the behaviour of the sun, moon and planets was very nearly as it is now, but that on rare occasions there were peculiar irregularities and discontinuities, so that the almanack gave us rules of the form 'in 99% of cases where the observations are such and such you can deduce that your position is so and so'. Furthermore, let us suppose that there were methods which enabled us, by direct and laborious calculation from the original astronomical data, not using the rough and ready tables of the almanack, to get our correct position in 100% of cases. Seafarers might use the almanack because they never had time for the long calculations and they were content with a 99% chance of success in calculating their positions. Would it not be absurd, however, if they *did* make the direct calculation, and finding that it disagreed with the almanack calculation, nevertheless they ignored it and stuck to the almanack conclusion? Of course the case would be altered if there were a high enough probability of making slips in the direct calculation: then we might stick to the almanack result, liable to error though we knew it to be, simply because the direct calculation would be open to error for a different reason, the fallibility of the computer. This would be analogous to the case of the extreme utilitarian who abides by the conventional rule against the dictates of his utilitarian calculations simply because he thinks that his calculations are probably affected by personal bias. But if the navigator were sure of his direct calculations would he not be foolish to abide by his almanack? I conclude, then, that if we change our suppositions about astronomy and the almanack (to which there are no exceptions) to bring the case into line with that of morality (to whose rules there are exceptions), Mill's example loses its appearance of supporting the restricted form of utilitarianism. Let me say once more that I am not here concerned with how ordinary men think about morality but with how they ought to think. We could quite well imagine a race of sailors who acquired a superstitious reverence for their almanack, even though it was only right in 99% of cases, and who indignantly threw overboard any man who mentioned the possibility of a direct calculation. But would this behaviour of the sailors be rational?

Let us consider a much discussed sort of case in which the extreme utilitarian might go against the conventional moral rule. I have promised to a friend, dying on a desert island from which I am subsequently rescued, that I will see that his fortune (over which I have control) is given to a jockey club. However, when I am rescued I decide that it would be better to give the money to a hospital, which can do more good with it. It may be argued that I am wrong to give the money to the hospital. But why? (*a*) The hospital can do more good with the money than the jockey club can. (*b*) The present case is unlike most cases of promising in that no one except me knows about the promise. In breaking the promise I am doing so with complete secrecy and am doing nothing to weaken the general faith in promises. That is, a factor, which would normally keep the extreme utilitarian from promise breaking even in otherwise unoptimific cases, does not at present operate. (*c*) There is no doubt a slight weakening in my own character as an habitual promise keeper, and moreover psychological tensions will be set up in me every time I am asked what the man made me promise him to do. For clearly I shall have to say that he made me promise to give the money to the hospital, and, since I am an habitual truth teller, this will go very much against the grain with me. Indeed I am pretty sure that in practice I myself would keep the promise. But we are not discussing what my moral habits would probably make me do; we are discussing what I ought to do. Moreover, we must not forget that even if it would be most rational of me to give the money to the hospital it would also be most rational of you to punish or condemn me if you did, most improbably, find out the truth (e.g. by finding a note washed ashore in a bottle). Furthermore, I would agree that though it was most rational of me to give the money to the hospital it would be most rational of you to condemn me for it. We revert again to Sidgwick's distinction between the utility of the action and the utility of the praise of it.

Many such issues are discussed by A. K. Stout in the article to which I have already referred. I do not wish to go over the same ground again, especially as I think that Stout's arguments support my own point of view. It will be useful, however, to consider one other example that he gives. Suppose that during hot weather there is an edict that no water must be used for watering gardens. I have a garden and I reason that most people are sure to obey the edict, and that as the amount of water that I use will be by itself negligible no harm will be done if I use the water secretly. So I do use the water, thus producing some lovely flowers which give happiness to various people. Still, you may say, though the action was perhaps optimific, it was unfair and wrong.

There are several matters to consider. Certainly my action should be condemned. We revert once more to Sidgwick's distinction. A right action may be rationally condemned. Furthermore, this sort of offence is normally found out. If I have a wonderful garden when everybody else's is dry and brown there is only one explanation. So if I water my garden I am weakening my respect for law and order, and as this leads to bad results an extreme utilitarian would agree that I was wrong to water the garden. Suppose now that the case is altered and that I can keep the thing secret: there is a secluded part of the garden where I grow flowers which I give away anonymously to a home for old ladies. Are you still so sure that I did the wrong thing by watering my garden? However, this is still a weaker case than that of the hospital and the jockey club. There will be tensions set up within myself: my secret knowledge that I have broken the rule will make it hard for me to exhort others to keep the rule. These psychological ill effects in myself may be not inconsiderable: directly and indirectly they may lead to harm which is at least of the same order as the happiness that the old ladies get from the flowers. You can see that on an extreme utilitarian view there are two sides to the question.

So far I have been considering the duty of an extreme utilitarian in a predominantly non-utilitarian society. The case is altered if we consider the extreme utilitarian who lives in a society every member, or most members, of which can be expected to reason as he does. Should he water his flowers now? (Granting, what is doubtful, that in the case already considered he would have been right to water his flowers.) As a first approximation, the answer is that he should not do so. For since the situation is a completely symmetrical one, what is rational for him is rational for others. Hence, by a *reductio ad absurdum* argument, it would seem that watering his garden would be rational for none. Nevertheless, a more refined analysis shows that the above argument is not quite correct, though it is correct enough for practical purposes. The argument considers each person as confronted with the choice either of watering his garden or of not watering it. However there is a third possibility, which is that each person should, with the aid of a suitable randomizing device, such as throwing dice, give himself a certain probability of watering his garden. This would be to adopt what in the theory of games is called 'a mixed strategy'. If we could give numerical values to the private benefit of garden watering and to the public harm done by 1, 2, 3, etc., persons using the water in this way, we could work out a value of the probability of watering his garden that each extreme utilitarian should give himself. Let a be the value which each extreme utilitarian gets from watering his garden, and let $f(1)$, $f(2)$, $f(3)$, etc., be the public harm done by exactly 1, 2, 3, etc., persons respectively watering their gardens. Suppose that p is the probability that each person gives himself of watering his garden. Then we can easily calculate, as functions of p, the probabilities that exactly 1, 2, 3, etc., persons will water their gardens. Let these probabilities be $p_1, p_2, \ldots p_n$. Then the total net probable benefit can be expressed as

$$V = p_1 (a - f(1)) + p_2 (2a - f(2)) + \ldots p_n (na - f(n))$$

Then if we know the function $f(x)$ we can calculate the value of p for which $(dV/dp) = 0$. This gives the value of p which it would be rational for each extreme utilitarian to adopt. The present argument does not of course depend on a perhaps unjustified assumption that the values in question are measurable, and in a practical case such as that of the garden watering we can doubtless assume that p will be so small that we can take it near enough as equal to zero. However the argument is of interest for the theoretical underpinning of extreme utilitarianism, since the possibility of a mixed strategy is usually neglected by critics of utilitarianism, who wrongly assume that the only relevant and

EXTREME AND RESTRICTED UTILITARIANISM 181

symmetrical alternatives are of the form 'everybody does X' and 'nobody does X'.[1]

I now pass on to a type of case which may be thought to be the trump card of restricted utilitarianism. Consider the rule of the road. It may be said that since all that matters is that everyone should do the same it is indifferent which rule we have, 'go on the left hand side' or 'go on the right hand side'. Hence the only *reason* for going on the left hand side in British countries is that this is the rule. Here the rule does seem to be a reason, in itself, for acting in a certain way. I wish to argue against this. The rule in itself is not a reason for our actions. We would be perfectly justified in going on the right hand side if (*a*) we knew that the rule was to go on the left hand side, and (*b*) we were in a country peopled by super-anarchists who always on principle did the opposite of what they were told. This shows that the rule does not give us a reason for acting so much as an indication of the probable actions of others, which helps us to find out what would be our own most rational course of action. If we are in a country not peopled by anarchists, but by non-anarchist extreme Utilitarians, we expect, other things being equal, that they will keep rules laid down for them. Knowledge of the rule enables us to predict their behaviour and to harmonize our own actions with theirs. The rule 'keep to the left hand side', then. is not a logical *reason* for action but an anthropological *datum* for planning actions.

I conclude that in every case if there is a rule R the keeping of which is in general optimific, but such that in a special sort of circumstances the optimific behaviour is to break R, then in these circumstances we should break R. Of course we must consider all the less obvious effects of breaking R, such as reducing people's faith in the moral order, before coming to the conclusion that to break R is right: in fact we shall rarely come to such a conclusion. Moral rules, on the extreme utilitarian view, are rules of thumb only, but they are not bad rules of thumb. But if we *do* come to the conclusion that we should break the rule and if we have weighed in the balance our own fallibility and liability to personal bias, what good reason remains for keeping the rule? I can understand 'it is optimific' as a reason for action, but why should 'it is a member of a class of actions which are usually optimific' or 'it is a member of a class of actions which as a class are more optimific than any alternative general class' be a good reason? You might as well say that a person ought to be picked to play

---

[1] [This paragraph has been substantially emended by the author. Ed.]

for Australia just because all his brothers have been, or that the
Australian team should be composed entirely of the Harvey family
because this would be better than composing it entirely of any other
family. The extreme utilitarian does not appeal to artificial feelings,
but only to our feelings of benevolence, and what better feelings can
there be to appeal to? Admittedly we can have a pro-attitude to anything, even to rules, but such artificially begotten pro-attitudes smack
of superstition. Let us get down to realities, human happiness and
misery, and make these the objects of our pro-attitudes and anti-
attitudes.

The restricted utilitarian might say that he is talking only of
morality, not of such things as rules of the road. I am not sure how
far this objection, if valid, would affect my argument, but in any
case I would reply that as a philosopher I conceive of ethics as the
study of how it would be *most rational* to act. If my opponent wishes
to restrict the word 'morality' to a narrower use he can have the word.
The fundamental question is the question of rationality of action
in general. Similarly if the restricted utilitarian were to appeal to
ordinary usage and say 'it might be most rational to leave Hitler to
drown but it would surely not be *wrong* to rescue him', I should again
let him have the words 'right' and 'wrong' and should stick to
'rational' and 'irrational'. We already saw that it would be rational
to praise Hitler's rescuer, even though it would have been most
rational not to have rescued Hitler. In ordinary language, no doubt,
'right' and 'wrong' have not only the meaning 'most rational to do'
and 'not most rational to do' but also have the meaning 'praiseworthy' and 'not praiseworthy'. Usually to the utility of an action
corresponds utility of praise of it, but as we saw, this is not always
so. Moral language could thus do with tidying up, for example by
reserving 'right' for 'most rational' and 'good' as an epithet of
praise for the motive from which the action sprang. It would be more
becoming in a philosopher to try to iron out illogicalities in moral
language and to make suggestions for its reform than to use it as a
court of appeal whereby to perpetuate confusions.

One last defence of restricted utilitarianism might be as follows.
'Act optimifically' might be regarded as itself one of the rules of our
system (though it would be odd to say that this rule was justified by
its optimificality). According to Toulmin (*The Place of Reason in Ethics*,
pp. 146–8) if 'keep promises', say, conflicts with another rule we are
allowed to argue the case on its merits, as if we were extreme utilitarians. If 'act optimifically' is itself one of our rules then there

will always be a conflict of rules whenever to keep a rule is not itself optimific. If this is so, restricted utilitarianism collapses into extreme utilitarianism. And no one could read Toulmin's book or Urmson's article on Mill without thinking that Toulmin and Urmson are of the opinion that they have thought of a doctrine which does *not* collapse into extreme utilitarianism, but which is, on the contrary, an improvement on it.

[10]

DISCUSSION

RULE-UTILITARIANISM: MERELY AN ILLUSORY ALTERNATIVE?

By Allan F. Gibbard

Nineteenth-century utilitarians like Mill, held that "actions are right in proportion as they tend to promote happiness, wrong as they tend to produce the reverse of happiness."[1] Two assumptions are involved here: first, that only happiness is desirable for its own sake, and second, that an action is right in proportion as it tends to promote what is desirable for its own sake. Neither of these two assumptions has had smooth going in later controversy. At the beginning of this century, G. E. Moore took strong exception to the belief that happiness alone is intrinsically good. He believed, for example, that enjoyment of what is evil or ugly is itself an evil, no matter how much happiness it causes.[2] It was still clear to him, however, that one ought to do what will result in the greatest possible intrinsic good. He thus accepted and made more explicit Mill's second implicit assumption. W. D. Ross in 1930 challenged even this belief that an action is right if it produces the most intrinsic good. He could not believe, for example, that it is always right to break a promise whenever one can thereby produce results which are intrinsically better.[3] In place of Moore's criterion for rightness, Ross proposed a list of seven "*prima facie* obligations", like the obligation of fidelity, some of which had nothing at all to do with producing intrinsically good results.[4]

Some of Ross's arguments may have real force. Suppose people who recognize the consequences of Moore's theory of right actions (which I shall refer to as *act utilitarianism*), and who examine their own convictions about moral questions like those posed by Ross, are unable to reconcile the two. What reason could they have to accept Moore's criterion over their own deep moral convictions? Attractive at first, Moore's act-utilitarianism may simply not be credible when we examine closely its consequences. Some philosophers who conceded that it was not credible, however, still could not believe that the connection between right means and desirable ends was as remote as Ross' seven principles would make it.

---

[1] J. S. Mill, *Utilitarianism*, ch. 2.
[2] G. E. Moore, *Principia Ethica*, p. 209.
[3] W. D. Ross, *The Right and the Good*, p. 34.
[4] Ibid., p. 21.

212   ALLAN F. GIBBARD

According to R. F. Harrod, the reason the act-utilitarian view yielded strange conclusions was, "There are certain acts which when performed on *n* similar occasions have consequences more than *n* times as great as those resulting from one performance. And it is in this class of cases that obligations arise."[5] For example, breaking a promise in one case might be beneficial, without affecting people's general confidence in promises. If people always broke promises when breaking them would produce more good than keeping them, however, then nobody could trust a promise. The whole social value of being able to make promises on which people can rely would be destroyed. "The test is always: Would this action, if done by all in similar relevant circumstances lead to the breakdown of some established method of society for securing its ends?"[6] With this test, Harrod accepts the view of earlier utilitarians that the goal of morality is to promote the good, but he seeks to avoid some of the disturbing consequences of their act-utilitarianism.

Harrod judges whether an action is right by considering the consequences of the whole class of like actions. Now Ross' complaint against act-utilitarianism is that it gives unreasonable answers to specific moral questions. For instance, act-utilitarianism tells us that if we have hired a boy to mow our lawn and he has done so, we should pay him only if we can find no better use for the money. If Harrod's view is to fare any better than act-utilitarianism against Ross' criticisms, it must give more reasonable answers to such specific moral questions.

R. B. Brandt argues, however, that under at least one possible interpretation, Harrod's theory would make exactly the same actions right and exactly the same actions wrong as does act-utilitarianism.[7] If a person asks a specific question, "What is the right action for me in this situation," then according to Brandt, either system will dictate the same answer if correctly applied. Now if Brandt interprets Harrod correctly, and if the system as he interprets it does have the same consequences as act-utilitarianism, then clearly Harrod's system cannot be an improvement over discredited act-utilitarianism, as it claims to be.

I shall not inquire whether Brandt's interpretation is correct, but simply state his interpretation and try to see whether it has the consequences he claims for it. To see the exact consequences of the Harrod theory, Brandt must of course state the theory as

---

[5] R. F. Harrod, "Utilitarianism Revised", *Mind*, vol. 45, p. 148.
[6] Ibid., p. 149.
[7] R. B. Brandt, "Toward a Credible Form of Utilitarianism", sec. 3, *Morality and the Language of Conduct*, ed. Castaneda and Nakhnikian.

clearly and unambiguously as possible. Harrod talks about "this action, if done by all in similar relevant circumstances", but it is hard to say when two actions are the same and when they are different. Brandt thinks things are clearer if instead of talking about what would happen if everyone in similar relevant circumstances performed "this action", we talk about what would happen if everyone conformed to a set of rules which prescribed "this action" in certain specified circumstances. "An act is right, if, and only if, it conforms with that set of general prescriptions for action such that, if everyone always did that thing among all those things he could do on a given occasion, which conformed with these prescriptions, at least as much intrinsic good would be produced as by conformity with any other set of general prescriptions." Thus, when we want to choose a right action in a specific situation, we must go through a two-stage process. In the first stage, we choose a set of prescriptions with ideal consequences if everyone obeys them all the time. The consequences are ideal if they are intrinsically at least as good as the consequences of everybody's obeying any other set of rules. Now the set of rules chosen will presumably tell what to do in all possible circumstances. Thus in the second stage, we see what the set of rules prescribes for the specific situation in question. Brandt labels this "a specious rule-utilitarianism"; for the sake of brevity, I shall call it simply *rule-utilitarianism.*

In contrast to rule-utilitarianism, Moore's sort of act-utilitarianism tells us at the outset what prescription to follow. "Do something, the consequences of which are at least as good intrinsically as those of any other act open to you." Of course, it should not be forgotten that how others have acted, are acting, or will act may very much affect what consequences an action will have.

Both utilitarianisms tell what is right in what Brandt calls an "objective" sense. Under either theory, an agent may have no way of knowing whether his action is right or wrong. If a person chooses the act which actually has the intrinsically best consequences, for example, it is right in the act-utilitarian sense even if he had no idea what the consequences would be. For this reason, whether an action is right in either sense may be more a matter of chance than of the agent's moral character.

The question at issue in this paper is whether rule-utilitarianism and act-utilitarianism do in fact have identically the same consequences for which actions are right and wrong. Brandt thinks he can show logically that the two utilitarianisms must be the

214   ALLAN F. GIBBARD

same in consequence. His logic does not depend at all on the nature or meaning of intrinsic good. The two criteria for rightness are formulated so that any concept at all of intrinsic good may be fitted into them. Brandt attempts to show that no matter what concept of intrinsic good one adopts, the two utilitarianisms logically must have the same consequences. We thus have a purely logical question, which can be settled without getting into any of the controversial areas of moral philosophy.

I believe I can show that Brandt's argument cannot be correct. I shall not do this by looking at his argument directly. Instead, I shall show examples of logically possible situations in which the two utilitarianisms turn out to have different consequences for action. If it is logically possible for the two systems to have different consequences for action, then it cannot also be logically necessary that they have the same consequences.

I can think of four possible senses in which rule-utilitarianism might reduce to act-utilitarianism. Let us call an action *RU-right* if it is right according to rule-utilitarianism as formulated above, and *AU-right* if it is right according to act-utilitarianism. Then Brandt might be claiming any or all of the following: (1). In any society, every AU-right action must also be RU-right. (2). In any society where all actions are AU-right, those actions are also RU-right. (3). In any society, every RU-right action must also be AU-right. (4). In any society where all actions are RU-right, those actions are also AU-right.

If for each of these four statements I can produce a logically possible situation where the statement does not hold, we will then have no logical reason for believing any of the statements.

The situations I sketch as counter-examples are a little far-fetched, but all that is required is that they be logically possible. Since life is complicated and the human mind is limited in its logical capacity, I will prefer simplicity to realism. Let us postulate a universe consisting of two people, Smith and Jones. To make their influence on each other as simple as possible, let them be placed in separate isolation booths, so that the actions of one can have no influence at all on the actions of the other. To make the action we are to judge as simple as possible, let a red push-button be installed in each isolation booth. The only action of moral significance open to either man will be to hold his push-button down at 10:00 a.m., or to refrain from doing so. With this sort of simple universe, we may hope to have definitive answers to questions of what is AU-right and what is RU-right, which would be impossible to answer in the near chaos of normal existence.

Let me then sketch a situation in this simplified universe where the first two senses of reduction will not hold. These senses are, it will be recalled, first, every AU-right action in any society is RU-right, and second, in a society where all actions are AU-right, all actions are RU-right. If we can imagine a situation where all actions are AU-right, but are not RU-right, then reduction of rule-utilitarianism to act-utilitarianism does not hold in either of these two senses. The situation will be as follows. Jones and Smith sit in their isolation booths with red push-buttons. If at 10:00 a.m. both are holding down their push-buttons, they receive cake and ice cream, which is intrinsically good. If only one of them is holding his push-button down, however, they both receive electric shocks, which is intrinsically bad. If neither of them is holding his button down, nothing happens.

Now suppose that at 10:00 a.m. Smith is not holding his button down. What AU-right action is open to Jones? To see which of the actions open to Jones is AU-right, we must examine the consequences of each action open to him, and judge which consequences are best. Now if Jones has his button depressed at 10:00 a.m., then since Smith is not holding his button down at that time, the results will be electric shocks. If Jones does not have his button depressed at 10:00 a.m., nothing happens, which is preferable to the electric shocks. In short, in this case where Smith does not have his button depressed, the result if Jones does not hold his button down is intrinsically better than the result if he does. Thus if Smith does not hold his button down, it is AU-right for Jones not to do so either.

Similarly, suppose that at 10:00 a.m. Jones is not holding his button down. Then if Smith does not hold his button down, nothing happens. The result is thus intrinsically better if he does not have his button depressed. Thus if Jones does not hold his button down, it is AU-right for Smith not to hold his button down.

We have established, first, that if Smith does not hold his button down, it is AU-right for Jones not to, and second, if Jones does not hold his button down, it is AU-right for Smith not to. Suppose neither has his button depressed at 10:00. Then each is performing an AU-right action given what the other is doing. This means that if either of the first two senses of reduction holds, the actions of both men must be RU-right also. Is this the case?

Suppose their actions were both in conformity with a set of prescriptions, universal conformity with which would produce a maximum of intrinsic good. Conformity by both is universal conformity, so a maximum of intrinsic good would be attained. This

216   ALLAN F. GIBBARD

means cake and ice cream would be served, since universal conformity to a set of prescriptions which included "Have your push-
button depressed at 10:00 a.m." would result in cake and ice
cream. Now the actions of the two men may be in conformity with
any number of sets of prescriptions, but this conformity does not
result in cake and ice cream. They are not both in conformity
with a set of prescriptions, conformity to which by everyone has
optimal results. Therefore our supposition cannot be true, and
their actions cannot both be RU-right. We concluded earlier that
their actions are both AU-right. We thus see that everyone's
actions in a society may be AU-right, without being RU-right.

Without this simplified example, the lesson it carries might
seem too paradoxical to be true. It is possible in a society where
everyone by acting in concert could make things better, that if
only a few people change their ways, things will be worse. In that
case, people will be AU-right not to change their ways, unless they
have some means of getting others to do so also. Thus each
individual may be doing the best he can do, given what the others
are doing, but the society collectively may not be producing as
much good as it could. While act-utilitarianism will sanction
people's actions in this case, rule-utilitarianism will not. Rule-
utilitarianism will demand that each person do what would be
best if everyone else were to co-operate, no matter how much
harm it does in a world where everyone else is not co-operating.
Whether this makes rule-utilitarianism or act-utilitarianism preferable I leave to the reader to decide. What this dilemma does
seem to stress is the necessity of institutions and methods of social
co-operation, even in a society of moral men.

In at least one far-fetched example, then the first two possible
claims that rule-utilitarianism reduces to act-utilitarianism do not
hold true. If Brandt argues, then, that either of these two claims
logically must hold true, his argument cannot be valid. Might he
not still have demonstrated, however, that reduction occurs in the
other direction? Can he have shown that the third reduction claim
holds true, every RU-right action is necessarily AU-right?

Returning to the situation of the red push-buttons, we may
recall that if both Smith and Jones have their buttons depressed
at 10:00 a.m., they achieve the greatest attainable good, the serving
of cake and ice cream. This is all that is required to make it RU-
right for Smith to hold his button down. No matter what Jones
does, if Smith has his button depressed, he will be in conformity
with a set of prescriptions consisting of the single prescription,
"Hold your red push-button down at 10:00 a.m.". Conformity by

everyone to this set of prescriptions would result in at least as much good as universal conformity to any other set of general prescriptions. It is RU-right for Smith to have his button depressed regardless of what Jones does.

Suppose Jones does not have his button depressed at 10:00 a.m. and Smith does. Smith's action, we have just seen, is RU-right. If, as Brandt may have argued, any action which is RU-right must necessarily be AU-right, then Smith's RU-right act of holding his button down must be AU-right. This, as we have seen before, is not the case. If Smith holds his button down, electric shocks result, while if he does not, nothing happens. The results are better if he does not hold his button down, and therefore holding his button down, even though RU-right, is not AU-right.

Now since we can imagine a situation in which an RU-right act would not be AU-right, there can be no valid logical argument showing that any RU-right act must necessarily be AU-right. Brandt cannot have proven reduction in this third sense, any more than he can have proven it in either of the first two senses. He cannot have demonstrated that every RU-right action must also be AU-right.

Now if Jones were doing the RU-right thing and holding his button down, then it would not be only RU-right for Smith to have his button depressed, but also AU-right. Smith's RU-right act is not AU-right only because Jones does not also do the RU-right thing. Rule-utilitarianism, then, allows people to keep following rules ideally suited for a morally perfect society, in a society which is not morally perfect. It seems to me that in any discussion of rule-utilitarianism it would be difficult to overemphasize this point: Rules suitable for a society where people always do the right thing may bring disaster if followed in a society where people sometimes do the wrong thing. If it would be immoral in an ideal society to steal a loaf of bread, then following a rule that anyone who steals a loaf of bread should be hanged will have no bad consequences in that ideal society, for the conditions for its application will never arise. In the ideal society, after all, no one would ever steal a loaf of bread. Suppose, then, we have a set of rules which, if followed, would result in an ideal society. We could add to this set of rules the rule that anyone who steals a loaf of bread unjustifiably shall be hanged, and let this new rule override anything to the contrary in the old set of rules. This new set of rules, if followed, would also produce an ideal society, for no one would ever steal a loaf of bread if the rules were followed, so no one would actually be hanged for stealing a loaf of bread.

218   ALLAN F. GIBBARD

In our ideal society, everyone who followed one set of rules would thereby be following the other set as well. Since, as we have seen, an ideal society would result if everyone obeyed the second set of rules, any action in conformity with the second set of rules is RU-right. But in any actual society where people do steal loaves of bread, it would be barbarous to follow a set of rules which called for hanging the unfortunate person.

We have seen, then, that when one person violates a set of rule-utilitarian prescriptions, another person who obeys the prescription may not be doing the AU-right thing. There remains the possibility that if everyone does the RU-right thing, then what they do will also be AU-right. Indeed this seems quite plausible, for if people are collectively producing the best attainable world, then each one separately must be producing the greatest amount of good open to him. What happens, however, when there are two incompatible ways in which the best attainable world could be attained?

Returning once again to Smith and Jones in their isolation booths, suppose that cake and ice cream will be served both, if both Smith and Jones have their buttons depressed at 10:00 a.m., and if neither one has his button depressed at that time. As in the previous example, if one of them has his button depressed and the other does not, electric shocks result.

Now in this example, there are a number of sets of prescriptions which satisfy the criterion for rule-utilitarian prescriptions, that universal conformity (i.e. by both of them) produces the greatest attainable good (cake and ice cream). One would consist of the prescription, "Have your red push-button depressed at 10:00 a.m.". If both follow this rule, they receive cake and ice cream. Conformity to this rule, then, is RU-right. It is therefore RU-right to have one's push-button depressed at 10:00 a.m. Another set of prescriptions, universal conformity to which would produce the most possible good, would consist of the prescription, "Do not have your red-push-button depressed at 10:00 a.m. If everyone follows this rule, cake and ice cream again results. Since this rule also satisfies the criterion for rule-utilitarian prescriptions, conformity to this rule is RU-right also. It is therefore also RU-right not to have one's push-button depressed at 10:00 a.m. In short, either course of action is RU-right.

If, then, at 10:00 a.m., Smith has his push-button depressed and Jones does not, they are both taking an RU-right course of action. Each of them is in conformity with a set of prescriptions, universal conformity with which would create the most possible good. They both receive electric shocks. Are their actions AU-right? The consequences of the action of one person, as Brandt points out, depend partly on what other people do. For this reason, whether a man's action has the best consequences, or in other words whether his action is AU-right, may depend on the actions of others. This is the case whether or not the man knows what action the others adopt. Now given that in our example Jones does not have his button depressed at 10:00 a.m., the consequences of Smith's holding his button down are electric shocks for them both. If Smith had refrained from holding his button down, the consequences would have been cake and ice cream. Clearly, given the context, Smith's action did not produce the best consequences in his power, and it was not AU-right for Smith to hold his button down. Both Smith and Jones take RU-right courses of action, but Smith's action (and for that matter, Jones' action) is not AU-right.

In short, when there are two ways to achieve the greatest good, but co-operation is needed to achieve it, rule-utilitarianism does not demand this co-operation. Different people may blindly conform to different sets of rules, each of which would work wonderfully if followed by everyone, and each will be RU-right. The results may be appalling. For example, it may not matter which side of the road people drive on, but it is important that they all drive on the same side. Conceivably then, everything any-one does in a society could be RU-right, without being AU-right in each case. There is no logical support for the fourth possible claim that rule-utilitarianism reduces to act-utilitarianism: That if everyone's actions are RU-right, they are also all AU-right.

In brief, it cannot be shown logically that rule-utilitarianism reduces to act-utilitarianism in any of the four senses of reduction which have occurred to me. If the reduction could be logically proven, then any counter-example to it would be logically self-contradictory. It is clear that the situations I have discussed, how-ever fantastic, are at least logically conceivable. Thus Brandt's argument, which tries to show that the reduction is logically neces-sary, cannot be valid.

We must not leap unthinkingly beyond this conclusion. We must remember, in the first place, that our conclusion concerns only Brandt's "spurious rule-utilitarianism." About the other sys-tems, Harrod's for example, which Brandt tried to discredit by showing rule-utilitarianism and act-utilitarianism equivalent, it says nothing. It has yet to be shown that any of these other theories is logically equivalent to rule-utilitarianism. Thus, while rule-utilitarianism definitely does not reduce to act-utilitarianism, no one should be shocked if Harrod's theory or one like it is shown to be equivalent to the act-utilitarian theory. We must realize in the second place that our conclusion does not prove rule-utilitarianism in any way preferable to act-utilitarianism. It does not, for example, mean that rule-utilitarianism gives any more weight to promise-keeping or obligations of gratitude than does act-utilitarianism. Instead, our discussion revealed that rule-utilitarianism can sanction a harmful response to a violation of the moral rules by someone else, such as hanging a person who wrongfully steals a loaf of bread. This being the case, rule-utilitarianism will have to be differently formulated if it is to merit serious consideration. Nevertheless, "spurious rule-utilitarianism" cannot be rejected simply on the grounds that it is logically equivalent to discredited act-utilitarianism.

University of Ghana.

[11]

DISCUSSIONS

"TWO CONCEPTS OF RULES"—A NOTE

By H. J. McCloskey

In his article, "Two Concepts of Rules",[1] John Rawls, by reference to the distinction between two types of rules, summary rules and rules defining a practice, claims to be able to set out a form of utilitarianism which will escape certain of the standard objections to utilitarianism. He illustrates his contention by reference to punishment and promise-keeping. This article has attracted a good deal of attention during the past 16 years, and is treated as essential reading for any serious student of utilitarianism. I wish here to argue that the argument of the article rests on a simple and evident fallacy.

Rawls' contention is that rules which define a practice, by contrast with summary rules which are generalizations about past decisions and past experience, are logically prior to the practice, and such that an act falling under the rule cannot be described without reference to the rule. Clearly there are rules of this kind, even though it may be disputed whether either of the examples Rawls gives, is an example of such a rule. (It is not my purpose here to discuss the latter issue. It is discussed fully enough in my article "An Examination of Restricted Utilitarianism").[2] Rawls is correct too in pointing to rules in games, e.g. in chess or in football, as examples of such rules, and to acts of the players, *qua* players, as examples of acts which can be described only by reference to the relevant rules. Consider the statement : ' Smith scored a goal '. Until we know the game concerned and its rules—football, soccer, hockey, or basketball—i.e., until we know the rules which define the act of scoring a goal, we do not know what Smith did.

Rawls uses this distinction to argue that exceptions to rules in practice which appear to have a utilitarian justification, cannot really have a utilitarian justification. Thus he argues that Carritt's example of an act of framing an innocent person in order to combat an outbreak of cruel crimes which appears to have a utilitarian justification, cannot in fact be justified even if Carritt's factual claim that such a murder would really reduce the occurrence of the crime in that particular situation were correct. Similarly a breach of a promise which appears to have good utilitarian consequences and which does not fall under one of the types of exceptions allowed by the rule in practice (which itself has a utilitarian justification as such) would in fact have no utilitarian justification. Rawls' argument is that such exceptions would change the practice to being a practice of a significantly different

[1] *Philosophical Review*, Vol. 64 (1955), pp. 3-32. Page references are to this article.
[2] *Philosophical Review*, Vol. 66 (1957), pp. 466-85.

kind, and one which would not have the same utilitarian justification. Punishment would be changed to telishment, where the latter lacks the utilitarian justification of the former (pp. 11-12), and the practice of promise-keeping, the point of which is " to abdicate one's title to act in accordance with utilitarian and prudential considerations in order that the future may be tied down and plans co-ordinated in advance " (p. 16) would become a different and less useful practice. Rawls supports these contentions with impressive reasons. None the less his claims here are also open to question, as I have argued in the article cited above. However, this too is not the issue I wish to press here.

The claim I am concerned to question, and that which is essential if Rawls' argument is to succeed is that to make an exception to the rule in practice is to change the practice. Here, possibly because he is misled by an analogy with chess (where the players are also the officials, adjudicators and legislators concerning the rules if they so choose), Rawls seems to confuse a number of types of exceptions with the least usual type of exception which occurs in respect of rules which define a practice. This can best be illustrated by reference to punishment and rules in games such as Australian Rules football. The types of exceptions which he assimilates to the one type, and which need to be distinguished are : (i) Exceptions permitted by the legislators and written into the rules by way of giving discretionary powers to the police and/or the judiciary. Rawls must, if his argument is to succeed, treat all exceptions by officials and private individuals as being of this type. (ii) Exceptions made by some, few, individual officials (umpires) without the knowledge or consent of the legislators and the majority of other officials, and where the individuals publicly express profound respect for the rule in practice as one which ought not to be infringed. (iii) Exceptions to the rule which defines the practice by some individual officials (umpires) which are in no way concealed but which are publicly known. (iv) Exceptions made in secret by private individuals (players of the game). (v) Exceptions made publicly by private individuals (players of the game).

Only exceptions of type (i) *must* involve a change in the rule in practice. Exceptions of type (ii), provided they are as described, the exception and not common practice, would not alter the nature of the practice nor the rule defining the practice. Exceptions of type (iii) would affect the rule in practice only if they were likely to be generally imitated. If they are not of common occurrence such imitation is unlikely. In any case, the practice, and the rule defining it, would change only after imitation of the exception became commonplace. Further, such exceptions as of kinds (ii) and (iii) are possible under the kind of rule of punishment (and promise-keeping) for which Rawls argues as being justifiable utilitarian rules. Consider the institution of punishment. Rawls defines punishment thus :

> A person is said to suffer punishment whenever he is legally deprived of some of the normal rights of a citizen on the grounds that he has violated a rule of law, the violation having been established by trial according to the due pro-

346   H. J. McCLOSKEY

cess of law, provided that the deprivation is carried out by the recognized legal
authorities of the state, that the courts construe the statutes strictly, and that
the statute was on the books prior to the time of the offense. (p. 10)

We know that under our rule in practice concerning punishment, which
is one of a large range of very different institutions of punishments which
would come under the description or definition of punishment set out by
Rawls, some of which are just and some unjust, discretionary power cannot
be withheld from the judiciary and the police. We know that under Australian rules concerning the institution of punishment, the judge can and even
must at times use his discretion, and that he can use it unfairly to influence
the jury against the accused whilst keeping his comments within what is
permitted by the law. We know how easy it is or would be for an unscrup-
ulous policeman to frame an individual, for example, by planting a drug on
him, and arresting him for possessing the drug. One does not have to be a
cynic to believe that some such immoral acts occur in one or other of the
Western democracies, all of whose systems of punishment conform roughly
with Rawls' definition of punishment. It is true that Rawls would not call
the punishment which results from such abuses of office by the judge or
policeman, punishment, but what is important here is that the institution
allows the exercise of such discretionary powers to the officials, and cannot
avoid doing so. Yet, unless abuses of power are widespread, the institution,
the rules which define the practice, do not change.

A reference to the game of football will illustrate the point that such
exceptions (abuses) do not change the practice, or in this case, the game.
An umpire, for example, a goal umpire, may as a result of accepting a bribe
decide for one match to count every doubtful goal or near miss by the Eagles
as a goal, and to score every doubtful goal by the Falcons as a point. This
is possible in a game such as Australian Rules football where the ball may
be kicked higher than the posts and still be deemed a goal if its course falls
between the line of the goal posts. It is deemed a behind—a point—if it
passes between the goal and point posts. Many decisions are very difficult
for the honest, conscientious umpire. The goal umpire is in the best position
to make the judgment, and because of the honesty of these umpires, their
judgment is generally respected by players and spectators alike even though
it is accepted that from time to time honest mistakes are made. Our corrupt
umpire would not alter the practice, in this case, the game. Examples of
type (iii) are evidently more common than the foregoing type in Australian
football. Some umpires deliberately do not penalize certain breaches of the
rules—this may be so as to keep the game flowing. Others interpret such a
rule as that the ball cannot be carried for more than 10 yards without
bouncing it, generously and allow the players to run 15 or even 20 yards
without penalty. Spectators and players accept such " interpretations " of
the rules, provided they are consistently applied. The rules of football have
not changed simply because one umpire at one ground has used his discretion—a discretion inseparable from his role as umpire—to interpret and

apply the rules in a certain way. It may be true that the game he umpires that day is not football as defined by the rules, and that it is different from the game played at another ground as a game of football. However, the rules in practice of Australian football remain what the legislators define them as being, and in the next round of games the players will, by and large, conform with and the umpires will, by and large, look upon the rules formulated by the legislators as standards or norms to obey or enforce as the case may be. To press the claim that the fact that the umpire cannot but have discretionary powers which may be mistakenly exercised changes the game, would involve allowing that perhaps the game of Australian football is never played—and similarly with the " games " of punishment and promise-making and keeping. Hart's discussion of what it is for legal and social rules to exist is relevant here.[3]

Exceptions of types (iv) and (v) are of the kind that most critics of utilitarianism, including possibly Carritt, have had in mind, especially in respect of punishment. (It is true that Carritt's wording of his example gives the impression that he is prepared to argue for discretionary power being given to the judiciary and/or the police, but his example need not be construed in that way. Certainly, it readily admits of restatement in terms of it being an individual utilitarian, a sincere and dedicated utilitarian such as Henry Sidgwick who is prepared to accept hypocrisy when it is demanded by utilitarian considerations, and who therefore is, as a private citizen, prepared to frame an innocent person to prevent evil consequences, whilst at the same time severely condemning perjury.) Such exceptions by no means alter the nature of the rule in practice. This is equally true of the publicly known exception as of the secret exception to the rule in practice. Publicly known exceptions to the rule, where the exception is based on utilitarian considerations, no more alter the rule than do prudential or selfish exceptions, which may be crimes, and punished as such.

The games analogy helps to bring this out. It is contrary to a rule of Australian football for one player to hold another except when the player held possesses the ball. It is a common practice for full-backs covertly to hold full-forwards by their shorts, and this, in order to promote what they see as the good, victory for their side. They commonly escape detection by the umpires. Yet this does not alter the rule in practice which defines the game, Australian football, for when detected, as with offences against the criminal law, the rule is applied. The ordinary citizen is in the position of the player and his secret or public illegal acts no more alter the rule than do the undetected or detected breaches of the rules of players of a game.

Players commonly infringe rules of the game, hopefully that they will not be penalized by the umpire, in order to win, just as ordinary citizens, for instance the doctor who in his own car and without police permission exceeds the speed limit in order to get a dying child to hospital, does in

[3]H. L. A. Hart, *The Concept of Law* (Oxford, 1961), Chs. IV and V.

respect of the law. Such acts—and there are many violators of traffic laws on utilitarian grounds—in no way alter the rule in practice, provided that there remains a general convergence of behaviour in conformity with the rule and provided the officials generally, usually, accept the rule as a norm or standard.

It is essential for Rawls' argument if it is to establish what Rawls seeks to establish, that exceptions of types (ii) to (v) be not simply assimilated to but identified with exceptions of type (i). The foregoing arguments would suggest that there is a vast difference between these types of exceptions, and hence that the version of rule utilitarianism which rests its case on Rawls' contention fails to establish what it seeks to establish, namely that it avoids certain of the difficulties of act utilitarianism.

La Trobe University.

Part V
A Collectively Satisfactory Theory?

[12]

IS ACT-UTILITARIANISM SELF-DEFEATING?[1]

THE normative principle that all acts are to be judged by their consequences—the principle of act-utilitarianism—has been subjected to a great deal of criticism, but continues to have adherents, of whom, I may as well say straightaway, I am one. Most of the criticism has been inconclusive because it has consisted of the outlining of unusual situations, in which the application of act-utilitarianism is said to give results which conflict with our "ordinary moral convictions." This method of argument can never move anyone who has greater confidence in the act-utilitarian principle than in his "ordinary moral convictions." Whenever the conflict is a real one, and not merely an apparent conflict, dependent on the omission of factors which the act-utilitarian can and should take into account, the genuine act-utilitarian will be prepared to jettison his "ordinary moral convictions" rather than the principle of act-utilitarianism.

The argument of Hodgson's *Consequences of Utilitarianism* is challenging precisely because it avoids this common approach. Hodgson recognizes the inconclusive nature of previous anti-utilitarian arguments. He advances a different kind of argument which, he confidently asserts, is capable of showing convincingly that the principle of act-utilitarianism is not a rational ethical principle. This makes the central argument of his book worthy of detailed consideration. This central argument is intended to show that

to act upon the act-utilitarian principle would probably have worse consequences than would to act upon more specific moral rules, quite independently of the misapplication of that principle [p. 3].

In fact, if this were true, it would still not quite refute act-utilitarianism. The two statements (*i*) "An act is right if and only if it would have best consequences" and (*ii*) "If people accepted (*i*) it would not have best consequences, even if they applied it correctly" are not inconsistent. Nevertheless, to establish the truth of (*ii*) would be seriously to embarrass the act-utilitarian, for he could hardly continue to advocate his doctrine. With this in mind, let us consider Hodgson's argument.

---

[1] D. H. Hodgson, *Consequences of Utilitarianism*. (Oxford, Clarendon Press, 1967.) Page references in the text are all to this book. In developing the views expressed in this review I have been assisted by discussions with various people, especially Professor R. M. Hare, Mr. D. Parfit, and Professor H. R. West.

ACT-UTILITARIANISM

Hodgson makes his attack on act-utilitarianism in the second chapter of his book. This is the crucial chapter. The remainder of the book is largely a working out of the application of the argument of this chapter with regard to, first, rule-utilitarianism, and second, the use of utilitarianism in the justification of legal decisions. For this reason I shall, in this discussion, concentrate on the argument of Chapter II.

Hodgson's formulation of the principle of act-utilitarianism, which I shall accept for the purposes of discussion, is as follows:

An act is right if and only if it would have best consequences, that is, consequences at least as good as those of any alternative act open to the agent [p. 1].

Hodgson, for convenience, uses "best" to mean "best or equal best," and I shall do the same.

In the second chapter, Hodgson considers the consequences of acting on the principle of act-utilitarianism in two different situations: when all the members of a society accept the principle, and when one is an individual acting in a society consisting mainly of people who are not utilitarians. The crucial points of his argument, however, are all raised by the case of a society in which act-utilitarianism is universally accepted, and so, for the sake of brevity, I will restrict what I have to say to this case.

Before presenting his arguments, Hodgson specifies carefully the circumstances of the society we are to consider. These circumstances represent, according to Hodgson, an "act-utilitarian's ideal." They are important, not just for Hodgson's own arguments, but also for possible counterarguments. I shall quote them in full.

[L]et us consider a society in which everyone accepts the act-utilitarian principle as his only personal rule, and attempts always to act in accordance with it. We assume that everyone is highly rational, sufficiently so to understand the implications of the use of act-utilitarianism (including those to be demonstrated in this section). We assume too that the universal use of act-utilitarianism and universal rationality is common knowledge, in the sense that everyone knows of it, and everyone knows that everyone knows, and so on. We leave open the possibility that everyone might always succeed in acting in accordance with his personal rule. We assume that there are no conventional moral rules in this society: everyone knows that everyone else attempts with high rationality to act in accordance with act-utilitarianism, and so no-one is concerned to criticise the conduct of others or to make demands of them [pp. 38-39].

Hodgson's arguments concern keeping promises and telling the truth. To take promise-keeping first: when we ask why we should be

PETER SINGER

more concerned to do something we have promised we would do, than to do an act which we just happen to have mentioned we might do, the standard act-utilitarian reply is that the person to whom we made the promise normally has expectations of the promised act being performed, which he would not have if the act had merely been mentioned as a possibility. It is, ultimately, because of these expectations that the performance of the promised act will have greater utility than the performance of the act which was mentioned as a possibility. But, Hodgson asks, would this be true in an act-utilitarian society of the kind specified? His answer is that it would not, because in such a society the promisee will know that the promise made to him will not be kept unless keeping it has best consequences. The fact that the act was promised will not lead to its performance having greater utility than it would have had, had it not been promised, unless the promisee will, because of the promise, have a greater expectation of its being performed than he would otherwise have had. The promisee will have good reason for this greater expectation only if he believes that the promisor believes that the act will be expected by him, the promisee, with greater expectation than it would have been, had it not been promised, but merely mentioned. The promisor will know this, and the promisee will know that he knows, and so on. A spiral has been set up which cannot be cut across. Any attempt to build up a basis for a greater expectation of the promised act is, Hodgson says, mere bootstrap-tugging. The expectation can have no rational basis, and hence there is no greater utility in doing something one has promised to do than there is in doing something one has merely mentioned one might do. So promising would be pointless in an act-utilitarian society.

A parallel argument applies to telling the truth. Imagine that A tells B: "X is Y." In an act-utilitarian society, B would have good reason to believe A only under the following conditions. If X were Y, it would, in A's belief, be best to tell B; if X were not Y it would, in A's belief, not be best to tell B that X is Y. These conditions will hold generally only if B likely to take the information conveyed as true, for only then will the utilitarian benefits which come from the conveying of true information—such as the possibility of making arrangements based on the information—be possible. But as B's taking the information to be true rather than false is a condition precedent of A's having good reason to tell B the truth, the situation is precisely similar to that of promise-keeping.

Hodgson concludes that for these reasons a society in which everyone

ACT-UTILITARIANISM

acted according to act-utilitarianism would be at a grave disadvantage compared to a society in which people acted on moral rules. For without promise-keeping and the communication of information there would be no human relationships as we know them. Hodgson emphasizes that this conclusion applies even if everyone applies act-utilitarianism correctly in the circumstances in which they are, but these circumstances—universal acceptance of act-utilitarianism and highly rational application of it—are in fact highly unfavorable to the production of good consequences.

One question that might be asked about Hodgson's ingenious arguments is whether he has himself considered sufficiently carefully all the effects which the circumstances of the society he has described would have. It will be recalled that Hodgson specified that in this society everyone adopts the principle of act-utilitarianism as his only personal rule, and attempts always to act in accordance with it. Under these circumstances, people would not act from the motives which most commonly lead people to make false promises and to tell lies—motives like self-interest, malevolence, pride, and so on. Nor would there be any need to make false promises or tell lies from utilitarian motives, in the sort of circumstances of which critics of utilitarianism are so fond: there would be no need to make consoling promises to dying people who wish their estates to be distributed in some way contrary to utility, since dying people would not wish this; no need, either, to tell a lie to save a man from his would-be murderer. Hodgson fails to see that there is any problem here. He writes of act-utilitarians breaking promises or telling lies without suggesting how doing so would bring about best consequences. His argument is based not on the existence of a reason for lying or breaking a promise, but on the absence of a sufficient reason for telling the truth or keeping a promise. This is significant, as we can see if we try to construct an example.

Let us imagine a case in which *A* has the choice of telling *B* the truth or a lie. *A* and *B*, we shall say, are working together in an office. (In constructing an example, it is impossible to avoid begging the question at issue to some extent. If Hodgson is right in saying that in an act-utilitarian society no communication would be possible, then offices and the other elements of this example would not be possible either. If this is considered a weakness, we might avoid the difficulty by assuming that, an instant before the events of my example take place, everyone in an until-then-normal society is miraculously converted to act-utilitarianism.) On this particular day, *B* intends to work overtime. His only means of transport home is by bus. If he misses the

PETER SINGER

bus, he will have to walk, which will make him very tired, waste time, and lead to his wife's worrying about him. In this situation, of which both *A* and *B* are aware, *B* asks *A*: "What time does the last bus go?" *A* knows the answer. Is it not in accordance with act-utilitarianism for *A* to tell *B* the correct time? Hodgson would reply that it would have better consequences for *A* to tell *B* the truth only if *B* were likely to take the information as true, and *B* would know that *A* would have no reason to tell the truth unless A believed that he, *B*, was likely to take the information as true, and so on. But consider the matter from *A*'s point of view. He has the choice of telling *B* the correct time, a fictitious time, or saying nothing. There is no possibility, barring extraordinary accidents, of any beneficial consequences arising from any course of action except telling *B* the correct time; but there is a fifty-fifty chance that telling *B* the correct time will lead to the beneficial consequences of *B* going to the bus stop at the right time. For even if there is no good reason for *B* to believe that *A* will tell him the truth, there is also no good reason for him to believe that *A* will tell him a lie, and so there is an even chance that *B* will take the information *A* gives him to be true. It is of course possible that if *A* tells *B* a fictitious time, *B* will treat this false information as false, but this cannot ensure, or even make it likely, that *B* will go to the bus stop at the right time. The point here is just that there is only one way for *A*'s statement to be true, but many ways for it to be false. Because of this, *A* has a reason for telling *B* the truth.

Once there is some reason for *A* to tell the truth, there is more than enough reason for him to do so. For *B*, being highly rational, will have thought of the considerations just pointed to, and will be aware that there is a reason for *A* to tell him the truth, and *A* will know this, and so on. So we get the Hodgson spiral working in the other direction, and *A* will have the normal utilitarian reason for telling the truth— that is, that *B* will take the information to be true and make arrangements based on its truth.

It might be objected that I have constructed an especially favorable case. In a real-life situation, would it not be possible that a lie would have best consequences? In the example, for instance, might it not be the case that *A* believes that great good will come if *B* works an hour longer than he would if he left to catch the last bus? If this is possible, would not *A* be right, on act-utilitarian grounds, to tell *B* that the last bus left an hour later than it really does leave?

This objection forgets that both *A* and *B* take act-utilitarianism as their personal rule and always try to act on it. So if it is the case that

ACT-UTILITARIANISM

the good of *B* working an extra hour outweighs the disutility of his having to walk home, all that is necessary to ensure that he does the extra work is that *A* explain this to him, thereby avoiding at least some of the disutility that would come from *A* telling *B* that the bus comes later than it really does—*B* will not have to wait unnecessarily, and he can telephone his wife so that she will not worry. So *A* still has no good reason for lying.

A different objection to my example might be that it depends on a question being asked to which there is only one true answer, and more than one false answer. Does our conclusion apply to other situations as well? In reply to this, one could say that it would seem to be possible to ask even ordinary questions, which would normally require a simple yes/no answer, in such a way as to make two false answers possible. If an office worker wished to know whether or not to reply to a letter, he could ask: "Shall I reply to this letter, file it, or make a paper dart out of it?" In this way the person addressed has a better chance of producing best consequences by saying what he really thinks best. Admittedly, if this were really necessary, act-utilitarianism would cause inconvenience, but it would not be disastrous, and it is certainly not clear that this inconvenience would outweigh the benefits of everyone's adopting act-utilitarianism.

In any case, there are other grounds for believing that in a society of act-utilitarians there would be sufficient reason for telling the truth in normal situations. Let us consider an example in which information is volunteered. I am walking along the street when *A* comes up to me and says: "There is a very good film on at the local cinema this week." How am I to take this remark? Is it possible that *A* wants me to go to the cinema for some reason, even though the film is very bad? Perhaps the cinema will have to close if it does not get good audiences this week, and the disutility of this outweighs the disutility of people being bored by the film. But this explanation will not do, for, as in the previous example, *A* could explain these facts to me, and I could buy a ticket without wasting my time by actually sitting through the film. Nevertheless, Hodgson might say, I cannot assume that *A* was telling me the truth. He may have been trying to warn me away from a very bad film, believing that I would take what he had told me to be false. This is not feasible either. Why would *A* have bothered to speak at all, since I am just as likely to take his remark to be true as to be false? Hodgson may claim that this is just his point. No one would have any reason to speak, and communication would cease. Before we accept this, however, consider the situation from the point of view of the

99

PETER SINGER

recipient of the information. Since by going through the business of inverting what *A* says to me—thinking to myself, "He says the film is good, but he may be telling a lie, so the film may be bad"—I am no more likely to arrive at the truth than if I take what *A* says at face value, why should I bother to invert it? Am I not just a fraction more likely to take it at face value? If I am, *A*, being highly rational, will know this, and will know that he is more likely to produce best consequences if he tells the truth, while I, being highly rational, will know this, and so expect *A* to tell the truth . . . and so we get the spiral unspiraling once again, and we have all the reason we need for telling the truth.

Analogously with the argument just made, we could also ask why *A* should not save himself the bother of inventing a lie by telling the truth, thus making it fractionally more likely that he would tell the truth, and reversing the spiral once again. Hodgson attempts to forestall this objection by saying that any disvalue involved in the need to invent a lie would be balanced by the satisfaction of exercising the skill of lying (p.43). Hodgson apparently has not noticed that the point is equally effective if made in regard to the recipient of the information, and his reply, which is not particularly convincing in the case of the person making the statement, would be quite implausible if made in respect of the recipient.

Hodgson does at one point suggest that even if it were possible to arouse expectations in the recipient that the information is true, it would not be possible to place much reliance on it, because it would still be better to tell a lie if the consequenences on the whole would be better—and since the recipient would know this, he would not have very strong expectations (p. 50). This again seems to overlook the fact that if everyone were an act-utilitarian most of the reasons, selfish and unselfish, which we would otherwise have for lying would not exist. Hence I believe that once the expectations can be aroused, at least as much reliance could be placed on them as is possible in our society at present, outside the circle of those we know to be sincere.

I have questioned only Hodgson's argument about truth-telling, but similar points could be made about his argument in respect of keeping promises. If there is little reason for making false statements, then there is little reason for making false statements of intention. But a promise implies, in some sense, a statement of intention, and whatever the promise adds to the statement of intention would not seem to affect the validity of the application of the previous argument about statements in general to the statements of intention implied by promises. In fact, it seems to me that a statement of firm intention to do an

ACT-UTILITARIANISM

act, coupled with a recommendation to the hearer to make arrangements based on the expectation that the intention be carried out, is just as useful as, if it is not equivalent to, a promise. If, because of unforeseen events, the "promisor" is in doubt as to whether doing as he said he intended to do will have best consequences, he must, as an act-utilitarian, take into account the expectations raised and arrangements which may have been made as a result of his statement of intention. This, of course, is as much as an act-utilitarian would ever want to say in defense of the institution of promising.

Quite apart from these objections to Hodgson's central argument, there is a more obvious one, which he does consider but not, in my opinion, refute. It is independent of the arguments I have put so far, and for the purposes of discussing it, we may assume that what I have said up to now has been mistaken.

The obvious objection is that if the situation were as Hodgson describes it, it would be justifiable on act-utilitarian grounds to take steps to form a social practice of telling the truth and making and keeping firm statements of intention (which I shall, for convenience, continue to call "promises"). Any steps toward the formation of these practices would have the good consequences of making desirable activities possible. Since telling the truth and keeping promises could help in the formation of these practices, while lying and breaking promises could not, this would give an additional reason for telling the truth and keeping promises. The spiraling effect would come into operation. This would ensure the rapid development of the practices. The informer or promisor would then have the dual reasons of preserving the useful practice and fulfilling expectations.

Hodgson seems to be aware of this kind of objection to his arguments. Yet his reply to it is puzzling:

Such steps could have good consequences, but, although perhaps justified by act-utilitarianism, they would amount to a partial rejection of act-utilitarianism and so would be inconsistent with our assumptions. These steps would amount to a partial rejection of act-utilitarianism, because the persons would be forming habits to do acts known not to be justified according to act-utilitarianism; and they could form these habits only if they resolved to refrain from applying act-utilitarianism in relation to these acts [p. 48].

I am puzzled by the statement that acts could be justified by act-utilitarianism, and yet amount to a partial rejection of act-utilitarianism. This looks like a contradiction. Perhaps Hodgson means that while the taking of steps to get the habit, or practice, established is

PETER SINGER

justified by act-utilitarianism, the practice itself is one of refraining from the calculation of consequences in respect of the particular acts, so that acts done in accordance with the practice may not be justified by act-utilitarianism. There are two points that may be made in reply to this. First, if acts may be justified because they help to get a practice established, surely they may also be justified because they help to preserve a useful, established practice. Second, Hodgson's admission that the acts which establish the practice may be justified by act-utilitarianism undermines the arguments he made earlier; for once the practice is established the point about lack of expectation, that promises will be kept and information given true, will not apply. Where there is a practice there are expectations, and the standard act-utilitarian justifications of keeping promises and telling the truth will operate.

It may be that in talking of "forming habits to do acts known not to be justified according to act-utilitarianism" Hodgson has in mind the formation of habits or practices of *always* telling the truth, and *always* keeping promises, no matter what the consequences. This would certainly be inconsistent with act-utilitarianism, but it would also be unnecessary. The benefits of communication and reliability may be gained without having such absolutist practices. All that is necessary is that there be habits of telling the truth and keeping promises unless there is a clear disutility in doing so which outweighs the benefits of preserving the useful practices and fulfilling the expectations aroused. It is, after all, an advantage of act-utilitarianism that it does not force us to reveal the hiding places of innocent men to their would-be murderers, or leave accident victims groaning by the roadside in order to avoid being late for an appointment we have promised to keep.

It might be more plausible to argue that it is the initial acts, before the practice has been established, and the expectations aroused, that would be contrary to act-utilitarianism. Hodgson does not argue this in the context of the passage we have been discussing, but in a subsequent discussion of the justification of a decision by a judge to punish an offender, Hodgson argues that although an unbroken record of punishment might deter potential offenders, such an unbroken record can never, on act-utilitarian grounds, get started. Hodgson's argument is that no single case can be a necessary or sufficient condition for such an unbroken record, because if we did not punish in any particular case, we could still have an unbroken record from the *next* case onward which would deter just as well [p. 93]. This argument seems to be

ACT-UTILITARIANISM

based on the assumption that the only consequences of an act which may be taken into account, in deciding whether that act is justified by the act-utilitarian principle, are those for which the act is a necessary or sufficient condition. (This assumption has, incidentally, been the basis of claims by other writers that act-utilitarianism cannot explain why we ought to vote at elections, or obey power restrictions, when failure to do so will not bring about the defeat of our candidate or a general power breakdown.) Although some act-utilitarian writers may have assumed that only consequences for which the act is a necessary or sufficient condition should be taken into account, there is no good reason for an act-utilitarian to do so. An act may contribute to a result without being either a necessary or sufficient condition of it, and if it does contribute, the act-utilitarian should take this contribution into account. The contribution that my vote makes toward the result I judge to be best in an election is a relevant consideration in deciding whether to vote, although it is, almost certainly, neither a necessary nor a sufficient condition of that result; for if this were not so, the act-utilitarian view would leave us with a result which was unconnected with the actions of any of the voters, since what is true of my vote is equally true of every individual vote. In the punishment case, the first act of punishing may be justified, on act-utilitarian grounds, by its probable contribution to an unbroken record of punishment which will have a deterrent effect. In the cases we were considering originally, an act of telling the truth or keeping a promise will normally have greater utility than would its opposite, because it has a reasonable chance of contributing to the beneficial consequences of setting up a desirable practice. Our act-utilitarians, being highly rational, would understand this, and so contribute to the establishing of the practice themselves, as well as expecting other act-utilitarians to do so. The expectations so generated would increase the utility of conforming to the practice, which would therefore become established very quickly.

It seems to me, then, that Hodgson fails to establish the challenging central thesis of his book; and as I have said, the remainder of the work is based on the arguments we have just been discussing. This does not mean that the later sections are without interest, once these arguments have been rejected. On the contrary, there is much here that is stimulating for anyone interested in rule-utilitarianism or the justification of legal decisions—particularly the latter topic, which takes up almost exactly half of the book's total length.

PETER SINGER

I should also say, perhaps, that in dissenting from Hodgson's conclusions I have not been concerned to deny that there are no problems at all, of the sort Hodgson raises, in being an act-utilitarian. There may be occasions when a person is handicapped by being known to be an act-utilitarian—for example, a doctor, who assures a seriously ill patient, depressed and fearful that he will die, that his condition is hopeful, is less likely to be believed if he is known to be an act-utilitarian than if he is known to believe that lying is always wrong. These occasions would, I think, be few enough and unimportant enough for the balance of advantage to favor act-utilitarianism. My concern has been to show that act-utilitarianism does not have the catastrophic consequences which Hodgson argues it would have.

PETER SINGER

University College, Oxford

[13]

Australasian Journal of Philosophy
Vol. 50, No. 1; May, 1972

DAVID LEWIS

UTILITARIANISM AND TRUTHFULNESS[1]

A demon has seized two highly rational act-utilitarians—call them 'You' and 'I'—and put them in separate rooms. In each room there are two buttons, a red one and a green one. The demon has arranged that by both pushing our red buttons or by both pushing our green buttons we bring about the Good; but by pushing one red button and one green button (or by pushing both buttons or neither button in one of the rooms) we bring about the Bad. The demon has made sure that we both know all the facts I have listed so far, that we both know that we both know them, and so on.

You manage to send me a message, and the message is 'I pushed red'. But, strange to say, that does not help. For I reason as follows. 'You are a highly rational utilitarian. You act in whatever way you think will have the best consequences, with no regard to any other consideration. This goes for sending messages: you send whatever message you think will have the best consequences, caring not at all about truthfulness for its own sake. So I have not the slightest reason to believe your message unless I have reason to believe that you think that truthfulness will have the best consequences. In this case, you must know that truthfulness has the best consequences only if I have some reason to believe you and to act accordingly. If not, there is nothing to choose between the expected consequences of truth and untruth, so you have no reason whatever to choose truth rather than untruth. I have not the slightest reason to believe you unless I have reason to believe that you think that I have reason to believe you. But I know that you—knowledgeable and rational creature that you are—will not think that I have reason to believe you unless I really do have. Do I? *I cannot show that I have reason to believe you without first assuming what is to be shown: that I have reason to believe you.* So I cannot, without committing the fallacy of *petitio principii*, show that I have reason to believe you. Therefore I do not. Your message gives me not the slightest reason to believe that you pushed red, and not the slightest reason to push red myself.' Arguing thus, I push at random. By chance I push green.

Such is the disutility of utilitarianism, according to D. H. Hodgson.[2]

We might better say: such is the disutility of *expecting* utilitarianism, and it is not sufficiently compensated by the efforts to maximize utility that fulfil the

---

[1] This research was supported by a fellowship from the American Council of Learned Societies.
[2] *Consequences of Utilitarianism* (Oxford University Press: Oxford, 1967), pp. 38-46.

David Lewis

expectation. Hodgson says that knowledgeable and rational act-utilitarians would have no reason to expect one another to be truthful, not even when the combination of truthfulness with expectation of truthfulness would have good consequences; so they would forfeit the benefits of communication. Similarly they would forfeit the benefits of promising; for an example of this, just change the message in my example to 'I will push red'. More generally, it seems that Hodgson's utilitarians would forfeit the benefits of all the conventions whereby we coordinate our actions to serve our common interests. The conventions of truthfulness and of promise-keeping are but two of these.

But to talk myself into ignoring your message 'I pushed red' is absurd. My example has no special features; it is just a simple and stark instance of the general situation Hodgson says would prevail among knowledgeable and rational act-utilitarians. I conclude that Hodgson is wrong in general. Where, then, is the flaw in my Hodgsonian argument that I ought to ignore your message? Every step up to the italicised one seems true, and every step beyond that seems false.

I think the argument went wrong when I tacitly assumed that I could not have reason to believe you unless I could show, using nothing but the facts set forth in the first paragraph—our situation, our utilitarianism and rationality, our knowledge of these, our knowledge of one another's knowledge of these, and so on—that I did have reason to believe you. But why must my premises be limited to these? I should not use any premise that is inconsistent with the facts of the first paragraph; but there is nothing wrong with using a premise that is independent of these facts, if such a premise is available.

The premise that you will be truthful (whenever it is best to instill in me true beliefs about matters you have knowledge of, as in this case) is just such a premise. It *is* available to me. At least, common sense suggests that it would be; and our only reason to suppose that it would not is the Hodgsonian argument we are now disputing. It is independent of the facts listed in the first paragraph. On the one hand, it is *consistent* with our rationality and utilitarianism, our knowledge thereof, and so on. For if you are truthful (except when it is best that I should have false beliefs), and if I expect you to be, and if you expect me to expect you to be, and so on, then you will have a good utilitarian reason to be truthful. You will be truthful without compromising your utilitarianism and without adding to your utilitarianism an independent maxim of truthfulness. On the other hand, it is not *implied* by our rationality and utilitarianism, our knowledge thereof, and so on. For if you are systematically untruthful (expect when it is best that I should have false beliefs), and if I expect you to be, and if you expect me to expect you to be, and so on, then you will have a good utilitarian reason to be untruthful. I am speaking, of course, of truthfulness and untruthfulness *in English*; I should mention that systematic untruthfulness in English is the same thing as systematic truthfulness in a different language *anti-English*, exactly like English in syntax but exactly opposite in truth conditions.

Therefore I should have decided that I did have reason to believe your message and to push red myself. This reason is admittedly not premised

Utilitarianism and Truthfulness

merely on our situation, our rationality and utilitarianism, our knowledge of these, and so on. But it is premised on further knowledge that I do in fact possess, and that is perfectly consistent with these facts.

Received May 1971

Princeton University

[14]

PHILOSOPHICAL LECTURE

PRUDENCE, MORALITY, AND THE PRISONER'S DILEMMA

By DEREK PARFIT

Read 16 November 1978

THERE are many theories about what we have reason to do. Some of these theories are, in certain cases, directly self-defeating. What does this show?

I

Consider first *the Prisoner's Dilemma*. You and I are questioned separately about some joint crime. The outcomes would be these:

	You confess	You keep silent
I confess	Each gets 10 years	I go free, you get 12 years
I keep silent	I get 12 years, you go free	Each gets 2 years

It will be better for each if he[1] confesses. This is so whatever the other does. But if both confess that will be worse for each than if both keep silent.

Let us simplify. It will be worse for each if each rather than neither does what will be better for himself. One case occurs when

> *Positive Condition*: each could either (1) give himself some benefit or (2) give the other some greater benefit,

and

> *Negative Condition*: neither's choice would be in other ways better or worse for either.

---

[1] 'He' means 'he or she' throughout.

When the Positive Condition holds, the outcomes would be these:

		You	
		do (1)	do (2)
I	do (1)	Each gets the lesser benefit	I get both benefits, you get neither
	do (2)	I get neither benefit, you get both	Each gets the greater benefit

If we add the Negative Condition, the diagram becomes:

		You	
		do (1)	do (2)
I	do (1)	Third-best for both	Best for me, worst for you
	do (2)	Worst for me best for you	Second-best for both

Part of the Negative Condition cannot be shown in this diagram. There must be *no reciprocity*: it must be true that neither's choice would cause the other to make the same choice. It will then be better for each if he does (1) rather than (2). This is so whatever the other does. But if both do(1) that will be worse for each than if both do (2).

When could there be no reciprocity? Only when each must make a final choice before learning what the other chose. This is not common. Nor would it ensure the Negative Condition. There might, for instance, be delayed reciprocity. Either's choice might affect whether he is later benefited by the other. We can therefore seldom know that we face a Two-Person Prisoner's Dilemma.

We can often know that we face a Many-Person version. One can be called *the Samaritan's Dilemma*. Each of us could sometimes help a stranger at some lesser cost to himself. Each could about as often be similarly helped. In small communities, the cost of helping might be indirectly met. If I help, this may cause me to be later helped in return. But in large communities this is unlikely. It may here be better for each if he never helps. But it would be worse for each if no one ever helps. Each might gain from never helping, but he would lose, and lose more, from never being helped.

THE PRISONER'S DILEMMA 541

Another case occurs when

> *Positive Condition*: each of us could, at some cost to himself, give to the others a greater total sum of benefits,[1]

and

> *Negative Condition*: there would be no indirect effects cancelling out these direct effects.

The Positive Condition often holds. If we are numerous, so does the Negative Condition. What each does would here be unlikely to affect what the others do.

The commonest examples are *Contributor's Dilemmas*. These involve *public goods*: outcomes which benefit even those who do not help to produce them. It can be true of each person that, if he helps, he will add to the sum of benefits. But his share of what he adds may be very small. It may not repay his contribution. It may thus be better for each if he does not help. This can be so whatever others do. But it would be worse for each if fewer others help. And if none help that would be worse for each than if all do.

Some public goods need financial contributions. This is true of roads, the police, or national defence. Others need co-operative efforts. When in large firms wages depend on profits, it can be better for each if others work harder, worse for each if he does. The same can be true for peasants on collective farms. A third kind of public good is the avoidance of an evil. This often needs self-restraint. Such cases may involve

> *Commuters*: Each goes faster if he drives, but if all drive each goes slower than if all take buses;
>
> *Soldiers*: Each will be safer if he turns and runs, but if all do more will be killed than if none do;
>
> *Fishermen*: When the sea is overfished, it can be better for each if he tries to catch more, worse for each if all do;
>
> *Peasants*: When the land is overcrowded, it can be better for each if he has more children, worse for each if all do.

There are many other cases. It can be better for each if he adds to pollution, uses more energy, jumps queues, and breaks agreements; but if all do these things that can be worse for each than if none do. It is very often true that, if each rather than none

---

[1] Or *expected* benefits (possible benefits multiplied by the chances that his act will produce them). In many of my later claims, 'benefit' could mean 'expected benefit'.

542   PROCEEDINGS OF THE BRITISH ACADEMY

does what will be better for himself, that will be worse for everyone.

II

Each may be disposed to do what will be better for himself. There is then a practical problem. Unless something changes, the actual outcome will be worse for everyone.

Let us use labels. Each has two alternatives: S (self-benefiting), A (altruistic). If all do S that will be worse for each than if all do A. But, whatever others do, it will be better for each if he does S. The problem is that, for this reason, each is now disposed to do S.

The problem will be partly solved if most do A, wholly solved if all do. A solution may be reached in one or more of these ways:

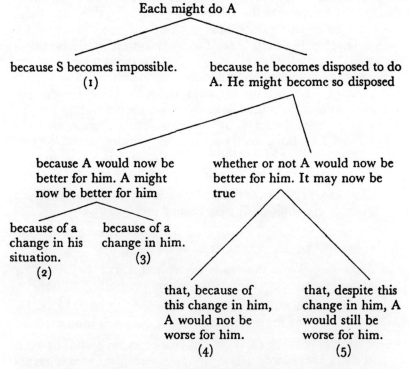

Each might do A

because S becomes impossible.
(1)

because he becomes disposed to do A. He might become so disposed

because A would now be better for him. A might now be better for him

whether or not A would now be better for him. It may now be true

because of a change in his situation.
(2)

because of a change in him.
(3)

that, because of this change in him, A would not be worse for him.
(4)

that, despite this change in him, A would still be worse for him.
(5)

(1) to (4) abolish the Dilemma. The altruistic choice ceases to be worse for each. These are often good solutions. But they are sometimes inefficient, or unattainable. We then need (5). This solves the practical problem. But it does not abolish the Dilemma. A theoretical problem remains.

THE PRISONER'S DILEMMA 543

In solution (1), the self-benefiting choice is made impossible. This is sometimes best. In many Contributor's Dilemmas, there should be inescapable taxation. But (1) would often be a poor solution. Fishing nets could be destroyed, soldiers chained to their posts. Both have disadvantages.

(2) is a less direct solution. S remains possible, but A is made better for each. There might be a system of rewards. But if this works all must be rewarded. It may be better if the sole reward is to escape some penalty. If this works, no one pays. If all deserters would be shot, there may be no deserters.

(1) and (2) are political solutions. What is changed is our situation. (3) to (5) are psychological. It is we who change. This change may be specific, solving only one Dilemma. The fishermen might grow lazy, the soldiers might come to prefer death to dishonour. Here are four changes of a more general kind:

> We might become *trustworthy*. Each might then agree to do A on condition that the others join in this agreement.
>
> We might become *reluctant to be 'free-riders'*. If each believes that many others will do A, he may then prefer to do his share.
>
> We might become *Kantians*. Each would then do only what he could rationally will everyone to do. None could rationally will that all do S. Each would therefore do A.
>
> We might become *more altruistic*. Given sufficient altruism, each would do A.

These are moral solutions. Because they might solve any Dilemma, they are the most important psychological solutions.

They are often better than the political solutions. This is in part because they do not need to be enforced. Take the Samaritan's Dilemma. It cannot be made impossible not to help strangers. Bad Samaritans cannot be easily caught and fined. Good Samaritans could be rewarded. But for this to be ensured the law might have to intervene. Given the administrative costs, this solution may not be worth while. It would be much better if we became directly disposed to help strangers.

It is not enough to know which solution would be best. Any solution must be introduced. This is often easier with the political solutions. Situations can be changed more easily than people. But we often face another Contributor's Dilemma. Few political solutions can be introduced by a single person. Most require co-operation by many people. But a solution is a public good, benefiting each whether or not he does his share in bringing it about. In most large groups, it will not be better for each if he does his share. His own contribution will not make enough difference.

This problem may be small in well-organized democracies. It may be sufficient here to get the original problem widely understood. This may be difficult. But we may then vote for a political solution. With a responsive government, there may even be no need to hold a vote.

The problem is greater when there is no government. This is what worried Hobbes. One example is the spread of nuclear weapons. Without world government, it may be hard to achieve a solution.

The problem is greatest when its solution is opposed by some ruling group. This is *the Dilemma of the Oppressed.*

Such Contributor's Dilemmas often need moral solutions. We often need some people who are directly disposed to do their share. If these can change the situation, so as to achieve a political solution, this may be self-sustaining. But without such people it may never be achieved.

The moral solutions are, then, often best; and they are often the only attainable solutions. We therefore need the moral motives. How could these be introduced? Fortunately, that is not our problem. They exist. That is how we solve many Prisoner's Dilemmas. Our need is to make these motives stronger, and more widely spread.

With this task, theory helps. Prisoner's Dilemmas need to be explained. So do their moral solutions. Both have been too little understood.

One solution is, we saw, a conditional agreement. For this to be possible, it must first be true that we can all communicate. If we are self-interested, this would seldom make a difference. In most large groups, it would be pointless to agree that we will make the altruistic choice, since it would be better for each if he breaks this agreement. But suppose that we are trustworthy. Each could now promise to do A, on condition that everyone else makes the same promise. If we know that we are all trustworthy, each will have a motive to join this conditional agreement. Each will know that, unless he joins, the agreement will not take effect. Once we have all made this promise, we will all do A.

In cases that involve only a few people, such a joint conditional agreement may be a good solution. But in cases that

THE PRISONER'S DILEMMA 545

involve large numbers it has little use. It will take some effort both to enable all to communicate and then to reach a joint agreement. But the agreement is a public good, benefiting each whether or not he helps to produce it. In most large groups, it will not be better for each if he helps. To this Contributor's Dilemma, trustworthiness provides no solution.

If we are reluctant to be free-riders, this problem is reduced. There is now no need for an actual agreement. All that is needed is an assurance that there will be many who do A. Each would then prefer to do his share. But a reluctance to free-ride cannot by itself create this assurance. So there are many cases where it provides no solution.

The Kantian Test could always provide a solution. This Test has its own problems. Could I rationally will either that none practise medicine, or that all do? If we refine the Test, we may solve such problems. But in Prisoner's Dilemmas they do not arise. These are the cases where we naturally say, 'What if everyone did that?'

The fourth solution is sufficient altruism. This has been the least understood. Each altruistic choice benefits others. But in Contributor's Dilemmas the benefit to each of the others may be very small. It may even not be perceptible. Some believe that such benefits make no moral difference. If that were so, rational altruists would not contribute.

It cannot be so. Consider *the Donor's Paradox*. Many wounded men lie out in the desert. Each of us has one pint of water, which he could carry to some wounded man. But if our pints are carried separately, much of the water would evaporate. If instead we pour our pints into a water-cart, there would be no evaporation. For rational altruists, this would be a better way of giving. Each wounded man would receive more water. But the pint that each of us contributes would now be shared between all these many men. It would give to each man only a single drop. Even to a wounded man, each drop of water is a very tiny benefit. If we ignore such benefits, we shall be forced to conclude that each of our contributions is now wasted.[1]

Let us next subdivide the moral solutions. When some moral motive leads someone to do A, what he does may either be, or not be, worse for him. This distinction raises deep questions.

[1] I follow J. Glover, 'It Makes No Difference Whether Or Not I Do It', *Proceedings of the Aristotelian Society, Suppl. Vol. 49* (1975). A similar argument could show that, when our acts may benefit or harm large numbers of people, we should not ignore very tiny chances.

But I shall simply state what my arguments assume. What is in our interests partly depends on what our motives are. If we have moral motives, it may therefore not be true that doing A is worse for us. But this might be true. Even if we know it is, we might still do A.

I am here dismissing four claims. Some say that no one does what he believes to be worse for him. This has been often refuted. Others say that what each does is, by definition, best for him. In the economist's phrase, it will 'maximize his utility'. Since this is merely a definition, it cannot be false. But it is here irrelevant. It is simply not about what is in a person's long-term self-interest. Others say that virtue is always rewarded. Unless there is an after-life, this has also been refuted. Others say that virtue is its own reward. This is too obscure to be easily dismissed—or discussed here.

To return to my own claims. Many Prisoner's Dilemmas need moral solutions. We must become directly disposed to make the altruistic choice. These solutions are of two kinds. Some abolish the Dilemma. In such cases, because of this change in us, it is no longer true that it will be worse for each if he does A. But in other cases this is still true. Even in such cases, we might do A. Each might do, for moral reasons, what he knows to be worse for him.

We often need moral solutions of this second kind. Call them *self-denying*. They solve the practical problem. The outcome is better for everyone. But they do not abolish the Dilemma. A theoretical problem remains.

III

It is this. We may have moral reasons to do A. But it will be better for each if he does S. Morality conflicts with self-interest. When these conflict, what is it rational to do?

On one view, it is the self-benefiting choice which is rational. This view lacks a good name. Call it *prudence*. If we accept this view, we will be ambivalent about self-denying moral solutions. We will believe that, to achieve such solutions, we must all act irrationally.

Many writers resist this conclusion. Some claim that moral reasons are no weaker than prudential reasons. Others claim, more boldly, that they are stronger. On their view, it is the altruistic choice which is rational.

This debate may seem unresolvable. How can these two kinds of reason be weighed against each other? Moral reasons

THE PRISONER'S DILEMMA   547

are, of course, morally supreme. But prudential reasons are prudentially supreme. Where can we find a neutral scale?

Some believe we do not need a neutral scale. They claim that, in Prisoner's Dilemmas, prudence is *self-defeating*. Even in prudential terms, morality wins.

Is this so? Call prudence

> *individually self-defeating* when it would be worse for someone if he is prudent,

and

> *collectively self-defeating* when it would be worse for each if all rather than none are prudent.

Prudence might be individually self-defeating. Either of these might be true:

> (1) It might be worse for someone if he acted prudently. When there is uncertainty, the prudent act may not be the one which turns out best.

> (2) It might be worse for someone if he was disposed to act prudently. This might be worse for him even if he always did what would be best for him. One example is the 'paradox of hedonism': happiness, if aimed at, may be harder to achieve.

In Prisoner's Dilemmas, neither of these is true. The bad effects are here produced by acts, not dispositions. And there is no uncertainty. It will be better for each if he acts prudently. It is the self-benefiting choice which is prudent; and, whatever others do, it will be better for each if he makes this choice. So prudence is not here individually self-defeating. But it is collectively self-defeating. If all act prudently, that will be worse for each than if none do.

Does this show that, if we all act prudently, we are irrational? We can start with a smaller question. Do our own assumptions show us this? Is our prudence failing even in its own terms?

We might answer: 'No. The prudence of each is better for him. It succeeds. Why is our prudence here collectively self-defeating? Only because the prudence of each is worse for others. That does not make it unsuccessful. It is not benevolence.' If we are prudent, we will of course deplore Prisoner's Dilemmas. These are not the cases loved by classical economists, where each gains from universal prudence. We might say: 'In those cases, prudence both works and approves the situation. In Prisoner's Dilemmas, prudence still works. Each still gains from his own prudence. But since each loses even more from the prudence of others, prudence here condemns the situation.'

This may seem an evasion. When it is worse for each if we are all prudent, it may seem that our prudence should condemn itself. Suppose that in some other group, facing the same Dilemmas, all make the altruistic choice. They might say to us: 'You think us irrational. But we are better off than you. We do better even in prudential terms.'

We could answer: 'That is just a play on words. You "do better" only in the sense that you are better off. Each of you is *doing* worse in prudential terms. He is doing what is worse for him.' We might add: 'What is worse for each of us is that, in our group, there are no fools. Each of you has better luck. His own irrationality is worse for him, but he gains even more from the irrationality of others.'

They might answer: 'You are partly right. Each of us *is* doing worse in prudential terms. But, though *each* is doing worse, *we* are doing better. That is not a play on words. Each of us is better off because of what we *do*.'

This suggestion looks more promising. Return to the simpler Two-Person Case. Each could either benefit himself (S) or give to the other some greater benefit (A). The outcomes would be these:

		You	
		do S	do A
I	do S	Third-best for each	Best for me, worst for you
	do A	Worst for me, best for you	Second-best for each

To ensure that neither's choice can affect the other's, suppose that we cannot communicate. If I do A rather than S, that will then be worse for me. This is so whatever you do. And the same holds for you. If we both do A rather than S, each is therefore doing worse in prudential terms. The suggestion is that *we* are doing better.

What makes this promising is that it contrasts 'each' with 'we'. In some claims, these are equivalent. It cannot be true that each is old but we are young. But in other claims they are not equivalent. It might be true that each is weak but we are strong. We *together* might be strong. Our suggestion is of this second kind. It might be true that, though each is doing worse in prudential terms, we together are doing better.

THE PRISONER'S DILEMMA 549

Is this true? Let us use this test. Our prudence gives to each a certain aim. Each does better, in prudential terms, if he more effectively achieves this aim. *We* do better, in the same terms, if we more effectively achieve the aim of each. This test seems fair. It might show that, if each does the best he can, we together could not do better.

What is the aim that our prudence gives to each? We might say, 'to act prudently'. This is true, but misleading. Some aims are fundamental. Others are derived from these. Call the former *goals*. When we are measuring success, only goals count. Suppose that we are trying to scratch our own backs. The goal of each might be that he cease to itch. We would then do better if we scratched each other's backs. But we might be contortionists: the goal of each might be that his back be scratched *by himself*. If we scratched each other's backs, we would then do worse.

If we are prudent, what is the goal of each? Is it that his interests be advanced, or that his interests be advanced *by himself*? If it was the second, we would not be prudent. Perhaps we are Nietzscheans, whose ideal is 'the fiercest self-reliance'. If we both do A rather than S, we would be doing worse in these terms. The interests of each would be better advanced. But neither's would be advanced by himself. Neither's goal would be achieved.

This Nietzschean ideal is not prudence. Both give each the aim of self-advancement. But only for Nietzscheans is this the goal. For the prudent, any act is a mere means. The goal is always the effect—whether this be pleasure, or some other benefit. (Nietzsche's 'blond beasts' were, it is said, lions. But, for them too, acting is a means. They prefer to eat what others kill.)

The goal of each person's prudence is the best possible outcome for himself. If we both do A rather than S, we make the outcome better for each. We cause the goal of each to be better achieved. We are therefore doing better in prudential terms. This confirms the suggestion made above. The prudent act is S. If we both act prudently, we are doing worse than we could even in prudential terms.

Does this show that our prudence here condemns itself? It may seem so. And it is tempting to contrast prudence with morality. We might say: 'Prudence breeds conflict, telling each to work against others. That is how universal prudence can be bad for all. Where prudence divides, morality unites. It tells us to work together—to do the best *we* can. Even on the scale provided by self-interest, morality therefore wins. This is what we learn from Prisoner's Dilemmas. If we exchange prudence for morality, we do better even in prudential terms.'

This is too swift. *We* do better, but *each* does worse. If we both do A rather than S, *we* make the outcome better for each, but *each* makes the outcome worse for himself. Whatever the other does, it would be better for each if he did S. In Prisoner's Dilemmas, the problem is this. Should *each* do the best he can for himself? Or should *we* do the best we can for each? If *each* does what is best for himself, *we* do worse than we could for each. But *we* do better for each only if *each* does worse than he could for himself.

This is just a special case of a wider problem. Consider any theory about what we have reason to do. There might be cases where, if each does better in this theory's terms, we do worse, and vice versa. Call such cases *Each–We Dilemmas*.

Some theories cannot produce such Dilemmas. We shall later see why, for certain theories, this is so. If a theory does produce Each–We Dilemmas, it is not obvious what this shows. Reconsider prudence. This tells each to do the best he can for himself. We are discussing cases where, if we all act prudently, we are doing what is worse for each. Prudence is here collectively self-defeating. But it is not obvious that this is a fault. Why should a theory be collectively successful? Why is it not enough that, at the individual level, it works?

We might say: 'But a theory cannot apply only to a single individual. If it is rational for me to act prudently, it must be rational for everyone to do so. Any acceptable theory therefore must be successful at the collective level.'

This involves a confusion. Call a theory *universal* if it applies to everyone, *collective* if it claims success at the collective level. Some theories have both features. One example is a Kantian morality. This tells each to do only what he could rationally will everyone to do. The plans or policies of each must be tested at the collective level. For a Kantian, the essence of morality is the move from *each* to *we*.

At the collective level—as an answer to the question, 'How should we all act?'—prudence *would* condemn itself. Suppose that we are choosing what code of conduct will be publicly encouraged, or taught in schools. It would here be prudent to vote against prudence. If we are choosing a collective code, the prudent choice would be morality.

Prudence is a universal theory, applying to everyone. But

it is not a collective code. It is a theory of individual rationality. This answers the smaller question that we asked above. In Prisoner's Dilemmas, where it is only collectively self-defeating, prudence does not condemn itself.

IV

Many bad theories do not condemn themselves. So the larger question remains open. In such cases, what it is rational to do?

It may help to introduce another common theory. This tells each to do what will best achieve his present aims. Call this *the instrumental theory*. Suppose that, in some Prisoner's Dilemma, my aim is the outcome which is best for me. On the instrumental theory, it is then the prudent choice which is rational. If my aim is to benefit others, or to apply the Kantian Test, it is the altruistic choice which is rational. If my aim is to do what others do—perhaps because I do not wish to be a free-rider—it is uncertain which choice is rational. This depends on my beliefs about what others do.

As these remarks show, the instrumental theory may conflict with prudence. What will best achieve my present aims may be against my own long-term self-interest. Since the two theories may conflict, those who believe in prudence must reject the instrumental theory.

They might point out that, even at the individual level, it can be self-defeating. It can produce intertemporal Dilemmas. These will be most common if I care less about my further future. Suppose that, at different times, I have conflicting aims. At each time I could either (1) do what will best achieve my present aims or (2) do what will best achieve, or enable me to achieve, all of my aims over time. On the instrumental theory, I should always do (1) rather than (2). Only so will I at each time do the best I can in instrumental terms. But over time I may then do worse, in these same terms. Over time, I may be less successful in achieving my aims at each time. (Here is a trivial example. At each time I will best achieve my present aims if I then waste no energy on being tidy. But if I am never tidy this may cause me at each later time to achieve less.)

Those who believe in prudence may appeal to such cases. They might say: 'The instrumental theory is here self-defeating. Even in this theory's terms, prudence is superior. The prudent act is (2). If you always do (2) rather than (1), you will more effectively achieve your aims at each time. If you are prudent, you do better even in instrumental terms.'

N n

Consequentialism

This is again too swift. I do better *over time*. But *at each time* I do worse. If I always do (2), I am at each time doing what will less effectively achieve the aims that I then have. (1) is what will best achieve these. Remember the interpersonal Dilemma. For the word 'we' substitute 'I over time', and for the word 'each' substitute 'I at each time'. In the interpersonal Dilemma, we do better only if each does worse than he could. In the intertemporal Dilemma, I do better over time only if at each time I do worse than I then could.

We must again distinguish two levels. The instrumental theory is here *intertemporally* self-defeating. But it does not claim to be successful at the intertemporal level. So it does not condemn itself. It is not a failure in its own terms.

Those who believe in prudence must claim that, none the less, it should be rejected. They might say: 'Any acceptable theory must be intertemporally successful. It is no defence that the instrumental theory does not claim such success. That merely shows it to be structurally flawed. If a theory is intertemporally self-defeating, this is enough to show that it should be rejected.'

This is a dangerous argument. If it refutes the instrumental theory that it is intertemporally self-defeating, why does it not refute prudence that it is collectively self-defeating? And if it is a good reply that prudence does not claim to be collectively successful, why can the instrumental theorist not make a similar reply?

As this shows, prudence can be challenged from two directions. This makes it harder to defend. Answers to either challenge may undermine answers to the other.

One challenge comes from moral theories. The other challenge need not come from the instrumental theory. It can come from theories which are more plausible. The instrumental theory has two features. It is *time-relative*: appealing to the agent's aims at the time of acting. And it is *purely instrumental*: it discusses only means, taking the agent's aims as given. According to this theory, no aim is irrational. Any aim can provide reasons for acting.

Other theories are time-relative, but not purely instrumental. One example is *the deliberative theory*. This appeals, not to the agent's actual aims at the time of acting, but to the aims he would then have, if he knew the facts and was thinking clearly. According to this theory, if an aim would not survive such deliberation, it does not provide good reasons for acting.

THE PRISONER'S DILEMMA 553

A deliberative theorist may add further claims. He may say that, even if they would survive this test, certain kinds of aim are intrinsically irrational.

Since it is time-relative, the deliberative theory may conflict with prudence. Someone may be thinking clearly, yet have aims which he knows to be against his own long-term self-interest. And we may deny that all such aims are thereby shown to be irrational. We may believe that there are many aims which are not less rational than the pursuit of self-interest. Some examples might be: benefiting others, discovering truths, or creating beauty. On a time-relative theory, what it is rational for me to do now depends on which among these many aims are the ones that I have now.

Those who believe in prudence must reject such theories. They must claim that reasons for acting cannot be time-relative. They might say: 'The force of a reason extends over time. Since I *will* have reason to promote my future aims, I have reason to do so *now*.' This claim is at the heart of prudence.

Many moral theorists make a second claim. They believe that certain reasons are not agent-relative. They might say: 'The force of a reason may extend, not only over time, but over different lives. Thus, if *you* have reason to relieve your pain, this is a reason for me too. *I* have a reason to relieve *your* pain.'

Prudence makes the first claim, but rejects the second. It may be hard to defend both halves of this position. In reply to the moralist, the prudent man may ask, 'Why should *I* give weight to aims which are not *mine*?' But he can then be asked, 'Why should I give weight *now* to aims which are not mine *now*?' He may answer by appealing to the intertemporal Dilemmas, where time-relative theories are intertemporally self-defeating. But he can then be challenged with the interpersonal Dilemmas, where his own theory is collectively self-defeating. The moralist might say: 'The argument for prudence carries us beyond prudence. Properly understood, it is an argument for morality.'

This is a tempting line of thought. But something else should be discussed first. At the interpersonal level, the contrast is *not* between prudence and morality.

V

It will help to draw some more distinctions. We have been considering different theories about rationality. We can describe such theories by saying what they tell us to try to achieve.

According to all these theories, we should try to act rationally. Call this our *formal* aim. We can ignore this here. By 'aims' we can mean *substantive* aims. We can describe moral theories in the same way. According to all these theories, we should try to act morally. Different moral theories give us different substantive aims.

We can next distinguish two ways in which a theory might be substantively self-defeating. Call this theory *T*, and the aims it gives us *our T-given aims*. Say that we *successfully follow T* when each succeeds in doing what, of the acts available, best achieves his T-given aims. Call T

> *indirectly self-defeating* when we will best achieve our T-given aims only if we do not try to do so,

and

> *directly self-defeating* when we will best achieve our T-given aims only if we do not successfully follow T.

Consider first a moral theory: Act Consequentialism, or *AC*. This gives to all one common aim: the best possible outcome. If we try to achieve this aim, we may often fail. Even when we succeed, the fact that we are disposed to try might make the outcome worse. AC might thus be indirectly self-defeating. What does this show? A consequentialist might say: 'It shows that AC should be only one part of our moral theory. It should be the part that covers successful acts. When we are certain to succeed, we should aim for the best possible outcome. Our wider theory should be this: we should have the aims and dispositions having which would make the outcome best. This wider theory would not be self-defeating. So the objection has been met.'

Could AC be *directly* self-defeating? Could it be true that we will make the outcome best only if we do not successfully follow AC? This is not possible. We successfully follow AC when each does what, of the acts available, makes the outcome best. This does not ensure that our acts jointly produce the best possible outcome. But, if they do, we must be successfully following AC. So AC cannot be directly self-defeating.

We can widen this conclusion. When any theory *T* gives to all agents *common* aims, it cannot be directly self-defeating. If we cause these common aims to be best achieved, we must be successfully following T. So it cannot be true that we will best achieve our T-given aims only if we do not successfully follow T.

What if T gives to *different* agents *different* aims? There may then be no way in which we can *best* achieve the T-given aims

THE PRISONER'S DILEMMA 555

of each. So we must change our definition. And we need our earlier distinction. Call T

> *directly individually self-defeating* when it is certain that, if someone successfully follows T, he will thereby cause his T-given aims to be worse achieved,

and

> *directly collectively self-defeating* when it is certain that, if all rather than none successfully follow T, we will thereby cause the T-given aims of each to be worse achieved.

Suppose that T gives to you and me different aims. And suppose that each could either (1) promote his own T-given aim or (2) more effectively promote the other's. The outcomes would be these:

	You	
	do (1)	do (2)
I do (1)	The T-given aim of each is third-best achieved	Mine is best achieved, yours worst
I do (2)	Mine is worst achieved, yours best	The T-given aim of each is second-best achieved

Suppose finally that neither's choice will affect the other's. It will then be true of each that, if he does (1) rather than (2), he will thereby cause his T-given aim to be better achieved. This is so whatever the other does. So we both successfully follow T only if we both do (1) rather than (2). Only then is each doing what, of the acts available, best achieves his T-given aim. But it is certain that if both rather than neither successfully follow T—if both do (1) rather than (2)—we will thereby cause the T-given aim of each to be worse achieved. Theory T is here directly collectively self-defeating.

If for 'T' we substitute 'prudence', we have just described a Prisoner's Dilemma. As this shows, nothing depends on the content of prudence. Such cases may occur when

> (*a*) theory T is *agent-relative*, giving to different agents different aims,

> (*b*) the achievement of each person's aim partly depends on what others do,

and

> (*c*) what each does will not affect what these others do.

556   PROCEEDINGS OF THE BRITISH ACADEMY

These conditions may hold if for 'T' we substitute 'common-sense morality'.

VI

Most of us believe that there are certain people to whom we have special obligations. These are the people to whom we stand in certain relations—such as our children, parents, pupils, patients, members of our own trade union, or those whom we represent. We believe we ought to help these people in certain ways. We should try to protect them from certain kinds of harm, and should try to give them certain kinds of benefit. Common-sense morality largely consists in such obligations.

Carrying out these obligations has priority over helping strangers. This priority is not absolute. We may not believe that I ought to save my child from some minor harm rather than saving a stranger's life. But I ought to protect my child rather than saving strangers from *somewhat* greater harms. My duty to my child is not overridden whenever I could do somewhat greater good elsewhere.

When I try to protect my child, what should my aim be? Should it simply be that he is not harmed? Or should it rather be that he is saved from harm by me? If you would have a better chance of saving him from harm, I would be wrong to insist that the attempt be made by me. This suggests that my aim should take the simpler form. Let us assume that this is so.

Consider *the Parent's Dilemma*. We cannot communicate. But each could either (1) save his own child from some harm or (2) save the other's child from another somewhat greater harm. The outcomes would be these:

		You	
		do (1)	do (2)
I	do (1)	Both our children suffer the greater harm	Mine suffers neither harm, yours both
	do (2)	Mine suffers both, yours neither	Both suffer the lesser harm

Since we cannot communicate, neither's choice will affect the other's. If the aim of each should be that his child not be harmed, each should here do (1) rather than (2). Each would thus ensure that his child is harmed less. This is so whatever the other does. But if both do (1) rather than (2) both our children will be harmed more.

Consider next those benefits which I ought to try to give my child. What should my aim here be? Should I insist that it be *I* who benefits my child, if I knew that this would be worse for him? Some would answer, 'No'. But this answer may be too sweeping. It treats parental care as a mere means. We may think it more than that. We may agree that, with some kinds of benefit, my aim should take the simpler form. It should simply be that the outcome be better for my child. But there may be other kinds of benefit, which my child should receive *from me*.

With both kinds of benefit, we can face Parent's Dilemmas. Consider *Case Two*. We cannot communicate. But each could either (1) benefit his own child or (2) benefit the other's child somewhat more. The outcomes would be these:

	You do (1)	do (2)
I do (1)	Third-best for both our children	Best for mine, worst for yours
I do (2)	Worst for mine, best for yours	Second-best for both

If my aim should here be that the outcome be better for my child, I should again do (1) rather than (2). And the same holds for you. But if both do (1) rather than (2) that will be worse for both our children. Compare *Case Three*. We cannot communicate. But I could either (1) enable myself to give my child some benefit or (2) enable you to benefit yours somewhat more. You have the same alternatives with respect to me. The outcomes would be these:

	You do (1)	do (2)
I do (1)	Each can give his child some benefit	I can benefit mine most, you can benefit yours least
I do (2)	I can benefit mine least, you can benefit yours most	Each can benefit his child more

If my aim should here be that I benefit my child, I should

242

Consequentialism

again do (1) rather than (2). And the same holds for you. But if both do (1) rather than (2) each can benefit his child less. Note the difference between these two examples. In Case Two we are concerned with what happens. The aim of each is that the outcome be better for his child. This is an aim that the other can directly cause to be achieved. In Case Three we are concerned with what we *do*. Since my aim is that *I* benefit my child, you cannot, on my behalf, do so. But you might enable me to do so. You might thus indirectly help my aim to be achieved.

Two-Person Parent's Dilemmas are unlikely to occur. But we often face many-person versions. It is often true that, if all rather than none give priority to our own children, that will either be worse for all our children, or will enable each to benefit his children less. Thus there are many outcomes which would benefit our children whether or not we help to produce them. It can be true of each parent that, if he does not help, that will be better for his own children. He can spend what he saves—whether in money, time, or energy—directly on them. But if none help, that will be worse for all our children than if all do. In another common case, each could either (1) add to his own earnings or (2) (by self-restraint) add more to the earnings of others. It will here be true of each that, if he does (1) rather than (2), he can benefit his children more. This is so whatever others do. But if all do (1) rather than (2) each can benefit his children less. These are only two of the ways in which such cases can occur. There are many others.

Similar remarks apply to all similar obligations—such as those to pupils, patients, clients, or constituents. With all such obligations, there are countless many-person versions of my three examples. They are as common, and as varied, as prudential Each–We Dilemmas. As we have just seen, they will often have the same cause. Here is another way in which this might be true. Suppose that, in the original case, it is our lawyers who must choose. This is the *Prisoner's Lawyer's Dilemma*. If both lawyers give priority to their own clients, that will be worse for both clients than if neither does. Any prudential Dilemma may thus yield a moral Dilemma. If one group face the former, another may in consequence face the latter. This can be so if we believe that each member of the second group ought to give priority to some members of the first. The problem comes from the giving of priority. It makes no difference whether this is given to oneself or certain others.

My examples all involve harms or benefits. But the problem

THE PRISONER'S DILEMMA 559

can arise for other parts of common-sense morality. It can arise whenever this morality gives to different people different duties. Suppose that each could either (1) carry out some of his own duties or (2) enable others to carry out more of theirs. If all rather than none give priority to our own duties, each may be able to carry out fewer. Deontologists can face Each–We Dilemmas. But I shall not discuss these here.

VII

What do such cases show? Common-sense morality is the moral theory most of us accept. According to this theory, there are certain things that each of us ought to try to achieve. These are what I call our 'moral aims'. We successfully follow this moral theory when each does what, of the acts available, best achieves his moral aims. In my cases it is certain that, if all rather than none successfully follow this theory, we will thereby cause the moral aims of each to be worse achieved. Our moral theory is here directly collectively self-defeating. Is this an objection?

Let us start with a smaller question. Could we revise our theory, so that it would not be self-defeating? If there is no such revision, ours may be the best possible theory. Since we believe our theory, we should ask what is the smallest such revision. So we should first identify the part of our theory which is self-defeating.

It will help to bring together two distinctions. One part of a moral theory may cover *successful acts*, on the assumption of *full compliance*. Call this part *ideal act theory*. This says what we should all try to do, simply on the assumptions that we all try, and all succeed. Call this *what we should all ideally do*.

Note next that, in my examples, what is true is this. If *all* of us *successfully* follow our moral theory, it will be self-defeating. It is our ideal act theory which is self-defeating. If we ought to revise our theory, this is the part that must certainly be revised.

The revision would be this. Call our theory *M*. In such cases we should all ideally do what will cause the M-given aims of each to be better achieved. Thus in my Parent's Dilemmas we should all ideally do (2) rather than (1). That will make the outcome better for all our children, and will enable each to benefit his children more.

Call this revision *R*. Note first that R applies only to those cases where M is self-defeating. If we decide to adopt R, we will need to consider how such cases can be recognized. I believe that they are very common. But I have no space to show this here.

Note next that R is restricted to our ideal act theory. It does not say what we ought to do when there are some others who do not follow R. Nor does it say what our aims should be when our attempts may fail. Nor does it say what dispositions we should have. Since these are the questions with most practical importance, it may seem that adopting R would make little difference. But this is not likely. If we revise this part of our theory, we shall probably revise the rest. Take the case of a public good which would benefit our children. One such good is the conservation of a scarce resource. Suppose that we are fishermen, trying to feed our children. We are faced with declining stocks. It is true of each that, if he does not restrict his catch, that will be better for his own children. This is so whatever others do. But if none restrict their catches that will be worse for all our children than if all do. According to R, we should all ideally restrict our catches. If some fail to do so, R ceases to apply. But it would be natural to make this further claim: each should restrict his catch provided that enough others do so too. We would need to decide what counts as enough. But, whatever we decide, adopting R would have made a difference. Failure to restrict our catches would now be at most a defensive second-best. Consider next the relation between acts and dispositions. Suppose that each could either (1) save his own child from some lesser harm or (2) save another's child from some greater harm. According to R, we should all ideally do (2). Should we be *disposed* to do (2)? If the lesser harms would themselves be great, such a disposition might be incompatible with love for our own children. This may lead us to decide that we should remain disposed to do (1). This would mean that, in such cases, our children would be harmed more; but, if we are to love them, this is the price they must pay. Such remarks cannot be made whenever M is self-defeating. It would be possible to love one's children and contribute to most public goods. Nor could such remarks cover all similar obligations—such as those to pupils, patients, clients, or constituents. It is therefore likely that, if we adopt R, we will be led to change our view about some dispositions.

We can now return to the main question. Ought we to adopt R? Is it an objection to our moral theory that, in certain cases, it is self-defeating? If it is, R is the obvious remedy. R revises M only where M is self-defeating. And the only difference is that R is not.

Remember first that, in these cases, M is *directly* self-defeating.

The problem is not that, in our attempts to follow M, we are somehow failing. That might be no objection. The problem is that we all *successfully* follow M. Each succeeds in doing what, of the acts available, best achieves his M-given aims. This is what makes M self-defeating. And this does seem an objection. If there is any assumption on which a moral theory should *not* be self-defeating, it is surely the assumption that it is universally successful followed.

Remember next that by 'aims' I mean substantive aims. I have ignored our formal aim: the avoidance of wrongdoing. This may seem to remove the objection. Take those cases where, if we follow M, either the outcome will be worse for all our children, or each can benefit his children less. We might say: 'These results are, of course, unfortunate. But how could we avoid them? Only by failing to give priority to our own children. That would be wrong. So these cases cast no doubt on our moral theory. Even to achieve our other moral aims, we should never act wrongly.'

These remarks are confused. It is true that, in these cases, M is not formally self-defeating. If we follow M, we are not doing what we believe to be wrong. On the contrary we think it wrong *not* to follow M. But M is substantively self-defeating. Unless we all do what we now think wrong, we will cause our M-given aims to be worse achieved. The question is: Might this show that we are mistaken? Ought we perhaps to do what we *now think* wrong? We cannot answer, 'No—we should never act wrongly.' If we are mistaken, we would *not* be acting wrongly. Nor can we simply say, 'But, even in these cases, we *ought* to give priority to our own children.' This just assumes that we are not mistaken. To defend our theory, we must claim more than this. We must claim that it is no objection to our theory that, in such cases, it is substantively self-defeating.

This would be no objection if it simply did not matter whether our M-given aims will be achieved. But this does matter. The sense in which it matters may be unclear. If we have not acted wrongly, it may not matter morally. But it matters in a way which has moral implications. Why should we try to achieve our M-given aims? Part of the reason is that, in this other sense, their achievement matters.

Someone might say: 'You call M *self*-defeating. So your objection must appeal *to* M. You should not appeal to some rival theory. This is what you have now done. When you claim that it matters whether our M-given aims will be achieved, you

562   PROCEEDINGS OF THE BRITISH ACADEMY

are merely claiming that, if they are not, the outcome would be
worse. This assumes consequentialism. So you beg the question.'
    This is not so. When our aims are held in common, call them
agent-neutral. Other aims are agent-relative. Any aim may be
concerned either with what happens or with what is done.
So there are four kinds of aim. Here are some examples:

	Concerned with	
	what happens	what is done
agent-neutral	that children do not starve	that children are cared for by their own parents
agent-relative	that my children do not starve	that I care for my children

When I claim that it matters whether our M-given aims will be
achieved, I am not assuming consequentialism. Some of these
aims are concerned with what we *do*. Thus parental care may
not be for us a mere means. More important, I am not assuming
agent-neutralism. Since our moral theory is, for the most part,
agent-relative, this would beg the question. But it need not be
begged.
    There are here two points. First, I am not assuming that what
matters is the achievement *of M-given aims*. Suppose that I could
either (1) promote my own M-given aims or (2) more effectively promote yours. According to M, I should here do (1)
rather than (2). I would thereby cause M-given aims to be, on
the whole, worse achieved. But this does not make M self-
defeating. I would cause *my* M-given aims to be *better* achieved.
In my examples the point is not that, if we all do (1) rather
than (2), we cause M-given aims to be worse achieved. The
point is that we cause *each of our own* M-given aims to be worse
achieved. We do worse not just in agent-neutral but in agent-
relative terms.
    The second point is that this can matter in an agent-relative
way. It will help to remember prudence, or *P*. In Prisoner's
Dilemmas, P is directly self-defeating. If all rather than none
successfully follow P, we will thereby cause the P-given aim of
each to be worse achieved. We will make the outcome worse
for everyone. If we believe in prudence, will we think this
matters? Or does it only matter whether each achieves his formal
aim: the avoidance of irrationality? The answer is clear.
According to prudence, acting rationally is a mere means. All

THE PRISONER'S DILEMMA 563

that matters is the achievement of our substantive P-given aims. What concerns us here is this. The achievement of these aims matters in an agent-relative way. To think it an objection that our prudence is self-defeating, we need not appeal to its agent-neutral form: Utilitarianism. Prudence is not a moral theory. But the comparison shows that, in discussing common-sense morality, we need not beg the question. If it matters whether our M-given aims will be achieved, this, too, can matter in an agent-relative way.

Does this matter? Note that I am not asking whether this is all that matters. I am not suggesting that the achievement of our formal aim—the avoidance of wrongdoing—is a mere means. Though assumed by consequentialists, this is not what most of us believe. We may even think that the achievement of our formal aim always matters most. But this is here irrelevant. We are asking whether it casts doubt on M that it is substantively self-defeating. Might this show that, in such cases, M is incorrect? It may be true that what matters most is that we avoid wrongdoing. But this truth cannot show M to be correct. It cannot help us to decide what *is* wrong.

Can we claim that our formal aim is all that matters? If that were so, my examples would show nothing. We could say, 'To be substantively self-defeating is, in the case of common-sense morality, *not* to be self-defeating.' Can we defend our moral theory in this way? In the case of some M-given aims, perhaps we can. Consider trivial promises. We might believe both that we should try to keep such promises, and that it would not matter if, through no fault of ours, we fail. But we do not have such beliefs about all of our M-given aims. If our children suffer harm, or we can benefit them less, this matters.

Remember finally that, in my examples, M is collectively *but not individually* self-defeating. Could this provide a defence?

This is the central question I have raised. It is because M is individually successful that, at the collective level, it is here *directly* self-defeating. Why is it true that, if we all do (1) rather than (2), we *successfully* follow M? Because *each* is doing what, of the acts available, *best* achieves his M-given aims. Is it perhaps no objection that *we* thereby cause the M-given aims of each to be *worse* achieved?

It will again help to remember prudence. In Prisoner's Dilemmas, prudence is collectively self-defeating. If we were choosing a collective code, something that we will all follow, prudence would here tell us to reject itself. It would be prudent to vote against prudence. But those who believe in prudence may think this irrelevant. They can say: 'Prudence does not claim to be a collective code. To be collectively self-defeating is, in the case of prudence, *not* to be self-defeating.'

Can we defend our moral theory in this way? This depends on our view about the nature of morality. On most views, the answer is 'No'. But I must here leave this question open.[1]

[1] Many other questions need to be discussed. How, for instance, is revision R related to agent-neutralism? I hope to say more in a book on self-defeating theories (to be written for the OUP). In preparing this Lecture I have been greatly helped by R. M. Adams, R. M. Dworkin, J. L. Mackie, D. Regan, and J. J. Thomson; also by B. Barry, S. Blackburn, D. Braybrooke, P. Bricker, L. J. Cohen, N. E. Davis, D. Dennett, M. G. J. Evans, P. Foot, J. P. Griffin, G. Harman, M. Hollis, S. Kagan, R. Lindley, P. Maddy, T. Nagel, R. Nozick, C. Peacocke, J. Raz, J. Sartorelli, T. Scanlon, F. Schick, A. K. Sen, J. H. Sobel, H. Steiner, and L. Temkin. My sections III and IV owe a great deal to T. Nagel, *The Possibility of Altruism* (Oxford, 1970). My section V owes much to D. Regan, *Utilitarianism and Cooperation*, (Oxford, 1980), D. Lyons, *Forms and Limits of Utilitarianism* (Oxford, 1965), and R. M. Adams, 'Motive Utilitarianism', *Journal of Philosophy*, 12 August 1976. My section II owes much to E. Ullman-Margalit, *The Emergence of Norms* (Oxford, 1977), D. Braybrooke, 'The Insoluble Problem of the Social Contract', *Dialogue*, March 1976, and F. Miller and R. Sartorius, 'Population Policy and Public Goods', *Philosophy & Public Affairs*, Winter 1979. The other publications to which I owe most are: K. Baier, 'Rationality and Morality', *Erkenntnis*, 1977; B. Barry, *Sociologists, Economists, and Democracy* (London, 1970); J. M. Buchanan, *The Demand and Supply of Public Goods* (Chicago, 1969); D. Gauthier, 'Morality and Advantage', *The Philosophical Review*, 1967, and 'Reason and Maximization', *Canadian Journal of Philosophy*, March 1975; G. Hardin, 'The Tragedy of the Commons', *Science*, 13 December 1968; R. M. Hare, 'Ethical Theory and Utilitarianism', in H. D. Lewis (ed.), *Contemporary British Philosophy* (London, 1976); M. Olson Jr., *The Logic of Collective Action* (Cambridge, Mass., 1965); A. Rapoport, *Fights, Games, and Debates* (Ann Arbor, 1960); T. Schelling, 'Hockey Helmets, Concealed Weapons, and Daylight Saving', *The Journal of Conflict Resolution*, September 1973; A. K. Sen, 'Choice, Orderings, and Morality', in S. Körner (ed.), *Practical Reason* (New Haven, 1974); J. H. Sobel, 'The Need for Coercion', in J. Pennock and H. Chapman (eds.), *Coercion* (Chicago, 1972); and J. Watkin, 'Imperfect Rationality', in R, Borger and F. Cioffi (eds.), *Explanation in the Behavioural Sciences* (Cambridge, 1970).

Part VI
Which Options are Relevant?

[15]

Utilitarianism and Alternative Actions

LARS BERGSTRÖM

STOCKHOLM UNIVERSITY

1. INTRODUCTION

We often want to find out, for some person P and situation S, what P ought to do (or ought to have done) in S. We are then assuming that there are in fact two or more alternative actions (or courses of action) open to P in S. If this assumption is not satisfied, there seems to be no point in asking what P ought to do in S. Some moral principles provide a general answer to questions of this kind, and some of these principles involve an explicit or implicit reference to the alternatives open to P in S. Such a reference is explicit, for example, in the following act-utilitarian principle:

(U) For every person P, situation S, and particular action a the following holds: if there are two or more alternatives open to P in S and if a is one of the alternatives open to P in S, then (i) a ought to be done (by P in S) if and only if, for every a' which is different from a and which is one of the alternatives open to P in S, the consequences of a are better than those of a', and (ii) a ought not to be done (by P in S) if and only if there is some a' which is one of the alternatives open to P in S and which is such that the consequences of a are worse than those of a'.

My formulation of this principle is somewhat more complicated than is usual, but there is nothing original about its content. It seems to be accepted, for example, by G.E. Moore in his book *Ethics*, and I believe that it corresponds quite well to the views held by many other utilitarians. In any case, I shall take (U) as a basis for my discussion in this paper.

In order to apply (U) we must be able to answer questions of the following kind: *Which* alternatives, if any, are open to P in S? I am inclined to believe that problems of this kind are much

237

more difficult than is ordinarily supposed. As a matter of fact, I
shall argue that we can probably never know what the alternatives
are in a given case, and that some of the problems involved here
are evaluative rather than empirical. The validity of these claims
depends, of course, upon the interpretation of the expression "the
alternatives open to P in S." This expression may be interpreted in
various ways. Some of these interpretations may be more reasonable than others, but it is important to notice that the reasonable-
ness of a given interpretation may vary with different purposes or
points of view. In the sequel, I shall work towards an interpretation
which is reasonable from the point of view of utilitarian principles
like (U). More precisely, I shall try to find an interpretation which
is at least fairly well in accordance with ordinary usage and relative
to which (U) is as acceptable as possible from a normative point
of view.

Most utilitarian principles provide criteria for the rightness,
wrongness, or obligatoriness of actions. One important and fairly
well-known distinction concerning the interpretation of "action" is
that between individual or *particular actions* on the one hand, and
action-types or classes of (particular) actions or *generic actions* on
the other. It should be noticed that (U) is applicable to particular
actions only. A particular action is associated with a definite agent
and a definite "occasion" or time-interval; it can be performed at
most once. Thus, if G is a generic action (e.g., smoking), P is a person, and t is a time-interval, then P's doing G at t is a particular
action. I use the letter "a" (sometimes with a subscript or super-
script) as a variable ranging over particular actions. If a is identical
with P's doing G at t, I say that P is the agent of a and that t is the
time-interval of a. Notice, that two particular actions may have
very different consequences even if they are instantiations of one
and the same generic action. From now on, when I speak of "actions," I am always referring to particular actions.

2. ALTERNATIVE-SETS

In order to facilitate my subsequent discussion of "alternatives," I shall now introduce some technical expressions. Thus, a_1
and a_2 will be said to be *agent-identical* (*time-identical*) if and
only if the agent (time-interval) of a_1 is the same as that of a_2.
An action a is said to be *performable* if and only if the agent of a
has (or had, or will have) it in his power to perform a. The expres-

sion "-a" denotes the particular "action" which consists in the forbearance to do a; and "$a_1 \cap a_2$" denotes the "action" which consists
in the performance of two agent-identical actions a_1 and a_2. (Notice,
that --a is the same as a. Moreover, the time-interval of -a is the
same as that of a, and the time-interval of $a_1 \cap a_2$ is the union of
the time-intervals of a_1 and a_2.) Two agent-identical actions a_1 and
a_2 are said to be *incompatible* if and only if $a_1 \cap a_2$ is not performable. Any agent-identical and performable actions a_1, a_2, . . . ,
a_n are to be *jointly exhaustive* if and only if -$a_1 \cap$ -$a_2 \cap$ . . . $\cap$ -a_n
is not performable. The notion of an "alternative-set" can then be
defined as follows:

Definition: The set A is an *alternative-set* if and only if the
following conditions are satisfied: (i) A has at least two members,
(ii) every member of A is a particular action, and the members of
A are (iii) agent-identical, (iv) time-identical, (v) performable,
(vi) incompatible in pairs, and (vii) jointly exhaustive.

The main thesis of this section can now be formulated thus:
From the point of view of (U), "the alternatives open to P in S"
should be interpreted in such a way that the alternatives open to
P in S constitute an alternative-set. This thesis may not be self-
evident, and I shall therefore comment upon each of the conditions
(i) through (vii) in order to show that they are all very plausible
in the given context.

(i) It seems almost analytically true that the alternatives open
to P in S should include at least two distinct alternatives. Besides,
(U) would not be applicable to the alternatives open to P in S
unless this condition is satisfied. Hence, it is quite innocent.

(ii) It may be less obvious that each of the alternatives open
to P in S should be a particular action. It might be objected, for
example, that the alternatives open to P in S may often include
forbearances, activities, courses of action, combinations of simultaneous actions, and so on, rather than single actions. However, I
propose to use "action" in such a wide sense that all of these possibilities are covered. (Moreover, actions in my sense need not be
intentional.) In other words, the important content of condition (ii)
is simply that each of the alternatives open to P in S is associated
with a definite agent and a definite time-interval. This is surely
reasonable from the point of view of (U), for many of the consequences of a given alternative may depend upon when and by
whom it is (or might be) performed.

(iii) Like the first two conditions, (iii) is probably quite uncontroversial. It seems very unlikely that anyone would deny that P must be the agent of each of the alternatives open to P in S; and these alternatives are clearly agent-identical if P is the agent of each of them. Moreover, (iii) is well in accordance with the standard formulations of utilitarianism.

(iv) We come now to the requirement that the alternatives open to P in S be time-identical. This requirement is not essential to the conclusions of this paper, but it seems reasonable from the point of view of (U), and it is probably implicit in many standard formulations of utilitarianism. To some extent, it may be supported by arguments of the following kind. Let it be taken for granted that a_1 is one of the alternatives open to P in S, that P is also the agent of another action a_2, that a_2 is performable, and that a_1 and a_2 are incompatible and jointly exhaustive. It may then seem tempting to say that a_1 and a_2 are the alternatives open to P in S. Suppose, however, that a_1 and a_2 are not time-identical. Several cases are possible here, but let us assume that the time-interval of a_1 includes, but is longer than, the time-interval of a_2. It may then be expected that P is the agent of some action a_3 such that $a_2 \cap a_3$ and $a_2 \cap -a_3$ are performable and time-identical with a_1. Suppose that the consequences of $a_2 \cap a_3$ are better than those of a_1, and that the latter are better than those of a_2. Given these assumptions, most act-utilitarians would presumably say that a_1 ought not to be done (by P in S). However, if a_2 were one of the alternatives open to P in S, then a_1 ought to be done according to (U)—provided of course that the incompatibility condition (vi) is satisfied. This result is surely unacceptable from a utilitarian point of view. Hence, it is important that a_2 is not one of the alternatives open to P in S, and this is guaranteed if we require that alternatives be time-identical.

(v) Most people would certainly agree that the alternatives open to P in S must be performable. This appears quite uncontroversial. The only trouble with this requirement seems to be its lack of precision. "Performable" (and, hence, "incompatible" and "jointly exhaustive") is defined in terms of "power," and the interpretation of the latter term is notoriously problematic. However, I shall not attempt to give a more precise meaning to "performable" in this paper.

(vi) The alternatives open to P in S should be incompatible in pairs or mutually exclusive. This requirement is of crucial importance in the present context, but it is also very reasonable. First of all, it seems to be sanctioned by ordinary usage. This claim is supported by several dictionaries. For example, according to *The Concise Oxford Dictionary*, "alternative" means "mutually exclusive"; and according to H. W. Fowler's *Dictionary of Modern English Usage*, the noun "alternative" means "set, especially pair, of possibilities from which *one only* can be selected" (my italics), or "either of such pair or any one of such set," or "second of such pair, the first being in mind," or "other of such a set, one at least being in mind." Second, and more important, it seems that (U) is definitely not acceptable, even from a utilitarian point of view, unless "alternatives" is interpreted in such a way that alternatives are incompatible. In particular, it follows from (U) that if *a* and *a'* are both among the alternatives open to *P* in *S*, and if the consequences of *a* are worse than those of *a'*, then *a* ought not to be done (by *P* in *S*). However, this is only acceptable if alternatives are incompatible. For if *a* and *a'* are not incompatible, then *a* ∩ *a'* is performable; and for all we know it might then be the case that *a* ∩ *a'* ought to be done (or, in other words, that both *a* and *a'* ought to be done). This is clearly inconsistent with the conclusion that *a* ought not to be done. Hence, from the point of view of (U) in particular, the alternatives open to *P* in *S* must be incompatible in pairs.

(vii) Finally, it seems quite obvious that (U) is only acceptable if "alternatives" is interpreted in such a way that the alternatives open to *P* in *S* are jointly exhaustive. This can easily be shown. It follows from (U) that if *a* and *a'* are the only alternatives open to *P* in *S*, and if the consequences of *a* are better than those of *a'*, then *a* ought to be done (by *P* in *S*). But this is only acceptable if alternatives are jointly exhaustive. If *a* and *a'* are not jointly exhaustive, then -*a* ∩ -*a'* is performable, and for all we know it might then be the case that -*a* ∩ -*a'* ought to be done (or, in other words, that neither *a* nor *a'* ought to be done). This is clearly inconsistent with the earlier conclusion that *a* ought to be done. Hence, from the point of view of (U), the alternatives open to *P* in *S* must be jointly exhaustive. I also believe that this requirement is well in accordance with ordinary usage, even if it is often forgotten in actual situations of choice.

I have now given what seems to be sufficient support for the thesis that, in the context of (U), "the alternatives open to *P* in *S*" should be interpreted in such a way that the alternatives open to *P* in *S* constitute an alternative-set in my sense. The validity of this thesis will be presupposed in the sequel.

3. RIVAL ALTERNATIVE-SETS

Let us say that A is an alternative-set *for* P in S if and only if A is an alternative-set, P is the agent of every action in A, and every action in A is performable by P in S. Of course, the alternatives open to P in S should constitute an alternative-set for P in S. Unfortunately, however, this does not take us very far when we want to determine the alternatives open to P in S, for there are probably very often, or perhaps even always, several rival alternative-sets for a given agent in a given situation. I shall now exemplify this claim.

Suppose that I am wondering whether I ought to work on this paper tomorrow (a_1) or to take a day off (a_2), and that $\{a_1, a_2\}$ is an alternative-set for me in the situation in question. It seems quite possible, however, that a_1 and a_2 may be performed in many different ways. For example, if I work on this paper tomorrow I may (a_3) or I may not ($-a_3$) re-write section 2. We may say that $a_1 \cap a_3$ and $a_1 \cap -a_3$ are different versions of a_1. In general, I shall say that a' is a *version* of a if and only if a' is different from but agent-identical and time-identical with a, and it is logically necessary that if a' is performed then a is also performed. Again, I may go to the theatre tomorrow night (a_4) or I may refrain from doing so ($-a_4$). Now, $a_1 \cap a_4$ is not a version of a_1, for these actions are not time-identical. However, let us say that a' is a *quasi-version* of a if and only if a' is agent-identical but not time-identical with a, and it is logically necessary that if a' is performed then a is also performed. It is clear that $a_1 \cap a_4$ and $a_1 \cap -a_4$ are different (and incompatible) quasi-versions of a_1. If I take a day off tomorrow I may take a trip into the country (a_5) or I may stay at home (a_6). If I take a trip into the country I may bring (a_7) or not bring ($-a_7$) my family. In other words, $a_2 \cap a_5$, $a_2 \cap a_6$, $a_2 \cap a_5 \cap -a_7$, and so on, are different versions of a_2. Now consider the following sets:

$A_1 = \{a_1, a_2\}$
$A_2 = \{a_1 \cap a_3, a_1 \cap -a_3, a_2\}$
$A_3 = \{a_1, a_2 \cap a_5, a_2 \cap -a_5\}$
$A_4 = \{a_1 \cap a_4, a_1 \cap -a_4, a_2 \cap a_4, a_2 \cap -a_4\}$
$A_5 = \{a_1 \cap a_3, a_1 \cap -a_3, a_2 \cap a_5 \cap a_7, a_2 \cap a_5 \cap -a_7, a_2 \cap -a_5\}$

It seems very plausible to assume that all these sets, as well as a great many others, are alternative-sets for me in the situation in question. In other words, it seems that I am confronted with several rival alternative-sets. But if this is the case, what *are* the alternatives open to me in the situation? For example, is a_1 one of the alternatives open to me? Or is $a_1 \cap a_3$ one of the alternatives? One thing is certain: both these actions cannot be among the alternatives open to me, for they are not incompatible. In general, the union of two or more alternative-sets is not itself an alternative-set. Hence, it seems that we have to make a choice among $A_1, A_2, \ldots, A_5, \ldots$, and so on. But which of these alternative-sets ought to be selected? Which is the "relevant" one? As far as I can see, there is no easy solution to problems of this kind.

It might be thought that the existence of rival alternative-sets is of no importance in practice. Thus, it might be held, for example, that it does not matter whether (U) is applied to A_1 or to A_2 or to . . . or to A_5. But such a view can hardly be accepted. It may perhaps be acceptable in some special cases, but it is probably not acceptable in general. Suppose, for example, that the consequences of a_1 are better than those of a_2, but that the consequences of $a_2 \cap a_5$ are better than those of a_1. This assumption is quite plausible. But then, if (U) is applied to A_1—i.e., if (U) is applied to a_1 and a_2 with the presupposition that these are the only alternatives open to me in the situation in question—it follows that a_1 ought to be done. On the other hand, if (U) is applied to A_3 it follows that a_1 ought not to be done. These normative conclusions are clearly inconsistent. Hence, it does indeed make a normative difference whether (U) is applied to A_1 or to A_2, even though both are alternative-sets for me in the situation.

The last point may be generalized. Let us say that two or more alternative-sets are *(U)-inconsistent* if and only if the normative conclusions which follow when (U) is applied to these alternative-sets are inconsistent. Thus, in my example, A_1 and A_3 are (U)-inconsistent. In general, it seems very reasonable to assume that *rival alternative-sets are often (U)-inconsistent*. It is not difficult to find plausible instances of this thesis. Let me mention just one more example of this. Suppose, that the consequences of $a_1 \cap a_4$ are better than those of any other action in A_4. This is plausible, for I may not be able to enjoy the theatre properly if I have taken a day off. If (U) is applied to A_4 it would then follow that $a_1 \cap a_4$ ought to be done. This is surely inconsistent with the statement that a_1 ought not to be done. Hence, A_4 and A_3 are (U)-inconsistent.

4. Relevant Alternative-Sets

Now, if rival alternative-sets are sometimes (U)-inconsistent, it seems extremely desirable from the point of view of (U)—as well as from the point of view of common sense—to have some criterion for distinguishing the "relevant" alternative-set for a given agent in a given situation. By saying that A is the *relevant* alternative-set for P in S I mean that A is an alternative-set which contains those and only those actions which are *the* alternatives open to P in S. In this section I shall consider the problem of finding a workable and normatively reasonable criterion which distinguishes relevant alternative-sets.

4.1. *Minimum Alternative-Sets*

Let us say that an alternative-set which contains only two distinct actions is a *minimum* alternative-set. Thus, for any action a which is a member of some alternative-set, $\{a, -a\}$ is a minimum alternative-set. In the case described in section 3 $\{a_1, a_2\}$ is a minimum alternative-set; there does not seem to be any practical difference between $\{a_1, a_2\}$ and $\{a_1, -a_1\}$.

Now it might be held that the relevant alternative-set for P in S is always a minimum alternative-set. I do not know whether anybody would seriously suggest this, but it seems that in practice people very often reason in accordance with this criterion. In actual situations of choice we often ask ourselves 'Shall I or shall I not do this?'. This suggests that we have a minimum alternative-set in mind.

I do not want to deny that minimum alternative-sets may be relevant in some cases; but, in general, the criterion that the relevant alternative-set for P in S is always a minimum alternative-set seems extremely unhelpful. With respect to the example described in section 3 it might be taken to suggest that $A_1 = \{a_1, a_2\}$ is the relevant alternative-set, but this may reasonably be doubted. Another minimum alternative-set for me in that situation is $\{a_2 \cap a_5, -(a_2 \cap a_5)\}$ and this set is presumably (U)-inconsistent with A_1 (given our earlier assumptions). In general, the criterion under discussion is clearly insufficient, for there are probably always several different minimum alternative-sets for a given person in a given situation. Indeed, there seems to be no reason for accepting it at all. I am inclined to maintain that we have to look for some other criterion.

4.2. *Maximum Alternative-Sets*

It might be held that the alternatives open to P in S are all those actions which are performable by P in S. Many people might regard this view as very reasonable or even self-evident, and it also seems that philosophers often write as if they would accept it. From the point of view of (U), at least, this suggestion is *prima facie* unacceptable, for the set consisting of all the actions which are performable by P in S is seldom if ever an alternative-set at all; hence, if (U) were applied to such a set, we would probably often get normative conclusions which are inconsistent. This can be seen, for example, in the case described in section 3. However, it might be held that it is possible to interpret "all those actions which are performable by P in S" in such a way that these actions do constitute an alternative-set. In particular, let us say that A is the *maximum* alternative-set for P in S if and only if A is an alternative-set for P in S and A has a greater number of members than any other alternative-set for P in S. It might be held that "all those actions which are performable by P in S" should be taken to refer merely to those actions which are members of the maximum alternative-set for P in S. Whether or not this is a reasonable interpretation, it might be held that the relevant alternative-set for P in S is always identical with the maximum alternative-set for P in S.

But this criterion, too, seems to involve certain difficulties. In particular, it seems far from obvious that there really is a unique and definite maximum alternative-set for a given person in a given situation. For one thing, this would presuppose that there is always a definite time-interval associated with a given person and situation, and this does not seem to be the case for any ordinary use of "situation." For example, in the situation described in section 3, it is hard to see whether a_1 or $a_1 \cap a_4$ (or neither of these actions) is time-identical with the actions in the maximum alternative-set for me in that situation (if there is such a set). It might of course be suggested, at this point, that "situation" should be defined in such a way that a reference to a definite time-interval has to be included in the very description of a situation. For example, it might be held that a situation is the state of the world (or the successive states of the world) within a particular time-interval. But even if this would guarantee the existence of a unique maximum alternative-set for every person and situation, it would probably not be acceptable from the point of view of (U). A given person would presumably then be more or less simultaneously confronted with a great many different maximum alternative-sets, and these would probably sometimes be (U)-inconsistent. For example, it might very well turn out that a_1 ought not to be done relative to one maximum alternative-set, but that $a_1 \cap a_4$ ought to be done relative to another. (In view of this, some people might be inclined to say that there is only one maximum alternative-set for a given person; in other words, it might be suggested that P's entire lifetime is the time-interval of the actions in the maximum (and relevant) alternative-set for P in every situation. Such a proposal would take us very far away from the intuitive content of ordinary utilitarianism. (U) would then pick out (sets of) "obligatory lives" rather than obligatory actions. Besides, (U) would hardly be normatively acceptable with this interpretation. Most of us have already deviated from our obligatory lives, and we may therefore be obligated to do certain actions which we ought not to have done if we had always done what we ought to do, but these actions ought not to be done according to this new version of (U).)

Moreover, there is probably seldom if ever a definite limit to the number of actions which a given person has it in his power to perform within a given time-interval. Hence, even if the problem of time-intervals were solved, the existence of maximum alternative-sets may reasonably be doubted. And even if there always is a unique maximum alternative-set for P in S, it seems fairly obvious that we can never determine such a set in practice. On the contrary, we can be pretty certain that any given set of actions is not a maximum alternative-set. Hence, the criterion under discussion here does not seem very promising.

4.3. *Personalistic Criteria*

It seems reasonable to assume that different persons may perceive different "alternatives" for a given agent in a given situation. Such differences may depend upon different interpretations of "alternative," but they may also depend upon differences in personality, accepted norms and evaluations, opinions as to what the situation in question is, and beliefs about the consequences of different actions. For example, if you have a greater power of imagination or a greater tolerance of complications than I have, you may "see" more alternatives than I do in a given case; if I maintain that a is one of the alternatives but you believe that two performable versions of *a* have significantly different consequences, then you might hold that these versions rather than *a* are among the alternatives. Again I may insist that *a* is an alternative on the ground that although the consequences of the versions of *a* are different they are equally valuable, and hence the versions need not be distinguished.

Now in order to determine the alternatives in a given case we might take somebody's intuitions or perceptions as a criterion or point of departure. Criteria which are constructed in this way may be called "personalistic criteria." For example, it might be held that the alternatives open to P in S are those actions which P is aware of and believes that he has it in his power to perform in S. Let us call these actions "the agent's alternatives" for P in S.

It seems quite possible that the agent's alternatives for P in S do not constitute an alternative-set. But we could perhaps transform the set consisting of the agent's alternatives into an alternative-set by means of certain rules. (We may require that the rules be "innocent" in the sense that they preserve as much as possible of the agent's intuitions.) Let us suppose that this could be done, and let us say that the results of this transformation is the *subjective* alternative-set for P in S. It might be held that the relevant alternative-set for P in S is always identical with the subjective alternative-set for P in S.

But this criterion is surely rather arbitrary. It is hard to see why the agent's perception should always be decisive. Moreover, in some cases there may be strong normative reasons for saying that the subjective alternative-set is not relevant; the criterion may lead to unacceptable normative conclusions when (U) is applied (for example, that a certain action ought not to be done even though some version of it has better consequences than every action in the subjective alternative-set).

As far as I can see it would be normatively unreasonable always to rely upon the agent's perceptions, partly because the agent may be stupid, unimaginative, and so on. It would perhaps be less unreasonable to rely upon the perceptions of so-called ideal observers. For example, it might be suggested that A is the relevant alternative-set for P in S if and only if A is an alternative-set for P in S, and for every ideal observer O, if O had carefully considered the question of what alternatives are open to P in S, and if O had at least as much information as anybody else about P, S, and the consequences of different actions performable by P in S, then O would have been willing to accept the view that the members of A are the alternatives open to P in S.

But even if this criterion is less arbitrary than the earlier one it seems to involve certain difficulties. For example, it seems quite possible that even if there are several alternative-sets for P in S, none of these satisfy the criterion. Different ideal observers may have different views. To a certain extent this seems to depend upon the characteristics that we require of an ideal observer. It seems reasonable to require that he be intelligent and imaginative. But to what extent? And should we also require that he accept (U)? Or that he accept the "correct" evaluations? If we require too much, nobody will be an ideal observer. If we require too little, there will be several ideal observers and these may have different views. We might modify the criterion so as to rely upon the views of the majority of ideal observers, but there may be no majority, or there may be a majority for more than one view. Besides, the view of some minority may be more "reliable" or normatively acceptable. Moreover, even if the ideal observers agree, they may have no definite opinion; several different alternative-sets may perhaps satisfy the criterion in a given case. Finally, even if there is always one and only one alternative-set which satisfies the criterion, we can probably never know what it is.

4.4 *Teleological Criteria*

From a utilitarian or teleological point of view it may be reasonable to say that the relevant alternative-set for P in S should in some way depend upon the relative value of the consequences of different actions which are performable by P in S. Consider, for example, the case described in section 3, and suppose that it is claimed that A_1 is the relevant alternative-set in that case. It seems that two different arguments may be advanced against this claim from a teleological point of view. First, it might be held that the claim is *normatively misleading*. For we may assume as before that the consequences of a_1 are better than those of a_2, but that the consequences of $a_2 \cap a_5$ are better than those of a_1; it may then be unacceptable from a utilitarian or teleological point of view to conclude that a_1 ought to be done, which would follow if A_1 were the relevant alternative-set. Second, there is a somewhat weaker objection to the claim that A_1 is relevant, namely that this claim is *normatively insufficient*. By this I mean, very roughly, that a_1 and a_2 are not sufficiently "specific"; there is too great a difference in value between the consequences of different versions or quasi-versions of these actions. What I ought to do is perhaps $a_1 \cap a_4$, but in order to arrive at this conclusion it is not sufficient to consider A_1.

Criteria which make the relevant alternative-set for P in S dependent upon the relative value of the consequences of different actions which are performable by P in S may be called "teleological criteria." I am in fact inclined to think that some teleological criterion should be accepted, and the ideas which lie behind the two arguments which have been sketched above may perhaps be used as a basis for such a criterion. Our problem may be roughly indicated as follows: granted that a minimum alternative-set is "too small" and that a maximum alternative-set (if there is such a thing) is "too large," how much should a minimum alternative-set be "expanded" in order to become relevant in a given case? Let us say that if A and A' are different alternative-sets, then A' is an *expansion* of A if and only if, for every a, a is a member of A only if a or some version or quasi-version of a is a member of A'. Thus, for example, in the case described in section 3, A_3 is an expansion of A_1, and we may also say that A_1 can be expanded into A_3. As mentioned above, one possible reason for saying that A_1 is not relevant is that A_1 is (U)-inconsistent with A_3. Hence, the following criterion might be suggested:

(1) If A is the relevant alternative-set for P in S, A' is another alternative-set for P in S, and A' is an expansion of A, then A and A' are not (U)-inconsistent.

If this criterion is too strong, one might weaken it as follows:

(2) If A is the relevant-set for P in S, A' is another alternative-set for P in S, and A' is an expansion of A, then either (i) A and A' are not (U)-inconsistent, or (ii) there exists some alternative-set for P in S which is an expansion of A' and which is not (U)-inconsistent with A.

Criterion (2) is surely reasonable, but it is perhaps too weak. Notice, for example, that with the same assumptions as above, A_1 would not be relevant if (1) is accepted (since A_1 is (U)-inconsistent with the expansion A_3), but it may be relevant if (2) but not (1) is accepted.

It seems that a claim to the effect that A is the relevant alternative-set for P in S is not normatively *misleading* as long as A

satisfies the condition mentioned in (1) or (2), but the claim may still be normatively *insufficient* in the sense roughly indicated above. In order to preclude this, the following additional criterion might be suggested:

(3) If A is the relevant alternative-set for P in S, A' is another alternative-set for P in S, A' is an expansion of A, a is a member of A, and a' and a'' are different versions or quasi-versions of a which are members of A', then the consequences of a' are the same as those of a''.

According to my own intuition, however, (3) is too strong. For example, it does not seem necessary to require that the consequences of a' are "the same" as those of a''; it may suffice if they are of (approximately) equal value. Besides, as long as (2) is satisfied, perhaps we need not bother to distinguish between different versions or quasi-versions of those actions which ought not to be done. Hence, the following criterion may be more reasonable:

(4) If A is the relevant alternative-set for P in S, A' is another alternative-set for P in S, A' is an expansion of A, a is a member of A, the consequences of a are at least as good as those of any other action in A, and a' and a'' are different versions or quasi-versions of a which are members of A', then the consequences of a' are (at least roughly) equally good as those of a''.

I am inclined to maintain that (4) is a reasonable criterion. However, it seems that (2) and (4)—as well as (1) and (4)—are insufficient; the conditions mentioned in these criteria are probably satisfied by a great many different alternative-sets for P in S. Hence, some further criterion is still needed for distinguishing the relevant alternative-set for P in S. If (2) and (4) are acceptable, the following might then be suggested:

(5) If A is the relevant alternative-set for P in S, A' is another alternative-set for P in S, and A is an expansion of A', then A' does not satisfy both of the conditions mentioned in (2) and (4).

It might perhaps be argued that there is always at most one alternative-set for P in S which satisfies both the conditions mentioned in (2) and (4) and the condition mentioned in (5); if this is correct, it might be held that this is the relevant alternative-set for P in S. In other words, but more roughly, it might be held that the relevant alternative-set for P in S is that alternative-set which is expanded as little as possible while still satisfying the conditions mentioned in (2) and (4).

I am not sure of whether the teleological criteria mentioned above are the most reasonable ones that may be constructed. But it seems to me that teleological criteria can be constructed which are more reasonable than other criteria. It should be noticed, however, that if the *value* of the consequences of different actions is essential —as it is according to teleological criteria—then the problem of determining the alternatives open to P in S is not a purely empirical one. From the point of view of common sense this may appear rather odd. Moreover, with a teleological criterion it seems that it would usually or always be impossible in practice to decide whether a given alternative-set is the relevant one for P in S (even if certain value-premisses are presupposed). There are at least two reasons for this. One is the same as that which seems to make it impossible to determine the maximum alternative-set for P in S: we can have no complete knowledge of all the actions which are performable by P in S. The other is that it is presumably impossible to determine the total consequences of a given action.

5. SUMMARY

My point of departure in this paper is a representative act-utilitarian principle, (U). The application of (U)—as well as the application of a great many other normative principles—presupposes some answer to questions of the form 'What are the alternatives open to the person P in the situation S?'; and a non-arbitrary answer to such a question presupposes some interpretation of "alternatives". I am ready to admit that the phrase "the alternatives open to P in S" may be interpreted in various ways, but I have argued that, from the point of view of (U), it should be interpreted in such a way that the alternatives open to P in S constitute an alternative-set (in my specific sense). However, this still leaves many possibilities open. I have argued that there are probably always several rival alternative-sets for a given person in a given situation, and I have suggested that these are presumably sometimes (U)-inconsistent. Hence, a satisfactory explication or clarification of "alternatives" seems to presuppose some criterion for distinguishing the "relevant" alternative-set in a given case.

I do not wish to pretend that I have found an acceptable criterion which can be used for this purpose. I have discussed various kinds of criteria, and all of them seem to involve certain difficulties. From the point of view of common sense, criteria in terms of minimum or maximum or subjective alternative-sets are perhaps the most reasonable; but I am inclined to maintain that some teleological criterion is more reasonable from a normative point of view.

If a teleological criterion is accepted—as I think it should be —then it seems that the following conclusions must also be accepted. First, it is not a purely empirical problem to determine the alternatives in a given case. Second, in practice we can probably never know what the alternatives are in a given case. These conclusions should not, in my view, be regarded as reasons against the acceptability of normative principles like (U); but they should make us more sensitive to some of the difficulties involved in the application of such principles.

(*Bibliographical note*: The main ideas of this paper have been presented in Chapter 2 of my book *The Alternatives and Consequences of Actions*, Stockholm 1966, which also contains further details and certain bibliographical references. The following more recent writings touch upon the same or similar problems: Dag Prawitz, "A discussion note on utilitarianism", *Theoria*, vol. 34 (1968); Lars Bergström, "Alternatives and utilitarianism", *ibid.*; Hector-Neri Castañeda, "A problem for utilitarianism", *Analysis*, vol. 28 (1968); Lars Bergström, "Utilitarianism and deontic logic", *Analysis*, vol. 29 (1968); Lennart Aqvist, "Improved formulations of act-utilitarianism", *Noûs*, vol. 3 (1969); Hector-Neri Castañeda, "Ought, value, and utilitarianism", *American Philosophical Quarterly*, vol. 6 (1969); and Dag Prawitz, "The alternatives to an action," *Theoria*, vol. 36 (1970).)

[16]

The Philosophical Review, XCV, No. 2 (April 1986)

OUGHTS, OPTIONS, AND ACTUALISM
Frank Jackson and Robert Pargetter

We often approach the question of what to do by identifying a set of alternative possible actions available to us, our options, and designating the best as what we ought to do. Questions can be raised about this approach; for instance, what to say about supererogation. This paper, though, is concerned with two problems that arise *within* the option approach, and which remain however questions about that approach are resolved. It can hardly be supposed that the option approach is *totally* misconceived, and, as will be apparent, our problems would arise for any approach to what agents ought to do (in the action guiding sense) which incorporated a ranking of available alternatives.

An option for an agent is an action or course of action possible for that agent. Our first problem is whether, in addition to what is possible for the agent, we sometimes need to take into account what the agent would actually do in certain circumstances. By *Actualism* we will mean the view that the values that should figure in determining which option is the best and so ought to be done out of a set of options are the values of what *would* be the case were the agent to adopt or carry out the option, where what would be the case includes of course what the agent would simultaneously or subsequently in fact do: the (relevant) value of an option is the value of what would in fact be the case were the agent to perform it. We will call the alternative view that it is only necessary to attend to what is possible for the agent, *Possibilism*. The main aim of this paper is to explore and defend *Actualism*.

Our second problem is how to select the right set of options in order to answer a given question about what ought to be done. The option approach says that what ought to be done is the best (or one of the best, but let's leave this inessential complication to one side) out of a set of options—but *which* set for *which* question about what ought to be done? Suppose we want to know if A is something an agent ought to do. Clearly A must be an option for the agent at (or over) whatever time it is, as must each member of the set out of which A needs to be best if it is to be something the agent ought to

FRANK JACKSON AND ROBERT PARGETTER

do; but is the set consisting simply of A and not-A the one to look at, or is it the set consisting of A and all specific alternatives to A, or should we be looking instead at whether A is an essential *component* of the best out of a set of maximally specific options which may not include A itself at all, or . . . ?

The two problems are separable. The first concerns how to evaluate an option for an agent. Actualism holds that you should evaluate an option by evaluating what would be the case were the agent to follow it (and so bears not just on what is best but also on what is second or . . . best). The second problem is how to select the set of options for evaluation. It is a selection problem, not an evaluation one. We will see, however, that an awareness of the existence of the second problem helps in meeting apparently decisive objections to Actualism as an answer to the first problem.[1]

We start on the first problem, holding the second in abeyance, by describing two helpful examples. We go on to defend Actualism's answers for them. We then note that Actualism has a certain consequence which might lead you to reject it,[2] but argue that it shouldn't. In the course of arguing this we offer a solution to the

---

[1] The first problem seems to have gone largely unnoticed until J. Howard Sobel, "Utilitarianism and Past and Future Mistakes," *Noûs* 10 (1976), pp. 195–219; Holly S Goldman. "Dated Rightness and Moral Imperfection," *The Philosophical Review* 85 (1977), pp. 449–487; and Richmond H. Thomason, "Deontic Logic and the Role of Freedom in Moral Deliberation," read to APA, 1977, and published in R. Hilpinen, ed. *New Studies in Deontic Logic* (Holland: Reidel, 1981), pp. 177–186. The matter is further pursued in Holly S. Goldman, "Doing the Best One Can," in A. I. Goldman and J. Kim, eds. *Values and Morals* (Holland: Reidel, 1978), pp. 185–214; P. S. Greenspan, "Oughts and Determinism: A Response to Goldman," *The Philosophical Review* 87 (1978), pp. 77–83; and I. L. Humberstone, "The Background of Circumstances," *Pacific Philosophical Quarterly* 64 (1983), pp. 19–34. Although they do not use the terms, Sobel and Goldman in her first paper are actualists, while Thomason, Humberstone, Greenspan and Goldman in her second paper are possibilists. The second problem seems to have gone largely unnoticed until Lars Bergstrom, *The Alternatives and Consequences of Actions* (Stockholm: Almquist & Wiksell, 1966). See also Sobel, "Expected Utilities and Rational Actions and Choices," *Theoria*, forthcoming, and the references therein. We are indebted here and elsewhere to very helpful correspondence with Sobel.

[2] It seems to have been what led Greenspan, *op. cit.*, to reject it, and is what leads Michael McKinsey, "Levels of Obligation," *Philosophical Studies* 35 (1979), pp. 385–396, to propose a complex series of obligations at different levels.

OUGHTS, OPTIONS, AND ACTUALISM

second, selection problem. In the final part of the paper we show, using earlier points, why two apparently decisive objections to Actualism fail.

I. Two Examples

We can sharpen and clarify the issue between Actualism and Possibilism with the example of Procrastinate, and the example of Jones.

Professor Procrastinate receives an invitation to review a book. He is the best person to do the review, has the time, and so on. The best thing that can happen is that he says yes, and then writes the review when the book arrives. However, suppose it is further the case that were Procrastinate to say yes, he would not in fact get around to writing the review. Not because of incapacity or outside interference or anything like that, but because he would keep on putting the task off. (This has been known to happen.) Thus, although the best that can happen is for Procrastinate to say yes and then write, and he *can* do exactly this, what *would* in fact happen were he to say yes is that he would not write the review. Moreover, we may suppose, this latter is the worst that can happen. It would lead to the book not being reviewed at all, or at least to a review being seriously delayed.

Should Procrastinate accept the invitation to review the book? Or if we suppose that he in fact declines—perhaps because he knows that he would not get around to writing the review—did he do the right thing in declining?

According to Possibilism, the fact that Procrastinate would not write the review were he to say yes is irrelevant. What matters is simply what is possible for Procrastinate. He can say yes and then write; that is best; that requires *inter alia* that he say yes; therefore, he ought to say yes. According to Actualism, the fact that Procrastinate would not actually write the review were he to say yes is crucial. It means that to say yes would be in fact to realize the worst. Therefore, Procrastinate ought to say no.

This case brings out the difference between Possibilism and Actualism, and it is the one we will principally discuss.[3] Our aim is to

---

[3]Similar cases are described in Sobel, Goldman and Thomason, *op. cit.* The case of Procrastinate is discussed breifly at the end of Frank Jackson,

FRANK JACKSON AND ROBERT PARGETTER

defend and explore Actualism's answer for it. (By Actualism's answer, we mean its answer as to what Procrastinate *objectively* ought
to do. It is thus strictly irrelevant whether Procrastinate believes or
knows he would never get around to writing the review, that being
relevant to the different, though closely related, questions of what
Procrastinate *subjectively* ought to do, and his *opinion* about what he
objectively ought to do.) It will, however, be useful to have before
us a second example which brings out the fact that the diachronic
nature of the case of Procrastinate is not essential to the discussion.

The case of Jones is described as follows by Holly Goldman:

> Jones is driving through a tunnel behind a slow-moving truck. It is
> illegal to change lanes in the tunnel, and Jones's doing so would dis-
> rupt the traffic. Nevertheless, she is going to change lanes—perhaps
> she doesn't realize it is illegal, or perhaps she is simply in a hurry. If
> she changes lanes without accelerating, traffic will be disrupted more
> severely than if she accelerates. If she accelerates without changing
> lanes, her car will collide with the back of a truck.[4]

Should she accelerate? According to Actualism the answer is yes.
We are told that she is going to change lanes regardless, that is, that
what she would do were she to accelerate is to accelerate simultaneously with changing lanes, and what she would do were she not
to accelerate is not accelerate simultaneously with changing lanes.
The former is better than the latter, hence she should accelerate.
According to Possibilism, all that matters is what is possible for
her—what she would actually do may bear on whether she in fact
does what she ought, but not on what constitutes what she ought to
do. Now what is best out of what is possible for her is to stay in lane
without accelerating, that requires not accelerating, and so she
ought not accelerate.

II. THE CASE FOR ACTUALISM'S ANSWER

There are four considerations which support Actualism's answer
that Procrastinate ought to say no, and we will note that each might

---

"On the Logic and Semantics of Obligation," *Mind*, forthcoming. That
paper focuses on "ought to be" rather than on "ought to do." The present
paper is an attempt at a more comprehensive discussion of the issues such
cases raise for "ought to do."

[4]"Doing the Best One Can," *op. cit.*, p. 186.

OUGHTS, OPTIONS, AND ACTUALISM

with suitable modifications be applied to the Jones case to give the answer that Jones ought to accelerate.

(i) Possibilism is arbitrary. It is true that saying yes is an essential part of the best extended course of action open to Procrastinate, namely, saying yes and later writing. This fact is the basis of Possibilism's declaration that Procrastinate ought to say yes. But it is *equally* true that saying yes is an essential part of the *worst* extended course of action open to him, namely, saying yes but failing to write the review. Surely then there must be more to say before the question of what Procrastinate ought to do is settled. *In themselves* the fact that saying yes is part of the best, and the fact that it is part of the worst shows nothing. The first points to the answer that Procrastinate ought to say yes, the second equally to that he ought to say no. Possibilism errs in allowing the first fact to settle the matter. By contrast, Actualism holds that we arbitrate between the two by reference to what Procrastinate would do were he to say yes, and would do were he to say no; and as in our case what would be the case were he to say yes would be worse, he ought not say yes and ought to say no.

Similarly, it would be arbitrary to hold that Jones ought not accelerate simply on the ground that not accelerating is part of the best, namely, not-accelerating-and-not-changing-lanes. For it is also part of the next to worst, namely, not-accelerating-while-changing-lanes.

(ii) Suppose Procrastinate turns to you for moral advice. He is not sure whether or not he will write the review should he say yes. You know he will not. (A common enough situation.) What is the correct thing to say to him? Obviously you tell him to say no—to suppose otherwise is to treat your knowledge as irrelevant—and no doubt the author of the book very much hopes you will succeed in persuading him to say no. If the *right* moral advice is to say no, if the author is entitled to hope that Procrastinate will say no, if we are all barracking for him to say no, then what else can we conclude but that he ought to say no? Were we barracking for him to be immoral? The author is hoping for immortality, not immorality. Similarly, if Jones has a passenger who knows that she is going to change lanes, her passenger may well fervently hope that she accelerates while changing lanes. Is her passenger hoping for Jones to do the wrong thing?

Notice that appeal to conditional obligation is beside the main

FRANK JACKSON AND ROBERT PARGETTER

point here. True, Procrastinate ought to say no given he would not write in time. That is common ground between actualist and possibilist regardless of whether or not Procrastinate would write in time. But that is *not* what Procrastinate was asking you about, for suppose when he turned to you for advice, all you said was "Given you wouldn't finish the review, you ought to say no." He would be fully entitled to complain "I know *that*. What I want to know is what I ought to do fullstop, not what I ought to do given. . . . Stop holding out on me." (Wouldn't you be impatient with a doctor who only said things like "Given . . . , you ought to have the operation," never "You ought to have the operation.")

(iii) Moreover, considerations to do with conditional obligation support that Procrastinate ought to say no. Detachment for conditional obligation is valid. If I ought to do X given Y, and Y is the case, then I ought to do X. If I ought to go to the doctor given I am sick, and I am sick, then I ought to go to the doctor. There would be little point in remarking on the conditional obligation otherwise. Now it is, as noted above, common ground that Procrastinate ought to say no given that were he to say yes, he would not write. It is the case that were he to say yes, he would not write. Ergo, he ought to say no.

It may be objected that though as a general rule if I ought to do X given Y, and Y is true, then I ought to do X, there can be exceptions when Y is a statement about a free, future act of mine.[5] If Y is about my genetic make-up, what I did yesterday, what the Prime Minister has done or will do, or generally about something outside my control, detachment is permissible; but if Y is about something within my control—most typically, some free act of mine in the future—the objection is that detachment can lead us astray—and, so possibilists' will say, does lead us astray in the case of Procrastinate. For his not writing should he say yes is a free, future act of his *ex hypothesi*.

This is a very unattractive position on detachment. Suppose I am wondering what I ought to do. I am, as one often is, fairly confident of what I ought to do *given* this, that, or the other: I know that I ought to pay the rates, given they are due; I know that I ought to

---

[5]This reply is explicit in Humberstone, *op. cit.*, and suggested in Thomason, *op. cit.* See also fn. 20, below.

OUGHTS, OPTIONS, AND ACTUALISM

take an umbrella, given it will rain; I know that I ought to vote for Hawke, given he will do the best job. Accordingly, I address myself to whether the rates are due, to whether it will rain, and to whether Hawke will do the best job. The position grants that all this is fine, but the one thing I must *not* address myself to is what I might freely do in the future. Even if I know that I ought to arrange for a taxi given I will drink too much tonight, it is wrong for me to ask myself whether I will in fact drink too much. That is to commit a deontic fallacy. Unless, of course, I am an uncontrollable drinker; in this case it is right to take it into account, for it would not then be a *free* future act. We submit that this is a *reductio*. Further, suppose I am judging of someone else whom I know will (freely) drink too much, that he ought to go by taxi. I am *not* judging merely that he ought to go by taxi *given* he will drink too much, for *that* judgment I could make in *ignorance* of whether or not he will drink too much. But if I can detach for him, how come he cannot detach for himself?

Similarly, Jones ought to accelerate; for she ought to given she is going to change lanes, and she is going to change lanes.

(iv) If anything is clear about the case of Procrastinate, it is that he ought not unduly delay the reviewing of the book. That is the basis for judging that his saying yes but failing to review would be the worst result. But what is unduly delaying the reviewing? Doing something which causes (in right way) the undue delaying of the reviewing of the book.[6] But *ex hypothesi* Procrastinate's saying yes would *be* doing something which causes the undue delaying of the reviewing of the book, hence, would *be* his unduly delaying the reviewing of the book. Thus, as his unduly delaying the review is something he ought not do, so is his saying yes. "They" are one and the same, and Possibilism's answer that he ought to say yes is wrong. Similarly, unduly disrupting the traffic in the lane she is going to change into is something Jones ought not do; but it is the same action in the case as described as not accelerating; hence, not accelerating is not, and accelerating is, what Jones ought to do.

[6]See, for example, Donald Davidson, "Agency," reprinted in his *Actions and Events* (Oxford: Oxford University Press, 1980). Even if you resist the view that unduly delaying the review and saying yes would be the same event and so the same action, it is hard to believe that they are sufficiently different to have different moral standings.

We have labored the case for Actualism, more particularly for its answers that Procrastinate ought to say no, and that Jones ought to accelerate, because Actualism has a consequence which is *prima facie* untoward. We hope to have motivated you to follow us in seeing how on examination it is not untoward but rather leads us to an appreciation of the second problem referred to at the beginning.

III. THE CONSEQUENCE

Actualists hold that Procrastinate ought to say no. We now argue that they must also hold that Procrastinate ought to say yes and then write. Or, to put the matter so as to avoid possible scope ambiguities, if actualists hold, concerning saying no, that Procrastinate ought to do it, actualists should also hold, concerning saying yes and then writing, that Procrastinate ought to do it.

Strengthening the antecedent is a counterfactual fallacy. Bad would follow Procrastinate saying yes, but this does not entail that bad would follow his saying yes and then writing; indeed good would follow that, though that would not have been what would have been the case had Procrastinate said yes. What most moved us to say that Procrastinate ought to say no is that what would then be the case is better than what would be the case had he said yes. But what would have been the case had he said yes and then written would have been better again. This fact, and the fact that he could have said yes and then written, are not at all affected by the fact that he would not as a matter of fact have written later had he said yes. We must not let the mere fact that someone would not do something show that they could not or ought not. The upshot then is that parity of reasons requires that we hold both that Procrastinate ought to say yes and then write, and that he ought to say no.

The position may be viewed as follows. It is common ground that saying yes and then writing is better than saying no, which in turn is better than saying yes and not writing. The controversy is over how to rank saying yes as against saying no. The actualist insists that the non-controversial ranking is, in itself, silent on this, as saying yes appears as a component both of a more specific option which is above saying no, and of one which is below it in the non-controversial ranking. Actualists obtain the answer to the controversial ques-

OUGHTS, OPTIONS, AND ACTUALISM

tion by using the empirical fact (what else could we use—necessary truths, empirical falsehoods?) that Procrastinate would not say yes and then write were he to say yes. Deleting the latter from the non-controversial ranking leaves saying no as the best out of what remains. But none of this impugns in any way the non-controversial ranking itself. It remains the case that saying yes and then writing is the best, and so the actualist must grant that Procrastinate ought to say yes and then write, along with holding that he ought to say no.

The corresponding consequence is perhaps even more obvious in synchronic cases. An actualist who holds that Jones ought to accelerate must also hold that Jones ought to not-accelerate-and-not-change-lanes. The reason for holding that accelerating is something she ought to do is essentially that it would be better than not accelerating, but it is also true that not accelerating simultaneous with not changing lanes is better than anything else available to her at the time. The reason accelerating is better than not accelerating is that both would be accompanied by changing lanes, but that leaves untouched the fact that not accelerating without changing lanes is best of all.[7]

There is a positive advantage to this consequence. Intuitively, Procrastinate meets some but not all of his obligations. He could do better, but he could do worse. According to the consequence this is the literal truth of the matter. He does one thing he ought, namely, say no; and fails to do one thing he ought, namely, say yes and later write. Nevertheless there are two lines of thought, each of which very much deserves an answer, that suggest that the consequence is

---

[7]We have treated the synchronic case of Jones in essentially the same way as the diachronic case of Procrastinate. It can however be argued that there is an important difference, a difference which makes it possible to resist the conclusion that Procrastinate ought to say yes and write, while admitting that Jones ought not accelerate and not change lanes. The basic idea is that saying yes and later writing is not an option in the relevant sense. Sobel, *op. cit.*, and Goldman in "Doing the Best You Can," *op. cit.*, both suggest this, though in different ways. We do not find the suggestion at all plausible, but for reasons that are irrelevant to the other arguments of this paper. If you are more sympathetic to this suggestion, you can read what follows as bearing only on what Actualists must say about synchronic cases; but notice that had our focus been on what Procrastinate *subjectively* ought to do, it clearly would have been wrong to give his writing the review given he says yes, no probability at all. We are indebted here to Peter Singer.

FRANK JACKSON AND ROBERT PARGETTER

unacceptable.[8] First, it is surely plausible that a person should be able to do all that he ought, but no one can do not-A, and also A and then (or simultaneously) B. Secondly, there is a widely discerned connection between what persons ought to do and the prescriptions or guidance we should give them. What sort of prescription is: Do not-A, and do A and then (or simultaneously) B? How could this possibly *guide* anyone, other than to the madhouse?

IV. DOING EVERYTHING ONE OUGHT

Perhaps no one who has ever lived has done everything he or she ought. But surely no ethical theory should make it impossible for someone to do everything he or she ought. Actualism implies that Procrastinate ought to say no, and that he ought to say yes and then write. It is impossible to do both. It seems we have a refutation of Actualism.

However, Actualism does make it possible for agents, including Procrastinate, to do everything they ought. To see this we need to bear two facts in mind: (a) the reason Procrastinate ought to say no is that even were Procrastinate to say yes, he would not write, and (b) the reason Procrastinate ought to say yes and then write is in part that Procrastinate *can* say yes and then write. Suppose Procrastinate did just this; then it would be false that were he to say yes, he would not write—the subjunctive conditional would have a true antecedent and a false consequent—but then it would be false that Procrastinate ought to say no. In that case he ought to say yes. So we see how according to Actualism Procrastinate *is* able to make it the case that he ought to say yes, namely, by saying yes and then writing. And he would in this case do all that he ought. Similarly, Jones ought to accelerate, and Jones ought to not-accelerate-and-not-change-lanes. But had she not-accelerated-and-not-changed-lanes, it would not have been the case that she ought to have accelerated. It would then have been the case that she ought to have not

---

[8]A third draws on the alledged distributivity of 'ought' over 'and', see, for example, Dag Prawitz, "A Discussion Note on Utilitarianism," *Theoria* 34 (1968), pp. 76–84, and Lars Bergstrom, "Alternatives and Utilitarianism," *Theoria* 34 (1968), pp. 163–170. But see our criticism of distributivity in Section VI, below.

OUGHTS, OPTIONS, AND ACTUALISM

accelerated, and so she would then have done all she ought (as far as this situation is concerned).[9]

There is an inclination to say that what Procrastinate *really* ought to do is say yes and later write, that it is *only* because he won't that he ought to say no. We can now say just what this amounts to, without conceding that strictly speaking it is false that he ought to say no. His obligation to say yes and then write *overrides* his obligation to say no in the following sense. If he were to fulfil his obligation to say yes and later write, then he would not have been obliged to say no. It is indeed the case that it is *only* because he would not fulfill the first that he has the second obligation. Likewise, the fact that Jones ought to not-accelerate-and-not-change-lanes overrides that she ought to accelerate. Had she done the first, it would not be the case that she ought to do the second, but not vice-versa.

In general, the situation can be viewed as follows. Consider an agent S at a time t, facing a set of courses of actions (or inactions) starting at t and finishing, say, when he finishes. Suppose the best course of action from t to the end is A_1-and-then-A_2- . . . -and-then-A_n. But suppose that were S to do, say, A_1-and-then-A_2, S would not *in fact* go on to A_3, A_4, . . . A_n, but rather would go on to complete A_1-and-then-A_2-and-then-C_3- . . . -and-then-C_m. Further, suppose that had S done B_1-and-then-B_2 instead of A_1-and-then-A_2, he would have gone on to complete B_1-and-then-B_2- . . . -and-then-B_p. And, finally, suppose that B_1-and-then-B_2- . . . -and-then-B_p is a better course of action from t to the end than A_1-and-then-A_2-and-then-C_3- . . . -and-then-C_m. In such a case Possibilism and Actualism give different answers. They agree that A_1-and-then- . . . -A_n ought to be done, but Possibilism holds that S ought to do A_1-and-then-A_2, while Actualism holds instead that S ought to do B_1-and-then-B_2. Nevertheless, S can do all that he ought. For he *can* do A_1-and-then- . . . -A_n; and if he did, it would then be the case according to Actualism that he ought to do A_1-and-then-A_2, and not B_1-and-then-B_2. Indeed, if S does A_1-and-then- . . . A_n, then S automatically does not only this thing that he ought, but everything that he ought—namely, A_1; and A_1-and-then-A_2; and

---

[9]A similar point in a different context has been made by Sobel, "Everyone's Conforming to a Rule," unpublished.

FRANK JACKSON AND ROBERT PARGETTER

A_1-and-then-A_2-and-then -A_3; and . . . .[10] S's obligation to do A_1-and- . . . A_n overrides all other obligations he is under. In fact, the things S ought to do according to Possibilism and those S ought to do according to Actualism are exactly the same in this special case. Possibilism gives the right answers for those who never put a foot wrong.

V. INCOMPATIBLE PRESCRIPTIONS

The question for Actualism is how to make sense of incompatible prescriptions, like one to do not-A along with one to do A and then B, directed simultaneously to the same agent. For no agent can fulfill such joint prescriptions.[11]

Our response is that prescribing, or at least prescribing that identifies what one ought to do, is more complex than has been generally realized. Take an example reasonably remote from the dispute between Possibilism and Actualism. I am ill. The best thing for me to do is to go to the doctor, the next best is to stay home, and the worst is to go to work. What should we prescribe for me, what ought I to do? It is too simple to say merely—go to the doctor. There is more to say than that. For if we said that I ought to go to the doctor and nothing further, staying at home and going to work

---

[10]We have simplified by supposing that there is one of the life-long courses of action which is best. If there are two, say X_1-and-then- . . . -X_n, and Y_1-and-then- . . . -Y_n, then both X_1- . . . -X_n, and Y_1- . . . -Y_n are permissible, [X_1- . . . -X_n or Y_1- . . . -Y_n] ought to be done; and if it *is* done, each of [X_1 or Y_1], . . . , [X_n or Y_n] ought to be done, and everything the agent ought to do, he or she does do. See also the appendix to Sobel, "Utilitarianism and Past and Future Mistakes," *op. cit.*

[11]But notice that this is a question for many possibilists as well. Few possibilists have been prepared simply to say that Procrastinate ought to say yes; they have felt the need to say more. Thus Goldman, "Doing the Best One Can," *op. cit.*, suggests we need orders of obligations. (See also McKinsey, *op. cit.*) In terms of our example Procrastinate's *primary* obligation is to say yes, while his *secondary* obligation is to say no. Now if both primary and secondary obligations are tied to prescriptions, their question is the same as ours, for they have clashing prescriptions exactly as we do; if on the other hand obligations are not tied to prescriptions in the first place, neither of us has a problem; while if primary obligations are prescriptive and secondary ones are not, we have a mystery.

OUGHTS, OPTIONS, AND ACTUALISM

would be, in terms of what I ought to do, exactly alike. Both would simply be things I ought not do. And it is not that simple. Clearly, what we have to say is that out of: going to the doctor, staying home, and going to work, I ought to go to the doctor; but out of: staying home, and going to work, I ought to stay home. Although staying home is not what I ought to do out of the larger set, it is what I ought to do out of the smaller set of options. And the moral is that, although incompatible prescriptions out of the same set of options are objectionable, there is nothing particularly puzzling in incompatible prescriptions out of different sets of options.

It would indeed be nonsensical to prescribe different and incompatible actions out of the same set, for that would make nonsense of the singling out nature of prescribing. But you can single out differently from different sets. The impossibility of my both going to the doctor and staying at home (and we could have made the impossibility logical by considering my going to the doctor instead of staying home, as opposed to my staying home) shows that they cannot be both what I ought to do out of the same set of options,[12] but they can be (and are) both what I ought to do out of different sets. Similarly, it is impossible to jog both regularly and occasionally; nevertheless, jogging occasionally may be the thing to do out of jogging occasionally and not jogging at all, while jogging regularly may be the thing to do out of jogging regularly and jogging occasionally. We can conclude, therefore, that the impossibility of doing A, as well as doing not-A and then (or simultaneously) B, does not refute the actualist's contention that they may both be what an agent ought to do, *provided* the corresponding prescriptions are out of different sets of options. But which sets of options? It is time to face up to the second, selection problem referred to at the beginning.

---

[12]Here and immediately above we are taking a position opposed to that of some who talk about moral dilemmas. See, for example, Bernard Williams, "Ethical Consistency" in his *Problems of the Self* (Cambridge: Cambridge University Press, 1973). In doing this we are making life harder for ourselves, but anyhow cases like those of Jones and Procrastinate are pretty clearly not instances of moral dilemmas.

FRANK JACKSON AND ROBERT PARGETTER

VI. THE SELECTION PROBLEM

We have said that the prescriptive element carried by 'S ought to do A' should be thought of as prescribing A out of a range of alternatives available to S.[13] This leaves open how to answer, for some given possible action, the question as to whether S ought to do it.

How is whether or not S ought to do A, recovered from facts about whether or not S ought to do A out if this or that set of options? The answer is by looking to the set consisting of the action in question and the action the agent would perform if he did not perform that action, that is, what he would do instead. Thus in the Jones case, concerning accelerating, she ought to do it. For out of accelerating and not accelerating, she ought to accelerate, and what she would do if she did not accelerate is, of course, not accelerate. In the case we have recently been discussing—where I am ill and face a choice, from best to worst, of going to the doctor, staying home, and going to work—the answer can depend on the sort of person I am. Consider staying home, ought I to do it? It depends on what I would do if I were to do something else. If what I would do if I did not stay home, would be to go to the doctor, the answer is no; staying home is then something I ought not do. But suppose I have a phobia about doctors, and as a result what would be were I not to stay home is that I would go to work. In that case the answer is yes; staying home is then something I ought to do. In either case, going to the doctor is something I ought to do; but in the first staying home is something I ought not do, and in the second it is something I ought to do. Surely this is the plausible result. If I ask you, "Ought I go to the doctor," you say yes without further ado; if I ask you should I stay home, your answer will depend on what you think I would do if I did not stay home. Indeed doesn't exactly this kind of thing happen when friends ask us whether they should stop smoking. We do *not* say yes to those we judge would start eating bagfuls of sweets, would give their families hell and so on, were they to stop. Stopping smoking is not something *they* ought to do,

---

[13]At whatever time it is; the times we mention explicitly in this section, however, are the times of acting, not the times as of which an action is an option for an agent.

OUGHTS, OPTIONS, AND ACTUALISM

because of what they *would* do were they to stop, despite the fact that it is *possible* for them to stop without all the trauma. Actualism comes into play not just in evaluating the options, but also in determining which options are to be evaluated.[14]

There is thus an unequivocal answer for each action concerning whether an agent ought to do it. For each A, it ought to be done by an agent just if what he would do if he did A is better than what he would do if he did not do A, that is, if it is what ought to be done out of the set of options consisting of what would be done if A were done, and what would be done if A were not done.

We said in the previous section that incompatible prescriptions directed simultaneously to the same agent are acceptable *provided* they are out of different sets of options. We can now say what the different sets are which make it possible for 'S ought to do A and B' and 'S ought to do not-A' to be true together. The first singles out A and B from: A and B, and what S would do if he did not do A and B; while the second singles out not-A from: not-A, and what S would do if he did not do not-A.

Of course, if 'S ought to do A and B' and 'S ought to do not-A' can be true together, we must deny distributivity over 'and':

(P)   If S ought to do A and B, then S ought to do A.

For even if 'S ought to do not-A' does not *entail* that it is false that S ought to do A, the cases we have given where 'S ought to do not-A' is true along with 'S ought to do A and B' are clearly ones where it is in fact false that S ought to do A.

We do not regard this as an objection. It has been widely recognized that there are apparent counter-examples to (P). Perhaps an overweight Smith ought to stop smoking and eat less, but it may not be true that he ought to stop smoking. For it may be that were he to stop smoking he would compensate by eating more. It is clear to many overweight smokers, and to their doctors, that they ought to stop smoking and eat less, while it is far from clear to them that they ought to stop smoking. And, to labor an earlier point, it will not do to say that *all* we need to say is that they ought not stop smoking given

---

[14]See Goldman, "Doing the Best One Can," *op. cit.*, fn. 3.

FRANK JACKSON AND ROBERT PARGETTER

they would compensate by eating more. They can know that *without* knowing whether or not they would compensate by eating more. Similarly, it will not do to say that *all* we need to say is that they ought not stop-smoking-and-eat-more. That also they can know without knowing whether or not they would compensate by eating more. What they are wondering about is not whether they ought to stop smoking given they would eat more, or whether they ought to stop smoking and eat more; for they know for sure without reference to whether they would in fact eat more, that the answer to these two questions is no. Rather, what they are wondering about is whether they ought to stop smoking.

The reluctance to concede the falsity of (P) derives from the existence of three initially very appealing general lines of argument for it.[15] The first starts from the fact that there is no difference between telling someone to do A and B, and telling them to do A and to do B. This, combined with the prescriptive nature of moral discourse, appears to lead straight to (P) (indeed to stronger, biconditional developments of it). There is, however, a difference between telling someone to do A and B out of one set of options, and on the other hand telling them to do A out of a second set and B out of a third. And, as we have seen, that is what is to the point in considering (P).

The second line of argument starts from the fact that if S does A and B, then S does A. Suppose that S does in fact do A and B, and that A and B is something S ought to do; then *in doing something S ought to do* S has *ipso facto* done A. How then could A fail to be something S ought to do? This is an entirely successful line of argument, but not for (P).

Instead, it establishes:

> (P*) If S ought to do A and B, and S does A and B, then S ought to do A.

The counter-examples to (P) highlight the difference between it and (P*). They are cases where were S to do A then S would not do B, and so are cases where S does *not* do A and B.

---

[15]Apart from the consideration considered and rejected above in Section IV. The argument that immediately follows is put particularly forcefully in Humberstone, *op. cit.*.

OUGHTS, OPTIONS, AND ACTUALISM

The third line of argument can be put as follows. If A and B is something S ought to do, then surely S is required to do A in some sense. But if we are right, A might fail to be something S ought to do; how then is there a requirement to do A? There is a requirement in the sense that if S does not do A, S *must* fail to do something he ought, namely, A and B. On the other hand, if S does A, S *may* do all that he ought; for that is consistent with his doing A and B, and if he does A and B, as we noted earlier, A cannot be something he ought not do, and he will do all that he ought to as far as these actions are concerned. That is, (P) must be distinguished from the unexceptional:

> (P**) If S ought to do A and B, and S does all he ought, then S ought to do A.

In our thinking about what we ourselves ought to do on some occasion it is easy to confuse (P) with (P*) or (P**). I reflect that I ought to pay the rates, and so that I ought to write a cheque and then mail it. I accordingly set myself to write the cheque. Aren't I working out that I ought to write a cheque from the fact that I ought to write a cheque and mail it? How then can (P) be fallacious? But I am implicitly taking for granted in my internal monologue that I will do all that I ought, including in this case writing a cheque and then mailing it. It is (P*) or (P**), not (P), which my monologue needs. (We are indebted here to a discussion with Aubrey Townsend.)

VII. A QUESTION DISTINGUISHED

Our focus has been on the conditions under which an *action* at a time ought to be done by some agent. Confusion can arise from failing to distinguish this question from the corresponding question for a *time*. As well as asking whether some action is one an agent ought to do, we can ask, for some given time, what an agent ought to do at it. For instance, we can ask, "What ought I to do on Tuesday?" To which the answer might be: read in the morning, go on and lecture in the afternoon, and so on. We urged that the first question should be approached by looking at the action and its alternative. In the case of the second question it is plausible that the

FRANK JACKSON AND ROBERT PARGETTER

set of alternatives to look at is all the different most relevantly specific actions[16] the agent might perform at that time, the narrowest options at the time, in the jargon of decision theory.[17] To see why this is plausible consider the Jones's case again. Suppose it is right now that she is changing lanes without accelerating. What should she be doing *right now*? Obviously, not changing lanes *and* not accelerating. If she asks just before acting what the right thing to do is, the plausible answer is, do not change lanes and at the same time do not accelerate. The most relevantly specific possible actions for her now are, from best to worst: not changing lanes and not accelerating, changing and accelerating, changing and not accelerating, not changing and accelerating. And we are plausibly nominating the best of these as what she ought to do now. Within the option approach, what else could we do? And surely if we answered her question as to what to do now by saying only, do not change lanes, we could rightly be accused of withholding information. Not changing lanes is only *part* of what she ought to be doing now, as any good driving instructor will tell us. Our claim is thus that if she asks "Tell me what to do now," the answer is "Do not change lanes and do not accelerate"—despite the answer to "Tell me whether or not to accelerate" being "Accelerate."

We are *not* saying here that you cannot answer the question as to whether not changing lanes is something Jones ought to be doing, but can only answer whether it is part of what she ought to be doing (to which yes is of course the answer). We *are* saying that this question is the *first* sort, not the second sort. If A-and-B is what an agent ought to do at a time (is the whole answer to the second sort of question), A cannot be, for A is only a part of A-and-B. When William and Mary ruled England, William was not the answer to who ruled England. But it may or may not be the case that A is

---

[16]Writing and mailing a cheque is more specific than writing a cheque; writing a cheque in blue ink instead of black and mailing it is more specific than either, but in a way which is (usually) irrelevant to value.

[17]See, for example, David Lewis, "Causal Decision Theory," *Australasian Journal of Philosophy* 59 (1981), pp. 5–30, see p. 4. Thus decision theory is not about whether a given action ought to be done, but about what ought to be done at or over a given time—and it is of course about what *subjectively* ought to be done.

OUGHTS, OPTIONS, AND ACTUALISM

something the agent ought to do (is an answer to the first sort of question).

The idea behind the option approach to what an agent ought to do is that it is what is best out of some range of options—that is, some range of actions possible for the agent. The second, selection problem is which set of options. To obtain the answer for a particular action as to whether S ought to do it, we let the *action* along with the agent determine the relevant set of options. And, in accord with our actualist sympathies, we made the set that consisting of the action and the action S *would* do instead. In order to obtain the answer for a particular time (or period of time) as to what S ought to do at that time, we let the *time* determine the set of options. It is the set of the most relevantly specific actions available to S at the time, and what ought to be done is the best out of that set. If the best is A_1-and- . . . -A_n, then A_1, for example, is not what ought to be done at the time. It is part of what ought to be done. A_1 may though be something that ought to be done, and will be if what S would do were he to do A_1 is better than what S would do instead if he did not do A_1.

There is therefore a difference between the Jones's case and Procrastinate's case (which may explain why some find Actualism's answer more persuasive in the latter). Saying no when the invitation arrives is something Procrastinate ought to do. It is also what he should do at that time, for at that time the relevant options are saying yes and saying no—he cannot write until later—and saying no is best (by Actualism, as saying yes would lead to a worse result). However, as we saw, though accelerating now is something Jones ought to do, what Jones ought to do now is not-accelerate-and-not-change-lanes. Saying no is both something Procrastinate ought to do, and what he ought to do when the invitation arrives; while accelerating is only something Jones ought to do, not what she ought to do right now. Correlatively, the cases differ in the extent to which they highlight the difference between Actualism and Possibilism. Saying no is, according to Possibilism, neither something that Procrastinate ought to do nor what he ought to do when the invitation arrives. Possibilism and Actualism disagree on both questions in this case. But in the Jones's case, they agree on one of the questions, namely what Jones ought to do right now. One thing that Possibilism and Actualism must always agree on, however, is

251

what an agent ought to do for the rest of his or her life, namely, the best option out of the set of the most relevantly specific options that occupy that period of time. For they could only disagree if that option were part of a more specific option of different value which would not in fact obtain were that option to be done by the agent. And in this special case there can be no such more specific option; we have *ex hypothesi* the most relevantly specific option for the period of time, and, for our agent, there is no more time.

We earlier denied (P). But (P) must not be confused with the evident truth:

(Q) If A and B is what S ought to do at t, then A is part of what S ought to do at t

or with the evident falsehood:

(Q*) If A and B is what S ought to do at t, then A is all of what S ought to do at t.

VIII. GOLDMAN'S TWO EXAMPLES AGAINST ACTUALISM

Holly Goldman gives two cases which led her to revise her allegiance to Actualism. The luckless Jones is the principal actor in both.

> Suppose a dog runs out into the road in front of Jones's car. If Jones honks, the dog will leap back off the road; if she swerves, she will miss hitting the dog, although her passenger will suffer a minor cut on the head. However, Jones does neither of these. . . . According to Principle 3, since she fails to honk, she ought at least to swerve. Also according to Principle 3, since she fails to swerve, she ought to honk. Thus Jones comes under two prescriptions, to honk and to swerve—but we can imagine that Jones is a poorly co-ordinated individual who *cannot* do both. . . . Dual application of Principle 3 generates pragmatically incompatible prescriptions. . . .[18]

This looks like a good objection, for Principle 3 is a principle an actualist should accept, it being that "Whether or not S ought to do

---

[18]"Doing the Best You Can," *op. cit.*, p. 189.

OUGHTS, OPTIONS, AND ACTUALISM

A depends on what act(s) S would perform at the same time as A, if he performed A,"[19] and it seems to lead to an objectionable equivocation over what Jones ought to do at the time.

There is, however, a subtle confusion in the alleged counterexample. Consider our earlier example where I faced the choice (in order from best to worst) of: going to the doctor, staying home, going to work; and suppose I say, "Given I am not going to go to the doctor, I ought to stay home." I am *not* saying that the obtaining of my not going to the doctor would make the order from best to worst: staying home, going to work, going to the doctor. My not going to the doctor would not make staying home best; going to the doctor would still be best. What I am saying, rather, is that if you take the original set of alternatives and delete my going to the doctor, then, out of the restricted set, staying home is best. By way of contrast, if I had said "Given my illness is not serious, I ought to stay home," I would be saying that were it the case that my illness is not serious, the order from best to worst would then be: staying home, going to the doctor, going to work. In the first case, what follows 'given' restricts; in the second, it re-orders.[20]

Now consider Goldman's example. The order from best to worst is: honk, swerve, hit the dog—the last being what Jones in fact does. Goldman says that Actualism forces us to say that "since she fails to honk, she ought *at least* to swerve" (our italics). Now it is true (independently of Actualism) that out of swerving, and hitting the dog, she ought to swerve. Read that way what Goldman says is correct (and her insertion of 'at least' suggests that reading). But read that way there is no problem for Actualism. That Jones ought to swerve out of: swerving, and hitting the dog, is consistent with that she ought to honk out of: swerving, honking, and hitting the dog. The incompatible prescriptions are out of different sets. On the other hand, if Goldman's claim is that Actualism forces us to say

---

[19]Ibid., p. 186.

[20]Confusing these two underlies an appealing but fallacious objection to detachment. "I ought to stay home given I am not going to the doctor; I am not going to the doctor, therefore, by detachment, I ought to stay home. But that's wrong. I ought instead to be going to the doctor." Reply. The first premise is not a statement of conditional obligation in the relevant sense. Note how it reads better with 'at least'—"I ought at least to stay home given I'm not going to the doctor."

FRANK JACKSON AND ROBERT PARGETTER

that Jones's failure to honk makes it the case that Jones ought to swerve out of: honking, swerving, and hitting the dog, her claim is false. Hence there is no equivocation over what Jones ought to do at the time. Swerving, honking, and hitting the dog, are the most relevantly specific options for her at the time. Hence what she ought to do out of them is what she ought to do at the time, accordingly that unequivocally is to honk.

Indeed the fact that Goldman's example is not a puzzle for Actualism, but a puzzle *simpliciter* is evident from the fact that what she claims follows from Actualism or Principle 3 is plausible *without recourse to either*. Both "since she fails to honk, she ought at least to swerve," and "since she fails to swerve, she ought to honk" sound correct as they stand and to invite *modus ponens*. The puzzle is solved by noting that both are correct, provided the first is read as saying that *deleting* honking leaves swerving as best *out of what remains*.

Goldman gives another counterexample by elaborating the earlier Jones's case. It was supposed that Jones would change lanes whether or not she accelerated. It was this that led to Actualism giving the answer that she ought to accelerate. Goldman rightly observes that if we add the supposition that it is also true that she would *not* accelerate whether or not she changed lanes, Actualism leads in the same kind of way to the result that she ought not change lanes. But accelerating along with not changing lanes is the worst result; it puts Jones's car under the truck. Goldman urges that "Clearly there is something wrong [with Actualism] . . . if it results in prescriptions for acts which are less good in combination . . . than other acts which the agent could perform instead."[21]

Our reply should be obvious from what has gone before. A doctor who says "Out of drug X and drug Y, take X, while out of drug V and drug W, take V," is not telling us to take both X and V. What is true is that, out of a *given* range of possible alternative courses of action, telling someone to do A and B is just the same as telling them to do A and to do B. This truth however should not be confused with the falsehood that prescribing A out of one set of alternatives, and prescribing B out of *another*, is tantamount to

---

[21]Ibid., p. 189.

OUGHTS, OPTIONS, AND ACTUALISM

prescribing A and B. Now in the elaborated Jones's case, Jones ought to accelerate (in the sense that it is something she ought to do, it is, of course, not what she ought to do at the time), and ought to stay in lane; but that is to prescribe accelerating out of accelerating and not, and to prescribe staying in lane out of staying in lane and not, and because these two prescriptions are out of different sets of options, there is no single prescription to both accelerate and stay in lane forthcoming from Actualism.

IX. Hindsight

It is now possible to give the central thrust of this paper very simply. There are *two* matters that need to be borne in mind when considering what ought to be done in terms of the option approach. One is the evaluation of the options. We have urged the plausibility of evaluating options in terms of what agents *would* do were they to adopt them. That is Actualism. The other matter is how to select the right set of options. That depends on exactly which question you want the answer to. If you want the answer for some action as to whether an agent ought to do it, look at the set consisting of the action and what the agent would do instead; if you want the answer as to what an agent ought to do at or during some time, look at all the maximally relevantly specific actions possible at or during that time. It then turns out that what at first appear to be decisive objections to Actualism are no objections at all.[22]

Monash University
La Trobe University

---

[22]We are indebted to discussions with John Bigelow, Michael Stocker, Len O'Neil, David Lewis and most particularly I. L. Humberstone, and to comments on an earlier draft from a referee.

Part VII
Which Consequences are Relevant?

[17]

Actual Consequence Utilitarianism

MARCUS G. SINGER

Utilitarianism, defined traditionally and most generally, is the doctrine that the morality of an action depends solely on its consequences. The general principle underlying this doctrine, as defined by Bentham and Mill, is that if the consequences are good the act is right and if the consequences are bad the act is wrong. Following Moore, a more precise formulation of this principle makes reference to the alternative actions open to the agent in the circumstances and thus provides, in a way, a comparative criterion of the morality of actions. On this basis, that act ought to be done which, of all the alternatives open to the agent in the circumstances, has the best consequences. And an act is right, as distinct from mandatory, if it produces or would produce at least as much good as any available alternative. So an act is wrong, according to this more precise formulation of the utilitarian doctrine, if there is some available alternative productive of better consequences; in other words, no matter how much good an act produces it is still wrong if it is or was possible to do something else productive of better consequences.

This last point is, I am satisfied, no part of Utilitarianism as advanced and understood by Bentham and Mill, and is one of the rather subtle (as distinct from explicit) modifications of traditional Utilitarianism effected by Moore. It is not the idea of available alternatives that is foreign to their way of thinking about the matter. It is rather the idea that an action may be productive of benefit and still be wrong, if the agent in the circumstances could have done something else that would have produced greater benefit. Thus Bentham says:

> An action . . . may be said to be conformable to the principle of utility, or for shortness sake, to utility (meaning with respect to the community at large) when the tendency it has to augment the happiness of the community is greater than any it has to diminish it. . . .
>
> Of an action that is conformable to the principle of utility one may always say either that it is one that ought to be done,

or at least that it is not one that ought not to be done. One
may say also, that it is right it should be done; at least that
it is not wrong it should be done: that it is a right action; at
least that it is not a wrong action.[1]

There is no hint here that one *ought*, or is obligated, to do that
act which, of all the available alternatives, would produce the
absolutely best consequences. It seems plausible to suppose that
for the classical utilitarians whether it is right or one ought to do
some action is a matter of degree, and one action can be 'more
right' than another, without the other being wrong.

Thus Hutcheson, whose influence on Bentham was considerable,
quite explicitly regarded the virtue of an action as a matter of
degree. 'In comparing the moral qualities of actions,' he says,

> in order to regulate our election among various actions
> proposed or to find which of them has the greatest moral
> excellency, we are led by our moral sense of virtue to judge
> thus; that in equal degrees of happiness, expected to proceed
> from the action, the virtue is in proportion to the number of
> persons to whom the happiness shall extend; (and here the
> dignity, or moral importance of persons, may compensate
> numbers) and in equal numbers the virtue is as the quality
> of the happiness, or natural good; or that the virtue is in a
> compound ratio of the quantity of good, and number of
> enjoyers. In the same manner, the moral evil, or vice, is as
> the degree of misery, and number of sufferers; so that, that
> action is best, which procures the greatest happiness for the
> greatest numbers; and that, worst, which, in like manner,
> occasions misery.[2]

I interpret this as meaning something like the following. An act
is good if it produces happiness for people, better if it produces
more happiness for a greater number of people, and best if it
produces the greatest happiness for the greatest number. But
although one act may be better than another it does not follow
that the other is wrong. And, though Hutcheson is quite explicitly
saying something about the virtue, the morality, of actions, he

1   Jeremy Bentham, *Introduction to the Principles of Morals and Legislation*
     (1789), ch. I, pars. 6 and 10.
2   Francis Hutcheson, *An Inquiry Concerning the Original of our Ideas of
     Virtue or Moral Good* (1725), sec. 3, par. 8 (in Selby-Bigge, *British
     Moralists, 121*).

actually does not use the language of *right* and *wrong*. Bentham
does, as does Mill. But what Mill says is 'actions are right *in
proportion* as they tend to promote happiness' (*Utilitarianism*,
ch. 2, par. 2, italics added). It is, so far as I know, an accident of
language that 'right' and 'wrong' have no comparative or super-
lative forms, as do 'good' and 'bad', and it is probably an accident
of philosophy, and perhaps the utilitarian tradition itself, that
'right' and 'wrong' in moral contexts came to be applied primarily
to actions and 'good' and 'bad' to have a wider scope. At any
rate, there is no implication in Mill's utilitarianism that one who
does something that would tend to promote happiness would be
doing something wrong if there were something else he could
have done that would have promoted more happiness; though
the latter may be 'more right', the former would not be wrong.

I shall not attempt here to trace out the implications of this
variation of utilitarian formulations. It seems likely that Moore
derived this modification of classical utilitarianism from Sidgwick.
For we find in Sidgwick the first explicitly comparative formulation of the principle of utility: 'By Utilitarianism,' Sidgwick
tells us, he means 'the ethical theory, that the conduct which,
under any given circumstances, is objectively right, is that which
will produce *the greatest* amount of happiness on the whole'.[1]
This presupposes, what Moore later made explicit, that comparison is made of the consequences of available alternatives, and
judgment made on that basis. It is not enough, in other words,
for there to be more happiness in the world after and as a consequence of one's action. One must also consider and compare the
consequences of other actions that could be performed in the
circumstances, and be prepared to forecast that that there is no
other action that could be performed in the circumstances that
would produce more happiness (have better consequences).

It is at this point that Moore introduces another modification
in the utilitarian doctrine, though it is not one that has been
generally adopted since nor is it one that has been much discussed.
Given that the morality of an action depends solely on consequences, as utilitarianism maintains, which consequences does it
depend on, the probable consequences, the actual consequences,
the intended, or what? Moore's answer is that it is the *actual*
consequences of an act that determine whether it is right or

1 Henry Sidgwick, *The Methods of Ethics* (7th ed.; London, 1907), p. 411
(italics added).

70   MARCUS G. SINGER:

wrong, for it is only on this basis that the objectivity of moral judgments can be assured. Results are 'the test of right and wrong', and 'right and wrong . . . always depend upon an action's actual consequences or results'. 'Suppose,' Moore says,

> that a man has taken all possible care to assure himself that a given course will be the best, and has adopted it for that reason, but that owing to some subsequent event, which he could not possibly have foreseen, it turns out *not* to be the best: are we for that reason to say that his action was wrong? It may seem outrageous to say so; and yet this is what we must say, if we are to hold that right and wrong depend upon the *actual* consequences.[1]

This is precisely what Moore does hold, and what he does say.

Bentham and Mill, so far as they thought about the matter at all, were thinking of the probable consequences, certainly not of the actual consequences. For one thing, they use the language of 'tendency.' For another, Bentham explicitly says that 'the tendency of an act is mischievous when the consequences of it are mischievous; that is to say, either the certain consequences or the probable.'[2] In any case, traditional utilitarianism is prospective, forward looking; it tries to provide a basis for determining what ought *to be* done. Actual consequence utilitarianism, in the nature of the case, is retrospective, it looks back, and provides at best a basis for judging what ought to *have been* done. Before the event we can only judge with some probability what the consequences will be, and there is always some appreciable chance that we shall be wrong. It is only after the event that we can determine, with reasonable certainty, what they actually were.

Actual consequence utilitarianism, then, maintains that one ought to do that act, of all the alternative acts open to one in the circumstances, that would *actually* have best consequences. It is not, on this view, sufficient for rightness that what one does would in all probability have best consequences. One may do something that on all the evidence available at the time of acting would very probably have consequences better than the likely consequences of all the available alternatives (best consequences), yet this would not make one's act right. Whether it is right or

1   G. E. Moore, *Ethics* (London, 1912; 1947 ed.), pp. 106–107, 118–119.
2   Bentham, op. cit., ch. XII, sec. 2.

ACTUAL CONSEQUENCE UTILITARIANISM 71

not depends on what *actually* happens, not on what one expected to happen, what was likely to happen, or what one intended to happen. If, owing to some unforeseen or even unforeseeable contingency, what one did turns out to have bad consequences— or merely consequences not as good as those of some alternative— then what one did was wrong. The estimates made beforehand may excuse one's conduct, one may not be culpable, but still what one did was wrong. For it actually brought about bad results.

Let us see how this works. One is in a situation in which one can choose to do any one of a number of mutually exclusive alternatives a_1, a_2,... a_n. Act a_1 would have, so far as one can determine at the time, consequences that are better than any alternative, and hence best on the whole. Act a_2 would have, so far as one can determine, consequences that are good, though not as good as those of a_1. Acts a_3 ... a_n, let us suppose, would have consequences, so far as one can determine at the time, that would be on the whole bad. According to traditional utilitarianism, it is all right to do a_2 and better to do a_1, and wrong to do any of the other alternatives. According to a more precise rendering of traditional utilitarianism, such as provided by Sidgwick, it is right to do a_1 and wrong to do any of the alternatives. But according to actual consequence utilitarianism, one ought to do that act which *actually has* best consequences, and what has so far been determined is only that a_1 would very likely, so far as available evidence goes, have best consequences, not that it *actually will*. It may, if you will, be said to be *probably right*, but it cannot be said to be right. After the act is performed, and is over and done with, and the returns are in, then we can look back and determine, as infallibly as human beings can make any determination, whether it was right or not. And after the act is performed, and is over and done with, we may look back and say, with benefit of hindsight, 'Ah, a_1 wasn't the right act after all; a_7 would have been.' For a_1 turns out to have had, though no one could have foreseen it at the time, very bad consequences, so bad in fact that almost any alternative would have been better.

Now there are certainly occasions when many of us judge after the fact, in the light of actual consequence utilitarianism— or something like it. Someone does something and after it is done we look back and decide that he should have done something else, since what he did didn't work out so well; so what he did was wrong. It had bad consequences, it turns out, so he should have done, and if only he had known perhaps he would have done, that other thing we were urging him to do all along. Hindsight, as we all know—or as we have all been told—is 20/20, and if only we have enough of it we can deliver nearly infallible judgments. After all, the returns are in on the act that was performed. Now we know what the consequences are, or were, whereas before the event we could only predict, with more or less probability, what they were going to be.

Well and good. This is the way we learn from and by experience and reflection on experience, and though it may not always be advisable or defensible, it is certainly coherent. But actual consequence utilitarianism is in a different state. It maintains that if a_1 turns out badly, if it actually turns out to have (or to have had) bad consequences, then one should not have done a_1, but something else instead, namely that alternative that would have had best consequences. And the trouble with it is that none of these alternatives have actually been performed, and if the criterion is that of the actual consequences, only one act, a_1, actually had consequences (or had actual consequences). If one maintains, as one can with benefit of hindsight, that the consequences of a_7, say, would have been better than the consequences of a_1 turned out to be, so it would have been better to have done a_7, that is not incoherent, but it is not actual consequence utilitarianism. On actual consequence utilitarianism only the *actual* consequences have a bearing on right and wrong. But the actual consequences can be determined only after the act, when the returns are in. And the returns can be in only on the one act that was actually performed, and can never be in on any of the alternatives. One can never say 'the actual consequences of a_2 (which was not performed) *were* . . .'; one can only say 'the actual consequences of a_2 would have been'. This is only to say something about what the consequences of $a_2 . . . a_n$ would probably have (actually) been, and is not to say anything about what they actually were. They were actually nothing, and they can now never be brought into existence.

In other words, actual consequence utilitarianism requires you to know the actual consequences of acts never performed, to compare with the actual consequences of the one performed. But if an act was never performed it has no actual consequences, hence it has no consequences, hence no comparison can be made, and

ACTUAL CONSEQUENCE UTILITARIANISM 73

hence, on this criterion, no judgment can be made. I conclude from this that actual consequence utilitarianism is incoherent, absolutely and totally and completely.

Even its defenders admit that before the fact actual consequence utilitarianism cannot provide a criterion for distinguishing right from wrong or determining what one ought to do, since there is no sufficiently reliable way of determining beforehand what the consequences will actually be. The most we can determine beforehand is what they probably will be. Thus defenders like J. J. C. Smart, who believe that 'the utilitarian criterion . . . is designed to help a person, who could do various things if he chose to do them, to decide which of these things he should do' are driven to such expedients as distinguishing between a *rational* act and a *right* act. The rational thing to do is that 'action which is, on the evidence available to the agent, *likely* to produce the best results', whereas the right action is the one that 'does *in fact* produce the best results'. So 'what is rational is to try to perform the right action, to try to produce the best results'.[1]

Such expedients, however, although they admit that 'the right action' cannot be identified in advance, except as a matter of probability, still presuppose that, on an actual consequence criterion, it makes sense to speak of it. It does not. There is no way of knowing, either in advance or afterwards, which action, of *all the available alternatives*, 'does *in fact* produce the best results'. For this notion of 'best results' is a comparative one, and there is no way of comparing the results of the act performed with the results of those not performed, since those not performed have no results. A judgment about an unrealized alternative must be a judgment about a hypothetical case, and consequently a judgment about what would probably have happened.

C. I. Lewis once drew a distinction in this connection which may be useful. Lewis suggested that we call an act *absolutely right* 'if its consequences *are* good—or more good than bad, or such as represent *that alternative which turns out best*'; *objectively* right if it probably would have best consequences; and *subjectively* right if the agent intends it to have best consequences.[2] What Lewis has to say on this matter is, I think, illuminating and

1 J. J. C. Smart, *An Outline of a System of Utilitarian Ethics*, in *Utilitarianism, For and Against*, by J. Smart and B. Williams (Cambridge, 1973), pp. 46, 47.
2 C. I. Lewis, *Values and Imperatives* (Stanford, 1969), pp. 35–38 (second set of italics added).

basically sound, but it does not make the notion of absolute rightness a coherent one. In so far as it involves comparison of the actual consequences of the act actually performed with the actual consequences of those not performed, it involves something impossible. For no alternative can 'turn out best'. Anthony Quinton has remarked, in reference to this concept, that 'Only the subsequent critic of action is in a position to determine what is absolutely right'.[1] But Quinton is concentrating on making the point that the agent, who has to decide what to do 'before any consequences have come about', cannot tell. Perhaps that is why he didn't notice that not even the subsequent critic of action is in such a position. No one could be.

Even though it is amply evident that actual consequence utilitarianism cannot provide a guide to conduct or a 'method for deciding what to do', as utilitarianism was traditionally meant to do, it may nonetheless be thought that it can provide an answer to the fundamental philosophical question of what makes right acts right. Yet, as has already been shown, it cannot. For, on the comparative principle in which actual consequence utilitarianism has in fact been embedded, the morality of an act depends on whether its consequences are in fact the best of all the available alternatives. But there can be no actual consequences of actions that are not performed, and *ex hypothesi* the available alternatives to the act that is performed are themselves never performed. Thus there is no way of determining the actual consequences of the alternatives. The most that can be done is to estimate, after the fact, what they would have been, now in the light of hindsight and very often in the light of more adequate

---

1   Anthony Quinton, *Utilitarian Ethics* (London, 1973), p. 49. Quinton was concentrating on making the point that 'something like rule-utilitarianism must be accepted by any theory which evaluates actions in the light of their consequences' (p. 48), or he might have seen the point I am urging here about the incoherence of actual consequence utilitarianism. Thus he says: 'Suppose ... that rightness is taken in what Lewis calls its absolute sense. In that case the most authoritative and least conjectural judgement about the rightness of an action will have to be made after the event. Now one form such a judgement could take is comparative. We have to compare the consequences of the action actually performed with those of the possible alternatives to it. But, since these, *ex hypothesi*, have not been performed, all that can be done is to work out what consequences it would be rational to expect that they would have had if they had been performed, that is what the general tendency is of actions of those possible, but in this case unperformed, kinds' (p. 50). Note that this is not to determine the *actual* consequences of these unperformed alternatives; it is to determine what they *probably would have been*, if. So these consequences are necessarily *hypothetical*.

information than was available beforehand. But this assessment is still a matter of probability, and there is no assurance of the requisite sort that the consequences of the unrealized alternatives would actually have been, if any of them had been chosen, what we after the fact believe they would have been. The controversial character of historical judgments about hypothetical situations attests to this. Though hindsight be 20/20, it cannot see in the dark.

Moore says:

> Suppose that a man has deliberately chosen a course, which he has every reason to suppose will not produce the best consequences, but that some unforeseen accident defeats his purpose and makes it actually turn out to be the best: are we to say that such a man, because of this unforeseen accident, has acted rightly?[1]

Moore concludes that, even though it sounds paradoxical, 'yet we must say it, if we are to hold that right and wrong depend upon the *actual* consequences.' And Moore is prepared to say it, because this is what he holds. Part of the paradox arises, I think, because there is a confusion here between *doing the right thing* and *acting rightly*. One in such a situation can by some stretch of language be said to have done 'the right thing,' or what 'turned out to be the right thing', but there is no sense in which he could be said to have 'acted rightly'. But apart from this, it is evident that Moore has not noticed that, although after the fact we can determine whether the consequences of an act were good or bad, in comparison with the situation existing before, nonetheless we cannot determine whether they were *best*, because this requires comparison with the consequences of its alternatives.

Perhaps this occurs because of the way in which Moore originally sets up the problem. For Moore consequences are the test of right and wrong, but then these must be consequences the act actually has rather than those it is believed to have or expected to have, for these are not consequences at all. Moore also takes it as 'self-evident' that

> *if* any being absolutely *knew* that one action would have better total consequences than another, then it *would* always

---

1   Moore, op. cit. p. 119.

be his duty to choose the former rather than the latter. But ... this hypothetical case is hardly ever, if ever, realized among us men. We hardly ever, if ever, *know for certain* which among the courses open to us *will* produce the best consequences. Some accident, which we could not possibly have foreseen, may always falsify the most careful calculations, and make an action, which we had every reason to think would have the best results, *actually* have worse ones than some alternative would have had.[1]

But we hardly ever, if ever, *know for certain* what results some alternative *would have had*, and although it may be that the action actually had worse results than some alternative would have had, it could not possibly have had worse (or better) results than any alternative *actually* had, and it is the latter situation that is required by actual consequence utilitarianism. The consequences 'some alternative would have had' are hypothetical, not actual, consequences.

It might be supposed that, despite these arguments, there is an interpretation in which actual consequence utilitarianism is not incoherent. This is the interpretation in which the utilitarian principle is understood in a non-comparative way, as saying simply that if the consequences are good the act is right and if the consequences are bad the act is wrong. We could, for instance, look back and say, 'We are worse off now as a result of that act', and decide that it was therefore wrong to have done it. Yet in every situation involving choice—and it is only these to which moral judgments are applicable—there is a choice between at least two alternatives, doing the act or not doing it. (In not doing something, of course, one is always doing something that is capable of being described.) And this being so, there is always at least an implicit comparison of the consequences of the act performed with the consequences that would have resulted if it had not been performed. It may be that we are worse off now since that act was performed. But it cannot *follow* that the act was wrong. For we must also consider what things would be like if it had not been performed. Things might be in a worse state. If so, then it was certainly better that the act was done even though we are all now worse off than we were before, because otherwise things would be still worse. But in maintaining this we cannot be talking about actual consequences.

1   Ibid. p. 118.

ACTUAL CONSEQUENCE UTILITARIANISM   77

A Note on the Literature

Although actual consequence utilitarianism is not widely held, it has been maintained by some influential figures, and there is no doubt that it, or something like it, plays a role in our common moral thinking (which, it should be evident, is not always very sound or admirable). It was, to my knowledge, first advanced and discussed by Moore in his *Ethics*, of 1912; it was foreshadowed in his *Principia Ethica* of 1903. It is currently held by J. J. C. Smart; and it has been defended by Lucius Garvin, in his *Modern Introduction to Ethics* (Cambridge, Mass., 1953), pp. 237–245. It is pretty much taken for granted, as essential to Utilitarianism, by Lars Bergström, in *The Alternatives and Consequences of Actions* (Stockholm, 1966); e.g., pp. 82 and 86; but Bergström is taking the theory presented in Moore's *Ethics* as his model, so this is not surprising. It is alluded to, though not discussed, by Richard Brandt in his *Ethical Theory* (Englewood Cliffs, 1959); there Brandt says that although it has considerable disadvantages, 'there would be a gain in consistency and neatness' (p. 381) if utilitarianism (or what he calls, and what after him so many others have come to call, 'act-utilitarianism') is interpreted on the actual consequence model. However, if the argument I have discovered is sound, this cannot be, since what is incoherent can be neither consistent nor neat. Surprisingly enough, it is also taken for granted as the appropriate formulation of the various utilitarian principles he distinguishes by David Lyons in *Forms and Limits of Utilitarianism* (Oxford, 1965, see pp. 26–27). But, after all, perhaps not so surprising, for it is only on an actual consequence interpretation, which we have now seen to be incoherent, that Lyons's ingenious and much admired arguments for the 'extensional equivalence' of 'act-utilitarianism' and what he calls 'general-utilitarianism' have any shred of plausibility.

UNIVERSITY OF WISCONSIN, MADISON

[18]

Decision-theoretic Consequentialism and the Nearest and Dearest Objection*

Frank Jackson

Our lives are given shape, meaning and value by what we hold dear, by those persons and life projects to which we are especially committed. This implies that when we act we must give a special place to those persons (typically our family and friends) and those projects. But, according to consequentialism classically conceived, the rightness and wrongness of an action is determined by the action's consequences considered impartially, without reference to the agent whose actions they are consequences of. It is the nature of any particular consequence that matters, not the identity of the agent responsible for the consequence. It seems then that consequentialism is in conflict with what makes life worth living. I take this to be one part of Bernard Williams's well-known attack on consequentialism.[1]

One way to reply to it would be to break the implicit connection between acting morally and living a life worth living. Doing what is morally right or morally required is one thing; doing what makes life worth living is another. Hence, runs the reply, it is no refutation of a moral theory that doing as it enjoins would rob life of its shape and meaning.

This is a chilling reply and I will say no more about it. My reply will be that consequentialism—properly understood—is perfectly compatible with the right actions for a person being in many cases actions directed toward achieving good consequences for those persons and projects that the agent holds dear. Consequentialism, I will argue, can make plausible sense of the moral agent having and giving expression in action to a special place for family, friends, colleagues, chosen projects, and so on and so forth.

* I am indebted to discussions with a number of audiences and to comments from Michael Smith. Peter Singer, Philip Pettit, and a referee (to whom I owe the title).

1. In, e.g., Bernard Williams. "A Critique of Utilitarianism," in J. J. C. Smart and Bernard Williams, *Utilitarianism: For and Against* (Cambridge: Cambridge University Press, 1973).

Ethics 101 (April 1991): 461–482

462 *Ethics* April 1991

I will start by explaining how, in my view, consequentialism should be understood. This explanation will help us sort out certain potential confusions in addition to providing the springboard for our reply to the nearest and dearest objection.

I should emphasize that I claim no great originality for my account of consequentialism. It is, I think, a natural extension of what, for instance, J. J. C. Smart had in mind all along (shorn of the commitment to a utilitarian construal of consequences), though he did not say it quite the way I will.[2] I hope that my way of putting things will make certain matters clearer.

UNDERSTANDING CONSEQUENTIALISM

Consequentialism approaches the question of whether an action is right or wrong in terms of a comparison of the possible outcomes of the action with the possible outcomes of each available alternative to that action. The notion of a possible outcome of an action is interpreted so as to include the action itself, and the comparison of the various outcomes is carried out in terms of a consequentialist value function. The interesting question of exactly what makes a value function warrant being described as consequentialist can here be left to one side. The details of the value function will not particularly concern us; any reasonable ranking of outcomes of the usual agent neutral kind will serve our purposes in what follows. Similarly, exactly how the available alternatives to the action in question are specified can be left vague. What will, however, concern us is how the values assigned to the outcomes feed into the determination of what ought to be done. We will be presupposing that the matter is approached in the usual maximizing way—classical consequentialism is our subject, not satisficing varieties thereof[3]—but that in itself leaves a major issue open, an issue which will turn out to be crucial for the argument of the article. This major issue can be most easily approached via a simple example.

The Drug Example, Mark 1

Jill is a physician who has to decide on the correct treatment for her patient, John, who has a minor but not trivial skin complaint. She has three drugs to choose from: drug A, drug B, and drug C. Careful con-

2. J. J. C. Smart, "An Outline of a System of Utilitarian Ethics," in Smart and Williams. It is arguable that something like the account can also be found in some classical presentations, e.g., Jeremy Bentham, *An Introduction to the Principles of Morals and Legislation* (London: Athlone, 1970); and Henry Sidgwick, *The Methods of Ethics*, 7th ed. (Chicago: University of Chicago Press, 1907), though other interpretations are very possible, and, as we will see, a much quoted passage from Sidgwick points in a quite different direction.

3. A satisficing variety is expounded in Michael Slote, *Commonsense Morality and Consequentialism* (London: Routledge & Kegan Paul, 1985), as worthy of serious attention. The discussion is set in the context of a general defense of satisficing, as opposed to optimizing or maximizing, approaches to decision theory.

sideration of the literature has led her to the following opinions. Drug A is very likely to relieve the condition but will not completely cure it. One of drugs B and C will completely cure the skin condition; the other though will kill the patient, and there is no way that she can tell which of the two is the perfect cure and which the killer drug. What should Jill do?

The possible outcomes we need to consider are: a complete cure for John, a partial cure, and death. It is clear how to rank them: a complete cure is best, followed by a partial cure, and worst is John's death. That is how Jill does, and also how she *ought* to, rank them. But how do we move from that ranking to a resolution concerning what Jill ought to do? The obvious answer is to take a leaf out of decision theory's book and take the results of multiplying the value of each possible outcome of each contemplated action by Jill's subjective probability of that outcome given that the action is performed, summing these for each action, and then designating the action with the greatest sum as what ought to be done. In our example there will be three sums to consider, namely:

Pr(partial cure/drug A taken) $\times$ V(partial cure)
+ Pr(no change/drug A taken)
$\times$ V(no change);

Pr(complete cure/drug B taken) $\times$ V(complete cure)
+ Pr(death/drug B taken)
$\times$ V(death); and

Pr(complete cure/drug C taken) $\times$ V(complete cure)
+ Pr(death/drug C taken)
$\times$ V(death).

Obviously, in the situation as described, the first will take the highest value, and so we get the answer that Jill should prescribe drug A. The obvious answer all along. The difference between a complete cure and a partial cure in the case of a minor skin complaint does not compensate for a significant risk of death, as we might say it in English.

Generalizing, the proposal is to recover what an agent ought to do at a time according to consequentialism from consequentialism's value function—an assignment of value that goes by total consequent happiness, average consequent preference satisfaction, or whatever it may be in some particular version of consequentialism—together with the agent's subjective probability function at the time in question in the way familiar in decision theory, with the difference that the agent's preference function that figures in decision theory is replaced by the value function of consequentialism. That is to say, the rule of action is to maximize $\Sigma_i Pr(Oi/Aj) \times V(Oi)$, where Pr is the agent's probability function at the time, V is consequentialism's value function, Oi are the possible outcomes, and

464   Ethics   April 1991

Aj are the possible actions. We can express the idea in English by saying that whereas decision theory enjoins the maximization of expected utility, consequentialism enjoins the maximization of expected *moral* utility.[4]

How else might one seek to recover what, according to consequentialism, a person ought to do from consequentialism's value function? Two alternatives to the decision-theoretic approach call for discussion.

We can think of consequentialism's value function as telling us what, according to consequentialism, we ought to desire. For a person's desires can be represented—with, of course, a fair degree of idealization—by a preference function which ranks state of affairs in terms of how much the person would like the state of affairs to obtain, and we can think of consequentialism as saying that the desires a person ought to have are those which would be represented by a preference function which coincided with consequentialism's value function. The other ingredient in the decision-theoretic account of what consequentialism says a person ought to do, the agent's subjective probability function, is an idealization of the agent's beliefs. Hence, the decision-theoretic account is one in terms of what the person ought to desire and in fact believes. But in addition to distinguishing what a person in fact desires from what he or she ought to desire, we also distinguish what a person in fact believes from what a person ought to believe. And in a sense of 'ought' which has a moral dimension—there is, for instance, such a thing as culpable ignorance. Hence, it might well be suggested that we should recover the consequentialist answer to what a person ought to do from the value function via what that person ought to believe rather than from what he or she in fact believes.[5]

However, the clearest cases of culpable ignorance can be handled in terms of what a person in fact believes. The decision problem which faces a doctor considering whether to prescribe a certain drug is not simply the choice between prescribing the drug and not doing so—though we may pretend that it is that simple in order to make some point that is independent of the complexities—it is more accurately described as the choice between: deciding now to prescribe the drug, deciding now against prescribing the drug, and postponing the decision until more information has been obtained and, on the basis of what one then knows, deciding between prescribing the drug and not prescribing

---

4. Decision theory comes in a number of varieties. For example, in some $Pr(Oi/Aj)$ is replaced by $Pr(Aj \rightarrow Oi)$. The points I wish to make here are independent of the particular variety. (Though I in fact favor the latter, which is indeed the most obvious way of capturing a *consequentialist* approach to matters provided the "$\rightarrow$" is read appropriately.) For a recent discussion of the varieties, see Ellery Eells, *Rational Decision and Causality* (Cambridge: Cambridge University Press, 1982). Incidentally, the preference function in decision theory is often referred to as a value function, but I will reserve the latter term for what an agent ought to prefer in the moral sense.

5. Smart appears to favor a proposal of this kind. See also Philip Pettit and Geoffrey Brennan, "Restrictive Consequentialism," *Australasian Journal of Philosophy* 64 (1986): 438–55.

the drug. Now, in the same way that prescribing the drug and not prescribing the drug have an expected moral utility, so does obtaining more information and doing what then has greatest expected moral utility; and we can investigate the conditions under which getting more information and doing what then has greatest expected moral utility has itself greater expected moral utility than either prescribing the drug or not prescribing the drug. It is easy to prove the following. Getting more information and then doing what has greatest moral utility has itself greatest moral utility provided the possible change in utility consequent on the new information when weighed by the probability of getting that new information is great enough to compensate for the effort and cost of getting the new information.[6] Thus, working solely with a person's subjective probability function, with what he or she actually believes, we can distinguish plausibly between cases where more information ought to be obtained and where we may legitimately rest content with what we have. Hence, it seems to me at least arguable that our approach to what a person ought to do according to consequentialism in terms of what he or she ought to desire and does in fact believe does not need to have the reference to what is believed replaced by a reference to what ought to be believed.[7] However, the bulk of what I have to say about the nearest and dearest objection to consequentialism is independent of this issue.

The other possible account of how to recover what a person ought to do from consequentialism's value function that we need to consider holds that a person's beliefs, rational or not, do not come into the picture. What is crucial is simply which action *in fact* has, or would have, the best consequences.[8] Many consequentialists write as if this was their view. In a well-known passage Sidgwick says "that Universal Happiness is the ultimate *standard* must not be taken to imply that Universal Benevolence is the only right . . . *motive* for action. . . . It is not necessary that the end which gives the criterion of rightness should always be the end at which we consciously aim."[9] Here it seems clear that he is assuming that what makes an act right—the criterion of rightness, as he puts it—is the extent to which it in fact achieves a certain end.[10] Similarly, Peter Railton dis-

6. For a clear presentation of the proof, see Paul Horwich, *Probability and Evidence* (Cambridge: Cambridge University Press, 1982), pp. 125–26.

7. For a more detailed development of this argument, see Frank Jackson, "A Probabilistic Approach to Moral Responsibility," in *Proceedings of the 7th International Congress of Logic, Methodology, and Philosophy of Science*, ed. R. Barcan Marcus et al. (Amsterdam: Elsevier, 1986), pp. 351–66.

8. Another approach in which the agent's beliefs do not come into the picture is one in which it is objective, one-place chances, rather than probabilities construed epistemically, of the various possible outcomes which matter, but I take the essentials of the critical discussion that follows to apply equally against this approach.

9. Sidgwick, p. 413.

10. And this is certainly how this passage is typically read; see, e.g., David O. Brink, *Moral Realism and the Foundations of Ethics* (Cambridge: Cambridge University Press, 1989), p. 257. And Brink is explicit in endorsing the idea that what makes an act right according

466   *Ethics*   *April 1991*

tinguishes *subjective consequentialism*, the doctrine that "whenever one faces a choice of actions, one should attempt to determine which act of those available would most promote the good, and should then try to act accordingly," from *objective consequentialism*, "the view that the criterion of the rightness of an act or course of action is whether it *in fact* would most promote the good," and goes on to argue in support of objective consequentialism.[11]

There are two problems with this proposal. First, it gives the intuitively wrong answer in the drugs case. In the drugs case, either it is prescribing drug B or it is prescribing drug C which is the course of action which would in fact have the best consequences—and Jill knows this, although she does not know which of the two it is—but neither prescribing drug B nor prescribing drug C is the right course of action for Jill. As we observed earlier, it is prescribing drug A which is the intuitively correct course of action for Jill despite the fact that she *knows* that it will *not* have the best consequences. We would be horrified if she prescribed drug B, and horrified if she prescribed drug C.

The second problem arises from the fact that we are dealing with an *ethical* theory when we deal with consequentialism, a theory about *action*, about what to *do*. In consequence we have to see consequentialism as containing as a constituitive part prescriptions for action. Now, the fact that an action has in fact the best consequences may be a matter which is obscure to an agent. (Similarly, it may be obscure to the agent what the objective chances are.) In the drugs example, Jill has some idea but not enough of an idea about which course of action would have the best results. In other examples the agents have very little idea which course of action would have the best results. This was the case until recently in the treatment of AIDS. Hence, the fact that a course of action would have the best results is not in itself a guide to action, for a guide

---

to consequentialism should be recovered from what in fact does or would happen. See also Fred Feldman, *Doing the Best We Can* (Dordrecht: Reidel, 1986).

11. Peter Railton, "Alienation, Consequentialism, and the Demands of Morality," *Philosophy and Public Affairs*, vol. 13 (1984), reprinted in *Consequentialism and Its Critics*, ed. S. Scheffler (Oxford: Oxford University Press, 1988), pp. 93–133, p. 113, my emphasis. All citations to Railton will be to that in Scheffler, ed. Railton (p. 113, n. 24) mentions the decision-theoretic approach in passing, and it is unclear going on the printed word how much substantive disagreement there is between us on the question of what, according to consequentialism, a person ought to do. However, very helpful discussion with Railton (February 1990) has made it clear to me that we are in substantive disagreement. What is, in any case, clear from the printed word alone is that we are in substantive disagreement over how to answer the nearest and dearest objection, for in the footnote he remarks that his arguments go through independently of whether or not the decision-theoretic approach is adopted, whereas, as will become very clear, our treatment of the nearest and dearest objection rests quite crucially on the adoption of the decision-theoretic approach. In Bart Gruzalski, "The Defeat of Utilitarian Generalization," *Ethics* 93 (1982): 22–38, a decision-theoretic approach is given a crucial role in assessing the relative merits of act and rule or generalized versions of utilitarianism.

to action must in some appropriate sense be present to the agent's mind. We need, if you like, a story from the inside of an agent to be part of any theory which is properly a theory in ethics, and having the best consequences is a story from the outside. It is fine for a theory in physics to tell us about its central notions in a way which leaves it obscure how to move from those notions to action, for that passage can be left to something which is not physics; but the passage to action is the very business of ethics.

Railton is well aware of the need to give an account of the passage to action, for he remarks that a "further objection [to objective consequentialism] is that the lack of any direct link between objective consequentialism and a particular mode of decision making leaves the view too vague to provide adequate *guidance* in practice." His reply is that "on the contrary, objective consequentialism sets a definite and distinctive criterion of right action, and it becomes an empirical question . . . which modes of decision making should be employed and when."[12] In short, Railton's proposal is, I take it, that the moral decision problem should be approached by setting oneself the goal of doing what is objectively right—the action that has in fact the best consequences—and then performing the action which the empirical evidence suggests is most likely to have this property.[13] However, this approach to the decision problem gives the wrong answers. I will illustrate the point with a modification of the drug example.

The Drug Example, Mark 2

As before, Jill is the doctor and John is the patient with the skin problem. But this time Jill has only two drugs, drug X and drug Y, at her disposal which have any chance of effecting a cure. Drug X has a 90% chance of curing the patient but also has a 10% chance of killing him; drug Y has a 50% chance of curing the patient but has no bad side effects. Jill's choice is between prescribing X or prescribing Y. It is clear that she should prescribe Y, and yet that course of action is not the course of action most likely to have the best results, for it is not the course of action most likely to be objectively right. It has only a 50% chance of being objectively right, whereas prescribing drug X has a 90% chance of being objectively right.

This example is one among many. Consider, for instance, the question of whether or not to place a bet on a horse race. Clearly, it is often the right thing to do not to place a bet. There may be no horse about which the bookies are offering good enough odds. And yet in declining to place a bet you know that you are pursuing the one course of action guaranteed

---

12. Both passages are from Railton, p. 117, my emphasis.

13. See also his earlier remarks on objective consequentialism "not blurring the distinction between the *truth-conditions* of an ethical theory and its *acceptance-conditions*" (ibid., p. 116). Feldman explicitly takes this approach to the moral decision problem.

468   *Ethics   April 1991*

not to have the best outcome. Your problem, of course, is that although you know that there is a course of action with a better outcome, you do not know which one it is.

In general it seems to me potentially misleading to speak of consequentialism as giving the moral agent the aim of doing what has the best consequences. If it means that the agent ought to do what has the highest expected value or moral utility, where value is determined consequentially, then of course there is no problem. But it is easy to slide into thinking that consequentialism holds that people should aim at the best consequences in the sense of trying to select the option with the best consequences, whereas in fact most of the time we should select an option which we know for sure does not have the best consequences. Most of the time we are in the position of the person who declines to bet. The right option to select is a "play safe" one chosen in the knowledge that it does not have the best consequences and in ignorance of which option does have the best consequences.

I argued that consequentialism must, as I put it, tell a story from the inside about how to recover what an agent ought to do from consequentialism's value function, a story in terms of what is in the agent's mind at the time of action. I thus am agreeing with Thomas Nagel's claim that "morality requires of us not only certain forms of conduct but also the motives required to produce that conduct."[14] For the proposal I borrowed from decision theory meets this constraint, because it is in terms of the agent's probability function, that is, in terms of the agent's belief state at the time of action. Indeed, the proposal I borrowed from decision theory can be viewed as an account of what an agent ought to do that yields an account of what an agent's motives ought to be, of how an agent's mind ought to be as far as the springs of action go. For, as we remarked earlier, we can view consequentialism's value function as an account of how an agent's preference function, the agent's desires, ought to be—the preference function ought to assign the same values to the various states of affairs as does the value function. Hence, when the proposal recovers what an agent ought to do from the agent's probability function combined with consequentialism's value function, this can be described as recovering what an agent ought to do from what the agent believes combined with what the agent ought to desire and, thereby, as yielding a theory of right motivation.

Although consequentialism of the decision-theoretic kind described here (henceforth, consequentialism) has built into its very account of right action, a doctrine about right motivation, it is not committed to any particular view about the mental *processes* an agent ought to go through in deciding what to do; indeed it is compatible with consequentialism

---

14. Thomas Nagel, *The View from Nowhere* (Oxford: Oxford University Press, 1986), p. 191. See also Williams, "A Critique of Utilitarianism," p. 128, though the focus there is on utilitarianism rather than on ethics in general.

that at least sometimes one ought not to go through anything that might naturally be described as a *process* of thought at all. It is, for instance, compatible with consequentialism that an agent ought to go through a distinctively deontological cast of thought before acting. The agent may, for instance, have a terrible track record in calculating likely consequences and have found out by bitter experience that he does better following simple rules; or perhaps he knows that the world is under the control of a demon who rewards people for thinking in the Kantian style.[15] But then the agent's probability function will give the probability that an act has good consequences given that it was reached by rule following (or given that it is the Kantian act) a high value, and feeding this into the expected value equation will give the rule-satisfying act (or the Kantian act) the highest expected moral utility.

Similarly, we can acknowledge the often made point that sometimes consequentialist considerations support not going through consequentialist *deliberations*.[16] It may be that acting spontaneously in the situation at hand is known to have the best results—ducking, swerving, smiling, playing a drop shot, and the like are commonly best done straight off as the spirit moves one and without further ado. But in such cases the conditional probability of good results given that one acts without further ado will be high, or at any rate higher than the probability of good results given one acts after deliberation, and so, consequentialism will give the right result that one should in such cases act spontaneously. In such cases the consequentialist should hold that one ought to be *consequentially motivated* although one should not consciously reason consequentially.

It might be objected that this is an impossible position for the consequentialist to take up, given our account of consequentialism. How can the probability function give a high value to good consequences conditional on spontaneous action? For probability here means the agent's subjective probability function, that is, the agent's beliefs in quantitative guise; and the whole point of these examples of spontaneous action is that the agent acts without thinking. Accordingly, it might be suggested, he or she will not have any beliefs of the needed kind. The agent will not, for instance, *believe* that ducking the blow will have good results. There will not be enough time for that thought, only time to duck instinctively. Consider, however, the familiar example in the philosophy of perception where you drive past an advertising billboard without consciously registering what is on the billboard. You are later asked what the billboard was advertising, and to your surprise you are able to answer. This shows that you have seen the billboard and what was on it, although you were not conscious of the fact. In the same way one who ducks believes that not ducking will have results that are unpleasant despite the fact that the

15. An example of Railton's, "Alienation, Consequentialism, and the Demands of Morality," p. 116.

16. See, for three examples among many, Railton; Smart, p. 43; and the helpfully detailed account of a number of different examples in Pettit and Brennan.

470   *Ethics   April 1991*

thought to that effect is not consciously entertained. Spontaneous action is not action without belief, it is action without the conscious reviewing of belief.

What is central here is the distinction between the immediate springs of action and the processes that lead up to the obtaining of those springs. Otherwise consequentialism can seem to face a dilemma. Suppose that consequentialism says nothing about the mind of the agent at all. It says merely that right action is action with property φ, for some consequentialist treatment of φ which pertains solely to what in fact would happen and not at all to what the agent thinks. In that case, consequentialism, as Williams puts it, "has to vanish from making any distinctive mark in the world," by which, I take it, he is, at least in part, making the point we made earlier that consequentialism must say something about right decision.[17] On the other hand suppose that consequentialism is expressed as a doctrine about how to go about making the morally right decision, as a variety of subjective consequentialism in Railton's terms, and suppose in particular that it says to think along φ lines. What then if thinking along φ lines is discovered to have bad consequences in certain situations?[18] Our decision-theoretic account of consequentialism disarms the second horn of the dilemma by answering that in such situations the agent ought not to think along φ lines, for the agent's beliefs will then include that thinking along φ lines in such situations has a low expected moral utility.

It is important to note that on our account, consequentialism is not committed to the view that maximizing expected moral utility is the right motive for action. A number of writers have made the point that doing something because you consider you ought to do it rather than doing it because you want to is, generally speaking, not the mark of the kind of person it is comfortable to be around. Being nice to someone solely because it is your duty to be nice to them is the kind of niceness we can all do without.[19] Michael Stocker sees this as a problem for what he calls "the standard view." As he puts it, "The standard view has it that a morally good intention is an essential constituent of a morally good act. This seems correct enough. On that view, further, a morally good intention is an intention to do an act for the sake of its goodness or rightness."[20]

17. Williams, "A Critique of Utilitarianism," p. 135. Also his otherwise rather dark remarks on pp. 134–35 about utilitarianism retiring or being left with nothing more than "total assessment from the transcendental standpoint" may be a way of expressing the idea that utilitarianism must at some level be a species of decision theory. I am indebted here to a discussion with Thomas Scanlon in 1988.

18. A similar point can arise for deontological theories of course. "Keep your promises" is not in itself a rule of decision, though "Keep what you *take* to be your promises" is. But what if you are know that you are very bad at remembering what it is that you promised to do?

19. For some convincingly detailed examples showing this, see Michael Stocker, "The Schizophrenia of Modern Ethical Theories," *Journal of Philosophy* 73 (1976): 455–66, and Railton.

20. Stocker, p. 462. Incidentally, on my view, consequentialism does not imply that a morally good intention is essential to a morally good act, at least if morally good act here

Perhaps this is true of some ethical views properly referred to as "standard," but it is not true of consequentialism as characterized here. The right motive for action on the consequentialist view is the agent's beliefs combined with desires that conform to the consequentialist value function, and the consequentialist value function *assigns no value as such to maximizing expected utility*. Take the drugs, mark 1 case. Prescribing drug A is the right thing to do because $\Sigma_i Pr(Oi/Aj) \times V(Oi)$ takes a maximum value when Aj is prescribing drug A. But this fact that it takes a maximum value does not then confer *additional* value on prescribing drug A. That would be double-counting. What ought to move a person to action according to consequentialism are desires which may be represented as ranking states of affairs in the consequentialist way, but maximizing expected utility is not a factor in this ranking.

Before we turn to how our account of consequentialism helps with the nearest and dearest objection, I need to note an annoying complication. I have been arguing for an interpretation of consequentialism which makes what an agent ought to do the act which has the greatest expected moral utility, and so is a function of the consequentialist value function and the agent's probability function at the time. But an agent's probability function at the time of action may differ from her function at other times, and from the probability function of other persons at the same or other times. What happens if we substitute one of these other functions in place of the agent's probability function at the time of action? The answer is that we get an annoying profusion of 'oughts'. Consider the drug case, mark 1. I said that the intuitively correct answer to what Jill ought to do is prescribe drug A, and so it is. But suppose Jill later conducts a piece of definitive research which establishes that with patients of John's blood type there is absolutely no chance that drug B will cause death, and in fact with such patients drug B is certain to effect a complete cure without any bad side effects. What will she then say about her past treatment of John, was it the right treatment or the wrong treatment? The natural thing to say would be something like, "By the light of what I now know, I ought to have prescribed drug B, but it would have been quite wrong to do so at the time." But if it would have been the wrong thing to do at the time, how can it be what she ought to have done?

I think that we have no alternative but to recognize a whole range of oughts—what she ought to do by the light of her beliefs at the time of action, what she ought to do by the lights of what she later establishes (a retrospective ought, as it is sometimes put), what she ought to do by the lights of one or another onlooker who has different information on the subject, and, what is more, what she ought to do by God's lights,

---

means what an agent ought to do. It is possible to do the right thing for the wrong reason. For an act which maximizes expected moral utility might also, as it happens, maximize expected highly immoral utility, and it might be that which prompts the agent to action. What is true is that doing an act for the right reason is sufficient but not necessary for it being what ought to be done *in the sense we are insisting is central in ethics*.

472 *Ethics April 1991*

that is, by the lights of one who *knows* what will and would happen for each and every course of action.[21] The last will be a species of objective ought of the kind that features in Railton's (and Brink's) account of objective consequentialism. I hereby stipulate that what I mean from here on by 'ought,' and what I meant, and hope and expect you implicitly took me to mean when we were discussing the examples, was the ought most immediately relevant to action, the ought which I urged it to be the primary business of an ethical theory to deliver. When we act we must perforce use what is available to us at the time, not what may be available to us in the future or what is available to someone else, and least of all not what is available to a God-like being who knows everything about what would, will, and did happen.

It might be tempting to conclude that my acknowledgment that there are a variety of oughts means that I am not really disagreeing with one who urges that what a person ought to do according to consequentialism is what *in fact* has the best consequences; we are rather talking past each other. However, the substantive issue remains of the need for a moral theory to elucidate the ought most immediately relevant to action, and of how this should be done, quite independently of whether or not the target notion is unambiguously captured by 'ought' in English.

A REPLY TO THE NEAREST AND DEAREST OBJECTION

The decision-theoretic way of understanding consequentialism gives a major role to the agent's subjective probability function. This fact is the key to our reply to the nearest and dearest objection. I think that the reply can be most easily grasped by leading up to it via two examples: the drug example, mark 3, and the crowd control example.

The Drug Example, Mark 3

In mark 1, Jill had three drugs, A, B, and C, and one patient. This time Jill has three patients, A, B, and C, and one drug, and only enough of that drug to administer to a single patient. Her choice in mark 1 was between drugs, her choice this time is between patients, but it is all the same a similar style of choice situation that faces her. For we are given that she knows that patient A will derive considerable benefit from the drug without being completely cured, and also that one or other of patients B and C would be completely cured by the drug. However, she also knows that one or other of patients B and C would be killed by the drug. She has no way of telling which of B and C would be the one completely cured and which would be the one killed. What ought Jill to do?

The answer obviously is to administer the drug to patient A, and this is of course the answer our decision theoretic approach delivers.[22]

---

21. There are also the various nonmoral oughts—prudential etc., but that is another, and here irrelevant, dimension of variation.

22. Assuming of course that getting more information and then acting is not a viable option.

Jackson   *Consequentialism and the Nearest and Dearest Objection*   473

The expected moral value attached to administering the drug to A is higher than that for administering to B and higher than that for administering to C, because the possibility of a rather better result in those two cases goes along with a significant chance of a very much worse result. Of course, Jill knows that there is a better course of action open to her in the sense of a course of action which would have better consequences than administering the drug to A, but her problem is that she does not know whether it is administering the drug to B or administering it to C which is that better course.

What do we learn from this example to help us with the nearest and dearest objection? Well, it would clearly be a mistake to accuse Jill of an illegitimate bias toward patient A when she gave the drug to him rather than the others. Jill is biased toward patient A in the sense that her actions are directed toward securing his good, but the explanation for this fact is not that her preference function gives a greater weight to a benefit for A rather than one for B or for C. The explanation lies in her probability function. Consequentialism demands of us an impartial preference function, for its value function gives equal weight to the happiness, or preference satisfaction, or pleasure, or share of the ideal good, or . . . of each individual, but what the example tells us is that the fact in and of itself that our behavior is directed toward securing the happiness, or preference satisfaction or . . . of a small group—our family, friends, and so on—does not in itself show that we have an illegitimately biased preference function by the standards of consequentialism. The explanation of the directed nature of our behavior may lie in our probability functions.

The question, then, for consequentialists is the following. Can the special regard we have for a relatively very small group of people—to the extent that it is morally justified—be explained probabilistically, in terms of our special epistemological status with regard to our nearest and dearest, rather than in terms of an agent-relative preference function? The drug example mark 3 does not show that the answer to this question is yes. What it shows is that this is the key question that we need to ask.

I do not have a decisive argument that the answer to this key question is yes. What I do have are two considerations that suggest that it may well be yes. The first I will introduce with the crowd control example.

The Crowd Control Example

Imagine that you are a police inspector who has been assigned the task of controlling a large crowd at a forthcoming soccer match. You have to choose between two plans: the scatter plan and the sector plan. The scatter plan is put to you in the following terms. "Each person in the crowd is of equal value. Any plan which told a member of the police squad to focus his or her attention on any particular person or group of persons would be immoral. Therefore, each member of the squad must roam through the crowd doing good wherever he or she can among as widely distributed a group of spectators as possible." The sector plan is put to you in the following terms. "Each member of the squad should

474   *Ethics*   *April 1991*

be assigned their own sector of the crowd to be their special responsibility. This way members of the squad will not get in each other's way, and will build up a knowledge of what is happening in their sector and of potential trouble makers in it, which will help them decide on the best course of action should there be trouble. Also we will avoid a major problem for the scatter plan, namely, the possibility that at some particular time there will be part of the crowd which no one is covering. Of course, the sector plan should be administered flexibly. Although, as a general rule, each squad member should confine his or her attention to their assigned sector, if things are going particularly badly in another sector, and it is clear that an extra helping hand would make a big difference, then a transfer of attention may well be justified."

The plan that we follow in day to day life is, of course, the sector plan. We focus on a particular group, our family, friends, and immediate circle, while allowing that we may properly neglect them if the opportunity arises to make a very big difference for the better elsewhere. As the point is sometimes put, though it would be quite wrong to neglect family and friends in order to achieve a small increase in welfare elsewhere, it would be quite proper to neglect them in order to achieve peace in the Middle East. And we can approach the question of whether probabilistic considerations can provide a justification from the consequentialist's point of view for our focusing on family and friends, by asking when the sector plan would be the right plan for a consequentialistically minded inspector to adopt.

The sector plan would be strongly indicated in the following circumstances. (a) When getting to know certain individuals is important for achieving good results. The scatter plan distributes any given squad member's attention very widely, making any detailed knowledge of the psychology of particular individuals difficult. If good results depend on such knowledge, then squad members should restrict themselves to a smaller group, as in the sector plan. (b) When achieving good results involves coordinating a series of actions. Sometimes an isolated action has little effect in itself. What is needed is an extended plan of action, with later actions chosen on the basis of positive and negative feedback from the results of earlier actions. Think of the contrast between a one shot drug treatment and an extended course of treatment with later drugs and dosages being chosen in the light of the effects of earlier treatments. (c) When achieving good results depends on setting up mutual trust and respect and understanding between individuals. The traditional "bobby on the beat" is a special kind of sector arrangement and rests on exactly this kind of point. (d) When there is a significant chance of different squad member's actions nullifying each other if directed toward the same people. When we are in a situation where "too many cooks spoil the broth," the sector plan is clearly superior to the scatter plan. (e) When there is an obvious way to assign police to separate sectors which coincides with their natural inclinations and enthusiasms, particularly when this fact is common knowledge. This reduces, and is known to reduce, the setting up costs of the sector plan by avoiding costly debate over who takes responsibility for which sector. It also increases the penalty consequent upon a squad member not policing their natural sector, by increasing the chance that that sector will remain unattended through other police wrongly assuming that it is attended.

Clearly, there is a great deal more to be said here, much of it to do with straight empirical facts.[23] But I hope that I have said enough to make it plausible that the sector plan is indicated in the kind of circumstances that apply in our day-to-day interactions with the world around us and the people in it. It *is* hard to know what actions will have good effects, and our opinions on the matter are much better founded in the case of people we know well precisely because we know them well. Achieving good results *is* very often a matter of coordinating a series of actions rather than scattering largesse around. Mutual trust and affection *are* important for good results. Too many cooks *can* spoil the broth when it comes to interacting in a beneficial way with one's fellow human beings. There *is* very obviously a group of people whose welfare we are naturally inclined to concern ourselves with, namely, those nearest and dearest to us. And, most important for our decision-theoretic approach to consequentialism, facts such as those just adumbrated are, I take it, pretty much common knowledge.

My suggestion, then, is that the consequentialist can reply to the nearest and dearest objection by arguing that the kind of direction of attention toward those we hold dear which is so characteristic of a worthwhile life can be explained without attributing a biased value function. It is instead a reflection of the nature of our probability functions, in particular, of the kinds of facts about the epistemology of achieving good consequences that we have been rehearsing. The suggestion is not of course that the kind of direction of attention we typically manifest *in fact* toward those we hold dear can be explained without attributing a biased value function. It is no objection to consequentialism that, according to it, we ought to do more than we in fact do for people we hardly know. We ought to do more for people we hardly know. We are too tribal. The suggestion is that a considerable degree of focus on our family and friends, enough to meet the demand that our lives have a meaningful focus, is plausibly consistent with living morally defensible lives according to consequentialism.

On Three Objections

1. Williams has argued that "it [consequentialism] essentially involves the notion of *negative responsibility:* that if I am ever responsible for anything,

---

23. See, e.g., the discussion of the allocation of responsibilities in Philip Pettit and Robert Goodin, "The Possibility of Special Duties," *Canadian Journal of Philosophy* 16 (1986): 651–76.

476   *Ethics*   *April 1991*

then I must be just as much responsible for things that I allow or fail to prevent, as I am for things that I myself . . . bring about. Those things must also enter my deliberations, as a responsible moral agent, on the same footing. . . . What matters [according to consequentialism] with respect to a given action is what comes about if it is done, and what comes about if it is not done, and those are questions not intrinsically affected by the nature of the causal linkage, in particular by whether the outcome is partly produced by other agents."[24]

If Williams is right, we are in trouble. The key idea behind our reply to the nearest and dearest objection was that the reflections we grouped under the heading of the sector plan made it plausible that a consequentialist ought to take special responsibility for what is within his or her ken, and that will obviously involve making *who* does something a very important matter in many cases—and that runs directly counter to Williams's claim that who does something is irrelevant for consequentialists. However, it is crucial here to bear in mind the distinction between value and expected value. Williams is right that consequentialism's value function gives no weight per se to who does something (and that no doubt was what he had in mind), but nevertheless who does something can be enormously important to the expected value of a course of action, and it is that which is crucial according to our account of consequentialism, and that is how who does something can "enter my deliberations." In particular, Smith may hold that it would, all in all, be better were A to obtain than were B to obtain, but it does not follow that Smith qua consequentialist should seek to bring about A rather than B. For Smith may hold, in addition, that someone else, Jones, knows more about the matter than he himself does and that Jones has good values. In such a case, the decision facing Smith is between he himself bringing about A rather than B, or instead leaving the decision to Jones as to whether or not to bring about A rather than B, and it is easy to show that the latter may have the greater expected moral utility for Smith. The crucial point is that, though for Smith the probability of good consequences given he does B is low, the probability of good consequences given *Jones* does B may be high because of Smith's opinion that Jones is best placed to make the decision. In general, in cases where we judge it best to leave a decision between A and B to the experts, as we say, although we may have ourselves a view as to which of doing A and doing B has the greatest expected value, leaving the matter to the experts may have the greatest expected value of all. Thus, *who* does something *can* be crucial according to consequentialism.

It might be replied on Williams's behalf that he did not have expected value in mind and that the point we have just made only holds for expected value. However, this would make nonsense of Williams's (correct)

---

24. Bernard Williams, "Consequentialism and Integrity," in Scheffler, ed., p. 31. Williams is, of course, supposing that *effects* due to the identity of the agent have been incorporated into the consequences.

insistence that consequentialism be an ethical *decision* theory and of the talk in the above quotation of how things "must enter my *deliberations*" (my emphasis).

2. Railton raises (as a preliminary to a reply), the nearest and dearest difficulty for consequentialism with the following example. "Juan and Linda . . . have a commuting marriage. They normally get together only every other week, but one week she seems a bit depressed and harried, and so he decides to take an extra trip in order to be with her. If he did not travel, he would save a fairly large sum that he could send Oxfam to dig a well in a drought-stricken village. Even reckoning in Linda's uninterrupted malaise, Juan's guilt, and any ill effects on their relationship, it may be that for Juan to contribute the fare to Oxfam would produce better consequences overall than the unscheduled trip."[25] It might be objected that what I have said so far in no way meets the objection posed by this example. But from the decision-theoretic point of view what is crucial is not that "it *may* be that for Juan to contribute the fare to Oxfam would produce better consequences," it is how likely it is to do so. And, of course, the effects of isolated acts of charity on the Third World are a matter of considerable debate, whereas Juan can be pretty certain of at least some of the effects of his making the unscheduled trip. It is important here to remember that the relevant consequence of sending, say, $500, should not be approached by asking what $500 will buy in the Third World, but by addressing the likely *differences* between what would we achieved by the sum Oxfam would have without Juan's $500, and what would be achieved by the sum with Juan's $500.[26]

What plausibly is obvious is that many of us in advanced Western societies could achieve a great deal more good if we devoted our energies to a systematic, informed program of transferring any excess wealth toward the Third World. I do not mean isolated donations of airfares, but neither do I mean just sending a lot more money until it really hurts. I mean becoming actively involved in and knowledgeable about what is going on in the Third World: learning how aid agencies work, which ones do good, which, knowingly or unknowingly, do harm; finding out exactly how villages use money sent to them; the effects outside money and services typically have on the local social and economic structures; and so on and so forth. But how can this observation possibly constitute a nearest and dearest objection to consequentialism? A person who behaved in the way that I have just described *would* be directing her attention to those nearest and dearest to her. For she would be paying special attention to a relatively small section of the world's population, and she would be

25. Railton, p. 120.
26. You may not like this way of approaching the consequences to be assigned to giving $500 to Oxfam, perhaps influenced by the examples in Derek Parfit, *Reasons and Persons* (Oxford: Oxford University Press, 1984), chap. 3, but that is a *different* objection—and in my view a tempting but mistaken one (see Frank Jackson, "Group Morality," in Philip Pettit et al., *Metaphysics and Morality* [Oxford: Blackwell, 1987], pp. 91–110).

478   *Ethics*   *April 1991*

giving a special place to her own projects, one of which would precisely be helping certain people in the Third World. For her, the people whose welfare she was particularly concerned with would be those people she had studied, and so got to know and understand, living in various villages in the Third World, as opposed to those living in the same house or the same neighborhood as she does.

3. It might well be objected that we can distinguish *two* nearest and dearest objections, and that I have replied to only one of them. One objection is, "How can consequentialists make sense of the fact that there is a relatively small group of people whose welfare plays a special role in our lives, given the agent-neutral nature of consequentialism's value function?" Our reply was that consequentialism should be viewed decision theoretically. The way right value translates into right action is through an agent's beliefs, and that when this is appreciated, empirical facts about our cognitive powers and situation make it plausible that our actions should be highly focused much of the time. The other objection is, "How can consequentialists make sense of it being the *particular* small group of people that it mostly is?" Perhaps consequentialism can make sense of there being a small group, but why the small group of family, friends, fellow citizens, and the like that it so often is?

One possible reply is that consequentialism cannot make sense of this but that that is no objection to it. We *are* outrageously tribal in our everyday morality and, hence, so much the better for consequentialism that it makes this clear. I cannot believe this. I grant that we are unduly tribal but not that we are outrageously so. I think that we can give a consequentialist explanation of why, for most of us, the special group is our family and friends in terms of empirical facts about human character and psychology.

One way you might draw on empirical facts about human nature is to argue that some particular action giving preference to family and friends in a way which goes against consequentialist principles is wrong but excusable in some sense because it is the exercising of a character which is good in consequentialist terms. This is William Godwin's claim about his famous example of your having to choose between rescuing Fenelon, a famous author and archbishop, and a valet who happens to be your own father, from a burning house: rescuing your father is the wrong action but at the same time the action which springs from the right character.[27] The idea is that although there is perhaps in theory a better character which would lead to the best action as judged consequentially, in practice such a character is not available to us, or at least not to most of us.

27. William Godwin, *Enquiry concerning Political Justice* (Oxford: Oxford University Press, 1971). The example is given on p. 71: the point about character was something of an afterthought prompted by the reception that greeted his answer that you ought to abandon your father (see p. 325). Railton takes a similar position on his example quoted earlier about a commuting marriage.

I think that there is an element of "ducking the question" about this reply. If the action which favors family and friends is right and consequentialism says that it is wrong, then consequentialism is false, and there's an end on it. If, on the other hand, the claim is that it is the action which favors family and friends which is wrong, then it is *that* which needs to be established, not facts about good character. Or perhaps what we are being offered is a *variant* on consequentialism according to which an action is to be judged not directly but via the status, judged consequentially, of the character which gives rise to it, but then we appear to be landed with a dubious compromise reminiscent of rule utilitarianism.[28] If consequences are the key in one place, why not across the board?

I am not here denying the correct and important point that some particular action may be wrong in consequentialist terms and yet spring from a character which is right in consequentialist terms.[29] I am denying that the point helps with the essentials of the nearest and dearest objection. For the consequences of having a character which gives a special place in one's affections and concerns to those persons who are closest to one are, in the main, consequences of the *manifestations* of such a character, that is, of the actions which are especially directed to the needs of those closest to one. Hence, a consequentialist justification of such a character presupposes a consequentialist justification of those actions—which returns us to the very question raised by the nearest and dearest objection. Of course it is not the case for every character trait that the consequences of possessing it are, in the main, the consequences of manifesting it. A major consequence of possessing a certain character trait may be that people know that you possess it, which knowledge may in turn have a major effect on their behavior without it ever being necessary to manifest that disposition. Being disposed to react with pointless violence on being attacked is an example; a nation's disposition to make a nuclear response to a major nuclear attack is another possible example familiar in the literature on nuclear deterrence. Our point, though, is that the character trait of being especially concerned with the welfare of those closest to us is, like most dispositions, known by and large through its manifestations and has its effects principally via those manifestations. I know that you are especially concerned about the welfare of your family because your actions display that concern. Hence, a consequentialist justification of that character trait awaits a consequentialist justification of those actions.[30]

28. Railton makes it clear that he is not offering such a variant. I am not so sure about Pettit and Brennan.

29. See, e.g., Railton; Sidgwick; and Parfit, sec. 14.

30. Nor am I denying the relevance of the distinction between evaluation of action and evaluation of character in explaining the very mixed feelings we would have toward a father who saved a stranger in preference to his daughter on the ground that he happened to know that the stranger was slightly more worthy of saving from an agent-neutral point of view. The distinction enables the consequentialist to explain the mixed feelings as a response to witnessing simultaneously the manifesting of a wrong character in a right action. I think that this is part of the purpose to which Godwin wished to put the distinction.

480   *Ethics   April 1991*

Be all this as it may, I think that points about character and human nature can be put to more direct work here. One's character can be a major factor in settling what consequences are likely, and so can be a major factor in settling what acts are right from the (act) consequentialist's point of view.

Some actions are such that they only have good results if they are followed up in the right way. Taking the first capsule in a course of antibiotics will only have good results if the remainder are taken at the right times; agreeing to write a book review will only have good results if you write the review in good time; going on a beach holiday will only have good results if you avoid getting badly sunburnt; and so on and so forth. In all these cases it is better not to start if you are not going to follow up in an appropriate way. From the consequentialist perspective whether action A ought to be done depends in part on what the agent would in fact do subsequent to doing A.[31]

This means that in deciding what to do here and now an agent must take account of what he or she will do in the future, and that involves taking very seriously questions of character. Do I have the persistence that will be called for, will I remain sufficiently enthusiastic about the project to put in the time required, will I be able to retain a sufficiently impartial outlook, will I be able to avoid the various temptations that will arise, and so on and so forth? For some of us in some situations these kinds of considerations count *against* attempting to secure benefits for our friends and family. We do better sometimes with people we are not so close to. Some men should most definitely not play doubles in tennis with their wives as partners. But as a rule we do better for reasons of character (that no doubt have an evolutionary explanation) with projects that involve family and friends rather than strangers. This is simply because we are much less likely to lose the enthusiasm required to see the project through to a successful conclusion when the project benefits people we have a particular affection for. Perhaps a mundane example will make the point clearer. Jones may be able, in principle, to do an equally good job of organizing the seminars in history or the seminars in philosophy for the forthcoming year. She has the required knowledge and contacts in both areas. She is however much more excited by philosophy

31. In Frank Jackson and Robert Pargetter, "Oughts, Options, and Actualism," *Philosophical Review* 95 (1986): 233–55, we argue that this is true in general, not just for consequentialism, provided only that consequences sometimes play a central role in determining what ought to be done. This view is controversial; see the extensive literature referred to therein. In Frank Jackson, "Understanding the Logic of Obligation," *Proceedings of the Aristotelian Society* 62, suppl. (1988): 255–70, I argue that the best way to understand what is going on is in terms of early actions of the agent being actions of early temporal parts. (In both papers the argument is conducted, for reasons of expository convenience, mainly in terms of what *objectively* ought to be done, rather than the decision theoretic ought that I have put in center stage here. I now think that this was an unfortunate choice of argumentative strategy: it obscured the point I have highlighted here—that ethics pertains most particularly to acting.)

than by history. In such a case, even prescinding from her own enjoyment, it may well be that she ought to take on the task of organizing the philosophy seminars. For, although she knows that she *could* do equally well at either, she knows that she *would* most likely do better if she takes on the philosophy program, and her knowledge of this fact should influence her to agree to take on the philosophy program rather than the history program.

We have seen that the good consequentialist should focus her attentions on securing the well-being of a relatively small number of people, herself included, not because she rates their welfare more highly than the welfare of others but because she is in a better position to secure their welfare. Typically, this will involve her in settling on a relatively extended program of action which will take some resolution and strength of character to carry forward successfully. Before she starts she knows, if she is at all like most of us, that the chances of success are much greater if she makes the relatively small group those who are her family and friends, rather than those she hardly knows. There are exceptions to this generalization about human psychology, perhaps Mother Teresa is one, perhaps Ralph Nader is another; from reports it seems that they have the ability to carry through a demanding program of action which benefits a group of people which, though tiny by comparison with the population of the world, is large by comparison with the circle of family, friends, and associates that provide the principle focus of action for most of us. They do not seem to be dependent on the kind of close personal relationships that are essential to keep most of us from being outrageously selfish.

CONCLUSION

Consequentialism tackles the question of what an agent ought to do in terms of the values of outcomes and assigns those values in an agent independent way, and yet the lives we consider worth living give a quite central place to certain of our fellow human beings. We have an agent relative moral outlook. My argument has been that the consequentialist can plausibly explain agent relativity in terms of the role probability plays in the recovery of what an agent ought to do from the consequentialist's value function. The injunction to maximize *expected* moral utility, when combined with the facts we listed under the heading of the sector plan, means that the consequentialist can accommodate our conviction that a morally good life gives a special place to responsibilities toward a smallish group. *Which* smallish group is another question, and here I argued that for most of us the group should be chosen tribally. Because of empirical facts about our natures, that choice decreases the chance that we will backslide.

One objection to consequentialism is that it conflicts with firmly held moral convictions, in particular concerning our obligations toward our nearest and dearest. It may be urged that my reply to this objection is seriously incomplete. For we can reasonably easily describe a possible

482 *Ethics April 1991*

case where the factors I mentioned as providing a justification in consequentialist terms for favoring one's nearest and dearest do not apply, and yet, according to commonsense morality, one should favor, or at the least it is permissible to favor, one's nearest and dearest.[32] My concern, though, has been to reply to the objection that consequentialism would, given the way things more or less are, render the morally good life not worth living. I take this to be the really disturbing aspect of the nearest and dearest objection to consequentialism. Consequentialists can perhaps live with the conflict with commonsense morality, drawing for instance on the notorious difficulties attending giving a rationale for its central features.[33] But it seems to me that they cannot live with the conflict with a life worth living, given the way things more or less are. That would be to invite the challenge that their conception of what ought to be done had lost touch with *human* morality.

32. I am indebted to David Lewis and Kim Sterelny for forcibly reminding me of this fact.

33. See, e.g., Shelly Kagan, *The Limits of Morality* (Oxford: Oxford University Press, 1989).

[19]

ARTICLES

An Objectivist's Guide to Subjective Value

Graham Oddie and Peter Menzies*

Oedipus killed his father and made love to his mother. Accepting Greek, and conventional, views on the morality of patricide and incest, Oedipus acted wrongly on both counts. But that is not the whole of the story. For it was precisely in the attempt to avoid these very wrongs that Oedipus so acted, believing in the light of the best evidence available to him that he was successfully avoiding them. Cases like this lead us naturally to a familiar distinction: between the objective and subjective notions of moral rightness. But which, if either, of these two notions is the primary one for moral theory, and what exactly are the relations between them? We address this question from within a broadly consequentialist framework, arguing for a version of objectivism which explains and justifies subjectivism where it is right and corrects it where it is wrong.

According to the consequentialist, the moral rightness of an option is related in some way to the value of its consequences. A major problem for the consequentialist is to explain the nature of this relation. In particular, is the morally right action the one with the best consequences, or is the morally right action the one which is best in the light of the agent's beliefs? The subjectivist claims that the primary notion for moral theory is given by what is best by the agent's lights (or, as we will say, what has greatest subjective value) regardless of what is actually the best.[1] The objectivist claims that the primary notion for moral theory is given by what is best (or, as we will say, what has greatest objective value) regardless of how things seem to the agent.[2]

* We wish to thank David Braddon-Mitchell, Frank Jackson, David Lewis, Hugh Mellor, Peter Milne, Joe Mintoff, Philip Pettit, and an anonymous referee for this journal for helpful conversations, correspondence, and criticism, which have influenced the argument and final shape of this article.

1. For a recent defense of decision-theoretic subjectivism see Frank Jackson, "Decision-theoretic Consequentialism and the Nearest and Dearest Objection," *Ethics* 101 (1991): 461–82.

2. For a defense of decision-theoretic objectivism, see D. H. Mellor, "Objective Decision Making," *Social Theory and Practice* 9 (1983): 289–309. Other philosophers

Ethics 102 (April 1992): 512–533

The version of objectivism which we will defend is this: the correct regulative ideal for the moral agent is that of maximizing objective value. In this sense the notion of value which is of primary significance for moral theory is an objective one. But it by no means follows that there is no role in moral theory for a suitable notion of subjective value. For an agent typically does not know the objective structure of the world and so cannot simply apply the injunction to maximize objective value in selecting an option. Accordingly, the objectivist must explain how an agent, given that his regulative ideal is that of maximizing objective value, is to select an option. We argue that an agent is justified in selecting an option on the basis of her best estimates of the objective values of the options; and we show that these estimates coincide with their subjective values under suitable conditions.

So the structure of the article is as follows. In the next section we set out the terms of the debate between the subjectivist and objectivist. In the section after that we explain the sense in which the concept of objective value has the primary role in moral theory. Next, we motivate, from the objectivist perspective, a selection rule by which an agent is justified in choosing among options, and in the following section we relate this objectivist rule to the standard subjectivist one. In the penultimate section we explore a subjectivist response, and in the final section we consider and disarm a seemingly persuasive objection to objectivism.

SUBJECTIVISM AND OBJECTIVISM CHARACTERIZED

The debate between the objectivist and the subjectivist presupposes two background consequentialist theses. The first is that the moral agent ought to select the most valuable option available to her. The second is that the relative value of an option is determined by the values and the probabilities of the outcomes of the option. To be specific, we will assume that the value of an option is given by the expectation of the value of the various outcomes of the option. Jointly these core theses are equivalent to the thesis that an agent should select the option with maximum expected value. From here on, for brevity we will identify the value of an option with the expected value of that option's outcomes.[3]

---

have defended objectivism though not in the decision-theoretic form that we prefer. See Peter Railton, "Alienation, Consequentialism, and the Demands of Morality," *Philosophy and Public Affairs*, vol. 13 (1984), reprinted in *Consequentialism and Its Critics*, ed. S. Scheffler (Oxford: Oxford University Press, 1988); and David Brink, *Moral Realism and the Foundations of Ethics* (Cambridge: Cambridge University Press, 1989).

3. We can relax the first (maximizing) thesis and still generate the dilemma: all we need to assume is that rightness is determined by, or supervenes on, value. Satisficing consequentialism, e.g., will still have subjectivist and objectivist versions. For a series of

514   *Ethics   April 1992*

Let us put aside, for the moment, the nature of the underlying function which assigns values to outcomes—for example, whether it is objective or subjective, and whether it is agent-relative or agent-neutral.[4] Even disregarding those aspects of the value function, the two core theses leave open a choice between two different kinds of probability, and thereby two different kinds of value possessed by the options. The subjective value of an option is given by the agent's degrees of belief (which we will call *credence*) together with the value of the possible outcomes of the act. The objective value of an option is given by the objective probability (which we will call *chance*) together with the value of the possible outcomes of the act.

Subjective and objective value thus differ in the nature of the probabilistic weights which, in conjunction with the values of outcomes, determine the value of the options. For subjective value we will employ the traditional Jeffrey account.[5] Where Cr is the agent's credence function, A is an option, the O_j are various possible outcomes, and Value is the function which assigns values to outcomes, the subjective value of A is given by:

$$SV(A) = \Sigma_j Cr(O_j/A)\text{Value}(O_j \& A).$$

Objective value, on the other hand, is given by chance together with value of outcomes. Where Ch is the actual conditional chance function, the actual objective value of A is given by:

$$OV(A) = \Sigma_j Ch(O_j/A)\text{Value}O_j \& A).$$

Putting this in a slightly more general form (of which OV is a special case), where $OV(A/K_i)$ is the objective value of A on the supposition that the hypothesis K_i is a full description of the relevant objective chances and Ch_i is the objective chance function according to the hypothesis K_i, we have:

$$OV(A/K_i) = \Sigma_j Ch_i(O_j/A)\text{Value}(O_j \& A).$$

There are two broad positions corresponding to the two kinds of value. The subjectivist claims that the kind of value which is of primary

arguments that value just is expected value, see Graham Oddie and Peter Milne, "Act and Value: Expectation and the Representability of Moral Theories," *Theoria* (in press).

4. The dispute between subjectivism and objectivism arises quite independently of the nature of the value of the outcomes. For example, the dispute arises in the same way for the theory of prudence as it does for the theory of morality: Is the prudentially right option the one which would be best for the agent in fact, or the one which the agent thinks would be best for her?

5. See Richard Jeffrey, *The Logic of Decision*, 2d ed. (Chicago: University of Chicago Press, 1983).

significance for moral theory, because it is the notion which determines
obligation, is subjective. The subjectivist claims that the regulative
ideal of the moral agent is always to perform the option with maximal
subjective value.

The objectivist claims that the notion of value which is of most
significance for moral theory, because it determines obligations, is
objective. The objectivism we will defend claims that maximizing objective value is the moral agent's regulative ideal.

A simple case illustrates the difference between the two kinds of
value and the two approaches based on them.

> *Case 1.*—Suppose that there are three drugs for a certain
> fatal condition: drugs A, B, and C. As it happens, drug A will
> definitely cure a particular patient but with some short-term and
> unpleasant side-effects. Drug C will definitely kill the patient in
> a way more painful and distressing than the original condition.
> But drug B is rather curious, and rather untypical of drugs in
> general. Its effect on the course of the disease depends upon
> certain chancy factors at the molecular level. In fact, with this
> particular patient there is a 50 percent chance that the desirable
> reactions will take place, and the disease halted in its tracks with
> the same short-term unpleasant side-effects that A has. But there
> is also a 50 percent chance that the drug will have the same effect
> as drug C. However, the doctor assigns a subjective probability
> of only 50 percent to A's curing the patient but a subjective
> probability of 100 percent to B's curing the patient. He prescribes
> B and the patient, unfortunately, dies.

According to the subjectivist, the doctor has done the morally right
thing; but according to the objectivist, the doctor has done the wrong
thing. The following case illustrates the converse situation.

> *Case 2.*—The medical and epistemic facts are as in case 1.
> But the doctor perversely chooses A, even though he assigns a
> subjective probability of 50 percent to the drug's leading to the
> patient's death. He does not believe it is the (morally) best action
> to perform, all things considered, but he has a whim to do some-
> thing risky with a patient he doesn't particularly like.

Again the subjectivist will come up with a single unequivocal judgment:
the doctor chose the consequentially wrong option, despite the fact
that he ensured the patient's recovery. The objectivist will disagree.

There is a third measure of value, and a third position riding on
it, which must be distinguished from both subjective and objective
conceptions of value. According to the third measure, the value of an
option in the case in which it is realized is the value of the actual
outcome the option (usually in conjunction with external chance factors)
produces; and in the case in which the option is not realized, its value
is the value of the outcome the option would have produced had that

516   *Ethics   April 1992*

option been chosen. Call this *actual-outcome value*. Actual-outcome consequentialism claims the agent ought to maximize the actual-outcome value of acts.

Already cases 1 and 2 undermine the thesis that the actual outcome, in a chancy moral set-up, is morally relevant at the moment of choice. For suppose the doctor knows all the chances involved and nevertheless chooses B. In fact the patient is lucky and survives, so that the actual outcome is exactly as it would have been under drug A. Still, reasonable subjectivists and objectivists would both say that the doctor subjected the patient to an unnecessary risk of fatality and, thereby acted wrongly.

To make actual-outcome consequentialism even more implausible one need only increase the probabilities of the bad outcome, thereby exaggerating the amount good luck contributes to the actual favorable outcome. The patient may or may not be grateful in such a case for the favorable outcome, but if he is, he should not be grateful that the doctor did the right thing. He should simply be grateful that he has had a lucky escape. What the doctor did was not responsible for his good fortune, even if it made his good fortune possible.[6]

A CRITIQUE OF SUBJECTIVISM

There are, in fact, different underlying motivations for subjectivism and these make for distinctive versions of the doctrine. Some consequentialists have embraced subjectivism because they think that the notion of objective value is incoherent or lacks applicability. For the purposes of this article we are assuming that the nature of the value function over outcomes is not in dispute between the subjectivist and the objectivist. So the kind of consequentialist who thinks the notion of objective value is incoherent must be construed as calling into question the notion of objective chance.

In our view the subjectivist who chooses to defend the view on these grounds puts herself at a disadvantage. For there is a considerable consensus among philosophers that there is a coherent notion of objective chance. It is true that there is controversy over the correct analysis of this notion: some favor a modal frequency interpretation; others favor a ratio of possible worlds construal; and others take it as

---

6. The distance between actual-outcome consequentialism and the expectation thesis can be narrowed. (We are grateful to an anonymous referee for making this point clear.) Suppose we think of an objective probability distribution over outcomes as itself an outcome, an outcome that is instrumentally valued or disvalued according to its expected value. Then each action would be valued according to its actual outcome. The doctor who lowers the objective probability of recovery, but where recovery (by chance) ensues, has failed to "produce" a good outcome because when chance is present one produces outcomes (other than the direct probability distribution itself) only by raising their objective probability relative to some relevant state, and in this case the comparison is taken to be the better drug.

an ontological primitive.[7] It is not, however, germane to our purposes to adjudicate between these rival interpretations. We need only the thesis that there is some coherent notion of objective chance. Clearly, commonsense judgments support the claim that there is such a notion. If you and I differ in the subjective probability we assign to a patient's recovering from a disease on being given a certain drug, we can nevertheless agree that there is some fact of the matter—some fact about objective chances—which determines which, if either, probability assignment is correct, or which is closer to being correct. This objectivity about chance implies an objectivity about expected value. If there is some fact of the matter about the probability of the drug curing the disease, then there is a fact of the matter about whether administering or not administering the drug has greater objective value.

A different, more plausible, kind of subjectivism allows the intelligibility and applicability of objective chance and of objective value of options but asserts that these concepts play no role, or only a secondary one, in moral theory. This position is sometimes supported by the claim that moral theory is principally concerned with providing a practical guide to action: we expect a moral theory like consequentialism to tell us what we should do in any given decision situation. Of its very nature, a practical guide to action must be one which an agent can have before her mind; that is, it must be one which employs only materials accessible to the mind of an agent. But typically agents do not know what the objective values of the options are because they do not know the relevant objective chances. For this reason alone, then, it would seem that the practical guide to action cannot proceed in terms of the objective values of the various options, it can proceed only in terms of the values guaranteed to be accessible to agents, namely, the subjective values.[8]

In response to this argument, we concede that one of the roles of moral theory is to provide a practical guide to action. But we would argue that it cannot do this without according a privileged position to the notions of objective chance and, by virtue of that, objective value. For we claim that there is a constraint of rationality governing the formation of the decision-relevant probabilities and values, a constraint of rationality which the subjectivist who grants the legitimacy of the objective notions will be hard put to deny. The constraint is

7. Bas van Fraassen offers a modal frequency interpretation of objective chance in his *The Scientific Image* (Oxford: Clarendon, 1980), chap. 6; Ronald Giere offers an interpretation in terms of possible worlds in "A Laplacean Formal Semantics for Single-Case Propensities," *Journal of Philosophical Logic* 5 (1976): 321–53. Karl Popper can be seen as taking chance as an ontological primitive in "The Propensity Interpretation of Probability," *British Journal for the Philosophy of Science* 10 (1959): 25–42.

8. As we understand it, this is the subjectivist position embraced by Jackson in "Decision-theoretic Consequentialism and the Nearest and Dearest Objection."

518 *Ethics* *April 1992*

that a rational moral agent will aim to bring her credences in line with the true objective chances and, thereby, to bring the values she assigns to options in line with their true objective values. Of course, this constraint is consistent with the fact that even a rational agent will not typically know what the values of these objective quantities are. But the constraint does enjoin the agent in these circumstances to employ her best estimates of these quantities. In other words, the constraint enjoins the rational agent to constrain her subjective credences by her best estimates of the true objective chances and, thereby, to constrain her decision-making values by her best estimates of the true objective values.

It is this constraint of rationality which gives the notion of objective value primacy, in moral theory, over the subjective notion. For the constraint embodies the thought that a rational agent should try to come as close as possible, by her lights, to the ideal of maximizing the objective value of her actions. Even though she may not know what these values are, her goal as a moral agent is to approximate them as far as she can. But how exactly is the rational agent to go about doing this? What precisely is to count as the agent's best estimate of the objective value of an option? We take up these questions in the next section.

AN OBJECTIVIST SELECTION RULE

The task before us is to provide a selection rule by which a rational agent, whose ideal. it is to maximize objective value, can, in the light of the information available to her, justifiably choose between alternative actions. A natural first thought is that the selection rule go something like this: select that option which is most likely, according to your subjective credences, to have maximal objective value.

Unfortunately, this suggestion is not correct, as can be seen from an example of Frank Jackson's.

> *Case 3.*—A doctor must decide on the correct treatment for a patient who has a serious skin complaint. Careful consideration of the literature has led her to the following opinions. Drug A will relieve the condition but will not completely cure it. One of the drugs B and C will completely cure the skin condition; the other will kill the patient, but there is no way she can tell which of the two is the perfect cure and which is the killer.[9]

In this case, the intuitively right answer that a selection rule must yield is that the doctor is justified in prescribing drug A: for the possibility that drug B or drug C might effect a complete cure is outweighed by the significant probability of death associated with them. But the proposed selection rule does not tell the doctor to prescribe drug A,

9. See ibid.

because given her credences A is the least likely of the three to realize maximal objective value.

The suggested selection rule tries to capture in too simple-minded a way the idea that a rational moral agent is justified in choosing among the alternative actions by estimating their objective values. As the example just described makes clear, one cannot explain these estimates simply in terms of the agent's distribution of credences over hypotheses about maximal objective value. The explanation misses the crucial point that the rational agent estimates the objective value of the actions by virtue of her estimates of the objective chances involved.

To clarify this point let us consider the way in which a rational agent should go about estimating the value of a chance function in a situation of incomplete information. Suppose you (a paradigm rational agent) wish to estimate the chance that a particular coin has of landing heads if tossed. While you do not know for sure what the chance is, you are certain that the coin is biased either 2:1 in favor of heads or 2:1 in favor of tails. In this situation, what is your best estimate of the chance that the coin will land heads if it is tossed? It is reasonable to suppose that your best estimate is obtained by taking a weighted average of the chances according to the different hypotheses, the weights being the credences you assign to these different hypotheses. For example, if you assign a credence of three-fourths to the hypothesis that the coin is biased in favor of heads and a credence of one-fourth to the hypothesis that the coin is biased in favor of tails, it is reasonable to suppose your best estimate of the chance is this:

$$Cr[Ch(H/T) = 2/3] \cdot 2/3 + Cr[Ch(H/T) = 1/3] \cdot 1/3 = 7/12.$$

Since you favor the hypothesis of bias in favor of heads it is obvious that your best estimate should be closer to that possibility than its rival, and that is the result delivered.

More generally, we propose the thesis that your best estimate of the chance of B given A is your *credence-mean estimate* of the chance of B given A. Specifically:

$$\Sigma_i Cr(K_i) Ch_i(B/A),$$

where Cr is your credence function, the K_is are hypotheses about the chance of B given A, and $Ch_i(B/A)$ is the relevant chance according to the hypothesis K_i.

This thesis is, in fact, an instance of the more general methodological thesis that an agent's best estimate of a magnitude X, in the light of his total information as represented by his credence function, is his credence-mean estimate of the magnitude. Suppose that an agent wants to estimate the magnitude X in the light of his total information.

520   *Ethics*   *April 1992*

He has to choose a value for X which, in some sense, minimizes error. Of course, only the actual value minimizes real error. But the agent has no access to the actual value apart from the information he has. Which value for X should he choose which will minimize the amount of error he can expect to make, given what he believes? Where x is the true value of X, $(x - y)^2$ is a plausible measure of the error in the estimate y. So the estimate which minimizes expected error minimizes the quantity: $\Sigma_x Cr(X = x)(y - x)^2$. By a simple and well known argument, the value of y which does so minimize expected error is just $\Sigma_x Cr(X = x) \cdot x$, that is, the credence-mean estimate of the magnitude.

In the light of these considerations, let us return to the problem of how to formulate the idea that a rational moral agent should choose among options on the basis of her best estimates of their objective values. As intimated earlier, the agent arrives at her best estimates of the objective values by estimating the chances involved. This suggests the idea of replacing the chances in the formula for objective value with the agent's best estimates of these chances. Making this substitution we obtain:

$$KV(A) = \Sigma_j [\Sigma_i Cr(K_i) Ch_i(O_j/A)] \text{Value}(A \& O_j).$$

We call this the formula for the K-value of the option A to emphasize the role played in it by the hypotheses about chance K_i. With a little more work, we can see how this formula captures the objectivist idea that a rational agent employs best estimates of objective value as her guide to decision-making. Rearranging the summands of (KV) we obtain the following:

$$KV(A) = \Sigma_i Cr(K_i)[\Sigma_j Ch_i(O_j/A) \text{Value}(A \& O_j)].$$

By the general definition of OV (objective value), this is tantamount to:

$$KV(A) = \Sigma_i Cr(K_i) OV(A/K_i).$$

This last formula says that the K-value of an option is the credence-mean estimate of its objective value. Given the general methodological result above, this means that the K-value that an agent assigns to an option represents her best estimate of its objective value. This is, of course, just the result we wanted. Accordingly, we propose that the selection rule that the objectivist should endorse is: select the act with maximal K-value.

There are several features worth noting about the formula for K-value and the accompanying selection rule.

First, the rule counts as a practical guide to action since it employs only materials accessible to the mind of an ordinary agent: unlike objective value, the K-value of an option can be determined by an agent who lacks complete information about the true configuration of chances in the world.

Second, the selection rule yields the intuitively right answer in Jackson's example—the answer that the doctor is morally justified in prescribing drug A. It is easy to see why this is so. In the example, the doctor divides her credence between the hypothesis that drug B effects a complete cure and drug C kills the patient, and the hypothesis that drug B kills the patient and drug C effects a complete cure. Accordingly, the K-value of the option of prescribing drug B, and also that of prescribing drug C, will be an average of the objective values of the option under each of the two hypotheses. Obviously, this average will be less than the K-value of prescribing drug A which, in virtue of the fact that the doctor is certain that drug A will effect a partial cure, is given by the value of the outcome of a partial cure for the patient.

Third, in many applications the relevant credences appearing in the formula are those of the agent at the time of decision. This is certainly the case when the agent invokes the rule of maximizing K-value as part of her decision-making procedure. It is also the case when one is assessing the moral blameworthiness of an agent. For example, a plausible conjecture is that an agent is judged worthy of blame for a wrongdoing if, or to the extent that, the K-value of the wrongful act was less than that of some other act available to her where the K-values of the acts are calculated in terms of the agent's credences at the time of the decision.[10] It is important, however, not to overlook the fact that an agent can assess the justifiability of her own actions after, as well as before, making the decision, and also the fact that the justifiability of an action can be assessed from our perspective as well as from the agent's perspective. The formula for K-value readily lends itself to these assessments. One simply plugs in the relevant credence: either the agent's credence function as it is at the time of the decision, or after the decision, or our own credence function rather than the agent's. But whichever person's credence function is being

10. This conjecture is a simple modification of a proposal made by Frank Jackson in "A Probabilistic Approach to Moral Responsibility," in *Proceedings of the Seventh International Congress of Logic, Methodology, and Philosophy of Science*, ed. R. Barcan Marcus et al. (Amsterdam: Elsevier, 1986), pp. 351–66. Of course, blameworthiness also involves important issues of culpable ignorance, issues which would require separate treatment. Jackson makes an interesting attempt to account for culpable ignorance without modifying his simple subjectivist model. But culpable ignorance is a common problem for both the objectivist and the subjectivist, and whatever plausible solution the subjectivist might have can also be used by the objectivist.

522 *Ethics April 1992*

used, the *K*-value assigned to an option represents that person's best estimate of the objective value of the option.

SUBJECTIVISM EXPLAINED

We have motivated, from an objectivist standpoint, a suitable objectivist selection rule. But what is the relationship between this objectivist selection rule and the subjectivist rule? This might be viewed as a particularly pressing question in light of the fact that the subjectivist selection rule is a very familiar one with well-understood formal properties.[11]

The answer to this question is comparatively straightforward: the *K*-value of an option is identical with its subjective value provided two assumptions hold true. We first state the two assumptions and then show that the two kinds of value coincide under these assumptions.

The first assumption is the *Principal Principle*. The Principal Principle (so-called by David Lewis) governs the way in which a rational agent's subjective credences should cohere with her beliefs about chance.[12]

> If Cr is the credence function of a rational agent, and $Ch_i(B/A)$ is the chance of B given A according to the hypothesis K_i, then $Cr(B/K_i \& A) = Ch_i(B/A)$.

In ordinary language, this says that if a rational agent is certain of a particular hypothesis about the chance of B given A—say, the hypothesis that the chance of B given A is x—and also certain of A, then the degree of belief she should have in B is also x.

The second assumption is what we call the *Independence Assumption*.

> Where Cr is the credence function of a rational agent, K_i is a hypothesis about the chance of B given A, and A is an option open to the agent, then $Cr(K_i/A) = Cr(K_i)$.

In ordinary language, this says that hypotheses about the chance of B given A are probabilistically independent of the option A. That is to say, the agent does not take performance of the action A to be evidence for or against any particular chance hypothesis.

---

11. See Jeffrey, *The Logic of Decision.*

12. See David Lewis, "A Subjectivist's Guide to Objective Chance," in *Studies in Inductive Logic and Probability*, ed. Richard Jeffrey (Berkeley: University of California Press, 1980), vol. 2, reprinted in Lewis's *Philosophical Papers* (Oxford: Oxford University Press, 1986), 2:83–113. Our formulation of the Principal Principle differs from Lewis's formulation in at least two respects: first, our formulation proceeds in terms of a subject's present (posterior-to-learning) credence function while Lewis's proceeds in terms of a subject's initial (prior-to-learning) credence function; second, our formulation concerns conditional credence and chance whereas Lewis's concerns absolute credence and chance.

These two assumptions imply that the K-value of the act A is identical with its subjective value. Let us start with the original formulation of K-value:

$$KV(A) = \Sigma_j[\Sigma_i Cr(K_i)Ch_i(O_j/A)]\text{Value }(A\&O_j).$$

Applying the Principal Principle, we can replace the quantity $Ch_i(O_j/A)$ with $Cr(O_j/K_i\&A)$ to obtain:

$$KV(A) = \Sigma_j[\Sigma_i Cr(K_i)Cr(O_j/K_i\&A)]\text{Value}(A\&O_j).$$

Applying the Independence Assumption, we can replace $Cr(K_i)$ with $Cr(K_i/A)$ to obtain:

$$KV(A) = \Sigma_j[\Sigma_i Cr(K_i/A)Cr(O_j/K_i\&A)]\text{Value}(A\&O_j).$$

Finally, a standard expansion theorem for conditional probability tells us that the bracketed expectation equals the conditional probability $Cr(O_j/A)$ so that we can obtain:

$$KV(A) = \Sigma_j Cr(O_j/A)\text{Value}(A\&O_j) = SV(A).$$

This result entails that the objectivist selection rule will yield the same prescriptions as the subjectivist rule in all decision situations in which the above two assumptions hold true. As we will argue, this constitutes an explanatory success for objectivism. Starting from the objectivist's position that the agent's ideal should be to maximize objective value, we can explain and justify the subjectivist selection rule, to the extent that it is indeed correct, and thereby explain whatever plausibility subjectivism has.

The coincidence of the K-value and subjective value might encourage the subjectivist to attempt a similar explanation of the plausibility of objectivism from a purely subjective standpoint. For does it not follow from the result that, provided that the two assumptions hold, an agent whose ideal it is to maximize subjective value will, as it happens, be selecting in accordance with her best estimates of objective value?

This line of argument can work for the subjectivist only to the extent that she can show either that the two assumptions required for the coincidence result always hold true, or that, when they do not hold and K-value and subjective value diverge, the subjectivist rather than the objectivist selection rule gives the correct recommendation.

The Principal Principle looks to be a safe assumption. Indeed, provided the subjectivist countenances propositions about chance at all, the principle is one which the subjectivist might well wish to embrace, since it formulates a purely internal coherence requirement. The problem for the first horn of the subjectivist dilemma is with the seemingly innocuous Independence Assumption, since this can be shown to fail in the case of Newcomb-like decision problems. In these problems, the objectivist selection rule diverges from the subjectivist rule. All that remains is to determine which of the two rules gives the correct recommendation in such cases. If it is the objectivist selection rule, then that demonstrates objectivism's explanatory priority, an explanatory priority which the subjectivist cannot invert.

Let us consider the original Newcomb problem to see how the Independence Assumption fails.[13] You have to make a choice about taking the monetary contents of two boxes that are put before you. (In order to change this from a mere prudential problem, we stipulate that whatever sums of money you receive as a result of your choice you will donate to a deserving charity and that no such charity will receive the money otherwise.) One box is transparent and you can see that it contains $1,000. The other box is opaque and you have been told that the contents of the opaque box have been determined on the basis of a prediction made yesterday by a predictor: if the predictor predicted you would take the contents of the opaque box alone, he put a million dollars in the box; if he predicted that you would take the contents of the transparent box as well as those of the opaque box, he put nothing in the opaque box. (The predictor is a Randian egoist who strongly disapproves of gratuitous acts of charity.) You know that the predictor is fairly reliable in that his predictions of the choices of other agents in this situation have been correct 75 percent of the time. You must decide between taking the contents of the opaque box alone and taking the contents of both boxes.

We will not plod through all the details of the calculation of the K-values and the subjective values of the two options. The crucial point is that, in calculating the K-expected value of, for example, taking both boxes, you have to consider the relevant chance hypotheses. One such hypothesis, call it K^*, is the following:

$$Ch(\text{Charity gets } \$1M + \$1,000/\text{I take both boxes}) = 1, \text{ and}$$
$$Ch(\text{Charity gets } \$1,000/\text{I take both boxes}) = 0.$$

This hypothesis about conditional chances is equivalent to the conjecture that there is a million dollars already in the opaque box. But your credence function may well make this hypothesis dependent on the action of your taking the contents of both boxes. If you were to learn that you will take both boxes, that may well, in the light of what you

13. Newcomb's problem was first discussed by Robert Nozick in "Newcomb's Problem and Two Principles of Choice," in *Essays in Honor of Carl G. Hempel*, ed. Nicholas Rescher (Dordrecht: Reidel, 1969).

know about the reliability of the predictor, lower your degree of belief that there is a million dollars in the opaque box, or equivalently, lower your degree of belief in the hypothesis K^*. In other words, your credences can reasonably be taken to be such that $Cr(K^*/\text{I take both boxes})$ is less than $Cr(K^*)$. The failure of the Independence Assumption for this chance hypothesis and for its rivals means that the rule of maximizing K-value yields a different answer from the rule of maximizing subjective value. Some elementary calculations show that the objectivist rule recommends taking both boxes, while the subjectivist rule recommends taking the opaque box alone. We assume that the objectivist two-box recommendation is the correct one in this particular version of Newcomb's problem.[14]

Independently of the concerns of this article, it is a fairly common complaint that the subjectivist rule goes awry in Newcomb's original problem as well as in more realistic decision problems. The common diagnosis has been that the subjectivist rule is not properly sensitive to the agent's beliefs about the causal structure of her decision situation. As rivals to the rule of maximizing subjective value, alternative selection rules have been proposed that are appropriately sensitive to the causal structure.[15] The objectivist rule we have presented is, in fact, a causally sensitive selection rule, since the chances which enter into the formula for K-value reflect the agent's causal beliefs. Indeed, it can be shown that this selection rule agrees with other causally sensitive selection rules in yielding the intuitively right prescriptions in a range of realistic decision problems.[16] But we motivated the rule of maximizing K-value in a way that had nothing to do with Newcomb problems. The fact that it is a causally sensitive selection rule able to handle all Newcomb problems provides, in our view, strong independent confirmation of

14. We make no claim about whether the objectivist recommendation is correct for other versions of Newcomb's problem, such as the version in which the decision-maker believes the predictor is infallible. We reserve our judgment about this particular version, since we believe there are reasons for thinking that it does not represent a genuine decision problem.

15. For a survey of these so-called causal decision theories, see David Lewis, "Causal Decision Theory," *Australasian Journal of Philosophy*, vol. 59 (1981), reprinted in his *Philosophical Papers*, 2:305–37.

16. The objectivist selection rule we have endorsed is identical, or very similar, to selection rules which several philosophers have developed to deal with Newcomb decision problems. It is identical to the rule Richard Jeffrey proposed in "Choice, Chance, and Credence," in *Philosophy of Logic*, ed. G. H. von Wright and G. Fløistad (Dordrecht: Nijhoff, 1980); and very similar to the rule endorsed by Jordan Howard Sobel in his "Probability, Chance, and Choice: A Theory of Rational Agency" (University of Toronto, unpublished manuscript). See also Jordan Howard Sobel, "Circumstances and Dominance in a Causal Decision Theory," *Synthese* 63 (1985): 167–202. For a discussion of the relation between the objectivist selection rule and other causally sensitive selection rules, see Peter Menzies, "Newcomb Decision Problems and Causal Decision Theory" (Ph.D. thesis, Stanford University, 1984), chaps. 4 and 5.

526   *Ethics   April 1992*

the original objectivist assumption: that maximization of objective value is the moral agent's regulative ideal.

AN ESCAPE ROUTE EXPLORED

There is one last escape route for the subjectivist here. In response to the argument of the previous section he could switch from the thesis that subjective value is the primary notion to the thesis that *K*-value is the primary notion. Call this position *K-subjectivism*. He could then make use of one half of our derivation (that part which uses the Principal Principle) to state *K* value in the following form:

$$KV(A) = \Sigma_j[\Sigma_i Cr(K_i)Cr(O_j/K_i\&A)]\text{Value}(A\&O_j).$$

K-subjectivism would appear to have a number of advantages. First, the above formulation of *K*-value seems to make no explicit references to the objective chance function. It explicitly mentions only notions which we have conceded are already available to the subjectivist (credence and value of outcome). The connection with chance and objective value is secured by the Principal Principle. From this starting point the subjectivist credentials of the notion of *K*-value seem to be as good as those of subjective value (*SV*).

Second, the selection rule based on this is, of course, identical to the objectivist's. So the *K*-subjectivist can deal with Newcomb problems.

Third, the *K*-subjectivist can apparently reverse our derivations and turn the objectivist explanation on its head. From his point of view, whatever plausibility objectivism might have had is explained by the following fact: that in (primarily) seeking to maximize *K*-value the agent is thereby selecting according to his best estimate of the objective value of options. The derivative role of objective value is explained by the primacy of the goal of *K*-value maximization.[17]

The response is an ingenious one, but it fails on two grounds. First, it is not quite accurate to claim that *K*-value so formulated makes no explicit reference to chances, since it is based on the partition by the K_i's, and these are hypotheses about conditional chance. What is true is that chances don't feature explicitly as weights in the expectation. But objective chances must play a privileged role in any formulation of *K*-value. Further, in any causal decision theory designed to solve Newcomb problems, causal notions, or some objective equivalent, will play a similarly privileged role.

Second, even if we ignore the privileged role accorded to chance, there is still a residual explanatory asymmetry which weighs in favor

17. This subjectivist response is a development of some criticisms made by Frank Jackson when we read an early version of this article at the Philosophy Society, Australian National University in November, 1990. However, we do not wish to imply that Jackson accepts this particular version of the response.

of objectivism. In the first instance the consequentialist is interested in the goodness of outcomes. Ultimately what he wants are objectively good outcomes. Given this, the objectivist aim of performing objectively good acts in order to produce objectively good outcomes has considerable plausibility. Given only partial knowledge of the objective values, the selection rule of choosing by maximal K-value is then naturally motivated by the argument from best epistemic estimates of objective value. The deductive links in this chain of reasoning can certainly be inverted by the K-subjectivist, but at least some of the explanatory power is lost in the process. This is because the starting points of the two positions have radically different degrees of inherent plausibility. It would be a brave subjectivist who claimed that what the consequentialist ultimately wants is not a good outcome but, rather, a world in which agents fulfill the subjectivist regulative ideal of choosing by K-value (as formulated above).

Maximization of K-value can, of course, be independently motivated by the desire to solve Newcomb problems. But such a motivation must concede that K-subjectivism lacks the initial plausibility of objectivism. And further, unlike objectivism, it cannot go on to claim the solution of Newcomb problems as a dramatic confirmation of its starting point—since the K-subjectivist motivates his starting point by its ability to solve those very problems.

Lastly the K-subjectivist, like all subjectivists, has no resources for explaining what is unsatisfactory with an agent's action when he selects by maximal K-value but, through gross inaccuracies in belief, thereby performs an action which falls far short of maximal objective value (as in case 1). The agent did what was best by his lights, period. Provided his lights are seriously enough askew any action at all, no matter how disastrous a contribution it makes to the value of the outcome, can be judged to satisfy fully the demands of morality. The objectivist can make a distinction. The agent's moral ideal is to maximize the objective value of his action, and in this the action he performed fell short of the mark. But the selection procedure he employed ensured that he was justified, given his epistemic situation, in making that choice.[18]

18. Of course the subjectivist could say that there is something wrong with the outcome of the morally good act in case 1 and might appeal to an objectivist parallel. If an agent does the objectively best act but external chance factors combine to produce a bad outcome, then the objectivist will approve of the act but lament the agent's bad luck. The subjectivist might claim that this is strictly analogous to his judgment on case 1. However, what this shows is that the objectivist has access to three distinct notions which the subjectivist collapses into two: justified/unjustified (depending on K-value), good/bad (depending on objective value), and lucky/unlucky (depending on external chance factors). Note also that the objectivist's distinction between being good and being justified may help to clarify the difference between a judgment on the agent from

TABLE 1
JACKSON'S CASE

Option	K_1	K_2	KV
A	5	5	5
B	10	−10	0
C	−10	10	0

AN OBJECTION DISARMED

We are now in a position to give more detailed consideration to Jackson's case (case 3). A similar case has been urged against objectivism by David Lewis.[19] The general structure of these cases is this: an agent has one moderately good option A (objective value of, say, +5), and two options, B and C, one with very high value, and the other with very low value (say, +10 and −10). The agent, while knowing the amounts of value at issue, doesn't know which of B and C is very good and which is very bad. Suppose that the agent divides her credence evenly between the hypothesis (K_1) that the objective values of B and C are +10 and −10, respectively, and the hypothesis (K_2) that they are the other way round. Thus, we have the values given in table 1. In this situation the morally justified act, the act which maximizes K-value, is not the act which maximizes objective value, and the agent knows that it is not.

Here K-value and subjective value coincide, and so according to the subjectivist by choosing A the doctor does the morally correct act in every relevant sense. What should the objectivist say? According to the objectivist, the ideal for the moral agent is that of maximizing objective value. But when the agent does not know which act maximizes objective value, the objectivist argues that she should be guided by her best estimates of the objective values of the options and that these are given by their K-values.

But this generates an objection to objectivism. How can K-value be the agent's best guide to objective value, if the act with maximum

---

a judgment on the act. The good agent will, presumably, choose according to his best estimate of the goodness of options, but the act he thereby chooses may still be a lousy one.

19. David Lewis, "Devil's Bargains and the Real World," in *The Security Gamble: Deterrence Dilemmas in the Nuclear Age*, ed. Douglas MacLean (Totowa, N.J.: Rowan & Allanheld, 1984), p. 154. In conversation Lewis has used such examples against a slightly different objectivist thesis: that subjective rightness is one's best epistemic guide to objective rightness (where subjective [objective] rightness is defined as maximal subjective [objective] value). Against that thesis the example is indeed decisive, since the agent knows in this case that the subjectively right act is not the objectively right act.

K-value is known not to have maximum objective value? Does the example not show that K-value is not the agent's best guide to objective value after all?

Certainly in this case K-value is not a terribly good estimate of objective value, because (*a*) it ranks A above both B and C by averaging the values of B and C; and (*b*) the agent knows that the option with greatest K-value does not have greatest objective value.

The second point is, of course, a quite general problem with taking the credence-mean estimate of a quantity to be one's best estimate of the quantity. This is just as much a problem for probabilities. In ignorance of the true chance, one can employ one's credence-mean estimate of chance as one's best estimate and still know that this estimate is not the real chance. A nice example of this concerns a coin the only information about which one has is that it is biased: that is, $Ch(H) \neq 1/2$. If one's credence function Cr distributes equally over all the other possibilities then, of course, $Cr(H) = 1/2$. The credence-mean estimate of the chance of heads is the only value which, on the information available, chance cannot be.[20]

What the objectivist needs in response to the argument is, on the negative side, a demonstration that the argument does not refute the thesis that K-value is the agent's best guide to objective value, and, on the positive side, an argument that by choosing to maximize K-value the agent is getting as close to maximal objective value as can be expected, given her information. We will deal with these in turn.

To deny that K-value is the best guide to objective value, it is not enough to show that it is not a terribly good guide. One must be committed to one or the other of two additional theses: (1) there is a better guide to objective value; or (2) K-value is not good enough in an absolute sense.

Take 1 first. There seems to be an implicit criterion of comparison of methods lying behind objection 1. Where M and N are such methods, the implicit principle seems to be this:

> M is a superior method for estimating objective value, with respect to a particular set of options, to a method N if the ordering induced by M is closer to the actual ordering than the ordering induced by N.

But of course a good method of estimation would have to satisfy desiderata other than this one. According to this principle alone the best "method" is that which orders options by their actual objective values: but clearly that is no method at all for ignorant agents such as ourselves. If the method is to be epistemically accessible to the agent

---

20. We would like to thank Peter Milne for drawing this example to our attention.

530   *Ethics   April 1992*

it must be appropriately sensitive to the agent's information. In particular it should satisfy the following condition of adequacy:

> If two options are epistemically indistinguishable, then any adequate method of estimation must assign them the same value.

It is clear that however one ought to cash out the notion of epistemic indistinguishability, *B* and *C* in our case are paradigm examples. So for a method *M* to be adequate it must assign the same estimated values to *B* and *C*. *K*-value is one such method. But to be superior to *K*-value a method would have to revise at least one of the judgments concerning the relative merits of *A* and *B*, of *A* and *C*, or of *B* and *C*. The only way of changing the ranking, while remaining adequate, would be to place both *B* and *C* above *A*. But then any advantage that is gained by correctly placing *B* above *A* is lost by incorrectly placing *C* above *A* as well. So no adequate method can be superior to *K*-value in this case.

Now 2. What could the absolute notion be? To deliver the criticism, it would presumably have to be something like this: in general the act with maximal *M*-value from a range of options must be the act with maximal objective value. But it follows pretty quickly from this that a method would have to be perfect in order to be good enough. It would have to yield the right objective value-ordering for any class of options. But that, as we have seen, would imply that only an omniscient agent has an adequate method of estimating objective values.[21] So the argument does not establish that *K*-value is not the agent's best guide to objective value, nor that it is not good enough.

Still, one might harbor a residual sense of uneasiness. Why, if maximizing objective value is the correct goal for the moral agent, should the agent choose by *K*-value when she knows (or even believes) that the option with maximal *K*-value is not the action with maximal objective value? Has not objective value been rendered obsolete?

The regulative ideal for the moral agent is to maximize objective value. But we have already noted two features of the ideal. First, it is an ideal which admits of degrees of realization, and there is an obvious and natural ordering of options with respect to the realization of the ideal. Those options with greater objective value are closer to the realization of the ideal than those options with less. As a result, a miss is not always as bad as a mile. Failing to achieve the ideal admits of degrees, and it is objectively preferable for the agent to perform an act with more objective value rather than less in those choices which do so fail. Second, the agent is not usually in the position of knowing

---

21. Let *S* be a set of options. Then if *A* is the member of *S* with maximal *M*-value, then it must be the member of *S* with maximal objective value. Now consider *S* − {*A*} and repeat the argument.

which option fully realizes the ideal. If we put these two features together, then it is clear that in attempting to realize the ideal the agent is not justified in selecting the option which, by her lights, has the greatest probability of fully realizing the ideal, since such an option may also have a significant probability of missing out by a large margin. Rather, the agent is justified in selecting the option which overall has the best prospects for objective value enhancement.

What is required is a demonstrable connection between maximal K-value, on the one hand, and overall objective value enhancement on the other. If an agent is to fall short of maximal objective value she clearly wants to do her best to minimize the shortfall. So, failing the ideal of maximizing value, the smaller the shortfall the better. In a situation of ignorance she does not, of course, know how to minimize the actual shortfall—that would be tantamount to knowing which option is in fact the best. But she can estimate how far each option is likely to fall short of maximal value, in the light of her information about objective chances: and her best estimate of that is just expected shortfall in the light of her beliefs. What we need to show is that the option with maximal K-value has the least expected shortfall from maximal objective value.

For each hypothesis about chances, K_i, there is an option with maximal objective value. The maximizing option will, of course, be different under different chance hypotheses and the objective value both of the maximizing option and of the option with maximal K-value may well be different under different hypotheses. So the shortfall of the option with greatest K value will also differ from one chance hypothesis to another. Let Max_i be the value of the maximizing option given that K_i is true. Let $S(A/K_i)$ be the amount by which the objective value of option A falls short of maximal objective value, given that K_i is true: $S(A/K_i) = \text{Max}_i - OV(A/K_i)$. The amount by which the objective value of option A can be expected to fall short of maximal objective value (the agent's best estimate of A's shortfall) is then a weighted average of the $S(A/K_i)$, where the weights are given by the agent's credences in the various hypotheses about chance. So to minimize estimated shortfall from maximal objective value (ES) the agent should choose the option which minimizes: $\Sigma_i Cr(K_i)S(A/K_i)$.

It is a simple matter to show that the expected shortfall of A is less than the expected shortfall of B if and only if the K-value of A is greater than the K-value of B: the higher the K-value the less the estimated shortfall from maximal objective value.[22]

22. $ES(A) > ES(B)$
   iff $\Sigma_i Cr(K_i)S(A/K_i) - \Sigma_i Cr(K_i)S(B/K_i) > 0$
   iff $\Sigma_i Cr(K_i)[\text{Max}_i - OV(A/K_i)] - \Sigma_i Cr(K_i)[\text{Max}_i - OV(B/K_i)] > 0$
   iff $\Sigma_i Cr(K_i)OV(B/K_i) - \Sigma_i Cr(K_i)OV(A/K_i) > 0$
   iff $KV(B) > KV(A)$.

532   *Ethics*   *April 1992*

TABLE 2

Option	K_1	K_2	S_1	S_2	KV	ES
A	5	5	5	5	5	5
B	10	−10	0	20	0	10
C	−10	10	20	0	0	10

NOTE.—S_i is the shortfall in case K_i.

It will be instructive to illustrate this simple result with Jackson's case. We can now see why, from the objectivist's viewpoint, the agent is justified in choosing drug *A*, knowing that it is not the objectively best option. Table 1 can be expanded to incorporate shortfall and estimated shortfall, as shown in table 2. Thus if (as seems reasonable) an agent whose ideal it is to maximize objective value is justified in minimizing the amount by which she can expect to fall short of maximal objective value, then she is justified in choosing by maximal *K*-value.

CONCLUSION

Maximizing objective value is the correct regulative ideal for the moral agent to adopt. This is the rational kernel of the objectivist's claim that agents ought to maximize objective value. But in view of the fact that an agent is often ignorant of the true configuration of chances, she is not always in a position to know how to go about obeying that injunction. The injunction itself is not an epistemically sensitive selection rule. In making her choices, an agent must use the partial information in her possession to provide best estimates, in the light of her information, of the objective value of her choices. It turns out that the best estimate of objective value is *K*-value. Further, by selecting the act with maximal *K*-value, the agent can expect to minimize shortfall from maximal objective value. So, given the objectivist regulative ideal, an agent is rationally justified in ranking options according to their *K*-value, and morally justified in choosing by maximal *K*-value. This is so even when she knows that the option with maximal *K*-value will not fully realize the ideal of maximizing objective value.

From this objectivist position we can explain the rational kernel, and hence the plausibility of, the subjectivist's regulative ideal: that of maximizing subjective value. The subjectivist selection procedure yields the morally justified option within a wide range of cases—those in which the Independence Assumption holds—because in those cases subjective value and the agent's best estimate of objective value coincide. But the pure subjectivist, the one who claims that maximizing objective value is not the moral agent's regulative ideal, cannot motivate switching to the use of *K*-value in cases where the Independence Assumption fails. Thus, where the subjectivist's selection rule gives the right results, the objectivist's selection rule not only yields the same but also explains the subjectivist's recommendation. Where the objectivist's selection rule gives the right result, and the subjectivist's fails, there is no purely subjectivist escape route. Thus it is that only the objectivist can provide a complete and adequate guide to the kind of subjective value that should direct the deliberations of the moral agent.

Part VIII
An Optimising or Satisficing Theory?

[20]

SATISFICING CONSEQUENTIALISM

Michael Slote and Philip Pettit

I—*Michael Slote*

Act-consequentialism is generally characterized as a certain sort of view about the relation between an act's rightness and its consequences. An act-consequentialist holds that states of affairs (outcomes, consequences) can be objectively or impersonally ranked according to their goodness and that any given act is morally right or permissible if and only if its consequences are at least as good, according to the impersonal ranking, as those of any alternative act open to the agent—the doing of an act being itself included among its consequences.[1] An act-utilitarian is, according to the prevalent conception, an act-consequentialist with a particular view about how states of affairs are to be impersonally ranked: roughly speaking, the goodness of states of affairs depends only on the well-being, happiness, satisfaction, utility, or desire-fulfillment of the individuals who exist in those states of affairs and one state of affairs is better than another just in case it contains a greater sum of individual utilities, or a greater overall balance of satisfaction over dissatisfaction.[2] Thus act-consequentialism holds that a right act must be optimific, and the act-utilitarian, in addition, that optimizing always means *maximizing* the sum of individual well-being, desire-fulfillment, etc. But these theses need not go together. Nowadays, it is by no means unusual for an (act-)consequentialist not to be a utilitarian and to hold, for example, that considerations of justice may affect the goodness of overall states of affairs without affecting the sum total of individual utilities.

Act-consequentialism itself, on the other hand, has been seen as a unitary moral conception by both defenders and critics. But

---

[1] For present purposes it will not, I think, be important to distinguish between acts and courses of action.

[2] This characterization ignores various forms of average utilitarianism. For a technically more precise elaboration of some of these distinctions, see A. K. Sen, 'Utilitarianism and Welfarism', *Journal of Philosophy* 76, 1979, pp. 463ff.

140   I—MICHAEL SLOTE

the claim that the rightness of an act depends on whether it produces the best consequences impersonally judged can in fact be broken down into a pair of claims that need not go together, and the major purpose of this essay will be to show how this is possible and, in consequence, to suggest a useful widening of the notion of (act-)consequentialism. The idea that the rightness of an act depends solely on its consequences, i.e., on how (impersonally) good its consequences are, is separable from the idea that the rightness of an act depends on its having the best consequences (producible in the circumstances); the second thesis entails the first, but not *vice versa*, yet standard conceptions of consequentialism entail both these theses. Roughly, then, consequentialism standardly involves the claim that the rightness of acts depends on whether their consequences are good enough together with the particular view that only the best possible (in certain circumstances) is good enough. And given this way of partitioning standard consequentialism, it is not perhaps immediately obvious why these two theses should naturally or inevitably go together. Could not someone who held that rightness depended solely on how good an act's consequences were also want to hold that less than the best was sometimes good enough, hold, in other words, that an act might qualify as morally right through having good enough consequences, even though better consequences could have been produced in the circumstances?

In what follows I shall try to give some of the reasons why someone might want to hold just this sort of view. It is a view that, to the best of my knowledge, has not been explicitly suggested previously; but I hope to show not only that there is nothing incoherent about it but also that it has attractive features lacking in standard act-consequentialism. Furthermore, it seems terminologically natural to treat any view that makes rightness depend solely on the goodness of consequences as a form of consequentialism, so once the feasibility of the idea that less than the best may be good enough becomes apparent, it will be appropriate to treat the view that rightness depends on whether consequences are good enough and that less than the best may sometimes be good enough as a form of consequentialism. The traditional or standard view that rightness depends on whether the consequences are the best producible in the circumstances will then most naturally be seen as a particular kind of consequentialism, rather than as constituting consequentialism *per se*.[3] And it will be natural to characterize this particular kind of consequentialism as 'optimizing consequentialism' since it holds that rightness depends on whether consequences are good enough and that only the best is good enough. By contrast, the new sort of consequentialist view just mentioned might appropriately be labelled 'satisficing consequentialism', if we may borrow from the recent literature of economics, where the notion of satisficing has been used to express the idea that (rational) economic agents may sometimes choose what is good enough, without regard for whether what they have chosen is the best thing (outcome) available in the circumstances.

Now the idea of satisficing (utilitarian) consequentialism deserves to be explored as a formal possibility quite apart from its intuitiveness or ultimate supportability; but in fact it can be made to appear of more than formal interest. Even those opposed to consequentialism and utilitarianism as moral theories have tended to think that (extramoral individualistic) rationality requires an individual to maximize his satisfactions or do what is best for himself;[4] but the recent economics literature concerning satisficing suggests the possibility of a non-optimizing form of individual rational choice, and by giving a brief philosophical elaboration of the idea of rational satisficing, I hope to make the idea of *moral* satisficing, and satisficing

---

[3] Surely, it would be terminologically odd to treat someone who affirmed what I am going to call 'satisficing consequentialism' as *denying* consequentialism, yet this is precisely what present-day terminology requires—see, for example, Bernard Williams 'A Critique of Utilitarianism', in Smart and Williams, *Utilitarianism: For and Against*, Cambridge University Press, 1973, p. 90.

Incidentally, the possibility of satisficing (act-)consequentialism is (I believe) unintentionally suggested by things said in the Introduction to Sen and Williams, eds., *Utilitarianism and Beyond* (Cambridge University Press, 1982, p. 3f.). At one point, consequentialism is simply characterized as a theory 'which claims that actions are to be chosen on the basis of the states of affairs which are their consequences . . .' and this is neutral as between optimizing and satisficing forms of consequentialism. However, the Introduction goes on to treat consequentialism as involving the production of optimal consequences and the possibility of consequentialist moral satisficing is never mentioned. Certainly, in Sen, *op. cit.*, consequentialism is *defined* in terms of optimal consequences.

[4] See, e.g., Rawls *A Theory of Justice*, Cambridge: Harvard, 1971, pp. 23ff., 416ff.

142 I—MICHAEL SLOTE

consequentialism in particular, seem more attractive.[5] It will turn out, furthermore, that ordinary or common-sense morality also regards acts that are less than the best (most beneficent) possible as sometimes good enough and so not morally wrong even apart from any sacrifices a better (more beneficent) act might require from the agent. And to the degree that common-sense morality allows for 'moral satisficing' in the area of beneficence (benevolence), the possibility of a satisficing form of (utilitarian) consequentialism is also underscored and made more appealing. After all, consequentialists have long sought for ways—rule utilitarianism, probabilistic act-utilitarianism, etc.— of reconciling their views (making them seem less out of line) with common-sense morality, and we shall see towards the end of this essay that satisficing consequentialism has a number of advantages, in terms of common-sense moral plausibility, over optimizing forms of consequentialism, utilitarian and non-utilitarian alike. We shall also see that prominent views about the object of and motivation behind morality that are taken to support optimizing consequentialism or utilitarianism support these views only in their most general form and are equally consistent with optimizing or satisficing versions. But first to the idea of rational individual satisficing.

I

Consider an example borrowed from the satisficing literature of economics, but treated in such a way as to emphasize its relevance to philosophical discussions of rationality, rather than its implications for economic theory. An individual planning to move to a new location and having to sell his house may seek, not to maximize his profit on the house, not to get the best price for it he is likely to receive within some appropriate time period, but simply to obtain what he takes to be a good or satisfactory price. What he deems satisfactory may depend, among other things,

---

[5] For relevant discussions in the economics literature of satisficing, see, e.g., H. Simon, 'A Behavioral Model of Rational Choice', *Quarterly Journal of Economics* 69, 1955, pp. 99-118; Simon, 'Theories of Decision Making in Economics and Behavioral Science', *American Economic Review* XLIX, 1959, pp. 253-83, *Administrative Behavior*, N.Y.: Macmillan, 1961, second edition; and R. Eyert and J. March, eds., *A Behavioral Theory of the Firm*, Englewood Cliffs, N.J.: Prentice-Hall, 1963.

on what he paid for the house, what houses cost in the place where he is relocating, and on what houses like his normally sell at. But given some notion of what would be a good or satisfactory price to sell at, he may fix the price of his house at that point, rather than attempting, by setting it somewhat higher, to do better than that, or do the best he can. His reason for not setting the price higher will not, in that case, be some sort of anxiety about not being able to sell the house at all or some feeling that trying to do better would likely not be worth the effort of figuring out how to get a better price. Nor is he so rich that any extra money he received for the house would be practically meaningless in terms of marginal utility. Rather he is a 'satisficer' content with good enough and does not seek to maximize (optimize) his expectations. His desires, his needs, are moderate, and perhaps knowing this about himself, he may not be particularly interested in doing better for himself than he is likely to do by selling at a merely satisfactory price. If someone pointed out that it would be better for him to get more money, he would reply, not by disagreeing, but by pointing out that for him at least a good enough price is good enough.

Such a person clearly fails to exemplify the maximizing and optimizing model of individual rationality advocated by utilitarians like Sidgwick and anti-utilitarians like Rawls. But I think he nonetheless represents a possible idea of (one kind of) individual rationality, and the literature of economic satisficing in the main treats such examples, both as regards individuals and as regards economic units like the firm, as exemplifying a form of rational behavior. It might be possible to hold on to an optimizing or maximizing model of rationality and regard satisficing examples as indications of the enormous prevalence of irrational human behavior, but this has typically not been done by economists, and I think philosophers would have even less reason to do so. For there are many other cases where satisficing seems rational, or at least not irrational, and although some of these are purely hypothetical, hypothetical examples are the stock-in-trade of ethical and moral-psychological theory even when they are of little or no interest to economists.

Imagine that it is mid-afternoon; you had a good lunch, and you are not now hungry; neither, on the other hand, are you sated. You would enjoy a candy bar or Coca Cola, if you had

144   I—MICHAEL SLOTE

one, and there is in fact, right next to your desk, a refrigerator
stocked with such snacks and provided gratis by the company
for which you work. Realizing all this, do you, then, necessarily
take and consume a snack? If you do not, is that necessarily
because you are afraid to spoil your dinner, because you are on a
diet or because you are too busy? I think not. You may simply
not feel the need for any such snack. You turn down a good
thing, a sure satisfaction, because you are perfectly satisfied as
you are. Most of us are often in situations of this sort, and many
of us would often do the same thing. We are not boundless
optimizers or maximizers, but are sometimes (more) modest in
our desires and needs. But such modesty, such moderation, need
not be irrational or unreasonable on our part.

In the example just mentioned, moderation is not functioning
as a means to greater overall satisfactions and is thus quite
different from the instrumental virtue recommended by the
Epicureans. The sort of moderation I am talking about is not for
the sake of anything else, indeed it may not be for its own sake
either, if by that is meant that it is some sort of admirable trait or
virtue. If one has the habit of not trying to eke out the last
possible satisfaction from situations and of resting content with
some reasonable quantity that is less than the most or best one
can do, then one has a habit of moderation or modesty as regards
one's desires and satisfactions, and it may not be irrational to
have such a habit, even if (one recognizes that) the contrary
habit of maximizing may also not be irrational. But if a
maximizer (optimizer) lacking the habit of moderation in the
above sense need not be immoderate in that ordinary sense of
the term that implies unreasonableness, then the habit of being
satisfied with less than the most or best may not be a virtue, even
if such moderation is also neither irrational nor an anti-virtue.[6]

---

[6] A person whose desires are moderate or modest might also be called 'temperate', but
what we have been saying about the habit of moderation is very different from what
Aristotle says about what he calls the virtue of temperance. On Aristotle's conception a
temperate individual has the right amount of desire for the right sorts of things, etc., and
such rightness, roughly, involves a mean between two less right extremes. But our talk of
moderation in the text above is not supposed to imply that taking more than moderation
would allow is in any way wrong or unreasonable. Moderation involves a mean between
extremes that are not necessarily (both) more undesirable than moderation itself is. And
it is possible to use the notion of 'temperance' or 'temperateness' in a similarly non-
Aristotelian and (relatively) value-free way.

SATISFICING CONSEQUENTIALISM   145

But if there is nothing irrational or unreasonable about maximizing, isn't the moderate individual who is content with less a kind of ascetic? Not necessarily. An ascetic is someone who, within certain limits, minimizes his enjoyments or satisfactions; he deliberately leaves himself with less, unsatisfied. The moderate individual, on the other hand, is someone content with (what he considers) a reasonable amount of satisfaction; he wants to be satisfied and up to a certain point he wants more satisfactions rather than fewer, to be better off rather than worse off; but there is a point beyond which he has no desire, and even refuses, to go. There is a space between asceticism and the attempt to maximize satisfactions, do the best one can for oneself, a space occupied by the habit (if not the virtue) of moderation. And because such moderation is not a form of asceticism, it is difficult to see why it should count as irrational from the standpoint of egoistic or extra-moral individual rationality.[7]

Now the kind of example just mentioned differs from the case of satisficing house selling in being independent of any monetary transaction. But the example differs importantly in another way from examples of satisficing mentioned in the literature of economics. Economists who have advocated the model of rational satisficing for individuals, firms, or state bodies have pointed out that, quite independently of the costs of gaining further information or effecting new policies, an entrepreneur or firm may simply seek a satisfactory return on investment, a satisfactory share of the market, a satisfactory level of sales, rather than attempting to maximize or optimize under any of these headings. But this idea of rational satisficing implies only that individuals or firms *do not* always *seek* to optimize and are *satisfied* with attaining a certain 'aspiration level' less than the best that might be envisaged. It does not imply that it could be rational actually to *reject* the better for the good enough in situations where both were available. In the example of house selling, the individual accepts less than he might well be able to get, but he doesn't accept a lower price when a higher bidder makes an equally firm offer. And writers on satisficing generally

---

[7] *Rational* satisficing seems to involve not only a disinclination to optimize, but a reasonable sense of when one has enough. To be content with much less than one should be is (can be) one form of *bathos*.

146   I—MICHAEL SLOTE

seem to hold that satisficing only makes sense as a habit of not
seeking what is better or best, rather than as a habit of actually
rejecting the better, when it is clearly available, for the good
enough. Thus Herbert Simon, in 'Theories of Decision
Making . . .' (*loc. cit.* n. 5), develops the idea of aspiration level
and of satisficing, but goes on to say that 'when a firm has
alternatives open to it that are at or above its aspiration level, it
will choose the best of those known to be available'.

However, the example of the afternoon snack challenges the
idea that the satisficing individual will never explicitly reject the
better for the good enough. For the individual in question turns
down an immediately available satisfaction, something he
knows he will enjoy. He isn't merely not trying for a maximum
of satisfactions, but is explicitly rejecting such a maximum. (It
may be easier to see the explicitness of the rejection if we change
the example so that he is actually offered a snack by someone
and replies: no thank you, I'm just fine as I am.) And I think that
most of us would argue that there is nothing irrational here.
Many of us, most of us, occasionally reject afternoon snacks,
second cups of tea, etc., not out of (unconscious) asceticism, but
because (to some degree) we have a habit of moderation with
regard to certain satisfactions. The hypothetical example of the
afternoon snack thus takes the idea of rational satisficing a step
beyond where economists, to the best of my knowledge, have
been willing to go.

At this point, however, it may be objected that the example
may be one of rational behavior but is less than clear as an
example of satisficing. The individual in question prefers not to
have a certain satisfaction and certainly deliberately rejects the
maximization of satisfactions, if we think of satisfactions as like
pleasures or enjoyments. But to the extent the individual rejects
an available satisfaction, he presumably shows himself to prefer
(or desire) not to have that satisfaction and so in some (trivial?)
sense is maximizing the satisfaction of his preferences (or
desires). More importantly, perhaps, it is not clear that the
moderate individual must think of himself as missing out on
anything *good* when he forgoes the afternoon snack. For although
he knows he would enjoy the snack, the very fact that he rejects
such· enjoyment might easily be taken as evidence that he
doesn't in the circumstances regard such enjoyment as a good

thing. In that case, he may be satisficing in terms of some quantitative notion of satisfaction, but not with respect to some more refined or flexible notion of (his own) individual good, and the example would only provide a counter-example to a rather crude maximizing ideal of rationality, not to the idea that it is irrational to choose what is less good for one when something better is available.

However, even if the enjoyment of a snack does count as a rejected personal good for the individual of our example, that fact may be obscured, both for him and for us, by the very smallness or triviality of the good in question. And so in order to deal with our doubts, it may, then, be useful at this point to consider other examples, more purely hypothetical than the present one, where the good forgone through satisficing is fairly obvious.

How do we react to fairy tales in which the hero or heroine, offered a single wish, asks for a pot of gold, for a million (1900) dollars, or, simply, for (enough money to enable) his family and himself to be comfortably well off for the rest of their lives. In each case the person asks for less than he might have asked for, but we are not typically struck by the thought that he was *irrational* to ask for less than he could have, and neither, in general, do the fairy tales themselves imply a criticism of this sort; so, given the tendency of such tales to be full of moralism about human folly, we have, I think, some evidence that such fairy-tale wishes need not be regarded as irrational. (In not regarding them as irrational, we need not be confusing what we know *about* fairy-tale wishes with what the individual *in* a given fairy tale ought to know.)

Now the individual in the fairy tale who wishes for *less* than he could presumably exemplifies the sort of moderation discussed earlier. He may think that a pot of gold or enough money to live comfortably is all he needs to be satisfied, that anything more is of no particular importance to him. At the same time, however, he may realize (be willing to admit) that he could do better for himself by asking for more. He needn't imagine himself constitutionally incapable of benefitting from additional money or gold, for the idea that one will be happy, or satisfied, with a certain level of existence by no means precludes the thought (though it perhaps precludes *dwelling* on the thought) that one will not be as well off as one could be. It merely precludes the

148   I—MICHAEL SLOTE

sense of wanting or needing more for oneself. Indeed the very
fact that someone could actually explicitly wish for enough
money to be comfortably well-off is itself sufficient evidence of
what I am saying. Someone who makes such a wish clearly
acknowledges the possibility of being better off and yet
chooses—knowingly and in some sense deliberately chooses—a
lesser but personally satisfying degree of well-being.[8] And it is
precisely because the stakes are so large in such cases of wishing
that they provide clearcut examples of presumably rational
individual satisficing. But, again, the sort of satisficing involved
is not (merely) the kind familiar in the economics literature
where an individual seeks something other than optimum
results, but a kind of satisficing that actually rejects the available
better for the available good enough. Although the individual
with the wish would be better off if he wished for more, he asks
for less (we may suppose that if the wish grantor prods him by
asking 'Are you sure you wouldn't like more money than that?',
he sticks with his original request). And if we have any sympathy
with the idea of moderation, of modesty, in one's desires, we
shall have to grant that the satisficing individual who wishes,
e.g., for less money is not irrational. Perhaps we ourselves would
not be so easily satisfied in his circumstances, but that needn't
make us think him irrational for being moderate in a way, or to a
degree, that we are not.[9]

II

Given the above discussion of the nature and justification of
rational satisficing, the way may be prepared for an examination

[8] He may feel it is better that he choose less, and this entails the thought that it is (in one
sense) better for him to choose less. But none of this need entail the thought that he will be
personally better off if he chooses less, that such a choice will be better for him in the
other natural sense of that expression. On this see my *Goods and Virtues*, Oxford: 1983,
ch. 3.
  Incidentally, our example requires us to assume that the wisher's choice is not
influenced by a (reasonable) fear of being corrupted by getting more than he in fact asks
for; but his non-optimizing attitude in fact shows a *certain kind* of present non-corruption.
[9] In fact, it is hard to see how any specific monetary wish can be optimizing if the
individual is unsure about his own marginal utility curve for the use of money. To that
extent, we are all *necessarily* satisficers in situations where we can wish for whatever we
want, unless, perhaps, we are allowed to wish for our own greatest future well-being in
those very terms. If satisficing were irrational, would that mean that anything other than
such an explicitly optimizing wish would be irrational?

of moral satisficing. But I shall not immediately proceed to a discussion of (the varieties of) satisficing consequentialism, because I believe we can make the strongest case for this new form of consequentialism by first pointing out the non-optimizing character of the common-sense morality of benevolence (beneficence).

Consider a manager of a resort hotel who discovers, late one evening, that a car has broken down right outside its premises. In the car are a poor family of four who haven't the money to rent a cabin or buy a meal at the hotel, but the manager offers them a cabin gratis, assuming (as we may assume for the sake of argument) that it would be wrong not to do so. In acting thus benevolently, however, she doesn't go through the complete list of all the empty cabins in order to put them in the best cabin available. She simply goes through the list of cabins till she finds a cabin in good repair that is large enough to suit the family. Imagine, further, that, as with examples of rational satisficing from the economics literature, she chooses the cabin she does because it seems a satisfactory choice, good enough, not because, as an optimizer, she thinks that further search through the list of cabins will not be worth it in terms of time expended and the likelihood of finding a (sufficiently) better cabin. In such circumstances, optimizing act-consequentialism or act-utilitarianism would presumably hold that the manager should look further for a better room. (Assume there is a better room and that she will easily find it if she proceeds further through the list.) But I think ordinary morality would regard her actions as benevolent and her choice of a particular room for the family in question as morally acceptable, not wrong. She may not display the optimizing benevolence that standard act-consequentialism would require, under the circumstances, but in ordinary moral terms she has done well enough by the family that is stranded and had no obligation to do any better.

The example illustrates the possibility of a morally acceptable satisficing benevolence that does not seek to optimize with respect to those benefitted (or those affected) by one's actions. But our earlier examples of rational individual satisficing extended the notion beyond the usual examples from the literature of economics to include cases where someone explicitly rejects a better (or the best) alternative; and the same possibility

150   I—MICHAEL SLOTE

in fact also exists in the area of moral satisficing. Thus consider
again our hotel manager and the travellers she benefits. They
have now moved to the cabin she has found for them and are all
hungry. But it is late; so the manager tells the lone remaining
waiter in the restaurant to bring out a meal for the travellers
from among the dishes that remain from dinner and that will not
be usable the next day. Assume that there are a large variety of
dishes, some more luxurious or splendid than others, and that
the waiter asks what, among these things, he should bring the
newly arrived travellers. The hotel manager may say: oh, just
something good and substantial, it needn't be too fancy or
elaborate. Alternatively, the waiter may ask whether he should
bring them the 'special dinner' and the manager may say: no,
there's no need for anything that fancy, just bring them
something appetizing and good. In either case, the manager
seems deliberately to be rejecting an alternative that stands a
good chance of being preferable to the poor family in question.
Most people prefer the 'special dinner', apart from its price, and
the manager has no reason to believe that her new guests are
particularly moderate or modest in their desires. Yet her reason
for choosing as she does may not be consideration for the waiter,
who may have the same amount of work to do whatever he
brings the family to eat, nor even less a snobbish sense of charity
that regards the 'special dinner' as too good for the family in
question. Rather, she may be expressing in her benevolent
actions a kind of moderation that she may also evince in her self-
regarding choices. And, again, I think common-sense would
regard such deliberately non-optimific benevolence as morally
acceptable, not wrong.

In addition, if I may appeal again to an even more
hypothetical example in order to underscore the similarity with
what was said earlier about self-regarding individual rationality,
consider a fairy-tale wish regarding people other than oneself. A
warrior has fought meritoriously and died in a good cause, and
the gods wish to grant him a single wish for those he leaves
behind, before he enters Paradise and ceases to be concerned
with his previous life. Presented with such an opportunity, may
not the warrior wish for *his family* to be comfortably well off
forever after? And will we from a common-sense standpoint
consider him to have acted wrongly or non-benevolently

SATISFICING CONSEQUENTIALISM 151

towards his family because he (presumably knowingly) rejected an expectably better lot for them in favor of what was simply good enough? Surely not.

But the warrior and hotel manager examples not only offer further illustration of the idea of satisficing benevolence, but also help to make clear that common-sense morality differs from standard optimizing consequentialism with regard to the morality of benevolence quite apart from issues concerning the amount of sacrifice one may correctly require from moral agents. In many familiar cases where (optimizing) act-consequentialism and act-utilitarianism diverge from common-sense morality with regard to what an agent may permissibly do, the former require that an agent benefit others even though doing so requires him to make a large personal sacrifice, whereas common-sense morality regards the agent as permitted to refrain from making such a sacrifice. But in the fairy-tale example of the dying warrior, the warrior who chooses less than the best for his family does not do so because a choice of something better would require too great a sacrifice. Neither choice would require *any* sort of personal sacrifice. And by the same token the hotel manager's personal sacrifice (if any) presumably stays constant however splendid a meal she decides to give the poor travellers. So the divergence between common-sense morality and standard (utilitarian) act-consequentialism with regard to such cases cannot be accounted for in terms of a disagreement over whether one can correctly require an agent to sacrifice his own desires, projects and concerns in the name of overall optimality. With regard to such cases they disagree, rather, as to how much good an agent may be morally required to do (for others) given a total absence, or constant amount, of agent sacrifice. Optimizing (utilitarian) act-consequentialism will hold that the moral agent must produce the best possible results in such circumstances, ordinary morality that producing sufficiently good non-optimal results may be all that is required.

Of course, this is not the only way in which common-sense morality diverges from optimizing act-consequentialism: ordinary morality also contains deontological restrictions on what an agent may permissibly do in the name of overall optimality. But the fact that common-sense morality allows a satisficing concern for good results, a less than optimific

152   I—MICHAEL SLOTE

beneficence, to be permissible in some cases where deontological restrictions are irrelevant (and where there is no issue of personal sacrifice on the part of the agent) suggests the possibility of a satisficing form of pure act-consequentialism. And since the plausibility of various forms of consequentialism partly depends on how far their implications diverge from the deliverances of ordinary moral intuition, this new form of consequentialism may turn out to have some distinctive advantages over traditional optimizing forms of consequentialism.

The idea of satisficing act-consequentialism is not, in fact, entirely new. It is to a certain extent anticipated, for example, by the sort of 'negative utilitarianism', proposed briefly by Karl Popper in *The Open Society and its Enemies*, according to which we have a moral duty to minimize suffering and evil, but no general duty to maximize human happiness. In the course of defending this doctrine, Popper claims, in particular, that the idea of relieving suffering has a greater moral appeal to us than the idea of increasing the happiness of a man who is doing well already. So Popper not only offers an example of non-optimizing consequentialism, but indicates that it can be based on 'satisficing' common-sense moral intuitions of the kind we ourselves mentioned above.[10]

But Popper suggests only one form of non-optimizing consequentialism, and it is a form attended by a number of serious difficulties. The presumed fact that adding to happiness has less moral appeal than relieving suffering hardly implies, for example, that our only duty is to relieve suffering. And the latter idea, which constitutes the essence of negative utilitarianism, seems to have the absurd consequence that we would do all that duty requires, if we painlessly destroyed all of suffering humanity.[11] Negative utilitarianism seems, then, to entail unacceptable views about when less than the best possible is good enough. But by virtue of its asymmetric treatment of

---

[10] See *The Open Society and its Enemies*, London: Routledge and Kegan Paul, 1974, vol. I, ch. 5, note 6; chapter 9, note 2. For another discussion of our common-sense satisficing moral intuitions, see R. M. Adams, 'Must God Create the Best?', *Philosophical Review* 81, 1972, pp. 317–32.

[11] The point is made by R. N. Smart in 'Negative Utilitarianism', *Mind* 67, 1958, p. 542f.

SATISFICING CONSEQUENTIALISM 153

human happiness and suffering it also rules out the possibility of morally permissible satisficing throughout a wide range of cases. Wherever the relief of suffering is in question, it demands that suffering be minimized; but common-sense morality is not in fact so demanding in this respect. A medic attending the wounded on the battlefield may attend to the first (sufficiently) badly wounded person he sees without considering whether there may be someone in even worse shape nearby, and from a common-sense moral standpoint such behavior seems perfectly acceptable. So although Popper's variety of satisficing consequentialism involves a fundamental asymmetry between good and evil, happiness and suffering, a less asymmetric form of such consequentialism may, for a number of reasons, be more attractive and intuitive. What was appealing, in our discussion of rational individual satisficing, was the idea of a reasonable sufficiency of good less than the best attainable. But this idea gains only imperfect expression in a moral theory like negative utilitarianism, which, among other things, treats the eradication of our suffering race as 'good enough' but not the behavior of the morally satisficing medic. What may be needed is a form of satisficing consequentialism with a more plausible conception of what counts as good enough, and it will help us towards such a theory if we consider another form of satisficing consequentialism that can be found in one of the great classics of utilitarian moral philosophy, Bentham's *An Introduction to the Principles of Morals and Legislation*.

The 1823 edition of the *Introduction* differs from that published in 1789 principally in regard to some clarificatory notes, and one of these notes discusses the Principle of Utility and interprets it as requiring that everyone seek the greatest happiness of those affected by his actions. But the unaltered main text of the book treats the Principle of Utility in quite a different (indeed incompatible) way as 'that principle which approves or disapproves of every action whatsoever, according to the tendency which it appears to have to augment or diminish the happiness of the party whose interest is in question: or, what is the same thing in other words, to promote or to oppose that happiness'.[12] The discussion in footnote presents a typical

---

[12] See the J. H. Burns and H. L. A. Hart edition of the *Introduction*, London: Methuen, 1970, pp. 11f. However, also see p. 282.

154   I—MICHAEL SLOTE

optimizing form of (utilitarian) act-consequentialism; but the
earlier main text says nothing about 'best' or 'greatest good',
and since an act may promote happiness without producing the
most happiness possible, in given circumstances, the earlier text
presents a kind of satisficing utilitarian act-consequentialism.
[As with Popper's discussion, a particular form of satisficing
consequentialism is advocated without the *general idea* of
satisficing (act-)consequentialism or (act-)utilitarianism being
mentioned.]

Now the form of satisficing consequentialism Bentham
advocates has some unfortunate features. If we take it quite
literally, his theory treats the rightness of any action as
dependent solely on the results of that single action; an act is
right even if it adds very little to the sum of human happiness
(the net balance of happiness over unhappiness) and even if an
alternative is available which is much more productive of
happiness. By the same token, an act is wrong if it subtracts from
the sum of human happiness, even when every available
alternative has worse results. (Given utilitarian notions of
consequences, it is easy to imagine such cases.) These implications do not square with ordinary moral intuitions, and they
are due to the *non-comparativeness* of the just-mentioned form of
consequentialism. Bentham's satisficing consequentialism regards an act as having produced *enough* good or happiness to be
right if it favourably alters the balance of happiness over
unhappiness even to the *slightest* extent, but if an alternative is
available which would produce much more good, we should
perhaps not normally feel that a slight addition to happiness was
(morally) good enough. The sufficiency of a slight contribution
to happiness would somewhat depend on what else was
available, and a comparative form of satisficing consequentialism
would require such alternatives to be taken into account in
judging what was good enough. An act producing only slight
good might not be judged good enough, even if some non-
optimific alternative act producing a great deal of good were
regarded as such. (The medic of our example would presumably
be wrong to go around simply applying bandages, even if that
would slightly ameliorate the situation; but he might still be
morally permitted to satisfice in the way mentioned earlier.)

Similarly, where an agent cannot avoid acting in such a way

as will lead to the decrease of human happiness, a non-comparative form of satisficing consequentialism, like Bentham's, must presumably treat whatever the agent does as wrong.[13] But it seems more plausible to take into consideration the alternatives to a given act and regard an act as having (circumstantially) good enough consequences if all its alternatives have worse consequences (for the sum of human happiness). So (some of) the difficulties of Bentham's satisficing consequentialist theory of right action are due to its insensitivity to the consequences of alternative actions, and we are thus pointed in the direction of some form of *comparative* satisficing act-consequentialism, in our search for a viable alternative to standard optimizing act-consequentialism.

Given, furthermore, our earlier plausible examples of moral satisficing with respect to the relief of suffering, it would seem that satisficing act-consequentialism does best to avoid the radical asymmetry between suffering and happiness entailed by Popper's negative utilitarianism, while at the same time remaining sensitive to the consequences of alternative actions. But having said as much, it would perhaps at this point be a good idea to consider some of the relative advantages and disadvantages of (plausible versions of) satisficing and optimizing act-consequentialism.

III

Some of the relative strengths of satisficing consequentialism most clearly appear in certain kinds of cases where an individual can through his own efforts do a great deal to relieve great human suffering. Consider a doctor who wants to help mankind, but is for personal reasons particularly affected by the plight of people in India—perhaps he is attracted to Indian art or religion or is very knowledgeable about the history of India. Now an optimizing (utilitarian) act-consequentialist would presumably say that a doctor who volunteered to work in India should

---

[13] Recent moral philosophy has taken very seriously the possibility that an agent might through no fault of his own be put in a situation of moral tragedy where he cannot avoid acting wrongly. But surely there are cases where anything one does will have bad consequences (in the permissive utilitarian sense of the term), yet where it is not wrong to perform an act with less bad consequences than any feasible alternative.

156   I—MICHAEL SLOTE

consider whether the suffering there is worse than in other
countries (and the opportunities to help great enough) so that by
going to India he is likely to do more good than he can do
elsewhere. And aside from the doctor's motivation and thought
processes, it will simply be wrong of him to go to India if some
other course of action would do more good for mankind, on any
usual optimizing act-consequentialist conception. But many
people who wish to relieve human suffering do not consider
whether their actions are likely to produce the greatest amount
of good possible. When they find a course of action that they
think will make a great (enough) contribution to the relief of
suffering and that can compel their personal allegiance and
energies, they may act accordingly, without considering whether
they might not do more good elsewhere. And such moral
satisficing does not, from a common-sense moral standpoint,
seem wrong; a person who has done a great deal to relieve
suffering would not normally be thought to have acted wrongly
because she could have done even greater service elsewhere.

   Now the reason why, in the present sort of case, less than the
best can seem good enough may have something to do with how
much good the satisficing individual does and/or aims to do.
The good he does is sufficiently great and sufficiently close to the
best he could do so as to make it implausible to deny the
rightness of his action(s). So for such situations it may well be
possible formally to elaborate the notion of enoughness as some
sort of percentage or other mathematical function of the best
results attainable by the agent. I shall not attempt to spell out
the details of any particular plausible way in which this might be
attempted. But if satisficing consequentialism has the sort of
initial plausibility I think it has, then the way will be open to
such a formal elaboration of enoughness and to a consequent
precision (over large ranges of cases) about what counts as a
morally permissible level of act-consequentialist satisficing.

   According to such satisficing act-consequentialism, then, an
agent may permissibly choose a course of action that seems to
him to do a great deal or a sufficient amount towards the relief of
human suffering without considering whether such action is
optimific in the relief of suffering among all the possible courses
of action open to him and without the course of action he chooses
actually being optimific. His sense of what counts as doing a

great deal, or a sufficient amount, towards the relief of suffering
may in part reflect what he knows about the most good that
agents can do in circumstances like his—and what he knows
generally about the world—but in doing the great good he does
he need not seek to do or actually succeed in doing the most good
possible. And, as we have seen, such a view of what an agent may
permissibly do comes closer to ordinary moral views about
benevolence than the usual forms of optimizing act-consequentialism.

One of the chief implausibilities of traditional (utilitarian)
act-consequentialism has been its inability to accommodate
moral supererogation. But a satisficing theory that allows less
than the best to be morally permissible can treat it as
supererogatory (and especially praiseworthy) for an agent to do
more good than would be sufficient to insure the rightness of his
actions. Thus, if the person with special interest in India
sacrifices that interest in order to go somewhere else where he
can do even more good, then he does better than (some plausible
version of) satisficing act-consequentialism requires and acts
supererogatorily. But optimizing act-consequentialism will
presumably not treat such action as supererogatory because of
its (from a common-sense standpoint) inordinately strict
requirements of benevolence.

Moreover, critics of optimizing consequentialism have recently tended to focus on one particular way in which such
consequentialism implausibly offends against common-sense
views of our obligations of beneficence. They have pointed out
that (optimizing) act-consequentialism makes excessive demands
on the moral individual by requiring that she abandon her
deepest commitments and projects whenever these do not serve
overall impersonally judged optimality. For example, it has
been held by Samuel Scheffler (and others) that it is unfair or
unreasonable to demand such sacrifice of moral agents, and by
Bernard Williams (and others) that such requirements alienate
individuals from their own deepest identities as given in the
projects and commitments they hold most dear, thus constituting
attacks on their integrity (integralness) as persons.[14] In the wake

---

[14] See, for example, Scheffler's *The Rejection of Consequentialism*, Oxford, 1982; and
Williams in Smart and Williams, *op. cit.*

158   I—MICHAEL SLOTE

of these criticisms, many philosophers have advocated rejecting act-consequentialism in favor of some more commonsensical moral view that makes it permissible to pursue non-optimific personal projects and commitments.

What I would like to suggest here, however, is that at least some of this moral accommodation of individual desires, commitments and projects can be accomplished within a (utilitarian) act-consequentialist framework. Satisficing act-consequentialism can permit a doctor to work in India, even if he could do more good elsewhere, as long as the amount of good he will do in India is judged to be sufficient. And this then permits the doctor to satisfy his special interest in or concern for things Indian while at the same time fulfilling all that morality demands of him. Similarly, a person interested in pure laboratory research might be permitted to pursue such research if it were likely to yield great practical benefits for mankind (rather than threaten human survival). Such consequentialism in effect then allows various sorts of *compromise* between the demands of impersonal morality and personal desires and commitments. To that extent, it allows greater scope for personal preferences and projects than traditional optimizing act-consequentialism does. However, it offers less scope than would be available on most common-sense views of what an agent may permissibly do. For ordinary morality would presumably allow an agent (capable of doing better) to pursue projects that do not contribute very much to overall human well-being, and satisficing consequentialism—unless it maintains a very weak view about what it is to do enough good—will rule such projects out.

However, none of the moral theories just mentioned offers an all-or-nothing solution to the problem of balancing personal projects and commitments against impersonal good. Although the point is somewhat obscured by Williams, even optimizing act-consequentialism allows for certain sorts of personal integrity, namely, integrity constituted by the desire precisely to produce the most good possible or by projects which indirectly produce the most good that a given agent can achieve. On the other hand, even anti-consequentialists who affirm some sort of common-sense permission to pursue non-optimific projects and commitments typically set limits on what sorts of projects may

SATISFICING CONSEQUENTIALISM 159

be thus pursued: the desire to rise in the Mafia is presumably not among them. But within these limits satisficing act-consequentialism occupies an intermediate position; it morally accommodates more kinds of personal preference and personal integrity than traditional optimizing act-consequentialism, but fewer kinds than common-sense anti-consequentialist morality would presumably allow. As such, however, it does offer act-consequentialists the possibility of moving closer to common-sense morality and accommodates a felt need to give greater weight to personal commitments and preferences, while retaining the advantages of a (utilitarian) act-consequentialist framework.[15]

In addition, the choice between satisficing and optimizing consequentialism represents a genuine and difficult problem not only at the level of act evaluation, but also in regard to motives, traits of character, and everything else that can be subjected to consequentialist moral assessment. Is a good (or right) motive, for example, one that has sufficiently good (but not necessarily best) consequences among some set of relevant alternatives or is it one that has the best consequences among such alternatives? The utilitarian and consequentialist evaluation of motives goes back at least as far as Bentham's *Introduction*, where it is said that motives are good if they produce pleasure or avert pain. Clearly, this represents an embryonic form of *satisficing* motive utilitarianism.[16] Something similar can also be found in Sidgwick's *The Methods of Ethics*[17] and in R. M. Adams's 'Motive Utilitarianism'.[18] And in point of fact satisficing forms of motive-utilitarianism and motive-consequentialism seem generally both more plausible and more interesting than any optimizing version I can think of. Act-consequentialists have

---

[15] In 'Evaluator Relativity and Consequentialist Evaluation' (*Philosophy and Public Affairs* 12, 1983, pp. 113–32), Amartya Sen has recently suggested (roughly) that an act's rightness may depend on whether it produces consequences that are best-from-the-standpoint-of-the-agent. Such a theory, despite the lack of historic antecedents, is arguably act-consequentialist and would permit the pursuit of individual projects. Unfortunately, it also seems to make such pursuit obligatory—perhaps this could be avoided by adopting a satisficing version of the theory.

[16] *Op. cit.*, p. 100.

[17] Seventh edition, p. 428.

[18] *Journal of Philosophy* 76, 1979, pp. 467–81.

160   I—MICHAEL SLOTE

had to grant, for example, that on many occasions a father who
gives preference to his own children out of love for them may
perform a morally wrong action in doing so, but they have
attempted to mitigate the harshness and common-sense implausibility of that judgment by adding that the motive of
paternal love may nonetheless be a morally good one because it
generally leads to good consequences. The father may do what is
wrong but he does so out of a morally good motive.[19] However, if
a motive had to be in some sense optimific in order to count as
morally good, then this irenic ascent (descent?) to the consequential morality of motives might easily fail of its purpose. Does
paternal love generally produce more good than the motive of
impartial benevolence, the love of mankind generally, and all
other relevantly alternative single motives? If, on the other
hand, we require of good motives only that they generally
produce (sufficiently) good results, paternal love need not
compete with these other motives in order to count as morally
good, so satisficing versions of motive-consequentialism have
distinct advantages, for an act-consequentialist and more
generally, over optimizing versions of motive-consequentialism.

But if that is so, a question concerning the consistency of
moral theories operating at different levels of evaluation
immediately arises. In 'Motive Utilitarianism' Adams raises the
question whether motive-utilitarianism (motive-consequentialism) is consistent with act-utilitarianism (act-consequentialism) and suggests, subject to certain qualifications, that they
are. But in the context of the present discussion and relative to
the assumption that one can consistently be both a motive-
consequentialist and an act-consequentialist, a further question
arises as to whether one can plausibly or consistently be a
satisficing consequentialist with regard to some objects of
consequentialist evaluation and an optimizing one with respect
to others. Can one, for example, reasonably be an optimizing
act-utilitarian but a satisficing motive-utilitarian?

To a greater or lesser extent, Bentham, Sidgwick, and Adams
all seem to have maintained precisely this combination of views,
but this may be due to their having ignored the possibility of

---

[19] Cf. Sidgwick, *op. cit.*, p. 428; Adams, 'Motive Utilitarianism'; and R. M. Hare,
Moral Thinking, Oxford: 1982.

satisficing act-utilitarianism rather than to any judgment that optimizing act-utilitarianism fits in well with satisficing motive-utilitarianism. (At the very end of this essay we shall briefly consider some possible reasons why satisficing consequentialism might easily be ignored or mistakenly ruled out.)

At the very least, the viability and independent plausibility of satisficing motive-consequentialism provide further motivation for satisficing act-consequentialism. They do something to allay fears that there must be something logically or conceptually wrong with any non-optimizing form of act-consequentialism and may even make it easier to regard satisficing versions of act-consequentialism as genuine competitors of the more familiar optimizing variety. Whether there may, in the end, be some sort of inconsistency or tension between optimizing act-consequentialism and satisficing motive-consequentialism is very difficult to judge, but in terms of sheer symmetry and simplicity, the superior plausibility of satisficing motive-consequentialism seems to recommend a preference for satisficing act-consequentialism as well.

IV

We come, finally, to certain views about the object (or purpose or goal) of morality and about the fundamental or ideal nature of moral motivation that may be thought to favor, indeed to mandate, optimizing, rather than satisficing, forms of (utilitarian) consequentialism. It has frequently been said, for example, that the object of morality is the general good or universal happiness, and such a view (barring any doubts one may have about morality's having any purpose or object at all) seems to imply that moral schemes—whether act-utilitarian, rule-utilitarian, motive-utilitarian, or any combination of these—must be optimific, e.g., directed towards the greatest happiness of the greatest number. (The problem whether this is best achieved by agent-indirection has no immediate relevance to the issue I am discussing.)

But to assume so would, in fact, be to confuse the general, or universal, happiness with the greatest possible general, or universal, happiness, and it should be clear—though our discussion of satisficing may help to make it clearer—that these things are not the same. Someone may aim at his *own* happiness

162   I—MICHAEL SLOTE

in a satisficing way, i.e., without aiming at his own greatest
possible happiness; and if someone's *sole aim in life* were to
become a good tennis player, it would hardly follow that she
aimed at becoming the best player in the world. (Even the latter
aim is a satisficing one, since it need not involve aiming to be as
good as possible relative to other players, e.g., in a totally
different class from everyone else. Some satisficing aims can
thus, somewhat misleadingly, be characterized by the use of
typical optimizing concepts like bestness.) By the same token it
hardly follows from the fact, if it is one, that morality aims at
universal well-being or happiness, that it does so in an
optimizing way. Yet a failure to distinguish universal happiness
or the general well-being from the greatest possible universal
happiness or general well-being is characteristic of the entire
utilitarian literature, and we find Sidgwick, for example,
constantly running these notions together (as well as identifying
the desire for one's own happiness alone, egoism, with the desire
for one's own greatest happiness).[20]

But from what we have seen, it is possible to aim at the general
happiness without aiming at the greatest general happiness.
And so it is possible to hold a satisficing form of act- (or act-and-
motive-)consequentialism consistent with what utilitarians and
others have wanted to say about the object of morality. (It is
equally possible to maintain a satisficing form of ethical egoism
without contradicting or undercutting the most familiar general
expressions of that doctrine.) In addition, the most familiar
characterizations of (utilitarian) moral motivation also fail to
give any preference to optimizing over satisficing forms of
consequentialism. For nothing in the idea of impartial, rational,
benevolence or of universal sympathy entails a desire for the
greatest possible human happiness; and even someone with the
highest degree of impartial rational benevolence or universal
sympathy may not always aim for the greatest happiness or well-
being possible, since it is possible for many (even all) individuals
to be satisficers about their own well-being and it is hardly clear
that the greatest possible benevolence or sympathy towards
(sympathetic identification with) them would require us to

---

[20] See Sidgwick, *op. cit.*, e.g., pp. 285–89; also p. 95. The confusion can also be found in
Mill's 'Utilitarianism'.

SATISFICING CONSEQUENTIALISM 163

desire their greatest well-being or thus the greatest general well-being of mankind.

It would seem, then, that satisficing (utilitarian) consequentialism cannot be excluded on the basis of those general characterizations of the purpose of morality and of moral motivation that have been used to defend (utilitarian) consequentialism generally and optimizing versions of (such) consequentialism in particular. And our whole previous discussion of satisficing individual rationality and of the satisficing elements in the common-sense morality of benevolence should clear the way to making satisficing (act-)consequentialism seem a genuine alternative to prevalent consequentialist views. However, I have here provided only the crudest sketch of how a plausible version of satisficing act-consequentialism might be formulated and perhaps the ultimate test of the whole notion of (consequentialist) moral satisficing will lie in how appealing more specific and detailed formulations eventually prove to be.

[21]

SATISFICING CONSEQUENTIALISM

Michael Slote and Philip Pettit

II—Philip Pettit

I

Consequentialism is usually defined by some formula like: one should always do what has the best consequences.[1] But there is an ambiguity in any edict of this kind and it has haunted consequentialist writing.

The ambiguity concerns the scope of the definite description 'what has the best consequences' *vis-à-vis* the scope of the predicate 'do'—or, *a fortiori*, the deontic operator 'should'. One reading gives the description wider scope, the other narrower.

Take doing something, P, to involve the intentional and direct pursuit of P. Intentional, so far as the goal is anticipated and desired. Direct, so far as the goal gives the agent his main orientation: he does not pursue it by aiming at another target, in the knowledge that thereby he can achieve P.

The wide-scope consequentialist formula prescribes with regard to what has the best consequences, that one should do that. It does not entail that the consequentialist goal should be direct; nor even that it should be intentional. The agent is to take a line that happens, whether or not he is aware of the fact, to yield the desired result.

The narrow-scope formula, on the other hand, supports both entailments. The agent is required to set out intentionally and directly in pursuit of what has the best consequences. He is to let himself be guided *ex ante* by the formula, not just allow his actions to be assessed by it *ex post*.

To pursue the best consequences is, by whatever metric one chooses, to maximize. Since the policy of satisficing is put

---

[1] See for example Joel J. Kupperman *The Foundations of Morality*, Allen and Unwin, London 1983, page 94. Kupperman is alive to the ambiguity I discuss and has useful things to say on the matter. The ambiguity shows up within the theory of justice in the distinction between utilitarianism considered as providing merely a 'criterion' of the just society and utilitarianism considered as also providing a 'charter'. On this distinction see my *Judging Justice* Routledge and Kegan Paul, London 1980.

166   II—PHILIP PETTIT

forward as an alternative to one of maximizing, it follows that
narrow-scope consequentialism must prohibit satisficing. The
wide-scope doctrine on the other hand need not do so. There
may be good reason why a wide-scope consequentialist—a
wide-scope maximizer, if you like—should prescribe a satisficing
policy.

Assume that there are cases where maximizing is a technically
feasible strategy. I wish to argue, with regard to those cases, for
the two following theses.

> A: There are good (if non-conclusive) reasons for any one
>   of which a wide-scope consequentialist might prefer a
>   satisficing to a maximizing policy.
> B: Unless some such reason obtains, satisficing is an
>   irrational policy for anyone, consequentialist or not, to
>   prefer.

The second thesis puts me in conflict with what Michael Slote
maintains in 'Satisficing Consequentialism'.[2] Besides defending
the theses, therefore, I shall also try to undermine his position.

II

The notion of satisficing derives from H. A. Simon.[3] It directs us
to a decision-making strategy of roughly the following form:

> (1) Set an aspiration level such that any option which
>   reaches or surpasses it is good enough.
> (2) Begin to enumerate and evaluate the options on offer.
> (3) Choose the first option which, given the aspiration
>   level, is good enough.

---

[2] Slote wishes to argue, not just that unmotivated satisficing is rational, but that the
narrow-scope consequentialist ought to drop the reference to 'best' (in favour of 'good
enough') and prescribe such a satisficing policy. I ignore this argument since it is
undercut by thesis B.

[3] See his *Administrative Behaviour*, Third Edition, The Free Press, New York, 1976; 'A
Behavioural Model of Rational Choice' *Quarterly Journal of Economics*, vol. 69, 1955;
'Theories of Decision Making in Economics and Behavioural Science' *American Economic
Review*, vol. 49, 1959; 'From Substantive to Procedural Rationality' in Spiro J. Latsis,
ed., *Methodological Appraisal in Economics*, Cambridge University Press 1976; 'On How to
Decide What to Do' *Bell Journal of Economics*, vol. 9, 1978; and 'Rational Decision
Making in Business Organizations' The Nobel Foundation, Stockholm 1978. I am
exercising some license in my characterisation of the satisficing strategy, since Simon
sometimes describes related but distinct policies as satisficing ones too.

SATISFICING CONSEQUENTIALISM 167

The policy described is meant to serve as an alternative to the following, maximizing sort of strategy:

(1) Enumerate all the options on offer.
(2) Evaluate each.
(3) Choose the best.

The main difference between the two kinds of policy is that whereas the maximizer insulates enumeration, evaluation and choice from each other, the satisficer allows them to interact. One evaluates as one enumerates and if a satisfactory option appears, one may choose before either task is complete.

The enumeration involved in each case will spell out the different salient alternatives before the agent.[4] It may be that to enumerate any alternative one must have looked ahead to enumerate all. In that case satisficing will be distinguished only in respect of evaluation.

As for that evaluation, there are three points to note. The first is that it is not relativized to a particular purpose or aspect. It represents, not what the agent would prefer in this or that context, but what he thinks is better or worse, all things considered.

Secondly, the evaluation of options is supposed, in line with the consequentialist perspective, to be derived from an evaluation of the likely consequences.[5] This assumption however is compatible with any of a variety of derivations: in the case of uncertain consequences, for example, the derivation may be by the rule of maximin, maximax, maximization of expected utility, or whatever.[6]

Finally, while the evaluation of options yields a preference

---

[4] I assume that there is no problem in recognising the features which ought to be ignored in spelling out alternatives, e.g., such features as acting with one's unused limbs in this position or that, acting at approximately 1 p.m. or a micro-second later. Both maximizers and satisficers are taken to have the relevant sense of salience. For the claim that only satisficers can appropriately enumerate alternatives see Alex Michalos 'Rationality between the Maximizers and the Satisficers' in K. F. Schaffner and R. S. Cohen (eds), *PSA 1972*, D. Reidel, Dordrecht-Holland 1974.

[5] I take the consequences to include the event in which the action itself consists. The case for such an inclusion can be found in Amartya Sen 'Evaluator Relativity and Consequential Evaluation' *Philosophy and Public Affairs*, vol. 12, 1983, pages 128 *et seq.*

[6] The usual consequentialist derivation is by maximization of expected utility. Simon seems also to endorse this.

168   II—PHILIP PETTIT

ordering which, so far as it goes, must be complete and consistent, it need not yield one which can be represented by a real-valued utility function.[7] It allows us to speak of maximizing —or satisficing on—preference fulfilment but not necessarily of maximizing utility.

III

Contrary to thesis A, it appears that there can be no good reason for a wide-scope consequentialist to satisfice, or to prescribe satisficing. There is a plausible argument to that effect.

Suppose that someone proposes a reason R for satisficing. If it is to engage the wide-scope consequentialist, then R must be a statement to this effect: that by pursuing a satisficing policy, seeking options with good enough consequences, an agent produces a beneficial side-consequence, C; and that acting so as to produce good enough directly intended consequences, plus the side-consequence C, is acting in a manner likely to bring about the best consequences overall.

But now an opponent of thesis A can argue as follows. If R holds, then trying to do what has good enough consequences will be promoting what has, or is likely to have, the best consequences. If the agent knows this, however, he can recast his policy as one of trying to do what has the best consequences. He can give up pursuing a satisficing policy and, taking account of consequence C as well as the results to which he had previously attended, adopt a strategy of maximization.

In fact, the opponent may urge, this is what any rational agent ought to do. No matter how important the realization of C is, there are bound to be circumstances in which the agent will think that its loss is more than balanced by the achievement of certain other results. In such a setting, satisficing will not produce what has the best aggregate consequences: R will fail. On the other hand, maximizing with a view to all the possible results, including consequence C, will guarantee that upshot. Thus the maximization strategy is, it appears, superior.

Thesis A is not undermined by this argument because one of the premises is false. This is the assumption that if a strategy is

---

[7] On the requirements for such representability see H. A. John Green *Consumer Theory*, 2nd edition, Macmillan, London 1976, Chapters 6 & 13.

SATISFICING CONSEQUENTIALISM 169

justified, in crucial part, by a side-consequence, C, then a similar justification is available for the strategy which differs only in casting C as a consequence to be intentionally and directly pursued.

The premise is false because, in Jon Elster's phrase, some justifying consequences are essential by-products.[8] The standard example is spontaneity. A particular strategy may be justified in part by the fact that the agent who pursues it will achieve spontaneity of character. It does not follow that we can equally justify the variant policy which elevates spontaneity to the status of a consequence intentionally and directly sought. One does not need to be a psychologist to recognize that someone who makes a regular concern of being spontaneous is unlikely to display that characteristic.

IV

Thesis A will be vindicated if we can identify a justifying side-consequence of satisficing which is essentially a by-product of the policy. It must be a consequence that cannot be pursued by an agent in such a way that the justification applies equally to the corresponding strategy of maximization. In fact there are a number of plausible candidates for the role. I will mention two.

One is the consequence that has always been invoked by Simon in support of the policy of satisficing. This is computational ease: the fact that decisions are made without the time and trouble required for enumerating and evaluating all possible options.

It is only reasonable to admit that in some circumstances at least, the gain in computational ease will compensate for any losses involved in satisficing. But is computational ease an essential by-product of satisficing? Can't an agent take direct, intentional account of the difficulty of going through a full enumeration and evaluation of alternatives and, maximizing his overall preference fulfilment, allow himself in appropriate cases to choose one of the options that satisficing might have selected?

---

[8] See his *Sour Grapes*, Cambridge University Press, 1983, Chapter 2. Elster does not give my argument for satisficing. He endorses the policy when maximization is not feasible. See pages 14 and 18.

170   II—PHILIP PETTIT

The approach suggested would have the agent raise himself to
a level above the enumeration and evaluation of first-order
options. Allowing for the benefit of computational ease, he
would first enumerate the short-cutting alternatives to that
standard strategy and then evaluate the different strategies
available. He would maximize at this higher level, opting for the
strategy which seemed best. Applying this policy then, he might
end up with a first-order option which would also attract a
satisficer.

In many areas such an approach will clearly be self-defeating.
To attempt to avoid computational costs by computing the
benefits of deviating from the ordinary procedure of enumeration
and evaluation may push such costs even higher. Computational
ease may be attainable then only by forswearing a certain sort
of maximizing computation. It may be essentially a by-product
of a strategy such as satisficing.[9]

The problem with computational ease derives from a regress.
The computational costs of maximizing at any level can only be
counted at the next level up. To weigh such costs in a
maximizing procedure, therefore, may be to engage further
costs that remain unweighed. Satisficing offers an exit from the
predicament.

A second side-effect which might be quoted in justification of
satisficing is the habit of moderation, the habit of making do
with less than the guaranteed optimum, which it encourages.
We may ascribe the sort of justification in question to Solon,
in view to his association with the maxim 'Nothing too
much'.[10]

The habit of moderation is certainly something beneficial, as

[9] This consideration is certainly in the spirit of Simon and is sometimes near to being
explicit in his writing. In his Nobel Foundation piece he writes for example 'In long-run
equilibrium it might even be the case that choice with dynamically adapting aspiration
levels would be equivalent to optimal choice, taking the costs of search into account. But
the important thing about the search and satisficing theory is that it showed how choice
could actually be made with reasonable amounts of calculation, and using very
incomplete information, without the need of performing the impossible—of carrying out
this optimizing procedure'. Section 2C.
[10] Richard Routley suggests this kind of justification in 'Maximizing, Satisficing,
Satisizing', Discussion Papers in Environmental Philosophy, Research School of Social
Sciences, Australian National University, Canberra 1983. I am indebted to his paper
for a number of lessons, including the reminder about Solon.

long tradition has it. Lacking a well-tempered character, a person is liable to display obsessive perfectionism, intolerance of the accommodations which life requires, and the like.

But is the habit of moderation essentially a by-product of a strategy such as satisficing? Arguably, yes. Consider the corresponding maximizer who puts a concern with the tempering of his own character into his calculations as to what is after all best. He does not have to raise himself to a level above ordinary enumeration and evaluation like his counterpart in the other case. He simply allows his overall evaluation of the options enumerated to be affected by their significance for moderation of character.

Such a person, for all that has been said, may turn out not to be moderate. On the contrary, he is required to be a perfectionist, if not about moderation, at least about the complex of values, including moderation, which dictates his ranking of options. Given that ranking, he can have nothing but the best; anything less is failure. The direct, intentional pursuit of moderation, under a maximizing brief, is self-defeating. The habit of moderation is an essential by-product. Or so it can plausibly be argued.

There is an important difference between Simon's and Solon's rationale for satisficing. We should comment on it, since the distinction is of relevance later.

If one satisfices for Simon's reason, then one always chooses the best from among the alternatives already enumerated and evaluated. Satisficing on such a ground is intentionally not maximizing but it is not intentionally sub-maximizing, as we might say. One does not seek the best but neither does one seek not-the-best.

Where one satisfices out of Solon's motive, this result is not assured. Suppose that for whatever reason the options enumerated and evaluated include a number which exceed the aspiration level; they may even be an exhaustive set. The evaluation will be based on all relevant considerations, since it is not relativized by aspect or purpose. But these considerations do not include the effect on the agent's habit of moderation. Thus, just as the agent sets himself ordinarily to satisfice in view of that effect, so he may set himself to choose less than the best—so long as it is good enough—in the sort of scenario envisaged.

172   II—PHILIP PETTIT

He may commit himself to a policy of sub-maximization.[11]

We have seen enough to be able to say that thesis A holds. There are at least two good reasons for either of which a wide-scope consequentialist might prescribe a satisficing policy.

V

We may turn now to thesis B: the claim that satisficing is an irrational policy to prefer, in the absence of a wide-scope consequentialist motive. I will argue that an unmotivated satisficer of the kind envisaged is committed to unmotivated sub-maximization and that this is profoundly irrational.

The unmotivated satisficer prefers a strategy guaranteeing only a good enough result to one ensuring the best. It is not that the enumeration and evaluation required to guarantee the best has costs such as Simon or Solon would count. It is just that the exercise is irrelevant, since a good enough option is preferred to the best.

This means that such a satisficer will have to support a policy of sub-maximization in any situation where all the options have been enumerated and evaluated. He will opt for less than the best, so long as it is good enough. In this he will resemble a certain sort of Solon-satisficer but the difference remains that he can have no reason for the line he takes. He will be an unmotivated sub-maximizer.

Unmotivated sub-maximization is an irrational policy to prescribe or pursue. This fact can be brought out in two ways.

Suppose that an agent ranks A above B, all things considered, and then chooses B without any motive of the Solon type. The irrationality of the policy first appears in the fact that whereas he could have given a reason for choosing A—it is in his view a better option—he can give no reason for choosing B.

It will not do for him to say simply that B is good enough. That might be a reason for him to go for B, if he were unaware of the nature or value of alternatives. It is not a reason for him to choose B rather than A.

---

[11] It is this fact, I believe, which leads Routley, *op. cit.*, to describe the strategy as satisizing rather than satisficing. I define satisficing independently of the rationale offered in support of it. Presumably the follower of Solon will not sub-maximize in the cases under consideration if he is quite sure that his desires, and therefore his overall ranking, are already moderate—and if he is confident that maximizing will not have an adverse effect on his established moderation.

SATISFICING CONSEQUENTIALISM 173

The second way in which the irrationality of the sub-maximization appears is even more striking. To evaluate A as better than B is to be disposed to choose A, other things being equal. For the Solon-satisficer who sub-maximizes other things are not equal. For the unmotivated sub-maximizer however they are. His strategy deprives the notion of evaluation therefore of its usual content. It is not clear what it can mean to rank A above B if when other things are equal one insists on choosing B.

VI

Thesis B is overwhelming, in my view, but it may be useful to pinpoint some reasons why it might be mistakenly rejected.

A crude reason would be that the sub-maximand is assumed to be, not fulfilment of one's preferences, but consumption of the main commodity involved in the options. One sub-maximizes, not in relation to a preference ranking of ice-creams, but rather a ranking of ice-creams by the quantity of the stuff they contain. On this assumption sub-maximization will appear to be so normal that no question may be raised about sub-maximizing without a Solon-like motive.

A slightly less crude reason for rejecting thesis B might be that the sub-maximand is taken to be the fulfilment, not of one's preferences all things considered, but only of one's preferences in a particular dimension. Sub-maximizing on one's aesthetic or hygienic or even moral ranking of options is unexceptionable. Thinking along these lines, a person might slip into thought-lessly condoning unmotivated sub-maximization.

These reasons are crude because even the sub-maximization that is mistakenly envisaged in each case is not pursued without motive. That has to be overlooked, if the mistakes are to have the effect of making unmotivated sub-maximization seem reasonable. A third reason why such a strategy might be condoned is more sophisticated.

This is the thought that even an unmotivated sub-maximizer has a meta-preference for choosing less than the best, that his choice will fulfil this meta-preference, and that it can therefore be represented as rational. At a level of second-order, pre-emptive preferences, it guarantees maximal satisfaction.

This sort of justification is circular. The unmotivated sub-maximizer prescribes the fulfilment of the meta-preference

174   II—PHILIP PETTIT

mentioned. But why? Not because that meta-preference exists anyhow, being inherited from nature or whatever. Nor because it is a meta-preference desirable on Solon's grounds. Rather, for the reason that fulfilling that meta-preference just is sub-maximizing. The circle is of small circumference.

VII

Enough has been said in direct and indirect support of our two theses. But the second thesis runs counter to something that Michael Slote maintains and I would now like to make some remarks on his position.

Slote countenances as rational, not just satisficing, but sub-maximization.[12] And not just any sort of sub-maximization, but in particular the kind unmotivated by a wide-scope consequentialist consideration. There is no question of saving computational costs or of practising an ascetic strategy.[13] One rejects what is best if one can otherwise get what is good enough.

In support of his view Slote argues that unmotivated sub-maximization is countenanced in common sense. You have the opportunity to enjoy a snack but you decide you are happy enough as you are. You have the chance to fulfil any wish for yourself or your family and you ask for a benefit well short of the optimum. You are in a position to offer food and hospitality to some people in need and you give less than the best. In each case he maintains that common sense will respect your decision as rational.[14]

The last example is best ignored. What is morally best, even if it seems to demand no special sacrifice, may not be that which the person regards as best all things considered. The final ranking may be affected by all sorts of non-moral considerations, such as the wish not to have to think too well of oneself or not to have to appear too saintly to others. What common sense applauds in this case is not clearly an instance of sub-maximization.

Of the other examples, the first is easily handled. You are

[12]See page 358, see chapter 20 of this volume for footnotes 12–17.
[13]See pages 357 and 358.
[14]See pages 355–361. With the first two examples Slote appeals to what we would intuitively say, with the third to what the common sense morality of benevolence would prescribe. I have cast both as appeals to what common sense would say.

SATISFICING CONSEQUENTIALISM 175

supposed not to have any ascetic motive, such as Solon would provide, for choosing less than what you regard as best. You are faced with a choice between having or forgoing a snack. You forgo it. What ground can there be then for saying that you nevertheless regarded having the snack as, all things considered, the better option? You may have realized, as Slote says, that you would enjoy the snack but clearly you still came to the conclusion that it was better to practise restraint. There is no evidence here of unmotivated sub-maximization.

Slote more or less concedes the case. 'Although he knows he would enjoy the snack, the very fact that he rejects such enjoyment might easily be taken as evidence that he doesn't in the circumstances regard such enjoyment as a good thing'[15]. Conceding this, he directs our attention to the remaining example.

The case is a fairy-tale one. 'The hero or heroine, offered a single wish, asks for a pot of gold, for a million (1900) dollars, or, simply, for (enough money to enable) his family and himself to be comfortably well off for the rest of their lives. . . . Someone who makes such a wish clearly acknowledges the possibility of being better off and yet chooses—knowingly and in some sense deliberately chooses—a lesser but personally satisfying degree of well-being'.[16]

In this case, as in the others, there is every reason to protest that the behaviour is not self-evidently an instance of unmotivated sub-maximization. The agent may be superstitious about asking for more. Or he may think it is wrong to use such an opportunity to become more than moderately rich. He may believe, all things considered, that it is best to be financially at the mean, or only just above it. Or he may even be infected by the wisdom of Solon. The possibilities are legion.

It should be clear that Slote's recourse to common sense is not likely to yield the conclusion he desires. We may concede that what common sense deems to be rational can hardly be denied that title. We may agree that common sense will judge the cases in question as he says it will. But we can always show, for every case presented, that it need not be taken, and may not be taken by common sense, to illustrate unmotivated sub-maximization. Against such a line of attack, thesis B will easily stand firm.

[15]Pages 358–9.
[16]Page 359.

176   II—PHILIP PETTIT

VIII

In conclusion, an *ad hominem* point against Slote. This is that the sub-maximizing strategy which he countenances imposes the same costs as maximizing, but without offering the same benefits. It gives us the worst of both worlds.

Slote implies that in order to sub-maximize, an agent needs to have enumerated and evaluated all the relevant options. What he endorses as rational therefore is a policy of mimicking the strategy of maximization up to the moment of choice. One enumerates all the salient alternatives; one evaluates each; and then one chooses something less than the best, provided it is good enough.

Slote commits himself to full-scale enumeration and evaluation of alternatives, because he maintains a maximizer's conception of how to evaluate options. He takes the measure of what is sufficiently good to be the distance from what is the best available; he takes sufficient goodness to be judged by a comparative metric.[17] If one has to compare an option with all the alternatives, in particular with the best, before one can tell that it is sufficient, then one must enumerate and evaluate all those alternatives before making one's choice.

The strategy which he countenances is a rare and perverse mixture. It requires that the agent should suffer all the pains of maximizing just in order to ensure that he does not enjoy its fruits. Such a strategy hardly constitutes a serious challenge to our thesis B.

NOTE

For useful comments and conversations I am indebted to a number of colleagues, some resident and some visiting, at the Research School of Social Sciences, Australian National University. I am particularly indebted to R. E. Goodin.

[17]See pages 366 and 368–9. Slote's emphasis on the comparative accounting of options is an endorsement of the economist's notion of opportunity costs.

Part IX
Beyond Common Sense?

[22]

SHELLY KAGAN

Does Consequentialism
Demand Too Much?
Recent Work on the
Limits of Obligation[1]

Consequentialism claims that an act is morally permissible if and only if it has better consequences than those of any available alternative act. This means that agents are morally required to make their largest possible contribution to the overall good—no matter what the sacrifice to themselves might involve (remembering only that their own well-being counts too). There is no limit to the sacrifices that morality can require; and agents are never permitted to favor their own interests at the expense of the greater good.

Our ordinary moral intuitions rebel at this picture. We want to claim that there is a limit to what morality can require of us. Some sacrifices for the sake of others are meritorious, but not required; they are supererogatory. Common morality grants the agent some room to pursue his own projects, even though other actions might have better consequences: we are permitted to promote the good, but we are not required to do so.

The objection that consequentialism demands too much is accepted uncritically by almost all of us; most moral philosophers introduce permission to perform nonoptimal acts without even a word in its defense. But the mere fact that our intuitions support some moral feature hardly constitutes in itself adequate philosophical justification. If we are to go beyond mere intuition mongering, we must search for deeper foundations. We must display the *reasons* for limiting the requirement to pursue the good.

1. The following works are reviewed in this essay: David Heyd, *Supererogation: Its Status in Ethical Theory* (Cambridge: Cambridge University Press, 1982); Thomas Nagel, "The Limits of Objectivity," in *The Tanner Lectures on Human Values*, vol. I, ed. Sterling McMurrin (Cambridge: Cambridge University Press, 1980), pp. 77–139; and Samuel Scheffler, *The Rejection of Consequentialism: A Philosophical Investigation of the Considerations Underlying Rival Moral Conceptions* (Oxford: Clarendon Press, 1982).

Nor is it sufficient to consider this issue in isolation: the arguments offered must cohere with the rest of what we want to defend about morality. The challenge is to provide a plausible defense that preserves the features which make the ordinary moral view a moderate one. A defense of the common view, obviously enough, must explain why it is sometimes permissible to refuse to perform some optimal act. But all those unwilling to embrace egoism must at the same time avoid arguments that rule out the possibility of there being any moral requirements at all. Thus the explanation must also account for the fact that sometimes a given optimal act *is* required by morality. Similarly, the account must capture the view that even when a given sacrifice is not required, it is nonetheless permissible—indeed, meritorious. Most arguments offered seem to be incompatible with these or other features of the common moral view, and therefore need to be rejected by those who wish to defend anything like that view.

Furthermore, discussions of the claim that consequentialism demands too much are often undermined by failure to distinguish this claim from the widely discussed objection that consequentialism permits too much—improperly permitting sacrifices to be *imposed* on some for the sake of others. Some theories include deontological restrictions, forbidding certain kinds of acts even when the consequences would be good. I will not consider here the merits of such restrictions. It is important to note, however, that even a theory which included such restrictions might still lack more general permission to act nonoptimally—requiring agents to promote the good within the permissible means. It is only the grounds for rejecting such a general requirement to promote the overall good that we will examine here.

I

David Heyd's *Supererogation* provides an instructive example of some of the problems I have just described. After presenting a historical survey of the place of supererogation in some major ethical theories, Heyd offers his own favored analysis of the concept. The details of Heyd's discussion, however, need not concern us, except for this: as the first systematic study of the subject of supererogation, one would expect Heyd to give particular care to justifying his view that some acts *are* supererogatory—optimal but not required. But *Supererogation* is a disappointing book.

When it finally addresses this task in its concluding chapter, instead of sustained argument we find a bewildering grab bag of incomplete thoughts. Like most who defend the existence of supererogatory acts, the intuitive appeal of this position seems to blind Heyd to the obvious inadequacies of his own discussion.

According to Heyd, the justification of supererogation has two "aspects": the negative aspect shows the justification for limiting what is morally required; the positive aspect shows "the value of non-obligatory well-doing as such" (p. 166). Heyd's summary of his argument suggests that each aspect is in turn supported by several considerations. Unfortunately, the actual presentation of the justifications makes no attempt to demarcate the boundaries of individual arguments, making the whole discussion difficult to keep straight. By my rough count, there are eleven arguments, offered in no particular order.[2] Several are actually no more than hints of arguments, and some may not even be meant as arguments at all. Furthermore, even the best of them have a half-baked quality about them, as though Heyd had desperately grabbed at anything at all that might support his case. Although there is no room here to review all of Heyd's arguments, I have reconstructed the more interesting ones, and given them names.

The Incommensurability of Reasons (pp. 170–71). Heyd claims that there are two types of reasons: reasons to promote overall human welfare, and reasons of "autonomy," which support the pursuit of one's own ends. Although the first sort of reason is *"morally* superior" to the second kind, the two types of reasons "cannot be compared in terms of strength." Thus it simply isn't generally true that promoting the overall good is backed by stronger or conclusive reasons—that is, that an agent "ought" to promote the good. If the agent chooses instead to act on the reasons that support promoting his own ends, this cannot be faulted from the standpoint of practical reasons; he hasn't failed to do what he *ought* to do.

By viewing the two types of reasons as incommensurable, Heyd would be able to explain why an agent might be free to perform some optimal act at great cost to himself, or to refrain, as he chooses. But such an

---

2. A guide to the perplexed (using my own labels): The Incommensurability of Reasons (pp. 170–71); The Good-Ought Gap (pp. 171–72); The Basicness of Rights (pp. 172–73); Coherence (pp. 173–74); Integrity (p. 174); The Minimalist Model of Morality (p. 174); Justice (pp. 174–75); The Intrinsic Value of Supererogatory Acts (pp. 175–76); Mill (p. 176); Good Samaritan Legislation (pp. 176–78); and Evidence of Concern (p. 179). Perhaps others would carve up the discussion differently.

account would make it impossible to explain how an agent could ever be *required* to promote the good—even at negligible cost to himself. Presumably in cases of this kind we want to say that the two sorts of reasons *can* be compared in terms of strength, and that reasons of autonomy have become so weak that they are conclusively outweighed. Yet how can supposedly incommensurable reasons become commensurable simply through variations in their magnitude? It just won't do for Heyd to support one part of his moral theory (supererogation) with a thesis that rules out another part of his moral theory (the existence of some requirements to aid; see, e.g., p. 90).

The Minimalist Model of Morality (p. 174). Morality, says Heyd, is not aimed at "the maximization of general good or happiness" but is rather "a means of securing some minimal conditions of cooperation and justice." Presumably only these minimal constraints on the autonomy of the individual are justified; beyond that, individuals have "the right to pursue their own ends" (p. 172). Heyd does not explicitly state how the minimal level is to be set, but he later seems to endorse the view that moral requirements "constitute the minimum required for the preservation of society" (p. 181; cf. p. 177).

Such a standard, however, would set morality unacceptably low: if I can save someone's life at no cost to myself, surely I am required to do so; but the preservation of society would not be threatened if no one ever fulfilled such obligations. Thus all but an egoist will recognize requirements to aid that go beyond those grounded by Heyd's minimalist model. Heyd may very well want to include a modest principle of aid as part of his model—but to do so is *ad hoc*. Once this is seen, and one realizes just how minimal a genuinely minimalist model of morality would be, the view should lose its appeal altogether. But at any rate, the minimalist conception cannot be used by one (such as Heyd) who wants to claim that the requirement to aid should be limited—but not nonexistent.

These first two arguments bring out nicely the importance of bearing in mind that ordinary morality lies precariously perched between *two* extremes. Many attacks on consequentialism can only be achieved by opening the door to egoism (or other overly minimal views); most of us, therefore, cannot consistently accept such arguments.

Justice (pp. 174–75). Heyd claims that "the non-utilitarian concept of justice serves both to counter utilitarian arguments for the punishment of an innocent individual and to support the distinction between duty and supererogation." Just as "individual persons should not be sacrificed for the promotion of overall happiness (as in the case of punishing an innocent man in order to save the lives of many others)," similarly "considerations of justice make it unacceptable to require any individual to work ceaselessly for the welfare of others."

This is an obscure argument. Who or what is supposed to violate justice when the individual is required to promote the overall good? Heyd does not say, and neither morality nor the individual himself seems an especially promising candidate for blame. Is it then *society* that acts unjustly— by requiring the promotion of the good, backing its requirements with social sanctions? This seems more promising: we have a straightforward case of imposing sacrifices on someone for the sake of others (*exactly* like punishing the innocent man). Other passages support this interpretation as well (e.g., pp. 166 and 176–77); but if this is indeed what Heyd has in mind it is simply beside the point. The immorality of *imposing* a sacrifice upon an individual is completely compatible with that individual's nonetheless being morally *required* to take the sacrifice upon himself. In effect, this third argument suffers from a confusion I mentioned earlier: the impermissibility of society imposing sacrifices might well be relevant to demonstrating that consequentialism *permits* too much; but it seems irrelevant to the question of whether consequentialism *demands* too much. Thus, even if it could be shown that it is unjust for society to coerce individuals into promoting the good, this would do nothing at all to support Heyd's view that the individuals themselves are free of such a moral requirement. (Heyd himself levels a similar objection against others; e.g., pp. 109–10.)

The Intrinsic Value of Supererogatory Acts (pp. 175–76). Since supererogatory acts go beyond what is required, their performance is "purely optional." Heyd believes that this makes such acts especially valuable. If he is right, this would give us a reason to reject a general requirement to promote the good. But what is this valuable feature? Heyd informs us that "some types of virtuous behaviour can be realized only under conditions of complete freedom and would be stifled under a more totalitarian concept of duty." This claim is never substantiated, however, for Heyd gives no clear statement of which virtues he has in mind. He does note that supererogatory acts display "individual preferences and virtues"; but surely doing one's duty can do the same. He also notes that the optionality of supererogation allows favoritism and partiality—but if these are "virtues" it is not clear to me that we should mourn their passing.

A more interesting possibility may be hinted at in Heyd's repeated suggestion that the special value of supererogatory acts consists in "their being totally optional and voluntary" (pp. 9; cf. pp. 18–19, 41–2, 53, 133). He never explains why this gives these acts special worth (other than the unhelpful allusions to virtue), but one possibility seems close to hand: since the supererogatory act goes beyond what is required, if an agent makes a sacrifice for another, he is doing it not because he must, but because he *wants to*. That is, his act is not done from duty—but out of concern for the one he aids. Thus Heyd may believe that supererogatory acts are (typically) done from an especially valuable kind of *motive* (cf. p. 177), which would be lost if duty were more encompassing.

Despite the initial appeal of this line of thought, however, it essentially depends on the assumption that if promotion of the overall good were morally required it would be impossible (or harder) to act out of this higher kind of motive. But there is no reason to believe such a claim. Being morally required to aid, after all, is perfectly compatible with being motivated by direct concern for those in need.

It seems, then, that Heyd's arguments repeatedly miss their mark: of the four we've examined, two are incompatible with Heyd's own views, one is irrelevant to his conclusion, and the last fails to deliver on its promise. In the end, I believe that all that can be salvaged from Heyd's discussion is the general suggestion that an adequate defense might contain both positive and negative elements: e.g., negatively, some considerations might point to the necessity of limiting moral requirements; positively, other considerations might indicate the desirability of doing so. Obviously, however, this suggestion does not itself indicate how this necessary defense might be provided.

In his closing paragraph, Heyd expresses doubts about whether basic disagreements in moral outook can be "resolved by rational argument"; and he asserts that he has not attempted to "prove" his "picture of man and of the nature of morality" (p. 183). Surely, however, we can at least ask that Heyd paint a coherent picture, instead of a series of inadequate sketches. It should be noted, furthermore, that the faults of Heyd's discussion are typical of most writing in this area. Although few philosophers

245   Recent Work on the
                                   Limits of Obligation

offer as *many* arguments as Heyd does, generally the particular arguments are just as weak. In the following sections, however, I will consider two works which are notable exceptions: each offers a sustained argument for the rejection of a general requirement to promote the good.

II

Thomas Nagel's "The Limits of Objectivity" is a rich and suggestive work in metaphysics and ethics. A series of three lectures, the first treats subjectivity and objectivity in the philosophy of mind, the second discusses the objectivity of values, and the third argues for the inadequacy of consequentialism.

In the second lecture, Nagel makes a key distinction between *agent-relative* and *agent-neutral* reasons (pp. 101–3). Roughly, an agent-neutral reason "is a reason for *anyone* to do or want something"—that is, it is a reason that applies to everybody, regardless of their particular circumstances or interests. If we judge that some state of affairs has agent-neutral value, "that means that *anyone* has reason to want it to happen." Agent-relative reasons, however, apply only to particular individuals; if we judge that something has agent-relative value, then we only believe "that someone has reason to want and pursue it if it is related to him in the right way (being in *his* interest, for example)." Much of the second lecture is devoted to arguing that there are at least *some* agent-neutral reasons; Nagel believes, for instance, that "*anyone* has a reason to want *any* pain to stop, whether or not it is his" (p. 108).

This is, of course, a controversial claim, but it won't be examined here, for it would certainly be accepted by the consequentialist. Indeed, it seems that consequentialism can be usefully viewed as the theory that the *only* reasons for action are agent-neutral ones (p. 119). Against this position, Nagel argues in the third lecture for the existence of genuine agent-relative reasons. "Deontological reasons" fall outside our topic. The existence of "reasons of autonomy," however, is directly relevant to the charge that consequentialism demands too much, for such reasons "would limit what we are *obliged* to do in the service of agent-neutral values" (p. 120). They spring from "the desires, projects, commitments, and personal ties of the individual agent, all of which give him reasons to act in the pursuit of ends that are his own" (p. 120).

Nagel writes:

> If I have a bad headache, anyone has a reason to want it to stop. But if for instance I badly want to become a first-rate pianist, not everyone has a reason to want me to practice. *I* have a reason to want to practice, and it may be just as strong as my reason for wanting my headache to go away. But other people have very little reason, if any, to care whether I become a first-rate pianist or not. Why is this?
>
> I think it is easier to believe in this distinction than to explain it (pp. 121–22).

It is indeed easy to believe in Nagel's distinction. But the question, as Nagel seems to recognize, is whether or not he can offer an adequate explanation of the distinction, and thus manage to defend our intuitions.

Before investigating this, however, it may be worth spelling out exactly how such agent-relative reasons bode ill for consequentialism's requirement to promote the overall good (a topic Nagel rushes over, pp. 124–25). Suppose, first, that my projects and interests did generate agent-neutral reasons, and only agent-neutral reasons. Since my projects would have agent-neutral value, not only would I have reasons to promote them, *everyone* would have such reasons; the promotion of my projects would count as part of the overall good. Since my projects would generate only agent-neutral reasons, however, I would have no *more* reason to promote them than would anyone else; the mere fact that they were *my* projects would give me no extra reason to favor them.

Suppose instead that my interests also generated agent-relative reasons (in addition to the agent-neutral reasons, if any). Then *I* would have reasons to promote my projects which not everyone else possessed; and if sufficiently strong, these extra reasons to promote *my* projects would override the agent-neutral reasons impinging on me. Thus it would be permissible, in some cases, to pursue my own projects at the possible expense of the overall good.

Nagel concentrates on denying that there is any agent-neutral value to the satisfaction of preferences per se (p. 124; there may be derivative value, since the frustration of desires can be painful, p. 123). This enables him to offer an indirect argument: since it is implausible to hold that *no* genuine reasons are generated, it must be agent-relative ones that are created by preferences (p. 125). Even if sound, I do not think such a *via negativa* will be especially illuminating. It may help establish the existence of agent-relative reasons, but it will not explain them. Furthermore, if the account in my two previous paragraphs is correct, the denial that there is any agent-neutral value to preference satisfaction per se seems an unnecessarily extreme thesis for Nagel to maintain, for the permissibility of favoring my own projects will be established so long as my preferences generate agent-relative reasons. There is no need to deny that they also generate agent-neutral reasons; it is simply that these must not exhaust their reason-giving force.[3] What is especially in need of explanation, then, is why agent-relative reasons are created. Unfortunately, given the needs of Nagel's indirect argument, the discussion focuses instead on explaining why agent-neutral reasons are *not* generated.

These are, perhaps, relatively minor complaints; but there is a more central difficulty with Nagel's account. Nagel's explanation of why it is sometimes permissible for an agent to promote his own interests, rather than sacrificing them for the overall good, is that agent-relative reasons will often outweigh the opposing agent-neutral reasons. Such an account, however, makes it mysterious how it could be permissible for the agent to *make* the sacrifice. Doing so, after all, would be in blatant disregard of the agent-relative reasons which, by hypothesis, outweigh the agent-neutral ones. In order to maintain the intuitive claim that the agent can make the sacrifice or refrain, as he chooses, it seems that Nagel will need a more complicated account of reasons than the one given here.

Nagel's problem is the complement of one that plagued Heyd. Heyd claimed that reasons of autonomy and reasons to promote the overall good are incommensurable. This enabled him to account for the agent's freedom to sacrifice his interests, or to refrain, as he chooses; but it ruled out the possibility of accounting for moral *requirements*. Nagel views agent-relative and agent-neutral reasons as commensurable, and thus can account for the existence of moral requirements; but he seems unable to account for the agent's ever having the *freedom* to sacrifice his interests if he chooses. It is far from clear whether a coherent account of reasons could manage to avoid both of these problems simultaneously.

Leaving this difficulty aside, let us now return to the earlier question:

---

3. If my projects lack agent-neutral value, then others have *no* direct reason to help promote them. This would provide a second way in which morality would be less demanding than most consequentialists believe it to be. But it would not show the inadequacy of consequentialism's requirement to promote the good; it would simply establish that it is an error to believe that preference satisfaction per se is *part* of the overall good.

Why does pain generate agent-neutral reasons, but the desire to be a pianist only agent-relative ones? Nagel distinguishes between involuntary desires, and those desires that are "adopted" or chosen (p. 122). His view is that, roughly, involuntary desires generate agent-neutral reasons, but adopted desires create only agent-relative ones. (This view was tacitly appealed to in the earlier argument for the agent-neutral value of the avoidance of pain, p. 109.)

Against those who claim that the satisfaction of an adopted desire has agent-neutral value, Nagel objects that "one would have to be deranged to think it *did* matter impersonally" (p. 123). Much of the rhetorical force of this reply, however, derives from the mistaken view that objects with agent-neutral value must be "good or bad in themselves" (p. 119; cf. p. 109). To say that an object is good in itself is presumably to say that its value does not depend upon anyone's desiring it; and it is admittedly much more plausible to hold that objects of adopted desires (typically) have value only because someone does desire them. But Nagel apparently overlooks the possibility that although an object's having value at all may depend upon its being desired by someone or the other, given that there *is* someone who desires the object, this generates agent-neutral reasons. This view is not at least obviously crazy, and so Nagel still needs to explain why adopted desires generate only agent-relative reasons.

In what appears to be the key passage, Nagel writes that when we look at adopted desires

> objectively, from outside, we can acknowledge the validity of the reasons they give for action, without judging that there is an agent-neutral reason for any of those things *to be done*. That is because, when we move to the objective standpoint, we are not *occupying* the perspective from which these values have to be accepted. Their diversity and their dependence on the history and circumstances of the agent insures this. From a point of view outside the perspective of my ambition to become a first-rate pianist, it is possible to *recognize* and *understand* that perspective and so to *acknowledge* the reasons that arise inside it; but it is not possible to *accept* those reasons as one's own, unless one adopts the perspective rather than merely recognizing it (pp. 122–23).

I must confess that I am unable to grasp what the argument or explanation is supposed to be here. The passage repeatedly asserts that if I do not share an adopted desire, I do not have—and indeed cannot have—a direct reason to promote the satisfaction of that desire. But I simply cannot see how Nagel gives any *explanation* of this. The trivial reminder that I do not share desires I do not share cannot in itself explain why such desires do not generate reasons binding upon me.

One possibility is that Nagel is tacitly assuming that an individual can have a reason to promote something only if he takes a (logically prior) interest in it. This would explain why unshared desires do not generate reasons; but such a Humean view seems to be in violation of the entire spirit of Nagel's enterprise, and is explicitly rejected elsewhere (e.g., p. 110).

A second possible explanation might stress the difference between involuntary desires—which are simply "evoked" (p. 109)—and adopted desires, which are chosen. Since in some sense it is my *fault* that I have adopted desires which may go unsatisfied, it might be suggested that this explains why others have no responsibility for helping me in this regard. (Compare the view that the guilty and the lazy do not deserve help in overcoming the troubles they have brought upon themselves.) I do not know if this account can be adequately developed and defended, but it would clearly go beyond anything Nagel has suggested.

Ultimately, then, Nagel's discussion is inadequate. Yet despite the failure in *detail* of Nagel's argument, I think that its general thrust is in the right direction. Nagel is concerned about the conflict between the objective and the subjective perspectives, and he is eager to emphasize the legitimate claims of the latter. Surely if an adequate defense can be provided for rejecting a general requirement to promote the overall good, that defense will be grounded in the existence and nature of the subjective standpoint. Nonetheless, it seems to me that "The Limits of Objectivity" does *not* provide an adequate argument along these lines. The most promising development of the Nagelian strategy, I believe, can be found instead in our final work.

III

Samuel Scheffler's *The Rejection of Consequentialism* is one of the most interesting works of moral philosophy that I have read in years. Starting from the reasonable view that "the salient features of *all* moral conceptions stand in need of principled motivation" (p. 121), the book is, as the subtitle indicates, "a philosophical investigation of the considerations underlying rival moral conceptions."

Three particular features engage Scheffler's attention: distribution-sensitive theories of the good; deontological restrictions; and what Scheffler calls *agent-centered prerogatives* which (within limits) permit the agent to perform acts, if he so chooses, that are less than optimal from an impartial perspective. Only the last will concern us here. Scheffler believes that he can offer a plausible rationale for rejecting consequentialism's general requirement to promote the good. As I've indicated, this rationale turns on the nature of the subjective or personal point of view.

Before turning to the rationale itself, let's look at the kind of agent-centered prerogative Scheffler finds most plausible. Consequentialism insists that an agent should act in accord with an impartial standpoint. In contrast, then, an agent-centered prerogative would make it permissible for the agent "to devote energy and attention to his projects and commitments out of proportion to their weight in the impersonal calculus" (p. 14). This basic idea is straightforward enough; but the particular passage where Scheffler describes the details of his prerogative is rather garbled. He suggests that a plausible prerogative

> would allow each agent to assign a certain proportionately greater weight to his own interests than to the interests of other people. It would then allow the agent to promote the non-optimal outcome of his choosing, provided only that the degree of its inferiority to each of the superior outcomes he could instead promote in no case exceeded, by more than the specified proportion, the degree of sacrifice necessary for him to promote the superior outcome (p. 20).

Taken literally, this passage seems to say that an act is permissible when the difference between two (obscure) magnitudes is less than or equal to some specified proportion. It is not at all clear what intuitive interpretation this formula could have.

Scheffler's lapse is unfortunate, for it does not seem difficult to understand the sort of prerogative that he probably meant to be describing. Imagine that I want to perform some act, S, rather than an alternative, O, because S is more in my interests. Consequentialism says I must weigh the interests of others just as heavily as my own; thus I can perform S rather than O only if the loss to others doesn't objectively *outweigh* the gain to me. Suppose, however, that I am permitted to count my own interests more heavily than others; in my calculations, let us say, I can magnify my benefits and losses, giving them up to M times their objective weight. Unlike consequentialism, where the size of the loss to others (of S rather than O) must be less than or equal to the gain to me, under such an agent-centered prerogative performing S rather than O would be permissible even in cases where the loss to others *does* outweigh the gain to me, provided that the size of the loss to others is less than or equal to M times the gain to me.

I believe that this is the sort of prerogative that Scheffler had in mind: I can justify certain nonoptimal acts, by giving my interests up to M times their objective weight; but I am not *required* to weigh my interests more heavily, and so I can still choose to sacrifice my interests and perform the optimal act. Furthermore, such a prerogative would differ from egoism, as Scheffler notes (p. 21),[4] for I would *not* be permitted to pursue my interests when the size of the loss to others would be greater than M times the gain to me.

There is, however, an important difficulty that Scheffler overlooks (pp. 23–5): such a prerogative will not only permit agents to *allow* harm, it will also permit agents to *do* harm in the pursuit of their nonoptimal projects (Scheffler readily permits optimal harmings). For the prerogative is only sensitive to the *size* of the loss to others, and not to whether the loss is caused by the agent's act. Thus, for example, it will apparently be permissible to kill my rich uncle in order to inherit $10,000. Lest it be suggested that a plausible M will avoid this result, bear in mind that most of us believe we would not be required to *pay* $10,000 in order to *save* the life of some stranger; any M large enough to save such results will obviously work in the former case as well. Such permissions to do non-optimal harm could be blocked by introducing deontological restrictions against harming, but Scheffler rejects these; nor does he offer any other rationale for limiting the prerogative to cases of *allowing* harm.

Let us now consider the proposed rationale for agent-centered prerogatives (of whatever form). Scheffler's exposition proceeds dialectically (see especially pp. 56–67), but the final outline of the argument seems to be this: 1) Each person has a point of view, the nature of which is

---

4. Provided that M is finite. Scheffler is wrong, however, to claim that such a prerogative would place restrictions on the *kind* of projects the agent can pursue (see p. 21; cf. pp. 18–19).

such that the individual's "own projects and commitments have a distinctive claim on his attention; he cares about them out of proportion" to their weight from an impersonal standpoint. In this sense, the personal point of view is "independent" of the impersonal standpoint (pp. 56–7). 2) Since an adequate morality must take account of the nature of persons, we should reject any moral principle "which ignores the independence of the personal point of view" (pp. 57–8). 3) There are, however, at least two different rational methods for taking account of the fact of personal independence (pp. 60, 63): (a) a "maximization" strategy, which is available to the consequentialist (pp. 58–61); and (b) the "liberation" strategy, which creates an agent-centered prerogative (pp. 61–2). 4) Since the liberation strategy is at least as adequate as the maximization strategy, we have a rationale for incorporating prerogatives: doing so "embodies a rational strategy for taking account of personal independence, given one construal of the importance of that aspect of persons" (p. 67).

Scheffler's conclusion is modest: he does not argue that it's *necessary* to include such prerogatives, but only that there is a plausible rationale for those theories which do (pp. 64–7). Whether this is so, of course, depends on the details of the liberation strategy; for the mere fact that a theory can be construed as *some* sort of response to the nature of persons does not in itself show that there is a rationale for responding in that way.

Consider, first, the maximization strategy. Despite its name, the core of this response is the recognition that personal independence "fundamentally affects the character of human fulfilment and hence the constitution of the individual good" (p. 60). Since abandoning one's projects can be especially hard, it is only plausible to "count the cost of such hardships in arriving at our overall assessments of relevant outcomes, thereby acknowledging the special concern people have for their projects *as their* projects" (p. 59). Consequentialists (whether correctly or not) go on to require the promotion of the overall good; but this sophisticated account of individual good should be accepted even by nonconsequentialists (cf. pp. 63–4, 123–24). There may be additional appropriate responses to personal independence as well, but at the very least the rationale for adjusting one's theory of the good seems clear and undeniable.

Matters are less clear with the liberation strategy. Scheffler claims that an agent-centered prerogative "takes account of the natural independence of the personal point of view precisely by granting it moral independence" (p. 62). Such a claim is misleading, however. Admittedly, any prerogative would give the personal point of view some freedom in practical deliberation from the constraints of the impersonal standpoint; nonetheless, like consequentialism, a limited prerogative is "unlikely to exhaust" (p. 61) the agent's own feelings about his projects. Thus nothing short of egoism would actually grant genuine moral independence to the personal point of view. If, like Scheffler, we want to reject egoism, we need a rationale for prerogatives that grant only *partial* moral independence.

Furthermore, Scheffler's central description of the rationale underlying the liberation strategy (p. 62) is obscure; and although other passages shed some light (pp. 64, 94, and 125–27), I believe the account remains fundamentally inadequate. In the liberation strategy, says Scheffler, the importance of the natural independence of the personal point of view "is conceived as stemming primarily from its impact on the character of human agency and motivation" (p. 94)—that is, people do not typically act in accordance with the impersonal standpoint. Scheffler suggests that "given *this* conception of the importance of the natural fact of personal independence, a moral view gives sufficient weight to that fact only if it *reflects* it, by freeing people from the demand that their actions and motives always be optimal from the impersonal perspective" (p. 62).

Thus, faced with the fact that people typically *don't* promote the overall good, the liberation strategy responds that morally they're not required to. But what is the underlying rationale for this response supposed to be? Surely Scheffler doesn't mean to be arguing that since people are going to do something anyway we might as well say that this is morally permissible—a quick road to egoism, and implausible to boot. Personal independence may constitute an implicit appeal for agent-centered prerogatives—but what is the rationale for *granting* this appeal? (Surely not the mere fact that the appeal is made.) Doing so is a response, to be sure, but why is it a *rational* response? Scheffler never raises these questions; but without answers, I don't see how we can accept his claim to have shown that the liberation strategy is a rational method for taking account of personal independence. Unlike the maximization strategy, Scheffler provides no genuine rationale at all for the liberation strategy.

Let me quickly suggest two possible approaches to providing such a rationale. The first would develop Scheffler's observation about the impact of personal independence on motivation and agency: it might be suggested, as a result, that a general requirement to promote the good would lack the motivational underpinning necessary for genuine moral requirements; and so moral theory must grant at least some sort of agent-centered prerogative. The second would stress the importance of personal independence for the existence of commitments and close personal relations: it might then be suggested that the value of such commitments yields a positive reason for preserving within moral theory at least some moral independence for the personal point of view. Neither of these approaches need lead to egoism; but I am not sure whether either of them can be adequately defended. Without some such approach, however, it seems that Scheffler fails to provide an underlying rationale for incorporating agent-centered prerogatives into moral theory. Like Nagel and Heyd, Scheffler's rejection of the general requirement to promote the good remains inadequately supported.

IV

In this essay I have examined three recent attempts to defend the view that (within limits) it is permissible for agents to pursue their own projects rather than the overall good. That all three attempts have proven inadequate should give pause to those who do not even feel the need to defend this common view. The shortcomings of a grab bag approach like Heyd's will not, perhaps, surprise us; but the failure of even the sustained attempts of Nagel and Scheffler should alert us to the difficulty of supporting the common belief. Indeed, if the intuition that consequentialism demands too much remains impossible to defend, we may have to face the sobering possibility that it is not consequentialism, but our intuition, that is in error.

   I am indebted to Thomas Nagel and Samuel Scheffler for valuable discussions of their work, and to the Editors of *Philosophy & Public Affairs* for criticisms of an earlier version of this essay.

[23]

*Utilitarianism and the Virtues**

PHILIPPA FOOT

It is remarkable how utilitarianism tends to haunt even those of us who will not believe in it. It is as if we for ever feel that it must be right, although we insist that it is wrong. T. M. Scanlon hits the nail on the head when he observes, in his article 'Contractualism and Utilitarianism', that the theory occupies a central place in the moral philosophy of our time in spite of the fact that, as he puts it, 'the implications of act utilitarianism are wildly at variance with firmly held moral convictions, while rule utilitarianism . . . strikes most people as an unstable compromise'.[1] He suggests that what we need to break this spell is to find a better alternative to utilitarian theories, and I am sure that that is right. But what I want to do is to approach the business of exorcism more directly. Obviously something drives us towards utilitarianism, and must it not be an assumption or thought which is in some way mistaken? For otherwise why is the theory unacceptable? We must be going wrong somewhere and should find out where it is.

I want to argue that what is most radically wrong with utilitarianism is its consequentialism, but I also want to suggest that its consequentialist element is one of the main reasons why utilitarianism seems so compelling. I need therefore to say something about the relation between the two theory descriptions 'utilitarian' and 'consequentialist'. Consequentialism in its most general form simply says that it is by 'total outcome', that is, by the whole formed by an action and its consequences, that what is done is judged right or wrong. A consequentialist theory of ethics is one which identifies certain states of affairs as *good* states of affairs and says that the rightness or goodness of actions (or of other subjects of moral judgement) consists in their positive productive relationship to these states of affairs. Utilitarianism as it is usually defined consists of consequentialism together with the identification of the best state of affairs with the state of affairs in which there is most happiness, most pleasure, or the maximum satisfaction of desire. Strictly speaking utilitarianism—taken here as welfare utilitarianism—is

* This is an expanded version of a paper delivered as the Presidential address at the Pacific Division Meeting of the American Philosophical Association on March 25th. 1983, and published in the *APA Proceedings and Addresses* 57 (November 1983). Much of the text is unaltered and the ideas are the same, but I hope to have explained myself more clearly this time around. I am grateful to the Officers of the APA for granting me the original copyright.

Among the many people who helped me to write the original version, Rogers Albritton and Warren Quinn in Los Angeles, and Rosalind Hursthouse, Gavin Lawrence, and David Wiggins in Oxford, all have my special thanks.

[1] T. M. Scanlon, 'Contractualism and Utilitarianism' in Amartya Sen and Bernard Williams, eds., *Utilitarianism and Beyond* (Cambridge, 1982), pp. 103-28.

left behind when the distribution of welfare is said in itself to affect the goodness of states of affairs; or when anything other than welfare is allowed as part of the good. But it is of course possible also to count a theory as utilitarian if right action is taken to be that which produces 'good states of affairs', whatever these are supposed to be; and then 'utilitarianism' becomes synonymous with 'consequentialism'. By 'utilitarianism' I shall here mean 'welfare utilitarianism', though it is consequentialism in one form or another that I shall be most concerned.

Although I believe that what is radically wrong with utilitarianism is its consequentialism, what has often seemed to be most wrong with it has been either welfarism or the sum ranking of welfare. So it has been suggested that 'the good' is not automatically increased by an increase in pleasure, but by non-malicious pleasure, or first-order pleasure, or something of the kind; in order to get over difficulties about the pleasures of watching a public execution or the pleasures and pains of the bigot or the prude.[2] Furthermore distribution principles have been introduced so that actions benefiting the rich more than they harm the poor no longer have to be judged morally worthy. Thus the criteria for the goodness of states of affairs have continually been modified to meet one objection after another; but it seems that the modifications have never been able to catch up with the objections. For the distribution principles and the discounting of certain pleasures and pains did nothing to help with problems about, e.g., the wrongness of inducing cancer in a few experimental subjects to make a substantial advance in finding a cure for the disease. If the theory was to give results at all in line with common moral opinion *rights* had to be looked after in a way that was so far impossible within even the modified versions of utilitarianism.

It was therefore suggested, by Amartya Sen, that 'goal rights' systems should be considered; the idea being that the respecting or violating of rights should be counted as itself a good or an evil in the evaluation of states of affairs.[3] This would help to solve some problems because if the respecting of the rights of the subject were weighted heavily enough the cancer experiment could not turn out to be 'optimific' after all. Yet this seems rather a strange suggestion, because as Samuel Scheffler has remarked, it is not clear why, in the measurement of the goodness of states of affairs or total outcomes, killings for instance should count so much more heavily than deaths.[4] But what is more important is that this 'goal rights' system fails to deal with certain other examples of actions that most of us would want to call wrong. Suppose, for instance, that some evil person threatens to kill or torture a number of victims unless we kill or torture one, and suppose that we have every reason to believe that he will do as he says. Then in terms of their total

---

[2] See, e.g., Amartya Sen, 'Utilitarianism and Welfarism', *Journal of Philosophy* 76 (1979), pp. 463–89.

[3] Amartya Sen, 'Rights and Agency', *Philosophy and Public Affairs*, 11 (1982), pp. 3–39.

[4] Samuel Scheffler, *The Rejection of Consequentialism* (Oxford, 1982), pp. 108–12.

outcomes (again consisting of the states of affairs made up of an action and its consequences) we have the choice between more killings or torturings and less, and a consequentialist will have to say that we are justified in killing or torturing the one person, and indeed that we are morally obliged to do it, always supposing that no indirect consequences have tipped the balance of good and evil. There will in fact be nothing that it will not be right to do to a perfectly innocent individual if that is the only way of preventing another agent from doing more things of the same kind.

Now I find this a totally unacceptable conclusion and note that it is a conclusion not of utilitarianism in particular but rather of consequentialism in any form. So it is the spellbinding force of consequentialism that we have to think about. Welfarism has its own peculiar attraction, which has to do with the fact that pleasure, happiness, and the satisfaction of desire are things seen as in some way good. But this attraction becomes less powerful as distribution principles are added, and pleasures discounted on an *ad hoc* basis to destroy the case for such things as public executions.

If having left welfarist utilitarianism behind we still find ourselves unable, in spite of its difficulties, to get away from consequentialism, there must be a reason for this. What is it, let us now ask, that is so compelling about consequentialism? It is, I think, the rather simple thought that it can never be right to prefer a worse state of affairs to a better.[5] It is this thought that haunts us and, incidentally, this thought that makes the move to rule utilitarianism an unsatisfactory answer to the problem of reconciling utilitarianism with common moral opinion. For surely it will be irrational, we feel, to obey even the most useful rule if in a particular instance we clearly see that such obedience will not *have the best results*. Again following Scheffler we ask if it is not paradoxical that it should ever be morally objectionable to act in such a way as to minimize morally objectionable acts of just the same type.[6] If it is a bad state of affairs in which one of these actions is done it will presumably be a worse state of affairs in which several are. And must it not be irrational to prefer the worse to the better state of affairs?

This thought does indeed seem compelling. And yet it leads to an apparently unacceptable conclusion about what it is right to do. So we ought, as I said, to wonder whether we have not gone wrong somewhere. And I think that indeed we have. I believe (and this is the main thesis

---

[5] The original version continued 'How could it ever be right, we think, to produce less good rather than more good?'. I have excised this sentence because in the context the use of the expression 'doing more good' suggested an identification which I was at pains to deny. At all times I have allowed *doing good* as an unproblematic motion, because although it does raise many problems, e.g. about different distributions of benefits, it does not raise the particular problems with which I am concerned. I want to insist that however well we might understand what it was to 'do as much good as possible' in the sense of producing maximum benefit, it would not follow that we knew what we meant by expressions such as 'the best outcome' or 'the best state of affairs' as these are used by moral philosophers. Cp. the discussion on page 202 of the present version of this paper.

[6] Op. cit., p. 121.

of the paper) that we go wrong in accepting the idea that there *are* better
and worse states of affairs in the sense that consequentialism requires. As
Wittgenstein says in a different context, 'The decisive movement in the
conjuring trick has been made, and it was the very one that we thought
quite innocent'.[7]

Let us therefore look into the idea of a good state of affairs, as this appears
in the thought that we can judge certain states of affairs to be better than
others and then go on to give moral descriptions to actions related produc-
tively to these states of affairs.

We should begin by asking why we are so sure that we even understand
expressions such as 'a good state of affairs' or 'a good outcome'; for as Peter
Geach pointed out years ago there are phrases with the word 'good' in them,
as, e.g., 'a good event' that do *not* at least as they stand have a sense.[8]
Following this line one might suggest that philosophers are a bit hasty in
using expressions such as 'a better world'. One may *perhaps* understand this
when it is taken to mean a 'deontically better world' defined as one in which
fewer duties are left unfulfilled; but obviously this will not help to give a
sense to 'better state of affairs' as the consequentialist needs to use this
expression, since he is wanting to fix our obligations not to refer to their
fulfilment.

Nevertheless it may seem that combinations of words such as 'a good
state of affairs' are beyond reproach or question, for such expressions are
extremely familiar. Do we not use them every day? We say that it is a good
thing that something or other happened; what difficulty can there be in
constructing from such elements anything we want in the way of aggregates
such as total outcomes which (in principle) take into account all the elements
of a possible world and so constitute good states of affairs? Surely no one can
seriously suggest that 'good state of affairs' is an expression that we do not
understand?

It would, of course, be ridiculous to query the sense of the ordinary things
that we say about its being 'a good thing' that something or other happened,
or about a certain state of affairs being good or bad. The doubt is not about
whether there is some way of using the words, but rather about the way they
appear in the exposition of utilitarian and other consequentialist moral
theories. It is important readily to accept the fact that we talk in a natural
and familiar way about good states of affairs, and that there is nothing
problematic about such usage. But it is also important to see how such
expressions actually work in the contexts in which they are at home, and in
particular to ask about the status of a good state of affairs. Is it something
impersonal to be recognized (we hope) by all reasonable men? It seems,
surprisingly, that this is not the case at least in many contexts of utterance
of the relevant expressions. Suppose, for instance, that the supporters of

[7] Ludwig Wittgenstein, *Philosophical Investigations* (Macmillan 1953, and Blackwell 1958), § 308.
[8] Peter Geach, 'Good and Evil', *Analysis* 17 (1956), pp. 33–42.

different teams have gathered in the stadium and that the members of each group are discussing the game; or that two racegoers have backed different horses in a race. Remarking on the course of events one or the other may say that things are going well or badly, and when a certain situation has developed may say that it is a good or a bad state of affairs. More commonly they will welcome some developments and deplore others, saying 'Oh good!' or 'That's bad!', calling some news good news and some news bad, sometimes describing what has happened as 'a good thing' and sometimes not. We could develop plenty of other examples of this kind, thinking for instance of the conversations about the invention of a new burglar alarm that might take place in the police headquarters and in the robbers' den.

At least two types of utterance are here discernible. For 'good' and its cognates may be used to signal the speaker's attitude to a result judged as an end result, and then he says 'Good!' or 'I'm glad' or 'That's good' where what he is glad about is something welcomed in itself and not for any good it will bring. But a state of affairs may rather be judged by its connection with other things called good. And even what is counted as in itself good may be said to be bad when it brings enough evil in its train.

Now what shall we say about the truth or falsity of these utterances? It certainly seems that they can be straightforwardly true or false. For perhaps what appears to be going to turn out well is really going to turn out badly: what seemed to be a good thing was really a bad thing, and an apparently good state of affairs was the prelude to disaster. 'You are quite wrong' one person may say to another and events may show that he *was* wrong. Nevertheless we can see that this quasi-objectivity, which is not to be questioned when people with similar aims, interests, or desires are speaking together, flies out of the window if we try to set the utterances of those in one group against the utterances of those in another. One will say 'a good thing' where another says 'a bad thing', and it is the same for states of affairs. It would be bizarre to suggest that at the races it really *is* a good thing that one horse or the other is gaining (perhaps because of the pleasure it will bring to the majority, or the good effect on the future of racing) and so that the utterance of one particular punter, intent only on making a packet, will be the one that is true.

This is not to say, however, that what a given person says to be a good thing or a good state of affairs must relate to his own advantage. For anyone may be *interested in* the future of racing, and people commonly are *interested in*, e.g., the success of their friends, saying 'that's a good thing' if one of them looks like winning a prize or getting a job; incidentally without worrying much about whether he is the very best candidate for it.

Now it may be thought that these must be rather special uses of expressions such as 'good state of affairs', because we surely must speak quite differently when we are talking about public matters, as when for instance we react to news of some far-away disaster. We say that the news is bad because a lot of people have lost their lives in an earthquake. Later we may say that things are not as bad as we feared and someone may remark 'that's a good thing'. 'A bad state of affairs', we might remark on hearing the original news about people dead or homeless, and this will usually have nothing to do with harm to us or to our friends.

In this way the case is different from that of the racegoers or the cops and robbers, but this is not of course to imply that what we say on such occasions has a different status from the utterances we have considered so far. For why should its truth not be 'speaker-relative' too, also depending on what the speakers and their group are *interested in* though not now on the good or harm that will come to them themselves? Is it not more plausible to think this than to try to distinguish two kinds of uses of these expressions, one speaker-relative and the other not? For are there really two ways in which the police for instance might speak? And two ways in which the robbers could speak as well? Are we really to say that although when they are both speaking in the speaker-relative way they do not contradict each other, and may both speak truly, when speaking in the 'objective' way one group will speak truly and the other not? What shows that the second way of speaking exists?

What thoughts, one may ask, can we really be supposed to have which must be expressed in the disputed mode? Considering examples such as that of the far-away earthquake we may think that we believe the best state of affairs to be the one in which there is most happiness and least misery, or something of the sort. But considering other examples we may come to wonder whether any such thought can really be attributed to us.

Suppose for instance that when walking in a poor district one of us should lose a fairly considerable sum of money which we had intended to spend on something rather nice. Arriving home we discover the loss and telephone the police on the off chance that our wad of notes has been found and turned in. To our delight we find that it was picked up by a passing honest policeman, and that we shall get it back. 'What a good thing' we say 'that an officer happened to be there.' What seemed to be a bad state of affairs has turned out not to be bad after all: things are much better than we thought they were. And all's well that ends well. But how, it may now be asked, *can* we say that things have turned out better than we thought? Were we not supposed to believe that the best state of affairs was the one in which there was most happiness and least misery? So surely it would have been *better* if the money had not been returned to us but rather found and kept as treasure trove by some poor inhabitant of the region? We simply had not considered that because most of us do not actually *have* the thought that the best state of affairs is the one in which we lose and they gain. Perhaps we should have had this thought if it had been a small amount of money, but this was rather a lot.

No doubt it will seem to many that there must be non-speaker-relative uses of words evaluating states of affairs because moral judgements cannot have speaker-relative status. But if one is inclined, as I am, to doubt whether propositions of this form play any part in the fundamentals of ethical theory there is no objection on this score. It is important however that the preceding discussion has been about propositions of a particular form and nothing has been said to suggest that all judgements about what is good and bad have speaker-relative status. I have not for instance made this suggestion for what Geach called 'attributive' judgements concerning things good or bad of a kind—good knives and houses and essays, or even good actions, motives or men. If there is some reason for calling these 'speaker-relative' the reason has not been given here. Nor has anything been said about the status of propositions about what is *good for* anyone or anything, or about that in which their good consists.

What has I hope now been shown is that we should not take it for granted that we even know what we are talking about if we enter into a discussion with the consequentialist about whether it can ever be right to produce something other than 'the best state of affairs'.

It might be suggested by way of reply that what is in question in these debates is not just the best state of affairs without qualification but rather *the best state of affairs from an impersonal point of view*. But what does this mean? A good state of affairs from an impersonal point of view is presumably opposed to a good state of affairs from *my* point of view or from *your* point of view, and as a good state of affairs from my point of view is a state of affairs which is advantageous to me, and a good state of affairs from your point of view is a state of affairs that is advantageous to you, a good state of affairs from an impersonal point of view presumably means a state of affairs which is generally advantageous, or advantageous to most people, or something like that. About the idea of maximum welfare we are not (or so we are supposing for the sake of the argument) in any difficulty.[9] But an account of the idea of a good state of affairs which simply defines it in terms of maximum welfare is no help to us here. For our problem is that something is supposed to be being said *about* maximum welfare and we cannot figure out what this is.

In a second reply, more to the point, the consequentialist might say that what we should really be dealing with in this discussion is states of affairs which are good or bad, not simply, but *from the moral point of view*. The qualification is, it will be suggested, tacitly understood in moral contexts, where no individual speaker gives his own private interests or allegiances a special place in any debate, the speaker-relativity found in other contexts thus being left behind. This seems to be a pattern familiar from other cases, as, e.g., from discussions in meetings of the governors of public institutions. Why should it not be in a similar way that we talk of a good and a bad thing to happen 'from a moral point of view'? And is it not hard to reject the conclusion that right action is action producing *this* 'best state of affairs'?

---

[9] Cp. footnote 5.

That special contexts can create special uses of the expressions we are discussing is indeed true. But before we proceed to draw conclusions about moral judgements we should ask why we think that it makes sense to talk about morally good and bad states of affairs, or to say that it is a good thing (or is good that) something happened 'from a moral point of view'. For after all we cannot concoct a meaningful sentence by adding just any qualification of this verbal form to expressions such as these. What would it mean, for instance, to say that a state of affairs was good or bad 'from a legal point of view' or 'from the point of view of etiquette'? Or that it was a good thing that a certain thing happened from these same 'points of view'? Certain interpretations that suggest themselves are obviously irrelevant, as, for instance, that it is a good state of affairs from a legal point of view when the laws are clearly stated, or a good state of affairs from the point of view of etiquette when everyone follows the rules.

It seems, therefore, that we do not solve the problem of the meaning of 'best state of affairs' when supposed to be used in a non-speaker-relative way simply by tacking on 'from a moral point of view'; since it cannot be assumed that the resulting expression has any sense. Nevertheless it would be wrong to suggest that 'good state of affairs from a moral point of view' is a concatenation of words which in fact has no meaning in *any* of the contexts in which it appears, and to see this we have only to look at utilitarian theories of the type put forward by John C. Harsanyi and R. M. Hare, in which a certain interpretation is implicitly provided for such expressions.[10]

Harsanyi for instance argues that the only *rational* morality is one in which the rightness or wrongness of an action is judged by its relation to a certain outcome, i.e. the maximization of social utility. The details of this theory, which defines social utility in terms of individual preferences, do not concern us here. The relevant point is that within it there appears the idea of an end which is the goal of moral action, and therefore the idea of a best state of affairs from a moral point of view. (It does not of course matter whether Harsanyi uses these words.)

Similarly Hare, by a more elaborate argument from the universalisability and prescriptivity of moral judgements, tries to establish the proposition that one who takes the moral point of view must have as his aim the maximization of utility, reflecting this in one way in his day-to-day prescriptions and in another in 'critical' moral judgements. So here too a clear sense can be given to the idea of a best state of affairs from a moral point of view: it is the state of affairs which a man aims at when he takes the moral point of view and which in one way or another determines the truth of moral judgements.

Within these theories there is, then, no problem about the meaning of

[10] See, e.g., John C. Harsanyi, 'Morality and the Theory of Rational Behavior', *Social Research* 44 (1977). Reprinted in Sen and Williams, op. cit., pp. 39-62, and R. M. Hare, *Moral Thinking* (Oxford, 1981).

204 *Philippa Foot*

expressions such as 'the best state of affairs from the moral point of view'. It does not follow, however, that those who reject the theories should be ready to discuss the pros and cons of consequentialism in these terms. For unless the arguments given by Hare and Harsanyi are acceptable it will not have been shown that there is any reference for expressions such as 'the aim which each man has in so far as he takes up the moral point of view' or *a fortiori* 'the best state of affairs from the moral point of view'.

If my main thesis is correct this is a point of the first importance. For I am arguing that where non-consequentialists commonly go wrong is in accepting from their opponents questions such as 'Is it ever right to act in such a way as to produce something less than the best state of affairs that is within one's reach?'[11] Summing up the results reached so far we may say that if taken in one way, with no special reference to morality, talk about good states of affairs seems to be speaker-relative. But if the qualification 'from a moral point of view' is added the resulting expression may mean nothing; and it may lack a reference when a special consequentialist theory has given it a sense.

In the light of this discussion we should find it significant that many people who do not find any particular consequentialist theory compelling nevertheless feel themselves driven towards consequentialism by a thought which turns on the idea that there are states of affairs which are better or worse from a moral point of view. What is it that seems to make this an inescapable idea?

Tracing the assumption back in my own mind I find that what seems preposterous is to deny that there are some things that a moral person must want and aim at in so far as he is a moral person and that he will count it 'a good thing' when these things happen and 'a good state of affairs' either when they are happening or when things are disposed in their favour. For surely he must want others to be happy. To deny this would be to deny that benevolence is a virtue—and who wants to deny that?

Let us see where this line of thought will take us, accepting without any reservation that benevolence is a virtue and that a benevolent person must often aim at the good of others and call it 'a good thing' when for instance a faraway disaster turns out to have been less serious than was feared. Here we do indeed have the words 'a good thing' (and just as obviously a 'good state of affairs') necessarily appearing in moral contexts. And the use is explained not by a piece of utilitarian theory but by a simple observation about benevolence.

This, then, seems to be the way in which seeing states of affairs in which

[11] See, e.g., Thomas Nagel, 'The Limits of Objectivity' in *Tanner Lectures*, vol. I (1980), p. 131, where he says that '... things would be better, what *happened* would be better' if I twisted a child's arm in circumstances where (by Nagel's hypothesis) this was the only way to get medical help for the victims of an accident. He supposes that I might have done something worse if I hurt the child than if I did not do it, but that the total outcome would have been better. It does not, I think, occur to him to question the idea of *things* being better—or *things* being worse.

people are happy as good states of affairs really is an essential part of morality. But it is very important that we have found this end *within* morality, and forming part of it, not standing outside it as the 'good state of affairs' by which moral action in general is to be judged. For benevolence is only one of the virtues, and we shall have to look at the others before we can pronounce on any question about good or bad action in particular circumstances. Off-hand we have no reason to think that whatever is done with the aim of improving the lot of other people will be morally required or even morally permissible. For firstly there are virtues such as friendship which play their part in determining the requirements of benevolence, e.g., by making it consistent with benevolence to give service to friends rather than to strangers or acquaintances. And secondly there is the virtue of justice, taken in the old wide sense in which it had to do with everything *owed*. In our common moral code we find numerous examples of limitations which justice places on the pursuit of welfare. In the first place there are principles of distributive justice which forbid, on grounds of fairness, the kind of 'doing good' which increases the wealth of rich people at the cost of misery to the poor. Secondly, rules such as truth telling are not to be broken wherever and whenever welfare would thereby be increased. Thirdly, considerations about rights, both positive and negative, limit the action which can be taken for the sake of welfare. Justice is primarily concerned with the following of certain rules of fairness and honest dealing and with respecting prohibitions on interference with others rather with attachment to any end. It is true that the just man must also fight injustice, and here justice like benevolence is a matter of ends, but of course the end is not the same end as the one that benevolence seeks and need not be coincident with it.

I do not mean to go into these matters in detail here, but simply to point out that we find in our ordinary moral code many requirements and prohibitions inconsistent with the idea that benevolence is the whole of morality. From the point of view of the present discussion it would be acceptable to describe the situation in terms of a tension between, for instance, justice and benevolence. But it is not strictly accurate to think of it like this, because that would suggest that someone who does an unjust act for the sake of increasing total happiness has a higher degree of benevolence than one who refuses to do it. Since someone who refuses to sacrifice an innocent life for the sake of increasing happiness is not to be counted as less benevolent than someone who is ready to do it, this cannot be right. We might be tempted to think that the latter would be acting 'out of benevolence' because his aim is the happiness of others, but this seems a bad way of talking. Certainly benevolence does not require unjust action, and we should not call an act which violated rights an act of benevolence. It would not, for instance, be an act of benevolence to induce cancer in one person (or deliberately to let it run its course) even for the sake of alleviating much suffering.

What we should say therefore is that even perfection in benevolence does

206 *Philippa Foot*

not imply a readiness to do anything and everything of which it can be said that it is highly probable that it will increase the sum of human happiness. And this, incidentally, throws some light on a certain type of utilitarian theory which identifies the moral assessment of a situation with that of a sympathetic impartial observer whose benevolence extends equally to all mankind.[12] For what, we may ask, are we to suppose about this person's *other* characteristics? Is he to be guided simply and solely by a desire to relieve suffering and increase happiness; or is he also just? If it is said that for him the telling of truth, keeping of promises, and respecting of individual autonomy are to be recommended only in so far as these serve to maximize welfare then we see that the 'impartial sympathetic observer' is by definition one with a utilitarian point of view. So the utilitarians are defining moral assessment in their own terms.

Returning to the main line of our argument we now find ourselves in a better position to see that there indeed is a place *within* morality for the idea of better and worse states of affairs. That there is such a place is true if only because the proper end of benevolence is the good of others, and because in many situations the person who has this virtue will be able to think of good and bad states of affairs, in terms of the general good. It does not, however, follow that he will always be able to do so. For sometimes justice will forbid a certain action, as it forbids the harmful experiment designed to further cancer research; and then it will not be possible to ask whether 'the state of affairs' containing the action and its result will be better or worse than one in which the action is not done. The action is one that *cannot* be done, because justice forbids it, and nothing that has this moral character comes within the scope of the kind of comparison of total outcomes that benevolence may sometimes require. Picking up at this point the example discussed earlier about the morality of killing or torturing to prevent more killings or torturings we see the same principle operating here. If it were a question of riding out to rescue a small number or a large number then benevolence would, we may suppose, urge that the larger number be saved. But if it is a matter of preventing the killing *by* killing (or conniving at a killing) the case will be quite different. One does not have to believe that all rights to non-interference are absolute to believe that *this* is an unjust action, and if it is unjust the moral man says to himself that he cannot do it and does not include it in an assessment he may be making about the good and bad states of affairs that he can bring about.

What has been said in the last few paragraphs is, I suggest, a sketch of what can truly be said about the important place that the idea of maximum welfare has in morality. It is not that in the guise of 'the best outcome' it stands *outside* morality as its foundation and arbiter, but rather that it appears *within* morality as the end of one of the virtues.

When we see it like this, and give expressions such as 'best outcome' and

---

[12] See Harsanyi, op. cit., Sen and Williams, op. cit., p. 39.

'good state of affairs' no special meaning in moral contexts other than the
one that the virtues give them, we shall no longer think the paradoxical
thought that it is sometimes right to act in such a way that the total outcome,
consisting of one's action and its results, is less good than some other
accessible at the time. In the abstract a benevolent person must wish that
loss and harm should be minimized. He does not, however, wish that the
whole consisting of a killing to minimize killings should be actualized either
by his agency or that of anyone else. So there is no reason on this score to
think that he must regard it as 'the better state of affairs'.[13] And therefore
there is no reason for the non-consequentialist, whose thought of good and
bad states of affairs in moral contexts comes only from the virtues themselves, to describe the refusal as a choice of a worse total outcome. If he does
so describe it he will be giving the words the sense they have in his opponents' theories, and it is not surprising that he should find himself in their
hands.

We may also remind ourselves at this point that benevolence is not the
only virtue which has to do, at least in part, with ends rather than with the
observance of rules. As mentioned earlier there belongs to the virtue of
justice the readiness to fight for justice as well as to observe its laws; and
there belongs to truthfulness not only the avoidance of lying but also that
other kind of attachment to truth which has to do with its preservation and
pursuit. A man of virtue must be a lover of justice and a lover of truth.
Furthermore he will seek the special good of his family and friends. Thus
there will be many things which he will want and will welcome, sometimes
sharing these aims with others and sometimes opposing them, as when
working differentially for his own children or his own friends.[14] Similarly
someone who is judging a competition and is a fair judge must try to see to it
that the best man wins. The existence of these 'moral aims' will of course give
opportunity for the use, in moral contexts, of such expressions as 'a good
thing' or 'the best state of affairs'. But nothing of a consequentialist nature
follows from such pieces of usage, found here and there within morality.

An analogy will perhaps help to make my point. Thinking about good
manners we might decide that someone who has good manners tries to avoid
embarrassing others in social situations. This must, let us suppose, be one of
his aims; and we might even decide that so far as manners is concerned this,
or something like it, is the only prescribed *end*. But of course this does not
mean that what good manners require of anyone is universally determined
by this end. A consequentialist theory of good manners would presumably
be mistaken; because good manners, not being solely a matter of purposes,
also require that certain things be done or not done: e.g. that hospitality not

---

[13] I have discussed examples of this kind in more detail in 'Morality Action and Outcome',
forthcoming in Ted Honderich, ed., *Objectivity and Value, Essays in Memory of John Mackie*. (Routledge
and Kegan Paul).

[14] See Derek Parfit, 'Prudence, Morality, and the Prisoner's Dilemma', *Proceedings of the British
Academy* 65 (1979), pp. 556-64, and Amartya Sen, 'Rights and Agency'.

208 *Philippa Foot*

be abused by frank discussion of the deficiencies of one's host as soon as he leaves the room.[15] So if invited to take part in such discussions a well-mannered person will, if necessary, maintain a silence embarrassing to an interlocutor, because the rule here takes precedence over the aim prescribed. Assuming that this is a correct account of good manners—and it does not of course matter whether it is or not—we can now see the difficulty that arises if we try to say which choice open to the agent results in the best state of affairs from the point of view of manners. In certain contexts the state of affairs containing no embarrassment will be referred to as a good state of affairs, because avoiding embarrassment is by our hypothesis the one *end* prescribed by good manners. But we should not be surprised if the right action from the point of view of good manners is sometimes the one that produces something *other* than this good state of affairs. We have no right to take an end from within the whole that makes up good manners and turn it, just because it is an *end*, into the single guide to action to be used by the well-mannered man.

This analogy serves to illustrate my point about the illegitimacy of moving what is found within morality to a criterial position outside it. But it may also bring to the surface a reason many will be ready to give for being dissatisfied with my thesis. For surely a morality is unlike a code of manners in claiming rational justification for its ordinances? It cannot be enough to say that we *do* have such things as rules of justice in our present system of virtues: the question is whether we should have them, and if so why we should. And the reason this is crucial in the present context is that the justification of a moral code may seem inevitably to involve the very idea that has been called in question in this paper.

This is a very important objection. In its most persuasive form it involves a picture of morality as a rational device developed to serve certain purposes, and therefore answerable to these purposes. Morality, it will be suggested, is a device with a certain object, having to do with the harmonizing of ends or the securing of the greatest possible general good, or perhaps one of these things plus the safeguarding of rights. And the content of morality—what really is right and wrong—will be thought to be determined by what it is rational to require in the way of conduct given that these are our aims. Thus morality is thought of as a kind of tacit legislation by the community, and it is, of course, significant that the early Utilitarians, who were much interested in the rationalizing of actual Parliamentary legislation, were ready to talk in these terms.[16] In moral legislation our aim is, they thought, the general good. With this way of looking at morality there reappears the idea of better and worse states of affairs from the moral point of view. Moreover consequentialism *in some form* is necessarily reinstated. For while there is

[15] It is customary to wait until later.
[16] See, e.g., Jeremy Bentham, *An Introduction to the Principles of Legislation* (1789), Chapter III, section 1.

room on such a model for rational moral codes which enjoin something other than the pursuit of 'the best state of affairs from the moral point of view' this will be only in so far as it is by means of such ordinances that the object of a moral code is best achieved.[17]

Thus it may seem that we must after all allow that the idea of a good state of affairs appears at the most basic level in the critical appraisal of any moral code. This would, however, be too hasty a conclusion. Consequentialism in some form follows from the premiss that morality is a device for achieving a certain shared end. But why should we accept this view of what morality is and how it is to be judged? Why should we not rather see that as itself a consequentialist assumption, which has come to seem neutral and inevitable only in so far as utilitarianism and other forms of consequentialism now dominate moral philosophy?

To counter this bewitchment let us ask awkward questions about who is supposed to *have* the end which morality is supposed to be in aid of. J. S. Mill notoriously found it hard to pass from the premiss that the end of each is the good of each to the proposition that the end of all is the good of all.[18] Perhaps no such *shared end* appears in the foundations of ethics, where we may rather find individual ends and rational compromises between those who have them. Or perhaps at the most basic level lie facts about the way individual human beings can find the greatest goods which they are capable of possessing. The truth is, I think, that we simply do not have a satisfactory theory of morality, and need to look for it. Scanlon was indeed right in saying that the real answer to utilitarianism depends on progress in the development of alternatives. Meanwhile, however, we have no reason to think that we must accept consequentialism in any form. If the thesis of this paper is correct we should be more alert than we usually are to the possibility that we may unwittingly, and unnecessarily, surrender to consequentialism by uncritically accepting its key idea. Let us remind ourselves that the idea of the goodness of total states of affairs played no part in Aristotle's moral philosophy, and that in modern times it plays no part either in Rawls's account of justice or in the theories of more thoroughgoing contractualists such as Scanlon.[19] If we accustom ourselves to the thought that there is simply a blank where consequentialists see 'the best state of affairs' we may be better able to give other theories the hearing they deserve.

Department of Philosophy   PHILIPPA FOOT
University of California at Los Angeles
Los Angeles, California 90024
U.S.A.

   [17] For discussions of this possibility see, e.g., Robert Adams, 'Motive Utilitarianism', *The Journal of Philosophy* 73 (1976) and Derek Parfit, *Reasons and Persons* (Oxford, Clarendon Press, 1984), pp. 24-8.
   [18] J. S. Mill, *Utilitarianism* (1863), Chapter IV.
   [19] John Rawls, *A Theory of Justice* (Cambridge, Mass., Harvard University Press, 1971); T. M. Scanlon, op. cit.

[24]

THE SCHIZOPHRENIA OF MODERN ETHICAL THEORIES *

MODERN ethical theories, with perhaps a few honorable exceptions, deal only with reasons, with values, with what justifies. They fail to examine motives and the motivational structures and constraints of ethical life. They not only fail to do this, they fail as ethical theories by not doing this—as I shall argue in this paper. I shall also attempt two correlative tasks: to exhibit some constraints that motivation imposes on ethical theory and life; and to advance our understanding of the relations between reason and motive.

One mark of a good life is a harmony between one's motives and one's reasons, values, justifications. Not to be moved by what one

* I wish to thank all those who have heard or read various versions of this paper and whose comments have greatly encouraged and helped me.

values—what one believes good, nice, right, beautiful, and so on—
bespeaks a malady of the spirit. Not to value what moves one also
bespeaks a malady of the spirit. Such a malady, or such maladies,
can properly be called *moral schizophrenia*—for they are a split
between one's motives and one's reasons. (Here and elsewhere,
'reasons' will stand also for 'values' and 'justifications'.)

An extreme form of such schizophrenia is characterized, on the
one hand, by being moved to do what one believes bad, harmful,
ugly, abasing; on the other, by being disgusted, horrified, dismayed
by what one wants to do. Perhaps such cases are rare. But a more
modest schizophrenia between reason and motive is not, as can be
seen in many examples of weakness of the will, indecisiveness, guilt,
shame, self-deception, rationalization, and annoyance with oneself.

At the very least, we should be moved by our major values and
we should value what our major motives seek. Should, that is, if we
are to lead a good life. To repeat, such harmony is a mark of a
good life. Indeed, one might wonder whether human life—good or
bad—is possible without some such integration.

This is not, however, to say that in all cases it is better to have
such harmony. It is better for us if self-seeking authoritarians feel
fettered by their moral upbringing; better, that is, than if they
adopt the reason of their motives. It would have been far better
for the world and his victims had Eichmann not wanted to do what
he thought he should do.[1]

Nor is this to say that in all areas of endeavor such harmony is
necessary or even especially conducive to achieving what is valued.
In many cases, it is not. For example, one's motives in fixing a flat
tire are largely irrelevant to getting under way again. (In many
such cases, one need not even value the intended outcome.)

Nor is this even to say that in all "morally significant" areas such
harmony is necessary or especially conducive to achieving what is
valued. Many morally significant jobs, such as feeding the sick, can
be done equally well pretty much irrespective of motive. And, as
Ross, at times joined by Mill, argues, for a large part of ethics,
there simply is no philosophical question of harmony or disharmony between value and motive: you can do what is right, obligatory, your duty no matter what your motive for so acting. If it is
your duty to keep a promise, you fulfill that duty no matter
whether you keep the promise out of respect for duty, fear of

---

[1] It might be asked what is better for such people, to have or lack this
harmony, given their evil motives or values; in which way they would be
morally better. Such questions may not be answerable.

losing your reputation, or whatever. What motivates is irrelevant so far as rightness, obligatoriness, duty are concerned.

Notwithstanding the very questionable correctness of this view so far as rightness, obligatoriness, duty are concerned,[2] there remain at least two problems. The first is that even here there is still a question of harmony. What sort of life would people have who did their duties but never or rarely wanted to? Second, duty, obligation, and rightness are only one part—indeed, only a small part, a dry and minimal part—of ethics. There is the whole other area of the values of personal and interpersonal relations and activities; and also the area of moral goodness, merit, virtue. In both, motive is an essential part of what is valuable; in both, motive and reason must be in harmony for the values to be realized.

For this reason and for the reason that such harmony is a mark of a good life, any theory that ignores such harmony does so at great peril. Any theory that makes difficult, or precludes, such harmony stands, if not convicted, then in need of much and powerful defense. What I shall now argue is that modern ethical theories— those theories prominent in the English-speaking philosophical world—make such harmony impossible.

CRITICISM OF MODERN ETHICS

Reflection on the complexity and vastness of our moral life, on what has value, shows that recent ethical theories have by far over-concentrated on duty, rightness, and obligation.[3] This failure—of overconcentrating—could not have been tolerated but for the failure of not dealing with motives or with the relations of motives to values. (So too, the first failure supports and explains the second.) In this second failure, we find a far more serious defect of modern ethical theories than such overconcentration: they necessitate a schizophrenia between reason and motive in vitally important and pervasive areas of value, or alternatively they allow us the harmony of a morally impoverished life, a life deeply deficient in what is valuable. It is not possible for moral people, that is, people who would achieve what is valuable, to act on these ethical theories, to let them comprise their motives. People who do let them comprise their motives will, for that reason, have a life seriously lacking in what is valuable.

These theories are, thus, doubly defective. As ethical theories, they fail by making it impossible for a person to achieve the good

[2] See my "Act and Agent Evaluations," *Review of Metaphysics*, xxvii, 1, 105 (September 1973): 42–61.

[3] See *ibid.* and my "Rightness and Goodness: Is There a Difference?," *American Philosophical Quarterly*, x, 2 (April 1973): 87–98.

in an integrated way. As theories of the mind, of reasons and motives, of human life and activity, they fail, not only by putting us in a position that is psychologically uncomfortable, difficult, or even untenable, but also by making us and our lives essentially fragmented and incoherent.

The sort of disharmony I have in mind can be brought out by considering a problem for egoists, typified by hedonistic egoists. Love, friendship, affection, fellow feeling, and community are important sources of personal pleasure. But can such egoists get these pleasures? I think not—not so long as they adhere to the motive of pleasure-for-self.

The reason for this is not that egoists cannot get together and decide, as it were, to enter into a love relationship. Surely they can (leaving aside the irrelevant problems about deciding to do such a thing). And they can do the various things calculated to bring about such pleasure: have absorbing talks, make love, eat delicious meals, see interesting films, and so on, and so on.

Nonetheless, there is something necessarily lacking in such a life: love. For it is essential to the very concept of love that one care for the beloved, that one be prepared to act for the sake of the beloved. More strongly, one must care for the beloved and act for that person's sake as a final goal; the beloved, or the beloved's welfare or interest, must be a final goal of one's concern and action.

To the extent that my consideration for you—or even my trying to make you happy—comes from my desire to lead an untroubled life, a life that is personally pleasing for me, I do not act for your sake. In short, to the extent that I act in various ways toward you with the final goal of getting pleasure—or, more generally, good—for myself, I do not act for your sake.

When we think about it this way, we may get some idea of why egoism is often claimed to be essentially lonely. For it is essentially concerned with external relations with others, where, except for their effects on us, one person is no different from, nor more important, valuable, or special than any other person or even any other thing. The individuals as such are not important, only their effects on us are; they are essentially replaceable, anything else with the same effects would do as well. And this, I suggest, is intolerable personally. To think of yourself this way, or to believe that a person you love thinks of you this way, is intolerable. And for conceptual, as well as psychological, reasons it is incompatible with love.

It might be suggested that it is rather unimportant to have love of this sort. But this would be a serious error. The love here is not merely modern-romantic or sexual. It is also the love among members of a family, the love we have for our closest friends, and so on. Just what sort of life would people have who never "cared" for anyone else, except as a means to their own interests? And what sort of life would people have who took it that no one loved them for their own sake, but only for the way they served the other's interest?

Just as the notion of doing something for the sake of another, or of caring for the person for that person's sake, is essential for love, so too is it essential for friendship and all affectionate relations. Without this, at best we could have good relations, friendly relations. And similarly, such caring and respect is essential for fellow feeling and community.

Before proceeding, let us contrast this criticism of egoism with a more standard one. My criticism runs as follows: Hedonistic egoists take their own pleasure to be the sole justification of acts, activities, ways of life; they should recognize that love, friendship, affection, fellow feeling, and community are among the greatest (sources of) personal pleasures. Thus, they have good reason, on their own grounds, to enter such relations. But they cannot act in the ways required to get those pleasures, those great goods, if they act on their motive of pleasure-for-self. They cannot act for the sake of the intended beloved, friend, and so on; thus, they cannot love, be or have a friend, and so on. To achieve these great personal goods, they have to abandon that egoistical motive. They cannot embody their reason in their motive. Their reasons and motives make their moral lives schizophrenic.

The standard criticism of egoists is that they simply cannot achieve such nonegoistical goods, that their course of action will, as a matter of principle, keep them from involving themselves with others in the relevant ways, and so on. This criticism is not clearly correct. For there may be nothing inconsistent in egoists' adopting a policy that will allow them to forget, as it were, that they are egoists, a policy that will allow and even encourage them to develop such final goals and motives as caring for another for that person's own sake. Indeed, as has often been argued, the wise egoist would do just this.

Several questions should be asked of this response: would the transformed person still be an egoist? Is it important, for the defense of egoism, that the person remain an egoist? Or is it important only that the person live in a way that would be approved of by an egoist? It is, of course, essential to the transformation of the person from egoistical motivation to caring for others that the person-as-egoist lose conscious control of him/herself. This raises the question of whether such people will be able to check up and see how their transformed selves are getting on in achieving egoistically approved goals. Will they have a mental alarm clock which wakes them up from their nonegoistical transforms every once in a while, to allow them to reshape these transforms if they are not getting enough personal pleasure—or, more generally, enough good? I suppose that this would not be impossible. But it hardly seems an ideal, or even a very satisfactory, life. It is bad enough to have a private personality, which you must hide from others; but imagine having a personality that you must hide from (the other parts of) yourself. Still, perhaps this is possible. If it is, then it seems that egoists may be able to meet this second criticism. But this does not touch my criticism: that they will not be able to embody their reason in their motives; that they will have to lead a bifurcated, schizophrenic life to achieve what is good.

This might be thought a defect of only such ethical theories as egoism. But consider those utilitarianisms which hold that an act is right, obligatory, or whatever if and only if it is optimific in regard to pleasure and pain (or weighted expectations of them). Such a view has it that the only good reason for acting is pleasure vs. pain, and thus should highly value love, friendship, affection, fellow feeling, and community. Suppose, now, you embody this utilitarian reason as your motive in your actions and thoughts toward someone. Whatever your relation to that person, it is necessarily not love (nor is it friendship, affection, fellow feeling, or community). The person you supposedly love engages your thought and action not for him/herself, but rather as a source of pleasure.

The problem is not simply that pleasure is taken to be the only good, the only right-making feature. To see this, consider G. E. Moore's formalistic utilitarianism, which tells us to maximize goodness, without claiming to have identified all the goods. If, as I would have it and as Moore agrees, love relations and the like are goods, how could there be any disharmony here? Would it not be possible to embody Moore's justifying reason as a motive and still love? I do not think so.

First, if you try to carry on the relationship for the sake of goodness, there is no essential commitment even to that activity, much less to the persons involved. So far as goodness is involved, you might as well love as ski or write poetry or eat a nice meal or . . . .

Perhaps it would be replied that there is something special about that good, the good of love—treating it now not qua good but qua what is good or qua this good. In such a case, however, there is again an impersonality so far as the individuals are concerned. Any other person who would elicit as much of this good would be as proper an object of love as the beloved. To this it might be replied that it is that good which is to be sought—with emphasis on the personal and individual features, the features that bind these people together. But now it is not clear in what sense goodness is being sought, nor that the theory is still telling us to maximize goodness.[4] True, the theory tells us to bring about this good, but now we cannot separate what is good, the love, from its goodness. And this simply is not Moore's utilitarianism.

Just as egoism and the above sorts of utilitarianisms necessitate a schizophrenia between reason and motive—and just as they cannot allow for love, friendship, affection, fellow feeling, and community—so do current rule utilitarianisms. And so do current deontologies.

What is lacking in these theories is simply—or not so simply—the person. For, love, friendship, affection, fellow feeling, and community all require that the other person be an essential part of what is valued. The person—not merely the person's general values nor even the person-qua-producer-or-possessor-of-general-values—must be valued. The defect of these theories in regard to love, to take one case, is not that they do not value love (which, often, they do not) but that they do not value the beloved. Indeed, a person who values and aims at simply love, that is, love-in-general or even love-in-general-exemplified-by-this-person "misses" the intended beloved as surely as does an adherent of the theories I have criticized.

The problem with these theories is not, however, with *other*-people-as-valuable. It is simply—or not so simply—with *people*-as-valuable. Just as they would do *vis-à-vis* other people, modern ethical theories would prevent each of us from loving, caring for,

---

[4] Taking love and people-in-certain-relations as intrinsically valuable helps show mistaken various views about acting rationally (or well). First, maximization: i.e., if you value "item" C and if state S has more C than does S', you act rationally only if you choose S—unless S' has more of other items you value than does S, or your cost in getting S, as opposed to S', is too high, or you are not well enough informed. Where C is love (and indeed where C is many, if not most, valuable things), this does not hold—not even if all the values involved are self-regarding. Second, paying attention to value differences, being alive to them and their significance for acting rationally: just consider a person who (often) checks to see whether a love relation with another person would be "better" than the present love.

and valuing ourself—as opposed to loving, caring for, and valuing our general values or ourself-qua-producer-or-possessor-of-general-values. In these externality-ridden theories, there is as much a disappearance or nonappearance of the self as of other people. Their externality-ridden universes of what is intrinsically valuable are not solipsistic; rather, they are devoid of all people.[5]

It is a truism that it is difficult to deal with people as such. It is difficult really to care for them for their own sake. It is psychically wearing and exhausting. It puts us in too open, too vulnerable a position. But what must also be looked at is what it does to us— taken individually and in groups as small as a couple and as large as society—to view and treat others externally, as essentially replaceable, as mere instruments or repositories of general and nonspecific value; and what it does to us to be treated, or believe we are treated, in these ways.

At the very least, these ways are dehumanizing. To say much more than this would require a full-scale philosophical anthropology showing how such personal relations as love and friendship are possible, how they relate to larger ways and structures of human life, and how they—and perhaps only they—allow for the development of those relations which are constitutive of a human life worth living: how, in short, they work together to produce the fullness of a good life, a life of eudaimonia.

Having said this, it must be acknowledged that there are many unclarities and difficulties in the notion of valuing a person, in the notion of a person-as-valuable. When we think about this—e.g., what and why we value—we seem driven either to omitting the person and ending up with a person-qua-producer-or-possessor-of-general-values or with a person's general values, or to omitting them and ending up with a bare particular ego.

In all of this, perhaps we could learn from the egoists. Their instincts, at least, must be to admit themselves, each for self, into their values. At the risk of absurdity—indeed, at the risk of complete loss of appeal of their view—what they find attractive and good about good-for-self must be, not only the good, but also and preeminently the for-self.

At this point, it might help to restate some of the things I have tried to do and some I have not. Throughout I have been concerned with what sort of motives people can have if they are to be

---

[5] Moore's taking friendship to be an intrinsic good is an exception to this. But if the previous criticism of Moore holds, his so taking friendship introduces serious strains, verging on inconsistencies, into his theory.

able to realize the great goods of love, friendship, affection, fellow feeling, and community. And I have argued that, if we take as motives, embody in our motives, those various things which recent ethical theories hold to be ultimately good or right, we will, of necessity, be unable to have those motives. Love, friendship, affection, fellow feeling, and community, like many other states and activities, essentially contain certain motives and essentially preclude certain others; among those precluded we find motives comprising the justifications, the goals, the goods of those ethical theories most prominent today. To embody in one's motives the values of current ethical theories is to treat people externally and to preclude love, friendship, affection, fellow feeling, and community—both with others and with oneself. To get these great goods while holding those current ethical theories requires a schizophrenia between reason and motive.

I have not argued that if you have a successful love relationship, friendship, . . . , then you will be unable to achieve the justifications, goals, goods posited by those theories. You can achieve them, but not by trying to live the theory directly. Or, more exactly, to to the extent that you live the theory directly, to that extent you will fail to achieve its goods.

So far I have urged the charge of disharmony, bifurcation, schizophrenia only in regard to the personal relationships of love, friendship, affection, fellow feeling, and community. The importance of these is, I would think, sufficient to carry the day. However, let us look at one further area: inquiry, taken as the search for understanding, wisdom. Although I am less sure here, I also think that many of the same charges apply.

Perhaps the following is only a special case, but it seems worth considering. You have been locked up in a psychiatric hospital, and are naturally most eager to get out. You ask the psychiatrist when you will be released; he replies, "Pretty soon." You find out that, instead of telling patients what he really believes, he tells them what he believes is good for them to hear (good for them to believe he believes). Perhaps you could "crack his code," by discovering his medical theories and his beliefs about you. Nonetheless, your further conversations—if they can be called that—with him are hardly the model of inquiry. I am not so unsure that we would be in a different position when confronted with people who engage in inquiry for their own sake, for God's glory, for the greatest pleasure, or even for the greatest good. Again, we might well be able to crack their codes—e.g., we could find out that some-

462   THE JOURNAL OF PHILOSOPHY

one believes his greatest chance for academic promotion is to find out the truth in a certain area. Nonetheless. . . .

(Is the residual doubt "But what if he comes to believe that what is most pleasing to the senior professors will gain promotion; and how can we tell what he really believes?" of any import here? And is it essentially different from "But what if he ceases to value truth as such; and how can we tell what he really values?"? Perhaps if understanding, not "mere knowledge," is the goal, there is a difference.)

It might be expected that, in those areas explicitly concerned with motives and their evaluation, ethical theories would not lead us into this disharmony or the corresponding morally defective life. And to some extent this expectation is met. But even in regard to moral merit and demerit, moral praise- and blameworthiness, the moral virtues and vices, the situation is not wholly dissimilar. Again, the problem of externality and impersonality, and the connected disharmony, arises.

The standard view has it that a morally good intention is an essential constituent of a morally good act. This seems correct enough. On that view, further, a morally good intention is an intention to do an act for the sake of its goodness or rightness. But now, suppose you are in a hospital, recovering from a long illness. You are very bored and restless and at loose ends when Smith comes in once again. You are now convinced more than ever that he is a fine fellow and a real friend—taking so much time to cheer you up, traveling all the way across town, and so on. You are so effusive with your praise and thanks that he protests that he always tries to do what he thinks is his duty, what he thinks will be best. You at first think he is engaging in a polite form of self-deprecation, relieving the moral burden. But the more you two speak, the more clear it becomes that he was telling the literal truth: that it is not essentially because of you that he came to see you, not because you are friends, but because he thought it his duty, perhaps as a fellow Christian or Communist or whatever, or simply because he knows of no one more in need of cheering up and no one easier to cheer up.

Surely there is something lacking here—and lacking in moral merit or value. The lack can be sheeted home to two related points: again, the wrong sort of thing is said to be the proper motive; and, in this case at least, the wrong sort of thing is, again, essentially external.[6]

---

[6] For a way to evade this problem, see my "Morally Good Intentions," *The Monist*, LIV, 1 (January 1970): 124–141, where it is argued that goodness and

SOME QUESTIONS AND CONCLUDING REMARKS

I have assumed that the reasons, values, justifications of ethical theories should be such as to allow us to embody them in our motives and still act morally and achieve the good. But why assume this? Perhaps we should take ethical theories as encouraging indirection—getting what we want by seeking something else: e.g., some say the economic well-being of all is realized, not by everyone's seeking it but by everyone's seeking his/her own well-being. Or perhaps we should take ethical theories as giving only indices, not determinants, of what is right and good.

Theories of indirection have their own special problems. There is always a great risk that we will get the something else, not what we really want. There are, also, these two related problems. A theory advocating indirection needs to be augmented by another theory of motivation, telling us which motives are suitable for which acts. Such a theory would also have to explain the connections, the indirect connections, between motive and real goal.

Second, it may not be very troubling to talk about indirection in such large-scale and multi-person matters as the economics of society. But in regard to something of such personal concern, so close to and so internal to a person as ethics, talk of indirection is both implausible and baffling. Implausible in that we do not seem to act by indirection, at least not in such areas as love, friendship, affection, fellow feeling, and community. In these cases, our motive has to do directly with the loved one, the friend, . . . , as does our reason. In doing something for a loved child or parent, there is no need to appeal to, or even think of, the reasons found in contemporary ethical theories. Talk of indirection is baffling, in an action- and understanding-defeating sense, since, once we begin to believe that there is something beyond such activities as love which is necessary to justify them, it is only by something akin to self-deception that we are able to continue them.

One partial defense of these ethical theories would be that they are not intended to supply what can serve as both reasons and motives; that they are intended only to supply indices of goodness and rightness, not determinants. Formally, there may be no problems in taking ethical theories this way. But several questions do arise. Why should we be concerned with such theories, theories that cannot be acted on? Why not simply have a theory that allows for harmony between reason and motive? A theory that gives determinants? And indeed, will we not need to have such a theory? True,

---

rightness need not be the object of a morally good intention, but rather that various goods or right acts can be.

our pre-analytic views might be sufficient to judge among index theories; we may not need a determinant theory to pick out a correct index theory. But will we not need a determinant theory to know why the index is correct, why it works, to know what is good about what is so indexed? [7]

Another partial defense of recent theories would be that, first, they are concerned almost entirely with rightness, obligation, and duty, and not with the whole of ethics; and, second, that within this restricted area, they do not suffer from disharmony or schizophrenia. To some extent this defense, especially its second point, has been dealt with earlier. But more should be said. It is perhaps clear enough by now that recent ethicists have ignored large and extremely important areas of morality—e.g., that of personal relations and that of merit. To this extent, the first point of the defense is correct. What is far from clear, however, is whether these theories were advanced only as partial theories, or whether it was believed by their proponents that duty and so on were really the whole, or at least the only important part, of ethics.

We might be advised to forget past motivation and belief, and simply look at these theories and see what use can be made of them. Perhaps they were mistaken about the scope and importance of duty and so on. Nonetheless they could be correct about the concepts involved. In reply, several points should be made. First, they were mistaken about these concepts, as even a brief study of supererogation and self-regarding notions would indicate. Second, these theories are dangerously misleading; for they can all too readily be taken as suggesting that all of ethics can be treated in an external, legislation-model, index way. (On 'legislation-model' see below.) Third, the acceptance of such theories as partial theories would pose severe difficulties of integration within ethical theory. Since these theories are so different from those concerning, e.g., personal relations, how are they all to be integrated? Of course, this third

---

[7] Taking contemporary theories to be index theories would help settle one of the longest-standing disputes in ethical philosophy—a dispute which finds Aristotle and Marx on the winning side and many if not most contemporary ethicists on the other. The dispute concerns the relative explanatory roles of pleasure and good activity and good life. Put crudely, many utilitarians and others have held that an activity is good only because and insofar as it is productive of pleasure; Aristotle and Marx hold of at least many pleasures that if they are good this is because they are produced by good activity. The problem of immoral pleasures has seemed to many the most important test case for this dispute. To the extent that my paper is correct, we have another way to settle the dispute. For, if I am correct, pleasure cannot be what makes all good activity good, even prescinding from immoral pleasures. It must be activity, such as love and friendship, which make some pleasures good.

point may not be a criticism of these theories of duty, but only a recognition of the great diversity and complexity of our moral life.[8]

In conclusion, it might be asked how contemporary ethical theories come to require either a stunted moral life or disharmony, schizophrenia. One cluster of (somewhat speculative) answers surrounds the preeminence of duty, rightness, and obligation in these theories. This preeminence fits naturally with theories developed in a time of diminishing personal relations; of a time when the ties holding people together and easing the frictions of their various enterprises were less and less affection; of a time when commercial relations superseded family (or family-like) relations; of a time of growing individualism. It also fits naturally with a major concern of those philosophers: legislation. When concerned with legislation, they were concerned with duty, rightness, obligation. (Of course, the question then is, Why were they interested in legislation, especially of this sort? To some small extent this has been answered, but no more will be said on this score.) When viewing morality from such a legislator's point of view, taking such legislation to be the model, motivation too easily becomes irrelevant. The legislator wants various things done or not done; it is not important why they are done or not done; one can count on and know the actions, but not the motives. (This is also tied up with a general devaluing of our emotions and emotional possibilities—taking emotions to be mere feelings or urges, without rational or cognitive content or constraint; and taking us to be pleasure-seekers and pain-avoiders— forgetting or denying that love, friendship, affection, fellow feeling, and desire for virtue are extremely strong movers of people.) Connected with this is the legislative or simply the third-person's-eye view, which assures us that others are getting on well if they are happy, if they are doing what gives them pleasure, and the like. The effect guarantees the cause—in the epistemic sense. (One might wonder whether the general empiricist confusion of *ratio cognescendi* and *ratio essendi* is at work here.)

---

[8] Part of this complexity can be seen as follows: Duty seems relevant in our relations with our loved ones and friends, only when our love, friendship, and affection lapse. If a family is "going well," its members "naturally" help each other; that is, their love, affection, and deep friendship are sufficient for them to care for and help one another (to put it a bit coolly). Such "feelings" are at times worn thin. At these times, duty may have to be looked to or called upon (by the agent or by others) to get done at least a modicum of those things which love would normally provide. To some rough extent, the frequency with which a family member acts out of duty, instead of love, toward another in the family is a measure of the lack of love the first has for the other. But this is not to deny that there are duties of love, friendship, and the like.

These various factors, then, may help explain this rather remarkable inversion (to use Marx's notion): of taking the "effect," pleasure and the like, for the "cause," good activity.

Moore's formalistic utilitarianism and the traditional views of morally good action also suffer from something like an inversion. Here, however, it is not causal, but philosophical. It is as if these philosophers have taken it that, because these various good things can all be classified as good, their goodness consists in this, rather than conversely. The most general classification seems to have been reified and itself taken as the morally relevant goal.

These inversions may help answer a question which afflicts this paper: Why have I said that contemporary ethics suffers from schizophrenia, bifurcation, disharmony? Why have I not claimed simply that these theories are mistaken in their denomination of what is good and bad, right- and wrong-making? For it is clear enough that, if we aim for the wrong goal, then (in all likelihood) we will not achieve what we really want, what is good, and the like. My reason for claiming more than a mere mistake is that the mistake is well reasoned; it is closely related to the truth, it bears many of the features of the truth. To take only two examples (barring bad fortune and bad circumstances), good activity does bring about pleasure; love clearly benefits the lover. There is, thus, great plausibility in taking as good what these theories advance as good. But when we try to act on the theories, try to embody their reasons in our motives—as opposed to simply seeing whether our or others' lives would be approved of by the theories—then in a quite mad way, things start going wrong. The personalities of loved ones get passed over for their effects, moral action becomes self-stultifying and self-defeating. And perhaps the greatest madnesses of all are—and they stand in a vicious interrelation—first, the world is increasingly made such as to make these theories correct; and, second, we take these theories to be correct and thus come to see love, friendship, and the like only as possible, and not very certain, sources of pleasure or whatever. We mistake the effect for the cause and when the cause-seen-as-effect fails to result from the effect-seen-as-cause, we devalue the former, relegating it, at best, to good as a means and embrace the latter, wondering why our chosen goods are so hollow, bitter, and inhumane.

MICHAEL STOCKER

The Australian National University

5

UTILITY AND RIGHTS*

DAVID LYONS

Two notions concerning the relation of rights to utilitarianism seem widely accepted, by both utilitarians and their critics. The first is that utilitarianism is hostile to the idea of moral rights. The second is that utilitarianism is capable of providing a normative theory about legal and other institutional rights. This chapter chiefly concerns the second thesis, and argues against it. But it also says something about the first. In previous writings I have challenged the first thesis,[1] but here I shall suggest that it is sound. The upshot is that utilitarianism has a great deal of trouble accommodating rights.

SCOPE AND PLAN OF THE ARGUMENT

By "utilitarianism" I mean the theory that the only sound, fundamental basis for normative (or moral) appraisal is the promotion of human welfare. But my argument has implications beyond utilitarianism in this limited sense. It extends in the first place to a number of normative views that are closely associated with utilitarianism but not equivalent to it, such as normative "economic analysis" in the law. Second, it extends to many other "goal-based" theories and perhaps to other normative theories as well. All of these theories have trouble with legal as well as with moral rights.

Outside ethical theory—in economics and fields that economics has influenced strongly[2]—traditional utilitarian terminology

108   DAVID LYONS

and doctrines have sometimes been displaced by new ones. To a great extent, this change represents an attempt to secure behavioristic foundations for normative doctrines. Sometimes, utilitarian terms have been given a self-consciously behavioristic interpretation, as when references to "pleasure" and "pain" are replaced by a concern for individuals' "preferences" or one's "willingness to pay." In other cases, normative doctrines have departed from traditional utilitarianism, largely because of worries about "interpersonal comparisons of utility." For example, the utilitarian requirement that the overall net balance of pleasure over pain be maximized has been replaced, in some quarters, by notions of "economic efficiency," some versions of which do not require us (even in principle) to compare the benefits conferred and burdens imposed on one individual with those conferred and imposed on others. The result is a doctrine that is by no means equivalent to traditional utilitarianism. I believe, nevertheless, that my argument applies to these modifications and descendants of utilitarianism. Economists and theorists working in other fields frequently take normative positions that are, for present purposes, similar to those found within the utilitarian tradition. The problems that I discuss in this chapter are, so far as I can see, problems for their theories as much as they are for utilitarianism.

Later on I shall suggest how these problems beset a much wider class of theories, including some that are opposed to utilitarianism. These problems concern rights. My argument requires, however, that we distinguish two broad categories of rights, which I shall call "moral rights" and "legal rights."

Some rights are thought to exist independently of social recognition and enforcement. This is what I think we usually mean by "moral rights." These include the rights that are sometimes called "natural" or "human," but are not limited to them. Natural or human rights are rights we are all said to have (by those who believe we have them) just by virtue of our status as human beings. They are independent of particular circumstances and do not depend on any special conditions. The class of moral rights is broader, since it includes rights that depend on particular circumstances or special conditions, such as promises. Moral rights, in general, do not depend on social recognition or enforcement, as is shown by the fact that they are appealed to even when it is not believed that they are enforced or recognized by law or by prevailing opinion.

Utilitarians are seen as hostile to moral rights; I shall call this *The Moral Rights Exclusion Thesis (Exclusion Thesis* for short). Economic theorists who embrace doctrines similar to utilitarianism tend to ignore (rather than reject) the idea of moral rights. Moral rights have little, if anything, to do with normative doctrines of this kind.[3]

Other rights presuppose some sort of social recognition or enforcement, the clearest case being rights conferred by law, including constitutional rights. I restrict my attention here to legal rights within this general class.

It is generally assumed that utilitarians have no difficulty accommodating legal rights and providing a normative theory about them; I shall call this *The Legal Rights Inclusion Thesis (Inclusion Thesis* for short). Normative theorists working within economics and policy studies are concerned with telling us which legal rights should be conferred, and take for granted that their theories are capable of accommodating such rights. I shall argue that they are mistaken.[4]

The main part of my argument may be summarized as follows. The Exclusion Thesis assumes that moral rights make a difference to evaluation of conduct by excluding a range of direct utilitarian arguments that might militate against conduct (but not when it involves the exercise of rights) or that might justify conduct (but not when it would interfere with the exercise of rights). I call this the normative force of moral rights. The Inclusion Thesis assumes, by contrast, that legal rights are morally neutral and lack such force. But, when legal rights are regarded as justifiable or morally defensible, they are regarded as having moral force. In other words, the idea that legal rights are morally defensible entails the idea of a moral presumption in favor of respecting them, even though it may not be useful to exercise them or may be useful to interfere with them in particular cases. The problem for utilitarianism, then, is whether it can somehow accommodate the moral force of justified legal rights. I argue that it cannot do so satisfactorily. Although there are often utilitarian reasons for respecting justified legal rights, these reasons are not equivalent to the moral force of such rights, because they do not exclude direct utilitarian arguments against exercising such rights or for interfering with them. Specifically, utilitarian arguments for institutional design (the arguments that utilitarians might use in favor of establishing or maintaining certain legal rights) do not logically or morally exclude direct utilitarian arguments concerning the exercise of, or interference with, such rights. As a consequence, evaluation of conduct from a utilitarian standpoint is dominated by direct utilitarian arguments and therefore ignores the moral force of justified legal rights. The utilitarian is committed to ignoring the moral force of those very rights that he is committed to regarding as having moral force by virtue of the fact that he regards them as morally justifiable.

BENTHAM'S APPROACH

Of the classical utilitarians, Bentham is the one whose approach is most directly analogous to that of contemporary economic theorists as well as that of utilitarians who wish to provide a normative theory of legal rights. He accepted The Exclusion and Inclusion Theses. And so it is useful to begin with his ideas.

We are often reminded that Bentham dismissed the very idea of natural rights as "nonsense." One reason, of course, was his rejection of certain doctrines associated with natural rights, such as the notion that they are conferred by nature or discovered by the pure light of natural reason. But Bentham in effect rejected moral rights generally, that is, rights that do not presuppose social recognition or enforcement.[5]

Bentham's most direct, official reason for rejecting moral rights derives from his analysis of statements about rights and obligations. He held that meaningful statements about rights must be understood as statements about beneficial obligations, and he held that statements about obligations concern the requirements of coercive legal rules. He held that one has a right if and only if one is supposed to benefit from another person's compliance with a coercive legal rule. It follows that he could not recognize rights that are independent of social recognition or enforcement, that is, moral rights.

These analytical doctrines have no straightforward relation

to Bentham's utilitarianism. His analysis of rights neither follows from a principle of utility nor entails it. Nevertheless, it is arguable that, given his utilitarianism, Bentham could not have accepted the idea that we have any moral rights. It would seem that his utilitarianism commited him to The Exclusion Thesis.

One might argue for the incompatibility of utilitarianism and moral rights as follows. Moral rights are not merely *independent of* social recognition and enforcement but also provide *grounds for appraising* law and other social institutions. If social arrangements violate moral rights, they can be criticized accordingly. Moral rights imply the establishment of institutions that respect them. But Bentham held that institutions are to be evaluated *solely* in terms of human welfare. Unless we assume that arguments based on moral rights converge perfectly with those based on welfare, it would seem that a utilitarian like Bentham would be obliged to reject moral rights.

This reasoning appears, however, to assume rather than prove The Exclusion Thesis. Why should we suppose that arguments based on moral rights diverge from welfare considerations? The answer has to do with the normative character of rights. If I have a right to do something, this provides *an argumentative threshold* against objections to my doing it, as well as a presumption against others' interference. Considerations that might otherwise be sufficient against my so acting, in the absence of my having the right, or that might justify others' interference, are ineffective in its presence.

Consider, for example, the idea that I have a right to life. This entails that I may act so as to save it and that others may not interfere, even if these acts or the results would otherwise be subject to sound criticism. I need not show that my life is valuable or useful, and the fact that my defending it would have bad overall consequences or is otherwise objectionable does not show that my defending it is wrong, or that others' interference is not wrong. My right provides a measure of justification for certain actions of my own, as well as limits to interference. I call this argumentative threshold character the *normative force* of moral rights.

This point is sometimes distorted by exaggeration. Note, however, that my right to life does not automatically justify any course of action whatsoever that may be needed to save it; nor does it absolutely block justification for other's taking my life. Rights are not necessarily "absolute." That is why I speak of thresholds that need to be surmounted.[6]

Let us apply this to utilitarianism. From the standpoint of this theory we are entitled to assume that considerations of welfare are morally relevant, so that the promotion of welfare to a minimal degree provides justification for a course of action. Considerations like these are incremental. However, minimal increments of utility are incapable of surmounting the argumentative threshold of my rights. I may defend my life even at *some* cost to overall welfare, and others may not interfere *just* because it would promote overall welfare to *some* degree if they did. In this way, the arguments that flow from moral rights appear to diverge from those predicated on the service of welfare. If one accepts moral rights, one cannot accept absolute guidance by welfare arguments. And so we have The Moral Rights Exclusion Thesis.

Similar considerations apply to normative doctrines in economics and other fields that are developed in terms like "economic efficiency." If one believes that institutions are to be evaluated solely in terms of their promotion of such values, and not in terms of independent rights, one cannot accept the idea that we have any moral rights.

Bentham's attitude toward legal rights was of course different. His analysis of rights in terms of the beneficial requirements of coercive legal rules allows for the possibility of legal rights. And the general idea that utilitarianism is compatible with legal rights is hardly controversial, being widely assumed in law, economics, and political theory. Much the same idea is presupposed by what is called "the economic analysis of law" (though only the normative versions of "economic analysis" interest us here).

The Legal Rights Inclusion Thesis assumes that institutions serving the general welfare or economic efficiency are capable of conferring rights. Critics of utilitarianism as well as critics of normative economic analysis (including those who believe we have moral rights) do not challenge this assumption. They may claim that utilitarian or economically efficient institutions would establish some rights that ought not to be established (such as certain property rights) or would violate some rights that ought to be respected (such as rights to privacy or to personal autonomy), but they do not claim that such institutions are incapable of conferring any rights at all.

This is a plausible assumption, at least when it is coupled with a morally neutral conception of legal rights, by which I mean a conception that generates no moral presumption that those rights should be respected. Furthermore, the idea that utilitarian and efficient institutions confer rights leaves plenty of room for opponents of utilitarianism and of normative economic analysis to criticize those institutions, on the basis of moral rights or other values.

I am sympathetic to the morally neutral conception of legal rights, for reasons such as the following. The law of a society may be understood as implying that people have certain rights. But the law may be outrageously unjust and hence the rights it confers morally indefensible. There is absolutely no moral presumption favoring respect for those legal rights conferred by chattel slavery. Circumstances may of course provide some reasons for respecting morally objectionable entitlements. Those on whom such rights may be conferred are, after all, human beings who can claim some measure of respect and consideration from others too. But, while these considerations may affect what we ought to do in the context of morally outrageous institutions, they do not show anything about the moral force of legal rights themselves. So I am prepared to say that, from the fact that I have a right conferred on me by law, *nothing follows* concerning what I or others may do. We might put this point by saying that *merely* legal rights have *no moral force*.

Some writers do not share my view of legal rights, though their reasons are unclear.[7] In any case, if I am wrong about legal rights in this respect, then all have moral force. If we could assume that, my argument would be simpler. Since I deny it, I must limit my attention to those legal rights with moral force. These are legal rights that are taken to be morally defensible, the rights conferred by laws that are supposed to be justified. Let us see what this amounts to.

LEGAL RIGHTS WITH MORAL FORCE

Suppose that Mary rents a house that comes with a garage for her car. Access to the garage is provided by a private driveway, which she alone is authorized to use. Sometimes, however, she finds someone else's car parked in the driveway, which prevents her from parking or leaving with her own car. This may be inconvenient or it may not. Whenever it happens, however, Mary's rights are not being respected by other individuals.

Mary's rights depend on social arrangements, and they are enforceable by legal means. They thus qualify as legal rights. I shall assume, however, that these rights are *not merely* legal. I am supposing, in other words, that the social arrangements presupposed by Mary's rights and their enforceability are justifiable; those institutions or their relevant parts are morally defensible. This does not seem an implausible assumption to adopt. From the fact that Mary's rights are not shared by others, for example, we cannot infer that they are morally objectionable. I would suppose that ordinary rights like Mary's can arise and be justified in otherwise unjust as well as just societies, though this is not required for the argument. Within a society in which people have fair shares of the resources and considerable freedom to decide how to use their respective shares, for example, some individuals, with needs that are different from Mary's, may reasonably decide to make arrangements that are different from hers. And in such a society there may be good reason to have rights like Mary's made enforceable by law. Of course, Mary's rights are meant only as an example. If one has objections to private parking arrangements, it should be possible to substitute another example for the purpose. It is useful, however, to choose *very ordinary* rights, which clearly depend on institutional arrangements and legal recognition or enforcement. What I think we can agree about Mary's rights applies to many other routine legal rights, that is, to those we think of as morally defensible.

Given the arrangements that Mary has made, she may use the garage and driveway as she wishes. She may permit others to use them or refuse to do so. Others may not use them without her permission. In other words, Mary's rights make a difference to what she and others may justifiably do.

The principal assumption I shall make is this. When we regard Mary's rights as morally defensible, on any basis whatsoever, we also regard them as having moral force. The differences that her rights make to evaluation of conduct obtain, not just in the eyes of the law, but also from a moral point of view. We may disagree about the conditions that must be satisfied if legal rights are to be morally defensible. But if we hold that Mary's rights are morally defensible, then we are committed to agreeing that they have such force. Utilitarians and nonutilitarians will disagree about the conditions that justify legal rights. This is compatible, however, with their agreeing that certain legal rights are morally defensible. And the latter entails, as I shall assume, that such rights have moral force. To deny that Mary's legal rights have such force is to deny that they are morally defensible.

Mary's rights make a difference even when they are infringed. If others encroach upon her rights thoughtlessly or for their own private convenience, for example, it is incumbent on them to apologize or even, perhaps, to compensate her for any inconvenience she has suffered as a consequence. If they fail to do so, then they act wrongly. If compensation should be offered, then Mary is free to accept it or refuse it, as she prefers.

Of course, Mary's rights are limited. The driver of an emergency vehicle on an urgent errand might justifiably block Mary's driveway without first obtaining Mary's permission—even, perhaps, in the face of her refusal to give permission. This holds from both a legal as well as a moral standpoint. And, to simplify matters here, I shall assume that the legal limits of Mary's rights correspond perfectly to what we should regard on reflection as their proper limits from a moral point of view. Limits like these on Mary's rights are compatible with the idea that her rights make a difference to moral arguments. We need not assume that Mary's rights are "absolute" and overwhelm all conflicting considerations. My point is simply that Mary's rights entail an argumentative or justificatory threshold. Certain considerations are capable of justifying encroachments on Mary's rights, but not all are. Let us look at this more closely.

If one regards Mary's moral position from a utilitarian standpoint, then one might be presumed to reason as follows. Mary is fully justified in exercising her legal rights only when and in a manner in which she can promote human welfare to the maximum degree possible, and others are fully justified in encroaching on Mary's rights in the same sort of circumstances and for the same sort of reason.

This reasoning may be framed in probabilistic terms. What

116   DAVID LYONS

may be thought required, then, is not that human welfare actually be promoted to the maximum degree possible, but that Mary's acts, when she exercises her rights, or the acts of those who encroach on them, be *most likely* to maximize human welfare (or something of the sort). This type of qualification will not, I think, affect the present argument, and I shall generally ignore it hereafter.

The utilitarian pattern of reasoning that I have sketched seems to clash with the idea that Mary's rights are morally defensible and thus have moral force. For it assumes that Mary's rights *make no difference* to what she and others may justifiably do, except insofar as the legal recognition of those rights changes circumstances so that certain possible courses of action have added utility or disutility. But this is not the way Mary's moral position is ordinarily viewed when it is assumed that her legal rights are morally defensible.

Suppose, for example, that a neighbor decides late at night to park his car in Mary's driveway, without obtaining her permission, in order to save himself a long cold walk from the nearest legal parking space. He might reason soundly that Mary is unlikely to be inconvenienced, since he shall move his car early the next morning. And that might turn out to be the case. Nevertheless, Mary might justifiably resent and complain of his presumption. Of course, Mary could reflect that she might have been seriously inconvenienced if an emergency had arisen during the night and she was unable to use her car. But it should not be assumed that her resentment would be justified solely by the possible inconvenience she might have suffered. For that might have happened even if she had given permission beforehand for him to use the driveway, in which case her resentment would not be warranted. Her belief is that her neighbor acted unjustifiably—that his action could not be justified simply by calculations of actual or probable utilities.

We can generalize these points as follows. Mary has the moral freedom to exercise her rights, within certain limits. Neither this freedom nor its limits can be explained by the utilitarian line of reasoning we have described. For example, Mary may act to her own disadvantage, without the prospect of compensating advantages to anyone else. Her rights also permit her some indifference to the effects of her choices upon others.

They permit her, for example, to inconvenience others while exercising her rights, without the prospect of compensating advantages to anyone, including herself. She need not act so as to maximize utility when she exercises her rights. Similarly, others may not act in certain ways without her permission, even if their doing so would maximize utility.

A utilitarian might object that he is not interested in Mary's rights as such but only in evaluation of her conduct and that of others. He might suggest that I have ignored the distinction between Mary's having rights and the conditions under which she justifiably exercises them. But I have framed my argument so as to respect that distinction. My point is not that Mary's rights completely determine what she and others may justifiably do but that her rights make a difference to the evaluation of her and others' conduct, a difference that unrestricted utilitarian reasoning cannot accept. The difference is not simple, since we cannot assume that Mary's rights are "absolute." In the present context, the difference amounts to this: from the mere fact that net utility would not be maximized by her exercising her rights, we cannot infer that her exercise of them is not justified; similarly, from the mere fact that net utility would be maximized by encroaching on her rights, we cannot infer that one is justified in encroaching on them.

One thing that complicates matters here is that Mary's rights, to be morally defensible, must have some foundation in human interests, needs, or welfare and are limited in turn by similar considerations. For this reason, utilitarian considerations are, *within limits*, relevant to a final determination of what Mary and others may justifiably do, which is bounded by a decent regard for others' welfare. Mary's decisions must give some respect to the interests of others, and what others may justifiably do is determined in part by the effects of their conduct upon people generally. Thus, despite her rights, Mary may not deny access to her driveway to someone in dire need, and others may use it without her permission if the need is pressing. But this is not to say that utilitarian reasoning *generally* determines how Mary and others may justifiably act. Let us suppose that *very substantial* utilities or disutilities outweigh the moral force of Mary's rights. We cannot infer from this that *minimal increments* of utility are sufficient to outweigh those arguments. To reason in that way

would assume that Mary's rights make no difference to moral
argument or, in other words, that her rights lack moral force.
But, if I am right, Mary's legal rights have moral force if they
are morally defensible.

It should be emphasized that I am assuming there is no moral
objection to Mary's having such special control over her garage
and driveway. I do not mean to suggest (and I have explicitly
denied) that any arbitrary arrangements that Mary might secure
under the law would have similar moral consequences. I would
not suggest, for example, that if the law gave Mary comparable
control over another human being—if, in other words, it
regarded her as the owner of a chattel slave—then she would
be morally free to decide, in a similar way, how to use that
person. Even if the law regarded Mary in that way, we might
reasonably deny that the legal arrangements make any difference to the way that Mary may justifiably behave, from a moral
point of view. But our example is not like that. I have deliberately
chosen to focus on an ordinary, mundane legal right that might
plausibly be regarded as morally defensible.

It is also important to emphasize that I have not been
discussing moral rights, that is, rights we are supposed to have
independently of social recognition or enforcement. Nor is it
suggested that Mary's rights arise of their own accord, without
any foundation in fact. What is suggested, rather, is that, given
the relevant facts in the social circumstances, which have to do
with Mary's unobjectionably renting a house with a garage
serviced by a driveway, she assumes a new moral position. She
acquires rights, and her acquired rights appear to function as
more or less stable moral factors with characteristic implications.

I have not claimed that there can be no utilitarian foundation
for Mary's rights. It might be argued, for example, that the
general welfare can be served by institutional arrangements that
provide Mary with such special control over her garage and
driveway. Let us now see how this argument would proceed,
and what it might prove.

UTILITARIAN INSTITUTIONS

Although Bentham is widely thought to be committed to the
pattern of utilitarian reasoning I have been discussing, he does

not seem to deal with problems of the sort we have considered. Bentham and those who follow in his footsteps, including those wedded to normative economic analysis, are concerned with the evaluation of law and social institutions. In this connection, Bentham applies the standard of utility, not to individual acts taken separately, but rather to the rules and institutions that he thinks of as conferring rights. Those favoring economic analysis use a standard of efficiency in a similar way. They criticize, evaluate, and recommend legal rules in terms of some value that the rules are supposed to serve. These theorists assume, in accordance with The Inclusion Thesis, that rights would be conferred by institutions they regard as justified.

It does seem plausible to suppose that institutions conforming to utilitarian requirements or to the dictates of economic efficiency would incorporate rights. In the first place, when we consider possible institutions, we naturally tend to model them on those with which we are familiar, and these are generally assumed to confer rights. In the second place, and most importantly for present purposes, it seems reasonable to suppose that institutions designed to serve the general welfare or economic efficiency are capable of satisfying a *necessary* condition for incorporating rights. That is, the rules of such institutions might confer the proper range of freedom and impose the appropriate restrictions upon others' behavior that correspond to rights like Mary's. I know of no general argument that could deny this possibility.

When Bentham assumed that rights would be incorporated in utilitarian institutions, he proceeded on the assumption that rights exist whenever coercive restrictions upon behavior serve the interests of determinate individuals. It is difficult to imagine how institutions supported by the best utilitarian arguments could fail to create some useful restrictions, and it is natural to suppose that some of these restrictions would be useful by serving or securing the interests of specific persons. So, on Bentham's theory, it would seem that such institutions confer rights.

Economic theorists have not devoted much attention to the question of what it is to have a right. But it is reasonable to suppose that they have been guided by some conception of rights like Bentham's.

But we cannot pursue the basic issue here within the framework constructed by Bentham. Our question is not whether rights as Bentham conceived of them can be reconciled to utilitarianism, nor whether rights as economic analysts conceive of them can be reconciled with the principles of economic efficiency. This is so for two distinct reasons.

In the first place, it could be said that Bentham took rights a bit too seriously. He inflated their normative force into coercive power. He imagined that, when I have a right, existing legal rules provide for their enforcement. But enforcement is not an essential feature of rights, not even legal rights. Rights can be recognized by law even when no legal provisions are made for their enforcement. Consider, for example, those civil rights of U.S. citizens that are based upon the "equal protection clause" of the Constitution. These rights went without enforcement for many years. The Civil Rights Acts and the Civil Rights Division of the U.S. Department of Justice were intended as means for securing these rights. Enforcement enhances these rights and establishes new "secondary" rights, but it does not create the basic constitutional rights themselves. Legal rights are not necessarily enforced, and their enforcement need not even be authorized. It follows that neither enforcement nor its authorization is an essential feature of legal rights. Bentham was mistaken. In consequence, at least part of the reason theorists sometimes think they have for concentrating upon legal rights while ignoring moral rights is an illusion.

In the second place, Bentham's analysis ignores the moral force of rights under justified institutions. The question that we face is whether utilitarianism or comparable theories can accommodate legal rights with moral force.

This qualification is important, and it does not prejudice our inquiry in any way that is unfair to utilitarianism or normative economic analysis. The institutions that a utilitarian or an economic analyst regards as fully justified are, presumably, his best candidates for institutions that create rights with moral force. If such a theorist regards some institutions as *justified* but he *cannot* accommodate the moral force of legal rights conferred by those institutions, then his theory is in trouble, faced with a kind of incoherence. On the one hand, he wishes to claim that the institutions he can justify would confer some rights. On the other hand, his basic theory does not allow him to accommodate the moral force possessed by legal rights in justified or morally defensible institutions. This is what I shall now try to show.

THE RELEVANCE OF DIRECT UTILITARIAN ARGUMENTS

The strategy of my argument is this. I shall suppose that a utilitarian or economic analyst believes that certain rights would be conferred by legal institutions that are justified by his basic normative principles. I take this to imply that the rights are to be regarded as morally defensible and thus that we can consider them as having moral force. I shall then try to show that this force cannot be accommodated by a normative position developed on the foundation of welfare or some comparable value such as economic efficiency.

For purposes of illustration, let us suppose that a utilitarian or economist believes that we can justify a set of institutions like those assumed in our example. Under the rules of those institutions, Mary has exclusive use of the garage and driveway attached to the house she is renting (though others' use of them is permitted under special circumstances, even without her permission). We shall assume, furthermore, that the freedom conferred by the rules on Mary and the obligations imposed by them on others match precisely what we should regard on reflection as the proper extent and limits of her rights when viewed from a moral standpoint. Mary is not required to worry generally about the utility of her actions or about economic efficiency when deciding how to use her garage or driveway or whether to permit others to use them. Nor are others expected to decide whether to use Mary's garage or driveway just on the basis of the utility of such conduct or its efficiency. And officials are not expected to decide on such grounds when they are called upon to apply or enforce the relevant, clear legal rules.

Unless something like this can be assumed, the idea that legal rights with moral force can be accommodated by a theory based on welfare or efficiency is defeated at the start. But the assumption appears reasonable. At least, I know of no general argument that could deny the possibility that such institutions as would be preferred by a utilitarian or by an economist might confer the proper range of freedom and the appropriate restrictions on others' behavior that correspond to the moral force of ordinary legal rights like Mary's. It should be emphasized, of course, that we are not supposing that such institutions would respect all rights that ought to be respected, including moral rights, which are independent of social recognition and enforcement, or that such institutions satisfy any other normative standards that a critic of utilitarianism or of normative economic analysis may endorse. These are concerns that a utilitarian or an economic analyst cannot be thought to share. Our strategy is to accept the normative approach of utilitarians and of economic analysts and to see where that leads us.

It must also be emphasized, however, that these assumptions do not settle the present issue. They imply only that such theories are capable of satisfying a *necessary* condition for accommodating legal rights with moral force. But our question is not whether utilitarianism or efficiency analysis could regard such institutions as justified or morally defensible. Our question is *what significance* such a theorist must attach to that fact when it comes to *evaluating conduct* in the context of those rules; for example, in determining how an official in such a system should behave.

A utilitarian or policy analyst might be thought to reason now as follows: "Institutions are justified if, or to the extent that, they promote human welfare or economic efficiency. Institutions ought to be designed so that official as well as private decisions will by and large promote such a value to the extent that this can be contrived. When that has been accomplished, conduct that is subject to the rules of those institutions can be justified only by reference to those rules. In other words, utilitarian and comparable arguments have their place, but they have no monopoly on justification. They do not always control the evaluation of conduct. When the rules are justified, they are to be followed. Their justified legal impact thus translates into moral force."

This is the approach John Rawls has suggested that a utilitarian would take to institutions that are justified on utilitarian grounds. In replying to the objection that utilitarianism allows the punishment of innocent persons, for example, he supposes that a utilitarian official who understands the utilitarian justification of the rules that he is charged with administering would abide by the rules.[8]

But the pattern of reasoning just sketched ignores some of the utilitarian considerations that are inevitably at work in particular cases that arise under such rules. For it is predictable that real social rules that are supported by the best utilitarian and economic arguments will require decisions in particular cases that would not most effectively promote welfare or efficiency. Such goals can sometimes be promoted more effectively by departing from the rules, or by changing them, than by following them. When that happens, a direct utilitarian or economic argument supports deviation from the rules.[9]

Suppose that a utilitarian official, or one who has adopted the precepts of normative economic analysis, is called upon to enforce the rules on Mary's behalf. He can understand perfectly the justification that he accepts for those rules. And his legal duty may be transparent. The rules vindicate Mary's claim, and he is legally bound to decide in her favor.

I do not see how such reasoning can settle matters for a utilitarian or economic-minded official. Suppose there are direct utilitarian or economic considerations on the other side—considerations sufficient to be appreciated by such officials, but not sufficient to surmount the justificatory threshold of Mary's rights. I do not see how our utilitarian or economic-minded official can regard these considerations as irrelevant to what he ought, ultimately, to do. He must regard them as providing arguments for deviating from existing rules, or for changing them, despite their justification. His primary aim, after all, is the promotion of welfare or efficiency. He must always consider arguments for promoting it directly, when he has the opportunity to do so. If so, he must be understood as prepared to violate Mary's legal rights—even though they are supposed to be morally defensible, from which it seems to follow that they have moral force and thus rule out unrestricted, direct, incremental utilitarian reasoning.

That is, a utilitarian official must be willing to reason as follows: "Mary's legal rights are clear, as is the utilitarian justification for allowing her to acquire such rights and to have them made enforceable by law. Even if this is an exceptional case, the same indirect utilitarian arguments continue to hold.

124   DAVID LYONS

Utilitarian legislators would be well advised not to modify the rules, should they have occasion to do so. These rules are as well designed, from a utilitarian standpoint, as any such rules can be. They cannot usefully be adjusted to take into account every special case that may arise under them. And, taking the utilitarian risks into account, it seems equally clear that welfare would be better served by not enforcing Mary's rights in this particular case." Acceptance of reasoning like this shows that such a theorist cannot fully accept the normative implications of his claim that Mary's legal rights are morally defensible. He cannot regard Mary's rights as making that difference to the evaluation of conduct that we supposed those rights do. For such reasoning cannot justify an infringement upon Mary's rights, though he is prepared to entertain it.

One might try to answer this objection in the following way: "An official who faces such a decision has more utilitarian reason to adhere to the rules than he has to depart from them. For an official who understands the utilitarian arguments for the rules appreciates that they assume general compliance on the part of officials as well as private citizens. This provides him with a general reason for believing that a departure from the rules is likely to do more harm than good. Furthermore, in any particular case it is likely that the direct utilitarian gains will be seen to be outweighed by the direct utilitarian costs of departing from the rules, resulting, for example, from frustrated expectations. It is therefore unreasonable to believe that a utilitarian official would depart from the rules instead of enforcing Mary's rights."

This argument requires that two points be made. In the first place, from the fact that a sound utilitarian argument is available for a legal rule it does not follow that utility will be maximized by adhering to the rules in each and every case. Conditions vary, and a sensitive utilitarian official will presumably be flexible. In the second place, the original argument can be understood as implying that officials *have an obligation* to comply with morally defensible rules that establish rights—an obligation that is not equivalent to the implications of direct utilitarian reasoning. Like Mary's rights, this obligation is not "absolute"; it can be overridden by substantial countervailing considerations. But, given Mary's rights and this corresponding obligation, direct, unrestricted, incremental utilitarian reasoning on the part of officials is ruled out. It is of course quite possible that direct utilitarian reasoning would yield conclusions that conform to Mary's rights; but this cannot be assumed. And the two modes of reasoning should not be confused.

A utilitarian might now reply in either of two ways. He might reject the pattern of reasoning that is entailed by talk of rights and obligations and maintain that we would be better off not to think in such terms. I do not address this issue here. My argument is meant to show certain difficulties that arise for utilitarian and comparable theories when they seek to *accommodate* rights (and obligations) under institutions they endorse.

Alternatively, a utilitarian might claim that a responsible utilitarian official would adopt a secondary principle (or perhaps a "rule of thumb") that requires him to adhere to the rules of utilitarian institutions. Such a principle, it may be said, is functionally equivalent to the idea that an official is under an obligation to adhere to the rules and to respect the rights they confer.

This line of reasoning seems, however, to concede the point at issue. To make it plausible, one must suppose that experience demonstrates that utility is best served in the long run if one reasons just as if one was under such an obligation. But systematic evidence to this effect is rarely, if ever, offered. A utilitarian who argues in this way appreciates the force of the original objection but retains the hope of *somehow* finding utilitarian arguments to meet it. He offers us no more than a promissory note, without any assurance that it can be honored.

Bentham never faced this issue squarely, and I do not think that Mill did either. They seem to assume either of two things: either that, once the rules are justified, they must be followed; or else that particular cases simply cannot arise such that the justified rules require one thing and the direct application of the utilitarian standard to those cases requires another. Bentham and Mill were, perhaps, prevented from considering such difficulties by the assumption that, once justified rules are established, the legal recognition of the rights they confer change circumstances so that certain possible courses of action have added utility or disutility. Thus, it may be thought that there is always sufficient utilitarian reason of a direct kind to

126   DAVID LYONS

argue against deviation from justified rules. But this, as I have
already suggested, cannot be assumed. Moreover, reasoning
like this does not meet the point of the objection, which is that
once those morally defensible rights are established, certain
modes of reasoning are *illicit*.

Economists have not faced this issue squarely either. This is
because they have not generally considered the implications of
their economic "analysis" when it becomes a normative position.
They are thus faced with a significant theoretical decision.
Either they shall consider efficiency the sole fundamental basis
for normative appraisals, of conduct as well as of institutions,
in which case they must accept the consequences of the foregoing
argument. Or they must accept the idea that there are other
values to be served, beyond economic efficiency, in which case
they must entertain the possiblity of rights and obligations that
are independent of social recognition and enforcement, rights
and obligations that justified legal institutions ought to respect.

The problem I have sketched may be summarized as follows.
Normative theories that are founded on certain values, such as
welfare or efficiency, quite naturally regard legal rules or
institutions as justified if they are supported by the best arguments in those terms. But such theories do not generate any
obligation to adhere to the rules that they regard as justified.
And they cannot do so unless they are restricted for just such
a purpose.

THE RELEVANCE OF RULE-UTILITARIANISM

A type of theory that might seem to meet this objection is
"rule-utilitarianism." In its relevant forms, rule-utilitarianism
limits the application of the standard of utility to rules or social
institutions and *requires compliance* with rules that are certified
as having the requisite utilitarian justification. I do not mean to
suggest that such a theory is incoherent. But, before proceeding
further, we should distinguish two types of rule-utilitarian
theory, only one of which is directly relevant to the present
argument.

One type of rule-utilitarian theory seeks to accommodate the
idea of moral obligations (and, derivatively, moral rights). It

concerns itself with the "ideal moral rules" for a community or an "ideal moral code."[10] Another type of rule-utilitarian theory is concerned with established laws that can be defended on utilitarian grounds. It concerns itself with obligations to comply with useful social institutions. The latter, not the former, is most relevant here. For we are concerned with the question what difference it makes, from a moral point of view, to have laws and social institutions that are morally defensible. A rule-utilitarian of the first type does not address himself to this question, at least not in any direct way. But a rule-utilitarian of the second type in effect addresses himself to this question. This is the sort of rule-utilitarianism suggested (though not endorsed) by Rawls.[11]

My point about this sort of theory is that it represents a qualified utilitarian position. It does not follow from the more basic idea, common to all forms of utilitarianism, that human welfare is to be promoted. Nor does it follow from the more specific idea that social rules are to be evaluated in utilitarian terms.

What can be understood to follow from the fact that an institution can be supported by the best utilitarian arguments? If it follows that the rules must be respected (or at least that there is a moral obligation to respect them), then the utilitarian has a basis for claiming that his theory accommodates legal rights with moral force. But not so otherwise. The question may be understood as follows. If a utilitarian believes that certain rules are justified on utilitarian grounds, does he *contradict* himself by supposing that direct utilitarian arguments for deviating from the rules may be entertained? I see no contradiction here. If so, the utilitarian cannot understand the legal impact of such rules automatically to translate into moral force, not even when those rules are supported by the best utilitarian arguments. He cannot regard the morally defensible rights under *utilitarian* institutions as having moral force.

If so, The Legal Rights Inclusion Thesis must be qualified drastically, so that it becomes a morally uninteresting platitude. It cannot be understood to say that utilitarianism and comparable theories accommodate legal rights with their moral force intact, even when those rights are conferred by rules regarded as justified under such theories. It can be understood to say only that utilitarianism and comparable theories accept the possibility of justified institutions with rights that must be regarded as *merely* legal, devoid of moral force. For these theories do not allow the rights conferred by justified institutions to make the requisite difference to the evaluation of conduct that such rights are ordinarily assumed to do.

We can apply this to Rawls's argument, in which he suggested that a utilitarian official would abide by the rules of institutions he regards as justified. We can understand Rawls's argument in either of two ways. He might be taken as suggesting that regarding rules as justified on utilitarian grounds *logically commits* one to abiding by their implications in particular cases. I have just tried to show that this is a mistake. Alternatively, Rawls might be understood as proposing that utilitarians *restrict their theory* so that it applies to rules or institutions but not to conduct under them. This is, I believe, a reasonable way of reading Rawls's suggestion, and the foregoing argument implies that it is the more generous of these two alternative readings.

For nothing in the idea that welfare is to be promoted restricts the application of the standard of utility to social rules or institutions. If such a restriction is *adopted* by a theorist who sees himself as working within the utilitarian tradition, that involves the *addition* of a factor that a utilitarian is not obliged to accept, either by the constraints of logic or by the normative implications of his theory. In the absence of such a factor, a utilitarian cannot ignore direct utilitarian arguments.

Imposing such a restriction on the idea that human welfare is to be promoted is either arbitrary or else is motivated by a desire to accommodate the moral force of rights and obligations under justified rules. In its relevant forms, rule-utilitarianism represents a compromise—a recognition that the utilitarian approach is incomplete at best and, unless it is restricted, cannot accommodate the moral force of morally defensible legal rights and obligations.

Similar considerations apply to normative theories based on the goal of economic efficiency. If the moral force of legal rights and obligations under justified institutions is to be accommodated, then those theories must be restricted. And restricting them reopens general questions about the standards to be used in evaluating institutions themselves.

It may be thought that I have overstated my case. I have suggested that a utilitarian (unless he restricts his theory to accommodate objections) will evaluate conduct by means of direct utilitarian considerations—in effect, by "act-utilitarian" reasoning. But, it may be objected, from the fact that an institution is supported by the best utilitarian arguments it must be thought by a utilitarian to follow that one has reason to conform to the rules of that institution. I have ignored, it may be said, the direct practical implications that the utilitarian justification of social rules or institutions has for a utilitarian.

If this were correct, then the most that could be claimed is that utilitarianism gives rise in such contexts to *conflicting* considerations. The foregoing reasoning would not show that direct utilitarian arguments concerning conduct are *excluded* by a utilitarian justification of the institutions within the context of which that conduct may take place. It would show only that such arguments must be weighed within utilitarianism against arguments flowing from the utilitarian justification of those institutions. Then the most that could be said for utilitarianism is either that one who follows its dictates would not violate the rights it regards as justified as often as my argument implies (thought he would violate them sometimes) or else that utilitarianism is indeterminate in such cases, in which event it would not require that such rights as it regards as morally defensible ought to be respected.

If they are sound, such consequences cannot offer much comfort to the utilitarian. But are they sound? I think not. To see this, we must distinguish between (1) a reason for maintaining an institution and (2) a reason for conforming to institutional rules. It is reasonable to suppose that the utilitarian justification of an institution provides a utilitarian with a reason of type (1), that is, a reason for maintaining that institution. But we cannot assume that a reason of type (2) likewise follows. The utilitarian justification of an institution provides a reason for conforming to that institution *only if* conformity to its rules is required, in the circumstances, for maintaining that institution. But this is just what we cannot assume. For it is possible for the rules to be violated (by officials or private individuals) without threatening the institution—more precisely, without threatening its utility. In such a case, the utilitarian justification of the institution

130   DAVID LYONS

provides the utilitarian himself with no reason for conforming to its rules—not when greater utility accrues to deviation from them.

Someone might approach this issue differently. One reason why indirect utilitarian considerations, concerning rules and institutions, do not converge with direct utilitarian considerations, concerning individuals' conduct, is that real social rules must be simple enough for the practical guidance of ordinary mortals and also typically involve social costs. These costs include sanctions designed to coerce officials and private individuals into following the law when they may be tempted to act otherwise. A person might therefore reason that an official would be strongly constrained to follow rules that are predicated upon serving human welfare when those rules have been properly designed. One might suppose that a utilitarian institution would be contrived so as to make it very undesirable for an official to depart from rules that he is charged with administering. Useful sanctions might seem to insure that Mary's rights would be respected.

But we cannot assume that such expedients will do the trick. In the first place, we cannot assume that maximally useful rules, or rules supported by the best utilitarian arguments, would always be sufficiently constraining to prevent deviation from them. In the second place, someone who is guided by utilitarian considerations should not be influenced so decisively by considerations of self-interest as this suggestion assumes. He should be willing to accept a risk himself, for the sake of serving the *general* welfare more effectively, as the direct utilitarian arguments that counsel infringements on Mary's rights show possible.

Alternatively, one might assume that an official would not deviate from rules that he is charged with administering, because he would think it *wrong* to do so. One might suppose, for example, that an official would regard himself as having accepted a position of public trust, which involves obligations that he cannot in good conscience ignore. He might see himself as morally bound by his commitment to adhere to the rules as he finds them. But, if we suppose that such a factor is at work in our example, then we are assuming, in effect, the influence of *non*utilitarian arguments. If the argument suggested here is to make any difference, it must be based on the idea of an independent obligation that does not follow from the considerations already canvassed. To have recourse to such obligations, however, is to concede that utilitarian principles need supplementation before we can secure a normative theory that is capable of accommodating ordinary legal rights with moral force.

EXTENSION OF THE ARGUMENT

As we have already observed, this argument would not seem limited to utilitarianism, but concerns also the relationship of rights to other closely related theories, such as economic analysis when offered as a normative approach to law or social policy. But the considerations that extend the argument that far suggest that it must extend much further.[12] The argument would seem to concern all "goal-based" theories that satisfy two conditions: (1) the goal or goals accepted by the theory as the basis for appraising institutions are capable of being served not only through institutional design but also by the actions of individuals when their conduct falls under the scope of the institutional rules; (2) the goal or goals do not (separately or together) entail some value that demands respect for rules that are favorably appraised in relation to them. The latter condition is vague, and I am not sure what sort of goal might fail to meet it. It simply seems necessary to allow that some goals might satisfy condition (1) but would also require respect for the rights conferred by institutions that serve those goals, in the way that welfare, happiness, economic efficiency, and the like do not.

To illustrate the way the argument might be extended—imagine that we dedicate a legal system to the service of social and economic equality—a useful example, since this value is often contrasted with utility and is believed to conflict with the latter in practice. The same sorts of problems concerning rights accrue to a theory based on promoting substantive equality as attach to one based on human welfare or economic efficiency. For the rules of institutions might be contrived to serve social and economic equality as far as it is possible for rules to do, but

132   DAVID LYONS

it would still be possible for social and economic equality to be
served (perhaps in small ways) by deviation from those rules in
particular cases. There is nothing about the basic value to be
served that requires respect for all the rights that may be
conferred by such institutions.

If we explored this issue further, we might find that a very
wide range of goal-based normative theories have the same
trouble with legal rights. We might also find that other sorts of
theories (e.g., "right-based" and "duty-based" theories) face
similar difficulties.

What all of this seems to show is that normative theories
require a more complex character than those we have considered
if they are to accommodate the moral force of legal rights under
justified institutions. Many theories fail to account for an
obligation to adhere to rules that are regarded by them as
justified. From the assumption that rules serve appropriate
values it does not seem to follow that there is the requisite sort
of obligation to adhere to them, an obligation that gives due
respect to the morally defensible rights conferred by those rules.

If a utilitarian (or other goal-based) theory of *moral* obligations
were possible, it might fill the gap just noted. It might explain
how we have moral obligations to comply with social institutions
that are predicated on serving the general welfare, for example.
We cannot assume that a utilitarian theory of moral obligations
would generate precisely this obligation, but the possibility of
a normative utilitarian theory of legal rights would be revived.

This development is ironic, for it rests the possibility of a
normative theory of *legal* rights upon the possibility of a theory
of *moral* obligations, though the former is usually thought to be
much less problematic than the latter. In any case, it brings us
round full circle. We began by noting the traditional utilitarian
attitude toward moral rights, embraced by Bentham, which is
similar to the traditional utilitarian attitude toward moral obligations (when obligations are not confused with whatever happens to be required by some sort of normative principle). Like
rights, obligations have a normative life of their own, with
implications that are neither reducible to, nor traceable by,
direct considerations of utility. It does not follow, however, that
a utilitarian theory of moral rights or obligations is impossible.

MILL'S THEORY OF MORAL RIGHTS AND OBLIGATIONS

In previous works I have offered a sympathetic reading of Mill's theory of morality and justice, in order to challenge the usual view that utilitarianism is incapable of accommodating either moral rights or moral obligations. (In recent years emphasis has been placed on rights, but obligations received more, and similar, attention a half century ago.) I would like now to summarize that argument briefly and show why it seems to fail. Considerations relevant to the main argument, concerning legal rights, apply here too.

Mill's theory is promising because (under the interpretation I have offered) his way of trying to accommodate moral rights and obligations is not a form of ad hoc revisionism motivated by the desire to evade substantive objections to utilitarianism. It is not a form of revisionism at all, but turns on a theory of the moral concepts, the relations among which establish constraints upon any normative theory. Instead of adopting (what has since been thought of as) the standard utilitarian approach to moral reasoning—instead of assuming that one is always required to promote a certain value to the maximum degree possible—Mill begins by sketching a stratified analysis of normative concepts.

Mill's general idea can be understood as follows. We can distinguish three levels of normative concepts and judgments. For present purposes, the bottom (most concrete) level concerns the rightness or wrongness, justice or injustice, morality or immorality of particular acts. The intermediate, second level consists of moral principles, which concern (general) moral rights and obligations. Judgments of right and wrong conduct at the bottom level are functions of moral rights and obligations, and of nothing else. (Since moral rights are assumed to be correlative to obligations, but not vice versa, this can be put solely in terms of obligations.) A particular act is right if and only if it does not breach a moral obligation, unless that obligation has been overridden by another obligation. But moral principles are not self-certifying; they turn upon values they somehow serve (Mill is least clear about this relation). The

134   DAVID LYONS

topmost level of normative judgments and concepts concerns the values that may be invoked to establish moral principles (which concern general moral rights and obligations). For Mill, of course, the value at work at this topmost level is human happiness or welfare. So, moral principles about general rights and obligations are supposed to have a direct relationship to the principle of utility. But judgments concerning the rightness or wrongness of particular actions have *no* such relation. Acts must be judged as right or wrong depending on whether they respect moral rights and obligations, and *never* on the basis of direct utilitarian reasoning.

This feature of Mill's reconstructed analytic theory is vital to the possibility of a utilitarian account of moral rights and obligations. It insures that Mill's theory does not collapse into act-utilitarianism. It insures, more generally, that the evaluation of conduct in his theory is not dominated by direct utilitarian considerations. Mill's way of insuring this is by conceptual analysis, which leads to the claim that moral concepts are so stratified that interactions are possible between adjacent levels but are absolutely prohibited between the top and bottom levels. Without this conceptual foundation, his theory would either collapse into act-utilitarianism or amount to just another, more or less arbitrary, revision of utilitarianism.

Mill's conceptual claims provide a necessary (though not a sufficient) condition for accommodating moral rights and obligations, if we assume that moral rights and obligations possess normative force (which Mill suggests). In the present context, that makes possible the hope that his theory will generate a moral obligation to conform to the actual rules of institutions that can be defended on utilitarian grounds, so that the theory will require respect for the rights conferred by such rules.

The success of Mill's theory thus turns upon the truth of his conceptual claims. But these seem stronger than the moral concepts can bear. It is plausible to hold that what is right or wrong is at least in part a function of moral rights and obligations (this is what is meant by the normative force of moral rights and obligations). But it is not so plausible to hold that the concepts involved *completely prohibit* the direct appeal to ultimate values, such as human welfare, when evaluating conduct. On the view I have ascribed to Mill—the one that promises a way of accommodating moral rights and obligations—someone who evaluates conduct by means of direct utilitarian arguments is guilty of a conceptual mistake. He is not reasoning unsoundly; he is reasoning *fallaciously*. But this appears excessive, to say the least; and yet nothing short of this will secure Mill's moral principles from being dominated by direct utilitarian considerations.

Consider, for example, our imaginary utilitarian official. When he takes into account the effects of his conduct on human welfare while trying to decide what to do, he does not seem to be confused or to be violating the constraints of the moral concepts. If he places too much weight upon direct utilitarian considerations, that may be a moral error, but it does not look like a conceptual mistake. As a utilitarian, it seems incumbent on him to consider the effects of his conduct on welfare. If so, we have no reason to believe that direct utilitarian considerations will not dominate his moral reasoning. Thus, we have no reason to believe that a satisfactory utilitarian theory of *moral* rights and obligations can be developed. So we have no reason to believe that a utilitarian would be obliged to respect the moral force of justified *legal* rights and obligations.

SUMMARY

A utilitarian might be assumed to reason as follows. "I will have no truck with 'moral rights,' which are figments of unenlightened moralists' imaginations. I am concerned with human welfare, with promoting it as far as possible, and I approve of social institutions to the extent they serve that purpose. Those institutions are morally defensible, and no others are. Under them, people have rights—not imaginary, toothless rights, but real, enforceable rights."

This was Bentham's attitude (though not Mill's), and it fits the normative thinking found most generally in the literature of "economic analysis." The trouble is, it ignores a central normative issue, what conduct is required or permitted by the theory that endorses those allegedly justifiable rights.

Economists might be excused for neglecting this issue—at least until it is pointed out to them—since they tend to think only about rules and regulations and to ignore how principles apply directly to individuals' conduct, perhaps because they have not approached their normative conclusions from a self-consciously normative standpoint. But utilitarians have no such excuse. As Bentham was aware, the aim of promoting some value like human welfare is as relevant to individual acts as it is to social institutions; the latter application does not rule out the former. But, unless utilitarianism is restricted, its direct application to conduct undermines respect for the very rights it wishes to endorse.

NOTES

* This is a revised version of a paper presented to the annual meeting of the American Society for Political and Legal Philosophy on January 4, 1980. An earlier version with a narrower focus, entitled "Utility as a Possible Ground of Rights," was published in *Nous*, 14 (March 1980), 17–28. In arriving at the views developed in these articles, as well as in revising them, I have been helped considerably by comments I have received from a number of individuals. These articles developed out of earlier presentations on the subject of utility and rights at the University of Texas, the University of Virginia, Colgate University, and Cornell University. On those occasions I sought to extend the utilitarian account of rights I had earlier extracted from John Stuart Mill's writings. Criticism of Mill's theory of moral rights led me to question the less controversial assumption about legal rights that is principally discussed here. I wish especially to thank John Bennett, Jules Coleman, Stephen Massey, Richard Miller, and Robert Summers for their comments on previous drafts.

1. See my "Human Rights and the General Welfare," *Philosophy & Public Affairs* 6 113–29 (1977) and "Mill's Theory of Justice," in A. I. Goldman and J. Kim, eds., *Values and Morals*, (Dordrecht: Reidel, 1978), pp 1–20.
2. See, e.g., Richard A. Posner, "Utilitarianism, Economics, and Legal Theory," 8 *J. Legal Stud.* 103–40 (1979) which also provides references to some of the relevant legal and economic literature.
3. It is sometimes suggested that economic analysis is capable of taking full account of competing normative claims, such as claims about justice or moral rights, by treating them as expressions of individuals' preferences (preferences frustrated when institutions

er cannot

would be regarded by such individuals as violating moral rights or breaching other moral principles). See, e.g., Guido Calabresi and A. Douglas Melamed, "Property Rules, Liability Rules, and Inalienability: One View of the Cathedral," 85 *Harv. L. Rev.* 1089–1128 (1972). But this is inadequate. Someone who claims, for example, that slavery is morally unacceptable because it violates basic human rights may be expressing a preference against slavery, but he is doing more than that. He is claiming in this context that considerations of efficiency alone *could not justify* slavery. The question to be faced is not whether slavery will frustrate preferences but whether that claim is true. To understand this as a question about preferences (even enlarging it to include the preferences of people other than those who embrace the claim) is to look at these matters from the standpoint of economic analysis, and thus to beg the very question at issue, namely, whether economically efficient institutions can be morally unacceptable *because* they violate rights.

4. It is sometimes suggested that when we speak of "moral" rights we are referring to rights that ought to be conferred and enforced by social institutions. On this view, a utilitarian's normative theory of institutional rights is equivalent to a theory of moral rights. This notion does not affect the present argument. I believe it, however, to be mistaken. To say that rights ought to be *respected* is not to imply that they ought to be *enforced* (even by extralegal institutions). Respect for rights can simply amount to doing what the corresponding obligations require, and from the fact that one is under an obligation (even an obligation correlative with another person's rights) it does not follow that any sort of coercion, strictly speaking, is justified for the purpose of insuring obligatory performances or penalizing nonperformance.

5. For Bentham's analysis of rights, see my "Rights, Claimants, and Beneficiaries," 6 *American Philosophical Quarterly*, 173–85 (1969), and H. L. A. Hart, "Bentham on Legal Rights," in A. W. B. Simpson, ed., *Oxford Essays in Jurisprudence* (Second Series) (Oxford: Clarendon Press, 1973), pp 171–201. Bentham did accept the idea of "natural liberties," but only in the sense that one is "free" to do whatever is not restricted by coercive social rules.

6. The sort of exaggeration cautioned against here is unfortunately suggested by Ronald Dworkin's speaking of rights as "trumps" against utilitarian arguments. See his "Taking Rights Seriously," in *Taking Rights Seriously* (Cambridge, Mass.: Harvard University Press, 1978), pp 184–205. But, as Dworkin makes clear, he does not assume that rights are generally "absolute"; see, e.g., pp 191–92. My suggestion that rights have normative (or moral) force derives from Dworkin's discussion, but differs from it in several

138   DAVID LYONS

ways. (1) I distinguish moral from legal rights and attribute moral
force to legal rights only when they are morally defensible or
justified. (2) The normative force of rights cannot be understood
simply in terms of their relation to utilitarian arguments but must
be considered more generally; my discussion attempts to allow
that. (3) Dworkin's distinction between "strong" and "weak" rights
corresponds roughly to the two aspects of normative force in my
discussion: "strong" rights provide obstacles to the justification of
others' interference, while "weak" rights provide justifications for
one's own behavior. Dworkin's argument seems to rely on both
aspects of the normative force of rights.

7. Dworkin seems to assume that all legal rights have moral force.
    See his "Reply to Critics," *Taking Rights Seriously*, pp 326–27.

8. See John Rawls, "Two Concepts of Rules," 64 *Philosophical Review*
    3–32 (1955).

9. This point does not depart from the main thesis of *Forms and Limits
    of Utilitarianism* (Oxford: Clarendon Press, 1965), in which I argued
    for the "extensional equivalence" of certain principles that I called
    "simple" and "general" utilitarianism. The extensional equivalence
    argument was extended to cover a limiting case of rule-utilitarian-
    ism—a theory (dubbed "primitive" rule-utilitarianism) in which no
    consideration is given to such things as the complexity or cost of
    rules. Rule-utilitarian theories that concern themselves with ordi-
    nary, manageable social rules were explicitly excluded from the
    scope of that argument. Thus, *Forms and Limits* argues, in effect,
    that direct and indirect utilitarian arguments are *sometimes* equiv-
    alent. Along with this chapter, however, it assumes that they are
    not always equivalent.

10. See, e.g., R. B. Brandt, "Some Merits of One Form of Rule-
    Utilitarianism," *University of Colorado Studies, Series in Philosophy*
    39–65 (1967).

11. In "Two Concepts of Rules," note 8, *supra*.

12. I owe this suggesttion to Jules Coleman.

[26]

Economics and Philosophy, 5, 1989, 167–187. Printed in the United States of America.

RIGHTS, INDIRECT UTILITARIANISM, AND CONTRACTARIANISM

ALAN P. HAMLIN
The University, Southampton, England

1. INTRODUCTION

Economic approaches to both social evaluation and decision-making are typically Paretian or utilitarian in nature and so display commitments to both welfarism and consequentialism.[1,2] The contrast between the economic approach and any rights-based social philosophy has spawned a large literature that may be divided into two branches. The first is concerned with the compatibility of rights and utilitarianism (or Paretianism) seen as independent moral forces (e.g., the debate on the possibility of a Paretian liberal[3]). This branch of the literature may be characterized as an example of the broader debate between the teleological and deontological approaches. The second is concerned with the possibility that substantial rights may be grounded in utilitarianism (or Paretianism) with the moral force of rights being derived from more basic commitments to welfarism and consequentialism. This branch of the

An earlier version of this essay was prepared during a visit to the Australian National University. This version has benefited from seminar discussion at A.N.U., the Universities of Adelaide and Flinders, Southampton and East Anglia. I am particularly grateful to Geoffrey Brennan, John Gray, Philip Pettit, Robert Sugden, Jack Wiseman, and the editors and referees of *Economics and Philosophy* for their helpful comments.

1. For definitions and general discussion of welfarism and consequentialism in related contexts see Sen (1979a, 1979b, 1985, 1987), Williams (1973), and the Introduction to Sen and Williams (1982).
2. Hamlin (1986) provides a critical overview of the economic approach and its relationship with rights.
3. For this debate, see Sen (1970, 1976, 1983) and the many references therein.

167

literature may be characterized as an exploration of the flexibility of the teleological approach, and, in particular, its ability to give rise to views more normally associated with the deontological approach. This essay is concerned with the second branch of the literature.

While the debate continues, the view that *directly* consequentialist and welfarist reasoning cannot support rights as anything more substantial than "socially useful illusions"[4] is widespread, and I shall support it in Section 3. Recently there have been a number of attempts to argue that *indirect* consequentialism and welfarism of one variety or another can succeed where their direct counterparts have apparently failed.[5] I wish to argue that the grounding of substantive rights in indirectly welfarist and consequentialist logic fails, but that this failure is instructive in that it suggests a more contractarian defense of rights might succeed.[6]

I use the term *indirect* consequentialism or welfarism in the spirit of Williams (1973) and others (Gray, 1984; Parfit, 1984; Regan, 1980; Sumner, 1987) to indicate a strategy that involves the identification of distinct levels of analysis such that direct consequentialism or welfarism is appropriate primarily, or only, at the highest and most abstract level. The direct application of the basic principle at this critical level is then argued to support the adoption of some distinct and strictly subsidiary principle at the lower, practical level. The indirectly utilitarian argument in support of substantial rights is that the proper consideration of the principle of utility at the critical level of analysis will lead to the adoption of substantial individual rights at the practical level. It is argument of this general form that this essay seeks to rebut. Indirectly consequentialist or welfarist strategies may fall outside of the rubric of indirect utilitarianism, and my argument is intended to encompass all such indirect strategies, although it will be convenient at several points in the argument to focus explicitly on the rather narrower class of indirectly utilitarian strategies.

My discussion will involve maintaining a distinction between the role of rights in social evaluation and their role in the determination of action. I shall also make use of a somewhat novel taxonomy of the status of rights within each of these roles in order to clarify my interpretation of "substantial" rights. The next section provides details of these elements of the argument. Thereafter, Section 3 characterizes the tensions

4. Rawls (1971, p. 28). For an influential statement of this position, see Lyons (1980, 1982).
5. See, for example, Gibbard (1984), Gray (1984), Griffin (1984, 1986), Hare (1981), the exchange between Mackie (1984) and Hare (1984), Harsanyi (1985a, 1985b), Pettit (1986, 1988), and Sumner (1987).
6. For alternative versions of the contractarian perspective on rights, see Buchanan (1975), Gauthier (1986), Hamlin (1986, 1989), Narveson (1984), Rawls (1971), and Sugden (1986). For relevant comparisons between utilitarianism and contractarianism, see Griffin (1986) and Scanlon (1982).

between rights and directly consequentialist and welfarist positions and identifies the range of strategies that might be deployed to escape these tensions. The critique of strategies involving indirect welfarism and consequentialism is contained in Section 4. Section 5 then sketches a contractarian approach to rights and indicates that it is not subject to the criticisms aimed at the indirectly utilitarian approach.

2. THE ROLE AND STATUS OF RIGHTS

The volume of literature devoted to the analysis of rights in recent years makes it abundantly clear that there are formidable difficulties in identifying the core of the concept of a right. Fortunately, most of the difficulties encountered in that literature are of little relevance in the present context. More precisely, I am concerned with just two aspects of the analysis of rights – their role and their status – and will discuss these in more detail later. I do not need to specify other aspects of rights with any precision, I could adopt the Hohfeldian distinctions between claims, liberties, powers, and immunities and phrase the discussion that follows in terms of these categories. Alternatively, I could adopt the distinction discussed by Sumner (1987) between rights as protected choices and rights as protected interests and utilize that vocabulary. Other possibilities exist: for example, much of what follows could be reworded in the language of duties rather than rights. However, I shall simply talk of rights throughout this essay (with one or two exceptions where further specification clarifies the discussion) leaving the reader to provide his or her own preferred qualification. The reason for this is that I believe that the arguments presented here apply – sometimes with minor amendment – to a wide variety of interpretations of the concept of a right, and I wish the arguments to be read in that general setting.

But I do need to be more specific regarding the role and status of rights. It is straightforward to distinguish two conceptual roles that may be played by rights (this is not intended to exclude other possible roles). First, rights may be directly involved in the evaluation of social states so that, for example, the violation of a particular right may influence the evaluation of society in a manner that is independent of any further consequences of that violation.[7] I term this the role of rights in evaluation. The second role then concerns the impact of rights on the determination of action so that, for example, the existence of a particular right may influence an individual's choice of action in a manner that is independent of any further consequences of the actions under consideration. I term this the role of rights in decision-making.

---

7. I shall follow the useful convention of referring to a justified transgression of a right as an *infringement*, and an unjustified transgression as a *violation*. Where justification is in doubt I shall use *transgression*.

In each of these roles the status of rights requires further specification. Direct consequentialism – which holds that decisions on actions are to be made solely by reference to the valuations (or expected valuations) of the social states that are consequent upon those actions – clearly imposes the restriction that the status of a right in its decision-making role is determined by its status in its evaluation role, in such a way that the status of the right must be identical in the two settings. But since consequentialism in this strong form is part of what is to be questioned in what follows, this restriction will not be imposed at the outset. Thus, the status of a right in the context of decision-making will be held to be conceptually independent of its status in the context of evaluation.

Status is an essentially quantitative concept. In both evaluation and decision-making, the status of a right may be conceived as lying on the continuum from zero to infinity. I intend to divide this range into just four regions. This proposed taxonomy of the status of rights focuses on the two endpoints of the continuum and on two alternative interpretations of the middle ground.

At one extreme lies the view that, in the context of decision-making, rights are complete constraints on action. The equivalent view in the context of evaluation holds that all rights are equally of infinite value in the sense that they are incommensurably prior to any other contributor to value. In this view, rights are not just "trumps" – each right is equally the ace of trumps. I shall refer to these views on the status of rights as *constraint rights* and *absolute rights*, respectively.[8] Clearly, a commitment to both absolute rights and direct consequentialism implies a commitment to constraint rights, but there will be other ways of arriving at the constraint-right view.

At the opposite extreme of the taxonomic scheme lies the view that, in the context of decision-making, rights are merely guides to those choices that may normally be expected to be good – "shadows cast by calculations of utility" in Gray's phrase (1984, p. 74). The equivalent view in the context of evaluation holds that rights are of no intrinsic value and are to be viewed purely instrumentally in the calculation of value. As a matter of terminology, I shall refer to these views on the status of rights as the *guide rights* and *instrumental rights*, respectively.

As usual, most interest focuses on the treatment of the middle ground. In the context of evaluation, the first possibility here may be termed the *goal-rights* approach, following Sen (1982). A goal-rights approach specifies rights observance as a goal standing alongside and commensurable with other goals, each of which contributes to social value. It is as if each right carries with it a moral reservation price that identifies the extent of the loss in social value attributable to the violation

---

8. This usage of absolute right is in accord with the usage in Feinberg (1978).

RIGHTS, INDIRECT UTILITARIANISM, AND CONTRACTARIANISM 171

of that right per se. Characterizing rights as goal rights clearly provides them with independent status in evaluation that is denied to an instrumental right. If absolute rights can be thought of as being equally the ace of trumps, then goal rights are cards like any others, each card with a specified face value to be played in a game with no trumps.

In Sen's original usage a goal-rights system operated in both the evaluative and decision-making roles. Sen was concerned to show, inter alia, that a goal-rights view at the evaluative level was sufficient to provide a consequentialist with good reason to take rights seriously at the level of decision-making. Given the different purpose here, I must depart from this usage. I will refer to the equivalent view in the context of decision-making as a *compensable-rights* view, indicating that the decision-maker will weigh the finite intrinsic value of a right in the decision calculus and infringe a right only if the gains from such action are sufficient to allow full compensation.

The alternative approach to the middle ground may be termed, in the context of evaluation, as the restricted-absolute-rights approach. This cumbersomely labelled approach operates by distinguishing two classes of argument and then claiming that a right is absolute (i.e., incommensurably prior) with respect to one class of argument, but offers only contingent protection (or no protection at all) against arguments of the other class. Detailed positions may vary in their identification of precisely which arguments are in which class, but they share the idea that rights are of incommensurably prior value over a restricted domain. In this way, restricted-absolute rights can be thought of as the result of holding an absolute-rights view in one domain and either an instrumental-rights or a goal-rights view in the complementary domain. For obvious reasons, I shall refer to the equivalent view of rights in the decision-making context as the *restricted-constraint* approach.

The restricted-absolute approach values rights above certain types of argument, regardless of their weight, while the goal-rights approach values rights above arguments of certain weights, regardless of their type. On the restricted-absolute-rights approach, the moral reservation price attaching to a particular right is not uniquely defined, but may vary between zero and infinity, depending on the precise comparison being made.

The taxonomy suggested here is summarized in Table 1. The taxonomy is exhaustive in the sense that any account of the status of a right (in either decision-making or evaluation) can be reduced to one of the four types identified or some combination of them. Each row of Table 1 indicates the linkage between evaluation and decision-making implied by direct consequentialism, so that a commitment to direct consequentialism binds the two columns together.

Having outlined this taxonomy, it is appropriate to conclude this section with some comments on the mapping between the categories it identifies and some of the views established in the literature.

172   ALAN P. HAMLIN

Table 1
Roles and Status of Rights

	Role of Rights	
	Evaluation	Decision-Making
Status of Rights	absolute	constraint
	restricted-absolute	restricted-constraint
	goal	compensable
	instrumental	guide

The Nozickian specification of rights seems to provide a clear example of the constraint-right approach and an equally clear example of a nonconsequentialist view that allows the separation of the role of rights in evaluation from their role in decision-making (Nozick, 1974). As Sen (1982) notes, Nozick's view is that "rights directly affect judgments of actions – and only of actions – rather than being embedded first in the evaluation of states of affairs and then affecting the evaluation of action through consequential links between actions and states" (p. 5). However, Nozick's (1974, p. 30n.) note to the effect that rights may be infringed (as opposed to violated) under threat of "moral catastrophe" suggests that rights are not strictly constraint rights and that some degree of consequentialist argument is allowed. If Nozick's claim is that rights are constraint rights only under normal circumstances, this leaves open the question of whether it is the *type* of an argument (*moral* catastrophe) that can render circumstances abnormal or the *weight* of an argument (moral *catastrophe*). If the former, Nozickian rights can be thought of as a variety of restricted-constraint right with consequentialist links to the restricted-absolute approach. If the latter, Nozickian rights would form a very special case of the compensable-rights approach, in which all rights were granted identical and very large reservation prices or weights, but where the logic of trading off rights against other goals is accepted in principle.

Lyons (1980) provides an example that can be adapted to further illustrate the difficulty involved in specifying rights as constraint rights subject to a requirement of normal circumstances. The example concerns Mary's right to use or not use her driveway and the resultant obligation on others not to block her access. Lyons (1980) suggests that "the driver of an emergency vehicle on an urgent errand might justifiably block her driveway without first obtaining Mary's permission, but that is a special case" (p. 21). But what makes it a special case? Two possibilities arise. The first relates to the presumption of Mary's consent. Faced with the impossibility of gaining Mary's actual prior consent, the emergency driver might – on reasonable grounds – believe that Mary would have given her consent and use this belief to decide on his action. This may well explain the driver's action. But it can only justify that action if the belief concerning Mary's consent is actually true, in which case we might say that the right is neither infringed nor violated, but merely anticipated.

The second possibility is more directly relevant to our present concern. The case of the emergency driver may be special simply because his claim overwhelms Mary's right, thereby indicating that Mary's right could not have been a constraint right at all. As with the general Nozickian right, the question of whether the right is actually a restricted-constraint right or a compensable right remains, but it only obscures this important question to claim that the right is a "constraint right in normal circumstances." This point will be of some importance in what follows, but for the moment we may simply agree with Feinberg (1978) that "if the right is absolute, then I possess it, and others are bound to me in appropriate ways in all circumstances *without exception*" (p. 97, emphasis in original), and extend the point to constraint rights in the nonconsequentialist setting.

Dworkin's (1977) characterization of rights is often taken to place him in the same position as Nozick.[9] Indeed, casting Dworkin's view into the category of constraint rights (absolute rights) seems plausible given the famous claim that: "Individual rights are political trumps held by individuals. Individuals have rights when, for some reason, a collective goal is not a sufficient justification for denying them what they wish, as individuals, to have or to do" (Dworkin, 1977, p. xi). However, further reading renders this categorization problematic. Recall Dworkin's terminology – a *principle* is an argument based on rights, while a *policy* is an argument based on a collective goal. We find that: "Rights may be less than absolute; one principle might have to yield to another, or even to an urgent policy with which it competes on particular facts. We may define the weight of a right, assuming it is not absolute, as its power to withstand such competition" (Dworkin, 1977, p. 92). This strongly suggests that Dworkin's view is more appropriately categorized as a goal-rights/compensable-rights view, in which some reservation prices or weights may be infinite, but where others are clearly both finite and commensurable with other values. The explicit reference to the differential weights of rights and their commensurability with both principles and policies rules out the possibility of a restricted-absolute/restricted-constraint interpretation of Dworkin's position.

A clear example of a restricted-constraint approach is provided by Rowley and Peacock (1975), who argue that rights are absolute and incommensurable with respect to arguments appealing to collective or nonindividuated goals, but may be infringed in order to respect greater rights. This view fits the common metaphor of trumps rather more neatly

---

9. For an argument in support of the similarity between Dworkin's and Nozick's views, see Pettit (1987).

than Dworkin's own view, since each right is held to trump all nonrights, while at the same time there is a strict hierarchy of rights within the trump suit.

3. WELFARISM, CONSEQUENTIALISM, AND RIGHTS

I have already noted that the force of direct consequentialism is to bind together the two columns of Table 1. The force of direct welfarism has an equally simple interpretation in that it enforces the instrumental-rights view in the context of evaluation.

I am here adopting the standard interpretation of welfarism as the requirement that a vector of measures of individual well-being, with one element for each relevant individual, exhausts the stock of ethically relevant information in any particular state of the world.[10] Interpreted in this way, it is immediately clear that welfarism contains both what has been called the principle of individual relevance, which may be crudely stated as the principle that anything that is good must be good for somebody (Hamlin and Pettit, 1989) and a commitment to the intra-personal commensurability of well-being. An alternative interpretation of welfarism that involves intrapersonal incommensurability – a variety of *types* of well-being – will be considered later in this section.

That welfarism enforces the instrumental-rights view is shown by the following argument. The principle of individual relevance denies that rights can have any intrinsic value over and above the value reflected in the well-being of individuals. This immediately rules out the possi-bility of goal-right status in evaluation, since the goal-right formulation requires rights to carry intrinsic value, and this requires a location of value other than individual well-being. Intrapersonal commensurability, then, denies the possibility of holding the well-being generated by rights observance to be lexically prior to well-being derived from other sources, and this, in turn, denies the possibility of either absolute- or restricted-absolute-right status in evaluation since these views of the status of rights in evaluation depend on the existence of patterns of lexical priority. Thus, since welfarism rules out all of the alternatives, the instrumental view of rights in evaluation is implied.

Direct welfarism is responsible for reducing rights to minimal status in the context of evaluation. Direct consequentialism, then, enforces the retention of that minimal status in the context of decision-making. This is the basic structure of all arguments that seek to demonstrate the inability of direct utilitarianism to ground substantial rights. Neverthe-less, it is often suggested that the relevant criticism of utilitarianism is that it "does not take seriously the distinction between persons" (Rawls,

10. This use of welfarism differs slightly from Sen's usage, which focuses on utility as a more restrictive concept than well-being; see Sen (1987, pp. 45–47) for example. For a discussion of alternative conceptions of well-being, see Griffin (1986).

RIGHTS, INDIRECT UTILITARIANISM, AND CONTRACTARIANISM **175**

1971, p. 27), so that it cannot "properly take rights and their non-violation into account" (Nozick, 1974, p. 28). This line of criticism suggests that it is the aggregative element in utilitarianism that is the cause of the inability to take rights seriously. For example, Gray (1984) writes: "the disparity between utility as an aggregative principle and the distributive character of principles about rights and justice . . . expresses a most fundamental divergence in the force of moral principles. . . . The impossibility of a utilitarian derivation of fundamental rights is only a consequence of this fundamental distinction" (p. 74). While not denying the importance of the distinction that concerns Gray, it seems inappropriate to ground the inability to derive substantial rights from direct utilitarianism in this distinction.

Strict Paretianism is an ethical stance that evaluates alternative states of the world in terms of a criterion of vector dominance, so that state A is socially preferred to state B if at least one individual prefers A to B, while no one prefers B to A. In the absence of such dominance states are declared to be noncomparable. The Pareto criterion can be defined in the presence of individual utilities that may be ordinal or cardinal and may or may not allow of interpersonal comparisons.[11] The Pareto criterion itself makes no use of interpersonal comparability and so does not require the existence of any aggregative measure of total well-being. Since the Pareto criterion retains commitments to both welfarism and consequentialism, it is instructive to review the possibility of grounding rights in a directly Paretian argument. For the sake of concreteness, I shall phrase this review in terms of a Hohfeldian liberty (or, alternatively, a right seen as a protected choice). It should be clear that minor variation in the argument will extend the conclusion to other conceptions of rights.

Consider A's right in X that entails A's authority over X in a manner delimited by the similarly limited rights of others. If this right is to be more than a guide right/instrumental right, we must recognize at least two further features of the right. First, in having the right, A must have some real choice concerning X. Feinberg (1980) puts this point clearly when he observes that "to have a right typically is to have some discretion or 'liberty' to exercise it or not as one chooses" (p. 156).[12] Second, in respect of the right being A's, we must recognize that A is placed in a relationship with X that is importantly different from the relationship that exists between B or C and X, where B and C have no rights in X.

The Paretian value judgment cannot ground these necessary features of a substantive right. To see this, we need only note that Paretianism

---

11. Discussions of a variety of assumptions concerning the measurability and interpersonal comparability of welfare can be found in d'Aspremont and Gevers (1977) and Roberts (1980).
12. Similarly "A right, as we have seen, has the function of assuring its holders a measure of autonomy over some specified domain" (Sumner, 1987, p. 150). See also Feinberg (1970).

tells us that uses of X to which B or C object (i.e., which reduce B's or C's utility) fail to pass the relevant criterion and so cannot be justified in directly Paretian terms. The point here is not that Paretianism is incompatible with the existence of substantial rights, but that Paretianism cannot itself ground substantial rights since it cannot grant A discretion over X in cases where B or C's interests suffer. Such situations will always be Pareto noncomparable.

This argument demonstrates that Paretianism, although it allows of a strict pattern of incommensurability between persons, is incapable of providing a direct basis for substantial rights and illustrates the more general proposition that welfarism and consequentialism are sufficient to reduce rights to minimal status in both evaluation and decision-making regardless of the view taken on aggregation.

Starting from a position that incorporates both direct welfarism and direct consequentialism – and so places us on the bottom row of Table 1 – what strategies might be adopted in attempting to take rights more seriously? Three suggest themselves. The first strategy is to deny the standard interpretation of welfarism. There are two interesting possibilities here. The first is to break with the principle of individual relevance and admit rights with intrinsic value over and above any value reflected in measures of personal well-being; this is essentially the strategy adopted by Sen in the goal-rights formulation.

The second possibility involves a move to an alternative interpretation of welfarism, which I shall refer to as *plural welfarism*, motivated by the claim that there are qualitatively distinct types of utility (Riley, 1986, and references therein; Sen, 1981). Under this alternative, each individual is characterized by a vector of well-being indicators, with social welfare being defined on the vector of such vectors. In this setting it may seem possible to construct an argument that rights are of special significance because of the *type* of utility associated with the satisfaction of rights claims, rather than the *quantity* of that utility.

A distinctively plural-welfarist account of rights must claim that the type of well-being generated by satisfaction of rights claims is incommensurably superior to other types of well-being. This claim of lexical superiority amounts to a claim that rights have absolute or restricted-absolute status, but I shall suggest that this claim falls far short of a convincing argument.

If the claim is a claim of fact – that people actually view their own well-being in this way – then it is merely an example of the contingent support for rights available under any interpretation of direct welfarism. If individuals' utility functions are such that the satisfaction of rights claims happens to provide superior well-being, where *superior* may mean either qualitatively or quantitatively better, then such rights claims will be supported. But such a contingency does not provide a welfarist (or plural-welfarist) grounding for rights as absolute or restricted-absolute rights since no argument is advanced as to why individuals will (or should) regard one type of well-being as incommensurably superior to another. The arguments against such intrapersonal incommensurability between aspects of well-being are well rehearsed by Griffin (1986).

If, on the other hand, the claim is a claim about the way in which a social welfare functional should utilize individual well-being data, the plural-welfarist account of rights again fails to ground rights in well-being. The problem here is that the structure of incommensurability is imposed on individuals and is not itself grounded in well-being. This is made particularly clear in Riley (1986, pp. 235–37), where the vector view of well-being is seen as an amoral framework onto which any particular morality can be superimposed by the "guardians" of that morality. In this context plural welfarism may provide a starting point for the attempt to incorporate substantive rights seen as independent moral principles within an otherwise welfarist position, but it cannot be held to provide any new arguments for the derivation of substantive rights from direct welfarism.

Direct welfarism, in either its normal or plural interpretations, cannot ground substantive rights. Absolute or restricted-absolute rights would require a general argument for intrapersonal incommensurability of a very particular form, and the prospects for such an argument seem bleak. Goal rights require abandoning the principle of individual relevance. For many this cost will be too high. In any event, strategies involving the denial of the standard interpretation of welfarism will not be pursued further in this essay.

The second strategy involves the denial of consequentialism, so that the status of rights in the context of decision-making is cut loose from the status of rights in evaluation. One variant of this strategy is the contractarian approach to rights, which concentrates on the possibility of the emergence of substantive rights from interpersonal agreement, rather than from some evaluation of overall social states. I shall pursue this strategy a little further in Section 5.

The third, and final, strategy to be considered here is the move from direct welfarism and consequentialism to indirect forms of these principles. This strategy forms the subject matter of the next section.

4. INDIRECT UTILITARIANISM AND RIGHTS

The first step in any indirectly utilitarian argument in support of substantial rights must be to establish that the directly utilitarian position is in some way self-defeating, so that adopting the principle of utility as a practical principle of decision-making yields outcomes that are less than optimal when evaluated by that same principle. Gray (1984) puts this point clearly, noting that: "Indirect utilitarianism embodies and exploits the apparent paradox that utility maximisation will not be achieved by adopting the strategy of maximising utility. Indeed, its central contention is that utility is best promoted if we adopt practical precepts which impose constraints on the policies which we adopt in pursuit of utility" (p. 74).[13]

When the general argument in favor of the indirect approach to utilitarianism is established, the next step consists of linking this approach specifically to substantial rights. This second step of the argument must show that the precepts for practical decision-making, derived from the critical consideration of the principle of utility, include rights and that the status of these rights in decision-making exceeds that of guide rights.

It is widely accepted that some accounts of indirect utilitarianism yield rights on an argument from uncertainty and fallibility, such rights are to be respected in situations where the truly utilitarian course of action is not clear. Such rights of thumb may be of considerable practical importance in a world of uncertainty and fallibility, but they cannot achieve a status greater than guide rights. Rather than dwell on this argument, which is forcefully put by Sumner (1987), I wish to consider two recent lines of indirect utilitarian argument, each of which claims to ground rights more substantial than guide rights.

The first is an argument from strategic interaction. In situations where the consequences of individuals' decisions depend on the contemporaneous decisions of others, there may arise coordination or other strategic problems that make it difficult for unconstrained individual action to result in socially optimal outcomes. The classic examples of such a situation include the prisoners' dilemma and the chicken and the hawk/dove game (see Elster, 1984; Schelling, 1960; Sugden, 1986). In this context, social rules or conventions may arise and act to precommit individual action so as to provide a possible escape from suboptimality. But the interpretation of a rule as a precommitment does not in itself ensure that the rule in question is elevated to a status in decision-making more substantial than that of a guide. Indeed, the essential nature of a precommitment strategy is that I undertake some action now that ensures that it will always be *in my interests* to follow a specified course of action or rule in the future; I do not follow that rule because I believe that such behavior has intrinsic value, or because the argument for rule observance is in any way incommensurable with other arguments, but simply because it is in my interest to do so *given my previous actions*. A fully credible precommitment has the property that even if the decision-maker engages in a full-scale evaluation of consequences in each case, he or she will always find it optimal to act in accordance with the rule.

It is the argument from strategic interaction that seems to lie at the

---

13. For more general discussion of possibly self-defeating theories, see Parfit (1984).

RIGHTS, INDIRECT UTILITARIANISM, AND CONTRACTARIANISM   **179**

heart of Gray's indirectly utilitarian defense of rights.[14] He argues that direct utilitarian calculation may erode conventional practices that are necessary to social cooperation, and that these practices should be supported on indirectly utilitarian grounds. He invests such practices with *second-order* utility, so that we should subscribe to them even where a directly utilitarian calculation would dictate that we should abandon them. At the same time, however, Gray (1984) argues that such social rules should not be subject to rigoristic application, so that the indirect utilitarian should see "social rules as more than rules of thumb and less than absolutist requirements" (p. 84). If successful, this argument would seem to pave the way for utilitarian support for compensable rights, where the second-order utility associated with each right plays the role of its intrinsic weight or reservation price.

On this view, the second-order utility associated with any particular social rule seems to be acting as a summary measure of the value of the more remote and indirect consequences of any act in breach of the rule. For example, if I fail to keep a promise, there are direct costs and benefits accruing to the individuals directly concerned, but there may also be remote and indirect costs and benefits associated with the reduction in the level of general promise-keeping and the consequent increases in uncertainty. These indirect consequences may often take the form of public goods or bads.

All of this is true, but it does not amount to an indirectly utilitarian account of rights that is noticeably stronger than that associated with rights of thumb. If there are remote and indirect consequences of an act to do with the support of valued social conventions, then, of course, these consequences should be included in any directly utilitarian evaluation of that act. The consequences may be indirect, but the utilitarianism remains direct.

Furthermore, if the same indirect consequences arise from many different actions (the indirect value of promise-keeping may be the same regardless of the particular promise in question), then it will be appropriate to utilize this constant value and so reduce the cost of calculation. Similarly, once uncertainty and fallibility are introduced, the second-order or indirect utility of an act can be viewed as an approximation acting to protect those values that might be particularly likely to be overlooked in any practical evaluation exercise. But, in all of this, the second-order utility is simply proxying ordinary utilitarian considerations rather than extending those considerations in such a way that grants the social rules or conventions any status in decision-making beyond that of guides.

14. Gray (1984, pp. 83–85), although it is possible to interpret Gray as offering the third type of argument to be considered later. In any event, Gray has moved away from indirect utilitarianism in his more recent thought (see Gray, 1989).

180   ALAN P. HAMLIN

The point here is simply that if the social rules, rights, or conventions are of purely instrumental status at the critical level of evaluation, as they must be in any directly or indirectly utilitarian framework, then the argument from strategic interaction offers no reason to raise their status in decision-making since the strategic value of rule observance can be accommodated within the status of guide rights offered by direct utilitarianism. The argument from strategic interaction reminds us that utilitarians should include *all* the consequences of an act in its evaluation, and that in an imperfect world, it may be sensible to proxy some of the valued consequences in practical decision-making. But it provides no basis for investing social rules or rights with value over and above that which can be directly grounded in the welfarist evaluation of the consequences of the operation of the rule or right in question. In this way, this line of argument fails to provide the basis for an indirectly utilitarian defense of rights with status greater than that of guide rights, but it does serve to emphasize the potential scope and importance of utilitarian guide rights.

The second line of argument to be considered here derives from the possibility that some particular valued consequences are, by their very nature, incapable of attainment by direct means. In the language developed by Elster (1983), they are consequences that are essentially byproducts (Chapter 2). This type of argument is developed explicitly by Pettit (1986, 1988; see also, Pettit and Brennan, 1986), and may be sketched as follows. The first and crucial step is to argue that there exist some consequences of value that can only arise as byproducts of a system of rights of some particular status; so that, for example, in the absence of a system of constraint rights, certain valued consequences are lost completely. Once this step is taken, the argument is relatively straightforward. If the byproduct consequences are sufficiently valued, it may be desirable at the critical level, and on purely utilitarian grounds, to select the constraint-right system as the only available means of achieving the desired ultimate consequences.

This line of argument clearly accepts that rights must be of instrumental status at the critical level; but the move of making higher status rights in decision-making a necessary condition for the achievement of desired consequences is intended to support the institution of such rights at the practical level, so that in the decision-making context individuals should act as if rights had inherent value even though they do not.

In questioning this line of argument, we may begin by viewing in more detail what it means for a benefit to be a byproduct of a right. Clearly, given the fundamentally welfarist framework, the benefit in question must be simply an increment in the well-being of one or more individuals, but how does such a benefit come about as a byproduct? The answer here is that the benefit must derive not from an action (or inaction) of some individual or group, but from the motivation that

RIGHTS, INDIRECT UTILITARIANISM, AND CONTRACTARIANISM 181

underlies that action. For example, if you refrain from intervening in some essentially private and self-regarding enterprise of mine, I will be in receipt of some benefit relative to the state of the world in which you intervene. But the level of the benefit may depend upon the reason for your nonintervention. If your decision was based on a utilitarian calculation that took account of my interests, then my benefit is seen to be contingent and insecure, while if your action was simply the uncalculating acceptance of a constraint, then my benefit may be quantitatively enhanced. Such an incremental benefit is then a byproduct of the constraint in the sense intended by Pettit.[15] It is the absence of calculation that is the key, and this immediately points to the inability of this line of argument to support a system of compensable rights. A compensable right, by its nature, does not absolve individuals from the responsibility of calculation; it simply provides another input to the calculation in the form of the reservation price of a rights infringement. Of course, the additional input might make the result of calculation obvious in some cases and so eliminate the need for detailed calculation, but this is very different from absolving the decision maker from calculation in principle, as required by Pettit. Clearly then a compensable-rights structure could not generate the sort of calculatively elusive byproducts required by the argument.

But equally it is implausible to suggest that full constraint rights could be supported by this argument, since the beneficial byproduct must be entirely commensurable with all other benefits and costs considered at the critical level, and the introduction of full constraint rights may imply costs in particular circumstances that may outweigh the value of the beneficial byproduct. Indeed, the implausibility of full constraint rights is accepted by Pettit, who suggests that rights derived from this line of argument will be constraints on action only in certain, normal circumstances.

However, we argued in Section 2 that the notion of a constraint right, which was operational only in normal circumstances, was underspecified to the point of incoherence, and that all such formulations should be reconstrued as either restricted-constraint rights, compensable rights, or some amalgam of the two. Now, since we have already ruled out compensable rights as being inconsistent with the requirement of a calculatively elusive byproduct, this leaves the restricted-constraint right as the only remaining possibility.

The difficulty in this remaining case lies in identifying, at the critical level, the type or class of argument that will resist the authority of the right and the type or class that will not. This difficulty seems insurmountable given the standard interpretation of welfarism at the critical

---

15. Pettit (1988) stresses the requirement of calculative elusiveness.

182   ALAN P. HAMLIN

level, since this denies the existence of different types of argument and insists that arguments differ only in their weight.

The alternative interpretation of welfarism as plural welfarism is again of relevance here. I argued earlier that the plural-welfarist position does not provide new arguments for the grounding of rights in direct welfarism. The question now is whether the plural-welfarist position, with its recognition of different types of utility, can assist in the grounding of restricted-constraint rights via the indirect strategy involving the essential byproduct argument.[16]

Of course, it is possible to imagine a case in which the utility deriving from the operation of a restricted-constraint-right system is not only essentially a byproduct of that system, but also of a type that is superior to at least some other types of utility. In this case, there will be an indirect grounding for a system of restricted-constraint rights, although it is scarcely needed since the directly plural-welfarist argument would apply in this case without the need of the byproduct argument. However, as in the case of direct plural welfarism, there is no reason to suppose that this case pertains. Rights are being elevated to restricted-constraint status on the assertion that they produce a superior type of utility, and this is little more than tautology. At best the plural-welfare view can offer only contingent support for substantive rights, and even then, it seems that the support is of a direct nature and does not fit well with the indirect strategy under present discussion.

We have reached an impasse. I have suggested three lines of argument that crosscut in such a way that none of the formulations of rights that carry status greater than guide rights can be derived by means of the byproduct argument from an underlying commitment to both welfarism and consequentialism at the critical level. Compensable rights are ruled out because they cannot provide a calculatively elusive benefit. Restricted-constraint rights are excluded because standard welfarism provides no basis for the identification of distinct types of argument, and plural welfarism fails to provide more than a contingent possibility. Full constraint rights are excluded by reference to the need to specify normal circumstances in the absence of any ability to argue that the byproduct benefits would necessarily exceed the potential welfare cost. It seems that if there are benefits that are essentially the byproducts of rights, they are beyond the reach of even indirect utilitarians.

Pettit (1987) offers a sketch of an argument that might be taken as a defense against this line of criticism (pp. 13–14). This counter-argument is that a right that is either a restricted-constraint right or a compensable right (or both) can still be regarded as a full constraint right over a restricted domain, so that within that domain one can imagine a non-

---

16. Pettit does not make any appeal to different types of utility or well-being in his argument.

calculative acceptance of the right that would then allow of the calculatively elusive byproduct. Whatever the formal attractions of this counterargument, it seems to have little real substance. It cannot provide the standard welfarist with a means of identifying alternative types of argument and so cannot ground a restricted-constraint right. And in relation to the compensable right, it seems to suggest that the fact that a calculation would reveal an action to be desirable allows us to view that action as being chosen without calculation. The point is simply that the practical individual cannot know whether any particular situation lies within the restricted domain or not unless he or she engages in the relevant calculation, and then the byproduct is already lost.

To the extent that Pettit's major concern is to display the possibility of a consequentialist derivation of rights, without major reference to welfarism, then, the argument presented here is not to be taken as critical. The nonwelfarist consequentialist can support substantive rights on the Pettit argument. But the abandonment of welfarism provides more direct access to other arguments for rights, as was briefly discussed earlier.

The basic problem with the indirectly utilitarian defense of rights highlighted earlier stems from the requirement of a strong link between the critical and practical levels of thought, or, in other words, between the critical evaluation of social states and the practical process of decision-making. Since the critical level involves both a particular substantive view of the social good, which is directly unsupportive of rights, and a view concerning the relationship between the good and that which should be chosen, it is overwhelmingly difficult to derive practical precepts that afford rights any substantial status. It is clear that if substantial rights are to be derived, rather than argued to be basic and independent moral considerations, the need is for greater flexibility at the critical level. I have already noted that this may be achieved by the suitable relaxation of welfarism, but in the final section of this essay, I want to sketch briefly an alternative and more contractarian defense of rights.

5. CONTRACTARIAN RIGHTS

In the space available, it is clearly impossible to do more than outline the possibility of a contractarian account of substantial rights, and so I shall limit my comments to presenting a sketch of the general structure of a contractarian theory of rights. In this way I hope to show that a contractarian approach to rights is at least plausible and, in particular, that it is not undermined by the type of arguments that I have deployed against indirect utilitarianism.[17]

17. More detailed comments on the relationship between contractarianism and rights can be found in the references provided in note 6, p. 168. The following sketch draws on Hamlin (1989).

I have already noted that the contractarian strategy involves breaking the link between social evaluation and decision-making, and so breaking with consequentialism. Welfarism is also inessential to the contractarian approach. Indeed, the critical level of analysis within contractarianism relates to the process of rational agreement rather than directly to a process of synoptic social evaluation. Of course, evaluation of some form may provide an input into the process of agreement, but synoptic evaluation is not basic to the contractarian approach.

The problem of rights in the contractarian framework is essentially the reverse of the problem of rights in the utilitarian framework. I have argued that the utilitarian finds substantial rights impossible to accommodate because of the relatively rigid specification of the critical level of evaluation. The contractarian, by contrast, locates the problem of rights at the practical level of decision-making.

It is relatively easy to see that it is at least plausible that individuals at the critical level of discourse may rationally agree that a system of substantial rights would be mutually beneficial (particularly when we remember that we are not restricted to a welfarist account of benefit), and this seems to be all that is required to provide a contractarian basis for substantial rights at the critical level. But, agreement to a system of substantial rights will only be rational if it is rationally expected that those rights will be influential at the practical level of decision-making. And there is nothing to ensure that individuals will comply with rules or rights just because they are grounded in some form of (hypothetical) agreement. Thus, the central problem of grounding rights within a contractarian framework is the compliance problem of ensuring that rights that are agreed to have substantial status at the critical level actually have substantial status at the practical level.

This difficulty in the contractarian foundation of rights is put in different terms by Sumner (1987), who stresses the point that any agreed structure of rights will only have moral status (i.e., substantial status, in my terms) if it is accepted that the circumstances in which the agreement was hypothetically made were themselves morally relevant. But, he argues, there must be some elements of the circumstances of agreement that are not themselves the outcome of agreement and so are not based in contractarianism. If this is true, contractarianism cannot provide a complete account of the foundation of substantial rights. Sumner's criticism is at base a version of the compliance problem, since it stems from the question of why any individual should accept the outcome of a contractarian agreement as a valid and substantial reason for practical action.

Two approaches can be taken to the compliance problem. The first is to take individual motivations and dispositions at the practical level of decision-making as fixed, and argue that any rights (or other rules) that are to be agreed at the critical level must be self-enforcing with respect to those fixed motivations and dispositions. For example, if individuals are taken to be own-utility maximizers at the practical level, a system of rights will only be complied with to the extent that rights-respecting actions generate maximal own utility.

Here, then, rights are once again reduced to the level of guide rights. The reason is clear. Just as welfarism at the critical level reduces rights to minimal status in evaluation, so utility maximization (or any other rights-disregarding decision theory) must reduce rights to minimal status in decision-making. If we are to have rights that are substantial at both the critical and practical levels, we must move away from such rigid specifications at both levels.

This, then, is the second possible approach to the compliance problem within the contractarian framework. On this approach the critical level includes the agreement of a set of rights and the rational choice of a set of dispositions that will encourage compliance with those rights and so internalize the agreed rights into the motivational structure of individuals at the practical level. These two aspects interact. It will only be rational to agree to a particular system of rights if the dispositions that will support those rights at the practical level are capable of being rationally adopted. This approach is equivalent to the idea that the circumstances of agreement are capable of being moralized from within the resources of contractarianism, so that the content of the agreement carries moral significance at the practical level.

Gauthier (1986) provides an example of this approach. There are difficulties with Gauthier's detailed argument, but the general line of argument merits further exploration, not least because perfect compliance is not required. Even if it were known at the hypothetical contract stage that the disposition to comply with a particular set of rights could be acquired only imperfectly, or only by some individuals, it might still be rational to agree to that set of rights if partial compliance holds out the prospect of mutual advantage.

This is not the place to pursue this line of argument.[18] The important point in the present context is that the arguments deployed here against any indirectly welfarist and consequentialist account of substantial rights gain no purchase against this contractarian argument.

REFERENCES

d'Aspremont, C., and Gevers, L. 1977. "Equity and the Informational Basis of Collective Choice." *Review of Economic Studies* 44:199–209.

Buchanan, J. M. 1975. *The Limits of Liberty*. Chicago: University of Chicago Press.

Dworkin, R. 1977. *Taking Rights Seriously*. London: Duckworth.

Elster, J. 1983. *Sour Grapes*. Cambridge: Cambridge University Press

———. 1984. *Ulysses and the Sirens*, Revised edition. Cambridge: Cambridge University Press.

Feinberg, J. 1970. "The Nature and Value of Rights." *Journal of Value Enquiry* 4:243–57. Reprinted in Feinberg, 1980.

---

18. Gauthier (1986) offers a very strong version of this argument; it is discussed and modified in Hamlin (1989) and criticized in Sumner (1987).

———. 1978. "Voluntary Euthanasia and the Inalienable Right to Life." *Philosophy and Public Affairs* 7:93–123. Reprinted in Feinberg, 1980.

———. 1980. *Rights, Justice and the Bounds of Liberty*. Princeton: Princeton University Press.

Gauthier, D. 1986. *Morals by Agreement*. Oxford: Oxford University Press.

Gibbard, A. 1984. "Utilitarianism and Human Rights." In *Human Rights*, edited by E. F. Paul, F. D. Miller, and J. Paul, pp. 92–102. Oxford: Basil Blackwell.

Gray, J. 1984. "Indirect Utility and Fundamental Rights." In *Human Rights*, edited by E. F. Paul, F. D. Miller, and J. Paul, pp. 73–91. Oxford: Basil Blackwell.

———. 1989. "Contractarian Method, Private Property and the Market Economy." *Nomos* 31. Forthcoming.

Griffin, J. 1984. "Towards a Substantive Theory of Rights." In *Utility and Rights*, edited by R. G. Frey, pp. 137–60. Oxford: Basil Blackwell.

———. 1986. *Well-Being*. Oxford: Oxford University Press.

Hamlin, A. P. 1986. *Ethics, Economics and the State*. Brighton: Wheatsheaf Books.

———. 1989. "Liberty, Contract and the State." In *The Good Polity*, edited by A. P. Hamlin and P. Pettit, pp. 87–101. Oxford: Basil Blackwell.

Hamlin, A. P., and Pettit, P. 1989. "Normative Analysis of the State: Some Preliminaries." In *The Good Polity*, edited by A. P. Hamlin and P. Pettit, pp. 1–13. Oxford: Basil Blackwell.

Hare, R. M. 1981. *Moral Thinking*. Oxford: Oxford University Press.

———. 1984. "Rights, Utility and Universalization, Reply to J. L. Mackie." In *Utility and Rights*, edited by R. G. Frey, pp. 106–20. Oxford: Basil Blackwell.

Harsanyi, J. 1985a. "Does Reason Tell Us What Moral Code to Follow and, Indeed, to Follow Any Moral Code at All?" *Ethics* 96:42–55.

———. 1985b. "Rule Utilitarianism, Equality and Justice." In *Ethics and Economics*, edited by E. F. Paul, F. D. Miller, and J. Paul, pp. 115–27. Oxford: Basil Blackwell.

Lyons, D. 1980. "Utility as a Possible Ground of Rights." *Nous* 14:17–28.

———. 1982. "Utility and Rights." *Nomos* 24:107–38.

Mackie, J. L. 1984. "Rights, Utility, and Universalization." In *Utility and Rights*, edited by R. G. Frey, pp. 86–105. Oxford: Basil Blackwell.

Narveson, J. 1984. "Contractarian Rights." In *Utility and Rights*, edited by R. G. Frey, pp. 161–74. Oxford: Basil Blackwell.

Nozick, R. 1974. *Anarchy, State and Utopia*. New York: Basic Books.

Parfit, D. 1984. *Reasons and Persons*. Oxford: Oxford University Press.

Pettit, P. 1986. "Can the Welfare State Take Rights Seriously?" In *Law, Rights and the Welfare State*, edited by D. Galligan and C. Sampford. London: Croom Helm.

———. 1987. "Rights, Constraints and Trumps." *Analysis* 46:8–14.

———. 1988. "The Consequentialist Can Recognise Rights." *Philosophical Quarterly* 38:42–55.

Pettit, P., and Brennan, G. 1986. "Restrictive Consequentialism." *Australasian Journal of Philosophy* 64:438–55.

Rawls, J. 1971. *A Theory of Justice*. Cambridge: Harvard University Press.

Regan, D. H. 1980. *Utilitarianism and Cooperation*. Oxford: Oxford University Press.

Riley, J. 1986. "Generalised Social Welfare Functionals: Welfarism, Morality and Liberty." *Social Choice and Welfare* 3:233–54.

Roberts, K. W. S. 1980. "Interpersonal Comparability and Social Choice Theory." *Review of Economic Studies* 47:421–40.

Rowley, C., and Peacock, A. 1975. *Welfare Economics: A Liberal Restatement*. Oxford: Martin Robertson.

Scanlon, T. 1982. "Contractualism and Utilitarianism." In *Utilitarianism and Beyond*, edited by A. K. Sen and B. A. O. Williams. Cambridge: Cambridge University Press.

Schelling, T. C. 1960. *The Strategy of Conflict*. Cambridge: Harvard University Press.

Sen, A. K. 1970. "The Impossibility of a Paretian Liberal." *Journal of Political Economy* 78:152–57.

RIGHTS, INDIRECT UTILITARIANISM, AND CONTRACTARIANISM **187**

———. 1976. "Liberty, Unanimity and Rights." *Economica* 43:217–45.
———. 1979a. "Utilitarianism and Welfarism." *Journal of Philosophy* 76:463–89.
———. 1979b. "Personal Utilities and Public Judgments: Or What's Wrong with Welfare Economics." *Economic Journal* 89:537–59.
———. 1981. "Plural Utility." *Proceedings of the Aristotelian Society* 81:193–215.
———. 1982. "Rights and Agency." *Philosophy and Public Affairs* 11:3–39.
———. 1983. "Liberty and Social Choice." *Journal of Philosophy* 80:5–28.
———. 1985. "Well-being, Agency and Freedom." *Journal of Philosophy* 82:169–221.
———. 1987. *On Ethics and Economics.* Oxford: Basil Blackwell.
Sen, A. K., and Williams, B. A. O. (editors). 1982. *Utilitarianism and Beyond.* Cambridge: Cambridge University Press.
Sugden, R. 1986. *The Economics of Rights, Co-operation and Welfare.* Oxford: Basil Blackwell.
Sumner, L. W. 1987. *The Moral Foundation of Rights.* Oxford: Oxford University Press.
Williams, B. A. O. 1973. "A Critique of Utilitarianism." In *Utilitarianism For and Against,* edited by J. J. C. Smart and B. A. O. Williams, pp. 77–150. Cambridge: Cambridge University Press.

Name Index